The Great Depression

UPDATED EDITION

EYEWITNESS HISTORY

The Great Depression

UPDATED EDITION

David F. Burg

☑®
Facts On File, Inc.

The Great Depression, Updated Edition

Facts On File, Inc.
An imprint of Infobase Publishing
132 West 31st Street
New York NY 10001

ISBN-10: 0-8160-5709-5
ISBN-13: 978-0-8160-5709-2

Library of Congress Cataloging-in-Publication Data
Burg, David F.
    The Great Depression / by David F. Burg. — Updated ed.
        p.   cm —(Eyewitness history)
    Includes bibliographical references (p.   ) and index.
    ISBN 0-8160-5709-5 (acid free paper)
    1. United States—History—1933–1945—Juvenile literature. 2. United States—History—1919–1933—Juvenile literature. 3. Depressions—1920—United States—Personal narratives—Juvenile literature. 4. New Deal, 1933–1939—Personal narratives—Juvenile literature. I. Title. II. Series.
        E806.B9 2005
        973.91—dc22   2004029126

Facts On File books are available at special discounts when purchased in bulk quantities for businesses, associations, institutions or sales promotions. Please call our Special Sales Department in New York at 212/967-8800 or 800/322-8755.

You can find Facts On File on the World Wide Web at
http://www.factsonfile.com

Text design by Joan M. Toro
Cover design by Cathy Rincon
Graphs by Sholto Ainslie

Printed in the United States of America

VB JT 10 9 8 7 6 5 4 3 2

This book is printed on acid-free paper.

In memory of Laura Roth Johnson and Floris Johnson Burg

NOTE ON PHOTOS

Many of the illustrations and photographs used in this book are old, historical images. The quality of the prints is not always up to modern standards, as in some cases the originals are damaged. The content of the illustrations, however, made their inclusion important despite problems in reproduction.

CONTENTS

PREFACE TO THE FIRST EDITION

Events of the present may be viewed as the past continuing to unfold. For whether we like it or not, and whether for good or ill, we are all vitally connected to the past, involved in it through its enduring influences on our lives. And if we doubt this statement, all we need to do is think about the personal legacy of our parents and grandparents in our own lives. We may escape from our ancestors, leave home forever and leave them to their deaths, but we only fool ourselves if we think we are truly free of them. The past does not necessarily predetermine present and future events; but if we remain ignorant of the past, then we cannot really understand the nature of our own lives now, and we increase the risk of dooming ourselves to allowing the past to decide the continuing course of events. That is, in order to influence how the present and future will develop, we must know the past—whether we speak of the collective human past or of our own personal lives. Surely that is reason enough to study history. Surely that is more than reason enough to study the era of the Great Depression, which has had such an enormous impact on subsequent events worldwide and on the lives of people we know personally.

So what can we confidently know about the past? Any historic work probably should contain a warning to the reader. For despite protestations of objectivity, historians inevitably bring some bias to their accounts. Quantitative analysis supposedly achieves objectivity; but interpretations of statistics depend upon the thesis the analyst has begun with, the nature of the questionnaire or other instrument used to gather data, and the formulas the analyst applies to the data, not to mention the final "massaging" the analyst performs. A thesis may prescribe outcomes by determining the questions asked; respondents sometimes misinterpret questions, give misleading answers, or even lie; analysts apply formulas that suit their own biases—we need only listen to how three different economists, let us say, interpret the same set of economic data in order to agree to the validity of this statement. If bias influences statistical analysis, then it seems most unlikely it would not enter into narrative history.

For one thing, sources can be misleading, frequently on purpose. For example, Herbert Hoover is known to have made numerous factual errors in his *Memoirs,* so anyone who uses them should be wary; but how does one know that in advance of reading them without knowledge of the subject and of historic commentary? Inaccuracy, of course, is common in memoirs—recollections are often faulty or self-serving. In addition, the historian who interprets the sources cannot help bringing personal biases to the interpretation. If the historian's biases are clearcut, then fair enough. For example, no reader will mistake that, in general, Robert S. McElvaine, in his highly readable *The Great*

Depression, evidences some disdain for the Hoover administration and some admiration for Roosevelt. Furthermore, concerning the historian's bias, there is an obvious problem involved in selecting materials and information. As the great historian Charles A. Beard, not one to hide his own biases, once commented, "Writing any history is jut pulling a tomcat by its tail across a Brussels carpet." Only those tufts of wool that snag in the claws get used, but the vastness of the carpet and the intricacy of its design remain unpenetrated. And there is still another problem. Regardless of how voluminous may be the writings, speeches, letters, memoirs, or recorded conversations any individual leaves for the researcher to peruse, finally that individual's ultimate motives and precepts remain elusive—sometimes they are purposely obscured, sometimes they are not even known to the individual. You cannot, after all, get inside another person's mind. Eleanor Roosevelt once said of her husband, the president, that she recognized he was a great man but that she did not really understand who he was.

So the absolute truth about the past events cannot be known, but we can at least approximate the truth closely enough to make knowledge of the past both amply reliable and highly useful for understanding the present. That's what I have hoped to achieve for readers in this book. The central format of the book—brief narrative overviews, chronologies and excerpts from sources—lends itself, I believe, admirably to such an achievement by allowing the reader to step into the era at any point. This format, along with the photographs, biographies, texts of sources, and bibliography, also allows readers plenty of scope for coming to their own understanding of the Great Depression. Readers of this book are not told, "Here is exactly what happened and this is how you should interpret it." We read usually on our own, privately, in silence, and the end result is of our own making. Reading a history is like reading a novel—it finally means whatever it means to you personally. Just so, readers of this book are left free to draw their own conclusions. But then, having said that, I think I must add one final warning: Even I might be biased. Make your own judgments.

PREFACE TO THE UPDATED EDITION

For this edition I have provided significant new material to both the narrative and the Eyewitness Testimony sections of every chapter as well as the biographies, and I have expanded the bibliography with scores of additional sources, including many published since the original edition of this book appeared. More than two dozen new photographs and charts have been added. And a modest update of the introduction also provides some reflection on the legacies of the New Deal informed by more recent scholarship.

To the narrative sections I have added extended commentary on the long-term effects emanating from the Treaties of Paris and Versailles that ended World War I; commentary on Gertrude Ederle's conquest of the English Channel and curious fads of the 1920s; a lengthy insertion on the possible causes of the Great Crash; a focus on the early achievements of Robert Hutchins Goddard; an overview of the tax rebellions of the early 1930s; material on the youths of America joining the ranks of the hoboes; expanded treatment of the experiences of African Americans and women during the depression years; a segment on the popularity of comic strips and comic books; a discussion of horse racing and the career of Seabiscuit; insights into the Roosevelts and the movie industry; and a sidelight on the development of major art collections by American entrepreneurs. The Eyewitness Testimony sections now contain new text reflecting the views of Eleanor Roosevelt; Irving Fisher and other prominent economists; reminiscing hoboes; Franklin D. Roosevelt in his fireside chats; and many other commentators. I sincerely hope that readers will find all of this new material both interesting and valuable.

ACKNOWLEDGMENTS

It is impossible to thank all of those whose work I have depended on in writing this book, so I would like to offer a blanket expression of appreciation to scores of historians who have published books and articles on the depression era. I would also like to thank, once again, the staff of the University of Kentucky M. I. King Library, whose resources have always proven a splendid benefit; I wish in particular to thank Thomas M. House for his help in the library's Photographic Archives, Special Collections. My thanks also go to the staff of the Library of Congress, most especially Michael Cooper of the library's Photoduplication Service. And, as always, I wish to thank my wife, Helen Rendlesham Burg, for her patience and support.

INTRODUCTION

FROM THE FIRST EDITION

Some events have had such profound and enduring impact on subsequent history that they emerge from the past as pivotal events, forming a definable break between what came before and what followed. The Great Depression of the 1930s stands out as such an event. Lasting for a decade, the depression and the enormous social, economic, and political changes it wrought altered the course of the entire remaining 20th century in ways that no one could have anticipated even as the 1920s were ending.

During the 1920s, American politicians and the general populace as well may have been especially myopic about foreseeing the likelihood of the coming depression—let alone its enduring effects. Preoccupied with that decade's economic surge, they appear in retrospect to have enthusiastically embraced the faith that the historic cycle of economic boom and bust had finally been overcome and that the new prosperity would last forever. Some knew better, of course. Among them, American farmers and blacks, who mostly endured the prosperous decade of the twenties, were struggling to survive. Others suddenly began to sense their faith's possible fragility when the Great Crash of the New York stock market occurred in the fall of 1929. Although economic decline did not begin precisely at that moment, the crash was a warning of things to come.

The collapse of prosperity that followed in the early thirties took an enormous toll. Millions of American workers lost their jobs, with no hope of finding other work that could maintain their livelihoods. Following the loss of work ensued lost savings, lost homes, lost security, lost pride, and lost hope for many who had never before experienced such extreme deprivation. Investors went bankrupt, banks failed, factories closed, corporations foundered, farmers lost their farms, sharecroppers lost everything. Politicians initially displayed confidence but offered no solutions. The majority of Americans who remained employed evidenced their compassion and caring through communal efforts to relieve the hunger and homelessness of the less fortunate. But private as well as state relief efforts have their limits, of course; and as the depression persisted through 1932, the demand for remedial action by the federal government grew. The hesitancy of President Herbert Hoover's administration to respond cost him reelection and swept Franklin Delano Roosevelt into the presidency.

Roosevelt's inauguration in March 1933 marked the beginning of an unprecedented political transformation. The federal government would now

xvii

assume varied roles that it had never before been expected to perform. Although lacking a defined vision of a comprehensive, long-term plan for change or of the potential outcomes his policies might effect, Roosevelt asserted the willingness to act, to experiment, and to improvise in hopes of overcoming the depression. His New Deal generated a vast array of economic and social programs that largely endure to this day and have influenced the life of every American alive during the past 70 years. These programs encouraged labor unionization; instituted regulation of banking and investment; promoted soil and forest conservation; funded massive public works projects; provided oversight for interstate commerce, communications, and transportation; established a process for subsidizing and controlling agricultural production; and, perhaps most important of all, created a social insurance system whose keystone is Social Security. The New Deal changed forever American social, economic, and political realities. Ironically, however, the bold experiment failed to end the Great Depression.

In Europe and Asia the depression provided the context for the burgeoning of extreme militaristic and nationalistic movements in Germany and Japan that culminated in World War II, with its eruption of terrible destruction, horror, and inhumanity. That war forced the United States to become not only a major participant in world events but also the primary defender of democratic and capitalistic systems in the cold war hostility with the Soviet Union (USSR) that followed. That protector and policeman role persisted until the hegemony of communism in the USSR and Eastern Europe began to unravel rapidly following the destruction of the Berlin Wall in 1989. But many remnants of the Great Depression endured through these cataclysmic events. As economic cycles of growth and recession have continued, for example, governments throughout the world have combatted the downturns with policies that were initiated during the depression years.

In the United States, opponents of the New Deal legacy have continuously battled against some federal and state programs it created—such as regulations of commerce and relief payments—and others spawned in later years through its ongoing momentum. Even now conservative candidates for the presidency and the Congress campaign as advocates of dismantling or drastically revamping these programs, while liberal candidates ardently defend them and propose their expansion. Both opponents and proponents thereby acknowledge that the New Deal's influence still pervades current U.S. social and economic systems.

Thus the ghost of the New Deal haunted the Capitol during the 1994 failed struggle to create a national health insurance system, a program the Social Security Act of 1935 had overlooked. And as the debate over passage of a balanced budget amendment to the Constitution proceeded in early 1995, opponents invoked the presumed sanctity of Social Security—expressing their fear its funding might be imperiled by the amendment—as ample reason to vote against it. Major conflict has focused on revising the "welfare system," whose initial programs emerged during the New Deal, and on scrapping funding for the arts, a New Deal innovation that was phased out before World War II and reemerged in altered form in the 1960s and 1970s. In just such ways, and others probably more significant and pervasive, perhaps beneficial or perhaps detrimental, the legacy of the Great Depression endures. And the events of 70 years past continue to unfold into the future.

FOR THE UPDATED EDITION

The overview presented in the original introduction still applies, as may be affirmed, for example, by the continuing debate over the future of the Social Security system. The administration of George W. Bush appears intent upon promoting revision of that system to allow wage earners who so desire to invest a certain percentage of their incomes that would be subject to the Social Security tax in private investments rather than having it subsumed into the Social Security fund. The impact such a change, if translated into law, would have on the Social Security system and on the retirement prospects for the so-called baby boomers generation remains to be seen.

Deserving of mention here is recent scholarship arguing that the New Deal, while widely viewed as having secured the primacy of traditional American political liberalism and the various reform programs its adherents had supported for many decades, actually subverted traditional liberalism in favor of a collectivist-oriented liberalism (in other words, socialist or marxist), a collectivist image of government, and the aggrandizement of power in the presidency. This is not entirely a new argument but actually a revival of objections presented during the New Deal era by both conservative opponents and disaffected liberals such as Senator Hiram Johnson, who at the time expressed grave concerns that the New Deal, perhaps especially during the years 1935 to 1938, was propelling the nation toward socialism and dictatorship. It should be pointed out, of course, that such concerns emerged within a background context of ascendant fascism and Stalinism in Europe and elsewhere.

This argument as currently stated is ably expressed by Gary Dean Best in his *The Retreat from Liberalism* (2002). Best points out that traditional liberals sustained their faith in capitalism and its ability to reverse the depression through revived and increased industrial production, while the new collectivist liberals—Felix Frankfurter prominent among them, Best says—embraced the view that capitalism was either moribund or dangerous (the latter evidenced by fascism in Italy and Germany) or both and therefore needed to be replaced by a collectivist system. The collectivist liberals had been persuaded by the advocacy of Harold J. Laski, well-known British Labour Party official and marxist, says Best. He quotes Rexford Tugwell as stating that these new liberals perceived Congress's sole purpose to be transferring "wide emergency powers" to the White House. "Thus," observes Best, "the Congress elected by the people was not regarded as a partner in government, nor even as part of a system of checks and balances, but as a rubber stamp on policies formulated without public debate by the White House junta." Best adds, "The subsidization of America under the New Deal for the sake of the leader's political fortunes obscured the loss of liberty that was taking place under it." To the extent that the collectivist liberal agenda succeeded, the New Deal failed totally in its efforts to remedy the depression, in Best's judgment. Whether Best's view has validity will likely be resolved by the debate that is certain to develop over future years. What can be said with certitude for now at least is that the collectivist liberal agenda Best outlines foundered upon congressional and judicial opposition and finally upon the pressing need for renewed dependence on America's capitalist production system to confront the challenges of war. In short, events beyond the collectivist liberals' influence or the president's control determined the outcome. Nevertheless, the issues of governmental checks and balances, the magnitude of presidential power, and rival visions of what the nation's government should be and do merit continuing argument—as they have since the administration of George Washington.

1

Prelude to Crisis
1919–1928

THE TREATY OF VERSAILLES

Although historians frequently cite 1929, the year of the Great Stock Market Crash, as the beginning of the Great Depression, they generally agree that the origins of the depression trace to the decade that preceded it and even to the cataclysm of World War I that predicated major events of the twenties and thirties. Certainly for the United States, World War I and its immediate aftermath, including the terms of the Treaty of Versailles, set the stage for subsequent trauma: the foundering of Woodrow Wilson's presidency, postwar disillusionment over the Allies' aims, American isolationism, the Red Scare, race riots, Prohibition, the emergence of the mob.

So the era of the Great Depression cannot be fully understood without first garnering at least some modest knowledge of the decade that preceded it. The Treaty of Versailles, finally signed on June 28, 1919, after months of haggling, is a good starting point. This controversial settlement partitioned the Austro-Hungarian Empire into autonomous states; awarded the Danzig (Gdańsk) corridor to Poland, dividing Prussia into separated areas; ceded Germany's Saar coal mines to France; mandated Allied occupation of the Rhineland for 15 years; granted the Allies the right to try Kaiser Wilhelm II for war crimes; awarded German colonies in Africa to the Allies; and imposed a monumental reparations bill on Germany—among other onerous stipulations. The only concession that President Woodrow Wilson had won at the Paris Peace Conference in his quest for a "just and honorable peace" based on his Fourteen Points was the creation of the League of Nations (a precursor to the United Nations). The harsh terms of the Treaty of Versailles, Great Britain's prime minister David Lloyd George observed at the time, predestinated a German hunger for revenge and set the stage for a larger war within 25 years.

Whether the Treaty of Versailles directly fomented the advent of World War II in Europe—and prevailing historical judgment argues that it did not—the treaty's terms, perceived by the Germans to be a "dictated peace" (*Diktat*), most certainly provided the catalyst for resurgent German nationalism and the political destabilization of the Weimar Republic during the 1920s. The treaty's stipulations bred the widespread view among Germans that their generals and politicians had betrayed them—that they had been "stabbed in the back" and

1

forced to accept a dishonorable peace settlement that violated Wilson's Fourteen Points, even though they had never actually been defeated. As peoples' actions and responses derive from their perceptions of reality, from what they believe to be true but more than likely is not, so for the Germans the prevailing view of the Diktat provided a compelling dogma that generated desires for exoneration, remediation, and vengeance. Adolf Hitler and other extremists would exploit these perceptions and desires aggressively. The Weimar Republic, plagued as well by severe economic turmoil and inflation resulting largely from the financial burdens imposed by the Treaty of Versailles, foundered as a consequence. Furthermore, in the Middle East, the Mediterranean, Asia, and Africa, the Peace of Paris and its related developments established conditions and mandates—including arbitrary boundaries for new nations in the Balkans, creation of Iraq under British control, denial of promised Arab independence, recognition of the Zionist movement's claims for inhabiting areas of Palestine, and other circumstances—whose repercussions continue to trouble the world to the present time.

Ironically, the one concession Wilson achieved, the League of Nations, proved to be his undoing. On July 10, the president personally delivered the Treaty of Versailles (264 pages in length) to the U.S. Senate; the treaty would have to be approved by a two-thirds vote. The Senate rejected the treaty in November and again in March 1920 on a second consideration. The major reservation to the treaty motivating his Senate opponents was recognition of and membership in the League of Nations.

Wilson, his health destroyed by his strenuous effort to secure ratification (he had traversed more than 8,000 miles in a single month of speech-making) and his stature reduced by the vitriolic comments of Senate opponents such as Henry Cabot Lodge and William E. Borah, was a broken man, unable to fulfill his duties after suffering a stroke.

PROHIBITION, RACISM, LABOR UNREST

Coincident with the struggle over the treaty came the onset of Prohibition. The Eighteenth Amendment to the Constitution secured ratification by the requisite number of states in January 1919. In October 1919, Congress passed the Volstead Act, enabling legislation for enforcement of Prohibition to begin in January 1920. The act defined an "intoxicating" beverage as one containing more than 0.5 percent alcohol and resulted in creation of the bootlegging industry to satisfy Americans' desire for stronger stuff. Gangster "Scarface" Al Capone moved from New York to Chicago to be in the right place to take best advantage of the boot-legging opportunities presented. Within a few years he had 700 hoodlums and the suburb of Cicero under his complete control.

Chicago was also the scene of one of the worst race riots of the century. Demobilized African-American troops, believing their contribution to the fighting had earned them a better stake in America, found a new spokesman for militancy in Marcus Garvey when they returned home from Europe and World War I. But whites had little desire to make concessions, and race riots broke out all over the nation in the summer of 1919. In the Chicago riot, which lasted 13 days, 38 people died and more than 500 were injured, mostly blacks. Partly in reaction to the riots but also reflecting a rising intolerance of immigrants, Jews, and Catholics, the Ku Klux Klan experienced a rebirth in the early twenties, gaining enormous political clout not only in the southern states but also in some states of the Midwest and even the Pacific Coast. Through the efforts of Edward Y. Clarke of the Southern Publicity Association and Imperial Wizard Hiram W. Evans, the Klan attained some 4.5 million members by the end of 1924.

The social and political tensions that racial animosity exposed were made worse by labor unrest in the fall of 1919 in the midst of a postwar depression that threw hundreds of thousands out of work while the cost of living spiraled upward. In September the Boston police went on strike, demanding higher wages and better working conditions. Subsequent riots and looting resulted in the intervention of the Massachusetts militia. The police capitulated and agreed to return to duty; but the police commissioner, supported by Governor Calvin Coolidge, dismissed them all and hired a new force. Also in September, 300,000 steelworkers, some belonging to the American Federation of Labor (AFL), began a nationwide strike to secure a shorter workweek—in some mills the workers toiled seven days a week, 12 hours each day. Violence followed in

Members of the Ku Klux Klan parading down Pennsylvania Avenue, Washington, D.C., 1926 *(Library of Congress)*

some mill towns, causing the dispatch of federal troops, and by the year's end the strike had failed. Coal miners belonging to the United Mine Workers of America (UMWA), led by John L. Lewis, struck for higher wages and a shorter workweek. A board of arbitration awarded the strikers a 27 percent wage increase but no reduction in hours.

THE 1920 ELECTION

The presidential election year of 1920 was a turning point in the United States. For one thing, it marked a milestone for American women, as the Nineteenth Amendment to the Constitution attained ratification in August, awarding women the right to vote in subsequent national elections. And those elections would offer a far broader choice than many previous ones. For example, in the presidential election of 1920 seven parties fielded candidates—Republican, Democratic, Farmer-Labor, Single Tax, Prohibition, Socialist Labor, and Socialist. The Socialists, originally one party, had split into two camps, with the courageous Eugene V. Debs heading the Socialist Party. Imprisoned by the Wilson government along with some 20,000 others for sedition because of his public opposition to World War I, Debs campaigned from his cell—the first imprisoned man ever to run for president—and received nearly a million votes.

Socialist activity worldwide, linked with the labor strikes in the United States, the perceived threat of communism resulting from the Bolshevik Revolution of 1917, and the deployment of Allied troops (British, French, and American) in Russia in 1919 to try to destroy the Bolsheviks and restore the czarist government, contributed to the Red Scare of 1920 and the resultant massive arrests of anarchists and other political agitators. Bomb plots abounded, fueling the scare. One bomb detonated on Wall Street in September 1920 caused 38 deaths. The so-called Palmer Raids—launched by Wilson's attorney general, A. Mitchell Palmer, and the Justice Department's new head of the Bureau of Investigation, J. Edgar Hoover, to suppress the "Reds"—rounded up thousands of suspected radicals, including hundreds of aliens who were summarily deported. Many Americans protested against the raids as violations of civil liberties.

The Republican candidate for president, Senator Warren G. Harding of Ohio, with Coolidge a vice presidential candidate, won the 1920 election handily with the promise of a return to "normalcy" following the tumult of war, revolution, race riots, labor unrest, and political hostility between president and Congress. His inauguration in March 1921 brought Republican dominance of the federal government and policies to encourage capitalist enterprise, ushering in the Roaring Twenties, sometimes referred to as the "age of excess." Ironically, it was the ostensibly conservative Harding who would pardon Debs, freeing him from prison, an act Wilson had adamantly refused to consider.

THE HARDING YEARS

The war years had brought prosperity, but the Harding presidency began in depression. The United States' gross national product (GNP, the total value of goods produced) had nearly doubled from $37.1 billion in 1902 to $73.3 billion in 1920, with commensurate increases in productivity in both agriculture and manufacturing. Union memberships soared along with the economic growth. Stimulants to the economy during the war years included booming exports of agricultural products, federal price supports for crops, loans to Great Britain and France, and greatly expanded demand for manufactured goods, especially war supplies and cars. Motor vehicle registrations rose from 468,000 in 1910 to more than 9.2 million in 1920. The federal budget increased tenfold, from $500 million in 1902 to $5 billion in 1920. Unfortunately the war had also generated $21 billion in federal debt. With the war's end, economic collapse ensued.

Perhaps hardest hit by the collapse were America's farmers. They had prospered during the war. Estimates indicate that the value of farm produce rose from $4 billion in 1914 to $10 billion in 1918, providing farmers with an

Secretary of the Treasury Andrew Mellon *(Library of Congress)*

enormous increase in income and purchasing power; many of them invested this windfall in more land, and land prices had skyrocketed, especially in the Midwest. Now as wartime demand for American produce dissipated and European farms began returning to production, the prices American agricultural products could command abroad began to fall. At the end of May 1920 the Harding administration announced the end of wheat price supports. Wheat subsequently dropped from $2.50 a bushel to under $1.00, and the prices of all other agricultural products soon dropped also. Farmers faced disaster—bankruptcies, foreclosures, dispossessions. They would experience little hope of recovery throughout the twenties, despite federal programs to provide low-cost loans and to impose higher tariffs on agricultural imports.

Big business, however, confronted a bright future. The corporations had stalwart champions in Harding's secretary of the treasury, Andrew W. Mellon, and secretary of commerce, Herbert Hoover. An unyielding opponent of progressive taxes, most certainly those created by the Wilson administration to help pay for the war, Mellon set about pressuring Congress to reduce taxes for corporations and the wealthy and to transfer the tax burden largely to those in the middle- and lower-income brackets. Business leaders could also take heart from Harding's approval of an act to rationalize the budget process by creating a budget director to advise the president on the annual budget and a comptroller general to audit all the government accounts. New legislation (the Fordney-McCumber Tariff Act) canceled the lower tariffs instituted by the 1913 Underwood Act, substantially increased tariffs on manufactured goods, and gave the president the authority, in some circumstances, to raise or lower tariffs as much as 50 percent (Harding would mostly raise them). American oil companies' interests in particular were favored by the Harding administration's policies, especially by approval of a revived treaty with Colombia that eased that nation's lingering disgruntlement over the United States' intervention to effect the independence of Panama. Both domestic and foreign policies, then, became means of benefiting American commercial interests.

Harding's presidency, most historians judge, marked a new record for nonachievement and corruption. Not that Harding was hopelessly incompetent; but he was, even by his own admission, some contend, out of his depth. Nor apparently was he corrupt personally, but he allowed his administration to be exploited by associates who were. Actually the judgment that Harding achieved little or nothing during his tenure as president may be overly harsh, given the brevity of his administration. His able secretary of state, Charles Evans Hughes, assisted by members of Congress as delegates to the Washington Conference held in November 1922, negotiated reductions in naval forces among Great Britain, Japan, the United States, France, and other nations; prohibition of the use of poison gases; and recognition of the rights of the signatories to their territories in the Pacific—a rare instance of international cooperation. The president secured congressional approval of the Sheppard-Towner Maternity Act, which provided federal funding to states that established health care programs for mothers and infants—social welfare legislation that anticipated New Deal proposals. Harding made four appointments to the Supreme Court—former president William Howard Taft, George Sutherland, Pierce Butler, and Edward Sanford—but none emerged as a distinguished jurist. Evidencing some enlightenment, especially compared to his Progressive predecessor who had appointed avowed racists to important posts in his administration, Harding publicly criticized the system of segregation in the South and sought passage of a law that would give federal courts jurisdiction over trials for lynchings.

As for corruption, that charge sticks. Cronies known as the "Ohio Gang" (Harding's home state) had succeeded in getting Harry M. Daugherty installed as attorney general. In this post Daugherty was able to provide protection to his bootlegger friends and defraud the government of funds from bonds. As head of the Veterans' Bureau, Charles I. Forbes apparently siphoned off $200 million from his agency through sales of supplies and through fraudulent land and construction deals. There were numerous other scandals. Most notorious of them all was the Teapot Dome scandal. Teapot Dome in Wyoming was the site of naval oil reserves that Albert B. Fall, Harding's secretary of the interior, managed to get control of from the navy in exchange for other reserves in California; Fall then accepted bribes to lease the Teapot Dome reserves to private firms. None of these scandals became known to the public until after Harding's sudden death in San Francisco on August 2, 1923.

COOLIDGE PROSPERITY

As vice president, Coolidge succeeded Harding. Since he largely shared his predecessor's economic views—Coolidge would declare succinctly that "the business of America is business"—there was no change in policy except for a new emphasis on honesty. All but one of Harding's cabinet officers retained their posts. The exception was the suspect Daugherty, who was replaced by Harlan Fiske Stone, whom Coolidge would later appoint to the Supreme Court. Under the authority of the Fordney-McCumber Act, Coolidge continued Harding's policy of raising tariffs on imports, which decreased American foreign trade and exacerbated the farmers' problems. This policy also crippled the European nations' ability to repay war debts. Nevertheless, the great economic boom of the twenties now replaced the postwar depression—except, unfortunately, for farmers, African Americans, and Hispanics. The depression, along with the ending of wartime government protection of each worker's right to join a union, had also diminished organized labor's influence in seeking better wages and hours, and the numbers of union members would fall through the remainder of the decade.

Having secured the blessing of America's business leaders, Coolidge easily won the Republican nomination for the presidency on the first and only ballot at the party's convention in 1924. As part of its platform, the party advocated opposition to nullifying war debts and to the League of Nations and acceptance of the World Court. At their convention the Democrats quarreled over the League of Nations and the Ku Klux Klan. The delegates fudged the League issue, rendering dead any hope of official American recognition of that institution. The conflict between urban and rural elements of the party over the Klan ended in stalemate, with no mention of the Klan in the platform. But the vehemence of the conflict exacted a heavy toll: It took 103 ballots to nominate John W. Davis, a lawyer from West Virginia and former congressman and ambassador to Great Britain. With the slogan "Keep Cool with Coolidge," an appeal to continuing the economic good times most Americans were experiencing, the president had no trouble defeating Davis and all the minor party candidates, including the popular Wisconsin liberal Senator Robert M. La Follette, candidate of the Committee for Progressive Political Action (CPPA).

Coolidge's decisive election enabled the success of his policies in Congress. Secretary Mellon finally got his way with taxes: The tax law of 1926 reduced both the federal surtax and estate tax rate from 40 percent to 20 percent and eliminated the gift tax—adding up to a boon for the wealthy. Business leaders persuaded Coolidge of the virtue of expanding credit, thereby fueling the economy. The money flowing into the financial network encouraged banks to buy government bonds and to loan investors funds for purchasing stocks and bonds, including European securities, and real estate. The banks also prompted installment buying (credit financing). However questionable the easy credit policies may have been—resulting in a growing burden of indebtedness and many uncollectible loans—they generated enormous prosperity in the United States and a semblance of it in Europe. Corporate net income in the United States surged from $8.3 billion in 1923 to $10.6 billion in 1928, a 28 percent increase. The great majority of Americans, again excepting the farmers, shared in the prosperity. Even industrial workers saw their earnings increase during these five years by 8 percent, while the average workweek shortened by nearly two hours to 45.7 hours. Average unemployment never exceeded 3.7 percent. The boom was enhanced by increased mechanization of production; cheaper electrical power; and new growth industries, such as automobiles, refrigerators, radios, and movies.

Continuing an anti-immigration policy begun by the Harding administration with the 1921 Emergency Quota Act, the Coolidge administration imposed further restrictions through still lower quotas based on national origins mandated by the Immigration Act of 1924, which reduced the average influx of immigrants from 700,000 per year to 300,000 (by 1927 to only 150,000) and effectively excluded Japanese immigration. The act generated resentment in Europe. Even Coolidge's adamant insistence on the repayment of war debts further irritated relations with the European nations, already distressed over high American tariffs.

Germany, reconstituted as the Weimar Republic following the war, defaulted on paying most of its reparations bills, but the burden of the payments it did make and the lingering effects of its war-shattered economy generated explosive inflation and threatened it with economic collapse. The Dawes Plan (named for Director of the Budget Charles Gates Dawes), put forth by the Americans and accepted by the Allies and Germany in September 1924, provided for a five-year graduated schedule of payments by Germany and reorganization of the German currency and the Reichsbank. The Coolidge administration fostered the plan, of course, because reparations payments would help the Allies pay their debts to the United States. Germany was able to meet the payment schedule, but only through borrowing heavily abroad (especially in the United States); and during 1925, the German economy finally began to show signs of ultimate recovery.

Such efforts to encourage prosperity abroad in order to sustain it at home were nearly the sum of the Coolidge foreign policy, given mostly to isolationism, except for continuing though lessening the United States' recurrent interventions in the affairs of the Latin American nations and the administration's involvement in two initiatives to engender world peace. The first peace initiative was a conference in 1927 at Geneva to discuss further reductions in naval forces that Coolidge sponsored in the wake of the so-called Locarno Treaty, a series of nonaggression agreements the Europeans had negotiated at Locarno, Italy—these included demilitarization of the Rhineland, German treaties to arbitrate differences with neighboring nations, and French mutual assistance pacts with Poland and Czechoslovakia. Unfortunately the French and Italians rejected participation in the Geneva conference, which meant only Great Britain, Japan, and the United States were involved and that nothing of substance was accomplished. The second initiative was a "declaration renouncing war as an instrument of national policy" and promising the resolution of disputes by "pacific means"; it was designed by Foreign Minister Aristide Briand of France and Secretary of State Frank B. Kellogg, who succeeded Hughes in 1925. The Kellogg-Briand Treaty, as it was known, became the Pact of Paris in August 1928 with the endorsement of 15 nations. Afterward it was signed by the Soviet Union, which the Wilson, Harding, and Coolidge administrations refused to recognize as a sovereign nation because of their opposition to communism.

PASTIMES AND PLEASURES

With developments abroad relatively peaceful and at home unusually prosperous, Americans turned to the pleasures afforded by automobiles, radio broadcasting, motion pictures, sports, and other indulgences. Americans' love affair with the car began in the twenties. By 1929 the automotive manufacturers were producing 4,455,000 cars per year (plus thousands of trucks and buses), and more than 23 million cars were registered to owners. The federal government did its share, by providing assistance to pay for constructing 190,000 miles of road. And the automotive industry had become the nation's most important business; its annual production at the end of 1930 was valued at $3.5 billion. The industry also fueled the growth of numerous other industries (steel, rubber, oil) and created new ones (service stations, garages, roadhouses)—all, of course, contributing to increased water, soil, and air pollution. The petroleum industry, for example, leaped ahead, stimulated by a 500 percent increase in the consumption of gasoline during the decade. But cars did not merely spur the economy; they caused major changes in the way Americans lived. Cars brought mobility to farmers, forced the revamping of city streets, accelerated the development of suburbs, and may have provided a major impetus for revolutionizing women's fashions (with skirts rising to knee length making it easier to get in and out of cars).

Although preeminent, cars were not the only fascination for Americans among changing modes of transportation. The airplane also commanded attention. More than likely, the interest derived largely from public enthrallment with the solo flight of Charles A. Lindbergh from New York to Paris in 1927 and the hero worship his feat evoked. Additional interest ensued when Amelia Earhart became the first woman aviator to make a solo transatlantic flight the following year.

It was during the twenties that radio was born. On November 2, 1920, KDKA in Pittsburgh, operated by the Westinghouse Electric Company, became the first broadcasting radio station in the nation. Twenty-one other stations had joined KDKA by 1922, and by 1929 there were 606 stations nationwide, about one-third of them controlled by either the National Broadcasting Company (NBC, founded in 1926) or the Columbia Broadcasting System (CBS, founded in 1927). Another new industry was born. Total annual sales of radios jumped from $60 million in 1922 to more than $842 million in 1929. In an effort to systematize broadcasting, Congress established the Federal Radio Commission in 1927 to award licenses and wavebands. The new radio network introduced regular broadcasting of news, religious services, sports, music, and entertainment programs. It offered regular broadcast features such as *Amos 'n' Andy,* Bing Crosby, Jack Benny, and Rudy Vallee and created a new means of advertising.

The burgeoning popularity of motion pictures during the twenties created yet another giant industry, including the construction of palatial cinemas in cities and towns throughout North America. Receipts from ticket sales more than doubled from $301 million in 1921 to $720 million in 1929 as average attendance climbed from 40 million to 80 million per week. By the end of the decade Adolph Zukor's Paramount Pictures alone controlled 1,600 movie theaters; Paramount's rivals Warner Brothers and Metro-Goldwyn-Mayer controlled hundreds more—all three firms were major film producers as well. Sound began creeping into the theaters by 1925, and in October 1927 Warner Brothers released the first movie with spoken dialogue plus singing, *The Jazz Singer,* starring Al Jolson. The star system had emerged, transforming actors such as Charlie Chaplin, Mary Pickford, Buster Keaton, Gloria Swanson, Greta Garbo, John Barrymore, and Douglas Fairbanks into celebrities as Hollywood assumed dominance in the international film industry.

Baseball continued as the national pastime—despite being rocked by stories revealing the scandal of the "fixed" 1919 World Series that occupied the sports pages in 1920. Annual attendance at major league games averaged between 9 million and 10 million throughout the decade. Babe Ruth was the king of the sport, hitting his record 60 home runs in 1927. That was also the year of the second heavyweight championship boxing match between Jack Dempsey and Gene Tunney—a Chicago rematch of the renowned 1926 fight that brought in $2.6 million. Bobby Jones was the star of the professional golf circuit; Bill Tilden, of tennis. Knute Rockne, coach of the Notre Dame University football team, held similar stature in his sport. To an unprecedented degree, Americans indulged themselves in spectator sports, but they also—men and now women as well—took up tennis, swimming, golf, and bowling on their own in increased numbers. Of some note, the swimming scene became transformed when, in September 1921, Atlantic City held its first Miss America Beauty Pageant, in which contestants introduced one-piece swimsuits that exposed the legs to above the knees.

On a quite different level, Gertrude Ederle excited public attention in 1926, when she became the first woman to swim the English Channel. Five men had preceded her in swimming the channel, but Ederle surpassed the record swim by more than two hours, despite encountering hard rains, turbulent waters, riptides, huge waves, flotsam, and even sharks. Following her return home to the United States, the 19-year-old reaped acclaim nationwide, with a

Babe Ruth *(Library of Congress)*

ticker-tape parade in her home city of New York, numerous celebrations and receptions, a meeting with President Coolidge, a vaudeville tour, and a role as herself in the movie *Swim, Girl, Swim.*

Fads seem to be an ever-present feature of American society, and, perhaps symptomatic of the decade's exuberance, the twenties witnessed a plethora of them. Some were bizarre, others punishing. Among the latter, marathon dancing propelled couples into at times hundreds of hours of dancing, resulting in extreme fatigue and incapacity. Perhaps the most bizarre of the 1920s fads, flagpole sitting emerged in Hollywood in 1924, when former sailor and inept boxer Alvin "Shipwreck" Kelly ensconced himself atop a flagpole for 13 hours, 13 minutes. The feat garnered Kelly so much publicity that he traversed the nation to replicate it in numerous cities. For the remainder of the decade Kelly's exploits inspired others, including many teenagers, to follow his example. By 1929 youngsters nationwide battled for fame as winners of the Juvenile Flagpole Sitting Championship of the World.

ARTS AND LITERATURE

The twenties marked a golden age in American literature and significant developments in painting, architecture, and music. The names alone of American writers of the "lost generation," so dubbed by Gertrude Stein, reveal the literary achievement: F. Scott Fitzgerald, Ezra Pound, T. S. Eliot, Ernest Hemingway, E. E. Cummings, Langston Hughes, William Faulkner, John Dos Passos, and Eugene O'Neill. They joined predecessors such as Willa Cather, Wallace Stevens, and Sinclair Lewis, who produced major works during the decade. In fact, all of Lewis's notable work—such parodies of the middle class as *Main Street, Babbitt,* and *Arrowsmith*—appeared in the twenties; he was the first American writer to receive the Nobel Prize in literature, in 1930. Theodore Dreiser's literary monument, *An American Tragedy,* also appeared in 1925. (On a rather different plane, but of long-term import, in 1922 DeWitt and Lila Wallace founded *Reader's Digest* in the basement of their Greenwich Village home; by 1940 the magazine would have a nationwide readership of 7 million.) This was also the era of the so-called Harlem Renaissance, a literary flowering centered in New York City's black community of Harlem. Among its most accomplished writers were James Weldon Johnson, Claude McKay, Countee Cullen, and Langston Hughes—and later Zora Neale Hurston. Painters and sculptors, such as Aaron Douglas, Meta Warwick Fuller, William H. Johnson, and Palmer Hayden were also involved. Harlem was also a major source of jazz creativity. In addition, historians and sociologists produced reinterpretations or seminal studies of life in America past and present, such as Charles and Mary Beard's monumental history *The Rise of American Civilization* (1927) and Robert and Helen Lynd's revealing study of life in a "typical" city, *Middletown* (1929).

Reflecting such European art developments as cubism, American painting moved in new directions. The famous photographer Alfred Steiglitz introduced the works of American abstractionists—Arthur Dove, Charles Demuth, and Georgia O'Keeffe—at his gallery in New York City. Other artists, such as George Bellows, Thomas Hart Benton, Edward Hopper, and Charles Sheeler, whose works more clearly reveal the preoccupations of the era, pursued a native realist tradition. The opening of the Museum of Modern Art in New York City in 1929, however, suggested the beginning of a more experimental art era. In architecture the skyscraper, invented by the Chicago school of architects (William LeBaron Jenney, Louis Sullivan, John Wellborn Root, and others) before the turn of the century, came into its own, not by way of new styles or developments but rather by its proliferation in cities across the continent. The popularity of Raymond Hood's Tribune Building (completed 1925) in Chicago and William Van Allen's Chrysler Building (completed 1930) and Shreve, Lamb & Harmon's Empire State Building (completed 1931) in New York symbolized the skyscraper's dominance and the prevailing taste as well. The decade was distinguished for advancements in building technology and height, though not in design. Nevertheless, Frank Lloyd Wright returned to the United States in 1922 after a four-year stay in Japan and resumed work here on a small scale at least, designing houses to suit the Southern California terrain. And immigrant European architects Raymond Schindler, Richard Neutra, William Lescaze, and Eliel Saarinen introduced new, unadorned, cubistic forms into American architecture though remaining relatively unknown during the decade.

In American music, achievement approaches that for literature. It was apt that F. Scott Fitzgerald christened the twenties the Jazz Age. Introduced through Dixieland jazz music in the war years, jazz flourished in new styles during the twenties. Paul Whiteman's orchestra made jazz a familiar sound nationwide after 1924. But the new jazz took its most fruitful inspiration from the blues performed by legendary African-American singers and performers such as Leadbelly (Huddie Ledbetter) and Bessie Smith. White musicians joined in. Jazz greats Louis Armstrong, Bix Biederbeck, Hoagy Carmichael, Duke Ellington, Fletcher Henderson, and Benny Goodman saw their careers blossom by mid-decade. It was the heyday of New York's Cotton Club and other night spots devoted to the new music. George Gershwin's career as a composer arose out of this jazz scene to attain fruition with *Rhapsody in Blue* (1924) and *An American in Paris* (1928). Musicals such as Sigmund Romberg's *The Student Prince* (1924) and *The Desert Song* (1926) and Jerome Kern's *Showboat* (1927) sustained the popularity of this genre. Classical music also burgeoned. The three most renowned music schools in the nation—Eastman in Rochester, New York; Juilliard in New York City; and Curtis in Philadelphia—were founded in the twenties. Well-known conductors such as Leopold Stokowski and Arturo Toscanini guided orchestras in major U.S. cities to international preeminence. These orchestras performed Aaron Copland's new compositions, some adopting jazz rhythms and themes.

CAUSES, SCIENCE, AND CRUSADES

Thus, beneath the surface calm of the Harding and Coolidge presidencies the nation evidenced fermenting cultural change. And many of the intellectuals involved in the literary and artistic developments of the twenties also became involved in other events that indicated fundamental tensions and conflicts in American society. Among the most noteworthy of these events were the trial and execution of Nicola Sacco and Bartolomeo Vanzetti and the trial of John Thomas Scopes. During the Red Scare period, a period in the 1920s of strong anticommunist sentiment, a shoe factory robbery in South Braintree, Massachusetts, resulted in two deaths. The Italian immigrant anarchists Sacco and Vanzetti were arrested, convicted, and sentenced to death for the crime. Intellectual leaders such as Harvard law professor Felix Frankfurter, novelist John Dos Passos, and poet Edna St. Vincent Millay protested the trial and sentencing as an injustice; despite their efforts, the two men were executed on August 23, 1927.

By contrast, not politics but religion formed the context of the 1925 trial of Scopes, accused of teaching the theory of evolution to his high school classes in Dayton, Tennessee, in violation of state law. Scopes was in fact guilty, he had broken the law to provide a test case of its constitutionality. The renowned lawyer Clarence Darrow, who had the year before successfully evoked an insanity plea that spared murderers Nathan Leopold and Richard Loeb from execution, came to town to defend Scopes. His opponent was William Jennings Bryan, frequent presidential candidate and Wilson's first secretary of state, whose intent was to uphold the Genesis creation myth and the sanctity of the Bible. The trial generated extensive newspaper coverage, with the caustic journalist H. L. Mencken on the spot to denounce Bryan's supporters as bigots. The jury found Scopes guilty. Despite the theatrics surrounding the trial, it highlighted the confrontation between science and religion.

Science, perhaps most notably the relatively new discipline of psychology, enjoyed a major vogue during the twenties. Sigmund Freud's theories on human sexuality contributed to changes in child-rearing techniques and sexual mores. J. B. Watson's behaviorist concepts emphasized the role of environmental influences in the development of personality. Carl Jung propounded theories of personality types, such as extroverts and introverts. In short, psychology inspired intense interest in behavioral and personality analysis. The cosmos itself also assumed new contours as the theories of Albert Einstein, who achieved worldwide renown with verification of his theory of relativity in 1919 and the award of the Nobel Prize in physics in 1921, revolutionized concepts of time, light, mass, and energy. Americans Robert Milliken and Arthur Compton won the Nobel Prize in physics in 1923 and 1927, respectively, enhancing the stature of scientific inquiry in the United States, where the sciences enjoyed increased emphasis in the curricula of colleges and universities, and student enrollments nearly doubled during the decade. The general high regard for scientific knowledge and method of course had some impact on traditional religious beliefs.

Still, religion continued as a major influence in American life, one that in many ways curiously mirrored the business climate of the 1920s. Fundamentalist denominations gained adherents during the decade, and the millionaire evangelist Billy Sunday retained his huge following. From his pulpit in the Tabernacle in Indianapolis or at revivals at Winona Lake and in major cities, he railed against socialists, immigrants, dancing, the "new woman," and other presumed threats to the stability of American society. In Los Angeles evangelism's promoter was Aimee Semple McPherson, who forged a national audience through radio broadcasts (on her own station) from her Angelus Temple, where in 1926 she founded the International Church of the Foursquare Gospel. In that same year she created a sensation by disappearing for more than a month. When she reappeared, she claimed she had been kidnapped, when actually she had been on an extended tryst with her married lover, but her flock never knew for sure and never lost faith in her leadership and healing. McPherson also created a business empire and a sizable fortune by presenting religion as Hollywood spectacle. Perhaps the greatest evangelist of the time, however, was the man who made a religion of business. That man was advertising entrepreneur Bruce Barton, whose reinterpretation of Christ's ministry, *The Man Nobody Knows,* was the bestselling nonfiction work in the nation in both 1925 and 1926. Ascribing to Jesus such qualities as "the will to success," Barton touted Jesus as "the founder of modern business." No wonder the twenties reaped such exceptional prosperity.

Americans' fascination with novel or exotic fads and diversions also materialized in the twenties. Mah-jongg, a Chinese game played with engraved tiles and adapted for Western use, was extremely popular, for example. People avidly followed reports on explorations of the chambers of Tutankhamen's tomb in the years following announcement of the tomb's discovery published in December 1922. In 1925 newspaper attention transformed the entrapment of Floyd Collins in a Kentucky cave into an ongoing headline story. It was perhaps the newspapers that set the tone for people's preoccupations. This was the period in which chains such as Scripps-Howard and Hearst gained control of papers in cities throughout the country and could thereby channel features, comics, editorials, and stories of their choice to a national readership—an inducement toward nationally shared tastes, interests, amusements, and preoccupations.

The frothy context of the 1920s—profound disillusionment with concepts of valor, honor, and service following the war; a fringe area of radical politics; strikes, racial conflicts, political and business scandals; Prohibition, bootlegging, organized crime; the huge popularity of cars, radios, movies, and the new values they entailed; the emergence of giant corporations and entirely new industries—supposedly caused a revolution in Americans' values, morals, and behavior. Certain changes are readily apparent, of course; others remain arguable. Organized crime, for example, effectively transformed crime into a corporate business, and its major source of revenue, bootlegging, changed American drinking habits: Before Prohibition beer had been the most favored drink; now hard liquor prevailed.

There was a clearly significant demographic change: The population grew from 106 million in 1920 to 123 million in 1930 and at the same time became largely urbanized—a dramatic shift from 54 million urban dwellers in 1920 to 69 million in 1930, while the farm population fell from 31.6 million to 30.4 million in the same period. The remaining 23.6 million lived in small towns.

City living in itself no doubt suggests differences in values and behavior. Fitzgerald, whose novels perhaps come as close as any fiction can to chronicling the life of this urban milieu, summarized the twenties in one sentence in his posthumously published work *The Crack-Up:* "It was an age of miracles, it was an age of art, it was an age of excess, and it was an age of satire." In many ways, then, it seemed an age that debauched or denied traditional values in all aspects of American life, not taking either itself or its legacy quite seriously; or at least it was an age perceived by many—both advocates and opponents of change—as a period of rebellion against the prevalent values of the prewar era. This perception of revolutionary change perhaps best suggested itself in the lives of women.

WOMEN'S EMANCIPATION

Women had gone to work in traditionally male jobs during the war, but they returned to homemaking afterward. Nevertheless, in the twenties, 2 million women entered the workforce, although mostly in nursing, teaching, clerical, and clerking jobs where their presence had long been accepted. Electric-powered, laborsaving machines—refrigerators, clothes washers, vacuum cleaners—eased the burden of women's traditional household duties, as did new products such as packaged and frozen foods. Other new products such as sanitary napkins and contraceptive devices—crusader Margaret Sanger founded the American Birth Control League in 1921—provided women greater independence. Women intellectuals embraced Sigmund Freud's concepts as a rationale for pursuing freer sexual behavior. Changes in women's fashions also reflected a growing liberalization of behavior, with hemlines rising above the knee and with exposed necks and shoulders. The "flapper" look defied prewar rules of decorum and in some states prodded legislators to introduce bills that would regulate skirt lengths and other features of women's clothing. Many women now felt comfortable smoking and drinking in public. They styled their hair in short "bobs" and wore makeup—overt rebellion against earlier standards. (Despite Prohibition, it was now chic to drink for both men and women; the speakeasies thrived as the public flouted efforts to enforce Prohibition, ineffectual as they were, and bootlegging became a major industry.) Beauty parlors mushroomed along with spectacular growth in the cosmetics industry, clearly indicating that the "new woman" took a keen interest in her appearance, with whatever sexual or moral overtones that suggested. Not all women joined in the revolution, of course. Some older feminists in fact chastised the young who embraced the "new woman" lifestyle as self-indulgent and indifferent to the struggle for women's equality. Perhaps the critics were right, as voting rights and greater independence in fact did not translate into increased involvement of women in public life, politics, or even voting.

THE 1928 ELECTION

In August 1927, as election year 1928 approached, Coolidge announced that he would not again seek the presidency, his for the asking. In June the following year the candidacy of the Republican Party fell to Herbert Hoover, a Quaker, a California engineer, a self-made millionaire, a nonpolitician who had never run for elective office but was highly regarded by the public for his humanitarianism as head of the American Relief Committee and the United States Food Administration during the war years and for his achievements as secretary of commerce. The Republican convention nominated Senator Charles Curtis of Kansas to be Hoover's running mate. The Democratic Party also convened in June and nominated Alfred E. Smith, governor of New York, product of the Tammany Hall political machine, Roman Catholic, and a strong foe of Prohibition. His running mate was Senator Joseph T. Robinson of Arkansas, a strong proponent of Prohibition. Smith's religion became an issue, costing him many votes among Protestants, and public contentment with prosperity served Hoover. The result was predictable: Hoover carried 40 states. He reappointed Mellon as secretary of the treasury; Henry L. Stimson became secretary of state. With prosperity now considered a permanent state, it appeared all Hoover had to do was more of the same—continue the Coolidge legacy. Unfortunately for him and the nation, for the world in fact, that would not prove possible.

ASIA AND EUROPE

While the majority of Americans, including the nation's leaders, pursued life in the twenties as if they preferred not knowing what was happening abroad, events in Asia and Europe moved slowly but in retrospect almost inexorably toward the crises that would erupt in the 1930s. As nationalism flared in China, where warlords battled among themselves for dominance and the formation of a unified central government seemed a very unlikely prospect, Japan assumed an ever larger role. The naval treaties of the early twenties had precluded the threat of a naval arms race between Japan and the United States while freeing the Japanese to assume effective control of the Pacific. By the late twenties they were the dominant influence in Manchuria. In Shanghai and Nanjing (Nanking), the military leader Chiang Kai-shek (Jiang Jieshi) was in control, espousing his intent to unify China. Communist leader Mao Zedong (Mao Tse-tung) had united with Chiang in the unification

Joseph Stalin *(Office of War Information, Library of Congress)*

effort but broke with him in 1927 following massacres of Communists by Chiang's forces.

In Europe ominous signs of possible traumas to come were evident. In Germany the Weimar government had been beleaguered by communist insurrectionists and paramilitary bands of right-wing radicals since its establishment in 1919. By early 1920 among the right, the National Socialist German Workers (Nazi) Party appeared with an obscure yet spirited propagandist named Adolf Hitler as spokesman. By the following summer Hitler had become his party's leader. In November 1923, trying to take advantage of economic instability resulting from hyperinflation, Hitler led an attempted coup (the so-called Beer Hall Putsch) in Munich. When the effort failed, he was tried and imprisoned in 1924 in Landsberg, where he would write *Mein Kampf,* a blueprint for the future Third Reich. By the end of the year, Hitler was set free, his book appeared in print in 1925, and the Nazi Party's membership grew slowly to the end of the decade. In 1928 the party captured only a dozen seats among the Reichstag's 491, but astute observers sensed something foreboding. Furthermore, by 1928 Joseph Stalin had emerged as sole leader in the USSR, and Benito Mussolini had solidified his power as Fascist dictator of Italy after being granted authority in 1926 to rule by decree. The players were in place for the tragic drama to come in Europe and Asia.

CHRONICLE OF EVENTS

1919

January 18: Delegates from 27 nations (there is no delegate from Russia) involved in the war against the Central Powers formally convene in Paris to discuss terms of a peace treaty to conclude the 1914–18 war (World War I). The Central Powers (Germany, Austria-Hungary, Bulgaria, and Turkey) have no representation at the conference. The defeated nations will each be presented with a separate treaty, concluded in a suburb of Paris, that contains the final terms for peace and be requested to accept them.

January 25: At the Paris Peace Conference, work begins on drafting a covenant for the League of Nations. President Woodrow Wilson of the United States chairs the committee selected to draft the covenant.

February 14: Delegates to the Paris Peace Conference complete a draft of the Covenant of the League of Nations.

May 7: Representatives of the German government, called to Versailles weeks earlier, receive the treaty containing the final terms for peace resulting from deliberations at the Paris Peace Conference.

June 28: German representatives at Versailles sign the peace treaty presented to them in May—they have no alternative. Among the many treaty conditions hateful to the Germans is Article 231, which forces them to accept sole and total responsibility for causing the war and all the losses resulting from it.

July 10: President Wilson presents in person the Treaty of Versailles to the U.S. Senate, in his speech focusing on the League of Nations as a matter of life and death concern to the future of humanity.

September 3: Wilson, stung by the criticism of his Senate opponents, leaves Washington, D.C., by railroad to begin a strenuous cross-country speaking tour of 17 states, taking his case for ratifying the peace treaty to the American people in a doomed effort to pressure the Senate.

September 11: Senators William Borah and Hiram Johnson begin a speaking tour to voice opposition to American participation in the League of Nations.

October 2: Having returned to the White House after his arduous speaking tour, Wilson suffers a stroke, leaving his left arm and leg paralyzed.

October 28: Overriding the president's veto of the previous day, Congress again passes the Volstead Act, a law providing for the enforcement of Prohibition.

November 19: Senate Democratic supporters of Wilson, joined by a number of Republicans, defeat a resolution of Senator Henry Cabot Lodge that contains 14 reservations to the Covenant of the League of Nations as a condition for ratification of the peace treaty.

1920

January 2: The Justice Department led by Attorney General A. Mitchell Palmer conducts largescale arrests of suspected communists and socialists. About 2,700 suspects are taken into custody by the time the Palmer Raids conclude.

January 8: At the Jackson Day dinner in Washington, D.C., the chairman of the Democratic Party reads a message from Wilson criticizing Senate opponents of the Treaty of Versailles and asserting that the majority of the American people favor the treaty. The president makes a plea for a national referendum on the treaty.

January 10: The League of Nations begins formal operations in Geneva, Switzerland.

January 16: The Volstead Act, empowering the Treasury Department to enforce the provisions of the Eighteenth Amendment to the Constitution prohibiting the manufacture, transportation, or sale of intoxicating liquors (0.5 percent alcohol by volume) officially takes effect.

February 7: Admiral Alexander Kolchak, leader of White Russian forces (loyal to the czar) supported by the Allies intent on defeating the Bolsheviks, is executed in Siberia. He had failed in military engagements with Soviet armies in his march toward Moscow and had fled to Siberia, hoping to find safety among the Allied forces there, but was betrayed by the Czech Legion that had fought for the Allies and was turned over to the Bolsheviks.

February 9: The Senate votes to reconsider the Treaty of Versailles and refers it back to the Foreign Relations Committee.

February 10: The Foreign Relations Committee presents to the Senate the committee's report on the Treaty of Versailles, still containing the 14 reservations of Senator Lodge regarding the League of Nations, which he and other opponents see as a threat to American independence.

February 13: At Wilson's request, Secretary of State Robert Lansing, who had disagreed with the president on policies at the Paris Peace Conference and on details of the League of Nations Covenant but had advocated ratification of the treaty by the Senate, resigns his position. Since Wilson's stroke Lansing has directed foreign policy and presided at cabinet meetings.

March 13: After President Friedrich Ebert and other members of the German Republic government flee Berlin for Dresden, rightist dissidents led by Wolfgang Kapp seize the Chancellory.

March 17: When military support fails to materialize, the Kapp Putsch collapses, and Kapp flees to Sweden. The Ebert government is restored, apparently assuring survival of the Weimar Republic, but the attempted coup arouses the government's suspicions of the military.

March 19: The Senate votes 49-35 in favor of ratifying the Treaty of Versailles with the Lodge reservations, falling short of the needed two-thirds vote. Thus both the treaty and the reservations opposed by Wilson fail to win approval. Technically the United States remains at war with Germany.

April 1: American troops, sent to Russia as part of the Allied effort to defeat the Bolsheviks, withdraw from Siberia.

April 4: General Anton Denikin, commander of the White Russian forces on the southern front, who had driven within 80 miles of Moscow before being routed by Bolshevik counterattacks, turns over the remnants of his command to General Baron Peter Wrangel in the Crimea and leaves for sanctuary in the United States.

April 15: In South Braintree, Massachusetts, robbers steal the payroll of a shoe factory and kill the paymaster and his guard.

May 5: New York City police arrest anarchists Nicola Sacco and Bartolomeo Vanzetti and charge them with the April 15 South Braintree robbery and murder. They will be sent to Dedham, Massachusetts, for trial.

May 8: The Socialist Party of America nominates Eugene V. Debs, currently in federal prison after being convicted of violating the 1918 Espionage Act, as the party's presidential candidate.

May 20: In a joint resolution of both houses, Congress declares an end to the war with Germany. An angry Wilson vetoes the resolution—a veto Congress fails to override.

June 8: The Republican Party Convention meets in Chicago and nominates Senator Warren G. Harding as presidential candidate; Governor Calvin Coolidge is his running mate.

June 25: The International Court of Justice is established at The Hague, Netherlands.

June 28: The Democratic Party Convention meets in San Francisco and nominates Governor James M. Cox as presidential candidate; Franklin Delano Roosevelt is his running mate.

July 2: In a joint resolution, Congress declares war with Germany and Austria-Hungary at an end, reserving all rights secured for the United States by war, armistice, and treaty. Wilson refuses to approve or sign the resolution.

August 26: The Tennessee legislature approves the Nineteenth Amendment to the Constitution, securing its ratification and granting women the right to vote in national elections.

November 2: Harding defeats Cox in the national election, winning the presidency.

November 30: General Wrangel has admitted defeat in the Crimea, and with the help of the French fleet, 150,000 White Russians—both civilians and military—have left for Constantinople (now Istanbul) and permanent exile. The Bolsheviks are in control of Russia.

December 2: Wilson and Leon Bourgeois, French member of the committee that drafted the Covenant of the League of Nations at the Paris Peace Conference, are awarded the Nobel Peace Prize for 1919.

December 23: The Better Government of Ireland Act proposed by British prime minister David Lloyd George is approved by the British Parliament; the law divides Ireland into the Irish Free State, with its own parliament, and Ulster, the six Protestant counties that become part of the United Kingdom of Great Britain and Northern Ireland. This division is unacceptable to Eamon De Valera, leader of the radical wing of the Sinn Fein independence movement, resulting in continuing civil war in Ireland.

1921

March 4: Warren G. Harding is inaugurated as president of the United States.

April 20: With the support of President Harding, the Senate overwhelmingly (69-19) ratifies the Thompson-Urrutia Treaty by which the United States makes amends to Colombia for instigating the

1903 revolution in Panama to gain control over the isthmus—in effect apologizing for the action and paying Colombia $25 million as reparations in exchange for concessions granting U.S. companies opportunity to invest in Colombian oil fields.

May 19: With Harding's signature, the Emergency Quota Act becomes law. It restricts the number of aliens of each nationality admitted to the country during a fiscal year to 3 percent of the number of foreign-born residents of that nationality based on the 1910 census.

May 27: Harding signs the Emergency Tariff Act, imposing enormously high tariffs on 28 agricultural items.

June 10: Harding signs the Budget and Accounting Act creating two offices: the director of the budget to help the president prepare annual budgets and the comptroller general to audit all government accounts. The act gives the president authority to appoint both officials.

June 21: Harding appoints Charles Gates Dawes as first director of the budget.

July 14: At the conclusion of the trial of Sacco and Vanzetti, the jury finds the defendants guilty of murder.

November 12: Postponed by one day so that delegates could attend entombment of the Unknown Soldier at Arlington Cemetery on November 11 (Armistice Day), the Washington Conference convenes to negotiate international arms limitations—representatives of the major European nations (except for Russia, which was not invited), China, and Japan attend.

1922

February 6: Delegates from the United States, Great Britain, France, and Japan at the Washington Conference sign a separate Four-Power Pact that recognizes the rights of the four nations in their island holdings in the Pacific Ocean and commits them to consulting on any controversies occurring in the Pacific. Also signed is the Five-Power Treaty, in which Italy joins the four nations already mentioned in agreeing to cease building battleships for 10 years and to reduce their fleets by fixed ratios and total tonnage (one article also commits the United States, Great Britain, and Japan not to build new fortifications or naval bases in the Pacific); and the Nine-Power Treaty, which recognizes China's independence and supports the Open Door policy but leaves virtually unchanged any concessions Japan and other nations enjoyed in China. The conference ends.

April 1: About 500,000 bituminous coal miners, led by the United Mine Workers of America (UMWA) and its president, John L. Lewis, go on strike after mine operators refuse to renew existing contracts and propose drastic wage cuts.

April 7: Secretary of the Interior Albert B. Fall secretly leases oil reserves at Tea Pot Dome in Wyoming to Harry F. Sinclair, representative of the Canada-based Continental Trading Company.

April 25: Fall secretly leases oil reserves at Elk Hills in California to Edward L. Doheny of the Pan American Petroleum Company.

June 30: Secretary of the Interior Fall is indicted for bribery and conspiracy.

July 1: Railway shopmen, threatened with decreased wages, go on strike, but members of the four major railway brotherhoods do not join them.

September 1: Attorney General Harry Daugherty secures a federal court injunction effectively making the railway shopmen's strike illegal and bringing it to an end.

September 19: Harding, a consistent opponent of granting a bonus to veterans for their services during the war, vetoes a bill passed by Congress that would have granted certificates for bonuses that could be redeemed immediately or held for 20 years.

September 21: Harding signs the Fordney-McCumber Act, which establishes the highest tariffs on imports in the nation's history to this time.

October 30: Menaced by the "March on Rome" of Benito Mussolini's *fascisti* (organized in March 1919 and having grown to 300,000 strong) and by the Italian army's incapacity to resist, King Victor Emmanuel has summoned Mussolini from Milan to assume the premiership and form a cabinet and a new government; the leader of the Fascists arrives triumphant in Rome.

November 7: Archaeologist Howard Carter reaches the sealed entrance to the tomb of Tutankhamen in Egypt.

December 30: Delegates to the Tenth Congress of Soviets, which becomes the First Congress of Soviets of the Union of Socialist Soviet Republics, ratify a treaty of union proposed by Stalin, officially creating the USSR.

Benito Mussolini *(Library of Congress)*

1923

January: On orders from President Raymond Poincaré, disgruntled because an economically blighted Germany has repeatedly failed to deliver on reparations payments to the Allies, French troops occupy the Ruhr region, supplier of four-fifths of Germany's coal and steel, thus further crippling the German economy.

March 25: The fifth Pan-American Conference meets in Santiago, Chile, to draft a treaty specifying that any controversy between American nations that is not resolved through diplomacy or arbitration will be submitted to a commission for settlement before military force is used.

April 9: The Supreme Court, in *Adkins v. Children's Hospital,* decides that a District of Columbia law limiting the workweek for women to 10 hours is unconstitutional.

June 20: Concerned about revelations of wrongdoing by members of his administration and the apparently declining popularity of his presidency, Harding sets out from Washington, D.C., with government officials and his wife on a nationwide speech-making tour to mend fences.

August 2: Harding, who has become ill on his speech-making trip in the West, dies during the night in his San Francisco hotel room, apparently as a result of a burst blood vessel in his brain.

August 3: Shortly before 3:00 A.M., Calvin Coolidge is sworn in as president by his father, a notary, at the family's home in Plymouth Notch, Vermont.

August 31: In the so-called Bucareli agreements, President Álvaro Obregón of Mexico commits his government not to expropriate subsoil holdings owned and developed by foreign firms prior to 1917—a boon to U.S. oil companies.

September 26: German chancellor Gustav Stresemann proclaims the ending of passive resistance efforts against the French in the Ruhr and plans to resume making reparations payments to the Allies.

October 22: German anger over French occupation of the Ruhr has led to riots; separatists seize public buildings at Aix-la-Chapelle and declare a Rhineland Republic, independent of both France and Germany.

November 8: Troops of the Nazi Party, led by Adolf Hitler (head of the party since July 1921) and General Erich Ludendorf (commander of the German armies during the war), stage the so-called Beer Hall Putsch in Munich.

November 9: The Beer Hall Putsch fails under police and military resistance; Ludendorf is arrested; Hitler, Hermann Goering, and other leading Nazis, some wounded, flee.

December 4: Secretary of State Charles Evans Hughes and representatives of the five Central American republics meet in Washington, D.C., in a conference intended to draft treaties to maintain the peace in Central America.

December 15: Coolidge announces appointment of Charles G. Dawes and two other members to a special committee of the Reparations Commission to devise a plan for curtailing inflation in Germany so that the German government can achieve solvency and begin paying reparations. In January, when the French seized control of the Ruhr, the German mark fell to a value of 18,000 to the dollar; by August, to 1 million; by November, to 4 billion—generating economic chaos and the total collapse of Germans' faith in their nation's economy.

1924

January 16: The McNary-Haugen Bill, intended to achieve "parity" in the prices of agricultural commodities, is introduced in both houses of Congress. It would create an Agricultural Export Corporation authorized to buy commodities in the U.S. markets. The corporation would set the prices of the U.S. commodities much higher relative to foreign commodities and sell them abroad for whatever prices they could bring—farmers would pay a tax to cover at least part of the differences in prices.

January 21: Vladimir Lenin, leader of the Bolshevik Revolution and of the Russian government, dies in Moscow. A struggle immediately begins between Joseph Stalin and Leon Trotsky to inherit Lenin's position of leadership of the Communist Party and the nation.

January 22: With the support of the Liberal Party, headed by H. H. Asquith, Ramsay MacDonald, head of the Labour Party, becomes both prime minister and foreign secretary of Great Britain, succeeding the Conservative Party's Stanley Baldwin, who had been prime minister only since May 22. MacDonald is the first Labour prime minister in history.

February 3: Former president Woodrow Wilson dies in Washington, D.C.

February 26: The treason trial of Hitler and other leaders of the Beer Hall Putsch begins in Munich.

April 1: The defendants in the Munich Beer Hall Putsch are sentenced to prison. In defending himself through the trial, however, Hitler has won adherents and received worldwide newspaper coverage.

April 9: The committee of the Reparations Commission proposes the Dawes Plan, named for Charles Dawes, which provides for a $200 million international loan to Germany, creation of a new German currency, and a series of graduated reparations payments by Germany.

May 19: Overriding Coolidge's veto, Congress again passes the Adjusted Compensation Act, which provides insurance policies to veterans against which they can borrow money (up to one-fourth of the policies' face value).

May 26: Coolidge signs into law the Immigration Act of 1924, which establishes the principle of "national origins" rather than census data as the basis for restricting immigration, effective in 1927—until then quotas will be reduced to 2 percent and based on the 1890 census. The intent is to reduce immigration from eastern and southern European nations.

June 3: The McNary-Haugen Bill suffers defeat in the House of Representatives.

June 10: Meeting in Cleveland, the Republican National Convention nominates Coolidge for the presidency, with Charles G. Dawes as his running mate.

July 4: In Cleveland the Committee for Progressive Political Action (CPPA) nominates Robert M. La Follette as its candidate for the presidency.

July 7: The Democratic National Convention, ending a tumultuous meeting in New York, nominates John W. Davis for president and Nebraska governor Charles W. Bryan, brother of William Jennings Bryan, for vice president.

July 11: The Communist Party nominates William Z. Foster as U.S. presidential candidate. The Socialist Party and other left-wing groups support La Follette, who will not accept Communist support.

September 1: The Dawes Plan, accepted by both Germany and the Allies, goes into effect.

November 4: Coolidge defeats both Davis and La Follette, polling more votes than both of his major opponents combined. His sweeping victory is reflected in the large Republican majorities gained in both houses. The Senate has 56 Republicans, 39 Democrats and one Farmer-Laborite; the House has 247 Republicans, 183 Democrats, two Socialists, and two Farmer-Laborites. In Great Britain Stanley Baldwin again becomes prime minister, as MacDonald resigns following loss of the Labour majority in Parliament.

December 20: Hitler is released from Landsberg Prison.

1925

January 30: An obscure young man named Floyd Collins begins exploring an underground passage in Sand Cave, five miles from Mammoth Cave in Kentucky, in hopes of discovering an attraction to draw tourists; a huge rock loosed by a cave-in pins his foot, and he lies trapped about 125 feet from an opening to the surface.

February 4: Charles Forbes, who was head of the Veterans Bureau until Harding (who had appointed him) asked him to resign in 1923, is indicted for fraud, conspiracy, and bribery.

February 16: After two weeks of hoopla initiated by a reporter for the *Louisville Courier-Journal* through a series of interviews with Floyd Collins that attracted hundreds of onlookers to Sand Cave, the trapped cave explorer dies.

April 27: Following the death of Friedrich Ebert, Field Marshall Paul von Hindenburg, co-commander of the German armies during the war, wins election as president of the Weimar Republic.

June 18: Robert M. La Follette dies.

July 10: The trial of John T. Scopes on charges of illegally teaching the theory of evolution begins in Dayton, Tennessee. He is defended by Clarence Darrow, representing the American Civil Liberties Union (ACLU); William Jennings Bryan takes part as the prosecutor and defender of the Bible.

July 21: The Scopes trial, referred to as the "monkey trial" because of its focus on the theory of evolution, comes to an end. The jury finds Scopes guilty, and the judge fines him $100.

July 26: William Jennings Bryan dies in Dayton, Tennessee.

December 1: Representatives of the European nations meeting in Locarno, Switzerland, sign several agreements—referred to as a whole as the Locarno Treaty—intended to ensure peace. A pact among Great Britain, France, Belgium, Italy, and Germany provides a guaranty for Germany's western boundary and for the demilitarization of the Rhineland. Another pact among France, Belgium, and Germany commits the signatories never to attack, invade, or begin a war with each other except with approval of the League of Nations or for some terrible transgression. Germany also agrees to arbitration treaties with all of her neighbors.

1926

January 27: The Senate votes 76-17 in favor of United States membership in the World Court, but with a series of five reservations (one by the Senate even curtailing the court's right to provide advisory opinions) concerning the court's authority that foredoom American participation.

May 9: Lieutenant Commander Richard E. Byrd of the U.S. Navy, accompanied by Floyd G. Bennett, flies from Spitsbergen, Norway, over the North Pole and back in 16 hours.

May 18: Evangelist Aimee Semple McPherson disappears; newspapers headline speculations of her drowning since she had been seen swimming in the ocean; 15,000 of her followers gather for a vigil at her Bible school in Los Angeles.

June 23: Aimee Semple McPherson reappears, walking out of the desert near Douglas, Arizona. She contends she was kidnapped and confined in a cabin, from which she escaped. Her story cannot be corroborated.

July 30: Mexican president Plutarco Elias Calles's government has decreed the nationalization of church property, prohibited religious teaching in private primary schools, expelled foreign nuns and clergy, and limited the numbers of practicing priests in each state. Now, in retaliation, the Roman Catholic hierarchy issues an interdict that places lay groups in charge of caring for churches and limits the rites clergy may perform in public.

August 6: Gertrude Ederle, a 19-year-old swimmer from New York City, swims the English Channel, becoming the first woman in history to do so. In addition, she sets a new record of 14 hours and 30 minutes for the crossing.

September 9: Germany is admitted to membership in the League of Nations.

September 18: A devastating hurricane (causing the deaths of 400 people and leaving 50,000 homeless) brings to a sudden end the already tottering Florida real estate boom, leveling poorly constructed developments on the east coast, leaving much of the Miami area in ruins, and exposing the financial weakness of many of the banks, city governments, and mortgaged investors involved. Prices of both land buildings had skyrocketed during the seven years following the war, driven up in many cases by unscrupulous speculators; Miami's population had grown from 30,000 in 1920 to 75,000 in 1925 as a result of the boom.

November 2: The midterm election significantly reduces Republican strength in Congress. In the Senate, the Republicans have only 48 members, while the Democrats have 47 and Farmer-Laborites have one member; in the House, however, the Republicans maintain a 237 to 195 majority over the Democrats.

1927

January 25: Following the strong advocacy of Senator William E. Borah, the Senate votes unanimously in favor of a resolution demanding that outstanding disputes with Mexico be resolved through arbitration. Sizable American public and political hostility has resulted from the Calles government's nationalization of church property.

February 10: Coolidge requests that the five nations that signed the Washington Five-Power Treaty (1922) convene in Geneva, Switzerland, in the late summer to negotiate additional limits to their naval strength.

February 11: The Senate passes the McNary-Haugen Bill.

February 17: The House passes the McNary-Haugen Bill, sending it to the president for signing.

February 25: Coolidge vetoes the McNary-Haugen Bill, denouncing its provisions for encouraging "one-crop farming" and overproduction, fixing prices for the benefit of a few farmers and processors, punishing those farmers who produced crops in quantities geared to market demand, creating resentment abroad through dumping cheap American farm produce, and imposing a tax that he considered unconstitutional. Congress fails to override the veto.

April: Coolidge taps Henry L. Stimson, William Howard Taft's secretary of war, for a special mission as his personal representative to negotiate a peace in Nicaragua. Civil war erupted there in 1925 after Coolidge withdrew U.S. Marines from Managua; and although Coolidge sent Marines back to the nation in summer 1926, the war continues.

April 6: French foreign minister Aristide Briand, in an address directed to the American people, declares France's willingness to join with the United States in signing a mutual agreement to outlaw war between the two countries. It is the 10th anniversary of the United States' declaration of war against Germany.

April 7: In New York City, Walter S. Gifford, president of American Telephone and Telegraph Company (AT&T), conducts a public showing of a new broadcasting medium, television. The television sets display pictures of Secretary of Commerce Herbert Hoover seated at his desk in his Washington, D.C., office.

April 9: Sacco and Vanzetti, after six years of appeals and public protests against the guilty verdict, are sentenced to death, despite the fact that Celestino Madeiros, a condemned criminal, had provided evidence that the South Braintree, Massachusetts, murder for which Sacco and Vanzetti have been found guilty was actually committed by the Morelli gang, of which Madeiros had been a member. The case cannot be reopened without the approval of the trial judge, Webster Thayer, who has adamantly refused to give consent.

April 25: Nicholas Murray Butler, president of Columbia University and of the Carnegie Endowment for International Peace and prominent Republican counselor, issues a formal acknowledgment of Briand's proposal.

May 20–21: Charles A. Lindbergh, intent on becoming the first person to fly solo across the Atlantic Ocean and to claim the prize of $25,000 established in 1919 by New York hotelier Raymond Orteig for doing so, lifts off his single-engine airplane, *The Spirit of St. Louis,* shortly before 8:00 A.M. on May 20 from the airstrip at Roosevelt Field outside New York City. He successfully completes the 3,610-mile solo flight in 33½ hours, landing at Le Bourget outside Paris to the acclaim of a crowd of spectators estimated at 100,000.

June 20: Briand sends to Washington, D.C., a draft treaty that would commit the United States and France to renouncing war "as an instrument of their national policy towards each other" and to settling all conflicts between the two nations by "pacific means."

June 20: In Geneva, Switzerland, headquarters of the League of Nations, the conference to discuss further reductions in naval armaments that Coolidge had called for in February convenes, but there is scant hope for its success since both Italy and France have rejected participation, leaving only Great Britain, Japan, and the United States involved.

August 2: While vacationing in the Black Hills of North Dakota, President Coolidge announces that he will not run for reelection in 1928.

August 23: Despite worldwide protests, Massachusetts governor A. T. Fuller, supported by a commission headed by President A. Lawrence Lowell of Harvard University, has refused to grant clemency to Sacco and Vanzetti, and the two Italian immigrants are executed.

October 6: In New York City cinema-goers witness the opening of *The Jazz Singer,* the first feature-length movie containing synchronized speech, as well as music and other sound—the first "talkie"—a production of Warner Brothers. The film stars Al Jolson, who delivers some dialogue and sings six songs, his theme song "Mammy" among them.

December 28: Neither Coolidge nor Secretary of State Frank B. Kellogg has welcomed Briand's proposed treaty because, as a bilateral agreement, it would commit the United States to an alliance with France, something the United States is not prepared to do. Their solution is to expand Briand's proposal by inviting "all the principal powers of the world" to sign an agreement renouncing war, and Kellogg now sends this counterproposal to Briand.

1928

January: Leon Trotsky, having been systematically stripped of power and influence by Stalin and even expelled from the Communist Party, is now exiled to Alma-Ata in Central Asia. Stalin is now the unchallenged dictator of the USSR.

January 11: U.S. secretary of state Kellogg begins to circulate among the governments of the major nations a draft of a treaty that would commit the signatories to renouncing war.

April 13: The Socialist Party of America nominates Norman Thomas as candidate for the presidency.

May 20: With the Weimar Republic's economy stabilized, right-wing parties make only a modest showing in the general elections. The Nazis poll 810,000 votes out of 31 million votes cast and win only 12 seats among the Reichstag's 491.

May 25: Both houses of Congress approve the Muscle Shoals Bill, the brainchild of Senator George Norris, which would authorize the federal government to operate an experimental fertilizer facility at Muscle Shoals, Tennessee, and sell any surplus power to city utilities—part of Norris's long-term effort to prevent commercial development of dams and power generation in the Tennessee Valley. Regarding the bill as socialistic, Coolidge vetoes it.

May 27: The Communist Party nominates William Z. Foster for president.

June 12: Meeting in Kansas City, the Republican National Convention nominates Herbert Hoover as the party's candidate for the presidency. His running mate is Senator Charles Curtis of Kansas.

June 26: In Houston, Texas, the Democratic National Convention chooses Alfred E. Smith, governor of New York, as the party's presidential candidate and Senator Joseph T. Robinson of Arkansas as vice presidential candidate.

August 27: Convened in Paris, France, representatives of 15 nations sign the Pact of Paris (also known as the Kellogg-Briand Pact), committing their nations to the renunciation of war "as an instrument of national policy" and to resolving all disputes by "pacific means." The pact is open to acceptance by all other nations.

November 6: Hoover defeats Smith by a popular vote of 21.4 million to 15 million; Thomas, the Socialist Party nominee, receives only 265,000 votes. The Republicans capture both houses of Congress by substantial margins—267 members to 163 in the House and 56 to 39 in the Senate. The Farmer-Laborites have one member in each house. Franklin Delano Roosevelt, chosen by Smith as his successor, wins the governorship of New York, but by a narrow margin.

November 7: Following Hoover's victory, both volume and prices on the New York Stock Exchange surge upward.

November 16: The boom in the stock market set off by Hoover's victory gains momentum, as 6,641,250 shares change hands—a new record far surpassing the previous one.

November 19: The victorious Hoover begins a goodwill tour of 11 Latin American nations.

December 17: Undersecretary of State J. Reuben Clark submits to Secretary of State Kellogg a memorandum that repudiates the Roosevelt Corollary (1904) to the Monroe Doctrine, which claimed for the United States the right to intervene unilaterally in the affairs of other nations in the hemisphere. The memorandum states that the Monroe Doctrine has no bearing on inter-American relations but was intended to guarantee the sovereignty of Latin American nations against European imperialism.

EYEWITNESS TESTIMONY

A living thing is born, and we must see to it what clothes we put on it. It is not a vehicle of power, but a vehicle in which power may be varied at the discretion of those who exercise it and in accordance with the changing circumstances of the time. . . .

It is a definite guaranty of peace. It is a definite guaranty by word against aggression. It is a definite guaranty against the things which have just come near bringing the whole structure of civilization into ruin.

Woodrow Wilson, chairman of the commission to draft a covenant for the League of Nations, in presenting the covenant to the Paris Peace Conference on February 14, 1919, in Senate Document 389 *(1919).*

Camels supply cigarette contentment beyond anything you ever experienced! You never tasted such full-bodied mellow-mildness; such refreshing, appetizing flavor and coolness. The more Camels you smoke the greater becomes your delight—*Camels are such a Cigarette revelation!* . . .

Freedom from any unpleasant cigaretty aftertaste or unpleasant cigaretty odor makes Camels particularly desirable to the most fastidious smokers.

R. J. Reynolds advertisement, in National Geographic Magazine *(September 1919).*

And it contains . . . a great charter of liberty for the workingmen of the world. For the first time in history the counsels of mankind are to be drawn together and concerted for the purpose of defending the rights and improving the conditions of working people—men, women, and children. . . . There is no other way to do it than by a universal league of nations. . . .

. . . Every great fighting nation in the world is on the list of those who are to constitute the League of Nations. I say every great nation, because America is going to be included among them, and the only choice my fellow citizens is whether we will go in now or come in later with Germany; whether we will go in as founders of this covenant of freedom or go in as those who are admitted after they have made a mistake and repented.

President Woodrow Wilson, on his nationwide tour supporting the Treaty of Versailles, in a speech at Omaha, Nebraska, September 8, 1919, in Baker and Dodd, The Public Papers of Woodrow Wilson *(1925–27).*

Sometimes people call me an idealist. Well, that is the way I know I am an American. America is the only idealistic country in the world.

President Woodrow Wilson, speech of September 8, 1919, at Sioux Falls, North Dakota, during his nationwide tour, in Baker and Dodd, The Public Papers of Woodrow Wilson *(1925–27).*

My objections to the League have not been met by the reservations. . . . Let us see what our attitude will be toward Europe and what our position will be with reference to the other nations of the world after we shall have entered the League with the present reservations written therein . . .

My friends of reservations, tell me where is the reservation in these articles which protects us against entangling alliances with Europe?

Senator William E. Borah, during Senate debate over ratification of the Treaty of Versailles with the reservations proposed by Senator Henry Cabot Lodge, November 19, 1919, in the Congressional Record *(1919).*

. . . if there are immense differences between individual Americans—for some Americans are black—yet there is a great uniformity in their environment, customs, temper, and thoughts. . . . To be an American is of itself almost a moral condition, an education, and a career. . . .

The circumstances of his life hitherto have necessarily driven the American into moral materialism. . . . The most striking expression of this materialism is usually supposed to be his love of the almighty dollar; but that is a foreign and unintelligent view. The American talks about money because that is the symbol and the measure he has at hand for success, intelligence, and power.

George Santayana, philosopher, 1920 essay "Materialism and Idealism in the American Character," from his book Character and Opinion in the United States *(1967).*

This is America—a town of a few thousand, in a region of wheat and corn and dairies and little groves . . . its Main Street is the continuation of Main Streets everywhere. . . .

Main Street is the climax of civilization. That this Ford car might stand in front of the Bon Ton Store, Hannibal invaded Rome and Erasmus wrote in

Oxford cloisters. What Ole Jensen the grocer says to Ezra Stowbody the banker is the new law for London, Prague, and the unprofitable isles of the sea; whatsoever Ezra does not know and sanction, that thing is heresy, worthless for knowing and wicked to consider.

Our railway station is the final aspiration of architecture. Sam Clark's annual hardware turnover is the envy of the four counties which constitute God's Country. In the sensitive art of the Rosebud Movie Palace there is a Message, and humor strictly moral.

Sinclair Lewis, novelist, introducing his subject, in the prefatory remarks of his novel Main Street *(1920).*

As an endless dream it went on; the spirit of the past brooding over a new generation, the chosen youth from the muddled, unchastened world, still fed romantically on the mistakes and half-forgotten dreams of dead statesmen and poets. Here was a new generation, shouting the old cries, learning the old creeds, through a revery of long days and nights; destined finally to go out into that dirty gray turmoil to follow love and pride; a new generation dedicated more than the last to the fear of poverty and the worship of success; grown up to find all Gods dead, all wars fought, all faiths in man shaken.

F. Scott Fitzgerald, novelist, from the conclusion of his first novel, This Side of Paradise *(1920).*

I am more and more under the opinion that for President we need not so much a brilliant man as solid, mediocre men, providing they have good sense, sound and careful judgment and good manners. All these Harding has.

Brand Whitlock, reform mayor of Toledo, Ohio, recording in his journal after Harding's nomination, quoted in Russell, The Shadow of Blooming Grove *(1968).*

At 73 he is a boss in the Senate, holding domination over a herd of miscellaneous mediocrities by a loose and precarious tenure. He has power, but men who are far beneath him have more power. At the great quadrennial powwow of his party he plays the part of bellwether and chief of police. . . . And when the glittering prize is fought for, he is shouldered aside to make way for a gladiator [Warren G. Harding] so bogus and so preposterous that the very thought of

him must reduce a scion of the Cabots to sour and sickly mirth.

H. L. Mencken, journalist and author, commenting on Senator Henry Cabot Lodge as chairman of the 1920 Republican National Convention, in the Baltimore Evening Sun *(June 15, 1920).*

Ain't I de Emperor? De laws don't go for him. You heah what I tells you, Smithers. Dere's little stealin' like you does, and dere's big stealin' like I does. For de little stealin' dey gits you in jail soon or late. For de big stealin' dey makes you Emperor and puts you in de Hall o' Fame when you croaks. If dey's one thing I learns in ten years on de Pullman ca's listenin' to de white quality talk, it's dat same fact. And when I gits a chance to use it I winds up Emperor in two years.

Character Brutus Jones, in Eugene O'Neill's play The Emperor Jones *(1921).*

Even if there is neither a biological nor a psychological justification for the popular belief in the inferiority of the Negro race, the social basis of the race prejudice in America is not difficult to understand. The prejudice is founded essentially on the tendency of the human mind to merge the individual in the class to which he belongs. . . . We find this spirit at work in anti-Semitism as well as American nativism, and in the conflict between labor and capitalism. . . .

For this reason there is no great hope that the Negro problem will find even a halfway satisfactory solution in our day. We may, perhaps, expect that an increasing number of strong minds will free themselves from race prejudice. . . . The weak-minded will not follow their example.

Franz Boas, anthropologist, in the essay "The Problem of the American Negro," in the Yale Review *(January 1921).*

I understand perfectly the feelings of Wilson. When he . . . realizes the suffering he has brought about, then he is being punished. It is he, not I, who needs a pardon. If I had it in my power I would give him the pardon which would set him free.

Woodrow Wilson is an exile from the hearts of his people. The betrayal of his ideals makes him the most pathetic figure in the world. No man in public life in American history ever retired so thoroughly discredited, so scathingly rebuked, so overwhelmingly impeached and repudiated as Woodrow Wilson.

Eugene V. Debs, Socialist Party leader, interview of February 1, 1921, in the federal prison at Atlanta, Georgia, a day after President Woodrow Wilson refused to grant him a pardon, quoted in Ginger, The Bending Cross *(1949).*

I have said to the people we meant to have less of government in business as well as more business in government. It is well to have understood that business has a right to pursue its normal, legitimate, and righteous way unimpeded, and it ought have no call to meet government competition where all risk is borne by the public Treasury. There is no challenge to honest and lawful business success.

President Warren G. Harding, addressing a special session of Congress, April 12, 1921, in the Congressional Record *(1921).*

God damn the continent of Europe. It is of merely antiquarian interest. Rome is only a few years behind Tyre and Babylon. The negroid streak creeps northward to defile the Nordic race. Already the Italians have the souls of blackamoors. Raise the bars of immigration and permit only Scandinavians, Teutons, Anglo-Saxons and Celts to enter. France made me sick. Its silly pose as the thing the world has to save. I think it's shame that England and America didn't let Germany conquer Europe. It's the only thing that would have saved the fleet of tottering old wrecks. My reactions were all philistine, anti-socialistic, provincial and racially snobbish.

F. Scott Fitzgerald, novelist, letter of May 1921, to his friend Edmund Wilson, from London, England, in Turnbull, ed., The Letters of F. Scott Fitzgerald *(1963).*

There are, of course, bad foreigners and good ones, good Catholics and bad ones, and all kinds of Negroes. To make a case against a birthplace, a religion, or a race is wickedly un-American and cowardly. The whole trouble with the Ku Klux Klan is that it is based upon such deep foolishness that it is bound to be a menace to good government in any community. Any man fool enough to be Imperial Wizard would have power without responsibility and both without any sense. That is social dynamite.

William Allen White, editor and author, letter to Herbert B. Swope, editor of the New York World, *September 17, 1921, in Johnson,* Selected Letters of William Allen White, 1899–1943 *(1947).*

The two old but still dominant parties appear to me to have utterly failed to grasp the economic import of the ordinary laborer and worker to industry and the health of the nation as an organism. They still seem to think that invested capital, however come by and into whatever slimy hands it may have fallen, is the be all and end all of government concern and duty. The unorganized as well as the organized worker everywhere becomes of less and less import. Is not this the legitimate opportunity of organized labor? For certainly the unorganized laborer is not unaware of this. Why is it then, that the voice of organized labor is never effectively heard in the councils of either of the old parties?

Theodore Dreiser, novelist, letter of October 4, 1921, to M. W. Martin, chairman of a group formed to prosecute policemen accused of killing four striking union members in Hammond, Indiana, written in Los Angeles, in Elias, Letters of Theodore Dreiser *(1959).*

To George Babbitt, as to most prosperous citizens of Zenith, his motor car was poetry and tragedy, love and heroism. The office was his pirate ship but the car his perilous excursion ashore.

Sinclair Lewis, novelist, in his novel Babbitt *(1922).*

Morals is connected with actualities of existence, not with ideals, ends and obligations independent of concrete actualities. The facts upon which it depends are those which arise out of active connections of human beings with one another, the consequences of their mutually intertwined activities in the life of desire, belief, judgment, satisfaction and dissatisfaction. In this sense conduct and hence morals are social; they are not just things which *ought* to be social and which fail to come up to the scratch. But there are enormous differences of better and worse in the quality of what is social. Ideal morals begin with the perception of these differences. . . . Human interaction and ties . . . can be regulated, employed in an orderly way for good only as we know how to observe them. And they cannot be observed aright, they cannot be understood and utilized, when the mind is left to itself to work without the aid of science.

John Dewey, philosopher and educator, in Human Nature and Conduct *(1922).*

Like Cato I say to this Senate, the I.W.W. [Industrial Workers of the World] must be destroyed! For they represent an ever-present dagger pointed at the heart of the greatest nation the world has ever known, where all men are born free and equal, with equal opportunities to all, where the Founding Fathers have guaranteed to each one happiness, where Truth, Honor, Liberty, Justice, and the Brotherhood of Man are a religion absorbed with one's mother's milk.

Voice, in Eugene O'Neill's play
The Hairy Ape *(1922).*

The question is—Has anybody a right to deny the Christian name to those who differ with him on such points and to shut against them the doors of Christian fellowship? The Fundamentalists say that this must be done. In this country and on the foreign field they are trying to do it. They have actually endeavored to put on the statute books of a whole state binding laws against teaching modern biology....

...There are many opinions in the field of modern controversy concerning which I am not sure whether they are right or wrong, but there is one thing I am sure of: courtesy and kindliness and tolerance and humility and fairness are right. Opinions may be mistaken; love, never is.

Harry Emerson Fosdick, associate minister at First Presbyterian Church in New York City and teacher at Union Theological Seminary, attacking the Fundamentalists in his essay "Shall the Fundamentalists Win," in the Christian Work *(June 10, 1922).*

[America] is not perfect, but it surpasses the accomplishments of any other people . . . Who can doubt that it has been guided by a Divine Providence? What has it not given to its people in material advantages, educational opportunity, or religious consolation? . . .

...The homely virtues must continue to be cultivated. The real dignity, the real nobility of work must be cherished. It is only through industry that there is any hope for individual development. The viciousness of waste and the value of thrift must continue to be learned and understood. . . . To these there must be added religion, education, and obedience to law.

Vice President Calvin Coolidge, speech in 1923, in
The Price of Freedom: Memorial Day
Speeches and Addresses *(1924).*

In America particularly, where competitive business and its concomitant, the sporting view of life, have reached their fullest development, there have come to

be two sorts of virtue. The greater virtue is to win; and meticulous questions about the methods are not in the best form provided the methods bring victory. The lesser virtue is to go out and die gracefully after having lost....

Thus we appear to search in vain for any really ethical basis of approval for competition as a basis for an ideal type of human relations, or as a motive to action. It fails to harmonize either with the pagan ideal of society as a community of friends or the Christian ideal of spiritual fellowship.

Frank H. Knight, University of Iowa professor, in his essay "The Ethics of Competition," in the Quarterly Journal of Economics *(August 1923).*

The public relations consultant is ideally a constructive force in the community. The results of his work are often accelerated interest in matters of value and importance to the social, economic or political life of the community.

The public relations counsel is the pleader to the public of a point of view. He acts in this capacity as a consultant both in interpreting the public to his client and in helping to interpret his client to the public. He helps to mould the action of his client as well to mould public opinion.

Edward L. Bernays, from his book Crystallizing Public Opinion *(1923).*

We saw jazz, already in the dives and moving into the speakeasies, set the tone and color of the country. . . . Jazz didn't change the morals of the early twenties. But it furnished the music, I noticed, to a change in manners and sexual ideas. Women wore less and wore it in a slipping, careless way on the dance floors. Every girl wore silk stockings—and many rolled them beneath the knees so that every sitting-down showed the American female thigh, nude and lush, anywhere from kneecap to buttocks. ("You just know she wears them," said the ads.)

Hoagy Carmichael, jazz musician and composer, in his memoir Sometimes I Wonder *(1965).*

Since the close of the last Congress the Nation has lost President Harding. The world knew his kindness and his humanity, his greatness and his character. He has left his mark upon history. He has made justice more certain and peace more secure. . . . But this is not the occasion for extended reference to the man

President Coolidge stands on the south lawn of the White House, February 26, 1925. *(Library of Congress, Prints and Photographs Division [LC-USZ62-32699])*

or is work. In this presence, among those who knew and loved him, that is unnecessary. But we who were associated with him could not resume together the function of our office without pausing for a moment, and in his memory consecrating ourselves to the service of our country. He is gone. We remain. It is our duty, under the inspiration of his example, to take up the burdens which he was permitted to lay down, and to develop and support the wise principles of government which he represented.

President Calvin Coolidge's opening words, in his first annual State of the Union message, delivered to a joint session of Congress, December 6, 1923, in Israel, ed., The State of the Union Messages of the Presidents, *vol. 3 (1966).*

Everything incongruous and inconsequent has its place in the unrolling of the comic film: love and masquerade and treachery; coincidence and disguise; heroism and knavishness; all are distorted, burlesqued,

exaggerated. And—here the camera enters—all are presented at an impossible rate; the culmination is in the inevitable struggle and the conventional pursuit, where trick photography enters and you see the immortal Keystone cops in their flivver, mowing down hundreds of telegraph poles without abating their speed . . . and at the height of the revel, the true catastrophe, the solution of the preposterous and forgotten drama, with the lovers reunited under the canopy of smashed cars, or the gay feet of Mr Chaplin gently twinkling down the irised street.

What I have said about Chaplin regards him as a typical slap-stick comedian. . . . The other practitioners of the art come out of his shadow, and some of them are excellent. What makes Chaplin great is that he has irony and pity, he knows that you must not have the one without the other; he has both piety and wit.

Gilbert Seldes, from his book The Seven Lively Arts *(1924).*

I have never viewed taxation as a means of rewarding one class of taxpayers or punishing another. If such a point of view ever controls our public policy, the traditions of freedom, justice, and equality of opportunity, which are the distinguishing characteristics of our American civilization, will have disappeared and in their place we shall have class legislation with all its attendant evils.

Secretary of the Treasury Andrew W. Mellon, in Taxation: The People's Business *(1924).*

He, too, appeared as a romantic figure. Benito Mussolini came like thunder on the right. . . .

Anyhow, that's how I saw the Duce and his Fascismo, as lightning that illuminated, in flashes, Russia and Germany, France, England—all Europe and, later, the United States. Mussolini took the method, the spirit, the stuff, of Bolshevism and used it to go—right. The method! Was that what the divine Dictator meant us to see—that there was a method, good either way? I, a broken liberal, had to answer that to explain it to my liberal girl [Steffens's future English wife], who believed, as I did still, a little, in majorities, in democracy, in liberty; and I had to see it as it happened, close up. I was there when Mussolini leaped into sight.

Lincoln Steffens, journalist who interviewed the Italian dictator in 1923–24 and lived in Italy from 1924 to 1926, in The Autobiography of Lincoln Steffens *(1931).*

Thus we have now the abounding freedom Eclecticism, the winning smile of taste, but no architecture. For Architecture, be it known, is dead. . . .

In the better aspects of eclecticism and taste, that is to say, in those aspects which reveal a certain depth of artistic feeling and a physical sense of materials, rather than mere scene-painting or archaeology, however clever, there is to be discovered a hope and a forecast. For it is within the range of possibilities . . . that out of the very richness and multiplicity of the architectural phenomena called "styles" there may arise within the architectural mind a perception growing slowly, perhaps suddenly, into clearness, that architecture in its material nature and in its animating essence is a *plastic art*.

Louis Sullivan, Chicago architect, in his 1924 book
The Autobiography of an Idea *(1956).*

Every year the candidates for the degree of *Doctor philosphiae* in America compose laboriously at least 3000 theses . . . but not one in a hundred contains any contribution to knowledge that is worth putting on paper. This is especially true in what is called the department of English. . . .

The brethren of the historical faculty have done better than the pedagogues in literature. Nine tenths of them, of course, are dull and dreadful asses engaged docilely in teaching Rotary Club and American Legion history, but there is also a respectable minority of more intelligent and enterprising fellows.

George Jean Nathan and H. L. Mencken, editors, in the
American Mercury *(May 1924).*

The test of our whole economic and social system is its capacity to cure its own abuses . . . If we are to be wholly dependent on government to cure these abuses we shall by this very method have created an enlarged and deadening abuse through the extension of bureaucracy and the clumsy and incapable handling of delicate economic forces. . . .

American business needs a lifting purpose greater than the struggle of materialism. . . . It lies in . . . a finer regard for the rights of others. . . . it lies in the organization of the forces of our economic life so that they may produce happier individual lives, more secure in employment and comfort, wider in the possibilities of enjoyment of nature, larger in opportunities of intellectual life.

Secretary of Commerce Herbert Hoover, speech delivered in Cleveland, Ohio, on May 7, 1924, in
The Hoover Policies *(1937).*

The next day, in talking with Josephus Daniels . . . I realized how deeply the religious issue had cut. In the committee he had voted for a specific naming of the Klan. "The truth is," said Daniels, "I felt so strongly I should have taken the floor and spoken in favor of the minority report [demanding clear denunciation of the Klan], but I found it painful even to vote against [William Jennings] Bryan."

The damage, deadly and certain, had been done, but as though the convention were determined to destroy the party's prospects completely, there was to be prolonged balloting ahead on the nomination. The contest had become disreputable. "My God," Theodore Dresier wrote me, "is this the meaning of Democracy?" The Republicans were laughing. The press was pouring oil on the flames. Thus hate grew. Something might have been saved from the wreck had both [William Gibbs] McAdoo and [Alfred E.] Smith withdrawn with a plea of harmony, but neither would budge an inch.

Claude Bowers, historian, politician, newspaperman and ambassador to Spain (1933–39), recalling the disastrous Democratic National Convention of 1924, in My Life: The Memoirs of Claude Bowers *(1962).*

In the three years he was Vice-President he made neither friends nor foes. Socially and politically, he was generally considered hopeless. He was as near nothing as any man we have ever had in that office. . . .

This is the man who became president last August. He is exactly the same man today that he was before. He has gained neither in mental range nor in moral strength. He is the identical Coolidge whom his party leaders a year ago thought too weak and nondescript to run again for the vice-presidency. Now, he is their candidate for the presidency. It sounds like a joke, but it isn't.

Frank R. Kent, syndicated columnist, writing about President Calvin Coolidge, in the
American Mercury *(August 1924).*

When the advocates of Prohibition urge that all laws must be enforced, they really refer only to the Prohibition laws. . . . Even the drastic Volstead Act has not prevented and cannot prevent the use of alcoholic beverages. The acreage of grapes has rapidly increased since it was passed and the price gone up with the demand. The government is afraid to interfere with the farmer's cider. The fruit grower is making money.

The dandelion is now the national flower. Everyone who wants alcoholic beverages is fast learning how to make them at home. . . . The folly of the attempt must soon convince even the more intelligent Prohibitionist that all this legislation is both a tragedy and a hoax.

Clarence Darrow, lawyer, writing about Prohibition, in the American Mercury *(August 1924).*

I do not know how you feel concerning Mr. [John W.] Davis and the National Election. However, if you are thinking of supporting Mr. Davis, would it be possible for you to speak at a few of our meetings on the international situation? We do so need speakers at our larger meetings who can speak with conviction on the subject of peace.

Eleanor Roosevelt, in a letter to women's rights leader Carrie Chapman Catt, September 17, 1924, soliciting her support for John W. Davis, in Schlup and Whisenhunt, It Seems to Me *(2001).*

The millennium is not yet here. The world has been made safe for democracy but democracy has not yet been made safe for the world. It is idle to speculate what might have happened had we entered the League of Nations. Much good has been accomplished by it, but a thoughtful man will pause before he says of a certainty that the kings and emperors have not been succeeded by autocrats.

Thomas R. Marshall, vice president of the United States from 1913 to 1921, in Recollections of Thomas R. Marshall *(1925).*

So far as the manual workers are concerned, we are again beginning to realize the old ideal of sound Americans,—equal prosperity for all classes and occupations, and that too, under liberty. The most serious menace at the present time is that of bootlegging in men, the bringing of immigrants over the Canadian and the Mexican borders. There is already an acute need for restriction of immigration from Mexico—a country that is doing nothing to provide better conditions for its own laborers and will continue to shift that burden on to us, so long as we are willing to accept it. We are rapidly creating another race problem by the wholesale importation of Mexican peons.

Thomas Nixon Carver, professor of political economy at Harvard University, from his book The Present Economic Revolution *(1925).*

There were Babylon and Nineveh: they were built of brick. Athens was gold marble columns. Rome was held up on broad arches of rubble. In Constantinople the minarets flame like great candles round the Golden Horn. . . . Steel, glass, tile, concrete will be the materials of the skyscrapers. Crammed on the narrow island the millionwindowed buildings will jut glittering, pyramid on pyramid like the white cloudhead above a thunderstorm.

John Dos Passos, novelist, in his novel Manhattan Transfer *(1925).*

That's what life is for most people, I reckon. . . . Just barren ground where they have to struggle to make anything grow.

The character Dorinda, in Ellen Glasgow's novel Barren Ground *(1925).*

Only an adequate large space on this earth assures a nation of freedom of existence. . . . The National Socialist movement must strive to eliminate the disproportion between our population and our area—viewing this latter as a source of food as well as a basis for power politics. . . . We must hold unflinchingly to our aim . . . to secure for the German people the land and soil to which they are entitled.

Adolf Hitler, in Mein Kampf *(1925).*

I looked up Hemingway. He is taking me to see Gertrude Stein tomorrow. This city is full of Americans . . . and they seem to be incapable of any sort of conversation not composed of semi-malicious gossip about New York courtesy celebrities. I've gotten to like France. We've taken a swell apartment until January. I'm filled with disgust for Americans in general after two weeks' sight of the ones in Paris—these preposterous, pushing women and girls who assume that you have any personal interest in them, who have all (so they say) read James Joyce and who simply adore Mencken. I suppose we're no worse than anyone, only contact with other races brings out all our worst qualities. If I had anything to do with creating the manners of the contemporary American girl I certainly made a botch of the job.

F. Scott Fitzgerald, novelist, letter of spring 1925, to Edmund Wilson, written in Paris, in The Letters of F. Scott Fitzgerald *(1963).*

His last battle will be grossly misunderstood if it is thought of as a mere exercise in fanaticism. . . . What moved him, at bottom, was simply hatred of the city men who had laughed at him so long, and brought him at last to so tatterdemalion an estate. He lusted for revenge upon them. He yearned to lead the anthropoid rabble against them . . . When he began denouncing the notion that man is a mammal even some of the hinds at Dayton were agape. And when, brought upon Clarence Darrow's cruel hook, he writhed and tossed in a very fury of malignancy, bawling against the veriest elements of sense and decency like a man frantic—when he came to that tragic climax of his striving there were snickers among the hinds as well as hosannas.

H. L. Mencken, journalist, commenting on William Jennings Bryan's conduct at the Scopes trial on the day following Bryan's death, in the Baltimore Evening Sun *(July 27, 1925), as revised for publication in the* American Mercury *(October 1925).*

Women have passed no laws. They have made no changes in party procedure, in campaign managements or tactics. They have affected to a slight degree the choice of candidates for important offices. They have not influenced party platforms or performances. Few are placed in appointive offices of power. . . .

What these facts indicate is simply this: There is no woman block. Those who thought that suffrage would mean that women would organize along sex lines, nominate women, urge special legislation, vote en masse have a right to be disappointed.

Emily Newell Blair, vice chairperson of the Democratic National Committee, discussing women in politics, in Harper's *(October 1925).*

Grand Rapids furniture is the product of the home for the home. It is made with the understanding of what the home is, what it means to our civilization and what it has contributed to human happiness. The home spirit, so characteristic of the city, is carried into its furniture. Hence, to have Grand Rapids furniture in your home is to brighten it with the home spirit and to share in the intelligence and taste that have distinguished Grand Rapids as "The Furniture Capital of America."

General advertisement for the furniture makers of Grand Rapids, Michigan, in The House Beautiful Furnishing Annual *(1926).*

Th' net incomes o' railroads in 1925 wuz th' greatest in all history, owin' perhaps t' th' thousands goin' by train t' th' factory t' drive home new cars.

Kin Hubbard, humorist and columnist, in Abe Martin: Hoss Sense and Nonsense *(1926).*

You know what's the trouble with you? You're an expatriate. One of the worst type. Haven't you heard that? Nobody that left their own country ever wrote anything worth printing. Not even in the newspapers.

. . .You're an expatriate. You've lost touch with the soil. Fake European standards have ruined you.

Statement by the character Bill Gorton to Jake Barnes, in Ernest Hemingway's first novel, The Sun Also Rises *(1926).*

In the finishing and furnishing of the house, utility and beauty must go hand in hand. Stationary features such as doors, windows, fireplaces, and stairs, together with movable objects of the most varied use,—curtains and rugs, chairs, tables, desks, and lamps,—are the raw material. Each of these must be serviceable, must be well adapted to its own particular use, or it becomes an absurdity. Each should also be well designed and, if possible, beautiful. But serviceability and even beauty in each piece are not enough to make a good interior. All the elements must combine harmoniously into an attractive whole. The full idea of "home" involves not only the comfort but the attractiveness. The full attraction will come only from consistency, order, harmony.

Fiske Kimball, architect, writing about interior design, in The House Beautiful Furnishing Annual *(1926).*

So popular has installment buying become, with purchasers as well as with manufacturers and merchants, that it is possible today to buy almost everything from candy to private yachts on the deferred payment plan. . . .

Many people are capable of wisely using this method of buying. Others are not. The danger to this latter class lies in the fact that they may get permanently ahead of their incomes, buying everything possible on time, and ultimately failing to make good on the payments when sickness or economic changes interrupt the smooth flow of their incomes. . . . Of course, there is no means of telling in advance how regular one's income is going to be.

Hawthorne Daniel, from his essay "Living and Dying on Installment," in World's Work *(January 1926).*

The Ku Klux Klan, in short, is an organization which gives expression, direction and purpose to the most vital instincts, hopes, and resentments of the old-stock Americans, provides them with leadership, and is enlisting and preparing them for militant, constructive action toward fulfilling their racial and national destiny. . . .

There are three of these great racial instincts. . . . These are the instincts of loyalty to the white race, to the traditions of America, and to the spirit of Protestantism, which has been an essential part of Americanism ever since the days of Roanoke and Plymouth Rock. They are condensed into the Klan slogan: "Native, white, Protestant supremacy."

Ku Klux Klan imperial wizard Hiram W. Evans,
from his essay "The Klan's Fight for Americanism,"
in North American Review
(March–April–May 1926).

There is no way of avoiding mention of Marcus Garvey among the conspicuous heads of Negro newspapers in America. At present Mr. Garvey is in that small section of Aframerica bounded by the walls of the Federal prison at Atlanta. Using the mails to defraud was the charge that sent him there. As Mr. Hearst directs the policies of his news-sheets from a hacienda in California, so does Mr. Garvey steer the course of the *Negro World* from his Southern retreat. The *Negro World* is a jumble of "back to Africa" rubbish. . . . Yet the man himself is a remarkable personality. He has inspired in his followers a hatred of all but the full-blooded Negro gentry. He has held audience with the Grand Goblin of the Ku Klux Klan himself. He has elevated himself to the supreme dictatorship of an African empire. He has created hundreds of colored knights and ladies.

Eugene Gordon, writing about African Americans in
journalism, in the American Mercury *(June 1926).*

Suppose that every month the best new book published were delivered to you by the postman, *just like a magazine.* . . . If such a book were sent to you every month, you could be *certain* that, without effort or trouble, you would always keep abreast of the leading books published throughout the year.

Advertisement for The Book-of-the-Month
Club, A New Unique Service, in the
American Mercury
(July 1926).

Both sexes are highly involved, directly and indirectly, yet the point of view of only one sex has entered thus far, to any appreciable extent, into the conduct of business. Is it unreasonable to hold that neither society at large nor the business world itself will profit greatly by our entrance into it, until we women, no longer content solely as understudies, shall offer, at whatever hazard, our own contribution—all we have gained through our special inheritance and experience—until we seek to supplement, rather than duplicate the parts in business that men play?

Anne W. Armstrong, Tennessee resident and former official
at Eastman Kodak Company, in Harper's
(August 1926).

. . . it cannot seriously be disputed that the ministry has fallen into public disregard and that the churches have decidedly lost prestige. Why?

Here in America for many reasons. Sect rivalry has given us numerous weak little congregations with poorly equipped ministry. . . .

Sect rivalry, moreover, emphasizes certain doctrines and practices which were never essentials of the faith, and ministers spend their time inculcating teachings, upholding standards of social conduct, or defending ecclesiastical judgments which should have been abandoned long ago. The multitude of rival sects makes for a narrow denominationalism, in some places bigoted in the extreme.

The Right Reverend Charles Fiske, D.D., Episcopal
bishop of central New York, on the declining status of the
church in society in Harper's *(October 1926).*

Christmas and a Radiola—one suggests the other. A real Christmas and a real Radiola—one of the sets containing all the new improvements that have set the world talking—but tried, tested and perfected. . . .

With the moderate terms that an RCA Dealer will arrange, you can easily greet Christmas morning with a Radiola! And it is a *permanent* investment, for it becomes a greater treasure as the great artists and singers of the world turn more and more to radio.

Advertisement for RCA radio sets, in National
Geographic Magazine *(December 1926).*

In fact, the present tendency appears to be to ascribe rather too much virtue and power to the Federal Reserve System. Some appear to believe that the . . . System is or should be a cure-all for economic ills:

that it should somehow stabilize commodity prices, prevent bank failures, suppress speculation, and eliminate the fluctuations of the business cycle. . . .

It is the business of the Reserve System to influence the amount of credit in use, and try to bring about a proper adaptation of the total volume of credit to the volume of business. . . . it is usually the member bank which exercises the initiative in putting additional Federal Reserve funds to work. . . . What the Reserve Banks do primarily is to fix the prices at which their funds may be purchased and in certain other ways influence the conditions under which their funds are used.

W. Randolph Burgess, assistant agent of the Federal Reserve Bank of New York, from his book The Reserve Banks and the Money Market *(1927).*

The proprietary rights of the United States in the Nicaraguan canal route, with the necessary implications growing out of it affecting the Panama Canal, together with the obligations flowing from the investments of all classes of our citizens in Nicaragua, place us in a position of peculiar responsibility. I am sure it is not the desire of the United States to intervene in the internal affairs of Nicaragua or of any other Central American republic. Nevertheless, it must be said that we have a very definite and special interest in the maintenance of order and good government in Nicaragua at the present time, and that the stability, prosperity, and independence of all Central American countries can never be a matter of indifference to us.

President Calvin Coolidge, message to Congress of January 10, 1927, justifying his sending of 2,000 marines to Nicaragua in response to a request by that nation's president, Adolfo Díaz, in the Congressional Record *(1927).*

The cumulative forces of the machine industry . . . widened in range and increased in momentum during the opening decades of the twentieth century. These forces made a steady growth in the volume and velocity of mass production the outstanding feature of American economy, with correlative influences on American slants of thought, modes of living, manners, and aesthetic expression. . . . At length the day arrived when in all the land save in out-of-the-way places, there could be found none but machine-made objects, duplicated by the ton, impersonal, standard-ized according to patterns adapted to fingers of steel, and circulated by publicity drives.

Charles A. Beard and Mary R. Beard, historians, in The Rise of American Civilization *(1927).*

There is only one mechanical invention which *has* created an entirely new medium—and the invention is, of course, the motion picture. . . .

It is only within the past few years that evidence has begun to accumulate which points beyond all possibility of doubt of a new art form. The old skeptics are gradually relenting in their indifference, while young enthusiasts, with the zeal of all neophytes, are only too ready to discover masterpieces in this or that picture—particularly when it is of German or Russian origin.

Alexander Bakshy, in Theatre Arts Monthly *(April 1927).*

Well, I have already say that I not only am not guilty . . . but I never commit a crime in my life—I have never steal and I have never kill and I have never spilt blood. . . .

. . . But my conviction is that I have suffered for things that I am guilty of. I am suffering because I am a radical and indeed I am a radical; I have suffered because I was an Italian, and indeed I am an Italian; I have suffered more for my family and for my beloved than for myself; but I am so convinced to be right that if you could execute me two times, and if I could be reborn two other times, I would live again to do what I have done already.

I have finished. Thank you.

Bartolomeo Vanzetti, final statement (April 9, 1927) before an appeals court that upheld the guilty verdict against himself and Nicola Sacco, in Fraenkel's The Sacco-Vanzetti Case, Vol. V *(1929).*

. . . you imply that there is conflict between religious loyalty to the Catholic faith and patriotic loyalty to the United States. Everything that has actually happened to me during my long public career leads me to know that no such thing as that is true. I have taken an oath of office in this state nineteen times. Each time I swore to defend and maintain the Constitution of the United States. . . . I have never known any conflict between my official duties and my religious belief. No such conflict could exist. Certainly the people of this state recognize no such conflict. They have testified to my devotion to public duty by electing me to the highest office within their gift four times.

New York governor Alfred E. Smith, responding to criticism of his Catholic faith, in the Atlantic Monthly *(May 1927).*

There's one thing I wish to get straight about this flight. They call me "Lucky," but luck isn't enough. As a matter of fact, I had what I regard as the best existing plane to make the flight from New York to Paris. I had what I regard as the best engine, and I was equipped with what were in the circumstances the best possible instruments for making such efforts. I hope I made good use of what I had.

Charles A. Lindbergh, aviator, describing his transatlantic flight during an interview after his arrival in Paris, in the New York Times *(May 23, 1927).*

Mrs. Burt's School for Tiny Tots 1–12 yrs.

Specialized care for young children. Sound education, music, dancing, thorough training.

Wide shaded lawns, swings, seesaws, sand piles, etc. Supervised outdoor play among happy little companions. Good food, home care, sympathetic understanding. Experienced physician and nurse.

Advertisement, in Theatre Arts Monthly *(June 1927).*

. . . a cry should go up from many million voices before the day set for Sacco and Vanzetti to die. We have a right to beat against tight minds with our fists and shout a word into the ears of the old men. We want to know, we will know—"Why?"

Heywood Broun, newspaper columnist, protesting the death sentence against Sacco and Vanzetti, in the New York World *(August 5, 1927).*

If the European list is abbreviated, it is short because the American list is so long. . . . It contains all the familiar names and many new ones, too, and ranges from O'Neill's *Marco Millions* to Anne Nichols' sequel to *Abie's Irish Rose.* It includes George Kelly's *Till the Day of Her Death,* Philip Barry's *John,* and very probably a new play by Sidney Howard. It finds George S. Kaufman and Edna Ferber collaborating on *The Royal Family.* . . . It shows Marc Connelly writing *The Gay Deceivers.* . . . It discloses that George M. Cohan has not been idle and that the result is *The Baby Cyclone.*

John Mason Brown, drama critic, in Theatre Arts Monthly *(October 1927).*

Wait a minute, wait a minute, I tell ya. You ain't heard nothing.

Singer Al Jolson, in the movie The Jazz Singer *(premiered October 6, 1927).*

This was my first sight of Aimee Semple McPherson. From it I received the impression, strengthened on many following occasions, that in this unique house of worship called Angelus Temple in the city of Los Angeles the Almighty occupies a secondary position. He plays an important part in the drama, to be sure; but center stage is taken and held by Mrs. McPherson. It is in her praise that the band blares, that flowers are piled high, that applause splits the air. It is to see her and hear her that throngs travel, crushed in the aisles of electric cars, elbow, and bruise one another as they shove at the doors of her Temple.

Sarah Comstock, journalist, from "Aimee Semple McPherson: Prima Donna of Revivalism," in Harper's *(December 1927).*

Today in Wall Street or the Baghdad Bazaar—now as when Judas betrayed Jesus for silver and Marco Polo found Chinese making banknotes of mulberry bark—men dream and talk of money. They talk more about it than of any other one thing. Could we, by some magic, at this instant catch all words being uttered in every tongue everywhere, the most frequent would probably refer to money and price.

William Atherton Du Puy, in National Geographic Magazine *(December 1927).*

Apply the idea of the unstable dollar to your own case. Suppose that you received before the War a dividend of four dollars per share, and that now you are receiving five dollars per share. Perhaps you cherish the idea that your dividend is now twenty-five per cent more than it used to be. But when you consider what your dividend dollar will buy, you will find that the real return to you is actually 12½ per cent less!

Work it out and see. The dollar of today, as compared with the dollar of 1913, is worth about 70 pre-war cents . . .; that is, it will buy about seventy per cent as much goods, on the average, as the dollar of 1913 bought. . . . Since each of these five present-day dollars is really only 70 cents, of pre-war standard, you will find that you actually have only five times 70 cents, or three dollars and a half, of pre-war standard.

Irving Fisher, renowned Yale University professor of economics, from his book The Money Illusion *(1928).*

. . . as a show-producer with unflagging power to draw she knows no equal. She is playwright, producer, director, and star performer in one; she keeps all her assistants . . . on their toes; and, in their midst, she plays her own role with an abandon that sweeps her hearers by hundreds to the altar. . . . Her Sunday evening service is a complete vaudeville program, entirely new each week, brimful of surprises for the eager who are willing to battle in the throng for entrance. In this show-devouring city no entertainment compares in popularity with that of Angelus Temple; the audience, whether devout or otherwise, concede it the best for the money . . . in town.

Sarah Comstock, writing about Aimee Semple McPherson in Harper's, *reprinted in* The American Scrapbook: The Year's Golden Harvest of Thought and Achievement *(1928).*

To keep the wealth value of the monetary unit stable, the banks must prevent any undue increase in their lending. As productive activity increases, the banks will permit a *proportional* credit expansion, so that there is an increased demand sufficient to absorb the increased output. If there is a pressure to borrow beyond this point in order to provide more working capital, the banks must check the borrowers by higher rates of interest or other means.

Ralph G. Hawtrey, from his book Trade and Credit *(1928).*

With but scant attention to it in many quarters, and distrusted and ridiculed in others, the infant automobile industry thus launched at the close of the century struggled on during the decade which followed, until in 1908 the then stupendous total of 60,000 cars was produced. In that year, W. C. Durant, then president of Buick, predicted that the time would come when a million automobiles a year would be made. He was laughed to scorn. . . . But eight years later, in 1916, more than a million cars were produced; . . . in 1923, well over three million; in 1925 and 1926, slightly over four million a year. Twenty-two million vehicles are now registered in this country. . . .

The factories which make motor cars and motor trucks now employ more than 375,000 persons, while directly and indirectly over 3,700,000 wage earners are engaged in producing and distributing automobiles, accessories, and parts. The capital invested in automobile factories in the year 1926 totaled over two billion dollars, while the yearly wages for the 375,000 workers well exceeded half a billion. Within a period of scarcely 30 years, the production of motor vehicles has become the largest of the country's manufactures, if the importance of these be measured by the wholesale value of their product. . . .

Ralph C. Epstein, assistant professor of economics and business organization at the University of Buffalo, from his book The Automobile Industry *(1928).*

It may yet remain to be determined whether science has proved a blessing or a curse. It is too soon to say, and the problem is too complicated. But certainly it is the fact that scientific "ideas" work so astoundingly in practical life which has given them such an enormous philosophical validity in the eyes of the people at large. Science in the opinion of the multitude has become something sacrosanct, and the average man to-day is as much a bigot about "science"—as he understands it—as the average man in Europe in the year 1000 was about the dogmas of the Roman Catholic Church, and for the same reason, namely, that he is breathing the air of the intellectual climate of his day.

James Truslow Adams, historian, in Harper's *(February 1928).*

Thus, one by one, at the conscious and unconscious behest of the white man, the old traditions hooked up with the colored man's peculiar appetites are booted on to the bunk heap. His natural human inclinations, talents, tastes, preferences, prejudices and predilections, along with the bunk, are ground under the flat foot of Aframerican inhibition. Chicken, watermelon, spirituals, chitlings, pigs' feet, bright colors, black faces, kinky hair, friendly congregating, the old-fashioned razor, pork chops,—all are now in the Index Expurgatorious of Aframerica. The Caucasians may snigger at all this as a new joke, but the "better class" colored folk will not. "Tis undignified to laugh, you know; the white man may think you boisterous."

Eugene Gordon, journalist on the staff of the Boston Post, *from "The Negro's Inhibitions," in the* American Mercury *(February 1928).*

Indignation, I believe, is the bad booze of controversialists. . . . Bryan was winning his fight against evolution until he allowed the cunning Darrow to lure him into indignation. Wilson was a hero until he started to bawl against the Senate. . . . The mob, which is the final arbiter in such matters, does not like indignant men. They strike it as funny. No doubt they really are. For though there may be ideas in this world worth suffering for and even dying for, it is hard to think of one that is worth getting indignant over. The Sacco-Vanzetti crusaders might have saved their babies if they had clung to the devastating austerity of Professor Felix Frankfurter and avoided the puerile yowling of striking garment-workers.

H. L. Mencken, journalist, editorial in the American Mercury *(February 1928).*

Smith is supposed to have horns and a tail out west. Kansas is one state, possibly the one state, that has made prohibition a success. But in general Kansas is the center of the world which Smith does not know and which does not know Smith. . . . If he comes to Emporia, to Kansas, the center of everything that is foreign to him, a rural population, an agricultural civilization, a population ninety per cent American-born of American parents, and sixty-five per cent born in Kansas, he will be facing a different audience. . . . It would do more for him politically than any other one thing he might possibly do to come with his message to a liberal state like Kansas and say it to our faces . . .

William Allen White, newspaper editor and author, letter of February 11, 1928, to Franklin D. Roosevelt, asking him to persuade Alfred Smith to address the Kansas State Editorial Association, in Johnson, Selected Letters of William Allen White, 1899–1943 *(1947).*

As to the practical difficulties in the way of enforcement, the agent ought to know more than any superintendent of the Anti-Saloon League. First of all, he points to the insufficiency of appropriations. The administrators of the various districts are allotted so much money, and with it they are expected to enforce the law. Invariably the fund is not large enough to permit the hiring of enough men or the provision of decent salaries to those who are hired. The result is an eternal skimping and a steady overworking of the men. It is not unusual for an agent to put in from sixteen to twenty hours a day and be expected to be on

the job with the rest of the world the following morning. Excessive fatigue is the result, and bad work.

Homer Turner, Prohibition agent, in the American Mercury *(April 1928).*

There are two ways of making money—one at the expense of others, the other by service to others. The first method does not "make" money, does not create anything; it only "gets" money—and does not always succeed in that. In the last analysis, the so-called gainer loses. The second way pays twice—to maker and user, to seller and buyer. It receives by creating, and receives only a just share, because no one is entitled to all. Nature and humanity supply too many necessary partners for that. True riches make wealthier the country as a whole.

Henry Ford, industrialist, in Forum *(October 1928).*

There has been revived in this campaign, however, a series of proposals which, if adopted, would be a long step toward the abandonment of our American system and a surrender to the destructive operation of governmental conduct of commercial business. Because the country is faced with difficulty and doubt over certain national problems—that is prohibition, farm relief, and electrical power—our opponents propose that we must thrust government a long way into the businesses which give rise to these problems. In effect, they abandon the tenets of their own party and turn to state socialism as a solution. . . .

By adherence to the principles of decentralized self-government, ordered liberty, equal opportunity, and freedom to the individual, our American experiment in human welfare has yielded a degree of well-being unparalleled in all the world. It has come nearer to the abolition of poverty, to the abolition of fear of want, than humanity has ever reached before. Progress of the past seven years is proof of it.

Herbert Hoover, Republican presidential candidate, from a final campaign address given in New York on October 22, 1928, in The New Day: Campaign Speeches of Herbert Hoover *(1928).*

But, as a matter of fact, football is more to the sports follower of this country than merely a game. It is at present a religion—sometimes it seems to be almost our national religion. . . .

This new religion has its dogma: the doctrine that only through so-called college spirit can a man be saved. According to this doctrine in its purest form, anything done for the purpose of bringing victory to the team is justifiable.

John R. Tunis, journalist, commenting on America's college football craze, in Harper's *(November 1928).*

Through his artistic efforts the Negro is smashing this immemorial stereotype faster than he has ever done through any other method he has been able to use . . . He is impressing upon the national mind the conviction that he is an active and important force in American life; that he is a creator. . . .

. . . I do not think it is too much to say that through artistic achievement the Negro has found a means of getting at the very core of the prejudice against him by challenging the Nordic superiority complex. A great deal has been accomplished in this decade of "renaissance." Enough has been accomplished to make it seem almost amazing when we realize that there are less than twenty-five Negro artists who have more or less of national recognition; and that it is they who have chiefly done the work.

James Weldon Johnson, poet and NAACP secretary, from his essay "Race Prejudice and the Negro Artist," in Harper's *(November 1928).*

I come to pay a call of friendship. In a sense I represent on this occasion the people of the United States extending friendly greeting to our fellow democracies on the American continent. I would wish to symbolize the friendly visit of one good neighbor to another. In our daily life, good neighbors call upon each other as the evidence of solicitude for the common welfare and to learn of the circumstances and point of view of each, so that there may come both under-

standing and respect which are cementing forces of all enduring society. This should be equally true amongst nations. We have a desire to maintain not only cordial relations of government with each other but the relations of good neighbors.

President-elect Herbert Hoover, speech in Honduras, November 26, 1928, during his tour of Latin America, in De Conde, Herbert Hoover's Latin-American Policy *(1970).*

No Congress of the United States ever assembled, on surveying the state of the Union, has met with a more pleasing prospect than that which appears at the present time. In the domestic field there is tranquility and contentment, harmonious relations between management and wage earner, freedom from industrial strife, and the highest record of years of prosperity. In the foreign field there is peace, the good will which comes from mutual understanding, and the knowledge that the problems which a short time ago appeared so ominous are yielding to the touch of manifest friendship. The great wealth created by our enterprise and industry, and saved by our economy, has had the widest distribution among our own people, and has gone out in a steady stream to serve the charity and business of the world. The requirements of existence have passed beyond the standard of necessity into the region of luxury. Enlarging production is consumed by an increasing demand at home and an expanding commerce abroad. The country can regard the present with satisfaction and anticipate the future with optimism.

President Calvin Coolidge, his sixth annual State of the Union message to Congress, December 4, 1928, in Israel, ed., The State of the Union Messages of the Presidents, *vol. 3 (1966).*

2

Fateful Year on
Wall Street
1929

HOOVER TAKES OVER

The year 1929 did not, of course, occur in isolation from the years that preceded it or those that followed. But in retrospect it stands out for people who experienced it and for historians as a watershed year because it climaxed in the drama surrounding the Great Crash of the stock market. And though it would be a while before the nature and extent of events leading into the Great Depression became revealed, 1929 seems inevitably to be cited as the turning point or the threshold to cataclysm.

The year began well enough, with the Coolidge administration continuing in office until the March 4 inauguration of Hoover; the economy was still growing; the GNP reached $204 billion in 1929, up from $128 billion in 1921. President-elect Herbert Hoover, who had taken elder statesman Elihu Root's advice on how to avoid the press and controversy, was on a six-week goodwill tour in South America with his wife and a diplomatic delegation. After his return and two weeks of meetings in Washington, D.C., Hoover left town again to enjoy some reclusiveness while choosing his cabinet. Among his choices were Henry L. Stimson as secretary of state, William D. Mitchell as attorney general, Charles Francis Adams as secretary of the navy, Ray Lyman Wilbur as secretary of the interior, Robert P. Lamont as secretary of commerce, and Andrew Mellon as secretary of the treasury—not all his first choices by any means. Overall they impressed observers as a reasonably capable lot. And with Hoover in the presidency and Mellon continuing at the Treasury, businessmen and investors felt confident that the Harding-Coolidge prosperity would continue.

The Wall Street bull market of increasing stock valuations, after a decline the previous December, had rebounded and expanded, driven by heavy buying, large infusions of money from corporations and investment trusts (similar to mutual funds), increased speculation, and margin borrowing (investors' use of credit from brokerage firms). Some economists and even some prominent stockbrokers—notably Paul M. Warburg of the International Acceptance Bank associated with Kuhn, Loeb and Company—were concerned about overspeculation. Warburg

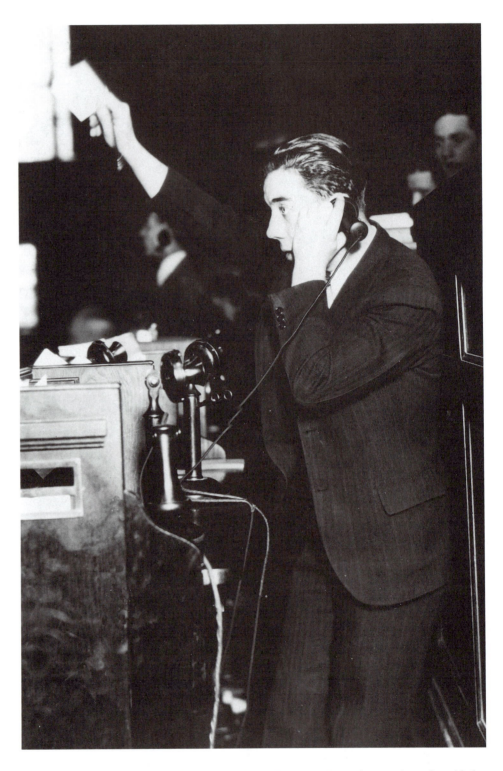

Stock exchange trader on the
telephone, January 24, 1929
(Library of Congress)

astutely argued for action by the Federal Reserve Board, warning that if the
overspeculation was not stopped, the stock market would collapse, generating a
national depression. But opponents of raising the discount rate (the rate member
banks of the Federal Reserve system pay in order to borrow money from the
federal system for lending to their own borrowers) and interest rates and opti-
mists preaching permanent prosperity prevailed.

It is not surprising, then, that in his inaugural address on March 4 Herbert Hoover voiced optimism. He depicted the nation as developing new social, political, and economic systems; advocated cooperation between government and business, with fairness of competition guaranteed through governmental regulation; and promised support for education, public health, and law enforcement. Although Hoover never inspired enthusiasm, he at least began with the public's confidence and respect. By all accounts, few men ever occupied the White House who were more intelligent, capable, efficient, humane, or committed. Hoover had proven himself a humanitarian through his food relief work during and after the war and an outstanding administrator both as head of the Food Administration and as Harding's and Coolidge's secretary of commerce. His competence was never in question. But there was something vital that he lacked. He had never been elected to any office before winning the presidency; he was not a politician. And so he never grasped the importance of his role in using the power of his office to influence, to cajole, and to bargain with congressmen, other politicians, and assorted other vested interests—a fatal shortcoming for a president. In fact, Hoover believed so thoroughly in the constitutional sanctity of the separation of powers among the three branches of government that he mostly remained aloof from trying to influence the development of legislation in Congress. To congressmen, cabinet members, and even the White House staff he seemed remote, stolid, and gloomy. He pursued a regimen that was a model of hard work, efficiency, and dedication but never of personal warmth or animation.

HOOVER'S VISION

Hoover had a clear understanding of the problems that he believed confronted the nation and also a clear idea of how he wanted to approach resolving them. He moved quickly in directing the Treasury Department to disclose to the public large refunds on taxes, in asking Congress to revise the graduated income tax scale to make it fairer to lower- and middle-income payers, and in ordering officers enforcing Prohibition to adhere to strictly legal tactics. He also directed the Justice Department to avoid harassing communists and other radicals, allowing them the freedom to demonstrate, and encouraged many proposals for prison reforms. He strongly supported oil conservation, added millions of acres to the national forests, provided power generated by federal dams to publicly owned utilities, and advocated construction of the St. Lawrence Seaway. He and Stimson envisioned implementing enlightened policies toward South America, independence for the Philippines, and naval arms reductions. Hoover also supported fairer treatment of American Indians and African Americans through funding and programs for the Bureau of Indian Affairs, invitations to the White House, and personal example. And he convened conferences or appointed commissions to study and to recommend programs addressing nearly every conceivable issue facing the nation's people. His approach to the presidency, then, evidenced a significantly greater activism than Coolidge had ever contemplated mustering. But unfortunately, Hoover was sitting on an economic time bomb ticking itself toward an explosion that obliterated his sincere reform efforts. The Great Stock Market Crash in October occurred when Hoover had been in office less than eight months. The massive economic decline that followed would change the focus of his administration as the nation faced social crisis.

SPECULATIVE FEVER

Although some of the causes of the Great Crash remain arguable, at least one, overspeculation, is clear-cut. Intimations of the ultimate eruption of speculative fever on Wall Street stretched as far back as 1920, when investors had rushed to be fleeced by Carlo Ponzi, and to 1925, when the boom in Florida real estate revealed itself to be a bubble. Certainly the imposing run-up in stock values from 1927 onward plainly evidenced the threat overspeculation posed not just to investors but also to banks and brokerages. Stocks rose consistently throughout the summer months of 1929, attaining a total market value of $67 billion (up from only $27 billion in 1925). From June through August the *New York Times* daily stock average climbed 110 points, advancing from 339 to 449, nearly a 25 percent increase in only three months. By contrast, in all of 1928, the average had climbed only 86.5 points. During this same three months General Electric common added 123 points to close out August at 391; American Telephone and Telegraph (AT&T), 94 points to 303; Westinghouse, 135 points to 286. Other stocks skyrocketed similarly. It did not require enormous insight to suspect that things were getting out of hand, yet such smart investors as Bernard Baruch publicly prophesied future momentum. (To his credit, Hoover tried to dampen speculation by sending an emissary to the banks in New York and by calling Richard Whitney, vice president of the New York Stock Exchange, to the White House to request that he take action—but to no avail.)

Despite the evident speculation occurring in the market, leading economists—many of whom continued buying stocks (and recommended that others do the same) as the decline proceeded—posited the view that stocks actually were not overpriced; in the years since the depression economists have often upheld this view while also conceding that no clear explanation for the dramatic stock market decline of October and November 1929 exists. Whereas common stocks increased in total value by 120 percent during the 1925–29 period, it can be argued that this dramatic rise merely reflected the actual prosperity of the time and the anticipation that it would not only continue but grow. In 1929 the price to earnings ratio (PE) of major industrial stocks slightly exceeded 15, up from an increase of 12 to 14 in 1928—all very much in line with the historic average ratio of roughly 16. (By contrast the PE of shares comprising the Standard & Poor's 500-stock index at the end of the year 2003 stood at 27, significantly higher than those ratios witnessed on the threshold of the Great Depression.) Furthermore, the production index reported by the Federal Reserve, which stood at 67 in 1921, rose steadily every year but 1924 to reach 118 in 1929—an annual increase of 3.1 percent during a period when commodity prices were falling—and climbed to 125 in June 1929.

Many corporations also evidenced huge earnings growth. While the common stock of United States Steel, for example, more than doubled in value between 1925 and 1929, reported per share earnings leaped from $9.20 to $21.20 over the same time span. As a consequence of strong growth in earnings, many corporations also raised their dividend payouts. Through 1929's first nine months 1,436 firms declared dividend increases, and corporate earnings reports in September and October remained positive. Total cash dividends, which amounted to $2.4 billion during the first nine months of 1928, increased to $3.1 billion during the comparable period in 1929, representing growth of nearly 30 percent. The GNP, as noted, also continued to increase from 1925 to 1929. These and other positive economic developments understandably could have well been interpreted as justifying stock prices. So what went wrong?

To a quite appreciable extent, government officials' comments about speculation created unease and may have caused many investors to withdraw funds from the market, triggering declines in stock prices. More pointedly, some commentators, including members of the Federal Reserve Board, blamed that board's "easy-money" policies, purportedly instigated by Benjamin Strong, governor of the Federal Reserve Bank of New York, who died in October 1928. But Strong's demise left the Federal Reserve system bereft of perhaps its most fiscally astute leader, and the system fell under the control of less capable men wracked with anxiety about "excessive speculation" in the stock market. Tacitly supported by President Hoover, who shared their anxiety, they began increasing the discount rate, with the Federal Reserve Bank of New York initiating an increase from 5 percent to 6 percent in February 1929, followed in August by the Federal Reserve Board's approval of adopting 6 percent for the entire system. With the higher rate in place, money flow for loans to stock brokers and to the construction industry, corporations, and small businessmen for reinvestment in capital goods declined; this may have been the real catalyst for collapsing stock prices. But, of course, even these explanations trace back to perceived overspeculation in the stock market.

The speculative fervor also became evident in the enormous increase in the numbers of investment trusts, which were created to sell shares to investors and then to invest the resulting funds in common or preferred stocks of individual companies, mortgages, bonds, debentures, or stocks of other investment trusts. (By investing in each others' stocks, the trusts were, in effect, pyramiding assets that existed only on paper.) In 1927, 300 such trusts existed; in 1928, 186 more were organized; in 1929, 265 more. And the amount of securities they sold to the public advanced from $400 million in 1927 to an estimated $3 billion in 1929. By the fall of 1929 their combined assets were estimated at $8 billion. The stocks of many trusts exceeded in value—in some cases by twice—the total worth of the investments they owned. The investment trusts were owned by commercial banks, stock brokerage firms, investment banking firms, and other investment trusts. Some were owned or controlled by persons of dubious integrity.

There were other warning signs. Contracts for new residential construction dropped throughout the year by a total of $1 billion from 1928, and fewer new houses meant fewer purchases of furniture, appliances, rugs, and other household items. Inventories, manufactured goods in storage awaiting purchase by retailers, increased threefold from half a billion dollars in 1928 to $1.8 billion in 1929—an ominous sign. As both of these statistics would suggest, consumer spending was in decline, dropping from an annual average increase of 7.4 percent during the preceding two years to an annual increase of only 1.5 percent during 1929. Consumers, the major driving force of the economy, were curtailing expenditures, perhaps because they felt financially overextended. And they probably were. During the four years from 1925 to 1929 outstanding installment credit rose from $1.38 billion to $3 billion, as most sales of cars, radios, and other durable goods were purchased on credit.

As a result, by July industrial production had begun to fall, and as the summer unfolded, the prices of wholesale commodities—metals, grains, cattle, lumber, textiles—registered continual declines. In response to these developments, the Federal Reserve Board finally moved to raise the discount rate from 5 percent to 6 percent in order to slow the flow of funds available for loans. But the net effect of this move would, rather ironically, be harsher for businesses, consumers, and farmers than for speculators since the rate of return on brokers' loans had been averaging from 6 percent to 12 percent, and the huge advance in stock prices would more than compensate for such an increase through the capital gains that could be achieved on the sale of inflated stocks. In short, the Federal Reserve Board's response was too late. It may, in fact, have had a negative psychological effect for some investors, giving them cause for worry.

THE GREAT CRASH

As they had for months, businessmen and bankers continued to speak optimistically of the economic future. Stock market speculation also continued, as revealed by the fact that brokers' loans—money used for margin buying—rose weekly. New York banks borrowed increasing sums from the Federal Reserve to provide for loans to investors. Prices rose, with many stocks on the New York Stock Exchange reaching their record highs on September 3. On that day, for example, General Electric closed at 396, AT&T at 304, Radio Corporation of America at 505, New York Central Railroad at 256, and United States Steel at 262. A downturn on September 5, in reaction perhaps to grave warnings by economist Roger Babson in a speech, prompted many investors to sell shares, but no panicky reaction followed, although the market became increasingly ragged and trended unevenly downward. During the third week of October the market began to reveal its soft underpinnings, and then on October 23, a severe break occurred. Extraordinarily heavy selling in the final hour of trading cranked the *New York Times* average down by 31 points to 384, erasing the gains made since June; individual major stocks declined by 10 to 40 points or more. Many investors with margin accounts received requests to post more collateral, as the value of the stocks on which they had borrowed funds no longer covered their outstanding loans.

Panic ensued on the morning of October 24—Black Thursday. Nearly 13 million shares, twice the previous record volume, went up for sale. By noon representatives of the major New York banks began assembling at the offices of J. P. Morgan and Company to discuss a response. They decided to pool their banks' resources to support the market; subsequently, Thomas W. Lamont, senior partner at the House of Morgan (J. Pierpont Morgan, Jr., was in Europe) announced that the banks would come to the rescue. At 1:30 P.M., Richard Whitney, vice president of the New York Stock Exchange and the House of Morgan's floor trader, entered the exchange and circulated among the traders, placing orders for about 20 different stocks. Confidence returned and prices moved upward. Some stocks actually ended the day with net gains. Trading was heavy on Friday and Saturday, but prices held, and bankers, politicians, and corporation presidents flooded newspapers and airwaves with positive pronouncements about the state of the economy and the future of the stock market.

On Monday the panic returned. The *New York Times* average lost 49 points, General Electric fell 48 points, AT&T dropped 34 points—and this time the bankers did not intervene. The next day, October 29, Black Tuesday, the fire storm struck again, culminating in the worst, most abrupt ruination Wall Street had ever experienced. By the end of the day more than 16.4 million shares had changed hands, and the *Times* average had fallen another 43 points. Even though the prices of many stocks actually bounced back from their lows of the day, the devastation was fearsome: General Electric and AT&T each dropped 28 points, for example. Worst hit were the investment trusts, with many losing half or more of their value on this single day. The declines continued. By mid-November the market had suffered a loss of $26 billion, or 40 percent of its value. But however grim the carnage of the final week of October and the early weeks of November, it really marked only the beginning. In the early months of 1930 the market stabilized, but in the spring and throughout many months to come it staggered on toward collapse; its deterioration would seem to be without end.

RESPONDING TO THE COLLAPSE

Secretary of the Treasury Mellon judged that the economy should be allowed to rectify itself, even if this meant total collapse as the prelude to eventual recovery. But President Hoover wished to avoid needless suffering and to contain the crisis. He called a series of November meetings with leaders of industry, labor, finance, railroads, public utilities, and agriculture to discuss how to respond and unfolded his plans for improving the situation. He advocated voluntary pledges from industrialists to sustain wages and prices, cooperation between industry and local governments to maintain spending on public building projects, increased federal expenditures for public works, efforts to loosen credit through the Federal Reserve system, stabilization of prices for agricultural products through programs of the Federal Farm Board, reduction of income tax rates, and a higher protective tariff.

During December, Congress, at Hoover's urging, passed a tax reduction act that the president signed into law. The act decreased tax rates from 1.5 percent to .5 percent on incomes below $4,000, from 3 percent to 2 percent on incomes of $4,000 to $8,000, and from 5 percent to 4 percent on incomes over $8,000. The rate for corporate profits would also drop one point from 12 percent to 11 percent. The reductions became retroactive for 1929 but were so small (to begin with, the previous tax rates had been very low) as to have negligible impact. The voluntary efforts of industry were also ineffective, as the economy had already been turning downward. And the proposal for a tariff increase, to be put in place through legislation passed in 1930, would prove to be an unqualified disaster. But for the time being, there did not appear to be an imperative reason to react vigorously to the Great Crash, as the economy's direction remained to be clarified in the future.

RIPPLE EFFECTS

The repercussions of the Great Crash on Wall Street extended well beyond the lives and fortunes of those immediately involved, of course. The actual numbers of stock owners were small: only about 4 million out of a total population of about 120 million. Of these 4 million, only about 1.5 million had large enough holdings to warrant accounts with brokerage firms. And the majority of these were small stockholders, with the largest investments, as might be expected, concentrated in the hands of higher-income earners. But however small their numbers within the larger population, these investors were a major source of much of the capital that in a normal stock market could end up being invested in new plants and equipment; with the value of their investments now liquidated, that capital source would disappear. Of immeasurable consequence also was the shocking nature of the crash and of the headlines that followed, which destroyed confidence, not just among investors but also among businessmen, professionals, corporation presidents, bankers, and the populace in general. And so the all-important consumers, anxious over the future, began to curb their spending.

There were repercussions abroad as well. For one thing, Wall Street had been a magnet for investment capital from abroad. As margin buying had mushroomed, the interest rates brokers charged for margin loans (call money) that they in turn borrowed from banks and corporations had kept pace, rising to as high as 20 percent. That kind of return was irresistible to foreign investors, who flooded money into Wall Street and suffered the consequences when the fall occurred. For Germany the consequences were most severe. Having attained stability during the four years from 1924 through 1928 after taming the fearful inflation of 1922–23, the Weimar Republic once again faced peril in 1929. Unemployment rose during the year. And after the Great Crash of the New York stock market the foreign credits that had helped fuel the German economy evaporated. Short-term loans were canceled; high tariffs stifled exports. Economic, social, and political conflicts increased. Leftist and rightist political movements gained adherents. Ominously, membership in the Nazi Party climbed from 108,000 in 1928 to 178,000 in 1929—an increase of 65 percent.

The Great Crash did not cause the worldwide depression that followed, but it did expose the underlying weaknesses of the U.S. and European economies. In the United States, agriculture had been in a depressed state for 10 years, with continual declines in exports, crop prices, and land values. Farm dwellers, who made up roughly a fourth of the population, may have wondered ruefully whether now the other three-fourths would share their experience. The boon of technology that created many jobs—in the automobile and related industries, for example—also had its downside. Railroads had suffered huge passenger losses to the lure of the car, with a resulting large decline in employment. The increased use of synthetic fibers created job losses in the textile industry. Unemployment and declining wages in some industries had resulted in a nearly one-third drop in union memberships so that unions lost clout, which in turn opened the door to more unemployment and wage cuts. Unemployment and lower wages translated into lower consumer spending. Many industries, spurred by consolidations effected through mergers, had been overexpanding and overproducing, resulting in both surplus capacities and inventories. These problems and more would now exact their toll.

That toll would be compounded here and abroad by the worldwide economic consequences of the crash and its aftereffects of cheapened currencies, high tariffs, import quotas, speculative excesses, and other policy errors. The United States had played a major role in the European economies, which had never returned to full strength after the war, by restricting trade through the maintenance of tariff barriers, even though imports accounted for only 4 percent of the American domestic market.

THE FARM AND THE CITY

Despite the impression left by the drama surrounding it, the stock market crash was not the only major story of 1929. There is more to American life than Wall Street, after all. As noted, a fourth of the populace lived on farms, where depression had struck in 1919 and lasted through the following decade. Neither Harding nor Coolidge had made any real effort to deal with the problems besetting agriculture. Hoover, by contrast, made agriculture a priority. Very nearly his first act as president was to call Congress into special session in April to draft legislation for a program to help farmers—the Agricultural Marketing Act.

At the time, the major problems of American agriculture were overproduction and low prices, compounded by the burdens of taxes and high costs for transportation and equipment. Congressmen representing western states and other farm areas wanted direct intervention by the federal government in the form of subsidies and tariffs on agricultural imports that would help relieve farmers of these burdens, as, in their view, high tariffs helped industry by reducing imports of manufactured goods.

But Hoover did not believe in direct government intervention and the bureaucracies it entailed. The Agricultural Marketing Act, as a result, created a Federal Farm Board whose sole purpose was to oversee distribution of loans to farm cooperatives at local, state, and regional levels. The purpose of these loans would be to assist farmers in efforts to reduce production and enhance marketing, which presumably would generate higher prices for their products. Hoover staunchly supported the concept of cooperatives as means by which farmers could help themselves—an approach he had advocated for 10 years. Unfortunately, despite Hoover's good intent, the program enacted was rather vague in both structure and purpose and proved ineffectual in addressing the agricultural depression. The plight of the farmers continued and even worsened, intensified by the unanticipated natural disaster of drought in the 1930s.

In urban areas developments and preoccupations that had emerged earlier in the decade showed little sign of lapsing. The great skyscraper building boom appeared intact. In New York the Chrysler Building neared completion, and construction of the Empire State Building, begun in 1928, continued the push toward ever higher buildings. Even Frank Lloyd Wright had joined the New York boom with the 1929 design of St. Mark's Tower (the building was never erected). In Chicago, birthplace of the skyscraper, the Palmolive Building, designed by Holabird and Root in the modern style, was under construction, as was the world's largest building at that time, the Merchandise Mart, designed by Graham, Anderson, Probst, and White.

Architecture was hardly alone in suggesting the appearance of the future. As the stock market crescendoed in summer 1929, Robert Hutchins Goddard, the father of modern rocketry who in 1919 had published his groundbreaking *A Method of Reaching Extreme Altitudes,* launched a steel cylindrical rocket, propelled by a liquid-fueled engine, a quarter of a mile skyward. Although hardly a great success, the venture attracted the interest of Charles A. Lindbergh, who began to help garner financial support for Goddard's continuing experiments. Industrialist and philanthropist Harry F. Guggenheim joined the effort, providing funding to Goddard through the Guggenheim Fund for the Promotion of Aeronautics. Both Lindbergh and Guggenheim would persist in their support, despite the press's ridicule of the scientist as "Moony" Goddard. The validity of Goddard's farseeing vision would be dramatically confirmed 40 years later with the successful Apollo moon shot, but well after his death.

In painting, the so-called Precisionists—Charles Sheeler, Joseph Stella, Charles Demuth, and others—had developed distinctly American works influenced by photography and the industrial landscape. (In the early thirties Sheeler would consummate this art form in his landscapes depicting the Ford Motor Company's River Rouge plant.) Georgia O'Keeffe in effect combined two art forms through her paintings of New York skyscrapers. And Edward Hopper had perfected his technique for interpreting American life in art through his paintings of houses and street scenes.

In literature, the decade was ending with a flourish. Sinclair Lewis published *Dodsworth.* William Faulkner produced two of his finest novels, *The Sound and the Fury* and *Sartoris.* Ernest Hemingway contributed *A Farewell to Arms;* Ellen Glasgow, *They Stooped to Folly.* Thomas Wolfe published his first novel, the monumental *Look Homeward, Angel.* The highly regarded critic Joseph Wood Krutch published *The Modern Temper;* humorist Ring Lardner, *Round Up.* Robinson Jeffers and Countee Cullen produced new volumes of poetry. Cullen was, of course, along with Claude McKay and W. E. B. DuBois, a major figure in the Harlem Renaissance—the flowering of African-American poetry, prose, and consciousness centered in Harlem during the twenties. Harlem was also the center for jazz music, which would move into an eclipse for several years in the wake of the Great Crash.

As for the two favored forms of entertainment, film and radio, they now shared the public popularity of sound. The talkies were beginning to displace silent films in the cinemas as new techniques allowed silent filming with separately recorded sound to be dubbed in afterward. King Vidor's *Hallelujah!* was among the first movies to adopt this technique. The sound for *In Old Arizona,* codirected by Raoul Walsh, was recorded mostly out of doors. Many devotees and film critics strongly, though futilely, resisted the move to sound, regarding it as corrupting the art of film.

There was no resistance to radio, however. In 1929 began weekly broadcasts of the *Old Gold–Paul Whiteman Hour,* whose popularity was enhanced by performances of The Rhythm Boys, a trio including Bing Crosby. At NBC *The Music Appreciation Hour* with Walter Damrosch, conductor of the New York Symphony, was in its second year of introducing an audience of millions to classical music and the voices of such opera stars as Ernestine Schumann-Heink and Rosa Ponselle. Among the most popular radio programs, however, were the variety show *The Fleischmann Hour,* with Rudy Vallee as host, and the nightly comedy serial *Amos 'n' Andy,* with Freeman Gosden and Charles Correll; both shows had been launched only the year before. Joining these shows in 1929, *The Rise of the Goldbergs,* starring Gertrude Berg, began its long, popular run. By now Graham McNamee had become the best-known announcer in radio through his broadcasts of the World Series and major news events. And H. V. Kaltenborn had established himself as a commentator on foreign affairs, broadcasting frequently from abroad. Radio programming had easily crossed the threshhold into more than two decades of enormous popularity.

These pursuits and pastimes remain overshadowed by the consequences of economic collapse that followed 1929. Whether in the White House or on Main Street, the disaster on Wall Street focused all attention on the state of the U.S. economy, for ultimately the economy's health—or lack of it—appears to be a determining factor in how people view other aspects of their lives. That conclusion's validity lies implicit in a statement in *Middletown,* the pioneering, seminal, and influential study of Muncie, Indiana, by sociologists Robert S. Lynd and Helen Merrell Lynd published in 1929. Of "Middletown" the Lynds observed, "Not only do those engaged in getting the living of the group predominate numerically, but as the study progressed it became more and more apparent that the money medium of exchange and the cluster of activities associated with its acquisition drastically condition the other activities of the people." In short, dollars and jobs determine the nature of home life, child-rearing, leisure activities, religious practices, and community involvement (the other concerns of the Lynds' study). If that is true, then clearly the effects of economic collapse would inevitably pervade every area of American life in the 1930s.

CHRONICLE OF EVENTS

1929

January 6: President-elect Herbert Hoover returns to Washington, D.C., after his tour of South American nations.

January 15: Supported by the view of the Committee on Foreign Relations that the pact will in no way interfere with existing treaties or oblige the nation to forgo its own self-defense or act against a violator, the U.S. Senate confirms the Pact of Paris without reservations by an 85-1 vote.

January 21: After two weeks of conferences with congressmen and numerous delegations, Hoover leaves Washington for Belle Isle, Florida, where he will polish his inaugural speech and think about his cabinet and other appointments.

February 11: An international committee assembles in Paris to revise the Dawes Plan for Germany's reparations payments. Owen D. Young, an American representative and head of General Electric, is chosen chairman, and the eventual agreement will be known as the Young Plan.

February 11: In Rome the pope's representative, Pietro Gasparri, and Benito Mussolini sign the Lateran Treaty, whereby the Italian government recognizes establishment of Vatican City as a sovereign and independent state and provides the papacy compensation for the seizure of the Papal States and the city of Rome in the 19th century; in exchange, the papacy accepts the government's right to control of the seized areas, excluding Vatican City.

February 13: Responding to the failure of the Geneva Conference and subsequent proposals by Coolidge for a five-year plan to expand the navy's fleet, Congress approves an act authorizing the construction of 15 light cruisers and one aircraft carrier.

February 14: Concerned that speculation in the stock market—specifically, margin buying—is becoming overheated, the New York Federal Reserve Bank recommends that the discount rate be raised an entire point, to 6 percent but the Federal Reserve Board has already made known its reluctance to raise rates.

February 14: In Chicago seven members of the O'Banion gang at the S. M. C. Cartage Company garage surrender to five men in police uniforms (actually members of the Torrio-Capone gang), who

Herbert Hoover was inaugurated president of the United States on March 4, 1929. He is shown here in a photograph that was probably taken the previous year. *(Library of Congress, Prints and Photographs Division [LC-USZ62-24155])*

line them up against a wall and shoot them dead—the so-called St. Valentine's Day Massacre.

March 4: Herbert Hoover is inaugurated president of the United States. In his inaugural address he advocates United States membership in the World Court. Hoover appoints Andrew Mellon as secretary of the treasury. Mellon has served in this post since the beginning of the Harding administration. Henry L. Stimson is appointed secretary of state.

March 25: Nervous investors begin unloading stocks on this final Monday in March. The Federal Reserve Board, finally reacting to concerns about the stock market, has been meeting daily in Washington, D.C., even on the preceding Saturday (March 23), but has issued no public statement. The meetings and the silence unsettle investors.

March 26: Following further inaction and silence by the Federal Reserve Board, the stock market falls again, sharply this time, the heavy volume exceeding

8 million shares of stock sold. But Charles E. Mitchell, director of the New York Federal Reserve Bank and chairman of National City Bank, expresses confidence to the press, asserting that National City will provide ample funds for loans; money rates decline and the market recovers.

March 27: National City Bank announces a commitment to keeping interest rates low by investing $25 million in the call market (future rights to buy stocks at fixed prices), and the threat that the Federal Reserve Board will raise rates dissipates.

April 12: Hoover sends a special message to Congress, convened in special session at his request to consider legislation dealing with the crisis in agriculture, but he makes no specific proposals on what the legislation should contain, leaving the outcome entirely to the will of Congress.

May 20: Fulfilling a commitment made in his inaugural address to tackle problems surrounding enforcement of Prohibition, Hoover appoints a Commission on Law Enforcement, with George W. Wickersham, who served as attorney general under President William H. Taft, as chairman. The other members are Newton D. Baker, secretary of war in the Wilson administration; U.S. circuit judge William S. Kenyon; and Roscoe Pound, dean of Harvard Law School. Hoover goes beyond his original commitment and charges the commission with reviewing the entire federal justice system.

June 5: Following a Labour Party victory in the May general election, Ramsay MacDonald returns as prime minister of Great Britain, succeeding Stanley Baldwin.

June 7: The Young Plan for German reparations payments is revealed to the affected nations. It reduces Germany's reparations burden to $8 billion at an interest rate of 5.5 percent to be paid in regular installments over a period of 58½ years; establishes the Bank for International Settlements at Basel, Switzerland, to handle the funds transfers; and terminates foreign controls over Germany's economy.

June 12: After weeks of argument and deadlock between the House and the Senate, the special session of Congress finally passes the Agricultural Marketing Act. The act establishes a Federal Farm Board to oversee a revolving fund of $500 million from which to dispense loans intended to assist farmers in reducing production and in marketing crops.

July 2: The White House Conference on Health and Protection of Children—a major conference typical of many similar meetings organized by Hoover and Secretary of the Interior Ray Lymon Wilbur to study and recommend policies on such issues as housing, oil conservation, education, and waste—convenes in Washington, D.C. Some 2,500 delegates concerned with child welfare attend.

July 24: In Washington, D.C., the Pact of Paris is officially declared in force worldwide. Besides the original 15 signatories, 31 other nations have now accepted and signed the treaty.

August 31: Representatives from 15 nations meeting at The Hague sign a preliminary draft of the Young Plan.

September 3: The Dow Jones Industrial Average reaches a record high of 381, an increase of 100 percent for the year to date. Individual stocks also reach record highs—American Telephone and Telegraph at $304, General Electric at $396, RCA at $505.

October 3: Gustav Stresemann, the Weimar Republic's foreign minister, wearied by his six-year effort to restore German stature, secure the republic's stability, and reduce the reparations burden, dies.

October 5: Hoover and British prime minister Ramsay MacDonald confer at the president's summer retreat at Rapidan, Maryland, and establish a mutual rapport and goodwill. They decide to pursue a cooperative effort to promote world peace, but their only substantive plan is to encourage another conference of the "Big Five" nations to negotiate further reductions in naval armaments.

October 7: The British government officially invites the governments of France, Italy, Japan, and the United States to a conference in London to discuss further limitations on naval armaments.

October 24 (Black Thursday): Following a 21-point drop in the Dow Jones average on October 23, panic selling ensues on Wall Street. Prominent bankers, including Thomas W. Lamont and J. P. Morgan, intervene with public statements of confidence to shore up the market, which recoups the day's losses.

October 24: The Fleischmann Hour, hosted by Rudy Vallee, debuts on the NBC radio network.

October 29 (Black Tuesday): After a big sell-off the previous day, when the Dow lost 13 percent of its value in the morning's trading, panic wreaks havoc on the New York Stock Exchange as a record 16.4 million shares change hands. The Great Crash of the stock market has begun.

October 29: The Farmers' National Grain Corporation, part of the Hoover program to salvage agriculture, is formed. The corporation's purpose is to loan money to its constituent cooperatives in the various states so they can buy wheat on the open market as a means of supporting the price of wheat that farmers may obtain.

October 31: The stock market rallies, with the *New York Times* average gaining 21 points. The Federal Reserve lowers the discount rate from 6 percent to 5 percent.

November 5: Democrat James J. Walker wins reelection as mayor of New York, defeating Republican Fiorello LaGuardia, whom the Democrats have excoriated as a socialist.

November 13: For the third day in a row, the stock market declines, with the *Times* average down 50 points over the last three days, closing at 224, a nearly 50 percent drop since September 3.

November 21: The president has called a series of conferences at the White House with leaders of industry, labor, finance, and agriculture to discuss the state of the economy. Today he meets with such industrial leaders as Henry Ford, Alfred P. Sloan, Pierre du Pont, and Owen D. Young, who issue highly optimistic statements afterward.

December 2: The regular session of the 71st Congress convenes. At the urging of the president, Congress begins consideration of a bill to reduce income taxes.

December 21: After conferring with a group of social scientists, who at his urging have submitted a plan for surveying all major aspects of American society to gather data that may be used for generating solutions to social problems, Hoover announces the appointment of the President's Committee on Recent Social Trends.

EYEWITNESS TESTIMONY

Our intellectual history thus conceived falls into three broad phases: Calvinistic pessimism, romantic optimism, and mechanistic pessimism. Between the first and the last lies the America of yesterday that shaped the American mind and American institutions; and with the submergence of that native world we are in the way of repeating here the familiar history of Europe, with its coercive regimentations reproduced on a larger scale and in more mechanical fashion . . . an industrialized society is reshaping the psychology fashioned by an agrarian world; the passion for liberty is lessening and the individual, in the presence of creature comforts, is being dwarfed; the drift of centralization is shaping its inevitable tyrannies to bind us with. Whether the quick concern for human rights . . . will be carried over into the future, to unhorse the machine that now rides men and to leaven the sodden mass that is industrial America, is a question to which the gods as yet have given no answer.

Vernon Louis Parrington, historian and professor, commenting on modern America, in the 1929 introduction to the second volume of his monumental study, published posthumously, Main Currents in American Thought *(1930).*

This is a day of specializing, especially with the doctors. Say, for instance, there is something the matter with your right eye. You go to a doctor and he tells you, "I am sorry, but I am a left-eye doctor; I make a specialty of left eyes." Take the throat business for instance. A doctor that doctors on the upper part of your throat he doesn't even know where the lower part goes to. And the highest priced one of all of them is another bird that just tells you which doctor to go to. He can't cure even corns or open a boil himself. He is a Diagnostician, but he's nothing but a traffic cop, to direct ailing people.

Will Rogers, humorist and author, in Ether and Me or "Just Relax" *(1929).*

Through Chance, we are each a ghost to all the others, and our only reality; through Chance, the hinge of the world, and a grain of dust; the stone that starts an avalanche, the pebble whose concentric circles widen across the seas.

Thomas Wolfe, in his novel Look Homeward, Angel *(1929).*

At the same time that secularization is lessening emotional resistance at some points, the very swiftness of the penetration of impersonal institutions like automatic machinery, electrical devices, and automobiles, has, however, multiplied occasions for emotional explosion in Middletown through discrepancies between these shouldering new ways and the other habits upon which they force themselves. One need only mention the new friction spots between parents and children incidental to the incorporation of automobile and movies into their world, or the emotional ramifications suggested above in connection with the advent and operation of automatic machinery among Middletown working men and their families.

Robert S. Lynd and Helen Merrell Lynd, sociologists, on the social effects of the "machine age," concluding their seminal study of Muncie, Indiana, in Middletown *(1929).*

The world breaks every one and afterward many are strong at the broken places. But those that will not break it kills. It kills the very good and the very gentle and the very brave impartially. If you are none of these you can be sure it will kill you too but there will be no special hurry.

Ernest Hemingway, in his novel A Farewell to Arms *(1929).*

Samuel Dodsworth was, perfectly, the American Captain of Industry, believing in the Republican Party, high tariff and, so long as they did not annoy him personally, in prohibition and the Episcopal Church. He was the president of the Revelation Motor Company; he was a millionaire; his large house was on Ridge Crest, the most fashionable street in Zenith; he had some taste in etchings; he did not split many infinitives; and he sometimes enjoyed Beethoven. He would certainly (so the observer assumed) produce excellent motor cars . . . but he would never love passionately, lose tragically nor sit in contented idleness upon tropic shores.

Sinclair Lewis, describing his protagonist, in his novel Dodsworth *(1929).*

With marked progress in individual industries, in an era of radical improvements in our economic life comparable to the Industrial Revolution, attended by singular good fortune in the expansion of foreign trade and achieving a dominant place in the firmament of international commerce and finance, with peace at home and abroad and with an administration in which the country has the greatest confidence, it is little wonder that those who buy stocks, who, in terms of the economist, are paying a present sum for an *infinite* series of future incomes, should be inclined to pay a rather high price. These people are placing a high value upon future increments of income and subjecting them to a low discount. They may be in error. It is for them to judge and most emphatically not for a body in Washington, no matter how wise and honorable and disinterested they may be. It must be reiterated that on the whole the individuals from whom flows that stream of evaluations, which has set present prices upon stocks, are among the best informed and most intelligent people in America.

> *Joseph Stagg Lawrence, professor of economics at Princeton University, from his book* Wall Street and Washington *(1929).*

Nearly all of us made promises we can't keep on account of the turn in Wall Street. I promised my wife a rope of pearls. I can't get the pearls but I have the rope—and I'm thinking of using it myself.

For a time the only thing that went up was the blood pressure of the speculators. And believe me, many a man was selling that short before the crash was over.

> *Eddie Cantor, comedian and singer, from his book* Caught Short! *(1929).*

The machine has brought community self-sufficiency to an end. This makes for greater productive efficiency when everything is going well, and for greater social disaster when everything is going ill. The reason the White armies were not able to subdue revolutionary Russia lay in the fact that the exposed nerves were few—each village could, in a pinch, maintain itself unaided. No such survival is now possible in the United States.

> *Stuart Chase, economist and social critic, from his book* Men and Machines *(1929).*

Perhaps the most fundamental difference, however, which exists between the American Catholic and his European brother lies in the comparative indifference which the former displays toward dogma. . . . He is little concerned with theological notions or with the

metaphysical background thereof. This indifference to dogma leaves him wholly unaware of the fact that in espousing democracy with such ardor, and in interpreting Catholicism in terms of democracy as he does, he has come perilously near aligning himself with the Modernists.

> *E. Boyd Barrett, journalist, commenting on the distinctiveness of American Catholicism, in the* American Mercury *(January 1929).*

If we assume that the pledges of the powers in the League [of Nations] Covenant and the Locarno treaties are lies . . . still the existence of the League makes more liable to exposure, and hence more difficult, such subterfuges, evasions, and double-dealing as those which eventuated in the World War. . . . The League is worldwide in its reach. . . . Even the United States is a member in spite of its myth of isolation. As an economic power, seen or unseen, present at every council table, as a signatory of the Kellogg peace treaty (assuming ratification), and as a master stakeholder in every play, the United States is in the League and it matters little whether or not its adhesion is indicated by parchment and seals. . . . If the League is a joke, it is a joke hated by all frantic nationalists who love wars and by all those Bolsheviks who hope to conquer mankind in the next world war.

> *Charles A. Beard, historian, in* Harper's *(February 1929).*

When a proud owner of a General Electric Refrigerator takes her friends in to see it, the first comment is apt to be "Why it's *so* quiet—you can barely hear it." . . .

The General Electric Refrigerator gives you the perfect refrigeration that does away with food spoilage and safeguards health. It provides a generous supply of ice, makes menu-planning so much easier, permits you to serve the sort of food that your guests will instantly recognize as perfect.

> *General Electric product advertisement, in* National Geographic Magazine *(March 1929).*

I have no fears for the future of our country. It is bright with hope.

> *President Herbert Hoover, inaugural address of March 4, 1929, quoted in Schlesinger,* The Crisis of the Old Order *(1957).*

For then, gentlemen, you must definitely become political. . . . You may then become hangmen of the regime and political commissars, and if you do not behave your wife and child will be put behind locked doors. And if you still do not behave, you will be thrown out and perhaps stood up against a wall.

Adolf Hitler, warning German army officers what to expect if communists take control of the government, in a speech delivered at Munich, March 15, 1929, quoted in Shirer, The Rise and Fall of the Third Reich *(1960).*

I contend that the talkies . . . are exercising a profoundly salutary influence upon the movie industry, and that the revolution which they caused will come to be known, in time, as a memorable Renaissance. They have shaken the insecure and essentially phony foundations of Hollywood. . . .

One would be inclined to shed tears of sympathy for the old order were this what it might appear to be: another triumph of the machine age, another victory of stuffy babbittry over charming, devil-may-care bohemianism. But it happens to be nothing of the sort. It is no more than the expected victory of a superior form of industrialism over an inferior one.

Robert Sherwood, playwright and movie critic, in the American Mercury *(April 1929).*

As I see it, the great weakness of the president is that he is over the heads of most of the people, that he has no time for small talk and petty politics; that he has not the ability to slap people on the back and tell them that they have done a good job. I hear it on every hand and it is giving me a great deal of concern. . . . Not withstanding the president's marvelous ideals there seems to be abroad a feeling that he is too much of a machine.

Mark L. Requa, a longstanding friend of Herbert Hoover, memo of May 27, 1929, quoted in Fausold, The Presidency of Herbert C. Hoover *(1985).*

It would be absurd to contend that America offers a simple problem to the observer . . . to see about one only Babbitts means that one is not an acute observer. But . . . as we penetrate below the surface of its social life, we begin to see that its civilization is . . . remarkable . . . for its extreme structural simplicity. This simplicity lies in the fact that it has come to be almost wholly a *business man's civilization.* . . .

Moreover, dealing inevitably with material things and with the satisfying of the world's material wants, the business man tends to locate happiness in *them* rather than in the intellectual and spiritual unless he constantly refreshes his spirit away from business during his leisure. . . .

Aside from narrowness of interests, the business man, from the nature of his major occupation, is apt to have short views and to distrust all others. . . .

Preoccupation with profit, again, tends to make a business man, as business man, blind to the aesthetic quality in life.

James Truslow Adams, historian, in Harper's *(July 1929).*

Southern statesmen may make a pretense of talking national and world politics, but it is only a pretense, for the thoughts and actions of every politician in the Southern States are inexorably limited, circumscribed, interdicted, shackled, handcuffed and muzzled by the omnipresent Negro question . . .

As much as anybody in the country the Negro wants to be a good American. . . . But he is also determined . . . to wear the rights as well as bear the burdens of American citizenship . . . I have said he will win. He must win not only for himself but for the South, because there cannot possibly be an enlightened, progressive and vital state of politics in the South unless the Negro does win. He must win for the nation, because if he fails, democracy in America fails with him.

James Weldon Johnson, secretary of the NAACP, in "A Negro Looks at Politics," in The American Mercury *(September 1929).*

Ponies galloping "wide open" down the field, mallets connecting right and left, the ball bouncing across the green turf—that's Polo, the smartest of all sports.

And whether it be at the polo game, the golf club, or in town, there you'll find Emerson's, the smartest of all hats.

Advertisement for Emerson's Hats of Fifth Avenue, New York, in Vanity Fair *(September 1929).*

Money rates remain at critical, uncomfortable and cramping levels, here and abroad. Security speculation has eaten nearly all of its credit cake. Stock prices are generally out of line with safe earnings expectations, and the market is now almost wholly "psychological"—irregular, unsteady and properly apprehensive of the inevitable readjustment that draws near.

Business Week, *article of September 7, 1929 (premier issue).*

We solicit conservative margin accounts based on purchases of stocks listed on the New York Stock Exchange . . . Our facilities, resources, and experience, developed through forty years of service to traders and investors, are placed at the disposal of individuals having satisfactory banking sponsorships.

Advertisement for Hornblower & Weeks, in Business Week *(September 7, 1929).*

Understand me, my friends, I again say that I am not speaking . . . against the protective system; but I do say in all sincerity that the protective system with reference to industrial schedules has grown and expanded until it has reached the point where it is practically an embargo, and by reason of that fact there is an inequality between the agricultural and the industrial interests, and it never can be otherwise so long as that continues.

Senator William E. Borah, leader of the Farm Bloc in the Senate, on September 26, 1929, arguing against the Hawley-Smoot Tariff Bill as inequitable to agriculture, in the Congressional Record *(1929).*

Its salient characteristic is a magnificent incapacity for the real, a Brobdingnagian talent for the fantastic. The very legend of the Old South, for example, is warp and woof of the Southern mind. The "plantation" which prevailed outside the tidewater and delta regions was actually no more than a farm; its owner was, properly, neither planter nor aristocrat, but a backwoods farmer; yet the pretension to aristocracy was universal. Every farm house became a Big House, every farm a baronial estate, every master of scant red acres and a few mangy blacks a feudal lord.

W. J. Cash, journalist, in "The Mind of the South," in the American Mercury *(October 1929).*

While brokers acknowledged that thousands of small traders undoubtedly had been completely wiped out, the senior partner of one of the largest commission houses stated that a tremendous amount of stock, having been held over a period of months, was sold at a profit. It was pointed out also that, while such a pre-

cipitous decline would have had disastrous results a few years ago, when margins of only about 10 percent were required, what with present margins of from 33 to 50 percent, both brokerage houses and banks were more than amply protected.

Minneapolis Star, *news story published the afternoon of "Black Thursday," October 24, 1929.*

The fundamental business of the country, that is, production and distribution of commodities, is on a sound and prosperous basis.

President Hoover, public statement of October 25, 1929, in Fausold, The Presidency of Herbert C. Hoover *(1985).*

The most disastrous decline in the biggest and broadest stock market of history rocked the financial district yesterday. In the very midst of the collapse five of the country's most influential bankers hurried to the office of J. P. Morgan & Co., and after a brief conference gave out word that they believe the foundations of the market to be sound, that the market smash has been caused by technical rather than fundamental considerations, and that many sound stocks are selling too low. . . .

[The break] carried down with it speculators, big and little, in every part of the country, wiping out thousands of accounts. It is probable that if the stockholders of the country's foremost corporations had not been calmed by the attitude of leading bankers and the subsequent rally, the business of the country would have been seriously affected. Doubtless business will feel the effects of the drastic stock shakeout. . . .

Under these circumstances . . . the entire financial district was thrown into hopeless confusion and excitement. Wild-eyed speculators crowded the brokerage offices, awed by the disaster which had overtaken many of them. . . .

Rumors, most of them wild and false, spread throughout the Wall Street district and thence throughout the country. One of the reports was that eleven speculators had committed suicide.

New York Times, *article of October 25, 1929.*

Wall St. Lays an Egg.

Famous front page banner headline run by the newspaper of stage and screen Variety *(October 30, 1929).*

When the first sharp shock of individual disillusionment and loss has passed away it will begin to dawn upon us that the collapse of "the greatest bull market of all time" is the best thing that has happened to American business in the past fifteen years. It marks the end, we hope, of a period of war disturbances, speculative enthusiasm and economic instability; the beginning, we are certain, of a period of steady, substantial development. The air has been cleared of unrealities and delusions; the road to real accomplishment is opened wide and far. Business will now see more clearly some of the things it had better not have done, and the many things that still remain to do.

Business Week, *editorial of November 2, 1929.*

Wall Street had gone into one tail spin after another. You would pick up a paper in the morning and read the stock report and you wouldent [sic] think there was that many "Minus" signs in the world. . . . It was just taking all the joy out of gambling. If it kept on like that it would discourage Gambling and that, of course, would be bad for the country (Thats [sic] what they said).

Will Rogers, humorist and author, column of December 1, 1929, in Rogers, How We Elect Our Presidents *(1952).*

The country has enjoyed a large degree of prosperity and sound progress during the past year with a steady improvement in methods of production and distribution and consequent advancement in standards of living. Progress has, of course, been unequal among industries, and some, such as coal, lumber, leather, and textiles, still lag behind. The long upward trend of fundamental progress, however, gave rise to over-optimism as to profits, which translated itself into a wave of uncontrolled speculation in securities, resulting in the diversion of capital from business to the stock market and the inevitable crash. The natural consequences have been a reduction in the consumption of luxuries and semi-necessities by those who have met with losses, and a number of persons thrown temporarily out of employment. Prices of agricultural products dealt in upon the great markets have been affected in sympathy with the stock crash.

President Herbert Hoover, first annual State of the Union message to Congress, December 3, 1929, in Israel, ed., The State of the Union Messages of the Presidents, *vol. 3 (1966).*

The President has great capacity to convince intellectuals. He has small capacity to stir people emotionally, and through the emotions one gets to the will, not through the intellect. He can plow the ground, harrow it, plant the seed, cultivate it, but seems to lack the power to harvest it and flail it into a political merchantable product. Probably he would fail terribly if he tried to do the other thing. He must be what he is. What he is is important and necessary, but I don't think he can sublet the job of emotional appeal. People going around talking to luncheon clubs don't get very far. Public sentiment isn't made that way. The intellectual appeal finally will win. It is a slower process, but probably surer.

William Allen White, editor and author, letter of December 3, 1929, to David Hinshaw, in Johnson, Selected Letters of William Allen White, 1899–1943 *(1947).*

In 1929, it was strictly a gambling casino with loaded dice. The few sharks taking advantage of the multitude of suckers. It was exchanging expensive dogs for expensive cats. There had been a recession in 1921. We came out of it about 1924. Then began the climb, the spurt, with no limit stakes. Frenzied finance that made Ponzi look like an amateur. I saw shoeshine boys buying $50,000 worth of stock with $500 down. Everything was bought on hope . . .

A cigar stock at the time was selling for $115 a share. The market collapsed. I got a call from the company president. Could I loan him $200 million? I refused, because at the time I had to protect my own fences, including those of my closest friends. His $115 stock dropped to $2 and he jumped out of the window of his Wall Street office. . . .

October 29, 1929, yeah. A frenzy. I must have gotten calls from a dozen and a half friends who were desperate. In each case, there was no sense in loaning them the money that they would give the broker. Tomorrow they'd be worse off than yesterday. Suicides, left and right, made a terrific impression on me, of course. People I knew. It was heartbreaking. . . .

On Wall Street, the people walked around like zombies. It was like *Death Takes A Holiday.* It was very dark. You saw people who yesterday rode around in Cadillacs lucky now to have carfare.

Arthur A. Robertson, industrialist and financier, in Terkel, Hard Times: An Oral History of the Great Depression *(1970).*

3
The Failure of Optimism
1930–1933

THE CATACLYSM BEGINS

As 1930 began the drama entered an intermission. The stock market actually stabilized and even recovered. The *New York Times* average, which had hit bottom in November, rose through the first three months of the new year; many major stocks regained as much as half of their price losses. But in April the intermission came to an end. The hard truth about the American economy began to emerge. The most apparent and earliest signs of serious trouble had long been evident in agriculture, already victimized by a decade of depression. Now the farmers' trauma would intensify.

The Federal Farm Board, created the year before, proved inadequate to the task of improving the market for farm produce. The Grain Stabilization Corporation established in February began to buy surplus wheat and to trade in futures, using funds provided by the Farm Board, but to no avail, as the flood of surplus production in the United States and in Russia, Canada, and Argentina battered wheat prices down to 80 cents a bushel. Midwestern farmers had borrowed money against their 1930 crop when wheat was selling for as much as a dollar a bushel. By January 1931 the price of wheat fell to 60 cents a bushel. The Grain Stabilization Corporation, its storehouses filled with grain purchased at prices over 80 cents per bushel and its funds depleted (in fact, its purchases left the Farm Board with a loss of $345 million), gave up the fight. By 1932 wheat would bring only 30 cents a bushel (it had sold for $3 a bushel in 1920). The story was the same for other crops: Corn fell to 15 cents a bushel, cotton to 5 cents. Steers brought 2.3 cents a pound; hogs, 3 cents. Adding to the farmers' plight, drought ravaged the Great Plains in 1930–31, destroying crops in the fields and condemning livestock to starve for want of feed. Farmers faced total ruin—crop and equipment losses, mortgage foreclosures, bankruptcy, dispossession.

Sensing impending disaster, corporate leaders, who in November 1929 had promised President Hoover they would do their best to maintain employment, production, investment, and wage levels, began to cut back on them all—retrenching to prepare for decline and thus, ironically, intensifying

the decline that came. In 1930 alone 1,345 banks failed. Investment in plants and equipment plummeted. From 1930 to 1931 corporations' investment in capital improvements dropped 35 percent. In 1932 such investment dropped another 88 percent to a mere $800 million, a nearly total collapse from the $16.2 billion level of 1929. The index of industrial production fell from a high of 119 in 1929 to only 68 in 1932, a staggering drop of nearly 43 percent. Consumers reacted in the same way as the corporate leaders, anxiously curtailing purchases and installment buying. As consumption fell, corporations cut production. As consumption and production both fell, unemployment rose. From a level of 3.2 percent in 1929, unemployment climbed to include virtually one-fourth of the workforce by 1933. Five million people were unemployed in 1930; by the end of 1932 the figure stood at 13 million. And those who were fortunate enough to retain jobs experienced cuts in their wages, as an 18 percent drop in prices from 1929 to 1933 erased corporate profits. Between 1929 and 1931, the GNP of the United States fell from $105 billion to $75 billion, a decline of roughly 29 percent in two

Breadline in Chicago, November 4, 1930 *(Library of Congress)*

years. Values on the stock market dissolved. The *New York Times* stock average that had closed at 224 on November 13, 1929, sank to only 58 by early July 1932. From September 1929 to July 1932 the stocks of leading corporations plunged downward—General Motors, from 73 to 8; AT&T, from 304 to 72; United States Steel, from 262 to 22—while the stocks of many investment trusts became worthless. The total value of all stocks listed on the New York Stock Exchange fell from about $89.7 billion on September 1, 1929, to about $15.6 billion on July 1, 1932. Clearly, the economy—agricultural, industrial, and financial—evinced not simply crisis but disaster of unprecedented magnitude.

GOVERNMENT FAILS THE TEST

As the economy foundered, powerless to right itself, so the federal government seemed powerless to ease the extent of the damage. For those who believed in a self-regulating market and the inevitability of business cycles assumed there was nothing the government should do. Secretary of the Treasury Mellon exemplified this view in a statement historians of the period often quote: "Liquidate labor, liquidate stocks, liquidate the farmers, liquidate real estate." The economy, he insisted, would heal itself in due course—some people might suffer a little in the meantime but presumably for the greater, long-term good. In contrast, President Hoover believed the government had to somehow be involved in effecting the cure but primarily as a cheerleader. Hoover's basic philosophy as a self-made millionaire and proponent of a supposedly free market tempered the nature of his response and limited the kinds of government initiatives he deemed appropriate.

As noted, Hoover had already made an effort to help the farmers through the Agricultural Marketing Act of 1929 and its offspring the Federal Farm Board, but commodity prices doomed this effort to failure. The National Business Survey Conference that the president had helped organize in November 1929 came to his support by preaching optimism and urging consumers to increase their expenditures. The consumers ignored the advice. After all, the business leaders' own actions in cutting wages and investments belied their optimistic declarations. Still Hoover pressed on with a public campaign of rosy pronouncements about the status of the economy while encouraging voluntarism and cooperation among business leaders, state and city governments, and local agencies as the appropriate resources for righting the economy and relieving hardship. The effort proved futile. As business declined so did state and local tax revenues so that the ability of government at these levels to provide relief soon reached its limits.

Hoover persisted. In fall 1930 he created the President's Emergency Committee for Employment (PECE), headed by Colonel Arthur Woods, with the purpose of generating positive thinking among the general public. Curiously, PECE never gathered any data about unemployment but issued optimistic statements about the adequacy of local relief efforts. Perhaps that is why it became desirable in August 1931 to rechristen PECE as the President's Organization for Unemployment Relief (POUR). Headed now by Walter S. Gifford, president of AT&T, POUR simply continued along the road PECE had followed.

On another front, fearing that the banking industry was fraying not only at the edges but at the center as well, Hoover continued to pressure the major banks to organize their own agency to assist their threatened fellow bankers. The financiers finally gave in, setting up the National Credit Corporation (NCC) in October 1931. Their institutions provided the NCC with $500 million intended to be used for buying assets of banks on the verge of insolvency—another voluntary endeavor that avoided government interference. But again the effort failed, to Hoover's dismay. By the end of the year the NCC had expended only $10 million because its cautious officials balked at using NCC funds to buy doubtful assets from failing banks, whose numbers were growing: 2,293 in 1931—a record.

THE HOOVER INITIATIVES

Faced with the failure of these various efforts, Hoover nevertheless remained obdurate in resisting proposals that the federal government intervene directly; he especially opposed providing federal relief payments to farmers and the unemployed. But the counsel offered by some of his advisers—in particular Eugene Meyer of the Federal Reserve Board and Ogden Mills, who would replace Mellon as secretary of the treasury in February 1932—began to have effect. Out of their suggestions, increased pressure from the banking industry, and the transformation of Hoover's own thinking, a new approach emerged. Hoover recommended to Congress the creation of the Reconstruction Finance Corporation (RFC), which Congress approved in an act passed in January 1932. The act authorized the RFC to be set up with initial funding of $500 million, underwritten by the Treasury, from which the new agency could advance loans to banks and other financial institutions, insurance companies, and agricultural credit associations. The RFC could also loan money to railroads if the loans were approved by the Interstate Commerce Commission (ICC). During the remainder of Hoover's presidency the RFC, originally headed by banker and former vice president Charles G. Dawes, dispensed more than $1.5 billion in loans to aid banks, mortgage loan firms, and railroads. These loans saved many financial institutions, at least temporarily, but the larger economy did not receive the hoped-for boost because the RFC's advances to financial institutions were not transformed into loans to commercial enterprises to stimulate new investment and production. As a result, in July 1932, Hoover welcomed the Emergency Relief and Construction Act, which provided increased funding to the RFC specifically for financing public works projects and even for making loans to state governments to subsidize their relief efforts—a significant shift for Hoover, though still short of accepting direct federal relief to individuals.

Hoover and others in government and business contended that the depression persisted because of the effects of economic disintegration overseas, especially in Europe, which resulted in a loss of markets for American goods and crops. Economic distress in Europe and Japan was severe certainly, with consequent repercussions for the United States, but American tariff policy deserved much of the blame. The Hawley-Smoot Tariff Act, proposed in 1929, passed by both houses of Congress in mid-June 1930, and signed into law by the president on June 17, proved badly misconceived. Alarmed by the prospect of its passage, more than 1,000 economists from 46 states had petitioned Congress to reject the tariff bill and Hoover to veto it if it passed. They argued that an increase in tariffs would harm American farmers, reduce exports, generate unemployment, prod other nations to increase tariff levels, and have still other negative consequences. The economists were right. Hawley-Smoot increased the already high tariffs imposed on raw materials by the Fordney-McCumber Tariff Act of 1922 by 50 percent to 100 percent and the ad valorem rate (proportioned to actual value of goods) from 33.22 percent to just over 40 percent. Among the effects of the new tariff schedule, as the economists foresaw, was a steep falloff in loans and investments by Americans provided to enterprises in other nations because the tariffs, as a deterrent to trade, were seen as jeopardizing returns on such investments, and so the declining European economies suffered further constriction. The tariff increase also strangled worldwide trade. The loss of credit and trade ravaged production and employment in all the trading nations, with the most severe consequences for Europe. At home, the lot of the farmers, who were supposed to be helped by the higher tariffs on agricultural imports, actually worsened. In short, Hawley-Smoot wreaked economic havoc at home and abroad.

FOREIGN RELATIONS

Eventually, of course, the worldwide depression that unfolded influenced international relations. Early on in the Hoover presidency, however, international relations were generally amicable, and Hoover set out to promote ways of augmenting the peace. In full agreement with the Pact of Paris, Hoover desired to see war not simply outlawed but eliminated. With British prime minister Ramsay MacDonald, who visited the president for policy discussions in October 1929, Hoover planned the London Naval Conference to bring together the "Big Five" nations (Great Britain, France, Italy, Japan, and the United States) to negotiate further reductions in naval armaments. The makeup of the American delegation to the conference, which convened in London in mid-January 1930, revealed the Hoover administration's sense of its potential significance. Secretary of State Stimson himself led the delegation, which included the Democratic leader of the Senate, Joseph T. Robinson, Republican senator David Reed, Secretary of the Navy Charles F. Adams, and Ambassador to the Court of St. James (Ambassador to England) Charles G. Dawes, among others. King George V opened the conference in the House of Lords. But things did not go well at the conference due to confusion over comparing technical capabilities of diverse ships and guns and because of enmity between Italy and France. In fact, Italy walked out. Japan also held out for a higher ratio of cruisers than it had been awarded in previous conferences. The final agreement, intended to remain in effect until 1936, raised Japan's ratio, granted Great Britain superiority in light cruisers and the United States in heavy cruisers, and all three nations equality in submarines. The U.S. Senate ratified the agreement in July.

In Japan the military, now moving toward effective control of the government, was not entirely pleased with the outcome of the London Naval Conference. But their attention turned elsewhere. As depression struck the island nation the military, with the support of the public, deemed it necessary to preserve markets for Japanese goods in Manchuria and China. The military also wished to check the growing nationalism in China represented by General Chiang Kai-shek's slowly consolidating military strength. And so the Japanese military plotted to take outright control of Manchuria. The "Mukden incident," as it was called, provided the pretext for invasion in September 1931. The incident involved purported sabotage of the South Manchurian Railway, owned by the Japanese, which the military used as an excuse to capture Mukden and from there to invade South Manchuria.

The invasion clearly violated the Nine-Power Treaty, the Pact of Paris, and the Covenant of the League of Nations—all to which Japan was a signatory. The response of Japan's fellow signatories, however, was hesitant because of the other countries' preoccupation with the depression and the political instability it spawned in Europe. League of Nations members also recognized that condemnation, sanctions, or threats of war would have negligible effect without American backing. The League Council passed a resolution in October advocating restoration of normal relations between Japan and China and another in November requesting Japan's withdrawal from Manchuria. Japan ignored both resolutions. In December the League Council voted to send a committee headed by Victor Alexander George Robert Lytton (Lord Lytton) to investigate events in the Far East. Secretary of State Stimson hoped the civilian government of Japan would rein in the military, but the government was by now too weak to do so. Hoover advocated using moral persuasion. By January 1932 the secretary of state had concluded that Japan's aggression demanded a more confrontational response. With Hoover's approval—in fact, it was Hoover who first thought of the response—on January 7 Stimson sent messages to the Japanese and Chinese governments apprising them that the United States would refuse to recognize any treaty or agreement on territorial changes they might enter into that violated existing treaties such as the Pact of Paris. This nonrecognition stance became known as the Stimson Doctrine. Two weeks later Japanese bombers and marines attacked Shanghai; and on February 18 the government of Japan recognized Manchuria, renamed Manchukuo, as an independent state—but which was under effective Japanese control.

Despite the ineffectiveness of the Stimson Doctrine, Hoover continued to oppose economic sanctions or stronger measures. On February 24, 1933, the League of Nations Assembly formally accepted the Lytton Report, submitted the previous October, which branded Japan's aggression inexcusable and advocated creation of an autonomous Manchuria. The Japanese delegates walked out.

No doubt of greater concern to the Atlantic-oriented American leadership than the Chinese-Japanese quarrel was the situation in Europe, where economic and political viability showed clear signs of unraveling as the first two years of the decade unfolded. War debts burdened Great Britain, France, and Germany. Britain and France depended on Germany's reparations payments for funds to repay their own war debts to the United States. Germany in turn depended on loans from the United States for funds to pay the reparations. Through this curious recycling of funds the United States in effect provided the money with which all three European nations paid their debts—new American loans paid the interest and principal on old American loans. But as the depression menaced all three republics' economies, the debt burdens became impossible to sustain.

The economic losses Great Britain had suffered in World War I prevented that nation from recovering its prewar industrial strength, and throughout the twenties it had lost ground to its competitors, primarily France and the United States, in world trade. When the Conservatives were in power, they fell well short of achieving their plan to transform the Commonwealth nations into a trade bloc that would supply Great Britain with raw materials in exchange for finished goods and services. When the Labourites were in power briefly in 1924 and 1929, they lacked sufficient strength in Parliament to effect nationalization of major industries such as railroads, coal, and steel. As a result, no clear-cut economic direction emerged during the decade. The depression hit Great Britain early and hard. In addition, the unsettling Irish civil war also preoccupied the British government. In August 1931 the Labour government headed by Ramsay MacDonald resigned to be replaced by a coalition government of Conservatives, Liberals, and Labourites still headed by MacDonald. In September the government jolted other nations by abandoning the gold standard underpinning the pound, which consequently fell in value. In early 1932 the government imposed protective tariffs and terminated debt payments to the United States. The government also signed agreements negotiated at the Ottawa Imperial Conference held in July and August that provided some exclusivity for trade within the Commonwealth—Canada called for the conference in retaliation for the Hawley-Smoot Tariff Act.

For France the depression descended more slowly. By 1929 the nation had recovered from a period of inflation in the mid-1920s caused by the financial burdens of rebuilding and war debts. Less industrial than Great Britain, France's economy held up fairly well until the second half of 1931, when the evaporating export market finally took its toll. Premier Pierre Laval visited Hoover in October to discuss reducing French payments for war debts but left empty-handed.

THE RISE OF THE FASCISTS

The depression claimed Germany as a major victim. The survival of the Weimar Republic became increasingly precarious during the first years of the decade. On the verge of stabilization politically as well as economically in 1929, the republic skidded toward economic collapse in 1930 and, two years later, the total dissolution of parliamentary government. Unemployment had already begun to increase as early as 1929. The American stock market crash that year and the financial crisis that ensued decimated Germany's export trade and forced factory closings so that unemployment in Germany quickly became severe. The coalition government headed by Social Democrat Hermann Müller failed in March 1930 over a dispute about the unemployment insurance fund. Heinrich Brüning, the Catholic Center Party's leader in the Reichstag (parliament) became chancellor. In an effort to save the parliamentary system, he asked President Paul von Hindenburg to dissolve the Reichstag in July and called for new elections in September. Unfortunately, the tactic backfired. Adolf Hitler's Nazi Party, seizing the opportunity the depres-

sion offered to exploit discontent, scored a triumph winning 107 seats in the new Reichstag, a gain of 95. The Communists also gained substantially, while the center democratic parties lost. The consequent internal quarreling rendered the parliament ineffectual and paralyzed Brüning's government. Brüning was forced to resign in May 1932, to be replaced by the devious, far-right Franz von Papen, who lacked a supportive political base. Papen's first act was to dissolve the Reichstag. In the elections at the end of July the Nazis made further gains, winning 230 seats. The republic rapidly disintegrated, with the senile Hindenburg manipulated by right-wing intriguers. Papen was forced out in November. And on the last day of January 1933, Hitler became chancellor of Germany.

Elsewhere in Europe, similarly ominous developments occurred. Benito Mussolini and his *fascisti* controlled Italy since 1923. In Austria, Germany's ally in World War I and at that time center of the former Habsburg empire, political turmoil had prevailed throughout the twenties—the opposing Christian Socialists and Social Democrats literally battled each other with their private armies. The failure of the Kreditanstalt, Austria's central bank, in May 1931, indicated things to come as the depression shattered that nation's economy. Supportive measures by the United States and other nations made little difference. Following a treaty with Mussolini in 1930, the Christian Socialists of

Adolf Hitler (third from right), with Hermann Göring (to Hitler's left), Ernst Röhm (to Hitler's right), Heinrich Himmler (to Röhm's right), and others at a Nazi rally in Nuremberg, Germany *(Library of Congress)*

Austria moved increasingly to the right; and after Hitler became chancellor of Germany, many of them openly embraced Nazism. In Hungary, also part of the former Habsburg empire, the Allies had crushed a Bolshevik government in 1919–20, and from 1921 to 1931 the prime minister, Count István Bethlen, ruled the nation. But the depression caused his demise, and fascists came to power. The former Habsburg states of Croatia and Serbia, wracked by mutual hostility throughout the twenties, became united again but only because King Alexander I imposed a dictatorship in January 1929 and renamed the nation as Yugoslavia. The military dictatorship that had come to power in Poland in 1926 simply tightened its authority as the depression hit. Generals also exercised whatever control existed in the tumultuous politics of Greece. One bright spot among the former belligerents of World War I was Turkey, Germany's ally during the war, which became a republic in 1922 and continued viably through most of the depression under the capable leadership of Mustafa Kemal, who adopted the name Kemal Atatürk in 1934. In Spain there was also cause for some hope. The dictatorship of General Primo de Rivera, in power since 1923, failed in 1930, partly as a result of the worldwide depression's impact, and the general died. By June 1931 a republican government began the process of adopting a constitution and electing a president and parliament, all in place by the end of the year. The army, awaited any opportunity to take control.

Hoover's Foreign Policies

Thoughtful Americans contemplating developments in Europe might have judged there was ample cause to worry about the future. As conditions deteriorated, especially in Germany, President Hoover decided on a bold step. In June 1931 he proposed a one-year moratorium on all intergovernmental debts. European governments greeted the proposal with relief, except for France. The French, worried that the moratorium's real purpose was to make it easier to collect on loans private American firms had made to Germany with funds that would have gone to reparations payments to France and the Allies, stalled and raised objections. But they finally came around on July 6. A week later the Darmstaedter und Nationalbank, one of Germany's major banks, failed. The Weimar government declared bank holidays and restrictions on transactions. The moratorium and a seven-nation agreement to continue credits to Germany had come too late.

In an effort to resolve the problems created by German reparations and other nations' war debts, the Allies called for a conference in Lausanne, Switzerland. It convened belatedly, in June 1932, by which time the untrustworthy Papen had become chancellor of Germany. The Allies agreed to reduce the reparations bill to only $715 million, which would be covered by bonds to be deposited with the Bank for International Settlements but not collected for three years—what amounted to cancellation of the debt. But the Allies also agreed not to ratify this plan until they had renegotiated the terms of their own debts with the United States. Hoover refused to admit the debts were uncollectable, and so the agreement was never ratified. Some nations—Great Britain, Italy, and Finland among them—did pay their December 1932 installments; but in the following years, all except Finland reneged.

Another conference, the Conference on the Reduction and Limitation of Armaments, that met in Geneva in February 1932, with 31 nations attending, might conceivably have produced some economic benefits, as it was intended to negotiate reductions in land armaments. At Hoover's behest, the American delegation submitted proposals calling for elimination of offensive weapons and reduction of armed forces to strength levels only one-third above what was needed for preserving internal order. The other delegations rejected these proposals. The conference adjourned in July, and shortly after it reconvened the following January, the hostility of the Hitler government confirmed the futility of its efforts. A World Economic Conference planned by Hoover and Ramsay MacDonald to meet in London in 1933 got derailed in the aftermath of Hoover's loss of the 1932 election.

In Latin America, the Hoover administration's approach fared much better than in the Far East or Europe, perhaps because of the goodwill generated by his tour of the region following the 1928 election, during which he enunciated his Good Neighbor policy, and perhaps because he and Stimson essentially agreed on an enlightened, cooperative stance toward relations with Latin American nations and maintained close contacts with their leaders. A memo prepared by Undersecretary of State J. Reuben Clark, Jr., and known as the Clark Memorandum repudiated the authority to intervene in Latin American nations' affairs that had been spelled out in the Roosevelt Corollary to the Monroe Doctrine. Formulated by President Theodore Roosevelt in 1904, the corollary appropriated for the United States the role of hemispheric policeman, duty bound to intervene in any of the Latin American nations evidencing "brutal wrongdoing" or "a general loosening of the ties of civilized society." The corollary clearly had extended the Monroe Doctrine beyond its original intent of preventing European nations from intervening in the hemisphere, as Clark concluded. Although the Clark Memorandum was not made public, Hoover accepted its import as consistent with the Good Neighbor policy. In consequence, the administration withdrew American forces from Nicaragua and planned to withdraw them from Haiti. The State Department in September 1930 also issued new criteria for official recognition of Latin American governments: that they be in de facto control, demonstrate intent to meet their international obligations, and propose to hold democratic elections within a reasonable time. Stimson also made a good faith effort to try to resolve territorial quarrels between Paraguay and Bolivia and Colombia and Peru. In what might be considered a tribute, when Franklin Delano Roosevelt became president, he embraced and perpetuated Hoover's Good Neighbor policy.

DISTRACTIONS AT HOME

While the Great Depression gripped their own nation and generated political strife abroad, most Americans who managed to avoid unemployment continued their lives much as before, concerned for the welfare of their fellow citizens, perhaps, but not much interested in the troubles of Europe or the Far East and certainly desirous that the United States avoid becoming entangled in international affairs. Americans felt they had enough to worry about. All the more reason to indulge in distractions that temporarily took the mind off the depression. Radio flourished: Some of the most popular shows in the history of broadcasting were introduced in the early thirties. News commentator Lowell Thomas made his first broadcast in September 1930; his program would continue for 46 years. *The March of Time,* presented by *Time* magazine, began broadcasting on CBS radio in March 1931, becoming the most popular news documentary in radio history (it continued until 1945). In May 1931, Kate Smith, "the queen of radio," debuted on CBS. On Christmas Day in 1931 began the still-continuing Saturday broadcasts of the Metropolitan Opera, with announcer Milton Cross. *The Chase and Sanborn Hour,* a variety series starring Eddie Cantor, joined the airwaves in September 1931. At the same time, Bing Crosby debuted on CBS. The following year, the comedy team of George Burns and Gracie Allen began their long-running program. *The Lone Ranger* premiered a year later in January 1933.

Both the radio and the press transformed the March 1932 kidnapping of Charles and Anne Lindbergh's baby son into a major news event—few crimes in American history have generated so much public attention. After the kidnapping from the Lindberghs' home in Hopewell, New Jersey, broadcasters and newspapers reported daily developments in the tragedy, escalated through payment of a $50,000 ransom and the involvement of racketeers, intriguers, and hoaxes. The tragedy's initial end came on May 12, when the baby's body was found in a wooded area less than six miles from the Lindbergh home, but it was not until fall 1934 that a suspect, Bruno Hauptmann, would be arrested and charged.

Another media event, although lacking the scope of attention given the Lindbergh case but more far-reaching in its import, centered on the trial of "the Scottsboro boys," nine young blacks arrested by the sheriff of Scottsboro, Alabama, in May 1931 and charged with raping two white women on a train. Unjustly charged (the evidence indicated that the two women, part-time prostitutes, had not been touched) and unjustly tried, the nine young men—all teenagers but one—were found guilty, and all but one, who was only 13, were sentenced to death. The case was appealed to the state supreme court. Although the National Association for the Advancement of Colored People (NAACP) hired Clarence Darrow to defend the young men, the Communist Party had already grasped the opportunity, and Darrow was obliged to withdraw and leave the defense to the party's International Labor Defense. The party used the case as a means of organizing African Americans in the South with some success. Protests arose throughout the United States and Europe; thousands signed and circulated petitions, including Albert Einstein, John Dos Passos, Theodore Dreiser, members of Parliament, and the German author Thomas Mann. The state supreme court upheld the sentence, and the case moved to the U.S. Supreme Court, which invalidated the convictions in a November 1932 decision, returning the case for retrial in a lower court. This drama would continue for years.

That other great distraction, the Hollywood cinema, entered a boom period. Five major studios—Metro-Goldwyn-Mayer, Twentieth Century–Fox, Paramount Pictures, Warner Brothers, and Radio-Keith-Orpheum (RKO)—owned the large national theater chains and dominated the industry. Every week 80 million customers filled the theaters—an amazing level of attendance considering that the entire populace numbered only about 128 million in 1930. Cinema-goers could experience the prototype gangster films *Little Caesar* (1930), *The Public Enemy* (1931), and *Scarface* (1932). Or they might prefer Ernst Lubitsch's movie musicals, among the first of their kind, *Monte Carlo* (1930) and *The Smiling Lieutenant* (1931), with Jeanette MacDonald and Maurice Chevalier. If wacky comedy appealed, they could see the Marx Brothers in *Animal Crackers* (1930) and *Duck Soup* (1932). And there was still Charlie Chaplin, who made the transformation to the talkies in *City Lights* (1931). Serious drama also achieved translation into film, with such examples as Eugene O'Neill's *Anna Christie* (1930) and Charles MacArthur and Ben Hecht's *Front Page* (1931). More sinister fare included film adaptations of novels such as *Dr. Jekyll and Mr. Hyde* (1932), directed by Rouben Mamoulian, or the classic *Frankenstein* (1931), with Boris Karloff as the monster, and *Dracula* (1931), starring Bela Lugosi as the count. There was also Lewis Milestone's 1930 rendering of Erich Maria Remarque's antiwar novel *All Quiet on the Western Front*.

Literary output in the United States, and therefore presumably readership, appears not to have fallen off during these first years of the depression. Celebrated poet Edwin Arlington Robinson produced two long works, *The Glory of the Nightingale* (1930) and *Mathias at the Door* (1931). Robert Frost's *Collected Poems* won the Pulitzer Prize in 1930, the same year that saw publication of Archibald MacLeish's *New Found Land* and Hart Crane's *The Bridge*. Edna St. Vincent Millay published *Fatal Interview,* a collection of love sonnets, in 1931. In the same year, E. E. Cummings produced a new collection of poems entitled *W (ViVa);* William Carlos Williams, *Collected Poems, 1921–1931;* and playwright Eugene O'Neill, one of his major works, *Mourning Becomes Electra.* T. S. Eliot's *Sweeney Agonistes* appeared in 1932. In fiction, William Faulkner produced three of his major works during these years: *As I Lay Dying* (1930), *Sanctuary* (1931), and *Light in August* (1932). James T. Farrell published *Young Lonigan,* the first volume of his trilogy about Studs Lonigan, in 1932. In short, these were years of major achievement in American letters. Perhaps validation of that achievement occurred with awarding of the Nobel Prize in literature in 1930 to Sinclair Lewis, the first American writer to receive the prize (many literary critics, however, believed it should have gone to Theodore Dreiser). It is noteworthy also that in the first years of the decade none of the authors mentioned attained best-seller status—that went instead to Pearl Buck for *The Good Earth* (1931) and Ellery Queen for two mysteries.

Other areas of the arts, however, did suffer from the depression's effects. If capital investment evaporates, then so also does construction. Consequently, although the two giant skyscraper projects already in process in New York, the Empire State and Chrysler Buildings, reached completion, few new architectural projects of significant size appeared in their wake. As a result of the decline in construction, nearly 85 percent of the nation's architects became unemployed. Among the few important building projects undertaken in these years, one noteworthy office tower, the Philadelphia Savings Fund Society Building, designed by George Howe and William Lescaze and erected in Philadelphia from 1929 to 1932, broke new ground as a forerunner of the so-called International Style that would transform America's cities throughout the next four decades. Similarly, Raymond Hood's designs for the unornamented Daily News Building (1930) and McGraw-Hill Building (1932) in New York suggested the direction that skyscraper styles would take, with successive stories set back rather than rising like a monolithic tower. The glass walls of the latter building also presaged the curtain walls (non-load-bearing walls hung on framed structures to hold glass, aluminum, and other materials) of the future. Hood was the first of a series of architects to work on Rockefeller Center, a complex of buildings begun in 1929 and completed in 1940—the most ambitious architectural project of the depression era. A major event of far-reaching influence occurred in New York when an exhibit organized by Henry-Russell Hitchcock and Philip C. Johnson and entitled "The International Style" (the source of the term) opened at the Museum of Modern Art in February 1932. The exhibit contained photographs and models of works by Walter Gropius, Le Corbusier, Ludwig Mies van der Rohe, Frank Lloyd Wright, and other modernists. In that same year, Wright and his wife founded the Taliesin Fellowship for architectural students at their home in Wisconsin. Wright also published *An Autobiography.*

Although the depression, for some reason, sent improvisational (or "hot") jazz into temporary limbo, American music at two poles—classical and proletarian—flourished. The decade began with creation of two new orchestras—in Indianapolis (1930) and Washington, D.C. (the National Symphony Orchestra founded by Hans Kindler in 1931). Also in 1931 Eugene Ormandy became conductor of the Minneapolis Symphony. Classical music concerts became a staple of radio. The Metropolitan Opera, which began weekly broadcasts in 1931, debuted Deems Taylor's *Peter Ibbetson* in February 1931 and Louis Gruenberg's *The Emperor Jones* (based on Eugene O'Neill's play) in January 1933. The first performance of African-American composer William Grant Still's *Africa, the Afro-American Symphony* occurred in 1930. Not surprisingly in a period of severe unemployment, hoboes, breadlines, and labor strife, proletarian music—political protest songs and union songs—proliferated. Among the memorable tunes were "The Death of Mother Jones" (1930), celebrating the life of the indomitable champion of American laborers Mary "Mother" Jones, and Florence Reece's "Which Side Are You On?"

Sports, as always, continued to be a major diversion from the troubles of daily life. Baseball remained the great American game, and one of its highlights occurred on October 1, 1932, when New York Yankee Babe Ruth hit a home run in the third game of the World Series against the Chicago Cubs at Wrigley Field, the hero's last series. What made the home run so memorable was the controversy (never settled) over whether Ruth gestured toward the bleachers, "predicting" he would hit the next good pitch into them—he already had two strikes. His teammate Lou Gehrig gave him a congratulatory handshake as he crossed the plate. In that same year the Olympics were held in Los Angeles, where Eddie Tolan, an African-American student at the University of Michigan, won both the 100-meter and 200-meter dashes. The 1932 Winter Olympics, held at Lake Placid, New York, inspired a vogue for skiing, not exactly an inexpensive sport for a depression-era public to embrace. An increasing number of Americans also took up bridge playing and bought Ely Culbertson's books on mastering the game.

THE POLITICAL TOLL

Despite these and many other diversions, the crippled economy remained the nation's primary preoccupation. Thus the ongoing depression would determine the outcome of the 1932 presidential election. Some foreshadowing of the election's outcome might have been gleaned from the congressional elections of 1930. In the House of Representatives the Republicans lost 52 seats, reducing their majority to two seats (218 to the Democrats' 216); by the time the 72nd Congress actually convened, deaths and the subsequent special elections had thrown the majority to the Democrats, with 220 seats to the Republicans' 214 (the Farmer-Laborites continued to hold one seat). The Republicans barely managed to retain control of the Senate, with 48 seats to the Democrats' 47 and one for the Farmer-Laborites. This outcome suggested public discontent with the Hoover administration's response to the depression, the drought, and other issues. The president found the election results saddening, but he was determine to maintain his conservative policies of little intervention and influence on congressional and state activities.

That response proved mistaken. The January 1931 report of the Commission on Law Enforcement and Observance (known as the Wickersham Commission for its chairman, George W. Wickersham) gave Hoover an opportunity to move in a new direction. The commission concluded that Prohibition was a failed effort. The battle to enforce Prohibition, said their report, was a failure; Prohibition had generated corruption, debilitated law enforcement generally and also the federal courts, and bred increasing public support for repeal of the Eighteenth Amendment. Two of the commission's 11 members favored repeal, two favored leaving the amendment intact, and seven favored keeping the amendment but with revisions. Although their conclusion did not provide Hoover with a clear-cut recommendation, it must have been obvious by now that Prohibition was beyond salvaging; many states were making little or no effort at enforcement, and the federal government could not do the job alone. But Hoover found the Wickersham Commission's report disappointing because of its criticism of enforcement, and he maintained his hardened opposition to repeal. It was not until August 1932 that he conceded to reality and announced that he would support repeal of the Eighteenth Amendment, making repeal inevitable since the Democratic Party platform also favored it. Once again, Hoover moved too late.

TAXES AND TURMOIL

In these early years of the depression a tax crisis emerged. During the 1920s property taxes had generated 90 percent of the levies by municipalities of more than 30,000 in population, and taxes on real estate, although now a lower percentage, still remained the main source of revenue in the early 1930s for state governments. During the depression's first three years, however, Americans' real income plummeted while nationwide unemployment reached 25 percent. Consequently, many property owners now lacked the wherewithal to pay their real estate taxes, and in some cities the delinquency rate reached 50 percent. Already in 1929 delinquency rates in Detroit and other major cities had risen to their highest levels of that decade, and now they ballooned. At the same time many states and localities struggled with increasing debt, and per capita debt rates also soared. As the tax burden on individuals doubled from 1930 to 1933, tax collections nevertheless fell; land values and new residential construction also collapsed, the latter by as much as 95 percent in some regions of the country. Farmers, long since financially crippled, saw their tax burdens double; multiple delinquencies ensued, reaching a 48 percent rate for all farm properties in Iowa, for example. Forced auction sales of farms resulted, leaving many farmers totally destitute.

As such calamities unfolded, not surprisingly, tax resistance burgeoned. In some rural areas armed farmers banded together to seize control of auctions and buy farms for a mere dollar apiece to return them to their owners, but this form of rural resistance evidenced itself only sporadically. In the cities the tax revolt assumed a more organized and more widespread nature. The National Association of Real Estate Boards (NAREB) established a Property Owners Division that founded local chapters of nonrealtor members nationwide. Dedicated to the cause of tax reduction, these chapters pursued aggressive tactics, including tax strikes, and, with the support of local NAREB boards, advocated reductions in government spending. In some locales they promoted new taxes—on incomes or gasoline, for example—to replace lost revenues resulting from decreasing property values. Taxpayers' leagues organized at county or city levels also became a major force in this antitax movement; by 1933 some 3,000 such leagues existed. Tax revolts that centered in such cities as Detroit, Chicago, New York, and Milwaukee garnered significant media attention.

The largest and most theatrical tax revolt developed in Chicago. Exacerbated by the city's traditional machine politics, tax inequities became viewed as a racket that favored the machine's supporters. Cook County had 446 distinct governmental entities, each with the autonomy to levy taxes, and the machine conspired with each to juggle assessments, rewarding supporters and punishing opponents. Efforts at reform in the late 1920s had failed, although average assessments had been reduced, and from May 1928 to July 1930 no general property taxes had been collected. But the Chicago City Council pressured the Joint Commission on Real Estate Valuation (JCREV) to devise a plan for solving the city's fiscal problems. In 1930 the JCREV formed the Citizen's Committee, chaired by Silas Strawn, chairman of retailer Montgomery Ward's board, to address the issue. The committee set up a subscription fund to pay for governmental needs only, creating consternation among the Republican administration of Mayor William "Big Bill" Thompson. It also mandated the so-called Strawn Plan, making 1928 taxes due in July 1930, 1929 taxes in February 1931, and 1930 taxes in November 1931, thereby imposing a sudden tax burden (three years' of taxes payable in a year and a half) on county residents.

The public reacted with rage and revolt. People were doubly angry because property values declined by 86 percent from 1927 to 1931, accompanied by a huge rise in foreclosures and a 70 percent decline in net income. Dismayed businessmen of the Loop (downtown Chicago) launched a tax resistance movement by forming the Association of Real Estate Taxpayers of Illinois (ARET) in May 1930. ARET advocated adding personal property to the tax rolls in order to reduce real estate taxes. It lobbied for an amendment to the Illinois Constitution allowing the legislature to classify property for taxation and thereby enforce the constitution's "uniformity amendment" specifying that all persons and corporations would pay taxes in proportion to the value of their properties. Voters rejected this approach, so ARET attacked the 1930 tax assessments and demanded that 1931 tax increases based on them be canceled.

The Illinois Tax Commission denied the demand in January 1931. ARET's losses instigated the Chicago tax strike.

ARET took its cause to court and won a judge's order that the Board of Review hear more than 30,000 taxpayer appeals; the board in turn appealed to the Illinois Supreme Court. Meanwhile the Cook County tax collector mailed out the tax bills for 1929. ARET urged all taxpayers to refuse to pay the bills until the state supreme court had ruled, and many complied on the grounds that if they paid any part of their taxes they became liable for the unpaid amount. (They may have gleaned a message from the federal government's successful 1931 prosecution of Chicago gangster Al "Scarface" Capone for tax evasion.) ARET strove on with its tax strike, rousing the wrath of newly elected Democratic mayor Anton Cermak and the opposition of all five Chicago newspapers. The tax strike gained increasing public support nevertheless, and ARET's membership grew as it urged taxpayers not to pay 1930 taxes and took to the radio to spread its message. Cermak and the newspapers launched a "pay your taxes" campaign; the mayor announced spending reductions and layoffs and accused the tax strikers of anarchy and treason. To reassure local creditors the Reconstruction Finance Corporation began extending loans to Illinois. The city moved to shut off water delivery to any tax strikers who owed more than $10,000 on their taxes. Then factionalism began to sunder ARET's membership, and a local judge issued an injunction that precluded ARET's February 1933 public meeting, sealed access to the organization's funds, and forbade future meetings or radio broadcasts. The Illinois Supreme Court fined ARET for practicing law without a license, and by the end of 1933 the tax strike organization entered receivership. Although ultimately a failure, the ARET-led tax strike had forestalled tax collections in Chicago for two years and provided a model for similar tax rebellions throughout the nation.

Meanwhile in Washington both the president and the Congress by the end of 1931 had adopted the view that new tax revenues had to be raised in order to balance the federal budget; Secretary of the Treasury Mellon estimated that the deficit would reach $1.5 billion by the end of 1933. The question was how to raise the revenues. The answer favored by the president and the Democratic leadership in Congress was to implement a sales tax, which would have had most serious impact on the finances of poorer Americans. After sales tax legislation was proposed, congressmen received floods of protest mail. In response they rebelled against the leadership, and some quite different legislation emerged from their deliberations. The Revenue Act of 1932, which Hoover signed into law on June 7, imposed the largest percentage tax increases in peacetime in American history—but on corporations and the wealthy. The corporate income tax rate became 1.75 percent; surtaxes on incomes exceeding $1 million became 55 percent; and estate taxes on legacies above $10 million became 45 percent. These increases affected only about 15 percent of the working public.

Growing unrest accented 1932. In Detroit unemployment was nearly 50 percent; the number of workers at the city's largest employer, the Ford Motor Company, fell to 50,000 by 1933 from a 1929 high of 174,000. On March 7, 1932, about 3,000 demonstrators brought together by Communist labor organizers marched through Detroit to gather at the Ford River Rouge plant in Dearborn, Michigan, to present a list of demands. In Dearborn police ordered them to turn back and fired tear gas when the marchers stood their ground. The marchers responded by throwing stones and dirt clods. Firemen sprayed freezing water on the crowd, and the police opened fire, killing one of the demonstrators. The other demonstrators retreated to a field, where police fire killed three more and wounded 50. Five days later 40,000 people attended the funeral, where a red banner bearing a portrait of Vladimir Lenin and the slogan "Ford Gave Bullets for Bread" was displayed.

THE BONUS ARMY

Probably more disturbing to the general public because it occurred in the nation's capital was the attack on the Bonus Army. The Bonus Expeditionary Force, or Bonus Army, originated in Portland, Oregon, in spring 1932, when a group of World War I veterans began a march to Washington, D.C., to pressure Congress into making immediate payments of "adjusted compensation certificates"—bonuses for wartime services that Congress had voted to award veterans, but not until 1945. Led by Walter W. Waters, a sergeant in the war and now an unemployed cannery worker, they road freight car rods and survived on handouts. They arrived in East St. Louis on May 21. Officials of the Baltimore and Ohio Railroad refused to let them board a freight train, so they uncoupled cars and put soap on the rails. The National Guard dispersed them. The incident gained national newspaper attention, attracting other veterans to the march. By June some 20,000 were encamped in a "Hooverville" of makeshift huts, as such sites were called, on the flats of the Anacostia River in Washington as Congress debated a bill introduced by Representative Wright Patman authorizing immediate payment of the bonuses.

The House passed the bill on June 15, but the Senate turned it down on June 17. Many of the veterans, despondent over the result, went home, but about 2,000, some joined by wives and children, stayed on at the flats. In the more than two months of the Bonus Army's encampment, not a single representative of the administration appeared to talk with them. On July 28, District of Columbia police were clearing some veterans from an abandoned building on Pennsylvania Avenue when one policeman, alarmed by an accident (a policeman slipped, firing his gun) fired his pistol, killing one veteran. No ruckus ensued, but Secretary of the Army Patrick J. Hurley used the incident as an excuse to send federal troops to evict the Bonus Army from the city. Commanded by General Douglas MacArthur, with his aide Major Dwight Eisenhower, the troops attacked marchers on the Anacostia flats with gas bombs and set fire to their huts. The veterans fled into Maryland. Although MacArthur had exceeded Hoover's orders by attacking the marchers, the president accepted responsibility and suffered the verbal stings of the editorialists. In the months leading to the election, Hoover could not afford any bad press.

THE 1932 ELECTION

The Republican Party's National Convention began in Chicago on June 14. The platform the party adopted rehashed old policies and proposals and fudged taking a stand on Prohibition. On June 17, the convention renominated Hoover and Curtis without opposition—but also without enthusiasm. The

Democratic National Convention presented quite a different spectacle. Politicians began arriving in Chicago the week after the Republicans left—a week early to do last-minute wheeling and dealing. New York governor Franklin Delano Roosevelt (frequently referred to as FDR) was the front-runner, with nearly a majority of votes but well short of the needed two-thirds. Leading a coalition against Roosevelt was the man Roosevelt had backed for the presidency in 1928, his former ally Alfred E. Smith, who was favored by John J. Raskob, former executive at DuPont and General Motors and current chairman of the Democratic National Committee. Roosevelt was fortunate in that the redoubtable Jim Farley managed his campaign. Farley and others, including publisher William Randolph Hearst, who sent messages from California, persuaded Speaker of the House John Nance Garner from Texas after the third ballot to release his delegates to Roosevelt—in return Garner would become the vice presidential candidate. The next day, July 1, Roosevelt won on the fourth ballot. The convention burst into emotional celebration. Smith, refusing to the last to release his delegates so the vote could become unanimous, stalked from the hall. Governor Roosevelt heard the results in Albany, New York, over his radio and made an unprecedented move: He wired the convention that he would fly to Chicago the next day to accept the nomination in person. In his acceptance speech delivered the evening of July 2, Roosevelt advocated massive relief, repeal of Prohibition, public works projects, a reforestation program, tariff reduction, and other departures from current policy. And he declared, "I pledge you, I pledge myself, to a new deal for the American people." Amid the cheers, the hall organ burst forth with "Happy Days Are Here Again."

Although the economy actually showed signs of improvement in the three months leading up to the election—there were increases in industrial production and employment, for example—the depression's effects had been so pervasive and so deep, with the GNP having fallen so low (nearly 30 percent from 1929), that only an enormous leap forward could have suggested genuine recovery was under way. Thus the prospects for the president's reelection looked hopeless. In Roosevelt's favor, following his reelection as governor in 1930, he had instituted some innovative reforms in New York aimed at combatting the depression. Since being stricken with polio in August 1921 and left permanently disabled, his public image, humanized by his valiant struggle to recover, also seemed more in tune with the sufferings of other people. FDR projected confidence, energy, compassion, even joyfulness, in contrast with the dour president. As governor, Roosevelt already had a strong group of advisers—including his so-called Brain Trust, the nucleus of which included Adolf A. Berle, Raymond Moley, and Rexford Guy Tugwell, whose counsel served him well both in governing and in politicking. In addition, he immediately replaced Raskob with Farley as chairman of the Democratic Party. Conservatives in the party, led by Smith and Garner, pressured Roosevelt to adopt policies not significantly different from Hoover's. Liberals such as Senator George W. Norris pressured him in the opposite direction. Most outspoken in the latter camp was Senator Huey Long from Louisiana. And although campaign money was not plentiful—many potential contributors were frightened away by the rhetoric of change—FDR could count on donations from such wealthy backers as Bernard Baruch, Pierre S. du Pont, William Randolph Hearst, and Joseph P. Kennedy.

Campaigning in the West, Roosevelt delivered an attention-getting speech, written by Berle, at the Commonwealth Club in San Francisco on September 23. In it he described a nation that had attained full development and was now in need of properly managing "existing economic organization to the service of the people." To do so meant reappraising the nation's values, focusing, for example, on husbanding natural resources rather than simply exploiting them. He described the government's role as the force for balancing the economic system. Although implying the need for basic change, these were hardly radical ideas. Still, as FDR traveled and campaigned throughout the nation, large crowds turned out to hear what he had to say. They also listened—and responded favorably—to his radio broadcasts. The response finally forced Hoover, who had planned to make only three or four speeches during the campaign, to leave the White House and join the public battle at the beginning of October. Perhaps in desperation, the president branded FDR as a proponent of radical change that would imperil the American way of life. For example, on the last day of October, in an impassioned speech at Madison Square Garden in New York City on the issue of protective tariffs—an issue on which Roosevelt had waffled in his speeches—Hoover declared, "The grass will grow in the streets of a hundred cities, a thousand towns; the weeds will overrun the fields of millions of farms if that protection be taken away." But however forceful Hoover's last-ditch campaigning, which mostly centered in the midwestern states, the die was already cast.

In the November 8 election Roosevelt achieved a landslide victory. Out of the total of 39.7 million votes cast, he won nearly 23 million votes, 57.4 percent of the popular vote, securing 472 electoral college votes. Hoover received close to 16 million popular votes and only 59 electoral votes, carrying only six states in the East. Socialist Party candidate Norman Thomas, many of whose supporters voted for Roosevelt in order to assure Hoover's defeat, received 885,000 votes (2.2 percent of the popular vote); Communist Party leader William Z. Foster, only 103,000. Roosevelt's overwhelming victory also secured the Congress for the Democrats. In the largest turnover of seats in many decades, they won 310 seats in the House, an increase of 90, and 59 in the Senate, an increase of 12.

The Interregnum

A disappointed Hoover returned to his duties, diminished but still president, trying haplessly to influence events in the last four months he had left to serve. On November 10 the ambassador from Great Britain requested that the United States defer his nation's next debt payment, due on December 15, and consider reducing both the principal and the interest rate. Hoover tried to involve the president-elect in resolving the issue. He invited Roosevelt to the White House for discussions. They met at the White House on November 22, along with Raymond Moley and Secretary of the Treasury Ogden Mills and talked about economic conditions and the possibility of appointing a commission to consider renegotiating debts. But Roosevelt remained noncommittal. The same outcome followed a second round of discussions at the White House on December 17, much to Hoover's chagrin. The two men met in January 1933 at Roosevelt's home at Hyde Park and also at the White House to discuss foreign policy issues with Secretary of State Stimson. Roosevelt left for a holiday at Warm Springs, Georgia, with nothing resolved.

In February both houses of Congress approved the Twenty-first Amendment to the Constitution repealing Prohibition and sent the amendment on to the states for ratification. At the same time, crisis erupted. The nation's banks were hemorrhaging in numerous states as anxious depositors made runs (withdrawing savings and other accounts) on their assets. Faced with the threatened failure of Detroit's banks, the governor of Michigan declared an eight-day bank holiday on February 14. The next day came the shocking news that an unemployed bricklayer named Joe Zangara had attempted to assassinate Roosevelt in Miami, firing a pistol from a distance of only 35 feet from the president-elect. Roosevelt was unharmed, but Mayor Anton Cermak of Chicago, who was beside FDR seeking a political favor from him, fell mortally wounded. On the 24th, the threat to Baltimore banks prompted the Maryland governor to declare a bank holiday. At the same time, witnesses questioned by Ferdinand Pecora at hearings before the Senate Banking and Currency Committee were revealing unethical behavior by some of the nation's leading bankers, including

Charles E. Mitchell of the National City Bank, that occurred before the Great Crash and even since—more cause for the public to feel panicky about the financial conditions of the banks. By March 2, some 10 additional states had declared bank holidays. In this critical situation, it is doubtful that many Americans noted that on February 27 a fire set by an incendiary had destroyed the Reichstag building in Berlin. Everyone was awaiting March 4, presidential inauguration day.

CHRONICLE OF EVENTS

1930

January 21: The London Naval Conference called by British prime minister Ramsay MacDonald convenes, with representatives of the "Big Five" nations attending. Secretary of State Henry L. Stimson heads the U.S. delegation, which also includes Secretary of the Navy Charles Francis Adams, Senate Democratic leader Joseph T. Robinson, Republican senators David Reed and Dwight W. Morrow, Hugh Gibson (ambassador to Belgium), and Charles G. Dawes (ambassador to the Court of St. James–Great Britain). King George V officially opens the conference.

February 24: Appointed by President Hoover and confirmed by the Senate, Charles Evans Hughes becomes chief justice of the Supreme Court, replacing William Howard Taft.

March 30: Following the collapse of Germany's coalition government, President Paul von Hindenburg appoints Heinrich Brüning as chancellor.

April 22: The London Naval Conference concludes. The compromises to which the conferees agreed give Great Britain superiority in light cruisers and the United States in heavy cruisers. Japan's cruiser and destroyer ratios with the other two nations' increase. Italy and France (France had demanded superiority over Italy) agree to disagree but oblige the other nations to limitations on the production of submarines—the United States and Great Britain had expressed willingness to cease production of submarines altogether—which actually give Japan parity in submarines. The new agreement is to remain in effect until December 31, 1936.

June 13: After months of debate followed by deadlock in a House-Senate conference, the conferees have reached agreement on the provisions of the Hawley-Smoot Tariff Bill. The Senate passes the bill by a vote of 44–42.

June 14: The House passes the Hawley-Smoot Tariff Bill by a vote of 222-153.

June 17: Even though he had expressed reservations about raising tariffs, Hoover signs the Hawley-Smoot Tariff Act into law. The act provides for the highest duties on imports in history. Duties for raw materials increase between 50 and 100 percent over those introduced by the Fordney-McCumber Tariff

Act of 1922. Average ad valorem rates rise to just over 40 percent—their previous level was 33.22 percent. The act provides no real relief for farmers, imposing duties on sugar and hides, for example, in which few farmers were involved, although those producing citrus fruits and cotton receive some aid.

July 18: At the chancellor's request, Hindenburg dissolves the German parliament, the Reichstag, after its members reject an austerity program proposed by Brüning. New elections will be held on September 14.

July 21: The Senate ratifies the London Naval Treaty by a vote of 58-9 during a special session of Congress called by the president to consider the treaty.

September 1: The Young Plan for payment of Germany's war reparations goes into effect. By the plan's terms, Germany's liability is limited to a little more than $8 billion, the interest rate on the debt is 5.5 percent, and regular payments are stretched over 58½ years. The plan also establishes the Bank for International Settlements at Basel, Switzerland, to assist Germany in making currency transactions.

September 14: National elections shatter Chancellor Brüning's hopes of securing a majority in the Reichstag, as both the Nazis and the Communists make major gains. The Nazis poll more than 6.9 million votes (against only 810,000 in 1928), earning 107 seats (up from 12); the Communists receive nearly 4.6 million votes (up from about 3.3 million in 1928) and 77 seats (up from 54).

September 23: Both United States Steel and Bethlehem Steel announce that they will cut the wages of those workers they still employ by 10 percent.

September 29: Lowell Thomas makes his radio debut as news commentator on CBS.

November 4: Congressional elections result in Republican losses. The Senate in the 72nd Congress will contain 48 Republicans, 47 Democrats, and one Farmer-Laborite. Republicans win 218 seats in the House, with 216 going to the Democrats and one to a Farmer-Laborite.

November 17: On this one day, 66 banks in Nebraska fail, most victims of the drought and the farming crisis.

December 2: The third session of the 71st Congress convenes.

December 12: The Bank of the United States in New York, with 400,000 depositors, fails.

1931

January 19: The Wickersham Commission on Law Enforcement releases its report, which focuses on Prohibition. The commission's findings indicate that Prohibition is a contentious issue among the public, whose support for enforcement has fallen away. Consequently, the commission's members, by a majority of seven to four, favor revising the Eighteenth Amendment. Two of the four in the minority favor repeal.

February 16: The House, by an overwhelming vote of 363-39, approves a bill that would provide early payment of bonuses to World War I veterans averaging between $225 and $500 per veteran.

February 19: Following the direction set by the House, the Senate approves the veterans bonus by a 72-12 vote.

February 26: Hoover votoes the bill passed by Congress that authorizes early payment of veterans' bonuses under provisions of the Adjusted Compensa-

Senator George W. Norris *(Library of Congress)*

tion Act that had been passed over Coolidge's veto in 1924.

March 3: Hoover vetoes the Muscle Shoals Bill, sponsored by Senator George Norris and approved by Congress in December, which authorize the federal government's operation of electrical power generation and distribution facilities at the Wilson Dam on the Tennessee River. Coolidge had pocket vetoed a previous incarnation of the bill in 1928. (The president must either sign or veto a bill within 10 days while Congress is in session; but if Congress adjourns before the 10 days expire, the president may leave the bill unsigned—a pocket veto—and thereby kill it.)

March 6: The March of Time, sponsored by *Time,* begins broadcasting on CBS radio.

March 6: The 71st Congress adjourns.

March 25: The sheriff of Scottsboro, Alabama, arrests nine young African American men and charges them with raping two white women on a train bound for Memphis from Chattanooga.

May 1: Kate Smith makes her radio debut on CBS, introducing what will become her theme song—"When the Moon Comes over the Mountain."

May 11: Officials of the Kreditanstalt, Austria's central bank, announce that the bank can no longer meet its obligations without aid from foreign banks, endangering world confidence in Austria's banking system.

June 16: As part of the European central banks' efforts to shore up the Kreditanstalt, the Bank of England provides the Austrian bank an advance of 150 million shillings.

June 18: Hoover receives a communication from President Paul von Hindenburg pleading for action to help salvage Germany's failing economy.

June 20: After securing support from leaders of Congress, Hoover calls for a one-year moratorium on payments on debts among the Allies and on German reparations payments.

July 6: Although initially opposed by the French government, Hoover's proposal for a moratorium on debts and reparations payments wins acceptance from the affected governments.

July 13: One of Germany's major banks, the Darmstaedler und Nationalbank, fails.

August 17: Hoover reconstitutes the President's Emergency Committee on Employment (PECE), which he had appointed in fall 1930, as the President's Organization of Unemployment Relief (POUR), headed by Walter S. Gifford, president of AT&T.

September 8: Concerned that many banks, large and small, are in peril of failing, Hoover calls Federal Reserve Board chairman Eugene Meyer to the White House and recommends creation of a private corporation among major solvent banks to provide credit to the imperiled smaller banks.

September 15: For the second time, Hoover calls Eugene Meyer to the White House to propose creation of a private credit corporation among solvent banks, specifying that they provide a loan pool of $500 million.

September 18–19: Alleging that the Chinese have sabotaged the Japanese-owned South Manchurian Railway, Japan sends troops to capture Mukden and to forcefully occupy large areas of South Manchuria.

September 21: After heavy withdrawals of gold from the Bank of England, threatening destruction of the bank's gold reserves, the MacDonald government announces Great Britain's abandonment of the gold standard.

September 22: Reacting to Japan's invasion of Manchuria, Aristide Briand, president of the League of Nations Council, sends telegrams to the Japanese and Chinese governments urging them to cease hostilities and withdraw their troops.

September 24: Secretary of State Stimson sends telegrams to the Japanese and Chinese governments in support of Briand's position. The Japanese install a puppet administration in Mukden.

October 16: Stimson, responding to a request from the League Council, authorizes Prentiss Gilbert, American consul general in Geneva, to attend the League of Nations' discussions of how to deal with the crisis in Manchuria.

October 23: French premier Pierre Laval begins a two-day visit in Washington, D.C., to discuss with Hoover the possibility of reducing the size of French war debt payments after the current moratorium on payments ends.

December 7: The 72nd Congress convenes. Deaths, including that of Speaker Nicholas Longworth, since the 1930 election and special elections to fill the resulting vacancies have given the Democrats a majority in the House—220 members to 214 for the Republicans and one for the Farmer-Laborites. In his State of the Union message the president, accepting

that the National Credit Corporation that arose out of his suggestions to Eugene Meyer is a failure, asks Congress to pass legislation creating the Reconstruction Finance Corporation (RFC) to provide federal loans to railroads, banks, and other enterprises.

December 10: Finally responding to an appeal from China following Japan's invasion of Manchuria in September, a clear violation of the Covenant of the League of Nations, the League Council votes to send a commission to the Far East to investigate. The commission is headed by Victor George Alexander Robert Lytton (Lord Lytton).

December 25: On Christmas Day the Metropolitan Opera initiates its Saturday radio broadcasts, introduced by Milton Cross. The company's first broadcast opera is German composer Engelbert Humperdinck's *Hänsel und Gretel.*

1932

January 2: Japanese troops occupy the city of Jinzhou (Chinchou), ending Chinese authority in Manchuria.

January 4: The Japanese army secures control of Manchuria.

January 7: Following several days of discussion with the president and his staff, Stimson sends a statement to the Japanese and Chinese governments informing them that the United States will not recognize any treaty or agreement between them that violates existing treaties, such as the Pact of Paris (which outlawed war) and the Nine-Power Treaty. The Stimson Doctrine, as it becomes known, is aimed at Japan.

January 12: Justice Oliver Wendell Holmes resigns from the Supreme Court. Hoover appoints Benjamin N. Cardozo as his replacement.

January 22: Congress approves an act authorizing creation of the Reconstruction Finance Corporation (RFC) to loan funds to banks, insurance companies, other financial firms, agricultural credit associations, and railroads—the latter only with approval of the Interstate Commerce Commission. The act provides for a pool of $500 million in RFC stock subscribed by the Treasury and grants the RFC authority to borrow $1.5 million more in tax-exempt instruments guaranteed by the federal government.

January 29: The Chinese government had responded to Japan's aggression by imposing a boycott against purchases of Japanese goods, which has proven quite effective. In retaliation Japanese naval vessels land marines to stage an unplanned attack on Shanghai that results in hundreds of Chinese dead.

February 2: After years of planning by a League of Nations "Preparatory Commission," a conference on disarmament convenes in Geneva. The 31 participants include the United States and the USSR. This new Geneva Conference focuses on land-based armaments.

February 2: Hoover signs the Reconstruction Finance Corporation Act.

February 10: "The International Style," a major architectural exhibit, opens at the Museum of Modern Art in New York City.

February 17: In response to concern over a severe decline in the Treasury's gold reserves and at the urging of Secretary of the Treasury Ogden Mills and the president, Congress approves the Glass-Steagall Act, which expands the securities eligible for discount by the Federal Reserve that back up 60 percent of the nation's currency, thus relieving the demands on the gold reserves, which back up 40 percent of the currency.

February 18: The Manchurian assembly supported by Japan declares the state's independence under the name Manchukuo and defines its boundaries, which include the province of Jehol, previously outside Japan's sphere of control. Japan formally recognizes the new state.

February 27: Hoover signs the Glass-Steagall Act.

March 1: The baby son of Anne and Charles A. Lindbergh is kidnapped, taken from his bed at their home in Hopewell, New Jersey.

March 3: Congress approves the Twentieth Amendment to the U.S. Constitution that eliminates lame-duck sessions of Congress and moves the presidential inauguration to January; the amendment is sent to the states to be considered for ratification.

March 7: A crowd of about 3,000, supported by representatives of the Communist Party, gathers in Detroit and marches to the Ford River Rouge plant in Dearborn, Michigan. Police order them to disperse; they refuse, and the police shoot tear gas into their midst. The marchers throw stones and clods. The police fall back to the factory; firemen spray the crowd with water. The police open fire, killing one demonstrator. The marchers fall back to a field, where three more are killed by police fire.

March 11: The League of Nations Assembly unanimously approves a resolution supporting the Stimson Doctrine of nonrecognition.

March 12: The dead from the River Rouge demonstration are ceremonially buried as about 40,000 look on.

March 23: Hoover signs into law the Norris-LaGuardia Anti-injunction Act. Provisions of the act assure workers the right to organize and to choose representatives for negotiations, while also restricting the use of federal injunctions against strikes and essentially outlawing "yellow-dog" contracts, which commit employees not to join a union.

April 2: An intermediary for the Lindberghs, Dr. John F. Condon, meets the apparent kidnapper in St. Raymond's Cemetery in the Bronx and delivers $50,000 in exchange for the information that the baby is safe on a boat at Martha's Vineyard. Lindbergh flies to Martha's Vineyard in a futile search.

April 10: Paul von Hindenburg wins a runoff election for the presidency of Germany, capturing 53 percent of the votes cast; Adolf Hitler comes in second, with nearly 37 percent of the votes.

April 14: At the behest of Chancellor Brüning, President Hindenburg issues a decree banning the SA, the Nazi private army known as the "Brownshirts."

May 12: The body of the Lindberghs' baby is found in a thicket less than six miles from the family's home.

May 15: Japanese prime minister Inukai Tsuyoshi, who had supported ending military operations in Manchuria, is assassinated, leaving the military in effective control of cabinet appointments and policy formation.

May 21: The Socialist Party nominates Norman Thomas as candidate for the presidency.

May 21: A group of unemployed veterans from Portland, Oregon, led by former sergeant Walter W. Waters, arrives in East St. Louis en route to Washington, D.C., by riding the rails. Their intent is to pressure the government to award veterans' bonuses early (they are not scheduled for distribution until 1945). After a conflict with the Baltimore & Ohio Railroad, they are rounded up by the National Guard and shipped out of the state on trucks. The incident receives press attention that attracts other veterans to join the advance on Washington of the Bonus Expeditionary Force, as they call themselves with mock humor.

May 28: The Communist Party nominates William Z. Foster for the presidency.

May 30: At President Hindenburg's request, Brüning submits his resignation as chancellor of Germany.

June 1: Hindenburg appoints Franz von Papen as chancellor to replace Brüning.

June 4: Chancellor Papen dissolves the Reichstag and calls for new elections on July 31.

June 6: At the Lausanne Conference convened to renegotiate Germany's reparations debt, the Allies accept reducing the debt to only $715 million, 90 percent below the amount established under the Young Plan.

June 7: Hoover signs into law the Revenue Act of 1932, which imposes the largest peacetime tax increase in history—to 55 percent in the surtax, to 1.75 percent in corporation taxes, and to 45 percent in estate taxes. The new taxes are expected to raise $1 billion.

June 14: The Republican National Convention begins in Chicago.

June 15: Feeling pressured by the Bonus Expeditionary Force, or Bonus Army, now swollen to 11,000 men and camped on the Anacostia River Flats, the House passes the Patman Bill, which authorizes immediate payment of the veterans bonus.

June 15: Papen lifts the ban on the Nazi SA.

June 16: The Republican National Convention nominates Herbert Hoover as the party's candidate for the presidency. Charles Curtis is again the nominee for the vice presidency.

June 17: The Senate rejects the Patman Bill. The Bonus Army, now numbering about 20,000, had assembled on the steps of the Capitol to await the vote. After it is announced, they sing "America" and return to their campsites. Some leave for home; others, many joined by their wives and children, determine to wait indefinitely.

June 27: The Democratic National Convention begins in Chicago.

July 1: On the fourth ballot, the Democratic Convention chooses Franklin Delano Roosevelt, governor of New York, as the party's nominee for the presidency. Speaker of the House John Nance Garner becomes the vice presidential nominee.

July 9: Meeting in Omaha, Nebraska, the Farmer-Labor Party National Committee nominates Jacob Coxey, leader of "Coxey's Army" in the march on Washington to seek relief during the 1893–94 depression, as their candidate for the presidency.

July 20: Papen deposes the constitutional Social Democrat government of the state of Prussia, appointing himself as German commissioner for Prussia.

July 21: Hoover signs into law the Emergency Relief and Construction Act. The law provides $1.5 billion in funding to be disbursed through the RFC for public works projects that would earn income and $300 million in loans as direct assistance to the states.

July 22: Hoover signs into law the Federal Home Loan Bank Act, which creates Federal Home Loan Banks authorized to provide discounted home mortgages.

July 31: In Germany's parliamentary elections, the Nazis win 230 seats, giving them the largest representation among the Reichstag's 603 members.

July 28: After an incident in which jittery policemen fire on some Bonus Army members, the District of Columbia commissioners ask the federal government to send troops to disperse the veterans. With Hoover's approval, Secretary of the Army Patrick J. Hurley dispatches army troops commanded by General Douglas MacArthur and his aide Major Dwight D. Eisenhower. They clear Bonus Army veterans from all downtown buildings and then drive them from the Anacostia Flats with tear gas.

August 11: Hoover publicly announces that he will support repeal of the Eighteenth Amendment to the Constitution, a position already advocated in the Democratic Party's platform.

August 30: At the convening of the Reichstag, the Centrists join with the Nazis to elect Hitler's lieutenant, Hermann Göring, president of the parliamentary body.

September 1: Under pressure from Governor Roosevelt because of scandals sullying the New York mayor's office that may threaten Roosevelt's campaign for the presidency, the flamboyant James J. Walker resigns.

September 12: Upon reconvening for its regular session, the Reichstag is once again dissolved.

October 4: The Lytton Commission, sent to investigate events in the Far East, releases its report, which describes the Japanese attack on Manchuria as inexcusable and recommends that Manchuria be made autonomous under Chinese sovereignty, with the political interests of the Japanese to be honored.

November 6: In the parliamentary elections, the Nazis lose 34 seats, reducing their numbers to 196, still the largest membership in the Reichstag.

November 7: The U.S. Supreme Court overturns the conviction of "the Scottsboro boys" (the nine young African Americans convicted of raping two white women), upheld by the Alabama Supreme Court in March, on the grounds that the defendants had been denied adequate counsel. The case will go back to the Alabama courts for retrial.

November 8: Franklin Delano Roosevelt triumphs overwhelmingly in the presidential election, capturing 57 percent of the popular vote and 472 electoral votes to Herbert Hoover's 59. Socialist Norman Thomas wins 2.2 percent of the popular vote.

November 19: Papen resigns as Germany's chancellor. Hindenburg offers the chancellorship to Hitler if he can muster a majority coalition in the Reichstag, but he cannot.

November 22: Hoover, Secretary of the Treasury Ogden Mills, and Roosevelt, accompanied by his adviser Raymond Moley, meet at the White House at the request of Hoover, who hopes to persuade the president-elect to cooperate with him in appointing a commission to deal with the issue of making adjustments in the Allies' debt payments; Roosevelt is noncommittal.

December 2: General Kurt von Schleicher becomes chancellor of Germany.

1933

January 5: Former president Calvin Coolidge dies.

January 9: Roosevelt and Stimson meet at Hyde Park, Roosevelt's home in New York State, so that the secretary of state can brief the president-elect on foreign policy.

January 20: Hoover, Roosevelt, Mills, and Moley meet for a second time at the White House. Roosevelt is insistent about divorcing the issue of the Allies' war debts from foreign policy issues and the economic crisis.

January 28: Chancellor Kurt von Schleicher, unable to form a Reichstag majority, submits the resignation of his government to President Hindenburg.

January 30: Adolf Hitler becomes chancellor of Germany.

January 30: *The Lone Ranger* debuts on radio station WXYZ in Detroit.

January 31: Edouard Daladier becomes premier of France, replacing Edouard Herriot, leader of the Radical Party.

February 3: A sufficient number of states have approved the Twentieth Amendment to the Constitution to secure its ratification. The amendment moves the time for swearing in members of Congress and the president to January of the year following their election.

February 14: The financial status of Detroit banks has become so critical that the governor of Michigan declares an eight-day bank holiday to provide time for devising a strategy for assuring their solvency.

February 15: While on a vacation and touring in his car through a park in the center of Miami, Florida, Roosevelt stops to give a brief speech to a crowd of about 20,000 and then pauses to talk with Anton J. Cermak, mayor of Chicago, who had approached the car. While they are talking, Joseph Zangara, an Italian immigrant, leaps onto a nearby park bench and fires five pistol shots at the president-elect. Roosevelt is unharmed, but Cermak falls fatally wounded.

February 16: The Senate votes to repeal the Eighteenth Amendment, which mandated Prohibition.

February 20: The House votes to repeal the Eighteenth Amendment. The Twenty-first Amendment, repealing Prohibition, therefore moves to the states for consideration.

February 21: In hearings before the Senate Banking and Currency Committee, Charles E. Mitchell, chairman of the National City Bank, and other witnesses reveal details of their own finances—such as receiving huge bonuses, making suspect stock trades, and avoiding income taxes.

February 24: The League of Nations Assembly, over the objection of Japan, adopts the Lytton Report (advocating creation of an autonomous Manchuria) and rejects recognition of Manchukuo. The Japanese delegates to the League walk out, never to return.

February 24: Responding to a run on banks in Baltimore, the governor of Maryland declares a bank holiday.

February 27: The building housing the German parliament, the Reichstag, burns, set ablaze by an arsonist.

February 27: Charles E. Mitchell resigns from the board of the National City Bank.

February 28: Blaming the Communists for the Reichstag fire, Hitler persuades Hindenburg to issue a decree suspending those sections of the Weimar constitution that guarantee civil liberties and personal rights on the grounds that the government needs a free hand to suppress Communist acts of terror.

March 2: Ten more states declare bank holidays. In the afternoon, President-elect Roosevelt and his entourage leave New York City, taking the ferry across the Hudson River, and board a Baltimore & Ohio Railroad train for the journey to Washington, D.C., for Roosevelt's inauguration.

EYEWITNESS TESTIMONY

The engineers turn out to be philologists. Their hands were not on the levers and steering wheels but on dictionaries. The ferocious processes of supply and demand have proved that they did not know any more about the financial structure than we did. Mr. Mitchell of the National City Bank, it is safe to say, was as perplexed as my barber—who was cleaned out on October 24. That solemn convention which took their chairs in the offices of J. P. Morgan and Company, pledged to "plug the air holes" and save the nation—did they know what forces had been loosed; where the deluge would end? They did not, and do not. Like the rest of us, they can only strive to keep smiling and hope for the best. The solid plateau of values was nothing but arrant non-sense—on all fours with the values of Florida swamps in 1926.

Stuart Chase, economist and social critic, from his book
Prosperity Fact or Myth *(1930).*

I believe that, in any civilised country today with a responsible government and a powerful central bank, it would be much better to leave management of the reserves of the central bank to its own unfettered discretion than to attempt to lay down by law what it should do or within what limits it should act. What the law—or, failing the law, the force of a binding convention—should attend to is the regulation of the reserves of the member banks, so as to ensure that the decision as to the total volume of bank money outstanding shall be centralised in the hands of a body whose duty it is to be guided by considerations of the general social and economic advantage and not pecuniary profit. . . . The legal reserves of member banks are, also, a means of making them contribute to the expense of the maintenance of the central reserves. But the legal reserves of the central bank merely lock away resources where they are useless, and the effective strength of a central bank entirely depends in practice on the amount of its *excess* reserves. Thus we have the paradox that the more strictly and conservatively the gold reserves of a central bank are prescribed by law, the weaker it is and the more utterly exposed to disastrous disturbances from every wind which blows. A central bank which was compelled to keep 100 per cent of its assets in gold would be not much better off than one which had no reserves at all.

John Maynard Keynes, British economist, in
A Treatise on Money: The Applied Theory
of Money *(1930, 1971).*

I backtracked a few hundred miles and did some harvesting in Kansas—"You can follow this wheat all the way into the Dakotas, if you want to go with it," I was told. When I finished in Kansas, I caught a train north through Nebraska into Wyoming and the Dakotas.
. . . Many times I road overnight on the top of boxcars. I'd take my belt, pass it under the runner on the catwalk, and hook it through my overalls. With no danger of falling off, I let the train rock me to sleep. I'd also hook myself on with my belt if I was riding on a tanker. It's awful tiresome bouncing up and down all night.

Reminiscence of Arvel Pearson, an Arkansan who lost his job at a coal mine in 1930, at age 15, and became a hobo, quoted in Uys, Riding the Rails *(1999).*

Many business men err, when first contemplating an advertising campaign, by conjuring up the mental image of a piece of copy that is, to them, a finished advertisement. Their thinking is introspective, resulting in a sort of glorified picture of "what *we* mean to the customer." Any enlightened salesman will agree that this attitude is wrong. The logical prior consideration is the prospective *customer*—what the customer wants to use, possess, or enjoy; what the customer wants to read, see, and be informed about. For lack of this insight, many advertisers commit the grave error of trying to tell the prospect what the advertiser wants him to know, instead of what the prospect wants to know.

Bernard Lichtenberg, vice president and director of advertising for the Alexander Hamilton Institute, and Bruce Barton, publicist and advertising executive, from their book Advertising Campaigns *(1930).*

Industrialism is the economic organization of the collective American society. It means the decision of society to invest its economic resources in the applied sciences. But the word "science" has acquired a certain sanctitude. It is out of order to quarrel with science in the abstract, or even with the applied sciences when their applications are made subject to criticism and intelligence. The capitalization of the applied sciences has now become extravagant and uncritical; it has enslaved our human energies to a degree now clearly felt to be burdensome. The apologists of industrialism do not like to meet this charge directly; so they often take refuge in saying that they are devoted simply to science! They are really devoted to the applied sciences and to practical production. Therefore it is necessary to employ a certain skepticism even at the expense of the Cult of Science, and to say, It is an Americanism, which looks innocent and disinterested, but really is not either.

John Crowe Ransom, Allen Tate, Robert Penn Warren, et al., from the introduction of I'll Take My Stand *(1930).*

The Depression's effects upon the home or family life in the United States were as varied as they were profound; but they can be put into two general categories: On the one hand, thousands of families were broken up, some permanently, others temporarily, or were seriously disorganized. On the other hand, thousands of other families became more closely integrated than they had been before the Depression.

The reason for these different effects due to the same cause was that the economic crisis, which came upon many families in all sections of the country with the force and suddenness of a cyclone, in most cases intensified the various antagonistic and affectional attitudes or reactions of one to the other among the individuals within the family groups. Sudden economic adversity made family life more dynamic.

Louis Adamic, immigrant from Yugoslavia and novelist, writing about 1930, in My America, 1928–1938 *(1938).*

It is notorious, for example, that in the late lamentable Presidential campaign, millions of copies of scurrilous pamphlets were circulated against Mr. Smith because he is Catholic. They were malicious to the last degree, and many of them were foul and obscene. And there was not a state in the union in which they were not distributed. . . . The mentality of those who wrote them and still more of those who believed them is beyond understanding. There seems to be no way to deal with such things except to endure them. But if bigots are all amenable to reason, we might ask them, "suppose the Catholics had retaliated in kind?" What if Catholics had deluged the United States with scur-

rilous and obscene Anti-Protestant propaganda? Of course we wouldn't. But suppose we did?

The Catholic World, *editorial of March 1930.*

Mr. Hoover is in genuine danger of becoming a silent and forgotten man, obscured by the trend of events and the glamour of his senatorial neighbors. We believe this would be exceedingly regrettable. Whatever may be his limitations, the President is possibly the most competent and national-minded among Washington politicians. He has the desire to work hard, to advance the common good, to satisfy in so far as he can the legitimate demands of his countrymen.

The Commonweal, *article of March 12, 1930.*

People, American people, no longer buy cars. They do not buy newspapers, books, foods, pictures, clothes. Things are sold to people now. If a territory can take so and so many Bogel cars, find men who can make them take the cars. That is the way things are done now.

Sherwood Anderson, author, in the Nation *(May 28, 1930).*

A procession of German Fascists was attacked today by Communists in the town of Unterbermgruen. . . . Adolf Hitler, the German Fascist leader, is snorting fire. . . . A cardinal policy of his now-powerful German party is the conquest of Russia. That's a tall assignment, Adolf. You just ask Napoleon.

News commentator Lowell Thomas, in his CBS radio debut broadcast, September 29, 1930, quoted in Henderson, On the Air: Pioneers of American Broadcasting *(1988).*

There is no country where the power of the dollar has not reached. There is no capital which does not take the United States into consideration at almost every turn. Conversely, there is no zone where our interests are not involved. Isolation is a myth. We are not isolated and cannot be isolated. The United States is ever present.

Officially, our government stays out of world organizations. We scorn the League of Nations; we continue to shy at the World Court. But such things count for less and less. We must deal with the world and the world must deal with us.

Edwin L. James, journalist, in International Digest *(October 1930).*

Al Capone's free soup kitchen, Chicago, November 18, 1930 *(Library of Congress)*

I am persuaded to write you, concerning aid to unemployment. I hope this movement will be speeded up so people in Pottstown will feel and know results before Cold weather comes upon us, the struggling starving working class under nourished Men. women. and children. It really is alarming that this so called prosperous Nation that we must suffer on acct [account] of a few men seeking power and rule . . . I am one of the men out of work but the rich don't care so long as they have full and plenty.

Anonymous man of Pottstown, Pennsylvania, letter of October 1930 to President Herbert Hoover, in McElvaine, Down & Out in the Great Depression: Letters from the "Forgotten Man" *(1983).*

I have eaten crow and swallowed my pride for ten years before the wastelanders, the lost generationers, the bitter-bitters, the futility people, and all other cheap literary fakes sicklied o'er with a pale coat of steer shit—but now I will hold my tongue no longer: I know what I know, and I have learned it with blood and sweat. I have lived alone in a foreign land until I could not sleep for thinking of the sights and sounds and colors, the whole intolerable memory of America, its violence, savagery, immensity, beauty, ugliness, and glory—and I tell you I know it as if it were my child, as if it had been distilled from my blood and marrow: I know it from the look and smell of the railway ties to the thousand sounds and odours of the wilderness—and I tell you I had rather have ten years more of life there than fifty years of Continental weak tea and smothering in this woolly and lethargic air, than a hundred years of shitty ex-patriotism.

Thomas Wolfe, novelist, letter of November 1930 to Alfred S. Dashiell, in Nowell, The Letters of Thomas Wolfe *(1956).*

Such poverty is not for the artist in America. They pay us, indeed, only too well. . . . But he [the writer] is oppressed ever by something worse than poverty—by the feeling that what he creates does not matter, that he is expected by his readers to be only a decorator or a clown, or that he is good-naturedly accepted as a scoffer whose bark probably is worse than his bite and who probably is a good fellow at heart, who in any case certainly does not count in a land that produces eighty-story buildings, motors by the millions, and wheat by the billions of bushels. And he has no institution, no group, to which he can turn for inspiration, whose criticism he can accept and whose praise will be precious to him.

Sinclair Lewis, novelist, speech of December 12, 1930, in Stockholm accepting the Nobel Prize in literature, in Address by Sinclair Lewis Before the Swedish Academy.

We have been and are even now under the spell of an illusion, a kind of popular superstition, of a type common enough in history. It is, in our case, a belief in the magical restoration of prosperity. Whereas up to the autumn of 1929 we had dreamed that depressions were abolished, we have since clung with passionate faith, worthy of some better object, to the idea that a boom and a crash and a recovery follow each other, like winter and summer, in a fixed cycle.

This belief in the automatic restoration of prosperity has made us for the time being a nation of fatalists. . . . Thus we have become more interested in prophesying the future than in preparing for it, in guessing than in governing, in wishing than in willing.

Walter Lippmann, newspaper columnist, from his book Notes on the Crisis *(1931).*

My facts and experience I interpret as meaning not only that this is the decadent stage of capitalism, but also that any and all reform is now, in the large, vain. In sum, it is, as I see it, much too late for any really

workable capitalistic or bank and corporation reform. . . . The rich are too rich; the poor are too poor. And the hour has come when some form of equitable sharing in the means of living—shall not only have to be considered but wisely and truly enforced.

Theodore Dreiser, editor and novelist, in Tragic America *(1931).*

A crowd of men and women, shouting that they were hungry and jobless, raided a grocery store near the City Hall today. Twenty-six of the men were arrested. Scores loitered near the city jail following the arrests, but kept well out of range of fire hose made ready for use in case of another disturbance.

The New York Times, *article of January 21, 1931, about Oklahoma City.*

The present administration has refused to follow the policy of Mr. Wilson and has followed consistently the former practice of this government since the days of Jefferson. As soon as it was reported to us, through our diplomatic representatives, that the new governments in Bolivia, Peru, Argentina, Brazil, and Panama were in control of the administrative machinery of the state, with the apparent general acquiescence of their people, and that they were willing and apparently able to discharge their international and conventional obligations, they were recognized by our government. . . .

Such has been our policy in all cases where international practice was not affected or controlled by preexisting treaty. In the five republics of Central America—Guatemala, Honduras, Salvador, Nicaragua, and Costa Rica—however, we have found an entirely different situation. . . . Those countries geographically have for a century been the focus of the greatest difficulties and the most frequent disturbances in their earnest course toward competent maturity in the discharge of their international obligations.

Secretary of State Henry L. Stimson, speech presented in New York to the Council of Foreign Relations, February 6, 1931, quoted in U.S. Department of State, Latin American Series *(1931).*

Several hundred men and women in an unemployed demonstration today stormed a grocery store and meat market in the Gateway district, smashed plate glass windows and helped themselves to bacon and ham, fruit and canned goods.

One of the store owners suffered a broken arm when he was attacked as he drew a revolver and attempted to keep out the first to enter.

One hundred policemen were sent to the district and seven persons were arrested as the leaders.

The New York Times, *article of February 26, 1931, about Minneapolis.*

I am firmly opposed to the government entering into any business the major purpose of which is competition with our citizens. There are national emergencies which require that the government should temporarily enter the field of business, but they must be emergency actions. . . . There are many localities where the federal government is justified in construction of great dams and reservoirs, where navigation, flood control, reclamation, or stream regulation are of dominant importance, and where they are beyond the capacity or purpose of private or local government capital to construct. In these cases power is often a byproduct and should be disposed of by contract or lease. But for the federal government deliberately to go out to build up and expand such an occasion to the major purpose of a power and manufacturing business is to break down the initiative and enterprise of the American people; it is destruction of equality of opportunity among our people; it is the negation of the ideals upon which our civilization has been based.

President Herbert Hoover, message to Congress on March 3, 1931, vetoing a bill that authorized the federal government to operate the power generation plants at Muscle Shoals on the Tennessee River, in the Congressional Record *(1931).*

It would seem that the economic crisis, the reduction of large classes of the German population to the level of the proletariat, and the unemployment of nearly five million persons, cannot go on for many more years without ruining the German nation as a whole. Here is a population . . . which in general is forced to be satisfied with an income barely sufficient for a minimum existence. . . . Thus vast sections of the people feel oppressed and bitterly discontented. . . .

Greater danger is threatening at the present time from the National Socialists, popularly called the Nazis. This movement comprises the large ranks of the disinherited and the *declasses*—middle class citizens, officials, officers and landowners. All of these deserve our sympathy and pity.

Erich Koch-Weser, German statesman and former member of the Reichstag, in Foreign Affairs *(April 1931).*

I spent five days in West Virginia. The situation in the coal fields is probably the most exciting anywhere on the industrial scene. The Communists are raising hell in Ohio and Pennsylvania, and in Harlan County, Kentucky, the operators have brought in the militia and are only holding the lid on by means of a reign of terror. . . . it takes a good deal of courage to go into that country, where shootings frequently occur and where just at present the atmosphere is full of uncertainty and suspicion, what with the authorities, the Communists, and the A.F. of L. . . .

My next stop was Chattanooga, what with the niggers and the mills one of the most squalid towns I have ever been in. The Scottsboro case has set the town agog, insofar as Southerners of that kind can be set agog. . . . The Scottsboro case itself is very difficult to unravel, because there is not only a defense and a prosecution but a double defense with the two lawyers very hostile to each other. . . . It's an extremely interesting case, however—on account of the Communist element something new, I suppose, in the South.

Edmund Wilson, writer and critic, letter of June 24, 1931, to John Dos Passos, in Edmund Wilson: Letters on Literature and Politics, 1912–1972 *(1977).*

For eighteen months, unemployment has been spreading poverty and acute suffering through industrial and agricultural areas alike. No one yet knows when the present economic disaster will be brought to an end. The illusory prosperity and feverish optimism which marked preceding years have given way to fearful economic insecurity and to widespread despair. . . . The administration's efforts to attain economic security have consisted of attempts to minimize the seriousness of the Depression, of bold assurances that steps which would restore prosperity were about to be taken, and of a woefully unsuccessful program to stimulate private or local agencies to undertake tasks which the administration was determined to shirk.

*Senator Robert M. La Follette, Jr., of Wisconsin,
in the Nation (July 15, 1931).*

At bottom, . . . we have far too many farmers and a dangerously inflated agriculture. The surplus farmers till millions of acres of inferior land which might better revert to forest and prairie. The first move toward a finer rural civilization must be to abandon about 70,000,000 of the 390,000,000 or more acres tilled last year. For on that immense area nobody can make a dollar, while those who try to do so only glut the market with underpriced commodities. . . . At least five million farmers—men, women, and children— must be forced out of their futile occupation; and the faster the better for all concerned. . . . As super-farming spreads, another five million must slowly shift to other work. For the super-farm can feed a man with the yield of three acres, whereas our noble quarter-section grubber must work nearly five acres to accomplish the same result.

*Professor Walter B. Pitkin, from an article entitled
"The Great Dirt Conspiracy" originally published in
Forum (August 1931), in which he advocated large-
scale farming (now known as agribusiness) as a means of
solving the nation's agricultural problems and paring its
27 million farmers, in Beard, ed., America Faces
the Future (1932).*

It seems to me that as things stand there is no normal economic solution of the present acute emergency in American industry. Hundreds of thousands of men, women and children are going to suffer terribly this winter in spite of all that the natural laws of economic change can do, however soon it may start, however rapidly it may move. Yet the situation is not hopeless, for if we can re-create the dynamic altruism outside of government which moved us during the war, we can harness forces that will bring relief and make us a better and nobler people.

*William Allen White, editor and author, letter to David
Hinshaw, August 10, 1931, in Johnson, Selected
Letters of William Allen White, 1899–1943
(1947).*

One way or the other, it is easy to exaggerate what has happened to America in the past two years. Easier still is to look out upon this groaning conti-nent—groaning under plenty—and decide there is nothing in our circumstances to justify the chute from the mad optimism of two summers ago to the profound pessimism of today. What we want, says James Truslow Adams, is perspective, the long view instead of the close-up. . . . But perhaps this is perspective: this new outlook upon the encroaching world, this first glance into the jungle of the future, this pause of doubt upon a road whereon we have met all sorts of hazards, but never before the question whether it was the right road going in the one desirable direction.

*Anne O'Hare McCormick, journalist, column of August
16, 1931, in the New York Times, quoted in Sheehan,
The World at Home: Selections from the Writings
of Anne O'Hare McCormick (1956).*

Several hundred homeless unemployed women sleep nightly in Chicago's parks, Mrs. Elizabeth A. Conkey, Commissioner of Public Welfare, reported today.

She learned of the situation, she said, when women of good character appealed for shelter and protection, having nowhere to sleep but in the parks, where they feared that they would be molested. . . .

The commissioner said the approach of Winter made the problem more serious, with only one free women's lodging house existing, accommodating 100.

The New York Times, article of September 20, 1931.

That there are grave imperfections in an economic order which makes possible the stark contrast of vast fortunes and breadlines is obvious. Society must turn its attention increasingly to the unsoundness of the present distribution of the national income, and to the control of the money-making spirit which lies behind it. Public sentiment must also turn against the amassing of property, especially through stock speculation, without regard for social consequences. New emphasis must rather be laid upon the Christian motive of service.

*From a statement issued by the convention of the
Protestant Episcopal Church convened in Denver in
autumn 1931, in Beard, ed., America Faces
the Future (1932).*

New Yorkers dominate the flow of Americans who have decided, at least for the time being, to cast their lot with the Russians. Pennsylvania, New Jersey, and Illinois show heavy quotas of recruits under the new call for "6,000 skilled workers," and Michigan, Ohio, California, and Massachusetts are well represented.

More than 100,000 applications have been received at the Amtorg's New York office for the 6,000 jobs. . . .

Three principal reasons are advanced for wanting the position: (1) unemployment; (2) disgust with conditions here; (3) interest in the Soviet experiment.

Business Week, *article of October 7, 1931.*

Somebody had blundered and the most expensive orgy in history was over.

It ended two years ago, because the utter confidence which was its essential prop received an enormous jolt and it didn't take long for the flimsy structure to settle earthward. And after two years the Jazz Age seems as far away as the days before the War. It was borrowed time anyhow—the whole upper tenth of a nation living with the insouciance of grand ducs and the casualness of chorus girls.

F. Scott Fitzgerald, novelist, in Scribner's *article of November 1931, quoted in* The Crack-Up *(1945).*

The cold truth is that the individualist creed of everybody for himself and the devil take the hindmost is principally responsible for the distress in which Western civilization finds itself—with investing racketeering at one end and labor racketeering at the other. Whatever merits the creed may have had in days of primitive agriculture and industry, it is not applicable in an age of technology, science, and rationalized economy. Once useful, it has become a danger to society. Every thoughtful businessman who is engaged in management as distinguished from stock speculation knows that stabilization, planning, orderly procedure, prudence, and the adjustment of production to demand are necessary to keep the economic machine running steadily and efficiently.

Charles A. Beard, historian, in Harper's *(December 1931).*

Attracted by smoke from the chimney of a supposedly empty summer cottage near Awana Lake . . . Constable Simon Glaser found a young couple starving. Three days without food, the wife, who is 23 years old, was hardly able to walk.

The couple . . . of New York, had been unemployed since their formerly wealthy employer lost his money, and several days ago they invested all they had,

except 25 cents for food, in bus fare to this region in search of work. Finding none, they went into the cottage, preferring to starve rather than beg. They said they had resigned themselves to dying together.

The New York Times, *article of December 25, 1931.*

A just and ideal economic order is, therefore, to the aspiring masses, as is the mirage to the worn traveler in the desert—a hope, whose realization appears perpetually to recede. Such an order or system must, apparently, in the circumstances of class interest and class prejudice, wait upon some development of intelligent understanding of the economic system we now have and of the economic forces at work in that system, on the part of those who are its victims. For, so long as the victims of the existing economic system do not understand the faults of the system against which they protest, well enough, specifically enough, and discriminatingly enough to make workable reforms . . . and so long as their revolts are likely to be guided by short-sighted selfishness, worth-while reform is hardly to be expected or hoped for. . . . the exploited masses are ordinarily in large part the dupes of the privileged interests as well as their own ignorance, and support, through their own prejudices and their own votes, those very economic policies by which they are laid under tribute.

Harry Gunnison Brown, professor of economics at the University of Missouri, from his book The Economic Basis of Tax Reform *(1932).*

Hence the only practical maxim for monetary policy to be derived from our considerations is probably the negative one that the simple fact of an increase of production and trade forms no justification for an expansion of credit, and that—save in an acute crisis—bankers need not be afraid to harm production by overcaution. Under existing conditions, to go beyond this is out of the question. In any case, it could be attempted only by a central monetary authority for the whole world: action on the part of a single country would be doomed to disaster. It is probably an illusion to suppose that we shall ever be able entirely to eliminate industrial fluctuations by means of monetary policy. The most we may hope for is that the growing information of the public may make it easier for central banks both to follow a cautious policy during the upward swing of the cycle, and so to mitigate the following depression, and to resist the well-meaning but dangerous proposals to fight depression by "a little inflation."

Friedrich A. Hayek, Tooke professor of economic science and statistics at the University of London, from his book Prices and Production *(1932).*

The stock market was full of bargain prices. About 1923, the bull market began its unprecedented climb. An ideal investor, buying an average assortment of stocks in 1926 and holding them till September 7, 1929, could have turned every $100 invested into $200—all in three years. . . . It was during substantially this period that investment trusts, having been a mania, became a full blown bubble. During the first nine months of 1929 they rose from 200 to 400 in number, taking in billions of their clients' money, to add to the two billion previously absorbed. During July they issued 222 millions of securities; during August, 485 millions; and September, 643 millions.

Naturally, brokers' loans kept pace with these opportunities. From October, 1928, to October 4, 1929, they increased by 50 per cent, reaching the record peak of nearly 9½ billions. This included "bootleg" loans which at the peak were by far the larger part.

Irving Fisher, renowned Yale University professor of economics, discussing excessive brokers' loans as one cause of the depression, from his book Booms and Depressions *(1932).*

The rise of the modern corporation has brought a concentration of economic power which can compete on equal terms with the modern state—economic power versus political power, each strong in its own field. The state seeks in some aspects to regulate the corporation, while the corporation, steadily becoming more powerful, makes every effort to avoid such regulation. Where its own interests are concerned, it even attempts to dominate the state. The future may see the economic organism, now typified by the corporation, not only on an equal plane with the state but possibly even superseding it as the dominant form of social organization. The law of corporations, accordingly, might well be considered as a potential constitutional law for the new economic

state, while business practice is increasingly assuming the aspect of economic statesmanship.

Adolf A. Berle, Columbia University law professor, and Gardiner C. Means, Columbia University economics professor, in The Modern Corporation and Private Property *(1932).*

I was much too young to sense what the Depression was doing to people like my mother and Oluf, or to realize what a heroic feat Uncle Allen was performing simply by keeping us all fed and sheltered. Having known nothing but hard times, I had no sense of the hopes that were being destroyed or the fear in which adults lived or the defeat my mother felt at Oluf's farewell words: "I am lost and going and not interested in anything any more."

Russell Baker, columnist, commenting on his family's life in Belleville, New Jersey, in 1932, in Growing Up *(1982).*

Our first concern was to create a character that the listener at home would associate with Portland's voice. . . . Over the microphone, Portland's voice sounded like two slate pencils mating or a clarinet reed calling for help. . . .

Most of the other radio couples—Burns and Allen, the Easy Aces, Fibber McGee and Molly and Ozzie and Harriet, to name a few—used their marital status and their domestic experiences for comedy purposes. They played themselves and their programs were almost weekly diaries that proved that they faced the same dilemmas that the average middle-class couple found confronting them in daily life.

Jack Benny and Mary Livingston were the exception. No mention was ever made in their dialogue that they were married. Mary's comedy was derived from reading frequent letters from home, criticizing Jack and his activities . . . and engaging in assorted sophisticated peccadillos.

Fred Allen, radio personality, discussing his first radio program, the Limit Bath Club Revue, *which premiered in 1932, in his memoir* Treadmill to Oblivion *(1954).*

Such was the general picture of the South in 1932. Everybody was either ruined beyond his wildest previous fears or stood in peril of such ruin. And the general psychological reaction? First a universal bewilderment and terror, which perhaps went beyond that of the nation at large by the measure of the South's lack of training in analysis. . . .

And along with this there went in the case of the masses a slow wondering and questioning, and in the end a gradually developing bitterness of desperation. . . . More completely and helplessly in the grip of social forces than Southerners had ever been before . . . they blamed the Yankee in the shape of Wall Street . . . muttered curses against the name of Morgan as the epitome of it.

W. J. Cash, journalist and writer, in The Mind of the South *(1941).*

We have a great many negro farmers, and practically all of them are tenants. Their ability to survive . . . depends upon the ability of the landlord to supply them with the necessaries of life. They have a system under which they make a contract with the landlord to cultivate his land for the next year and in the meantime he feeds them through the winter, and at the end of the year they gather their crops and pay for their supplies and rent, if they are able to do so . . .

In a very large percentage [of cases] the landlord is now unable to finance these tenants for another year. He is unable to get the supplies. He has no security and no money. . . .

Men are actually starving by the thousands to-day, not merely in the general sections that I refer to, but throughout this country as a whole. . . .

The situation has possibilities of epidemics of various kinds. Its consequences will be felt many years. The children are being stunted by lack of food. Old people are having their lives cut short.

Congressman George Huddleston of Alabama, testimony during hearings on federal aid for unemployment relief before a subcommittee of the Senate Committee on Manufactures, January 5, 1932, in the Congressional Record *(1932).*

While I was in Oregon, the *Portland Oregonian* bemoaned the fact that thousands of ewes were killed by the sheep raisers because they did not bring enough in the market to pay the freight on them. And while Oregon sheep raisers fed mutton to the buzzards, I saw men picking for meat scraps in the garbage cans in the cities of New York and Chicago. I talked to one man in a restaurant in Chicago. He told me of his experience in raising sheep. He said that he had killed 3,000 sheep this fall and thrown them down the canyon, because it cost $1.10 to ship a sheep, and then he would get less than a $1 for it. He said he could not afford to feed the sheep, and he would not let them starve, so he just cut their throats and threw them down the canyon.

Oscar Ameringer, Oklahoma City newspaper editor, testimony before a House subcommittee of the Committee on Labor, February 1932, in the Congressional Record *(1932).*

One thing is certain. This is no ordinary real-estate development. For here, on land largely owned by Columbia University and leased by John D. Rockefeller, Jr., is rising what we have been told is to be a cultural center for New York, if not for the whole United States. Out of this stony pit . . . is to emerge a "new and shimmering city of soaring walls and challenging towers," "a great cultural and architectural monument" . . . the enterprise will bring economic advantages: being "the greatest building project in the history of the world," . . . For this is Radio City—or, as we are now told we should call it, Rockefeller City.

Frederick Lewis Allen, editor of Harper's, *in* Harper's *(April 1932).*

Seen on Park Avenue the other day: A Rolls-Royce, green, slim and elegant, sporting a pair of orange tinted "license" plates bearing the legend "Repeal the 18th Amendment"!

I . . . found out that these plates can be had for 50c the pair from WONPR (pronounced Wonpurr): the Women's Organization for National Prohibition Repeal from their headquarters at 485 Madison Avenue, New York.

Judge, article of April 16, 1932.

All passionate goodness is forever unreconciled to an ethically senseless world.

Non-theistic humanists, trying to content themselves with their slogans like "Morals minus Religion," would better take the measure of this towering fact. They can have morals minus religion—for a while. They may even lead a whole generation of intellectuals into morals minus religion; but, in the end, they will be hoist with their own petard. The very goodness they have achieved, the more serious it is, will the more certainly press up into religion, and religion with its sustaining resources will press back into it, and the two blend in one response to life's meaning as a whole.

Harry Emerson Fosdick, clergyman, in Harper's *(May 1932).*

Everybody you talk to would rather hear about Capone than anybody you ever met. What's the matter with an age when our biggest gangster is our greatest national interest? Part is the government's fault for not convicting him on some real crime.

Will Rogers, humorist, quoted in The Catholic World *(May 1932).*

I want to say to you that the situation of the Chicago schoolteachers has been critical for the past year. A year ago we went into the summer vacation period with two months' back salary unpaid. This year . . . we will go into the summer vacation with six months' unpaid salaries.

Twenty million dollars today is owing the teachers, 14,000 teachers, of Chicago. That is an average of $1,400 for each teacher in the Chicago school system that that community owes to the teachers. . . .

I say to you that we have reached the breaking point.

Irwin A. Wilson, president of the Chicago Principals Club, testimony on unemployment before a Senate subcommittee of the Committee on Manufacturers, May 9, 1932, in the Congressional Record *(1932).*

When I appeared before the Subcommittee . . . last December, I stated that there were 238,000 persons out of work in Philadelphia and that we estimated unemployment in the city in ordinary times to be between 40,000 and 50,000. There are now 298,000 persons out of work. In other words . . . it is six times normal unemployment.

In December I told you that 43,000 families were receiving relief. Today 55,000 families are receiving relief.

In December our per family grant was $4.39 per week per family. It is now $4.23 per family. Of this $4.23 per family, about $3.93 is an allowance for food. This is about two-thirds of the amount needed to provide a health-maintaining diet.

Karl de Schweinitz, executive secretary of the Philadelphia Community Council, from testimony on unemployment before a Senate subcommittee of the Committee on Manufactures, May 9, 1932, in the Congressional Record *(1932).*

The season that is almost over has already gone into Broadway's records as the unhappiest, financially, since the "boom" days of fabulous memory came to a crashing conclusion. Red ink adorns the ledgers of most managers who have challenged the fates. Gloom shrouds the Lambs Club. Dark playhouses yawn emptily, and even the theatrical labor unions are stirring uneasily, though not yet offering any concessions. . . . Excepting here and there a manager who has a hit . . . all agree that these are very black days indeed, and that they promise to continue indefinitely.

John Hutchens, in Theatre Arts Monthly *(June 1932).*

I do not believe in routine charity. I think it is a shameful thing that any man stoop to take it, or give it. I do not include human helpfulness under the name of charity. My quarrel with charity is that it is neither helpful nor human. The charity of our cities is the most barbarous thing in our system, with the possible exception of our prisons. What we call charity is a modern substitute for being personally kind, personally concerned, and personally involved in the work of helping others in difficulty. True charity is a much more costly effort than money-giving.

Henry Ford, industrialist, in Literary Digest *(June 11, 1932).*

The next day when the nominating speeches were made I watched the demonstration for Hoover with some amusement. Most delegates looked as though scourged to the task. Heavy faces, sour faces, without expression, certainly without enthusiasm or conviction. Baloons were released to the ceiling, but they helped very little. Most amusing was the insistence of the band on playing "California, here I come, *right back where I started from.* . . ."

The artificiality of the demonstration was shown when the chairman held up his hand for silence and it came with the suddenness of a shock. No one could have attended that convention without being convinced that the next President would be nominated in the Democratic convention.

Claude Bowers, journalist and historian, commenting on the June 14–16, 1932, Republican National Convention, in My Life: The Memoirs of Claude Bowers *(1962).*

The multitude does not blame the politicians for the depression. The guilt for that has been firmly fastened on the bankers. What is resented in the men of politics, and resented with a unanimity that may unseat them all, is their solemn levity, pussyfooting, resourcelessness, the unbearable habit of "playing politics."

Anne O'Hare McCormick, journalist, column of June 26, 1932, in the New York Times, *quoted in Sheehan,* The World at Home: Selections from the Writings of Anne O'Hare McCormick *(1956).*

The extreme slackness and narrow range of trading is, of course, discouraging to the Street [stock market], which has to be satisfied with very small pickings from the professional short-term operations that make up the sum total of market activity today. But the quiet, steady action of the market is a fairly clear sign that all trace of hysteria has disappeared and that it is resting on its oars awaiting definite signs of business improvement, undismayed by bad earnings and with little fear of future shocks.

Article of Business Week, *July 27, 1932.*

If there is truth in this analysis, it is not strange that while the masses in the United States now appear to be inert and nonrevolutionary, there are revolutionary fears in high places, and the chief vocal opposition to the existing regime comes from a few writers and technical experts. This is precisely what we would expect. Ideas of revolutionary implication are bound to arise first among the best educated and those near to power, not among those who are in the depths of penury and hopelessness.

George Soule, economist and editor, in Harper's *(August 1932).*

But 1,000 homeless veterans, or 50,000 don't make a revolution. This threat will pass and be forgotten. . . . Next day the Bonus leaders would come, the slick guys in leather puttees; they would make a few speeches and everything would be smoothed over. They would talk of founding a new Fascist order of khaki shirts, but this threat, too, can be disregarded; a Fascist movement, to succeed in this country, must come from the middle classes and be respectable. No, if any revolution results from the flight of the Bonus Army, it will come from a different source, from the government itself. The army in time of peace, at the national capital, has been used against unarmed citizens—and this, with all it threatens for the future, is a revolution in itself.

Malcolm Cowley, author and editor, in the New Republic *(August 17, 1932).*

The difference will be made by the Emergency Relief Act. Or rather by the fact that the Emergency Relief Act exists. For the act itself with its $300 million for direct relief loans to the states is neither an adequate nor an impressive piece of legislation. But the passage of the Act . . . marks a turning in American political history. And the beginning of a new chapter in American unemployment relief. It constitutes an open and legible acknowledgement of governmental responsibility for the welfare of the victims of industrial unemployment. And its ultimate effect must be the substitution of an ordered, realistic, and intelligent relief program for the wasteful and uneconomic methods . . . employed during the first three years of the depression.

There can be no serious question of the failure of those methods. For the methods were never seriously capable of success. They were diffuse, unrelated, and unplanned. The theory was that private charitable organizations and semi-public welfare groups . . . were capable of caring for the casuals [casualties] of a worldwide economic disaster.

Fortune, *article of September 1932.*

So, as the prices of stocks and commodities begin to rise once more and hope springs again in the breast of American business, we say its job, and our job, is but begun. These things can mean nothing, they are mere numbers in the mouth or marks on paper, if men in America are not at work, in the deepest sense of the word. The ten million who stand idle on Labor Day, 1932, are the most colossal challenge to the energy and intelligence of any generation that has lived, and we who believe in the power of American business cannot evade it.

Business Week, *editorial of September 14, 1932.*

A squad of patrolmen staged a polite raid last night on the residents of a new suburban development. The policemen, with apologies and good feelings on both sides, arrested for vagrancy twenty-five inhabitants of Hoover Valley, the shantytown that sprang up in the bed of the old lower reservoir of Central Park near the Obelisk. . . .

Hoover Valley . . . sprang up during the Summer months but it was only during the last four weeks that the men who made their homes in the southern end of the lower reservoir built more permanent structures. Seventeen shacks, all of them equipped with chairs, beds and bedding and a few with carpets, were erected.

. . . Twelve shacks, some of them less pretentious, are being built in back of the seventeen, which were set out in a row called "Depression Street."

The New York Times, *article of September 22, 1932.*

Clearly, all this calls for a reappraisal of values. A mere builder of more industrial plants, a creator of more railroad systems, an organizer of more corporations is as likely to be a danger as a help. The day of the great promoter or the financial Titan, to whom we granted anything if only he would build or develop, is over. Our task now is not discovery or exploitation of natural resources, or necessarily producing more goods. It is the soberer, less dramatic business of administering resources and plants already in hand, of seeking to reestablish foreign markets for our surplus production, of meeting the problem of underconsumption, of adjusting production to consumption, of distributing wealth and products more equitably, of adapting existing economic organizations to the service of the people. The day of enlightened administration has come.

Franklin Delano Roosevelt, speech at the Commonwealth Club of San Francisco, September 23, 1932, during his presidential campaign, in the New York Times *(September 24, 1932).*

Fifty-four men were arrested yesterday morning for sleeping or idling in the arcade connecting with the subway through 45 West Forty-second Street, but most of them considered their unexpected meeting with a raiding party of ten policemen as a stroke of luck because it brought them free meals yesterday and shelter last night from the sudden change in the weather. . . .

The work of fingerprinting and making necessary comparisons with police records required so much time that Magistrate Renaud postponed the men's trials on disorderly conduct until this afternoon. This insured them sleeping quarters for the night and more free meals today.

The New York Times, *article of October 7, 1932.*

In the words of the Democratic national platform, the federal government has a "continuous responsibility for human welfare, especially for the protection of children." That duty and responsibility the federal government should carry out promptly, fearlessly, and generously.

It took the present Republican administration in Washington almost three years to recognize this principle . . . for at least two years after the crash, the only efforts made by the national administration to cope with the distress of unemployment were to deny its existence.

Franklin D. Roosevelt, campaign speech delivered October 13, 1932, in Rosenman, The Public Papers and Addresses of Franklin D. Roosevelt, *vol. 2 (1938–1950).*

This campaign is more than a contest between two men. It is more than a contest between two parties. It is a contest between two philosophies of government. . . .

Our economic system has received abnormal shocks during the past three years, which temporarily dislocated its normal functioning. These shocks have in a large sense come from without our borders, but I say to you that our system of government has enabled us to take such strong action as to prevent the disaster which would otherwise have come to our nation. It has enabled us further to develop measures and programs which are now demonstrating their ability to bring about restoration and progress.

. . . This election is not a mere shift from the ins to the outs. It means deciding the direction our Nation will take over a century to come.

President Herbert Hoover, campaign speech delivered at Madison Square Garden in New York City, October 31, 1932, in Myers, The State Papers and Other Public Writings of Herbert Hoover *(1934).*

Optimism, the ancient faith and folly of the American people, has got some dreadful wallops from the Depression, but there is still enough of it left to go round. It takes, of late, the form of touching confidence that the taxpayer, in the long run, will profit by the present discontents—that the cost of government will be somehow abated and the tax burden reduced. This is precisely as sensible as believing that next week will have seven Tuesdays—no less and no more. The plain fact is that government is costing us more every day, Depression or no Depression.

H. L. Mencken, editor in the American Mercury *(November 1932).*

November, 1932, will in future be one of the landmarks in American political development, almost as 1800 and 1828 were. This is not the risky thing, a prophecy; it is already an undeniable fact. Whether . . . the election was meant only to turn the Republicans out and change the ruling party, the actual effect was different from any such change ever made before, except on the eve of a war, and already it is seen to be obviously revolutionary in many unexpected ways. Its further developments cannot be predicted, but they are certain to come.

Charles Willis Thompson, journalist, in the Commonweal *(November 30, 1932).*

As we went from picket line to picket line the talk harked back continually to 1776 when other farmers blockaded the highways. Up in James they had a "battle" with deputies last Wednesday. . . . Over in Stevens in South Dakota, across the Missouri to Nebraska, we find similar groups of farmers who talk of "revolution." These farmers feel that they have a historic mission. The word "revolution" occurs often among them, but what they mean is a farmers' revolt. They do not understand revolution in the communist sense. They think of themselves as fighting the banking interests of the East or the "international bankers" about whom they are perpetually talking.

They have sat still for years and seen prices of food and animals which they have raised slide down the hill to ruin. The bread lines in the cities grew, and the numbers of unemployed swelled to millions while their fruit rotted on the ground because there was no market for it. Now they are out to do something about it.

Mary Heaton Vorce, writer and frequent contributor to Harper's, *in* Harper's *(December 1932).*

At least 25,000 families in our country and more than 200,000 boys and young men are reported by the United States Children's Bureau and the National Association of Travelers' Aid Societies as recruits in the present transient army. Because of the difficulties which lie in the way of a "head-to-head" census, these figures are generally conceded as telling only a part of the story. . . .

It is impossible to travel across any country, to live in box cars or "jungles," as the camp sites near railroad yards are called, or even in municipal shelters, without meeting men whose influence is destructive. All too easily impressionable young people thrown into these environments without home guidance or direction pick up the vices and crimes of the underworld—gambling, stealing, drug addiction, prostitution and sexual perversion.

Newton D. Baker, secretary of war in the Wilson administration, in the New York Times *(December 11, 1932).*

As nearly as I can learn, we did not have enough votes on our side.

President Herbert Hoover, commenting wryly on his recent election defeat during a speech at the Gridiron Club, December 12, 1932, quoted in Fausold, The Presidency of Herbert C. Hoover *(1985).*

Although the death rate is low, there is much evidence that the health of many children is being adversely affected by the prolonged depression. For example, hospitals and clinics report an increase in rickets among children; in New York City, where relief for the unemployed has probably been more nearly adequate than in any other of the largest cities, the city Health Department reports that 20.5 per cent of the school children examined were suffering from malnutrition in 1932.

Grace Abbott, head of the Department of Labor Children's Bureau, from "Children and the Depression: A National Study and a Warning," in the New York Times *(December 18, 1932).*

A thorough study of the attitudes and activities of the Negro reveals a clear trend toward greater racial solidarity and militancy in the struggle for status. Of course, all Negroes in the United States are not acutely race conscious or extremely militant. The majority of southern Negroes are, perforce, still stark realists, more interested in getting their daily bread and in getting along with white people than in open espousal of an "equal rights" crusade. Yet the agitation by the militant northern wing, plus the process of higher education, is slowly leavening the whole mass of Negro opinion and it is probably only a matter of time until the masses of the Negroes swing into the militant column....

It takes no prophet to foresee that when the militant spirit among Negroes has become strong in all sections, the strain upon race adjustments will be greater than it has ever been before. There will be need of patient and tactful statesmanship on both sides. Between the militant Negro group and the conservative white group the possibilities for racial clashes will greatly increase, and their prevention depends upon the extent to which a technique of interracial peacekeeping can be worked out.

T. J. Woofter, Jr., research professor at the Institute for Research in Social Science, University of North Carolina, from his book Races and Ethnic Groups in American Life *(1933).*

We know from sad and very bitter experience just how this competition of underpaid labor breaks down the whole wage scale.

The result is that the fiber of the nation is being steadily weakened; self-respect, courage, and initiative are being destroyed in millions of homes by years of idleness, malnutrition, and despair. We must check this national degradation at any cost. To continue present industrial competition in reducing the standards of American living, and present competition in reducing the standards of charitable relief ... and present competition in reducing quality or quantity of necessary public services is simply to engage in competitive suicide. That we are engaged in it, anyone can see; and certainly we are getting a demonstration of what it means in this country today.

Donald R. Richberg, lawyer for the Railway Labor Executives Association, from testimony in January 1933 before the Senate on providing cooperative state and federal relief for unemployment, in the Congressional Record *(1933).*

When informed that Calvin Coolidge, known as "Silent Cal" because of his extreme reticence, had died (January 5, 1933), author Dorothy Parker quipped, "How can you tell?"

Recorded in The Algonquin Wits *(1968) by R. E. Drennan.*

America and Japan stand at deadlock on Manchuria. Japan will not yield. If America yields it will be for the first time on any important measure of foreign policy on which it has taken a positive stand, and it will be on something, moreover, that lies deeper than prestige or present material interest. What then? By every historical analogy, by all political precedent, Japan and America are today where England and Germany were in, say, 1907. If they drift, if the forces now making are allowed to gather, then by every precedent they will come to the same culmination. If we really are concerned about world peace we shall not worry ourselves about machinery and treaties and conferences and commissions. We shall face this fact and deal with it in time.

Nathaniel Peffer, Columbia University professor, in Harper's *(February 1933).*

No longer need parts or pieces be counted laboriously by hand ... nor yards, gallons or units of measurement. The International Accounting Scale does this work with such speed, economy and accuracy as to make the manual method a waste of time and money....

Wherever counting of similar parts, pieces or other units of measurement is routine work, the International Accounting Scale is a profitable investment. It is particularly valuable in inventorying, preparing piece-work payrolls, filling customers' orders, and handling stock.

Advertisement for International Business Machines Corporation, in Business Week *(February 8, 1933).*

Through the citizen's mind run many things. He sees an army of bankrupts, victims of ever-returning depressions; he remembers a miner's time sheet, showing monthly wages due $31.88, minus $22.00 for "transfers." Support a family on this for a month! He remembers the advice given to salesgirls working long hours for $9.00 a week: "If that isn't enough to live on, get yourself a boy friend." ... He remembers skilled workmen who have been out of work, not since the depression began, but through the boom. The citizen can only ask himself: What will this army do if the barriers give way? Will they not demand retribution?

George R. Leighton, member of Harper's *staff, in* Harper's *(March 1933).*

Probably Mr. Hoover realizes the handicap of certain of his qualities, for over and over he explains to those blithe spirits who wish him to start a Billy Sunday campaign for this, that or the other needed public measure: "I can't be a Theodore Roosevelt," or "I have no Wilsonian qualities"—speaking not in pride but with regret. It was with these limitations that he met Congress, treating Congress as a political institution, as a branch of government rather than as a collection of average Americans chiefly interested in returning to Washington every two or six years with the acclaim of their constituencies.

Hoover could not charm these men, could not bind them to him. A certain deep integrity of self-respect stayed his blandishing hand. And his manner chilled Washington.

William Allen White, editor and author, in the Saturday Evening Post *(March 4, 1933).*

Many all-American bands got lost in the shuffle of unemployed feet. The public stayed home and made do with what they had. They listened to the sweet and simple radio music: the Vallee-Lombardo schmaltz. No one would have any of us. . . .

There was a kind of desperate urgency that took over all of us in the early 1930's; everyone who could tried to shut out personal loss, the depression . . . not a place for a jazz composer to be trapped in. But there I was.

Hoagy Carmichael, jazz musician, in his memoir Sometimes I Wonder *(1965).*

4

The First New Deal
1933–1934

THE BANK CRISIS

It is almost as if 1933 actually began on March 4. The prevailing view at least accepts that the inauguration day marked a dramatic shift in U.S. government and politics. At about 11:00 A.M., President Hoover and President-elect Roosevelt departed from the north portico of the White House for the drive to the Capitol. There they witnessed the swearing in of Vice President Garner in the Senate Chamber. At noon both men entered the inaugural stand, where Chief Justice Charles Evans Hughes administered the oath of office to Roosevelt. The new president delivered a historic address containing the memorable words, "So, first of all, let me assert my firm belief that the only thing we have to fear is fear itself—nameless, unreasoning, unjustified terror which paralyzes needed efforts to convert retreat into advance." Following the inaugural address, Hoover shook his successor's hand and journeyed to Union Station to board the train for New York City, where he would stay at the Waldorf-Astoria Hotel and remain available if the new president needed his services. His services were never requested, and soon Hoover would leave New York to traverse the continent and rejoin his family in Palo Alto, California. The New Deal era had arrived.

There was little time for the new president and his family and associates to celebrate; the bank crisis demanded immediate attention. Roosevelt's cabinet was in place to help the president tackle the present crisis. Most involved in that process perhaps was the new secretary of the Treasury, William Woodin. But tackling the economic problems would also be part of the task confronting Secretary of Commerce Dan Roper, Secretary of Labor Frances Perkins (the first woman cabinet member ever appointed) and Secretary of Agriculture Henry A. Wallace, who persuaded Rexford Guy Tugwell to serve as assistant secretary. Cordell Hull was secretary of state; Harold Ickes, secretary of the interior; George Dern, secretary of war; and Claude A. Swanson, secretary of the navy. Homer Cummings was attorney general. As postmaster general Roosevelt had chosen James A. Farley. On the evening following the inauguration all were sworn in at the White House by Justice Benjamin Cardozo—the first time an entire cabinet had been sworn in at one time.

President Franklin D. Roosevelt
(seated, center) with his cabinet
(Library of Congress)

On his first full day in office Roosevelt had in hand drafts of two proclamations prepared in the rough before he had reached Washington, D.C. He
issued the first one that day, calling Congress into special session to convene on
March 9, by which time Secretary Woodin had promised to have an emergency
banking bill drafted for presentation to the Congress. On the next day, March
6, Roosevelt issued the second proclamation, declaring a national bank holiday
that temporarily closed all the banks and regulated the exporting of gold on
the basis of provisions in the Trading with the Enemy Act, a law enacted in
October 1917. On March 8, Roosevelt held his first press conference, attended
by more than 100 reporters. He stated his intention that all his conferences
would be open, with free discussion and spontaneous questions. He discussed
the banking crisis, projecting confidence, assurance, joviality. He answered
questions, explaining that some of his comments were meant as "background"
and some were to be considered "off the record." At the conference's end the
reporters burst into applause. That night Senators Robert M. La Follette, Jr.,

and Edward P. Costigan visited FDR at the White House in an effort to persuade him to take the opportunity presented by the crisis to nationalize the
banks—a position supported by other liberal members of Congress as well. But
Treasury Secretary Woodin, aided by Ogden Mills, had already secured the
cooperation of major bankers hastily called to Washington to prepare a plan for
saving the banks. Roosevelt believed it best to salvage the system, failure
though it was, in order to ease public fears.

The next day at noon Congress convened in special session. The House
immediately took up discussion of the Emergency Banking Bill drafted by
Woodin and, ironically, Mills and other former advisers of Hoover, after it was
read by the chairman of the Banking and Currency Committee; no other
members saw it. Debate was limited to 40 minutes. By 4:00 P.M., the Emergency Banking Act had passed by unanimous vote. It went to the Senate,
where Huey Long proposed an amendment that his colleagues shouted down.
The Senate passed the bill by a 73-7 vote before 7:30 P.M. Rarely, and never in
recent years, had Congress acted with such dispatch. Certainly Congress, even
when controlled by his own party, had never responded so expeditiously to any
request of President Hoover. The new Congress apparently shared the new
president's sense of urgency.

The Emergency Banking Act removed the United States from the gold
standard and outlawed exports of gold except by those agencies licensed by the
Treasury Department. The dollar would no longer be redeemable in gold, and
anyone owning gold was to turn it in at a Federal Reserve bank: The bank
would pay $20.67 an ounce. This move would give the government greater
control over the supply and value of the dollar. The law empowered the
comptroller of the currency to reorganize threatened national banks and the
Reconstruction Finance Corporation (RFC) to purchase banks' preferred
stock or assume banks' debts. It also authorized the Federal Reserve to accept
shakier investments from member banks as part of the discounting system. Federal inspectors from the RFC, the Treasury, and other agencies would investigate banks as they reopened and implement the new law. The emergency
legislation had the desired effect, calming depositors' fears and providing banks
a respite while confidence returned. To solidify this gain, Roosevelt addressed
the American people over the radio on March 12 in the first of his famous
"fireside chats," explaining what the finance officials were doing and assuring
his listeners that any bank open on March 15 had the support of the government. Over the following two weeks people returned hundreds of millions of
dollars in savings and other deposits that they had withdrawn. The crisis passed.

THE HUNDRED DAYS

On the day following approval of the banking act FDR sent a second message
to Congress citing the need to achieve a balanced budget on the grounds that
the $5 billion deficit run up by the Hoover administration invited bankruptcy
and aggravated the depressed economic conditions, including unemployment.
He requested authorization to cut $400 million from payments to veterans and
$100 million from the wages of federal employees. Although the Democratic
caucus in the House opposed this proposal, as did most liberals in both houses,
the sense of emergency and the desire to accommodate the president won out.

The House passed the bill (the Economy Act) the next day, March 11, and the Senate on March 15. On March 13, the president sent a message to Congress requesting an amendment to the Volstead Act that would permit the brewing of 3.2 beer—that is, beer containing 3.2 percent alcohol (.5 percent was the limit under the act). The House passed the amendment act on March 14; the Senate on March 16. On the day the Senate passed the bill, Roosevelt sent to Congress his message on legislation dealing with agriculture. And so within two weeks of Roosevelt's inauguration, the flurry of activity and legislation that would highlight the "Hundred Days" introducing the New Deal already roared forward.

By the time the special session adjourned on June 15 the Congress and the president had generated a broad spectrum of laws and programs to combat the depression. At the end of March the Civilian Conservation Corps Reforestation Relief Act became law. In creating the Civilian Conservation Corps (CCC), the act provided for one of the New Deal's most popular and memorable programs. Young men aged 17 to 24 from families on relief found work at camps run by the U.S. Army, earning $30 per month, as well as food, clothing, shelter, and educational opportunities in exchange for planting trees, repairing national park facilities, building reservoirs and bridges, and performing other diverse jobs serving the nation. By mid-June, 1,300 CCC camps had been set up under the overall administration of Robert Fechner, former vice president of the American Federation of Labor (AFL). By the end of the summer 300,000 young men were at work. About one-tenth of the recruits were African Americans.

In April the government officially abandoned the gold standard. In May five major pieces of legislation took effect—three of them on May 12. One was the Federal Emergency Relief Act, which provided $500 million in grants to the states for relief funds to help the unemployed; Roosevelt appointed Harry Hopkins to head this effort. The Agricultural Adjustment Act authorized unprecedented involvement of the federal government in agricultural production and marketing. Through a system of national planning and financial incentives, the Agricultural Adjustment Administration (AAA), created within the Department of Agriculture, entered into agreements with farmers to reduce production of cotton, wheat, corn, and other crops—farmers received payments for plowing under crops or planting less acreage—and to remove cattle from the market—the AAA bought 6 million hogs to slaughter for this purpose. (Lowered production, it was assumed, would result in higher prices.) The Thomas Amendment to the act gave the president broad power to devalue the dollar by as much as 50 percent, to issue $3 billion in paper money, and to remonetize silver (make it legal tender) to inflate values—a proposal Roosevelt did not support. The AAA program, to say the least, was controversial; Secretary of Agriculture Wallace, for example, found the hog program quite distasteful however necessary as an emergency measure. Part of the agricultural package was the Emergency Farm Mortgage Act, which authorized the sale of $2 billion in tax-exempt government bonds to provide funds for the Federal Land Banks to use for refinancing farm mortgages and also provided funds to the RFC to help farmers repurchase foreclosed lands.

In late May the Tennessee Valley Authority Act became law. The act marked the final success of Senator George Norris's multiyear struggle to prevent private development of Muscle Shoals as a source of hydroelectric power in favor of public development—in fact, it expanded the scope of the senator's plan. The Tennessee Valley Authority (TVA), established to oversee the program, would be concerned not just with development but also with flood control, soil conservation, and reforestation—a master national plan for the entire Tennessee River watershed that would involve several states in a program to serve public ends. Roosevelt appointed a three-man board to oversee the TVA: Arthur E. Morgan as chairman, Harcourt A. Morgan, and David Lilienthal. Another act that became law in late May, the Securities Act, mandated that all brokerage and investment firms that sold stocks and bonds to the public must file annual full-disclosure statements with the Federal Trade Commission (FTC), with both civil and criminal penalties for firms failing to do so.

Roosevelt signed six more acts into law in June. The Wagner-Peyser Act created the United States Employment Service within the Department of Labor and provided matching federal grants to states providing funds to set up local employment offices. The Home Owners' Loan Act authorized the federal government to refinance mortgages, creating the Home Owners' Loan Corporation (HOLC), with funding from the RFC and HOLC bonds specially channeled for this purpose. The act provided that the holder of a defaulted mortgage could turn it over to the government in exchange for a guaranteed government bond. Thus the act's provisions helped both home owners and real estate mortgage issuers—the former through refinancing mortgages, the latter through the bond exchange.

Probably the most "far reaching" (Roosevelt's own depiction) piece of New Deal legislation, the National Industrial Recovery Act thrust the federal government directly into the workings of the corporate world. The act encouraged industrial cooperation by suspending the antitrust laws and allowing industries to join together in formulating codes to encourage competition and to specify fair labor standards, including minimum wages. It guaranteed workers the right to organize for collective bargaining, choosing their own unions, and outlawed union-busting contracts. It also created the National Recovery Administration (NRA) to organize the drafting of codes and the Public Works Administration (PWA), with a budget of $3.3 billion, to construct highways, public buildings, and other facilities. Roosevelt appointed General Hugh Johnson to head the NRA and Secretary of the Interior Ickes to head the PWA. The Glass-Steagall Act, the fourth act passed in June, forbade commercial banks from involvement in investment banking (buying and selling stocks and bonds) in the hope of dampening speculation and raised the level of capital assets national banks were required to maintain. It also created the Federal Deposit Insurance Corporation (FDIC) to insure individual bank deposits up to $2,500 and withdrew authority to buy and sell government securities from the private Federal Reserve banks, conferring that authority on the Federal Reserve Board. (It should be noted that Roosevelt reluctantly accepted the FDIC, whose major champion was Republican senator Arthur H. Vandenberg.) The Farm Credit Act reorganized all government farm loan efforts under the Farm Credit Administration headed by Henry Morgenthau, Jr. Thus the FCA would administer the refinancing of farm mortgages, using funds provided under the Emergency Farm Mortgage Act approved in May. Finally, the Railroad Coordination Act created a new federal agency, the Coordinator of Transportation, whose task was to attain improvements in organization and cooperation among the nation's railroads.

A Program of Government Intervention

Clearly the plethora of legislation generated by the president and Congress in the Hundred Days constituted an unprecedented interjection of the federal government's power and influence into the private sector, both corporate and individual, and not only into the private sector but into the public sector at the state and local levels as well. That interjection violated, or at least overturned, the conservative principles and policies of the preceding Republican administrations and of many financiers and industrialists. But so eager was the entire nation to overcome the depression that the vast majority, even among those who disagreed philosophically with New Deal policies, welcomed the Roosevelt administration's initiatives as acceptable, desirable, necessary. The president, refusing to embrace the overtly socialistic proposals of some of his backers (for example, the nationalization of banks advocated by Senators Robert M. La Follette, Jr., and Edward P. Costigan), had apparently made it clear that the New Deal intended to salvage the economic system—not revolutionize it—through reform, cooperation, and experimentation. Nonetheless, the Hundred Days pushed the United States in the direction of national economic planning and centralization.

Circumstances justified many of the New Deal's programs—or at least some drastic measures—as genuinely necessary to salvaging endangered enterprises, notably banking and agriculture. For banking and the finance and securities industries as a whole, provisions of the Emergency Banking Act, the Economy Act, the Securities Act, and the Glass-Steagall Act had the effect of restoring adequate stability and even a certain confidence that the nation's financial institutions would revive and regain their soundness. Saving agriculture, however, proved a more problematic undertaking.

The Farm Crisis and the AAA

Agriculture had been in jeopardy for many years, its withering traumas mostly ignored by the federal government. Following an entire decade of decline in the 1920s, farmers had suffered a further one-third fall in net income just over the three years after the Great Crash. In desperation Midwest farmers began agitating. In March 1933 the Farmers' Holiday Association had threatened a general strike unless Congress acceded to its demands by early May. Near the end of April farmers in La Mars, Iowa, protesting mortgage foreclosures, had dragged a judge from the courtroom, threatened him with hanging, and mauled him. There were many other such rebellious incidents. Not surprisingly, then, farmers welcomed the New Deal's initiatives. Nevertheless, although initially pleased by the price support programs created by the Agricultural Adjustment Administration, farm state leaders and individual farmers would in many cases have second thoughts about those programs in action. Secretary of Agriculture Wallace, whose father had been secretary before him and whose life witnessed a heritage of devotion to farming, would eventually have some misgivings of his own. He had, of course, played a major role in drafting the

Agricultural Adjustment Act and totally approved of the AAA's goal to cut back production in order to restore balance to the agricultural market. In his view the effects of the AAA would be as much social as economic. He was right. In September 1933, Wallace, faced with the problem of overproduction of cotton and hogs, was obliged to order that 10 million acres of cotton be plowed under and that 6 million piglets and 200,000 sows be slaughtered to prevent their going to market. Even though the Federal Surplus Relief Corporation, which he, Hopkins, and Ickes organized in October, distributed to the hungry 100 million pounds of pork resulting from the slaughter, Wallace conceded that the policy of crop and livestock destruction to support prices was an ignoble one for "any sane society." Many farmers agreed, finding such acts an admission of the market's failure as well as morally questionable while people went hungry and unemployed.

Secretary of Agriculture Henry A. Wallace *(Library of Congress)*

An immediate problem in implementing the AAA program occurred with Roosevelt's appointment of George N. Peek to head the agency. Peek believed that the appropriate way to handle the agriculture crisis was the approach espoused in the old McNary-Haugen Bill, whereby the federal government would buy crop surpluses at inflated prices and funnel them into the export market. Peek abhorred the policy of controlling production by reducing acreage under cultivation and fought constantly with Wallace. After months of haggling, in December 1933 Roosevelt forced Peek to resign. But Peek's tenure had created a somewhat rocky start for the AAA. Peek had also been distressed that the general counsel for the Department of Agriculture and the AAA, recruited by Wallace, was Jerome N. Frank, a corporation lawyer from Chicago and New York City. Frank, in turn, recruited other liberal, urban-oriented lawyers, among them Abe Fortas, Adlai Stevenson, and Alger Hiss.

As a means of underwriting the AAA allotment program, the government set up the Commodity Credit Corporation in October 1933. The CCC began by loaning money to cotton farmers who had agreed to join the crop reduction program, accepting their crops as collateral. Since the CCC approach seemed viable, it was quickly extended to wheat, corn, barley, peanuts, and an array of other commodities. It was assumed that as farmers adjusted production and market prices rose farmers would sell their new crops at the higher prices and pay off the loans. Unfortunately prices never recovered sufficiently during the thirties to fulfill the assumption, and the CCC ended up with huge storehouses filled with the commodities.

Whatever its defects, the AAA definitely affected the lives of millions of farmers. By spring 1934 more than 4,000 committees were in place nationwide recruiting farmers for the allotment program. Three million farmers signed up, thereby contracting with the government to reduce acreage under cultivation. Southern cotton farmers alone withdrew 10 million acres from cultivation. Through 1936 the AAA contributed $1.5 billion in subsidies to farmers enrolled in the program. Unfortunately, the AAA's herculean effort failed to resolve the farm crisis. Critics complained that by basing subsidies on acreage the allotment program mostly aided large commercial farmers—large landowners could withdraw areas with poor soil from planting while continuing to plant fertile acres and still collect the subsidies. Certainly AAA did nothing to relieve the plight of tenant farmers, sharecroppers, and other poor farmers. In fact, in the South, where landlords controlled the AAA committees, reductions in cotton acreage forced tenants and sharecroppers off the land. In response, Arkansas sharecroppers and farm laborers, black and white, joined together in July 1934 to form the Southern Tenant Farmers Union, led and supported by the Socialists, whose leader Norman Thomas spoke out against the inequities of the AAA in the South. When general counsel Frank and his liberal cohort at AAA joined the advocacy for the sharecroppers, however, Roosevelt purged them from the administration for defying official policy. The sharecroppers were left to the mercies of the landlords.

THE DUST BOWL

The dust bowl, as the Great Plains region came to be called because of the severe drought in the 1930s, had a greater effect on driving up commodity prices by 50 percent in 1934 than the AAA did—a grim irony, as the great drought also destroyed both farmland and farmers. Over the three years the AAA program was in place, into 1936, farmers' income increased 50 percent while their total indebtedness fell by $1 billion. But by the end of the decade, parity (the ratio to prices received in 1909–14) reached only 80 percent. Not until 1941 did farm income, spurred by the World War II market, exceed the severely depressed level of 1929. And by then farmers had already endured more than 20 years of deprivation.

Many farmers, of course, bore responsibility for their own plight as a result of their overexpansion during World War I (inflating land values that collapsed) or through improper cultivation and conservation practices. Farmers in the Great Plains region reaped the bitter harvest of both during the years of the dust bowl. The cyclical rainfall of this region results in periods of drought—in fact, in the pre–Civil War era, the plains were referred to as the Great American Desert. The twenties had been kind, with ample precipitation. But the thirties reversed the cycle. There were pockets of drought in 1931; in 1932 the drought spread; in 1933 it intensified; and in 1934 it settled across the entire region from Kansas to Colorado and northern Texas, affecting a dozen states. During summer 1934 the temperature exceeded 100 degrees for 36 consecutive days in Oklahoma. In May of that year heavy winds joined the drought, blowing the sun-baked soils into huge dust clouds extending for miles: Dust from the wind storms even filtered into cities as far away as the eastern seaboard. In previous centuries the tall grasses of the Great Plains had held the soil fast during the drought cycles, but the grasses had disappeared, overgrazed by cattle or

Dust storm in Baca County, Colorado, 1935 *(Library of Congress)*

Dust drifted around a farmhouse in Oklahoma, April 1936; photo by Arthur Rothstein *(Library of Congress)*

plowed under as farmers overcultivated the land. Now in 1934 the winds drifted fine, dry soil like snow, darkening the sun at midday, burying fences, barns, and houses. Thousands of farm families, dispossessed by dust and foreclosures, packed their belongings and moved on, some to the cities, others to California—the great caravan of "Okies" (so-named because many of these families were from Oklahoma) that would continue to the end of the decade. But many stayed, their hopes raised by New Deal programs, although some became militant and spoke ominously of revolution. Eventually, the farmers would benefit from New Deal conservation programs.

THE CCC AND THE TVA

As the depression gathered steam, transiency mushroomed; men and boys, joined sporadically by girls feigning to be boys, hit the rails and the roads. Some 250,000 teenagers traversed the nation during the peak depression years. They left their homes for diverse reasons: In some cases to relieve their parents of the burden of their maintenance, in other cases to escape the afflictions of a home life scarred by the effects of unemployment and impoverishment; some sought work and others adventure. The army of young hoboes presented a special concern for both society and government, because these youths not only lost the long-term benefits of education but also subjected themselves to such immediate potential dangers as injury or death on the freight trains and brutalization, including rape, at the hands of older hoboes. The federal government launched investigations of the "youth problem," revealing that closed schools provided a major cause of transiency among the young. For many the 1933–34 school year was reduced to a single term as strained economic resources forced communities to close their schools; more than 25,000 teachers lost their jobs; and hundreds of thousands of youths found themselves totally idle: 40 percent of American high school–age students had no schools to attend by 1935. The Civilian Conservation Corps was one of the federal government's answers to this "youth problem."

The CCC, as well as the Tennessee Valley Authority, also evidenced Roosevelt's genuine and long-term commitment to conservation, and both constituted major successes for the First New Deal. Although some criticism emerged concerning the almost militaristic regimentation at the CCC camps, overall this was the New Deal's most praised and popular program. Through the course of the depression, until World War II, the CCC provided 2.5 million young men with jobs and self-respect. At its peak in 1935 the CCC had half a million young men in its camps—many of whom came from major cities and were given their first experience of nature and outdoor living by CCC. These young men provided the nation an ongoing legacy of restored forests; improved national parks, campgrounds, and beaches; small dams, watersheds, and other flood control projects; new bridges and fire towers; and a host of other conservation benefits. Roosevelt, personally devoted to the CCC, hoped to make the program a permanent part of the American scene.

Although world events would bring an end to the CCC in July 1942, the TVA became one of the permanent legacies of the First New Deal. The TVA embodied Roosevelt's long-term belief in the planned use of land resources. It promoted soil reclamation and conservation, and its dams not only generated hydroelectric power to be harnessed for the region's development but also fostered flood control to prevent erosion and the loss of topsoils. The TVA also instituted educational programs for the region's residents. Not the least of the TVA's achievements was involving the people of the valley in its procedures. Although the chairman, Arthur E. Morgan, took a paternalistic view of the mission and particularly the execution of the programs of the TVA, favoring comprehensive economic, educational, and social plans and programs for the region effectively imposed by the administration, the view of the two other board members, David Lilienthal and Harcourt A. Morgan countered this effort at centralization with what they advocated as "grass roots democracy." They advocated that the TVA operate as a regional agency, working with local groups (not, however, utility companies) to implement the agency's programs. The agency's actual regional planning, then, proved minimal, but it served the region nonetheless well in providing power, fertilizers, soil conservation, reforestation, flood control, bookmobiles, recreational lakes, and other benefits.

THE NRA'S IMPACT

What perhaps at the time seemed the most innovative and comprehensive New Deal program, the National Recovery Administration actually had antecedents in Hoover's policies and a tentative prognosis as well. It was an ambitious although rather muddled program to promote cooperation (a basic Hoover concept) among business, labor, government, and the public. The NRA definitely entailed federal interference in the marketplace, but the nature and extent of that interference were not clear immediately—not until the agency's head, General Hugh Johnson, revealed the NRA's direction. Since economic planning and balance constituted the key ideas of the NRA, the first order of business involved each industry's drafting of a code of conduct regarding wages, work conditions, production, and pricing to which all its participants would have to adhere. On the face of it, such a code would necessarily be imperious, restrictive, and monopolistic—but would it be constitutional? Johnson's NRA provided the muscle to elicit creation of the codes (through negotiation, not imposition) and to compel adherence to them. In pushing cooperation, the NRA effectively suspended the antitrust laws while to some extent accepting the fixing of prices (400 industry codes prohibited selling "below cost").

In exchange for these concessions to promote commerce, the business leaders assumed the obligation to establish minimum wages and hours, to improve working conditions, to eliminate child labor, and to accept workers' rights to collective bargaining and to choose a union (the last being a stipulation of Section 7(a) of the National Industrial Recovery Act). Not every company chose to go along, of course. Among major industries, the automobile manufacturers and coal operators resisted adopting codes, but both groups finally acceded in the late summer of 1933—the automakers at the end of August, all except Henry Ford, who remained adamantly opposed to the NRA, and the coal operators in mid-September. Johnson devised a means of subtle persuasion emphasizing patriotism: Those companies in the program would display a sign containing the NRA Blue Eagle and the words "We Do Our Part," and all consumers would know that these were the preferred firms to buy from. Another persuasive means also involved public relations: parades, songs, and speeches extolling optimism and future economic recovery. But the NRA program made negligible or, at best, only temporary headway in rectifying the depression. Production and employment did rise in summer 1933, as industrialists, freed from competitiveness by the NRA codes, anticipated price increases for their goods. But, ironically, higher prices in effect counteracted wage increases and discouraged consumption so that by fall things were largely back to where they had been. Once more, optimism, a Hoover remedy, had failed.

A CHANGED ATMOSPHERE

Optimism was not a total failure this time, however. Roosevelt's own optimistic and confident demeanor had a positive impact—the effect of a forceful personality, no doubt, when contrasted with the dour Hoover. The sense that the new administration was at least doing something also inspired hope among many. The Socialist leader Norman Thomas, in fact, judged that the Roosevelt activism had saved the nation from serious social unrest. And, of course, government spending had beneficial effects. For example, the Reconstruction Finance Corporation under the direction of Jesse Jones became the nation's largest banking and investment institution, shoring up private banks' capital, thus making funds available for loans by buying their preferred stock; making mortgages and loans available through a host of subsidiaries, including the Commodity Credit Corporation, the Electric Home and Farm Authority, and the Federal National Mortgage Association; and stimulating increases in exports through loans dispensed by the Export-Import Bank. In time, spending on public works would also have a positive impact on the economy.

For at least one group of Americans, however, hopelessness prevailed. Blacks quickly discovered that they could expect no amelioration of their economic or social degradations from the New Deal. Despite some declarations of good intentions, Hoover had continued the federal government's denial of office appointments, educational or social services programs, or simple justice for blacks, who had suffered the institutional racism of the Wilson administration and its Republican successors only to experience continuing denial and disdain. Through their own efforts African Americans had achieved some progress during the 1920s and early 1930s nevertheless. Some three-quarters of a million had abandoned the South for residence in northern cities, where they continued to confront racial discrimination yet gained major improvements in their lives: significant declines in death and infant mortality rates and increases in life expectancy and greatly increased levels of school and college attendance and literacy, for example. In moving north they had also escaped the permanent poverty, peonage, and Jim Crow repressions of the South. In the North they could also vote, and blacks had begun to win election to local offices in Chicago, Cleveland, Detroit, New York City, and Philadelphia.

Despite being ignored by three successive Republican administrations, blacks nevertheless had voted overwhelmingly for Hoover's reelection in 1932, as Roosevelt's record revealed no hint of accommodation whatsoever for black interests—he and his closest advisers wanted desperately to retain the Democratic Party's southern block, after all. And in the Congress that convened in 1933 most major chairmanships and sizable numbers of votes resided in southerners' hands, so that proposing an antilynching law or any other civil rights legislation would mean, New Dealers believed, the certain defeat of bills and programs to address what the administration saw as the most pressing social and economic problems, overriding any African-American concerns. Blacks had only two advocates in the Roosevelt administration: Secretary of the Interior Harold Ickes and First Lady Eleanor Roosevelt, whose efforts others, including FDR, initially disregarded. The depression consequently continued to weigh more heavily on African Americans, long victimized by racism and poverty, than on any others, as they lost their jobs with no prospect of reemployment in even the most menial and ill-paying jobs, which unemployed whites commandeered. Black tenant farmers, sharecroppers, and laborers in the South spiraled downward into total destitution; many futilely sought refuge in the region's cities, where by 1932 over half had no employment of any kind. Even those New Deal programs that might have helped blacks failed them because inequities inhered in their provisions and administration. In the CCC, for example, young blacks composed only 5 percent of the enrollees in 1933 (rising to 6 percent in 1934) despite the fact that their unemployment rate was twice that of white youths; and acreage restrictions imposed by the AAA forced the majority of southern black farmers out of cotton raising, actually increasing their desperation. African-American leaders concluded that the First New Deal was in fact a "raw deal" for blacks.

PUBLIC WORKS PROGRAMS

In November 1933, after prodding by his staff and discussion with relief administrators in the Midwest (including Judge Harry S. Truman in Missouri), Federal

Emergency Relief Administration head Harry Hopkins convinced the president that a federally operated work relief program was needed, as Secretary of the Interior Ickes's Public Works Administration was slow to start. Hopkins announced on November 15 that the new agency, the Civil Works Administration (CWA) under his administration, would undertake to employ 4 million people within a month. It was not until mid-January of 1934, however, that Hopkins achieved his goal, with the CWA then employing 4,230,000 at minimum wage. During its brief lifetime, CWA workers built or helped rehabilitate thousands of roads, schools, airports, and playgrounds. The CWA hired about 50,000 teachers to teach in rural schools and in urban adult education classes. It also hired writers and artists to make use of their skills. But over the course of a few months the CWA program cost the government a billion dollars. Deeply concerned over the costs and the possibility the program might create a permanent subsidized workforce, Roosevelt ordered Hopkins to terminate the CWA by spring 1934. The dismantling began in the South in February, to follow warmer weather northward. Many objected, as the CWA had proven very popular with local businesspeople, workers, and officials as well as liberals in Congress.

THE NRA FOUNDERS

The NRA would also face dismantling, or at least major revision, but in its case because of acknowledged failure. Everyone, it seems—consumers, businesspeople, union leaders, and politicians—had turned against the NRA by the beginning of 1934. Consumers were discontented over higher prices. Businessmen found the codes and government interference burdensome. Unions expressed strong disappointment that Section 7(a) of the National Industrial Recovery Act (NIRA), clearly intended to foster unionization, had not worked to their advantage because industries had subverted them through the formation of "company unions"—only John L. Lewis's United Mine Workers of America (UMWA) had expanded during 1933. And many politicians, even among the Democrats, deplored the NRA as an example of dictatorial government or as a promoter of monopolies. In response to the criticisms, Roosevelt in early March created the National Recovery Review Board, chaired by Clarence Darrow, to investigate the NRA codes. The Darrow board began to deliver its conflicting reports in May. They condemned the codes as monopolistic and advocated resurrecting the antitrust laws and a competitive marketplace, while at the same time damning competition as "savage" and "wolfish." NRA administrator Hugh Johnson responded by denouncing and castigating Darrow. Although displeased, Roosevelt admitted something was amiss at the NRA and that Johnson had to go. He secured Johnson's resignation in September and replaced him with Donald Richberg.

GOLD, SILVER, AND THE DOLLAR

While the newly created agencies (AAA, CCC, TVA, RFC, CWA, and NRA) evolved or faltered, the administration pursued other courses as well. The First New Deal did not come to an end with the Hundred Days. One tactic that offered some hope of shoring up efforts to reverse the depression, especially with agricultural products and other potential exports, involved manipulating the price of gold, which underpinned the value of the dollar and other currencies. Roosevelt found attractive the ideas of Professors George Warren and Frank Pearson, the so-called Gold Dust Twins, who argued that the government could increase the prices of farm and other commodities while stimulating trade by driving up the value of gold through ongoing purchases on the open market at ever-increasing prices, which would depreciate the value of the dollar. So beginning in late October 1933, Roosevelt, Secretary of the Treasury Morgenthau, and the RFC's Jesse Jones, joined frequently by Professor Warren, met each morning at the White House to decide what price the government would pay for gold that day, thus anticipating slowly driving up the price. Many in the administration opposed this policy as ill-conceived, including James Warburg and Dean Acheson, and either resigned or lost their jobs as a result. In fact, the policy did fail to attain its ends. In January 1934, Roosevelt stopped the gold purchases and signed the Gold Reserve Act, which empowered him to set the official price of gold. He did so—at $35 per ounce—thereby depreciating the value of the dollar. (The official price would remain at this level until 1971.)

A reluctant Roosevelt also gave in to Senator Key Pittman of Nevada, another advocate of depreciating the dollar in order to inflate prices, who had secured an international agreement at the otherwise failed London Economic Conference that committed the United States to purchasing large quantities of silver for four years. So in December 1933 the president announced that the federal government would buy the nation's annual output of silver for the next four years at a rate of 64.5 cents per ounce—nearly a third higher than the going market price—a nice boon for the silver producers certainly. But the so-called silverites wanted more. In spring 1934 they mustered enough support in both houses of Congress to pass legislation that would further boost the price of silver. Roosevelt had no choice but to give in. The Silver Purchase Act of June 1934 directed the secretary of the treasury to buy silver until either the price on world markets reached $1.29 or the government's holdings equaled one-third of its monetary (gold) reserves. The cost of the purchase program would be borne by issuing silver certificates (dollars redeemable in silver metal). So the silver-producing states at least reaped some benefit, but the policy failed to inflate prices of other goods.

Similarly, the administration acceded to the wishes of other interest groups or devised legislation that would benefit them in ways that reflected Lilienthal's "grass roots democracy" approach. One example, the Taylor Grazing Act of 1934, introduced by Congressman Edward T. Taylor of Colorado and strongly supported by Secretary of the Interior Ickes, placed regulation of grazing on public lands with the Interior Department (it had been under the Forest Service). The act designated 80 million acres of grasslands whose use would be administered through mutual agreements devised by stockmen and the Interior Department in cooperation. Of course, arrangements that favored special interest groups could also result in those groups' holding an inordinate amount of power, by demanding favorable treatment in exchange for their political support.

OPPOSITION TO THE NEW DEAL

By 1934 some vocal opposition, particularly among bankers and business leaders, began to emerge. Roosevelt had not intended to alienate the business community, but he was convinced of the need to impose regulation on the finance industry. Consequently, in February 1934 he sent Congress a message requesting legislation mandating regulation of the stock exchange. The financial community responded with hostility, led by the somewhat discredited Richard Whitney, president of the New York Stock Exchange, who insisted that his was "a perfect institution." (Four years later, in 1938, Whitney would be arrested and charged with grand larceny.) The Securities Exchange Act passed despite the opposition of the business community and became law in June. The act created the Securities and Exchange Commission as a regulatory agency of the federal government, imposed restrictions on insider trading, required the filing and full disclosure of complete information on all securities being traded, and provided for regulation of margin requirements (the cash amount a customer must provide when borrowing from a broker to buy a stock—margin is a percentage of the stock's value) in an attempt to discourage speculation. Other acts also became law in June: the Communications Act, establishing the Federal Communications Commission (FCC) to regulate the radio, telegraph, and cable industries; the Railway Labor Act and the Railroad Retirement Act, which established pensions for railway workers; and still others. In addition, Roosevelt appointed the first National Labor Relations Board, chaired by Lloyd K. Garrison (Francis Biddle would replace him in November), whose main purpose was overseeing compliance with Section 7(a) of the NIRA (concerning unionization of workers).

These and other developments in 1934 constituted major additions to New Deal programs. They apparently tipped the balance of goodwill and aroused the opposition. Concerned that the New Deal programs wreaked havoc on the budget by building in deficit spending, Budget Director Lewis Douglas resigned in protest at the end of August. That same month the American Liberty League was founded in the District of Columbia. Ostensibly intended to provide an organizational voice for New Deal opponents from any party or background, the Liberty League's core strength came from conservative Democrats and industrialists. Among its six officers, four were Democrats. Jouett Shouse, a former member of the Democratic National Committee, was president, supported by Alfred E. Smith, Irenee du Pont, and John J. Raskob, a Du Pont corporate executive and former national chairman of the Democratic Party. Member backers included Alfred P. Sloan of General Motors, J. Howard Pew of Sun Oil, and Edward F. Hutton of General Foods.

LABOR MILITANCY

Potential trouble for the New Deal emerged from other sources as well. In 1934 many labor organizations, frustrated that Section 7(a) of the NIRA had failed in its intended effect to spur unionization, turned to the tactics of massive strikes and increased militancy. In 1934 about 1,800 strikes erupted, involving nearly 1.5 million workers. Some major strikes resulted in street warfare and bloodshed. In Minneapolis the local organization of the Brotherhood of Teamsters, led by a member of the International Workers of the World (IWW), staged a crippling strike intended to shut down the city's transporta-

Haddon Heights, New Jersey,
October 17, 1934; photo by Mark
Benedict Barry *(Library of Congress)*

tion system and end the rule of the open shop (no unions allowed) enforced by
the employers' Citizens Alliance. The Citizens Alliance formed a "citizens'
army" in opposition to the strikers, and a clash in May left two of this "army"
dead. In July two strikers were killed and 65 wounded in a fight with police.
But, backed by the governor and a general strike, the Teamsters' local finally
won its fight, securing the right to organize the transportation workers. A similar showdown occurred in July in San Francisco, where the longshoremen, led
by Harry Bridges, struck the docks. On July 5 police gunfire left two strikers
dead and many wounded. But Bridges persisted, organizing a general strike
that even shut down the city's small businesses. The strike ended in arbitration
that gained the longshoremen the right to unionize and most of their other
demands. In many strikes, however, the workers ended up losers; and the hostility the strikes generated revealed the smoldering potential for genuine class
warfare in America's cities.

SINCLAIR, TOWNSEND, LONG, AND COUGHLIN

The discontent found different outlets elsewhere. In California some leading
Democrats persuaded longtime Socialist Upton Sinclair to change his party
allegiance in 1933 and run for governor in 1934. The novelist advocated a
utopian approach through his End Poverty in California (EPIC) program outlined in *I, Governor of California,* published in 1933. His production-for-use
program entailed the state's purchasing of unused lands, on which the unemployed could then grow their own food, and of unused factories, in which the
unemployed could make their own shoes, clothes, and other goods. These land

and factory colonies would become self-governing under worker management. Sinclair won the Democratic nomination for governor in August 1934. But as his campaign attracted a growing following not only in the state but nationwide and his chances for election improved, opponents in business, movies, and publishing mounted a slashing attack on his record as a radical reformer. Leaders from varied backgrounds, from film mogul Louis B. Mayer to evangelist Aimee Semple McPherson, joined in the attack. Originally sympathetic to Sinclair's campaign, Roosevelt backed away from him as the attacks continued. Sinclair lost the November election by a quarter of a million votes and went back to his writing.

California had another reformer, Dr. Francis E. Townsend, whose program attracted national attention. Townsend conceived surplus workers to be a problem contributing to the perpetuation of the depression, and he proposed a plan that would both alleviate this problem and benefit the elderly at the same time. He first outlined his plan in a letter to the *Long*

Senator Huey P. Long *(Library of Congress)*

Beach Press-Telegram in September 1933. The plan was simple: The federal government would provide a monthly pension of at least $150 to everyone over the age of 60 with the condition that the money had to be spent. The pensioners would be removed from the labor force and their spent pensions would increase consumption, thus generating jobs for younger people. The government would raise the money for the pensions through a national sales tax. Following the response to his letter, Townsend, joined by his brother and a former business associate named Robert Earl Clements, incorporated Old Age Revolving Pensions, Ltd., in January 1934 to raise money and promote the plan—by now the proposed pension had risen to $200 per month, to be spent within 30 days of receipt. In August Clements began organizing local Townsend clubs throughout the nation. By January 1935 the organization had a weekly newspaper, which gained a readership of 200,000 by the end of the year. Also in January, Congressman John S. McGroarty of California introduced a Townsend Plan bill in the House. But after economists pointed out that the plan's annual pension disbursements would add up to $24 billion, nearly half the national income and twice the current amount of all federal, state, and local taxes combined, the bill was defeated.

Among the reformers, Senator Huey Long, the demagogue from Louisiana, represented an apparently growing and genuine threat to the Roosevelt administration. Long had supported Roosevelt in the 1932 election, but the legislation of the Hundred Days, especially the NIRA, aroused his opposition and ill will. He denounced Roosevelt as a tool of banking interests and announced his own program to save the nation. Long saw redistribution of wealth as the solution, and in February 1934 he launched a national political organization to foster it under the guidance of Gerald L. K. Smith, an erratic former preacher and Klansman. Long's program, known as Share Our Wealth, entailed in essence the liquidation of all personal fortunes exceeding about $3 million. The government would then provide an annual income of at least $2,000 to each family along with a $5,000 allowance for buying a home, a radio, and a car. Long also advocated old-age pensions, public works, a minimum wage, a shorter workweek, and other measures that proved highly attractive. Promoted by the sensationalizing Smith, Share Our Wealth grew rapidly, with Smith claiming 27,000 clubs and 7 million adherents by 1935—no doubt an exaggeration but nonetheless a cause for concern among the New Dealers.

By the end of 1934 one of the New Deal's most outspoken supporters, Father Charles Coughlin, priest of the Catholic Church of the Little Flower in a Detroit suburb, was beginning to sound more and more like the opposition. At this time, through his radio broadcasts, Coughlin had an enormous following sometimes estimated at well over 30 million listeners—he received more mail even than President Roosevelt. During the 1932 campaign he had urged his listeners to vote for Roosevelt. In the spring of 1934 he was still saying that he would never change his view "that the New Deal is Christ's deal." He and the administration, however, fell out over the silver issue; and Coughlin began criticizing Roosevelt and Morgenthau, even though as late as the fall he still professed his overall support for the administration. But a critical shift occurred in November, when Coughlin announced the founding of the National Union for Social Justice. The organization's agenda included nationalization of utilities and other industries, an annual wage, and other measures based on the view that capitalism was beyond saving. Coughlin spoke ominously of what he perceived as the administration's willingness to turn the nation over to "international bankers."

FASCISTS AT HOME AND ABROAD

More openly menacing than Father Coughlin were the homegrown advocates of fascism. William Dudley Pelley typified such right-wingers. Headquartered in Asheville, North Carolina, Pelley created yet another organized movement, the Silver Shirts, with its own publication entitled *Liberation* and its own publishing house. Founded on the last day of January 1933, the Silver Shirts grew to include member groups throughout the nation that absorbed Pelley's views from the publications he disseminated. Pelley saw evidence of "the international Jewish conspiracy" everywhere, and he railed against the "Dutch Jew Rosenfelt" (meaning FDR) and the horde of Jews he believed controlled the government. Similar native fascist groups held such views in common while openly embracing Nazism.

Adolf Hitler was, of course, Pelley's inspiration—the Silver Shirts were named in honor of Hitler's SS guard and founded the day after Hitler became chancellor of Germany. On January 30, 1933, President Paul von Hindenburg appointed Hitler chancellor because there seemed no alternative. The devious Franz von Papen had been unable to obtain a parliamentary majority after the November 1932 election, and the equally devious General Kurt von Schleicher had fared no better in trying to put together a coalition government. Papen helped arouse both businessmen and Nazis in support of a coalition with Hitler as chancellor and himself as vice chancellor. Even though nearly two-thirds of the German electorate had voted against the Nazis in November, Hindenburg accepted the view that this new government would neutralize the Communists, exclude the Socialists, and keep Hitler in line as part of a conservative coalition. It was a fateful choice.

Hitler used the February 27 burning of the Reichstag, which he blamed on the Communists, as an excuse to suspend civil liberties, claiming this was necessary for the government to combat the "threat" to the state that the German public believed to be real. Even so, in the March elections he called, the Nazis secured only 44 percent of the votes cast, but no matter: Supported by his National Socialist Party and the Catholic Center, Hitler obtained a parliamentary vote on March 23 granting him the power to promulgate laws. With that authority in his grasp, he began a relentless consolidation of his control over the army, the bureaucracy, and the separate German states. In April he authorized dismissal of Jewish officeholders and boycotts of Jewish merchants, resulting in mob attacks on Jews and their shops throughout Germany. In May he had the unions shut down and their leaders sent to concentration camps. In July the National Socialist Party became the only legal political party in Germany. On June 30, 1934, known as the "Night of the Long Knives," Hitler had Ernst Röhm and hundreds of other potential rivals and opponents in the party murdered. When Hindenburg died in August 1934, Hitler assumed the office and powers of the presidency. He was now dictator of the Third Reich.

ROOSEVELT'S FOREIGN POLICIES

Although Roosevelt privately expressed concern about Japanese aggression in China and about the potential menace of Nazism, he took a hands-off view of the Far East and showed few outward signs of worry about the rise of Hitler. Roosevelt learned early on of Hitler's ruthlessness and intentions from both the U.S. consul general and the ambassador in Berlin. But Roosevelt did not know how to respond, especially since the United States did not belong to the League of Nations, which with American leadership might at least have voted for some kinds of sanctions. Moreover, Roosevelt received constant reminders of the isolationist views of powerful congressmen and senators. The revelations and accusations of wartime profiteering during World War I by armaments makers and bankers, along with vilifications of Woodrow Wilson, arising out of the 1934 committee investigation authorized by the full Senate and headed by Senator Gerald Nye, also made it difficult to suggest any course of action that even implied the possibility of a future military confrontation with any nation. (The Nye committee's investigation was instigated by a *Fortune* article on the armament manufacturers.)

In addition, Roosevelt did not regard foreign affairs as demanding major attention; in fact, he evinced the prevailing American isolationism in his public statements—he had even abandoned Woodrow Wilson's vision and voiced disapproval of American participation in the League of Nations in his campaign speeches. In May 1933, FDR did advocate international economic cooperation in a speech, and he supported the United States' participation in the London Economic Conference convened in June. But Roosevelt's opposition to stabilizing the values of currencies prevented any useful agreement stemming from the meeting, and his July message scolding the assembled nations sabotaged the conference altogether. The failure of the conference meant a permanently lost opportunity to achieve international cooperation in trying to effect solutions to the depression. The Reciprocal Trade Agreements Act of March 1934 authorized the president to negotiate mutual agreements with other nations and to raise or lower tariffs by 50 percent in response to their concessions, but these agreements had to be arrived at through the slow process of one-to-one talks.

The Roosevelt administration foreign policy did reveal initiative with the decision to officially recognize the Soviet Union, which marked a major departure from the policy steadfastly held to by the four preceding administrations. There was some hope that a market might be found for American goods in the USSR, which in addition might serve as a counterpoint to possible threats by Germany or Japan—both earlier foes of Russia. After secret negotiations, Soviet representative Maxim Litvinov arrived in Washington, D.C., in November 1933. In a series of 11 letters and one memorandum that he and Roosevelt exchanged, the two nations reestablished diplomatic relations, and the USSR agreed to limit Communist propagandizing in the United States while guaranteeing Americans religious freedom in the USSR. Before Litvinov's return home, executives of some of the nation's major businesses, such as the Morgan and Chase banks, treated him to a banquet at the Waldorf-Astoria in New York City.

In Latin America Roosevelt initially appeared inclined to return to the United States' old interventionist role. He even sent ships to Cuba in 1933

Secretary of State Cordell Hull
(Library of Congress)

when a junta (a group of military officers) seized control of that nation's government, but no troop landing resulted, and the government failed in January 1934 because the United States refused to recognize it. Subsequently, Roosevelt and Secretary of State Cordell Hull revived the Good Neighbor policy espoused by President Hoover. At the Seventh International Conference of the American States held in Montevideo, Uruguay, in December 1933, Hull had supported a resolution that no state had a right to intervene in any other state's affairs. In May 1934, the American and Cuban governments signed an agreement abrogating the Platt Amendment of 1903 that had awarded the United States the right to intervene in Cuba's internal affairs. In exchange, however, Cuba conceded to the United States the right to keep the naval base at Guantánamo Bay. As further evidence of the administration's goodwill, in August the last remaining American marines were withdrawn from Haiti after a 19-year occupation.

THE PURSUIT OF HAPPINESS

Some Americans were paying attention to events abroad—in New York City, for example, 20,000 people rallied to protest Hitler's criminal behavior and persecution of Jews—but the vast majority appeared indifferent to the affairs of Europe. After all, the Great Depression continued, and that meant worry enough for most. To relieve their worries, Americans pursued the pleasures already afforded them in the twenties, with the addition that now they could legally drink beer, wine, and liquor. On the radio they could listen to the humorous political commentary of the beloved Will Rogers (a staunch isolationist), the continuing comic escapades of George Burns and Gracie Allen or of Amos and Andy, or fresh new radio comics Jack Benny and Fred Allen. For serious commentary, they had Lowell Thomas; for religious discourse, Father Coughlin and Aimee Semple McPherson. The greatest escape, of course, was movies. In 1933 audiences could enjoy the humorous antics of W. C. Fields in *You're Telling Me* and *It's a Gift* or the chorus lines of *42nd Street* and *Gold Diggers of 1933;* and in 1934, the enormously popular Frank Capra comedy *It Happened One Night*. The thriller of 1933 was *King Kong,* featuring the great ape's rampage in New York City that climaxed atop the Empire State Building. Greta Garbo was the reigning queen. She had made her "talkies" debut in the 1930 film version of Eugene O'Neill's *Anna Christie* and starred in *Queen Christina* in 1933. Most pleasurable of all, perhaps, audiences could enter the world of music, dance, and romance portrayed in the first two films of the long series Fred Astaire and Ginger Rogers starred in—*Flying Down to Rio* (1933) and *The Gay Divorcee* (1934)—which invariably evoked opulence in the midst of depression.

Although an exposition would seem an unlikely event in the depths of a depression, Chicago staged the Century of Progress in 1933 to celebrate the 100th anniversary of the city's founding and to improve the local economy. The city had a precedent: 40 years before in the midst of one of the worst depressions in American history, it had hosted the truly magnificent World's Columbian Exposition, arguably the greatest world's fair in history. Like its predecessor, the Century of Progress exposition made money, but it lacked the distinction of its forebear. The buildings were diverse, and some reflected International Style design, but not with compelling artistry. Regrettably, the fair's organizers had failed to involve Frank Lloyd Wright in any capacity. Although dedicated to showcasing the marvels of the applied sciences, the exposition's most lingering memory for many visitors may have been the suggestive fan dance of Sally Rand.

THE 1934 ELECTION

The fact that movies and the Century of Progress exposition, both to some extent presenting fantasy worlds, attracted such huge audiences suggests something about Americans' attitudes during these years. What is suggested may be as simple as a refusal to concede the field to reality or perhaps, on the other hand, a renewal of hope. Whatever the case, the First New Deal had obviously won many converts among the public, for despite the continuing depression, the protests of Huey Long and other opponents, and rantings of radical movements, the electorate went to the polls in November 1934 and did something unprecedented. Normally in off-year elections the party in power loses a sizable number of seats in Congress. Instead, in 1934, the voters gave the Democrats a majority of 322 in the House, reducing the number of Republicans by 13 to a total of 103—their lowest percentage representation in the House in Republican Party history. In addition, Farmer-Laborites and Progressives won 10 seats. The story was still worse for the GOP in the Senate, where the Democrats increased their numbers to 69, taking nine seats from the Republicans and securing the largest representation they had ever had in the Senate. Such overwhelming Democratic control of Congress appeared to presage legislative triumphs for the New Deal during the next two years.

CHRONICLE OF EVENTS

1933

March 4: Franklin Delano Roosevelt is inaugurated president of the United States.

March 5: Roosevelt issues a proclamation calling Congress into a special emergency session to be convened on March 9.

March 5: In Germany's parliamentary election, the Nazis secure 44 percent of the total vote and 288 seats; with their allies the Nationalist Party attaining 8 percent of the vote and 52 seats, they achieve a majority by 16 votes in the new Reichstag.

March 6: Roosevelt issues a proclamation declaring a national bank holiday and restricting the export of gold.

March 8: President Roosevelt holds his first press conference. He tells the more than 100 assembled reporters that he wants such conferences to be open and freewheeling, with some remarks intended as "background" and others "off the record." He discusses the banking crisis and answers all questions. At the end, the reporters applaud.

March 9: The special session of Congress convenes at noon. The chairman of the House's Banking and Currency Committee reads aloud to the assembled representatives the contents of the only copy of the Emergency Banking Bill available—by four o'clock they have unanimously approved it. The Senate begins debate on the House version of the bill and passes it by 7:30 P.M. with a 73-7 vote.

March 10: Having outlined his economic plans to congressional leaders the night before (after signing the Emergency Banking Act), Roosevelt now sends a special message to Congress deploring the government's $5 billion deficit as a cause of unemployment and depression and advocating fiscal belt-tightening to achieve a balanced budget.

March 12: President Roosevelt holds the first of his "fireside chat" radio broadcasts, explaining the government's support for the banking industry under the terms of the Emergency Banking Act. The listening audience is an estimated 60 million people.

March 13: Congress receives a message from the president requesting passage of an amendment to the Volstead Act that would legalize 3.2 beer (3.2 percent alcohol). The House passes the Economy Act authorizing cuts in veteran's payments and federal wages, including the president's salary.

March 13: Joseph Goebbels becomes Germany's minister of propaganda.

March 14: The House approves an act (the Beer Tax Act) amending the Volstead Act to allow brewing of 3.2 beer.

March 15: The Senate approves the Economy Act.

March 15: The securities markets, closed since the beginning of the bank holiday, reopen on a confident note.

March 16: The Senate approves the Beer Tax Act amending the Volstead Act.

March 16: Roosevelt sends Congress a message proposing national planning for agriculture.

March 21: Roosevelt sends a message to Congress requesting acts creating a civilian army to work in the national forests, a public works program, and federal grants to the states to support relief.

March 23: Prodded by Chancellor Adolf Hitler, the Reichstag, convened only two days before, approves the so-called Enabling Act, which in effect grants dictatorial powers to the chancellor and his cabinet.

March 27: By executive order the president reorganizes the government's agencies involved with farm credit into a single agency, the Farm Credit Administration, and appoints Henry Morgenthau, Jr., to head it.

March 27: The Japanese government announces Japan's intention to withdraw from the League of Nations.

March 31: The president signs into law the Civilian Conservation Corps Reforestation Relief Act, establishing the Civilian Conservation Corps (CCC) to provide jobs for young men in camps operated by the U.S. Army.

March 31: The Hitler government ends the independence of the German states, reconstituting their parliaments with Nazi majorities in accordance with the results of the March Reichstag elections.

April 1: Hitler proclaims a national boycott of Jewish-operated businesses. Acts of violence against Jews and attacks on their properties occur in cities throughout Germany.

April 5: Roosevelt issues an executive order creating the CCC.

April 6: The Senate passes a bill sponsored by Senator Hugo Black of Alabama that would mandate a 30-hour workweek by barring from interstate commerce all goods produced in plants where the workweek went beyond 30 hours. The president opposes the measure, so the administration immediately begins work on a counterproposal.

April 7: Beer is sold and consumed legally in the United States for the first time since Prohibition began in 1920.

April 7: Hitler issues guidelines specifying that officials who do not support the Nazis may be dismissed from office and Jewish officials may be dismissed on the basis of stipulations in a special "Aryan paragraph." Officials in the governments of individual states who oppose the Nazis are also dismissed.

April 10: Roosevelt sends a message to Congress requesting legislation to create the Tennessee Valley Authority (TVA) with the mandate to create a master plan for development of dams, reservoirs, and hydroelectric power generation throughout the entire Tennessee River Valley region.

May 2: German government agents occupy labor union headquarters, confiscate their funds, and arrest leading union officials, sending many to concentration camps; all German workers become united in the German Labor Front.

May 12: Roosevelt signs into law three pieces of legislation: the Agricultural Adjustment Act, the Emergency Farm Mortgage Act, and the Federal

Cotton sharecropper Bud Fields and his family at home in Hale County, Alabama, shown in a photo by Walker Evans, 1935 or 1936. *(Library of Congress, Prints and Photographs Division [ppmsc 00234])*

Emergency Relief Act. The first establishes the Agricultural Adjustment Administration (AAA) to create an allotment program for farm products, the second authorizes the Federal Land Banks to refinance farm mortgages, and the third provides $500 million in grants to the states for relief.

May 16: Roosevelt issues a public statement advocating international economic cooperation and currency stabilization.

May 18: Roosevelt signs into law the Tennessee Valley Authority Act, which authorizes creation of the TVA and a national plan for developing the entire Tennessee River watershed region.

May 27: The Securities Act becomes law. It requires filing of disclosure statements by all firms that sell stocks and bonds.

June 6: The Wagner-Peyser Act becomes law, authorizing the United States Employment Service within the Department of Labor and matching grants to states to set up similar local employment agencies.

June 12: The London Economic Conference originally planned by Hoover and British prime minister Ramsay MacDonald, convenes; representatives of 66 nations attend. King George V opens the proceedings.

June 13: The Home Owners' Loan Act becomes law, creating the Home Owners' Loan Corporation (HOLC) to provide funds from the Reconstruction Finance Corporation (RFC) and the sale of bonds for refinancing home mortgages.

June 16: Roosevelt signs into law four pieces of legislation: the Glass-Steagall Banking Act, the National Industrial Recovery Act, the Farm Credit Act, and the Railroad Coordination Act. The first forbids commercial banks from selling securities and, through an amendment presented by Senator Arthur Vandenberg, creates the Federal Deposit Insurance Corporation (FDIC) to provide funds for insuring bank deposits up to $2,500. The second establishes a Public Works Administration (PWA) with a fund of $3.3 billion for construction of highways, military facilities, and public buildings; authorizes trades groups to generate fair competition codes; and guarantees workers the right to organize for collective bargaining, outlawing antiunion contracts. The third law authorizes the Farm Credit Administration to consolidate all credit programs for agriculture. The fourth authorizes the new federal office of Coordinator of Transportation to

encourage improved organization and cooperation in the railway industry.

June 16: The special session of Congress adjourns, exactly 100 days after the session began.

July 3: Roosevelt sabotages the London Economic Conference by objecting to efforts to stabilize world currencies that he asserts would preclude the administration's efforts to increase commodity prices, publicly repudiating an agreement approved by Raymond Moley (FDR's representative) at the conference and lecturing the other nations on fiscal responsibility—an about-face from his May message that outrages the European leaders.

July 8: Roosevelt appoints Harold Ickes as administrator of the PWA.

July 11: By executive order Roosevelt establishes the Emergency Council (renamed the National Emergency Council in November).

July 14: The Reichstag passes a law forbidding the establishment of any new political parties in Germany, decreeing the National Socialist (Nazi) Party to be "the only political party in Germany."

July 20: Germany and the Vatican agree to the Reich Concordat intended to resolve differences between policies of the Nazis and the Roman Catholic Church; the agreement guarantees the freedom and autonomy of the church.

July 30: The National Planning Board—a three-man advisory board—is established within the PWA to provide recommendations for long-range policies.

August 5: General Hugh S. Johnson, head of the National Recovery Administration (NRA), establishes the National Labor Board, composed of six members (three representing labor and three representing industry) to assist in handling labor disputes arising out of NRA approaches to recovery.

August 10: Roosevelt issues an executive order requiring that purchases by all government agencies be placed with suppliers who adhere to NRA codes.

August 27: The automobile manufacturers, one of the last holdouts among the nation's top 10 industries, finally agree to adopt an NRA code. Ford is the only exception.

September 18: The bituminous coal operators, last of the 10 major industries to do so, accept formation of an NRA code for their industry.

October 2: Eugene O'Neill's *Ah, Wilderness!* opens at the Guild Theatre in New York City, with George M. Cohan playing the lead role.

October 14: Hitler announces Germany's withdrawal from the Disarmament Conference and from the League of Nations. He also dissolves the Reichstag, calls for a national plebiscite on the decision to leave the League, and issues secret orders to prepare German armed forces to resist any armed attack.

October 16: By executive order Roosevelt establishes the Commodity Credit Corporation within the RFC as an agency of the price support program for agricultural products. It will loan money to farmers who agree to remove lands from production.

October 19: Roosevelt decides to adopt the proposal of Professors George Warren and Frank Pearson, known as the Gold Dust Twins, to purchase gold on the open market at increasing prices as a means of spurring foreign trade, devaluing the dollar, and pumping up the prices of commodities.

October 25: Roosevelt, Secretary of the Treasury Morgenthau, and RFC administrator Jesse Jones, joined often by George Warren, begin daily morning meetings at the White House to decide on the price to be paid for gold during the day.

November 7: Maxim Litvinov, representing the government of the USSR, arrives in Washington, D.C., for discussions with the State Department and the president concerning normalization of relations between the USSR and the United States.

November 12: In the plebiscite on German withdrawal from the League of Nations, 95 percent of the voters support Hitler's decision.

November 15: Having convinced Roosevelt of the need for a federally operated work relief program, Harry Hopkins, head of the Federal Emergency Relief Administration (FERA), announces creation of the Civil Works Administration (CWA), with the goal of employing 4 million people by mid-December.

November 16: President Roosevelt and Maxim Litvinov exchange letters and a memorandum formally restoring diplomatic relations between the United States and the USSR. Diplomatic relations had been broken off following the 1917 Bolshevik Revolution.

December 5: The Twenty-first Amendment to the Constitution, repealing the Eighteenth Amendment (Prohibition) secures ratification by the states.

December 16: Roosevelt issues an executive order authorizing the National Labor Board to investigate and help resolve labor-management disputes.

December 19: By executive order Roosevelt creates the Electric Home and Farm Authority within the RFC to administer a program to stimulate purchases of electrical appliances.

December 21: Accepting an international agreement of the London Economic Conference, Roosevelt issues a proclamation committing the U.S. government to purchasing the nation's output of silver at a rate of 64.5 cents per ounce (21 cents above the current market price) for the next four years.

December 26: At the Seventh International Conference of American States being held in Montevideo, Uruguay, Secretary of State Hull votes in favor of a resolution asserting that no state has a right to intervene in the affairs of any other state—an affirmation of the Good Neighbor policy.

December 30: Roosevelt issues a proclamation returning all state-chartered banks not belonging to the Federal Reserve system to the jurisdiction of state banking authorities.

1934

January 1: Dr. Francis E. Townsend of Long Beach, California, in partnership with Robert E. Clements, founds Old Age Revolving Pensions, Ltd., which advocates Townsend's plan for the federal government to provide every citizen over 60 years old with an allowance of $200 per month (to be financed by a sales tax) that must be spent within 60 days. This, he argues, would provide an enormous stimulus to the economy while opening up jobs to younger Americans.

January 15: Roosevelt sends a message to Congress proposing devaluation of the dollar, fixing it at 50–60 percent of its gold value.

January 24: Townsend and his associates file articles of incorporation for Old Age Revolving Pensions, Ltd., to promote the Townsend Plan for federal pensions for those over 60.

January 26: Germany and Poland announce the signing of a 10-year nonaggression pact.

January 30: Roosevelt signs into law the Gold Reserve Act, authorizing the president to establish the official value of gold.

January 31: With the authority granted by the Gold Reserve Act, Roosevelt sets the price of gold at $35 per ounce, thus reducing the dollar to 59.06 percent of its previous gold content.

February 2: Roosevelt issues an executive order establishing the Export-Import Bank as a part of the RFC to stimulate foreign trade through granting or guaranteeing private loans.

February 6: Culminating the so-called Stavisky Affair, riots promoted by fascist groups erupt in Paris, resulting in 15 rioters being killed by police near the Chamber of Deputies; 1,500 are injured. (Alexander Stavisky had marketed worthless bonds; he was found dead in January, supposedly a suicide victim, but right-wing groups propounded that he had been murdered to prevent exposure of the involvement of government ministers and parliamentarians.) Repercussions of the Stavisky Affair and the riots will bring down the month-old administration of Premier Edouard Daladier.

February 9: Responding to charges of fraud in the system of contracting with private firms for carrying air mail, Roosevelt issues an executive order authorizing the U.S. Army Air Corps to carry the mail. He also sends a message to Congress requesting legislation to authorize government regulation of the stock exchange.

February 15: Under orders from Roosevelt, who is concerned over the huge amounts of money the CWA program costs and convicted it will not be needed beyond the spring, Harry Hopkins begins to disband CWA workers in the South, intending to continue the dismantling of CWA northward as warmer weather appears, until the agency ceases to exist and its efforts are subsumed by FERA.

March 2: Roosevelt sends a message to Congress requesting the president be granted authority to negotiate agreements on tariffs.

March 7: By executive order Roosevelt creates the National Recovery Review Board to investigate the danger of monopolies being formed as a result of the codes being adopted by industries cooperating with the NRA. Clarence Darrow will serve as chairman.

April 21: The Bankhead Cotton Control Act becomes law, providing use of increased taxes as a means of forcing resistant cotton farmers to enroll in the production control program.

April 24: The Roosevelt administration begins making public the names of persons or organizations speculating in silver futures. Among them is Father Coughlin's Radio League of the Little Flower.

April 30: The chancellor of Austria, Christian Socialist Engelbert Dollfuss, who had suspended the parliament and banned the Austrian Nazi Party in spring 1933, now establishes himself as a fascist dictator.

May 1: The Communist Party's May Day parade in New York City attracts the largest crowds in the party's history, as disaffected American workers and intellectuals find the party's policies increasingly appealing and its membership grows.

May 4: Darrow's National Recovery Review Board submits its first report to NRA head Hugh Johnson. The report concludes that giant corporations dominate the NRA codes program, stifling unions, small corporations, and public interests.

May 9: After employers in San Francisco refuse to accept local longshoremen's intent to join the International Longshoremen's Union as their bargaining agent—a right conferred by terms of the National Industrial Recovery Act—the city's longshoremen go on strike, led by Harry Bridges.

May 12: Minneapolis truck drivers call a strike after the Citizens' Alliance, an association of employers in Minneapolis, consistently refuses to deal with the local of the Teamsters Union, even though the National Industrial Recovery Act specifies that all workers have the right to organize.

May 22: Roosevelt sends a message to Congress requesting legislation with guidelines for Treasury Department purchases of silver.

May 22: In Minneapolis 20,000 people gather in the central marketplace, both supporters and opponents of the truck drivers' attempts to unionize. A fight ensues, resulting in the deaths of two special deputies of the Citizens' Alliance.

May 24: The Municipal Bankruptcy Act becomes law.

May 29: The United States and Cuba sign a treaty abrogating the Platt Amendment that had claimed the United States' right to intervene in Cuban affairs. The new treaty grants the United States the right to have a base at Guantánamo Bay, however.

June 6: Roosevelt signs into law the Securities Exchange Act, creating the Securities and Exchange Commission to administer the regulatory provisions of the Securities Act of 1933 on margin requirements, disclosure of information on securities, and prevention of insider trading.

June 8: Roosevelt sends a message to Congress reiterating his commitment to creating a program of social insurance but at the same time he suggests that drafting of legislation for such a program be deferred until the winter.

June 12: The Reciprocal Trade Agreements Act becomes law, authorizing the president to negotiate raising or lowering existing tariff rates by as much as 50 percent with any country that will enter into a reciprocal trade agreement.

June 14: Hitler flies to Venice for his first meeting with Benito Mussolini.

June 18: The Indian Reorganization Act becomes law, authorizing adoption of new constitutions providing for self-governance for tribal reservations that grant women the right to vote. The law also ends allotments of land to individual Indians; authorizes the Indian Office to consolidate previous allotments of lands into tribal ownership and to buy lands for Indians who have none; empowers tribes that incorporate to buy, manage, and dispose of property; encourages economic development through a revolving credit fund for Indians; and provides federal funding for Indian youths to pursue vocational or college educations. Oklahoma and Alaska Indians are exempted from the act's provisions because of opposition in Congress.

June 19: The Silver Purchase Act becomes law, committing the government to purchasing silver until the Treasury's holdings become equal in value to one-third of its gold reserves or until the price of silver on world markets reaches $1.29 per ounce—inflating prices and creating a windfall for silver producers.

June 20: The Communications Act becomes law, creating the Federal Communications Commission (FCC) to regulate the radio, telegraph, and cable industries.

June 27: The Railroad Retirement Act becomes law, establishing pensions for railway workers.

June 28: The Kerr-Smith Tobacco Control Act becomes law, providing the use of taxes to coerce tobacco farmers to join the production control system. The National Housing Act also becomes law, establishing the Federal Housing Administration to insure loans by private lenders to middle-income families for renovating existing homes or building new ones. In addition, the Taylor Grazing Act becomes law, setting aside up to 80 million acres of

public grasslands for cattle grazing under the regulatory administration of the Interior Department. By executive order Roosevelt establishes the Committee on Economic Security, headed by Secretary of Labor Frances Perkins, to generate a program for social insurance by December.

June 29: Roosevelt appoints a National Labor Relations Board within the NRA.

June 30: By executive order Roosevelt creates the National Resources Board with Secretary of the Interior Harold Ickes as nominal chairman but with control of programs and staff centered in the National Planning Board headed by Frederic A. Delano.

June 30: SS troops (an elite Nazi corps), presumably under orders from Hitler, assassinate Ernst Röhm, head of the SA (the Nazi militia), and more than 150 members of the SA. They also kill other presumed opponents of Hitler, including former chancellor Kurt von Schleicher and Gregor Strasser, who had recruited Joseph Goebbels for the Nazis.

July 3: The Hitler government proclaims that the murders carried out on June 30 were acts in "self-defense of the state."

July 5: In San Francisco the employers send policemen to try to reopen the docks at the Embarcadero, closed by the longshoremen's strike. Violence leaves two strikers dead and many wounded. The National Guard moves into the city to restore order.

July 12: Teamsters, who had earlier struck the docks in San Francisco in support of the longshoremen, now strike the entire city.

July 16: After a respite in the conflict over unionization of truck drivers in Minneapolis—they had compromised on indirect representation by the Teamsters—the drivers vote to strike again. In San Francisco members of other unions join the Teamsters and longshoremen, walking out of their jobs and imposing a general strike on the entire city.

July 20: The general strike in San Francisco collapses; the longshoremen agree to accept arbitration of their grievances.

July 22: In Chicago, outside a cinema on Lincoln Avenue, a group of agents from the Federal Bureau of Investigation (FBI) gun down John Dillinger, bank robber and the FBI's "public enemy number one."

July 25: Austrian Nazis seize control of government buildings in Vienna and assassinate Chancellor Engelbert Dollfuss, an opponent of Anschluss (the merging of Austria with Germany). Kurt von

Schuschnigg succeeds to the chancellorship and promises to continue Dollfuss's policies.

August 2: German president Paul von Hindenburg dies at age 87. Hitler obliges the members of the Reichswehr (the Regular Army of the Weimar Republic) to swear total allegiance to him as supreme commander of the reconstituted Wehrmacht (armed forces). Hitler abolishes the title of president and announces that from now on he will assume the duties of the president, taking the titles fuehrer, Reich chancellor, and commander in chief. He also begins rebuilding the navy and air force.

August 19: In a plebiscite called to affirm Hitler's assumption of the presidency—and in fact total control of the government and armed forces—90 percent of the voters approve.

August 21: After the imposition of martial law and still more bloodshed and arrests of leaders of both the union and the Citizens' Alliance, the Minneapolis employers finally acquiesce in the truck drivers' joining the Teamsters Union.

August 22: Prominent Democrats and Republicans disaffected with the New Deal found the American Liberty League in Washington, D.C., to promote opposition to Roosevelt administration policies.

August 28: Upton Sinclair, novelist, reformer, and founder of End Poverty in California (EPIC), alarms New Dealers by winning the primary election for Democratic candidate for governor of California.

August 31: The United Textile Workers Union calls a nationwide strike.

September 18: The Soviet Union officially joins the League of Nations.

September 24: Hugh Johnson, at the president's request, submits his resignation as administrator of NRA.

September 27: The governments of France, Great Britain, and Italy issue a joint declaration in support of Austrian independence.

October 9: Croatian terrorists kill Foreign Minister Louis Barthou of France and King Alexander of Yugoslavia in Marseilles.

November 11: Father Coughlin announces formation of the National Union for Social Justice.

December 1: Sergei M. Kirov, Communist Party boss of Leningrad and a protégé and ally of Joseph Stalin in the Politburo, is assassinated. This first attempt since 1918 to kill a party leader triggers scores of executions and the incarceration of thousands.

Eyewitness Testimony

The land of the free and the home of the brave! Home of the slave is what they ought to call it—the wage slave ground under the heel of the capitalist class, starving, crying for bread for his children, and all he gets is a stone! The Fourth of July is a stupid farce!

. . . No, you can celebrate your Fourth of July. I'll celebrate the day the people bring out the guillotine again and I see Pierpont Morgan being driven in a tumbril!

The character Richard, in Eugene O'Neill's play
Ah, Wilderness! *(1933).*

He sat down on a bench. . . . Still thinking of tents, he examined the sky . . . like a stupid detective who is searching for a clue to his own exhaustion. When he found nothing, he turned his trained eye on the skyscrapers that menaced the little park from all sides. In their tons of forced rock and tortured steel, he discovered what he thought was a clue.

Americans have dissipated their racial energy in an orgy of stone breaking. In their few years they have broken more stones than did centuries of Egyptians. And they have done their work hysterically, desperately, almost as if they knew that the stones would some day break them.

The character Miss Lonelyhearts, in Nathanael West's
novel Miss Lonelyhearts *(1933).*

The brilliance of the [Treasury] Secretary's [Andrew W. Mellon] tax policies in prosperous years was badly tarnished when the winds of adversity blew upon them. Nothing in his eleven years of incumbency though reflected less credit on the Secretary's sagacity than the rather shabby political trick into which he had been forced by the frantic occupant of the White House on November 13, 1929. . . . Unhappy Herbert Hoover thrust forth statement after statement, to no good effect. On November 13 he had called on the Wizard of the Treasury. Secretary Mellon must make a statement. But it must not merely be a thing of words, it must breathe and assure confidence by its internal evidence.

He did. The purport of his statement was that the President, the Secretary and Roy A. Young of the Federal Reserve Board—choicest of choice minds—had come together to consider the country's tax problem in the light of present conditions. They had pondered the meaning of the stock market flurry and had ruled it out as unimportant to the country's fundamental position. Business was not only good, it would be better. Therefore, there would be tax reductions for 1930.

Harvey O'Connor, in his book Mellon's Millions
(1933).

It was becoming clear that inflation in some form was the only remedy for the depression. Rather than leave an opening to crude inflationism, conservative financial opinion brought support to the group which advocated inflation in a limited and technically manageable form, that is to say, open market purchases to whatever extent might be necessary to correct the deflation that had occurred since 1929, and to raise the price level to what it had been in that year. That is the policy that has come to be known as "reflation." It was recognised that it might involve a renewed loss of gold, and legislation was passed at the end of February, 1932 (the Glass-Steagall Act), enabling the Federal Reserve Banks to include Government securities in the cover for their note issues.

Ralph G. Hawtrey, from his book The Gold Standard
in Theory and Practice *(1933).*

The Hoover debacle, now passing quietly into history, was of such colossal proportions that it has driven the right hon. gentleman quite out of politics—a good thing for him, for his party, and for his country. He was, for all his virtues, a bird of evil from the start.

H. L. Mencken, journalist, in the American Mercury
(January 1933).

Mr. Roosevelt's high skill at the art of practical politics is an important asset in a President, but potentially, however, it is also a great weakness. His agility and adroitness at the business incline him not infrequently to play politics when a direct and forthright course would be more statesmanlike. An instance of this sort of thing was his sharp rebuke to Rabbi Stephen S. Wise and the Rev. John Haynes Holmes for their demand on him that he oust from office the grafting Tammany leaders. Another was his sidestepping of important questions during the presidential race—for example, foreign affairs—because there was no pressure on him to declare his views. . . . This was undoubtedly good politics, but it was certainly not a very high order of statesmanship.

Robert S. Allen, journalist, in the American Mercury
(January 1933).

It takes more than a Depression to stop the national extravaganza known as major-league baseball. The sixteen clubs have already begun preparation for the six-months battle which, even in these hard times, has a box-office value of $10,000,000. The season will see 1,232 games, beginning in mid-April and finishing at the end of September, and they will attract an average of 7,500 patrons a game. There will follow the World series, which has a minimum value of $600,000. The first four clubs to finish in each league share in the World Series jackpot.

Arthur Mann, sports writer, in the American Mercury *(March 1933).*

It is possible that when the banks resume a very few people who have not recovered from their fear may again begin withdrawals. Let me make it clear to you that the banks will take care of all needs except of course the hysterical demands of hoarders—and it is my belief that hoarding during the past week has become an exceedingly unfashionable pastime in every part of our nation. It needs no prophet to tell you that when the people find they can get their money—that they can get it when they want it for all legitimate purposes—the phantom of fear will soon be laid. . . . I can assure you, my friends, that it is safer to keep your money in a reopened bank than it is to keep it under the mattress.

President Franklin D. Roosevelt, from his fireside chat of March 12, 1933, in Buhite and Levy, FDR's Fireside Chats *(1992).*

This is the fact that overshadows all other facts in Washington today: Once more there is a government. The capital is experiencing more government in less time than it has ever known before. Always a chameleon city, changing its color with every President, it is now as tense, excited, sleepless and driven as a little while ago it was heavy and inactive. There is an element of fantasy in the contrast between the frantic hurry of today and the torpor on the Hill, the isolation of the President, during the comatose months of the interregnum.

Anne O'Hare McCormick, journalist, column of March 19, 1933, in the New York Times, *quoted in Sheehan,* The World at Home: Selections from the Writings of Anne O'Hare McCormick *(1956).*

The Administration policy in dealing with the banks is to telescope future grief into one brief spasm of agony. Unless prices were to be raised by a considerable degree of inflation, it was inevitable that a great many banks would have to close. Their suspension would be spread out over months, or a year, with business increasingly paralyzed by this creeping terror, wondering where it would strike next. . . .

What has been done so far inspires hopes for business upbuilding. The Administration must press on now to a thorough reform. But time is of the essence.

Business Week, *editorial of March 22, 1933.*

The Insull holding company structure was a skyscraper of many stories. The income-producing properties rested in the cellar, and the floors above were occupied by various gradations of holding companies up to the top, where Insull Utility Investments and Corporation Securities Co. held sway. It has now been revealed that not only was the top floor vacant, but all the others, occupied by similar fictitious legal personalities, as well. When creditors forced their way into Insull's labyrinthine corporate structure, they found literally nothing more than empty desks and stacks of account books. Whatever there had been was pawned away; everything else was worthless paper.

N. R. Danielian, investigator of holding companies for the House Committee on Interstate and Foreign Commerce, in the Atlantic Monthly *(April 1933).*

The extraordinary degree to which the country has become conscious of Huey P. Long since his entrance into the United States Senate, not so many months back, makes his case a particularly interesting one. A year or so ago this tough young fellow, with his loud mouth and boorish ways, was just a local Louisiana politician who had achieved national notoriety through his clownish performance as Governor. . . . To-day he is a national figure and a party factor, holding his state in the hollow of his hand, a recognized force in the nomination of a President of the United States, the only Senator with three votes instead of one, not a man to be lightly dismissed or shoved aside.

Frank R. Kent, journalist and political commentator, in the Atlantic Monthly *(April 1933).*

President Roosevelt has done his part: now you do something.

Buy something—buy anything, anywhere; paint your kitchen, send a telegram, give a party, get a car, pay a bill, rent a flat, fix your roof, get a haircut, see a show, build a house, take a trip, sing a song, get married.

It does not matter what you do—but get going and keep going. This old world is starting to move.

Charles Edison, president of Thomas A. Edison, Inc., in West Orange, New Jersey, notice posted on the firm's walls, in Time *(April 3, 1933).*

We spent a good deal of time at the Cabinet meeting today discussing the cuts required of us by the Director of the Budget. I think there was a feeling that this Department was entitled to some consideration when I showed what the cuts would mean, as far as the Indian Office and the National Parks and various Negro activities are concerned. I was especially grati-

Secretary of the Interior Harold L. Ickes *(Library of Congress)*

fied when Vice President Garner spoke up frankly to say that he thought it would be a mistake to cut down on the Negro activities, and one or two others agreed with him.

Secretary of the Interior Harold L. Ickes, diary entry of April 4, 1933, in The Secret Diary of Harold L. Ickes, *vol. 1 (1953).*

Prohibition was beaten in the end, not by the wets but by the drys. . . . This civil war reached a climax at the time of the stock market collapse, and simultaneously the dry brethren lost most of their income, for it came mainly from well-heeled saints with a pious weakness for games of chance. Without money, they were reduced to harassing the morons in the Bible schools. Presently the Prohibition agents sold out to the bootleggers, and the holy cause was on its last legs.

I suspect that its great hero, the late Lord Hoover, had a good deal to do with its discrediting.

H. L. Mencken, journalist in the American Mercury *(May 1933).*

There is general agreement among the leading businessmen who have appeared before the congressional hearings that something must be done to regulate hours, pay, production, and prices. Even more convincing are the results of a questionnaire conducted by Cornell. Most of the leading businessmen questioned felt that the times demand drastic reorganization designed to reduce to a minimum the effects of the business cycle, to increase the stability of employment, and to insure adequate purchasing power. A minimum wage is necessary to prevent the unscrupulous from exploiting labor. Any plan devised to reach these ends must have in mind raising the standard of living of the country as a whole.

Business Week, *editorial of May 10, 1933.*

In adjusting our production of basic foods and fabrics, our first need is to plant and send to market less wheat, less cotton, less corn, fewer hogs, and less of other basic crops whereof already we have towering surpluses, with no immediate prospect of clearance beyond the seas. The act authorizes the secretary of agriculture to apply excise taxes on the processing of these products and to pay the money thus derived to farmers who agree to enter upon programs of planned production, and who abide by that agreement. . . .

This effort we will continue until such time as diminishing stocks raise prices to a point where the farmer's buying power will be as high as it was in the prewar years, 1909 to 1914.

Secretary of Agriculture Henry A. Wallace, radio address of May 13, 1933, explaining the basic purposes of the Agricultural Adjustment Act, in the Wallace papers at the Library of Congress.

Germany is entirely ready to renounce all offensive weapons if the armed nations, on their side, will destroy their offensive weapons. . . . Germany would also be perfectly ready to disband her entire military establishment and destroy the small amount of arms remaining to her, if the neighboring countries will do the same. . . . Germany is prepared to agree to any solemn pact of nonaggression, because she does not think of attacking but only of acquiring security.

German chancellor Adolf Hitler, speech to the Reichstag, May 17, 1933, responding to a call for disarmament by President Roosevelt, in Shirer The Rise and Fall of the Third Reich (1960).

Your Big Boss [Roosevelt] is doing a splendid job. I am scared stiff about him. Every day, as he handsprings lightly over the first page, tossing the world on his toes, I am jostled by a fear that he will fall down, but he has not fallen down so far. And the fine thing about it, of course, is that he has established good will enough now so that he can make some mistakes. March 4, the American people did not care what a man did so long as he did something. And since March 4, there has been something doing and mostly something doing in the right direction. But if his foot slips now they are going to count it against him.

William Allen White, editor and author, letter of May 23, 1933, to Harold L. Ickes, in Selected Letters of William Allen White, 1899–1943, vol. 1 (1947).

I cut out my regular appointments today because I had to attend a hearing with the Public Lands Committee of the House in support of a bill that I had introduced to give this Department power to regulate grazing on the public range. This bill passed the House at the last regular session but didn't get through the Senate. Recently, with the approval of the

President, I had it reintroduced. The public range is being overgrazed to an alarming extent. Part of it has already been destroyed and there will be more of this until there is some control. Some of the Western states are opposed to it because their stockmen in their greed want to turn their flocks and herds onto the range without the aye, yes or no of anyone. Secretary of Agriculture Wallace also appeared in behalf of the bill.

Secretary of the Interior Harold L. Ickes, diary entry of June 7, 1933, in The Secret Diary of Harold L. Ickes, vol. 1 (1953).

There should be made, without any preliminary publicity, a really expert and searching study of the income tax law. It is obvious that the law works badly, and yet it is equally obvious that it must not only be preserved as the chief source of revenue but must be used also for the social purpose of altering the distribution of wealth. If this is to be done, the law itself has to be made simpler to administer, simpler to observe and simpler to understand. . . . The administration, I believe, should prepare itself for a really thorough house-cleaning and reconstruction of the tax laws.

Walter Lippmann, newspaper columnist, letter of June 16, 1933, to Raymond Moley, in Blum Public Philosopher: Selected Letters of Walter Lippmann (1985).

During the two-year period of 1931–32, in this formerly prosperous Iowa county, twelve and a half per cent of the farms went under the hammer, and almost twenty-five per cent of the mortgaged farm real estate was foreclosed. And the conditions in my home county have been substantially duplicated in every one of the ninety-nine counties in Iowa and in those of the surrounding States.

We lawyers of the Corn Belt have had to develop a new type of practice, for in pre-war days foreclosure litigation amounted to but a small part of the general practice. In these years of the depression almost one-third of the cases filed have to do with this situation. . . .

To one who for years has been a standpatter . . . the gradual change to near-radicalism, both in himself and in those formerly conservative property owners for whom his firm has done business down the years, is almost incomprehensible, but none the less alarming.

Remley J. Glass, lawyer, in Harper's *(July 1933).*

To defend, either by word or intimation, a thing so anti-American as polygamy would put in jeopardy all this prestige and hard-won amity with the Gentiles. So the Mormon Church has done the politic thing: it has banned plural marriage. True, it was required by Federal statute to repudiate the principle; but it should be remembered that it might have gone on with the practice through the devious channels of the underground. Its authorities finally had the good sense to supplement the legal prohibition with a church decree.

Yet it is a fact . . . that a considerable remnant of polygamy is still a part of the under strata of Mormonism.

Louis W. Larsen, Mormon educator and advertising executive, in The American Mercury *(July 1933).*

There is a clear way to reverse that process [economic decline]: If all employers in each competitive group agree to pay their workers the same wages—reasonable wages—and require the same hours—reasonable hours—then higher wages and shorter hours will hurt no employer. Moreover, such action is better for the employer than unemployment and low wages, because it makes more buyers for his product. That is the simple idea which is the very heart of the Industrial Recovery Act.

On the basis of this simple principle of everybody doing things together, we are starting out on this nationwide attack on unemployment. It will succeed if our people understand it . . . There is nothing complicated about it and there is nothing particularly new in the principle.

President Franklin Delano Roosevelt, in his third fireside chat, July 24, 1933, in Rosenman's The Public Papers and Addresses of Franklin D. Roosevelt *(1938–50).*

It can hardly add to our self-esteem to realize that here in the United States, except for favored areas, we have reached merely the hunger point in caring for the unemployed. Relief standards in many localities have taken no account of rent, light, fuel, or clothes. "You can freeze a man to death as surely as you can starve him to death," said a relief worker from West Virginia at a Washington hearing last winter.

Helen Hall, writer who visited coal mines in Wales and West Virginia, in the Atlantic Monthly *(August 1933).*

We had a cabinet meeting this afternoon. The Cuban situation is very tense and we spent a good deal of time considering it. . . . While I was in the President's office this morning, he gave orders to have messages sent to the captains of all American ships lying off Cuba forbidding them to land marines or sailors for the protection of property alone. He said that only danger to lives would justify anyone's being landed. . . . The question of intervention was discussed very fully in the Cabinet meeting, but it seemed clear that the decision of everyone, from the President down, was against intervention unless it was actually forced upon us.

Secretary of the Interior Harold L. Ickes, diary entry of September 8, 1933, in The Secret Diary of Harold L. Ickes *vol. 1 (1953).*

I have always been able to provide fairly well for my family, but in the past three years my salary has been on a constant decline, but still I am thankful I have a position.

. . . and this is the reason for me writing you; Winter coming on, no coal in our coal bin, and the children needing warm clothes to go to school. Two children in Grammer [sic] School, and two in High School. Cannot even give my wife the necessary medical attention she should have.

Anonymous man of St. Louis, Missouri, letter of October 23, 1933, to President Roosevelt, in McElvaine, Down & Out in the Great Depression: Letters from the "Forgotten Man" *(1983).*

In certain quarters it is asserted that Mr. Roosevelt's New Deal is nothing other than the first stage of an American movement toward Fascism. . . .

Philosophically, Fascism is a movement whose leaders are civilians in riding boots. Politically, it is an entirely new type of tyranny, both personal and demagogic—a tyranny which for the first time in history exploits the mob spirit in an era of universal suffrage and gives to the supreme leaders irresponsible power as limitless as that of the modern state. In contrast to this picture, we now see in America a leader who has never played the role of hero or savior. . . .

In spite of the novelty of Mr. Roosevelt's experiment, perhaps the most appropriate term for this new American way of grappling with social and economic unrest is still the good old word "democracy."

Max Ascoli, exiled Italian law professor, in the Atlantic Monthly *(November 1933).*

During the 1932–33 term the deflation gathered momentum so rapidly that many communities had to close their schools. By the end of last March nearly a third of a million children were out of school for that reason. But the number of children, shocking as it is, does not tell the story so vividly as does the distribution of the schools. Georgia had 1,318 closed schools with an enrollment of 170,790, and in Alabama 81 percent of all the children enrolled in white rural schools were on an enforced vacation. In Arkansas . . . over 300 schools were open for *sixty days or less during the entire year. . . .*

These are, of course, States which . . . have always lagged educationally. But consider the case of Ohio, which formerly was near the other end of the procession. According to authentic information . . . practically every school in the State had to shorten its term. Numbers of county schools shut down at the end of seven months.

Avis D. Carlson, resident of Witchita and frequent contributor to Harper's, *on the closing of schools caused by the inability to pay teachers, in* Harper's *(November 1933).*

Agriculture first felt the present depression in 1920. With agriculture prostrate at the end of 1932, and with the cities sharing in the depression, at last, many distribution margins remained as wide as in 1929. Between 1929 and 1933 city incomes fell one-third; farm income, already low, fell two-thirds; but distribution spreads stayed wide. It is informing to note that of the fifteen leading corporations in point of earnings in 1932, nine dealt in food or tobacco.

Industry and the distribution trades in general, like agriculture in general, are over-extended, sprawling, struggling more or less helplessly amid insane duplications of effort and blind, destructive competition. . . . Wealth has become overcentralized, too narrowly circulated. . . . The New Deal proposes, for the sake of all, that money be put forth more freely in

farm prices and city wages, to breed again. The great effort is to start money moving from the bottom up.

Director of the Agricultural Adjustment Administration (AAA) Chester C. Davis, in Review of Reviews and World's Work *(December 1933).*

I am very happy to inform you that as a result of our conversations the government of the United States has decided to establish normal diplomatic relations with the government of the Union of Soviet Socialist Republics and to exchange ambassadors.

I trust that the relations now established between our peoples may forever remain normal and friendly, and that our nations henceforth may cooperate for their mutual benefit and for the preservation of the peace of the world.

President Franklin D. Roosevelt, letter of November 16, 1933, to Maxim Litvinov, official envoy of the USSR, formalizing their agreement on official recognition of the USSR, in Rosenman, The Public Papers and Addresses of Franklin D. Roosevelt *(1938–1950).*

III. The reputation of *Ulysses* in the literary world, however, warranted my taking such time as was necessary to enable me to satisfy myself as to the intent with which the book was written, for, of course, in any case where a book is claimed to be obscene it must first be determined whether the intent with which it was written was what is called, according to the usual phrase, "pornographic," that is, written for the purpose of exploiting obscenity.

If the conclusion is that the book is pornographic, that is the end of the inquiry and forfeiture must follow. But in *Ulysses,* in spite of its unusual frankness, I do not detect anywhere the leer of the sensualist. I hold, therefore, that it is not pornographic.

Judge John M. Woolsey, United States District Court for the Southern District of New York, decision of December 6, 1933, lifting the ban on the importation of James Joyce's masterpiece Ulysses *(1922), in* Federal Supplement, V *(1934).*

The members of the firms of J. P. Morgan and Company and Drexel and Company held twenty directorships in fifteen great banks and trust companies, with total assets of $3,811,400,000. They held twelve directorships in ten great railroads, with total assets of $3,430,000,000. They held nineteen directorships in thirteen public-utility holding or operating companies, with total assets of $6,222,000,000. They held six directorships in as many great insurance companies, with total assets of $337,000,000. They held no less than fifty-five directorships in thirty-eight industrial corporations, with total assets of $6,000,000,000. In grand total, they held 126 directorships in 89 corporations with total assets of twenty billions—incomparably the greatest reach of power in private hands in our entire history.

Nor was this all. On the boards of these eighty-nine corporations upon which the Morgan partners sat as directors, they came into regular and close relationship with 537 fellow directors, drawn from all fields of commerce. Many of these hundreds of fellow directors . . . were thus brought within the orbit, at least, of the Morgan influence.

Ferdinand Pecora, justice of the New York Supreme Court, commenting on findings of the 1933–34 hearings by the Senate Banking and Currency Committee, for which he served as legal counsel, from his book Wall Street under Oath *(1939).*

Had that same attitude [valuing safety and reasonable price] been taken by the purchaser of common stocks in 1928–1929, the term investment would not have been the tragic misnomer that it was. But in proudly applying the designation "blue chips" to the high-priced issues chiefly favored, the public unconsciously revealed the gambling motive at the heart of its supposed investment selections. These differed from the old-time bank-stock purchases in the one vital respect that the buyer did not determine that they were worth the price paid by the application of firmly established standards of value. The market made up new standards as it went along, by accepting the current price—however high—as the sole measure of value. Any idea of safety based on this uncritical approach was clearly illusory and replete with danger. Carried to its logical extreme, it meant that no price could possibly be too high for a good stock, and that such an issue was equally "safe" after it had advanced to 200 as it had been at 25.

Benjamin Graham, lecturer in finance at Columbia University, and David L. Dodd, assistant professor of finance at Columbia University, from their book Security Analysis *(1934).*

We'd left because there wasn't a prayer of getting a job in our home town [Jackson, Nebraska] and we heard that we could earn money picking fruit on the coast. Four nights and three days later we arrived at Spokane, Washington. The depot had an unloading dock four city blocks long, where they stripped the boxcars and loaded the freight onto trucks. We were told that there were over two thousand hoboes on the dock that night.

I still had three of my four dollars left. We went to an eatery on Skid Row. For fifteen cents we got a pork chop with hash brown potatoes and a cup of coffee.

There was absolutely nothing for us in Spokane. We rode a freight out the next morning taking the advice of hoboes who told us to go south toward Oregon. At Pasco, Washington, we were offered jobs picking strawberries. You're bent over all day long and if you worked your brains out, you couldn't make a dollar at the price they gave us per basket. One day of that and we quit.

Reminiscence of Tiny Boland, who left home in 1934 at age 14 with three friends to ride the rails and seek work, quoted in Uys, Riding the Rails *(1999).*

Obviously, then, the whole principle [of equality of treatment] falls to the ground if we raise tariffs to such a height as to shut out foreign goods regardless of the economy of their production abroad. . . . This is exactly what the Hawley-Smoot Tariff did in 1930. . . . The fact that a general upward tariff revision was undertaken in the United States upon a great range of foreign specialties which we do not and cannot produce in quantities approaching the needs of our consumption; that fact that the highest tariff in the world, at a time when international economics and finance demanded that our tariff be lowered, was raised to still greater heights; the fact that a great number of duties approached and exceeded the value of the article upon which they were imposed; the fact that foreign countries were convinced that the United States was determined to shut out their products and that payments to this country must be made in gold and not in goods and services—these are the important points in question. Equality of treatment to them [other nations] became devoid of meaning; it became a unilateral concession which we demanded of them.

Joseph M. Jones, Jr., from his book Tariff Retaliation *(1934).*

This appetite for yellow metal assumed a wide variety of forms:

... (b) Cooperation between central banks to alleviate gold strain, and to maintain a gold exchange standard for many countries, broke down. ...

(e) Mal-distribution of gold was accentuated by abnormal influences upon the balance of payments of most countries. The sudden cessation in 1929 of foreign lending by leading capital-exporting countries, the pressure on Germany to create an export surplus sufficient to pay reparations, the burden of the international war debts, and the introduction of higher tariff walls in creditor countries—all of these factors disarranged the equilibrium of payments between countries. It took gold away from countries which needed it most and gave gold to countries which needed it least. The net effect, therefore, was to intensify demand for gold relative to supply and to exert deflationary pressure on the world price level.

(f) Gradually the abnormal hunger for gold spread to private individuals and led to a wave of hoarding. This wave was especially strong in the United States from 1930 to 1933, but in 1933 it became important in Europe.

Lionel D. Edie, from his book Dollars *(1934).*

Western civilization, because of fortuitous historical circumstances, has spread itself more widely than any other local group that has so far been known. It has standardized itself over most of the globe, and we have been led, therefore, to accept a belief in the uniformity of human behaviour that under other circumstances would not have arisen. ...

The white man has . . . never seen an outsider, perhaps, unless the outsider has been already Europeanized. . . . The uniformity of custom, of outlook, that he sees spread about him seems convincing enough, and conceals from him the fact that it is after all an historical accident. He accepts without more ado the equivalence of human nature and his own culture standards.

Ruth Benedict, anthropologist, in her most famous work, Patterns of Culture *(1934).*

The central theme of the exposition was the growth of science and its application to industry and the arts of life. The development of the basic sciences—mathematics, physics, chemistry—was skillfully shown. Among the applications of science, chief emphasis was laid upon communication—the telephone, radio, the timid beginnings of television, the ocean liner, the railroad, the automobile. In striking contrast to these technical marvels, however, the most popular exhibit was that illustrating the human reproductive process—a series of jars in which were shown specimens of the human embryo in various stages of development.

Robert Morss Lovett, University of Chicago professor, commentary on Chicago's 1933 Century of Progress exposition, in Current History *(January 1934).*

In another and more important way, too, the psychologists disappointed their hopeful readers. Science, in the modern popular conception, is more than factual; it is our last remaining form of magic. And, because psychologists were accepted as scientists, they were believed to be able to work the same kind of legerdemain upon the human mind that the modern surgeon works on the human body, or the engineer upon cold, inhuman steel. But psychology, for all its theories, has performed no miracles. It has renamed our emotions "complexes" and our habits "conditional reflexes," but it has neither changed our habits nor rid us of our emotions. We are the same blundering folk that we were twelve years ago, and far less sure of ourselves.

Grace Adams, in the Atlantic Monthly *(January 1934).*

Secretary Wallace has pointed out in public speeches that the choices open to us are these: to increase foreign purchasing power in the United States by accepting at least one billion dollars more imports than we did in 1929; or to take from forty to seventy million acres out of production; or to take a middle course, admitting perhaps a half a billion more of imports, and returning some land, but not the whole of the forty to seventy million acres, to the public domain. The first alternative . . . would throw the main burden of readjustment on industry and a lesser burden on agriculture; the second alternative would throw an enormous burden on agriculture as well as industry; the third, or compromise, alternative would distribute the burden. By no one of the alternatives do we escape from the necessity of great adjustment.

Walter Lippmann, newspaper columnist, in Foreign Affairs *(January 1934).*

Mr. Roosevelt proposed in his speech that the NRA and a lot of these other government regulated business ethics would be made permanent. Well that was a terrible blow to some business men. They had figured they would only be required to be honest by the government till the emergency was over.

Will Rogers, humorist and author, column of January 4, 1934, in How We Elect Our Presidents *(1952).*

But President Roosevelt is the first statesman in a great capitalist society who has sought deliberately and systematically to use the power of the state to subordinate the primary assumptions of that society to certain vital social purposes. He is the first statesman deliberately to experiment on a wholesale scale with the limitation of the profit-making motive. . . . He is the first statesman who . . . has placed in the hands of organized labor a weapon which, if it is used successfully, is bound to result in a vital readjustment of the relative bargaining power of Capital and Labor. He is also the first statesman who, the taxing power apart, has sought to use the political authority of the state to compel, over the whole area of economic effort, a significant readjustment of the national income.

Harold J. Laski, Labour Party supporter and professor of political science at the London School of Economics, in the Atlantic Monthly *(February 1934).*

The President talked to me rather at length today about the lynching bill. As I do not think you will either like or agree with everything that he thinks, I would like an opportunity of telling you about it, and would also like you to talk to the President if you feel you want to. Therefore, will you let me know if you are going to be in Washington before long?

Eleanor Roosevelt, in a letter to Walter White, executive secretary of the NAACP, May 2, 1934, quoted in Schlup and Whisenhunt, It Seems to Me *(2001).*

We had an interesting Cabinet meeting on Friday. . . . I was particularly interested in the discussion of the drought conditions in the Middle West. The situation is extremely serious there. . . . Rex Tugwell, who was substituting for Henry Wallace, said that Department of Agriculture experts thought that we were about half through a fifteen-year cycle. In any event, the people in the drought country are apparently facing a terrible situation next winter, during which relief will have to be extended on a broad scale.

Secretary of the Interior Harold L. Ickes, diary entry of May 28, 1934, in The Secret Diary of Harold L. Ickes *vol. 1 (1953).*

The emancipation of woman is an accomplished fact, but man is still plodding along in his traditional grooves. He has never thought of woman as woman—that is, a thinking, feeling creature entirely separate from himself. He continues to think of her as mother, wife, daughter, Good Woman, Bad Woman—always woman in relation to him, never woman as statesman, lawyer, doctor, financier, entirely dissociated from him. He is still living under the delusion that men are somehow superior to women, which leads him personally to the necessity of endeavoring to appear so. It gets him into no end of trouble, is rather a nuisance to everybody, and is on the whole palpably unfair. Isn't it time he was emancipated from this obsession and given a chance to lead his own life?

Pringle Barret, Wellesley graduate and wife of a physician, in the Atlantic Monthly *(June 1934).*

The notion that, if the government would retire altogether from the economic field, business, left to itself, would soon work out its own salvation, is, to my mind, foolish; and, even if it were not, it is certain that public opinion would allow no such thing. This does not mean that the administration should not be assiduously preparing the way for the return of normal investment enterprise. But this will unavoidably take time. When it comes, it will intensify and maintain a recovery initiated by other means. . . .

I conclude, therefore, that, for six months at least, and probably a year, the measure of recovery to be achieved will mainly depend on the degree of the direct stimulus to production deliberately applied by the administration. Since I have no belief in the efficacy for this purpose of the price and wage-raising activities of NRA, this must chiefly mean the pace and volume of the government's emergency expenditure.

John Maynard Keynes, British economist, commenting on New Deal policies for overcoming the depression, in the New York Times *(June 10, 1934).*

We seek the security of the men, women, and children of the nation.

That security involves added means of providing better homes for the people of the nation. That is the first principle of our future program. The second is to plan the use of land and water resources of this country to the end that the means of livelihood of our citizens may be more adequate to meet their daily needs. And, finally, the third principle is to use the agencies of government to assist in the establishment of means to provide sound and adequate protection against the vicissitudes of modern life—in other words, social insurance.

President Franklin D. Roosevelt, fireside chat of June 28, 1934, in Rosenman, The Public Papers and Addresses of Franklin D. Roosevelt *(1938–1950).*

Who is she . . .

. . . this beautiful woman whom men avoid; whom other women do not envy?

She is the woman whose person is unpleasant because of underarm perspiration odor.

She is quite unconscious of this unpleasantness. She believes that because she is scrupulous about her daily bath, perspiration can do no harm. . . .

It's not worth taking a chance on when you can play safe so easily. With Mum!

Advertisement for Mum deodorant, a product of Bristol-Myers, in Ladies' Home Journal *(July 1934).*

Unemployment among scientifically and technically trained men has been, and is, acute. The plight especially of the technically trained young men, who have received an expensive education and who are essential to the future life of the country, is pathetic. This has arisen from general decrease in engineering activity, and has been accentuated by the reduction of research and the dropping of research personnel for emergency budgetary reasons by large industries and by universities. The present drastic reduction in the scientific work of the Government bureaus, in order to balance budgets, has added significantly to this unemployment, and places upon the Government a considerable responsibility to extend its measures for emergency unemployment relief to scientific workers.

From an unsuccessful proposal that the federal government provide massive financial support for scientific research, Report of the Science Advisory Board: July 31 to September 1, 1934 *(Washington, D.C., 1934), pp. 269–274.*

I swear to God this holy oath that I shall offer total obedience to the Fuhrer of the German Reich and Nation, Adolf Hitler, the supreme commander of the Wehrmacht, and that I shall be prepared, as a brave soldier, to lay down my life at any time.

Oath required of German soldiers on August 2, 1934, and thereafter, in Questions on German History *(1984).*

When you drive through the Middle West droughty country you try not to look at the thrusting out ribs of the horses and cows, but you get so you can't see anything else but ribs, like hundreds of thousands of little beached hulks. It looks like the bones are rising right up out of the skin. Pretty soon, quite gradually, you begin to know that the farmer, under his rags, shows his ribs, too, and the farmer's wife is as lean as his cows, and his children look tiny and hungry.

Meridel LeSueur freelance writer, in the American Mercury *(September 1934).*

I have been hoping for some time that General Johnson would resign or be forced out. I think he has been a heavy load for the Administration to carry. The first part of his job he did well. . . . He aroused enthusiasm throughout the country, he was a past master at carrying on the type of ballyhoo campaign that was necessary to put NRA across, but when it came to settling down to administrative work, he seemed to be a total loss. He never appeared to be able to get out of his head that it wasn't all to be ballyhoo. He was so used to streaming headlines on the front pages of the papers that he had to keep reaching for those headlines, with the result that he said and did many reckless things.

Secretary of the Interior Harold L. Ickes, diary entry of September 27, 1934, in The Secret Diary of Harold L. Ickes, *vol. 1 (1953).*

To those people who say that our expenditures for public works and for other means for recovery are a waste that we cannot afford, I answer that no country, however rich, can afford the waste of its human resources. Demoralization caused by vast unemployment is our greatest extravagance. Morally, it is the greatest menace to our social order. Some people try to tell me that we must make up our minds that for the future we shall permanently have millions of unemployed. . . . I stand or fall by my refusal to accept as a necessary condition of our future a permanent army of unemployed.

President Franklin D. Roosevelt, from his fireside chat of September 30, 1934, in Buhite and Levy, FDR's Fireside Chats *(1992).*

May I state confidentially, and ask you not to reveal its source . . . that [Georgia governor] Talmadge had planned up until a week ago (and may still be planning unless he has been fully conciliated by the President) one of the dirtiest anti-Negro campaigns

Drought-stricken farm in Oneida County, Idaho, June 1936, Farm Security Administration; photo by Arthur Rothstein *(Library of Congress)*

that has been promoted in recent years in the South. . . . It is his idea, I understand, to oppose the present Senator [Richard B.] Russell. Talmadge's whole program has been, up until this last minute, anti-administration and as silly as it might seem to one in the North the theoretical favoritism shown the Negro in connection with the Recovery program would be the biggest issue he would offer Georgia "Red Necks." . . .

This is all ridiculous because first of all the Recovery program has not functioned fairly among Negroes in the South. Secondly, Russell is no particular friend of the Negro. What I imagine will happen if and when Talmadge launches his campaign against Russell will be that Russell's defense . . . will be an attempt to exceed Talmadge

in the bitterness of his attack on the Negro from some other front.

Eleanor Roosevelt, in a letter of November 28, 1934, to Walter White, executive secretary of the NAACP, concerning information she had received about the plans of Governor Herman Talmadge of Georgia, quoted in Schlup and Whisenhunt, It Seems to Me *(2001).*

There are those who tell us that we should not have work relief. They say that straight relief is cheaper. No one will deny this contention. It costs money to put a man to work. Apparently, to the advocates of direct relief, the primary object of relief is to save the government money. The ultimate humane cost to the government never occurs to them of a continued situation through which its citizens lose their sense of independence and strength and their sense of individual destiny. Work for the unemployed is something we have fought for since the beginning of the administration and we shall continue to insist upon it. It preserves a man's morale. It saves his skill. It gives him a chance to do something socially useful.

Let me say again that we should allow ourselves no smug feelings of charity at this holiday season to know that the federal government is attempting to take care of the actual physical wants of 18 million people. We are merely paying damages for not having had a thought about these things many years ago.

Harry L. Hopkins, head of the Federal Emergency Relief Administration, radio address of December 31, 1934, in Vital Speeches of the Day *(New York, December 31, 1934).*

Sometimes their talk about the Depression was shaded with anger, but its dominant tones were good humor and civility. The anger was never edged with bitterness or self-pity. Most often it was expressed as genial contempt toward business, labor, government, and all the salesmen of miracle cures for the world's ailments. Communists were "crackpots" and "bomb throwers." Father Coughlin and Huey Long were "rabble-rousers." The German-American Bund with its Nazi swastikas, "a bunch of sausage stuffers." Benito Mussolini, "the top Wop." Not even the New Deal escaped. In Belleville, men on the government's W.P.A. payroll were usually seen leaning on shovels. The initials W.P.A., Uncle Allen said, stood for "We Poke Along."

Russell Baker, columnist, describing his family's conversations, in Growing Up, *(1982).*

5

The Second New Deal
1935–1936

THE SUPREME COURT V. THE NEW DEAL

The Roosevelt administration's effort to revise the failed programs of the preceding two years or to devise new programs to replace them in the continuing pursuit of a remedy for the Great Depression, constituted the Second New Deal. That some of the First New Deal's programs failed was a disappointment for the administration, but it could hardly have been a surprise. Even before receiving the nomination as the Democratic candidate, Roosevelt had tentatively committed his presidency to improvisation: In a famous speech to the graduating class at Oglethorpe University in May 1932, he had proclaimed that "the country demands bold, persistent experimentation." And that is exactly what the First New Deal had provided. FDR pursued a pragmatic approach: Try something and see whether it works; if it does not work, then try something else. But this sort of pragmatism, however bold and experimental it may have appeared, was clearly within the American political tradition. The First New Deal was distinctive in its massive expansion of the federal government's role in the economy, but it was not revolutionary. It appeared revolutionary enough, however, to arouse fear, trembling, and rage among some segments of the American populace. The failures of the New Deal were both predictable and welcome to these opponents.

In 1935 the New Deal's momentum foundered on an obstacle—much to the relief of the growing opposition. That obstacle was the Supreme Court. As the year opened the Court rendered a decision in *Panama Refining Company v. Ryan,* referred to as the "hot oil" case. The Court declared one section of the National Industrial Recovery Act (NIRA) invalid because it awarded legislative duties to the president exceeding his executive powers. In response, the administration induced Congress to circumvent the Court by passing the Connally Act, which outlawed shipments of oil that surpassed state production codes—that is, "hot oil"—and thus restored the effect of the NIRA section found unconstitutional. Then on May 27 (called Black Monday by New Dealers), the Court handed down a unanimous verdict in the case of *A. L. A. Schechter Poultry Corporation et al. v. United States*—known as the "sick chicken" case because

Schechter was accused of selling diseased chickens to retailers. Once again the Court found the NIRA invalid, this time as a violation of the Constitution's commerce clause granting Congress the power to regulate commerce with foreign nations and "among the several States" but not within any single state. The decision not only sentenced the National Recovery Administration (NRA) and its extensive programs to death but also raised the clear threat that future Supreme Court decisions based on the commerce clause could dismantle the entire New Deal.

That threat became all the more real in 1936 when Court decisions increasingly revealed a 5-4 split, with a conservative majority frequently headed by Chief Justice Hughes. In January 1936, another decision by the Court crippled a New Deal program. The Court decided in *United States v. Butler* that the tax imposed on processing by the Agricultural Adjustment Administration

Chief Justice Charles Evans Hughes
(Library of Congress)

(AAA) was unconstitutional on the grounds that it provided an illegitimate use of the government's power to levy taxes. The Court ordered that $200 million already collected from processors be returned to them, thus gutting the AAA's program to control crop production. As a result this decision also presaged the collapse of crop prices and imperiled the Roosevelt administration's budget, creating the need to find new sources of revenue. (Nor did it help the budget when Congress passed, over the president's veto, a bill providing $2 billion in veterans bonus payments in 1936.) In February 1936, in the *Ashwander* case, the Court did uphold the Tennessee Valley Authority's (TVA) mandate to distribute power from Wilson Dam but left the TVA open to further challenge by not ruling on the agency's legitimacy. In May, in the case of *Carter v. Carter Coal Company,* the Court invalidated the entire Guffey-Snyder Act, which dealt not only with coal production levels but also with wages, hours, and collective bargaining. The Court also invalidated the Municipal Bankruptcy Act and a New York law establishing minimum wage standards for women (the latter decision elicited widespread dismay and consternation). Every decision, it seemed, necessitated some response from the Roosevelt administration to salvage threatened programs. Moreover, the first two years of the New Deal had already passed, yet the depression remained intact. It seemed as though new or different programs were necessary.

SOCIAL SECURITY AND OTHER MAJOR PROGRAMS

The administration rose to the challenge with the extensive legislative program of the Second New Deal. Many commentators had expected Roosevelt to begin advocating moderate concepts in 1935 that would placate opponents in business and industry, but in fact the administration shifted toward more radical measures. As the year began Roosevelt proposed a massive public employment program that would put 3.5 million jobless Americans to work. The Emergency Relief Appropriation Act, which became law in April, provided the administration with nearly $5 billion for this program. Roosevelt placed Harry Hopkins in charge as administrator of the new agency, the Works Progress Administration (WPA). Although some of the WPA's undertakings proved of doubtful worth, the agency would be responsible during its life for building or renovating thousands of schools, hospitals, and playgrounds. Its National Youth Administration (NYA), founded in June 1935, provided grants to young people in exchange for work as a means of keeping them in school and also job training programs to occupy unemployed youths. And in August the WPA created the Federal Art, Federal Music, Federal Theatre, and Federal Writers' Projects that made invaluable contributions to America life by promoting the arts publicly and provided work to such aspiring writers and painters as Ralph Ellison, John Cheever, Saul Bellow, Richard Wright, Jackson Pollock, Yasuo Kuniyoshi, and Willem de Kooning.

Also in January the president asked Congress to pass legislation to establish a social security program. Robert Wagner and David Lewis introduced the administration's bill in the Senate and the House. The House passed the bill in April; the Senate, in June. Roosevelt signed the Social Security Act into law on August 15. A landmark law, it established a national old-age insurance system that would provide annuities to retired persons aged 65 and older funded

Senator Robert F. Wagner *(Library of Congress)*

through payroll taxes; it also established an unemployment insurance system administered by the states. The system had certain flaws—not all workers were covered, it reduced spending power by taking money from wage earners, hitting especially hard those who made less—but it was nevertheless momentous for solidifying, through the creation of an ongoing government program, full recognition of the concept that society bears responsibility for the poor, elderly, and unemployed.

In February, Senator Wagner introduced a bill that would establish the National Labor Relations Board as both a permanent and an independent federal agency with authority to oversee workers' elections of their own agents for collective bargaining and to curtail "unfair labor practices" (such as, firing of union members) by businesses. Initially Roosevelt opposed the bill, but after negotiating certain changes with Wagner in May, he came to support it. The bill the president signed into law on July 5, the National Labor Relations Act (or the Wagner Act), provided the federal government's full support for workers' right to organize and obligated employers to accept union organization of their employees and facilities. The act constituted a significant victory for organized labor.

Still other major pieces of legislation besides the Social Security Act achieved enactment in August. The most significant of these were the Public Utility Holding Company Act (Wheeler-Rayburn Act) and the Wealth Tax Act (Revenue Act of 1935). Through the provisions the administration had proposed for the Public Utility Holding Company Act Roosevelt hoped to completely dismantle the huge electric utility combinations, or holding companies, that managed to avoid state regulatory oversight. The original draft of the bill contained a so-called death sentence that authorized the Securities and Exchange Commission (SEC) to terminate all utility holding companies after January 1, 1940. Strenuous opposition to the "death sentence" arose in Congress, primarily in the House, generating an extended struggle between the two houses and intense lobbying by the utility industry, whose chief spokesman was Wendell Willkie, president of Commonwealth and Southern Corporation. The House defeated the "death sentence" following lobbying so unethical that both houses of Congress called for investigation of the companies' tactics (Hugo Black conducted the hearings for the Senate). The controversy finally resulted in a compromise bill that nevertheless provided for dissolving companies that were two times removed from actual operations and gave the SEC discretionary power to dissolve others not determined to be operating in the public interest, so the attack on the size of the combinations as such remained intact.

The Revenue Act, originally intended to provide a redistribution of wealth, also evoked controversy and opposition. The president had proposed increasing inheritance taxes and graduated income taxes for the wealthy and taxes on corporations' income based on their levels of income. Senator Huey Long welcomed the proposal as an affirmation of Share Our Wealth's tenets, but harsh criticism erupted from many businessmen and newspapers, including Roosevelt's old ally William Randolph Hearst. Senator La Follette became the bill's champion in the Congress. When finally passed, however, the act had been stripped of the inheritance tax and any meaningful graduated tax on corporate incomes. It did increase the top personal income tax rate from 59 percent to 75 percent while also hiking surtaxes and estate and gift taxes, thus exacerbating a spreading enmity against the Roosevelt administration among the wealthy. By the time an exhausted Congress adjourned in August the Second New Deal had secured a huge array of new legislation, including laws dealing with soil conservation, banking (enhancement of the Federal Reserve system), and codes for coal production. Those major acts signed at the end of the session and the Wagner Act (National Labor Relations Act) of July formed the highlights—a pinnacle in the administration's social policy.

THE PACE SLACKENS

The year 1936 proved tame by contrast. Probably the major piece of legislation passed during the year was the Rural Electrification Act signed into law in

May. This legislation, introduced in the Congress by Senator George Norris and Congressman Sam Rayburn, reconstituted the Rural Electrification Administration (REA), established the year before as part of the Public Works Administration (PWA), as an independent agency and mandated that the REA's loans to fund electrification go whenever possible to nonprofit organizations rather than to private utilities. The utilities, which had resisted cooperating with the REA in bringing electricity to rural areas, strenuously fought against approval of the bill. The act's becoming law therefore constituted a further blow to the private utilities' control over the production and delivery of electric power. In a similar vein, the Walsh-Healey Public Contracts Act, which obligated all industries doing business with the federal government to adhere to NRA standards for wages, hours, and working conditions, became law in June—a response to the *Schechter* case in the effort to keep NRA principles alive. And in late February, Congress enacted the Soil Conservation and Domestic Allotment Act, based on the 1935 Soil Conservation Act, in an effort to salvage a vestige of the AAA's crop allotment program (now rendered dormant by the *Butler* case). The new conservation act created a program of payments to farmers for removing land from cultivation of major crops, such as corn and wheat, in order presumably to restore soil fertility.

Steel mill workers' houses and privies in Birmingham, Alabama, March 1936. Farm Security Administration photo by Walker Evans *(Library of Congress)*

Congressman Sam Rayburn *(Library of Congress)*

POLITICAL OPPONENTS OF THE NEW DEAL

Perhaps 1936 saw less legislative action because time was needed for the nearly revolutionary laws and programs approved in the previous year (sometimes referred to as the Second Hundred Days, as well as the Second New Deal) to take effect, but more than likely the relative calm stemmed from the fact that a presidential and congressional election loomed in November. Anticipation of the election surfaced by mid-1935, when Democratic politicians grew concerned that Huey Long posed a threat to Roosevelt's reelection. Long's Share Our Wealth clubs grew rapidly in numbers throughout 1934 and 1935, reaching a peak of perhaps 27,000 clubs with an estimated membership of 8 million, evidencing his popularity and adding to the speculation that he might mount a third-party candidacy. Jim Farley estimated that Long could poll as many as 6 million votes in a run for the presidency. But whatever potential threat Long represented ended abruptly in September 1935. While in Baton Rouge asserting his control over the state legislature, Long was killed by an assassin, Carl Austin Weiss, who shot him down at the entrance to the capitol's rotunda. Long's bodyguards responded with a fusilade that left more than 60 bullet holes in Weiss's head and body. Two days after the attack, on September 10, Long died. Gerald L. K. Smith tried to perpetuate Long's legacy, but, bereft of its charismatic leader, Share Our Wealth began to wither away.

Father Charles Coughlin, by 1935 openly hostile to the Roosevelt administration, and his National Union for Social Justice offered a different kind of threat. Long might have been considered an offbeat exponent of the American populist tradition, but Coughlin's pronouncements sounded increasingly fascist. What remained of his populism found expression in his advocacy of farm relief and inflation and in his attacks on banks and bankers; he favored government ownership of banks. These attacks also revealed Coughlin's mounting anti-Semitism. The Roosevelt administration tried to counter Coughlin's appeal by emphasizing his suspect speculations in silver futures and by assigning Hugh Johnson and Harold Ickes to denounce his ideas. Exasperated at last by Congress' failure in May 1936 to pass a bill sponsored by Representative William Lemke and Senator Lynn Frazier that would have thrown $8 billion newly minted dollars into refinancing farm mortgages, Coughlin joined in a rather curious trinity with Gerald L. K. Smith and Dr. Francis Townsend to form the Union Party. In June the party chose Lemke as its candidate for the presidency. In the meantime schism broke the Socialist Party into two camps, as about a third of the party's members split off to form the Social Democratic Federation; Norman Thomas once again was the Socialist Party candidate. The Communist Party, taking its cue from Moscow, forsook its hostility to both the New Deal and the Socialists, with party leader Earl Browder advocating something akin to a Popular Front for America in the guise of a farmer-labor party.

THE 1936 ELECTION

These varied developments meant that the Republicans would emerge as the only truly serious threat to Roosevelt's chances of winning reelection. Well before the party's national convention met in Cleveland in early June, Governor Alfred M. Landon of Kansas appeared to have the nomination locked up. The only Republican to win election as governor in a state west of the Mississippi River in 1932, Landon represented the liberal wing of his party. An admirer of Woodrow Wilson and supporter of the League of Nations, he had in fact agreed with many of the principles and programs of the New Deal, although he was an arch conservative in fiscal policy. Early on he won the support of William Randolph Hearst and his publications. And despite opposition at the convention, Landon handily gained the nomination. Frank Knox, editor of the *Chicago Daily News,* received the nomination for the vice presidency.

There was no real doubt that Roosevelt would be renominated when the Democrats met in Philadelphia later in the month, with Garner once again as his running mate. Both men presented their acceptance speeches to an effusively partisan crowd at Franklin Field on June 27. An unexpected drama occurred when the president, supported by his son James, painstakingly made his way to the podium in the glare of spotlights. Thrown off balance as he

Governor Alfred M. Landon *(Library of Congress)*

paused to shake hands with poet Edwin Markham, he tottered on his steel braces and fell, scattering the pages of his speech. Although shaken and angry, the president, helped to his feet and brushed off by his aides, recovered, shook Markham's hand, and proceeded to the podium, where with composure he presented one of the most enthusiastically received speeches of his career. It contained the still resonant line: "This generation of Americans has a rendezvous with destiny."

Among the advantages favoring Roosevelt in the election was a revived, or reviving, economy—nearly always a decisive factor for American voters. Since 1933 unemployment had fallen by about half from a peak of perhaps 13 million. Total income had also risen by more than 50 percent—advancing from nearly $40 billion in 1933 to nearly $65 billion in 1936. Corporate profits had more than doubled. And the Dow Jones Industrial Average (DJIA), a formulated combined value of 30 major stocks reflecting the stock market's overall value, had gained 80 percent during the three years. The recovery, however, made no difference to the majority of corporate leaders, who by now voiced hostility to Roosevelt, denouncing him for what they perceived to be socialistic policies combined with aggrandizement of dictatorial power in the presidency.

The American Liberty League, founded in the late summer of 1934, had become an advocacy group for this view. The league's president, Jouett Shouse,

President Franklin D. Roosevelt (holding the arm of his son James for support) speaking in Bismarck, North Dakota, during a tour of drought areas, August 1936. Farm Security Administration photo by Arthur Rothstein *(Library of Congress)*

had served as chairman of the Democratic Party Executive Committee. Other conservative Democrats supporting the league included John Jacob Raskob, former chairman of the Democratic National Committee, and Alfred E. Smith, the Democratic candidate for president in 1928. Financial backing came from prominent leaders of industry. The league's denunciations of Roosevelt became so strident as the election approached, however, that many Democrats who had become discontented with the New Deal reacted by turning against the league and returning to Roosevelt's support. A speech Smith presented at a league dinner near the end of January 1936 was particularly offensive to New Dealers, providing Roosevelt with ammunition for the campaign and leading to the league's decline from a peak membership of 125,000 as disaffected supporters abandoned the organization, which disbanded in 1940.

Street scene in Middlesboro, Kentucky, October 1935; photo by Ben Shahn *(Library of Congress)*

Coal miners on a Sunday in
Morgantown on Scott's Run, West
Virginia, October 1935; photo by
Ben Shahn *(Library of Congress)*

On the eve of the election the *Literary Digest* poll, which had accurately forecast the outcome of the 1932 election, predicted that Landon would capture 32 states with a total of 370 electoral votes and thus handily win the presidency, with Roosevelt securing only 16 states and 161 electoral votes. Polls based on statistical samplings by George Gallup and Elmo Roper, however, predicted a Roosevelt win. FDR's close political adviser Jim Farley assured the president that Landon would carry only two states, Maine and Vermont. The election day results revealed the most overwhelming victory in the nation's history to that time. As Farley had predicted, Roosevelt carried every state but Maine and Vermont, winning a record 61 percent of the popular vote and 523 electoral votes (the largest electoral college percentage since 1820) to Landon's eight. The popular vote was about 27.5 million to about 16.7 million, with Lemke receiving only 882,000 and Thomas only 187,000. The results in the congressional elections registered the same outcome: The Democrats would hold huge majorities of 333 seats to the Republicans' 88 in the House and 75 to 16 in the Senate. A chastened Father Coughlin announced his withdrawal from politics.

THE SPANISH CIVIL WAR AND OTHER THREATS

The election results no doubt reflected Americans' general satisfaction with New Deal domestic policies, but they probably also revealed approval of Roosevelt's public assurances of the government's desire to find means of precluding U.S. involvement in wars overseas. During the third and fourth years of his first term Roosevelt became increasingly concerned over the direction of events in Europe and Asia, where the potential for large-scale war appeared to be growing. Most obvious was the increasing menace posed by Germany, as Hitler pursued massive rearmament in violation of the Treaty of Versailles. But the governments of France and Great Britain adopted a policy of restraint toward Hitler on the grounds that the chancellor could eventually be brought round to securing a peaceful Europe—after all, in his public pronouncements he stressed Germany's desire for peace. And although Roosevelt sought to conceive ways of attaining a collective security that might contain the German threat, his efforts evoked indifference from the leaders of France and Great Britain and contempt from Hitler, who perceived Roosevelt as restrained by American isolationist sentiment. In March 1935, Hitler renounced the Treaty of Versailles, publicly announced creation of the Luftwaffe (air force), and decreed mandatory military service, with the goal of creating a peacetime army numbering nearly half a million. And in March 1936, German troops occupied the Rhineland.

These blatant treaty violations elicited ineffectual responses from the French and British governments, which also took a noncommittal attitude toward Italy's menacing of Ethiopia. France and Great Britain did initially involve Italy in efforts to isolate Germany, but their final payoff to Italy became, in effect, to acquiesce in the conquest of Ethiopia. Italian troops invaded the African nation in October 1935 and completed the conquest the following May. As if intent on further tweaking the British and French, Mussolini allied himself with Hitler in late October 1936 to form the Rome-Berlin Axis. Following the rebellion of Spanish troops in July 1936 against the republican government in Madrid, the Axis hastened to support the Spanish rebels, led by General Francisco Franco. Both powers recognized the legitimacy of Franco's Nationalist government in October. As the civil war in Spain proceeded, the Germans provided Franco tanks, armaments, and air support (the Condor Legion), and Italy sent armaments and more than 60,000 troops. Thus the Spanish civil war began to shape itself into something like a dress rehearsal for a larger war.

As for the democracies, the British persuaded the French to join in a policy of noninvolvement, with the French sealing their common border with Spain to cut off arms shipments and both nations thereby evidencing their desire to conciliate Hitler and Mussolini. All the U.S. government could offer in response was the Neutrality Acts, which prohibited transport of armaments to belligerent nations on American vessels and authorized the president to deny protection to Americans who traveled on the ships of nations involved in war. Powerful isolationist blocs in both houses of Congress opposed American intervention of any sort. Proposals to create an economic embargo—on shipments of oil to Italy, for example—evoked no support from Roosevelt or among the other democratic nations' governments.

NEUTRALITY AND NONINVOLVEMENT

These policies of nonintervention, noninvolvement, and neutrality rested easily with the American people as a whole; the isolationists in Congress knew their constituencies. Roosevelt did gain the funds and authority to pursue a program of shipbuilding in order to slowly expand the U.S. fleet in the Pacific—even the Japanese government had no objection to that. But any overt effort he might make to persuade the American people that developments in Europe and Asia suggested it would be prudent to prepare for war, or at least for self-defense, appeared not simply futile but politically suicidal. If anything, the Nye committee findings on the shadiness of war profiteering by armaments makers during the Great War of 1914–18 reinforced the prevalent view that war was a nasty business the United States should forgo the next time: let the Europeans deal with their problems while Americans carried on in Fortress America, protected by the wide expanses of the Atlantic and Pacific Oceans.

Roosevelt nevertheless tried to sound warnings whenever possible. While on a 3,000-mile trip through the West begun in September 1935, the president visited the San Diego Exposition. There on October 2, the same day Mussolini gave the orders to invade Ethiopia, he presented the final speech of his tour and warned of the dangers of impending war. The next day he underscored the need for the nation to bolster its defenses by boarding the USS *Houston* out of San Diego harbor to witness naval exercises—the first president ever to do so. Roosevelt also intently pursued ensuring the security of the American hemisphere, which he genuinely feared might become vulnerable to a determined Hitler. He continually expounded the Good Neighbor policy, which became a priority in 1936 when Roosevelt fostered the Inter-American Conference dedicated to discussing means of safeguarding peace in the hemisphere and to inspiring a similar conference in Europe. The Inter-American Conference convened in Buenos Aires, Argentina, in December 1936, and Roosevelt's attendance in person was intended as a message to both Germany and Japan. The foreign powers did not get the message, however, nor did the people of the United States, where newspaper played up the throngs and fetes that greeted the president on various stops during his voyage to the South American country rather than the political implication of the conference.

HOLLYWOOD REIGNS

The American people, in looking inward to resolve the distresses of the depression and to avoid the problems besetting other nations, had numerous attractions—again, some have suggested escapes—to choose among. But none compared to the allure of film. The thirties marked Hollywood's golden age. During the decade, the studios produced more than 5,000 feature-length films. Americans flocked to the theaters in astonishing numbers despite the deprivations of the depression, purchasing 60 to 80 million tickets weekly. Film genres that had emerged from Hollywood at the beginning of the decade continued their popularity in mid-decade and beyond. For example, gangster films remained popular, with stars like Edward G. Robinson and James Cagney—who portrayed hardened criminals in earlier films—now sometimes in the roles of police officers or FBI agents and sometimes still portraying hardened criminals. This was the period of director Frank Capra's greatest popularity: In 1936 he gave moviegoers *Mr. Deeds Goes to Town,* in which the hero, played by Gary Cooper, is a decent common man whose humane values contrast sharply with those of the film's villain, a rapacious businessman. A similar juxtaposition of values occurred in that year's possibly most memorable film, Charlie Chaplin's *Modern Times.* Chaplin portrayed his classic little tramp character confounded by an industrialized society in which machines rule humans, despotic executives tout an inhuman efficiency, the helpless unemployed starve, children become destitute and orphaned, and the American Dream appears a mockery.

Some movies, of course, offered no message, providing simply fun and romance; for example, in their 1936 hit *Swing Time,* Fred Astaire and Ginger

This photo by Walker Evans shows Main Street in Macon, Georgia, March 1936. *(Library of Congress)*

Rogers still danced through a wealthy world unreal to most. The Marx Brothers, the great comedy team success of the decade, produced the popular *A Night at the Opera* in 1935. Another comedy team, Stan Laurel and Oliver Hardy, already a success in the silent movie era, continued their film antics. In fact, a raft of comedians entertained audiences at the movies in these years— W. C. Fields, Will Rogers, Jimmy Durante, Marie Dressler, Bob Hope. Mystery movies and thrillers were also successful. Alfred Hitchcock produced three thrillers in 1935–36: *The 39 Steps, Secret Agent,* and *Woman Alone.* Also noteworthy, in 1935 appeared the first feature-length movie filmed in Technicolor, *Becky Sharp,* directed by Rouben Mamoulian.

In the field of literature some familiar names maintained a certain prominence. In 1936 another of William Faulkner's masterpieces, *Absalom, Absalom!,* was published. That same year one of the most popular books in American history appeared, the blockbuster *Gone with the Wind,* Margaret Mitchell's only novel, which became a best-seller not only during 1936 but ever since. A new proletarian protest literature that emerged from the travails of the Great Depression, with a focus on labor strife, found a strong voice in

John Steinbeck's short novel *In Dubious Battle*, published in 1936; Steinbeck had already gained some renown with his 1935 novel about Mexican laborers, *Tortilla Flat*. Proletarian themes had come to the stage as well, notably in Clifford Odets's 1935 drama *Waiting for Lefty*, with its advocacy for the working class. International recognition of the achievement and stature of serious American drama occurred in 1936 when the Nobel Prize in literature was awarded to Eugene O'Neill—the second American to be so honored. Currently playing in New York City were productions of Lillian Hellman's *The Children's Hour*, which had opened in fall 1934; Robert Sherwood's *Idiot's Delight*, starring Alfred Lunt and Lynn Fontanne; Langston Hughes's *Mulatto;* George Bernard Shaw's *Saint Joan*, starring Katherine Cornell; and Laurence Housman's *Victoria Regina*, with Helen Hayes, who played the queen, and Vincent Price.

Listening to the radio remained a shared passion nationwide. Ventriloquist Edgar Bergen with his dummy Charlie McCarthy debuted on Rudy Vallee's *The Fleischmann Hour* in December 1936 to instant and durable success, joining the likes of the already well-established Fred Allen, George Burns and Gracie Allen, and Jack Benny. Major Edward Bowes's *Original Amateur Hour* entered the airwaves in 1935 as another vehicle for introducing new talent to listeners, although except for Frank Sinatra and Beverly Sills, the talent remained amateur. And in sports broadcasting, long a staple of radio, Walter "Red" Barber, perhaps the greatest baseball announcer in broadcast history, was now established as the voice of the Cincinnati Reds (in 1939 he would move to New York to cover the Brooklyn Dodgers).

Another nationally shared passion, perhaps especially noteworthy because of its seeming incongruity with hard times, the newspaper comic strip, or the comics (popularly called "the funnies"), experienced a golden era following the depression's onset. Although the first comics appeared in the 1890s (notably the *Yellow Kid* and the *Katzenjammer Kids*), they had not become a fully established American phenomenon until about 1920 and following, with such strips as *Gasoline Alley* (1919), *Popeye* (1919), *Winnie Winkle* (1920), *Little Orphan Annie* (1924), *Tarzan* (1929), and others—some intended as depictions of reality and others presenting satire, parody, or fantasy. But during the 1930s the comics greatly increased in both numbers and subjects, now including science and space fiction, detective adventures, domestic comedy, and drama; some incorporated major innovations, with ongoing story lines and the adaptation of cinematic techniques. Chic Young's social comedy *Blondie* first appeared in 1930; Chester Gould's detective strip *Dick Tracy*, in 1931; Alex Raymond's space fantasy *Flash Gordon*, in 1933; Milton Caniff's adventure tale *Terry and the Pirates* and Al Capp's southern satire *Li'l Abner*, both in 1934.

The funnies inspired the 1933 advent of comic books as presentations of aggregate strips. By 1935 comic books came into their own and thereafter spawned such specialized offerings as *Detective Comics* (1937) and *Action Comics* (1938), the latter notable as the birthplace of *Superman*. These varied comic strips and books both reflected and reinforced prevalent American cultural norms. Reading them constituted a shared experience for Americans from coast to coast. With this experience they imbibed reassurances of democratic ideals, long-term economic opportunities, and freedoms afforded to

the majority—as well, of course, as the inevitable ultimate triumph of good over evil. Many of the comic strips and books of the era, like the movies, may be adjudged mediums of escape from pressing problems. But as the Japanese marauded in China and menace intensified in Europe, a number of comic strip creators in effect sent their characters to war, thereby helping to prepare American readers for an impending deeper involvement in overseas events. Some science fiction strips even proved prescient: For example, *Buck Rogers,* which first appeared in 1929, presented its title character talking about an "atomic bomb" in 1939. The funnies of the 1930s, then, clearly conveyed themes that often belied the humor evinced in their popular name.

THE 1936 OLYMPICS

Despite economic woes, the modern Olympiad, a revival of the ancient games initiated in 1896, with winter games added in 1924, continued through the depression years. One of the most dramatic sports events of the depression decade occurred at the 1936 Olympic Games held in Berlin. The great American track athlete Jesse Owens, who had set or equaled six world records while on the Ohio State University track team (100-yard dash, 220-yard dash, 220-yard high hurdles, broad jump, 100-meter run, and 200-meter run) won four gold medals. Owens and nine other African-American athletes competed at the Berlin Olympics, and nine of them won gold medals. Disgusted at such an exhibition of athletic prowess that shattered the notion of Aryan superiority, Hitler left the stadium before the awards ceremony. Although Americans generally applauded this Olympic triumph, the irony is that Owens and his black compatriots would return to a homeland where they had little hope of obtaining equality of opportunity. Although Eleanor Roosevelt staunchly advocated civil rights for blacks, the president made no move toward accommodating blacks' aspirations or providing federal support for eliminating the discriminatory Jim Crow laws or other barriers—presumably out of anxiety over the prospect of losing the Democratic Party's power bases in the South.

PROGRESS AGAINST THE DEPRESSION

The administration had achieved some real gains in the struggle against the depression. By 1936, the economy showed genuine signs of revival. Unemployment had declined to about 13 percent of the workforce as opposed to nearly 25 percent in 1933; the GNP had recovered to a per capita level of $650

This photo by Walker Evans shows a street in the black section of Tupelo, Mississippi, March 1936. *(Library of Congress)*

This photo by Arthur Rothstein shows a hobo jungle in St. Louis, Missouri, March 1936. *(Library of Congress)*

(it had stood at $619 in 1930 and only $485 in 1933); and production had doubled since 1932 (this increase was due in great part to technological advances, however). Of course, it remained arguable whether these gains resulted from New Deal programs or a cyclical rebound or some other cause. Despite the signs of recovery, the depression was certainly far from over: 3.5 million people received some form of relief, and 9 million remained unemployed, with many factories still closed or on reduced production schedules. Roosevelt and the New Dealers would, nevertheless, take credit for the economic improvements—it was an election year, after all—and the president's enormous win against Landon would convince him that he had the strong support of the people and thus a clear-cut mandate for whatever policy changes he wished to make. He would carry that conviction into the new year.

CHRONICLE OF EVENTS

1935

January 17: In *Panama Refining Company v. Ryan,* known as the "hot oil" case, the Supreme Court decides by an 8-1 vote that Section 9(c) of the National Industrial Recovery Act (NIRA) improperly grants legislative power to the executive branch of the federal government. This section provides the president authority to prohibit interstate transportation of oil in amounts exceeding those permitted under state laws—a means of limiting production, an NIRA goal.

January 17: The president sends a message to Congress requesting legislation to provide a social security system.

January 27: In accordance with the terms of the Treaty of Versailles, a plebiscite is held in the Saar region to determine whether the inhabitants want to join Germany, remain under the administration of the League of Nations, or join France. More than 90 percent of those voting choose joining Germany.

February 18: In three suits known as the "gold cases," the Supreme Court decides by a vote of 5-4 that a law passed by Congress in 1933 voiding the federal government's obligation to redeem government bonds in gold (substituting instead legal tender currency) is unconstitutional but that bondholders have no right to sue for reimbursement.

February 22: President Roosevelt signs into law the Connally Act, which prohibits the shipment of "hot oil"—that is, oil produced in excess of state production codes—thus, in a more carefully worded act, restoring the federal government's oil policy formerly outlined in Section 9(c) of the NIRA.

March 1: The Saar region rejoins Germany.

March 12: Roosevelt sends a message to Congress requesting legislation to regulate utility holding companies.

March 9: Hitler announces the creation of the Luftwaffe (German air force).

March 16: Hitler decrees a law providing for universal military service and creation of a peacetime army of about 500,000. The Reich has been secretly rearming, as France and Great Britain know, but with this law Hitler openly and blatantly defies provisions of the Treaty of Versailles.

March 17: The League of Nations intervention to resolve a dispute over a part of Ethiopia's border with Somalia (an Italian possession) that had been requested by Emperor Haile Selassie of Ethiopia reaches an impasse, and the League turns the issue over to Great Britain and France for resolution.

March 19: Roosevelt requests that the Senate Special Committee Investigating the Munitions Industry, chaired by Senator Gerald P. Nye, draft legislation providing for U.S. neutrality.

April 8: Roosevelt signs into law the Emergency Relief Appropriations Act, providing $4.8 billion to create jobs through public works projects.

April 13: Roosevelt signs into law the Johnson Act, which forbids loans by private firms or the government to nations that have defaulted on war loans to the United States government.

April 19: The House of Representatives, by a vote of 371-33, passes the Social Security Bill.

April 27: Roosevelt signs the Soil Conservation Act, authorizing policies and expenditures to combat soil erosion and creating the Soil Conservation Service, in response to the Dust Bowl.

April 30: By executive order, Roosevelt creates the Resettlement Administration with the purpose of moving impoverished farmers off of worn-out lands and resettling them in areas of fertile soil and providing them with equipment and guidance for undertaking proper farming techniques. He places Rexford Guy Tugwell in charge of the program.

May 6: In the case of *Railroad Retirement Board v. Alton Railroad Co.,* the Supreme Court decides by a 5-4 vote that the Railroad Retirement Act of 1934 is unconstitutional on the grounds that the pensions it mandates exceed the authority of the interstate commerce clause while also violating the Fifth Amendment.

May 6: By executive order Roosevelt establishes the Works Progress Administration (WPA) as the vehicle for overseeing the public works projects mandated by the Emergency Relief Appropriations Act. He places Harry Hopkins in charge.

May 11: By executive order Roosevelt establishes the Rural Electrification Administration as part of the public works program and places Morris Cooke in charge.

May 16: The Senate passes the pro–workers rights Wagner Bill by a vote of 53-12.

May 21: Hitler makes a major speech to the Reichstag, repeatedly proclaiming Germany's desire for peace and renouncing any territorial or other claims concerning France, Poland, and Austria.

May 27: In the landmark case of *A. L. A. Schechter Poultry Corporation v. United States,* referred to as the "sick chicken" case, the Supreme Court, in a unanimous decision, invalidates the NIRA, saying it is an unconstitutional extension of federal authority into intrastate commerce and grants legislative powers to the executive branch of the federal government.

May 31: During a press conference Roosevelt deplores the Supreme Court's decision in the *Schechter* case as a "horse-and-buggy definition of interstate commerce" that hamstrings the government's ability to provide assistance to any group, including business.

June 7: In preparation for November elections, the National coalition government of Great Britain is reorganized, with Stanley Baldwin replacing Ramsay MacDonald, now in failing health, as prime minister.

June 18: The British and German governments reach an agreement limiting naval armaments.

June 19: The House of Representatives passes the Wagner Bill. The Senate, by a vote of 76-6, passes the Social Security Bill. Roosevelt sends a message to Congress requesting legislation imposing higher graduated taxes on the wealthy and on corporations.

June 26: By executive order Roosevelt creates the National Youth Administration within the WPA to provide work grants so that students can continue their educations and to provide temporary jobs for unemployed youths.

July 5: Roosevelt signs the Wagner Act (the National Labor Relations Act) into law. The act awards workers the right to organize and to join unions for collective bargaining purposes, unimpeded by employers; in addition it reestablishes the National Labor Relations Board as an independent agency to conduct elections by workers choosing a collective bargaining agent and to ensure that employers do not engage in "unfair labor practices."

July 14: In response to the threat of fascism and after months of negotiations, the leaders of France's Socialist, Communist, and Radical Parties—Léon Blum, Maurice Thorez, and Édouard Daladier—march together in the Bastille Day parade in Paris, officially sealing their joining together to form the Popular Front.

August 2: The WPA establishes the Federal Art Project, the Federal Theatre Project, the Federal Music Project, and the Federal Writers' Project.

August 12: By executive order Roosevelt creates a new Electric Home and Farm Authority (EHFA),

replacing the previous EHFA; the agency's purpose is to provide financing for the purchase of electrical appliances, especially in rural areas.

August 15: Roosevelt signs into law the Social Security Act, which creates a national system of old-age insurance designed to provide workers over 65 with retirement annuities based on the levels of their previous earnings and paid for by taxes on wages. The act also establishes an unemployment insurance program but leaves its organization and administration to the separate states.

August 23: Roosevelt signs the Banking Act of 1935 into law. The act authorizes the president to appoint seven members of the new board of governors of the Federal Reserve System, each for a term of 14 years; gives the board authority to approve the chief officers of regional banks in the system; provides the board with greater authority over discount rates and reserve requirements; establishes a Federal Open Market Committee of seven board members and five bank members of the system to oversee open market operations; and requires all large state banks to join the system by July 1942 if they wish to participate in the Federal Deposit Insurance Corporation (FDIC) system.

August 27: The first session of the 74th Congress adjourns.

August 28: Roosevelt signs into law the Public Utility Holding Company Act, which disbands utility holding companies two steps removed from actual operating companies and empowers the Securities and Exchange Commission (SEC) to eliminate large utilities that are not operating in the public interest and to supervise the financial transactions of utilities.

August 30: Roosevelt signs into law the Guffey-Snyder Bituminous Coal Stabilization Act, which guarantees collective bargaining for miners, mandates uniform wages and hours, establishes a national commission to set prices and control production levels, provides for closing marginal mines, and creates a tax on production to support rehabilitating laid-off miners. The president also signs into law the Wealth Tax Act (or Revenue Act of 1935), which increases taxes on estates, gifts, and capital stock; sets up an excess profits tax for corporations; and hikes the surtax level.

August 31: Roosevelt signs into law a first Neutrality Act, which imposes a mandatory six-month embargo against shipment of arms to belligerents, granting the president authority to define what are "implements of war" and to decide when an embargo should take effect; it also empowers the president to prohibit shipment in U.S. ships of war materials to belligerents and to deny protection to American citizens traveling aboard ships of belligerent nations.

September 8: Following a day of overseeing the work of the Louisiana legislature in the capitol in Baton Rouge, Huey Long leaves the building's rotunda, headed for the governor's office, when Carl Austin Weiss steps from the shadows and shoots him in the stomach. Long's bodyguards kill Weiss and rush the senator to the hospital.

September 10: Huey Long dies.

September 15: The Hitler government institutes the so-called Nuremberg Laws, which strip Jews of German citizenship and forbid marriage or extramarital relations between Jews and Aryans.

October 2: While on a tour in the West, the president presents a speech at the San Diego Exposition in which he warns of the growing threat of war overseas and pledges to maintain U.S. neutrality.

October 3: After rejecting a proposal by Great Britain and France that would actually result in Ethiopia's becoming a protectorate of Italy as a reso-

lution of the Ethiopia-Somaliland border dispute, Italy invades Ethiopia from Somalia and Eritria. Under the authority of the Neutrality Act, President Roosevelt bans the shipment of arms to either side.

November 14: The National coalition government wins reelection in Great Britain.

November 16: The WPA establishes the Historical Records Survey to make inventories of local government records nationwide.

December 8: British foreign minister Sir Samuel Hoare and French premier Pierre Laval sign an agreement offering Italy the cession of large parts of Ethiopia.

December 18: Public outrage in Great Britain over the terms that Hoare and Laval have offered to Italy concerning Ethiopia forces Hoare's resignation.

1936

January 6: The Supreme Court announces the decision (a vote of 6–3) in *United States v. Butler et al.,* declaring unconstitutional the taxes imposed on processors of farm products by the Agricultural Adjustment Administration.

Families of evicted sharecroppers in Parkin, Louisiana, January 1936. *(Library of Congress)*

January 19: Pierre Laval loses majority support in parliament and resigns as premier of France.

January 20: King George V of Great Britain dies. The Prince of Wales succeeds to the throne as Edward VIII.

January 25: At an American Liberty League dinner in Washington, D.C., attended by 2,000 people, former Democratic presidential candidate Al Smith delivers a speech containing such extreme condemnation of Roosevelt that support for the league begins to dwindle in reaction.

February 10: The Hitler government institutes a law forbidding the courts to interfere with the activities of the Gestapo (secret state police), placing the Gestapo above the law and sanctioning whatever actions it takes.

February 17: The Supreme Court announces the decision (an 8–1 vote) in the case of *Ashwander et al. v. Tennessee Valley Authority.* The decision affirms the right of minority stockholders in a public utility to bring suit against corporate officers who cooperate with the Tennessee Valley Authority's (TVA) policies and thereby challenge the terms of federal law. At the same time, the decision affirms the constitutional authority of the TVA to operate and to distribute power from the Wilson Dam.

February 29: Roosevelt signs into law a second Neutrality Act that extends the provisions of the first act by an additional 14 months and mandates that the president expand any embargo to include nations that enter a war already in progress; the act also prohibits making loans to belligerent nations. The president also signs the Soil Conservation and Domestic Allotment Act, a response to the Supreme Court's *United States v. Butler et al.* decision. The act provides payments to farmers who plant clover, soybeans, and other crops that restore soil fertility in place of commercial crops, such as wheat and corn, that deplete the soil.

March 7: German troops cross the border and begin the occupation of the Rhineland, which by the terms of the Treaty of Versailles and the Locarno Pact is supposed to remain permanently demilitarized.

March 29: In a German national plebiscite, 98.7 percent of the voters approve Hitler's foreign policies.

April 3: Following an unsuccessful appeal and other delays, Bruno Hauptmann is electrocuted in Trenton, New Jersey, for the kidnapping and murder of the Lindbergh baby.

April 6: In the case of *Jones v. Securities and Exchange Commission* the Supreme Court 6–3 decision calls into question the commission's administrative policies but does not challenge the SEC's constitutionality. The SEC's mandate is to regulate the stock market and protect investors.

April 18: Louis Howe, the president's long-standing and most trusted personal and political adviser, dies after an extended illness.

May 5: Italian troops enter Addis Ababa, the capital of Ethiopia.

May 9: Having conquered Ethiopia, Mussolini announces in Rome that King Victor Emmanuel of Italy is now emperor of the African nation.

May 18: In *Carter v. Carter Coal Company* the Supreme Court decides that the entire Guffey-Snyder Bituminous Coal Stabilization Act of 1935 is unconstitutional, even though only a small part of the act, dealing with pricing and fair trade, is under challenge in this suit.

May 20: Roosevelt signs into law the Rural Electrification Act, which makes the Rural Electrification Administration (REA) a separate agency, not part of the relief or public works programs, and establishes the principle that the REA's loans to bring electricity to farms should preferably go to nonprofit agencies.

May 25: The Supreme Court rules the Municipal Bankruptcy Act invalid as an infringement of the states' right to deal with cities—the act permitted municipalities to seek debt readjustments in federal bankruptcy courts when so authorized by state laws.

June 1: In *Morehead v. Tipaldo,* the Supreme Court (again by a 5–4 vote) invalidates a New York State law that establishes a minimum wage for women.

June 5: Following elections in May in which the Popular Front won 57 percent of the vote and 386 seats out of 608 in the parliament, Léon Blum, leader of the Socialist Party (the largest group in the Popular Front), becomes premier of France. Blum is the first Socialist and the first Jew ever to hold the office.

June 11: The Republican National Convention meeting in Cleveland, Ohio, nominates Alfred M. Landon, governor of Kansas, as the party's candidate for the presidency. Colonel Frank Knox is the vice presidential nominee.

June 19: Republican congressman William Lemke of North Dakota announces his candidacy for the presidency as the nominee of the Union Party recent-

The home and family of a Utah coal miner, near Price, Utah, shown in a photo by Dorothea Lange, March 1936. *(Library of Congress, Prints and Photographs Division [USF34-T01-9009-C])*

ly formed by Father Coughlin, Gerald L. K. Smith, and members of Dr. Townsend's movement.

June 20: Roosevelt signs into law the Robinson-Patman Act (Federal Anti-Price Discrimination Act), which prohibits wholesalers or manufacturers from providing rebates or discounts to large buyers such as chain stores.

June 22: Roosevelt signs into law the Revenue Act of 1936, which imposes moderate graduated taxes on the undistributed earnings of corporations.

June 22: The Democratic National Convention convenes in Philadelphia to renominate Roosevelt and Garner.

June 26: Roosevelt signs into law the Oklahoma Indian Welfare Act, which extends the terms of the Indian Reorganization Act of 1934 to Oklahoma Indians.

June 27: Roosevelt delivers a dramatic speech accepting the Democratic nomination for the presi-

dency before a crowd of more than 100,000 assembled in the Franklin Field stadium in Philadelphia; the speech contains the resonant and long-remembered phrase of Americans having "a rendezvous with destiny."

June 30: Emperor Haile Selassie appears before the League of Nations in Geneva to advocate support for Ethiopia's resistance to Italy.

June 30: Roosevelt signs into law the Walsh-Healey Public Contracts Act, which stipulates that all industries having contracts with the federal government must adhere to the standards for wages, hours, and working conditions that had been established by the National Recovery Administration (NRA).

July 4: The League of Nations officially cancels the sanctions imposed against Italy following the invasion of Ethiopia, in effect accepting the Italian conquest.

July 16: Reacting to political chaos and street fighting between right-wing and left-wing groups in Spain since the victory of the leftists in the February election, General Francisco Franco stages a military revolt in Morocco. (He was in command of Spanish troops on the Canary Islands, announced the revolt, and flew to Morocco to lead that garrison in invading Spain.)

July 17: Military garrisons throughout Spain join Franco's rebellion, marking the beginning of the Spanish civil war.

August 8: Bowing to pressure from the government of Great Britain—which has declared that if French support of the Loyalists against Franco's Nationalists in the Spanish civil war leads to war between Germany and France, Great Britain will not support France—the French government closes the border with Spain to any shipments of arms.

October 21: In Berlin the German and Italian foreign ministers sign a secret protocol committing the two nations to pursue a common policy in foreign affairs.

October 24: Germany and Italy agree to recognize the government established by the Nationalists (Franco's forces) in Burgos, Spain.

October 31: Roosevelt concludes his presidential campaign with a rousing speech at New York City's Madison Square Garden that contains a slashing attack on the "organized money" that opposes him.

This photo by Arthur Rothstein shows mountain people in Garrett County, Maryland, 1936. *(Library of Congress)*

November 1: In a public statement Mussolini refers for the first time to a Rome-Berlin "Axis" as a new force in European affairs.

November 3: Election results give Roosevelt a record victory, as he carries every state but Maine and Vermont and wins virtually 61 percent of the popular vote and 523 electoral votes to only eight for Landon.

Democrats also secure enormous majorities in Congress: 333 to 88 in the House and 75 to 16 in the Senate. Minority parties secured 16 House seats and four Senate seats.

November 25: In Berlin representatives of the German and Japanese governments sign the Anti-Comintern Pact, agreeing not to conclude any treaties with the USSR without mutual consent and to consult on how to respond if the USSR attacks one or the other nation.

December 1: Having traveled to South America aboard a cruiser to attend a conference of 21 Latin American nations, President Roosevelt opens the conference in Buenos Aires, Argentina.

December 5: The Eighth All-Union Congress of the Soviets approves a new constitution (replacing the 1924 constitution) for the Soviet Union drafted by a committee headed by Stalin; the new constitution grants universal suffrage to all citizens over 18.

December 11: In a dramatic radio broadcast to the British people and the world, King Edward VIII announces his abdication from the throne.

December 12: The Duke of York succeeds to the throne of Great Britain as George VI; he grants the title duke of Windsor to the former king.

EYEWITNESS TESTIMONY

It was a strangely altered world in which the former lords of creation now found themselves. The economic initiative had definitely passed from Wall Street to Washington—at least for the time being—and many of their one-time instruments of power had been blunted or taken away from them.

The House of Morgan, for example, was now no longer permitted to issue securities; it was simply a bank of deposit. Other private banking houses, too, had been compelled to make the choice between deposit banking and investment banking; most of them—including Kuhn, Loeb & Co. and Dillon, Read & Co.—had chosen to issue securities and forego deposits....

Yet it is curious to note the extent to which the fundamental trend toward concentration of economic power was continuing. The big corporations were relatively stronger than ever before. In 1929 the 200 biggest corporations in the country had controlled ... some 49 per cent of all non-financial corporate wealth. By the beginning of 1932 ... the proportion had increased to about 55 per cent.

Frederick Lewis Allen, from his book The Lords of Creation *(1935).*

In the past, wars have frequently helped to break the economic deadlock of depressions. This has been because they have called for large expenditures by governments for munitions, equipment and supplies. This has stimulated trade and revived employment, and it has been made possible because people will gladly give to governments enormous sums for the prosecution of war and for the destruction of their fellow men which they will not permit that government to spend for constructive aid to themselves. It is also true that wars have indeed frequently grown out of depressions and have been used both consciously and unconsciously by peoples and by governments as a means of getting out of the tragic dilemma of wide-scale unemployment. Professor M. H. Cochran is, indeed, largely right when he maintains that in recent times wars have been started by governments more to quiet discontent at home than because the foreign conflicts of interest between nations become insoluble, and that war is made to serve as a political red herring to divert people's minds from the internal issues which concern and

divide them.... Finally, the high emotional tension which a depression creates is also conducive to war, which temporarily at least clears the air and creates for a time a more or less united front among the people.

Paul H. Douglas, then professor of economics at the University of Chicago and later U.S. senator from Illinois, from his book Controlling Depressions *(1935).*

NRA came as a blessed alleviation of the dog-eat-dog rule of the Antitrust Acts. This does not mean that there is no competition or even any improper limitation of competition under NRA. It means only that competition must keep its blows above the belt, and that there can be no competition at the expense of decent living. The only price limitations in NRA, outside of three (or at most four) special cases, are limitations against making a practice of selling at less than cost of production for the purpose of destroying competition or of preventing competition based on the degradation of human labor.

Administrator of the National Recovery Administration (NRA) General Hugh S. Johnson, in The Blue Eagle from Egg to Earth *(1935).*

The church is in bondage to capitalism. Capitalism in its contemporary form is more than a system of ownership and distribution of economic goods. It is a faith and a way of life. It is faith in wealth as the source of all life's blessings and as the savior of man from his deepest misery. It is the doctrine that man's most important activity is the production of economic goods and that all other things are dependent upon this. On the basis of this initial idolatry it develops a morality in which economic worth becomes the standard by which to measure all other values and the economic virtues take precedence over courage, temperance, wisdom and justice, over charity, humility and fidelity. Hence nature, love, life, truth, beauty and justice are exploited or made the servants of the high economic good. Everything, including the lives of workers, is made a utility, is desecrated and ultimately destroyed.

H. Richard Niebuhr, clergyman, in The Church Against the World *(1935).*

The movies, however ... have a weekly attendance of 77,000,000 people in the United States, with

28,000,000 under twenty-one and 11,000,000 thirteen and under. These minors average an attendance of at least once a week and in many cases, two, three, four and more times a week. Scarcely surprising that movies change the manners and affect the mores. . . .

Similarly, large percentages of girl inmates in an institution for sex delinquents rightly or wrongly attribute to the movies a leading place in stimulating cravings for an easy life, for luxury, for cabarets, roadhouses and wild parties, for having men make love to them and, ultimately, for their particular delinquency. Male adolescents, likewise, testify to using certain types of movies as excitants for arousing and stimulating the passions of girls. . . . As a mass form of entertainment this obviously has social consequences highly undesirable.

Henry James Forman, in Our Movie Made Children *(1935).*

But this was the reason why these things could never be forgotten—because we are so lost, so naked and so lonely in America. Immense and cruel skies bend over us, and all of us are driven on forever and we have no home . . . and all of our lives is written in the twisting of a leaf upon a bough, a door that opened, and a stone.

For America has a thousand lights and weathers and we walk the streets, we walk the streets forever, we walk the streets of life alone. . . .

It is a fabulous country, the only fabulous country; it is the one place where miracles not only happen, but where they happen all the time.

Thomas Wolfe, in his novel Of Time and the River *(1935).*

Radio, used to its full technical and scientific capacity, and guided by wise and far-reaching vision, would be a valuable instrument for bringing the world to a new international understanding and technique. . . . The written and spoken word will be immensely powerful in this regard. . . . And in this whole matter of building up a far-reaching international understanding, music could play a clarifying and inspiring part. By bringing East and West into touch with each other, radio can endlessly stimulate the flow of ideas and the expression of life in art.

Leopold Stokowski, conductor of the Philadelphia Orchestra, in the Atlantic Monthly *(January 1935).*

Well, ladies and gentlemen, America, all the people of America have been invited to a barbecue. God invited us all to come and eat and drink all we wanted. He smiled on our land and we grew crops of plenty to eat and wear. He showed us in the earth the iron and other things to make everything we wanted. He unfolded to us the secrets of science so that our work might be easy. God called: "Come to my feast."

Then what happened? Rockefeller, Morgan, and their crowd stepped up and took enough for 120 million people and left only enough for 5 million for all the other 125 million to eat. And so many millions must go hungry and without these good things God gave us unless we call on them to put some of it back.

Senator Huey Long of Louisiana, advocating his Share Our Wealth program, radio broadcast of January 1935, in the Congressional Record.

Please Mrs. Roosevelt, I do not want charity, only a chance from someone who will trust me until we can get enough money to repay the amount spent for the things I need. As a proof that I am really sincere, I am sending you two of my dearest possessions to keep as security, a ring my husband gave me before we were married, and a ring my mother used to wear. . . . If you will consider buying the baby clothes, please keep them [rings] until I send you the money you spent. It is very hard to face bearing a baby we cannot afford to have . . . and still there is no money for the hospital or clothing.

Pregnant housewife in Troy, New York, letter of January 2, 1935, to Eleanor Roosevelt, in McElvaine, Down and Out in the Great Depression: Letters from the "Forgotten Man" *(1983).*

The work itself will cover a wide field, including clearance of slums, which for adequate reasons cannot be undertaken by private capital; in rural housing of several kinds, where, again, private capital is unable to function; in rural electrification; in the reforestation of the great watersheds of the nation; in an intensified program to prevent soil erosion and to reclaim blighted areas; in improving existing road systems and in constructing national highways designed to handle modern traffic; in the elimination of grade crossings; in the extension and enlargement of the successful work of the Civilian Conservation Corps; in nonfederal work, mostly self-liquidating and highly useful to local divisions of government; and on many other projects which the nation needs and cannot afford to neglect.

President Franklin D. Roosevelt outlining his proposals for the Second New Deal, message to Congress, January 4, 1935, in the Congressional Record *(1935).*

Expect nothing fancy and look for no miracles from Listerine Tooth Paste. It won't cure pyorrhea. It won't correct acid mouth. It won't revitalize your gums. It will, however, clean your teeth better than ordinary dentrifices and at a surprising saving of time and money. Millions of people have found these homely virtues to be worthwhile.

Advertisement for Listerine Tooth Paste, in the Saturday Evening Post *(January 5, 1935).*

The third possibility—joint action of government and business, with the government representing not only the public interest but also the specific interests of labor and consumer groups—would probably provide the most effective available method for getting the interests of the nondominant economic groups represented in the immediate future.

On the other hand, the government would thereby be placed in the position of playing a dual role. In behalf of the public interest it should act as arbiter between conflicting interests; as representative of labor and consumer interests it should play a partisan role. It would be most difficult for the government to perform this partisan role, for it would be constantly under pressure from business, the strongest of the economic interest groups . . . and even if this present administration . . . succeeded in acting on behalf of the nondominant groups, there is neither guarantee nor likelihood that the political commitments of future administrations would permit them so to act.

Gardiner C. Means, economist, advocating centralized economic planning in a report to the Senate, January 17, 1935, in the Congressional Record *(1935).*

It is overwhelmingly important to avoid any danger of permanently discrediting the sound and necessary policy of federal legislation for economic security by attempting to apply it on too ambitious a scale before actual experience has provided guidance for the permanently safe direction of such efforts. The place of such a fundamental in our future civilization is too precious to be jeopardized now by extravagant action. It is a sound idea—a sound ideal. . . .

Three principles should be observed in legislation on this subject. In the first place, the system adopted, except for the money necessary to initiate it, should be self-sustaining in the sense that funds for the payment of insurance benefits should not come from the proceeds of general taxation. Second, excepting in old-age insurance, actual management should be left to the states, subject to standards established by the federal government. Third, sound financial management of the funds and the reserves and protection of the credit structure of the nation should be assured by retaining federal control over all funds through trustees in the Treasury of the United States.

President Franklin D. Roosevelt, calling for legislation to establish unemployment compensation, old-age benefits, aid to dependent children, and increased funding for public health agencies, message to Congress, January 17, 1935, in the Congressional Record *(1935).*

Discussing the advisability of giving President Roosevelt a blank check for nearly $5 billion for work relief is about as profitable as debating the weather. There doesn't seem to be much that anyone can do about it no matter what opinion he may hold. . . .

But at least, such contemplation should serve to emphasize the fact that the inescapable burdens of the future will be lightened materially if we are able to induce a government policy that hastens the revival of private business and ends political recovery efforts.

Business Week, *editorial of February 2, 1935.*

The President had up for discussion the need of Harry Hopkins for more money. He wondered whether it would be well to permit Congress to pass a bill giving Hopkins the necessary relief money and another bill to provide for the continuance of Fechner's CCC camps. In the end the decision was to stand by the original bill appropriating $4,880,000,000 for work relief. I must say that the President seemed to me to be distinctly dispirited. I have never seen him in quite such a state of mind. He looked tired and he seemed to lack fighting vigor or the buoyancy that has always characterized him. I came away not at all reassured as to his ability to fight his program through.

Secretary of the Interior Harold L. Ickes, diary entry of February 28, 1935, in The Secret Diary of Harold L. Ickes, *vol. 1 (1953).*

The danger of being projected into the World Court seems for the moment to have passed. . . . The administration's idea of sneaking us into the World Court in a hurry was a legislative trick. But the President's card was trumped and the trick taken by the team of Father Coughlin and Mr. Hearst. Father Coughlin's five millions of adherents and Mr. Hearst's followers (perhaps largely the same) swamped the telegraph offices and deluged the desks of the senators with protests, and the plan for swift disposal of the World Court question went awry.

The Catholic World, *editorial of March 1935.*

The intention of the Administration to socialize the electric light and power industry has been obvious from the beginning. A new development of policy goes a bit further. Forthright and official steps are now being taken to sovietize the industry.

Some time ago President Roosevelt notified the governors of the states that he would send them suggested drafts of model bills, by the passage of which state legislatures might cooperate with the New Deal. Among 11 such bills Secretary Harold L. Ickes has included 3 intended to legalize the taking over of electric utilities by the people and providing corporate organizations and funds for the job.

Business Week, *editorial of March 23, 1935.*

The New Deal has sometimes been pictured as a kind of academic brain storm. This is, of course, either a humorous or a malicious attribution. No group of pallid professors huddled around a desk in order to concoct its main features; nor did President Roosevelt invent it. His sense of history has been accurate and so he has understood and taken advantage of the progressive drift. . . . The policies which are spoken of as new have an entirely honorable lineage in American history; they are an expression of the American faith.

Rexford G. Tugwell, Brains Trust adviser to the president, in the Atlantic Monthly *(April 1935).*

The relief load has remained constant in spite of recovery chiefly because there is an exhaustion of savings and assets among the unemployed and among what might be called the casualties of the depression, because the criterion of need has been raised and the stigma of relief partially removed. The relief load could be cut down by cutting down the criterion of relief and by restoring the stigma of relief. If the country wishes to say, for example, that the average need a month should be $18 rather than $28, and if it wishes to say that the $18 shall be given in such a way as to humiliate the recipient, the relief load will diminish drastically and immediately. . . .

It would be possible to keep the destitute from dying of starvation and from freezing to death at very much less cost. It would be possible to spend very much more and still the destitute would not be rolling in luxury. What is being spent is something more than what the destitute must have to exist and much less than what most of them need for an American standard of life.

Walter Lippmann, newspaper columnist, from a column entitled "The Relief Load" *(April 16, 1935), in Nevins, ed.,* Interpretations, 1933–1935 *(1936).*

The program for social security that is now pending before the Congress is a necessary part of the future unemployment policy of the government. While our present and projected expenditures for work relief are wholly within the reasonable limits of our national credit resources, it is obvious that we cannot continue to create governmental deficits for that purpose year after year after year. We must begin now to make provision for the future. . . . It [the social security program] proposes, by means of old-age pensions, to help those who have reached the age of retirement to give up their jobs and thus give to the younger generation greater opportunities for work and to give to all, old and young alike, a feeling of security as they look toward old age.

President Franklin D. Roosevelt, from his fireside chat of April 28, 1935, in Buhite and Levy, FDR's Fireside Chats *(1992).*

In response to a summons from the White House, Hopkins, Walker, and I met the President at two-fifteen for a session of over an hour. It was clear from the questioning that the President had read the memorandum on public works and work relief that I had left him yesterday and had been impressed by it. . . . He frankly recognized the impossibility of PWA bidding for projects against WPA. Frank Walker insisted that there was a great deal of confusion in the minds of the public, that they didn't know with whom to file their applications. Harry Hopkins scoffed at this suggestion but I came to the support of Walker, insisting that there was not only confusion throughout the states but even here in Washington.

Secretary of the Interior Harold L. Ickes, diary entry of June 27, 1935, in The Secret Diary of Harold L. Ickes, *vol. 1 (1953).*

Mrs. William Wetmore (*Right*): "Everywhere you go people are smoking Camels. Their smoother, richer flavor seems to fit in with the gayer, pleasanter life we are leading again."

Camels are mild in the best sense of the word— mild in flavor and, even more important, so mild you can smoke all you want. . . .

See if you don't agree with Mrs. Allston Boyer, Miss Dorothy Paine, Mrs. William Wetmore, and the other discerning women who have learned that in cigarettes the cost of the tobaccos and the skill of blending them are all-important.

Advertisement for Camels in Stage *(August 1935).*

People are still interested in the 6 million pigs that were killed in September of 1933. . . .

I suppose it is a marvelous tribute to the humanitarian instincts of the American people that they sympathize more with little pigs which are killed than with full-grown hogs. Some people may object to killing pigs at any age. Perhaps they think that farmers should run a sort of old-folks home for hogs and keep them around indefinitely as barnyard pets. This is a splendid attitude, but it happens that we have to think about farmers as well as hogs. And above all we must think about consumers and try to get a uniform supply of pork from year to year at a price which is fair to farmer and consumer alike.

Secretary of Agriculture Henry A. Wallace, defending the Agricultural Adjustment Administration's programs, radio broadcast of November 12, 1935, in the Wallace Papers at the Library of Congress.

Just who profited from the last war? Labor got some of the crumbs in the form of high wages and steady jobs. But where is labor today, with its 14 million unemployed? Agriculture received high prices for its products during the period of the war and has been paying the price of that brief inflation in the worst and longest agricultural depression in all history. Industry made billions in furnishing the necessities of war to the belligerents and then suffered terrific reaction like the dope addict's morning after. War

and depression—ugly, misshapen, inseparable twins—must be considered together. Each is a catapult for the other. The present worldwide depression is a direct result of the World War. Every war in modern history has been followed by a major depression.

Senator Bennett Champ Clark of Missouri, advocating support of the Neutrality Acts, in Harper's Monthly *(December 1935).*

The tragedy of this generation is that it has no faith. They do not rebel because rebels must have a glowing faith in something. Our boys and girls neither believe nor disbelieve.

They have courage and they have hope, not because they draw on spiritual strength; not because they trust in God; or country; or even in themselves; but because they are young. The future is dun and black with fog. They are bewildered, as men at sea in an open boat without compass or chart. They do not dare not to hope.

Maxine Davis, from her portrait of American youth The Lost Generation *(1936).*

There is little in the data we have examined to support the belief that deliberately enforced increases in the quantity of money will produce a sound and lasting economic recovery. As just remarked, the largest part of the money supply moves with or after business activity, not before it. A "moderate" enforced expansion of the money supply therefore seems likely to have little effect on current business activity. . . . A large and continued expansion, on the other hand, will undoubtedly raise prices, but also seems extremely likely to bring on such a contraction of the real volume of economic activity, ending in virtual collapse, as took place in many European countries after the war. These considerations bear forcefully on the political and other proposals now current, which insist that "reflation," "inflation," or some similar method offers a sure and quick weapon for forcing a sound economic recovery. An examination of the recorded facts, both for the period since 1930 and for earlier years, does not lead one to place great confidence in these proposals.

James W. Angell, professor of economics at Columbia University, from his book The Behavior of Money *(1936).*

The jacal on the left is where this Mexican family formerly lived; the new house was built through a Resettlement Administration loan. This photo by Arthur Rothstein, taken in April 1936, shows rehabilitation clients. *(Library of Congress, Prints and Photographs Division [USF34-002910-D])*

It may be that the next two or three years (or even longer) may be years of comparative revival. But it is impossible to feel any confidence in a continuance of stability. . . . The probability of peace and progress in the next half-century is not very great. . . .

2. Why is this? There are two main reasons.

In the first place comes the danger of war. . . . So long as we could believe that the great body of people in civilised countries hated war and would be prepared to do anything to avoid it, it was possible to view the growing diplomatic tensions in Europe and elsewhere with the belief that these were minor difficulties which patience and goodwill could eliminate. The Nazi revolution has dispelled that illusion. We now know that . . . we have to live out our lives side by side with men whose conceptions of the true ends of life are fundamentally different from our own—men to whom the kindly virtues of peace are contemptible and for whom the destruction of life is a better thing than its preservation.

Lionel Robbins, professor of economics at the University of London who coined the term the Great Depression *to define a depression whose severity was unprecedented in history, from his book* The Great Depression *(1936).*

Socialized industries, each a law unto itself, cannot plan for work, leisure, security, and abundance for all unless there is over them a general economic planning council to prepare a master plan. This council is the general staff in the war against poverty. It is the expert arm of government, subject to general decisions of Congress or the electorate as to policy, but free from interference in detail.

Norman Thomas, Socialist Party leader in After the New Deal, What? *(1936).*

[A]nd out of the westcoast haze comes now and then an old man's querulous voice

advocating the salestax,

hissing dirty names at the defenders of civil liberties for the workingman;

jail the reds,

praising the comforts of Baden-Baden under the blood and bludgeon rule of Handsome Adolf (Hearst's own loved invention, the lowest common denominator come to power out of the rot of democracy) . . .

a spent Caesar grown old with spending

never man enough to cross the Rubicon.

Characterization of William Randolph Hearst, in John Dos Passos's novel The Big Money *(1936).*

"Then I'll tell you. I think that in time the Jim Bonds [people of mixed race—white and black] are going to conquer the western hemisphere. Of course it won't quite be in our time and of course as they spread toward the poles they will bleach out again like the rabbits and the birds do, so they won't show up so sharp against the snow. But it will still be Jim Bond; and so in a few thousand years, I who regard you will also have sprung from the loins of African kings. Now I want you to tell me just one thing more. Why do you hate the South?"

The character Shreve in William Faulkner's novel Absalom, Absalom! *(1936).*

The basic point of departure is the fact that the business of a consumer society is able . . . to furnish from within itself the materials and conditions of its own success. It is one institutional structure which grows by what it feeds on and feeds on itself. For its intent can never be anything but democratic abundance. Founded on the wants of the consumer, it mounts and spreads as they multiply and diversify. This means that "the store" can grow without limit. It is not bound like the producers' organizations of the producer economy by inner and outer competition. Producer societies, no matter how democratically conceived and organized, are always restricted to their own exclusive development: They tend automatically toward monopoly; their prosperity rests on scarcity.

Horace M. Kallen, professor at the New School for Social Research, advocating consumer cooperatives in The Decline and Rise of the Consumer *(1936).*

"But in my little experience the end is never very different in its nature from the means. Damn it, Jim, you can only build a violent thing with violence."

"I don't believe that," Jim said. "All great things have violent beginnings."

"There aren't any beginnings," Burton said. "Nor any ends. It seems to me that man has engaged in a blind and fearful struggle out of a past he can't remember, into a future he can't foresee nor understand. And man has met and defeated every obstacle, every enemy except one. He cannot win over himself. How mankind hates itself."

Exchange between two of the main characters, in John Steinbeck's novel In Dubious Battle *(1936).*

The *Studies* are now to be . . . generally available in four compact volumes. Thus my work enters a further phase. . . . It is today almost universally accepted, when it is not actively urged, that definite knowledge of so deeply vital a subject is necessary for all, and that without it life must remain perilous. Nor is mere information enough; there is always a lurking peril. With all the information available, the sexual life can never be easy. Here, as elsewhere, discipline is needed as well as knowledge, and art as well as discipline. That is the reason why we must continue to study the problems of sexual psychology.

Havelock Ellis, English physician and author, commenting on his "Studies in the Psychology of Sex," in the American Mercury *(January 1936).*

Almost never has a successful dramatization . . . followed more implicitly the chiaroscuro of the novelist's art. Pauline Lord, Ruth Gordon, Raymond Massey, its three stars, have assumed the minds and hearts of a living folk history rather than important stage roles. Miss Lord is the wife who crushes Frome with her whining; her brooding, sullen jealousy; the iron of her will.

. . . As Mattie, the gay, affectionate waif who loves church socials, the stars, bright ribbons, and Ethan Frome, Ruth Gordon plays with a radiant and touching simplicity which climbs above even her own high acting career. Mr. Massey makes the tortured bewilderment of Ethan, caught in the web of his poverty, his love, the inexorable tentacles of his wife's possessive spirit, as actual as the shadows across his gaunt face.

Ruth Woodbury Sedgwick, reviewing the Owen and Donald Davis stage adaptation of Edith Wharton's novel Ethan Frome, *in* Stage *(February 1936).*

The history of these past three years will be written in the future as the history of an American revolution which was engineered and carried on under the unseeing eyes of one hundred and thirty million citizens. In the guise of a More Abundant Life and a New Deal for the Forgotten Man, a collective system of government and economy which combines many of the predominant features of both fascism and communism has been introduced as a substitute for traditional democracy. It is unquestionable that, but for the growing storm of opposition now sweeping upon the Administration from all sections of the country, Dr. Tugwell and his fellow revolutionaries would have been successful in their scheme.

Senator Lester J. Dickinson of Iowa, in the American Mercury *(February 1936).*

The President told me on Friday that he would be reelected all right, but that the next four years would be very tough ones, with a crisis in 1941. It told him I hoped that something would be done during the next four years to build up a leader who could carry on the work of this Administration. He said that he believed there would be a realignment of parties.

Secretary of the Interior Harold L. Ickes, diary entry of February 9, 1936, in The Secret Diary of Harold L. Ickes, *vol. 1 (1953).*

My husband and I had a rare treat Wednesday night in listening to Marian Anderson, a colored contralto, who has made a great success in Europe and this country. She has sung before nearly all the crowned heads and deserves her great success, for I have rarely heard a more beautiful and moving voice or a more finished artist. She sang three Schubert songs and finished with two Negro spirituals, one of which I had never heard before.

Eleanor Roosevelt, from her "My Day" newspaper column for February 21, 1936, quoted in Chadakoff, Eleanor Roosevelt's My Day *(1989).*

The generation which is now beginning to feel the oats of maturity has little respect for our national lawmakers. It knows no great figures in Congress, although there is occasionally some praise for Borah, Glass, and Norris. Most of Congress is ungrammatical, pedestrian, small. Youth is disillusioned about these men who should be its leaders; they cannot lead because they are too susceptible to pressure groups.

They follow haphazardly—and the young people of the country not only are unled, but they have no respect for leadership. It's all a racket, they say.

George E. Sokolsky, journalist, in the Atlantic Monthly *(March 1936).*

Wage earners and employers have shown a growing disposition to avail themselves of the fair and impartial services of these government boards. They are really set up for the purpose of keeping industrial peace for the benefit of employers and workers and in the public interest. These agencies will gather authority as the years go on; and as the spirit of cooperation between employers and employees continues to grow, as they become increasingly aware that it is in their interest and in the interest of the public as well, we will find the good offices of these boards being sought more and more as a voluntary substitute for long and costly strikes and lockouts.

Secretary of Labor Frances Perkins, commenting on the National Labor Relations Board and other federal agencies, in Annals of the American Academy of Political and Social Science *(March 1936).*

Collective bargaining, whether voluntary or involuntary, must be recognized as a method of employee-employer relationship which enjoys governmental sanction and support, which labor, organized or unorganized, approves, and which capital can no longer oppose. No matter what else comes of the New Deal, collective bargaining, in some form, will be congealed into the American industrial system.

George E. Sokolsky, journalist, in the Atlantic Monthly *(March 1936).*

The only issue is Roosevelt. Is he a hero, as his parasites allege, or a quack, as I have argued here? The answer will be heard on election day. Every vote will be cast either for him or against him. His opponent will be only the residuary legatee, the innocent bystander.

H. L. Mencken, journalist, in the American Mercury *(March 1936).*

Speaking of comedy reminds me—there are seven varieties this month, only one of which deserves your undivided attention. . . . The name, *Desire.* The players, Gary Cooper, Marlene Dietrich. The director, Frank Borzage. Result, comedy of the sophisticated gender

This 1936 photo by Dorothea Lange shows a migrant agricultural worker's family. It includes seven hungry children and their 32-year-old mother. Their father was a native Californian and the image is shot in Nipomo, California. *(Library of Congress, Prints and Photographs Division [USF 34-T01-9097-C])*

and the first one since *It Happened One Night* to capture that romantic sprightliness that has been the aim of every director of comedies in Hollywood for the past two years.

> *Katherine Best, film critic, in* Stage *(April 1936).*

The control of every single branch of German culture is complete. It begins, not by censoring what actually appears, but by determining who shall be the creators and transmitters of culture. No publication, no concert platform, no publishing house, no theater, no gallery, is open to any writer, artist, or musician, who has not first of all run the gauntlet of the Propaganda Ministry. One may not exhibit a picture, or present a play, or perform on the piano, or write in the papers and magazines, unless one is a member of the established "chamber." One cannot get into the chamber if one is suspected of being a heretic. And the very first test is a blood test—one must be able to prove a blood stream uncontaminated by non-Aryan admixture.

> *Dorothy Thompson, journalist, in* Foreign Affairs *(April 1936).*

Such were the major reasons for the collapse of the Roosevelt myth in 1935. Early this year, following the sweeping decision of the Supreme Court outlawing the AAA and uprooting the vital principle of much New Deal legislation, other incidents developed. . . .

So we are now in for a deluge of superlatives about showmanship. That is, until the show closes. Then, perhaps, we will have to admit that the President is not the accomplished actor we now think he is. But the political sagacity myth is a thing of the past. Under the strains of opposition, in the face of the first adversity, the master politician cracked up. Perhaps Mr. Roosevelt can't take it.

Ashmun Brown, journalist, in the American Mercury *(April 1936).*

Wearing our shade hats, with handkerchiefs tied over our faces and vaseline in our nostrils, we have been trying to rescue our home from the accumulation of wind-blown dust which penetrates wherever air can go. It is an almost hopeless task, for there is rarely a day when at some time the dust clouds do not roll over. "Visibility" approaches zero and everything is covered again with a silt-like deposit which may vary in depth from a film to actual ripples on the kitchen floor. I keep oiled cloths on the window sill and between the upper and lower sashes. They help just a little to retard or collect the dust.

Caroline A. Henderson, a farmer with her husband in Oklahoma for 28 years, in the Atlantic Monthly *(May 1936).*

Six months ago Federal Theatre was a theory, a plan, a wild surmise. Today it is a far-flung reality with two hundred producing groups and a personnel of over 12,000—one of the largest government-sponsored theatres in the world. Its New York record to date shows seven major productions of which four have played to full houses. Fifty-seven per cent success is a high average in a business that accepts seventy-three per cent of failures in a season, but to compare Broadway and Federal Theatre in anything but the most general terms is unfair to both. Federal Theatre could

Home in a section inhabited by blacks and whites in Charleston, West Virginia, September 1936. *(Library of Congress)*

never produce an *Idiot's Delight;* Broadway could never sell, at fifty-five cents top, so beautiful and dignified a production as that given T. S. Eliot's *Murder in the Cathedral.* The cost of Federal Theatre productions cannot be reckoned on the same balance sheet as those of the commercial producer. Where Federal Theatre has the advantage of a fixed salary scale, set for all WPA workers alike, it has the disadvantage of having little or no choice in casting; it cannot hire and fire at will, its working hours per day are short and it must make up by long and patient rehearsals for the inequalities in its acting groups.

Rosamond Gilder, associate editor, in Theatre Arts Monthly *(June 1936).*

Neither Old Dealer nor New Dealer, it appears, has courage to assail the international bankers, the Federal Reserve bankers. In common, both the leaders of the Republicans and the Democrats uphold the old money philosophy. Today in America there is only one political party—the banker's party. In common, both old parties are determined to shambattle their way through this November election with the hope that millions of American citizens will be driven into the no-man's-land of financial bondage.

Father Charles Coughlin, Catholic priest and political activist, endorsing William Lemke, candidate of the Union Party, radio address of June 19, 1936, in Vital Speeches of the Day *(1936).*

Mr. Roosevelt himself holds that he has not deviated by a hair's breadth from the course he set in his inauguration speech. In his own view he is still "a little left of center," and he declares categorically that he intends to follow exactly the same direction in the next four years. To go straight center is to stand still, he explains, and stand-still agreements are only for financial and political bankrupts. To go right of center is to go back; to go left of center is to make progress. "Right" and "Left" he considers convenient omnibus words for hurried journalists, and the fact that Socialists and stand-patters alike repudiate the New Deal seems to him convincing proof that he has hewed pretty close to the line which just leans away from the middle.

Anne O'Hare McCormick, journalist, column of June 21, 1936, in the New York Times, *quoted in Sheehan,* The World at Home: Selections from the Writings of Anne O'Hare McCormick *(1956).*

Governments can err, Presidents do make mistakes, but the immortal Dante tells us that divine justice weighs the sins of the cold-blooded and the sins of the warm-hearted in different scales.

Better the occasional faults of a Government that lives in a spirit of charity than the consistent omissions of a Government frozen in the ice of its own indifference.

There is a mysterious cycle in human events. To some generations much is given. Of other generations much is expected. This generation of Americans has a rendezvous with destiny.

President Franklin D. Roosevelt, acceptance speech at the Democratic National Convention, June 27, 1936, quoted in Schlesinger, The Politics of Upheaval *(1960).*

In the whole of the Western Hemisphere our good-neighbor policy has produced results that are especially heartening.

The noblest monument to peace and to neighborly economic and social friendship in all the world is . . . the boundary which unites the United States and Canada. . . . Mutual trust made that frontier. To extend the same sort of mutual trust throughout the Americas was our aim. . . .

Throughout the Americas the spirit of the good neighbor is a practical and living fact. The twenty-one American republics are not only living together in friendship and in peace—they are united in the determination so to remain.

President Franklin D. Roosevelt, speech at Chautauqua, New York, August 14, 1936, in Peace and War: United States Foreign Policy, 1931–1941 *(1943).*

As everyone knows, Hollywood is in politics up to its neck. When Upton Sinclair was running for Governor of California, important movie interests produced a series of fake newsreels in which actors were dressed up as tramps and announced from the screen that they had come to California to live off the state government. Actresses were made up as housewives and interviewed . . . stating their intention of voting against "the Bolshevist Sinclair." . . . The incessant militarism and propaganda tone in general of certain newsreels, notably those of the ubiquitous Mr. Hearst, is notorious.

The New Republic, *article of August 19, 1936.*

Some ten thousand followers of Father Coughlin came to Cleveland's public auditorium last week—twenty thousand to his Sunday mass-meeting in the Cleveland Stadium—and went partially insane. They indulged in cries, shrieks, moans, rolling of the eyes and brandishing of the arms. . . .

Father Coughlin . . . repeatedly apologized for having called the President "Franklin Double-Crossing Roosevelt" before the Townsendites, and nervously evaded reports that he had been reprimanded by Rome. . . . "If I can't deliver my radio audience—and that's 9,000,000 voters—if I can't deliver them for Lemke and O'Brien in November, I'm through," he told the press. "I'll be a washout, and I'll quit broadcasting."

Jonathan Mitchell, writer on social, political, and economic subjects and Washington, D.C., resident, in the New Republic *(August 26, 1936).*

There are those who fail to read the signs of the times and American history. They would try to refuse the worker any effective power to bargain collectively, to earn a decent livelihood, and to acquire security. It is those shortsighted ones, not labor, who threaten this country with that class dissension which in other countries has led to dictatorship and the establishment of fear and hatred as dominant emotions in human life.

President Franklin D. Roosevelt appealing for the labor vote, from his fireside chat of September 6, 1936, in Buhite and Levy, FDR's Fireside Chats *(1992).*

It may be difficult to convince the rank and file of the American public today that most of the job-giving and wage-paying institutions of American industry are suffering from an attack on so called [sic] "economic royalists" and that the credit system which keeps

The Amoskeag Manufacturing Company was one of the largest textile factories in the world and employed many people in the town of Manchester, New Hampshire, from its opening in 1809 until December 1935, when it closed. This photograph shows factory workers' housing near Canal Street in Manchester in 1936. *(Library of Congress, Prints and Photographs Division [LC-USF33-T01-854-M-2])*

business alive is being undermined by an assault on the "money changers in the temple." But the simple lesson of the effect of destructive taxation and subversive tax spending on jobs and income is understandable and easily told. Business must tell that story simply, honestly and repeatedly.

Business Week, *editorial of September 19, 1936.*

No doubt there are those who argue that the great blanket appropriations made to the President, the largest being for $4,800,000,000, were necessary at the time to meet the conditions which then existed. Even if that be granted, the effect was disastrous upon the spenders themselves. They lost their sense of values, became intoxicated with the power to spend such vast sums. . . .

It has been said that the Administration acts as if it were willing to give the whole Treasury away, "trying to enrich everybody by impoverishing everybody else."

The Saturday Evening Post, *editorial of October 3, 1936.*

The President got on the subject of "prima donnas." He said that Ray Moley, while saying favorable things about him, said them in such a way as to hurt. . . . He also said that he had to send for Joe Kennedy every few days and hold his hand. Then he went on to talk about Rex Tugwell. He remarked that no one connected with him or the Administration had been subjected to such criticism as Rex had. Yet Rex had never whimpered or asked for sympathy or run to anyone for help. He had taken it on the chin like a man. The other day the President thanked him for the way he had stood up under fire.

Secretary of the Interior Harold L. Ickes, diary entry of October 9, 1936, in The Secret Diary of Harold L. Ickes, *vol. 1 (1953).*

The people of America have no quarrel with business. They insist only that the power of concentrated wealth shall not be abused.

We have come through a hard struggle to preserve democracy in America. Where other nations in

This photo by Dorothea Lange shows a migratory workers' camp on the American River near Sacramento, California, November 1936. *(Library of Congress)*

other parts of the world have lost that fight, we have won.

The businessmen of America and all other citizens have joined in a firm resolve to hold the fruits of that victory, to cling to the old ideals and old fundamentals upon which America has grown great.

President Franklin D. Roosevelt, campaign speech in Chicago, October 14, 1936, quoted in Rosenman, The Public Papers and Addresses of Franklin D. Roosevelt *(1938–1950).*

Well, honestly, have you ever known the state of journalism to sink to such an abyss of imbecilic foolishness as it has in some of these papers in recent months? I can't believe it when I read it. Such irreconcilable things and systems and ideas as Communism, Fascism and Socialism are lumped together in one indiscriminate wad and hurled wildly in the direction of the President. The other night on the radio I heard a speaker accuse Mr. Roosevelt of all three of them in the same breath. About the only thing I have not heard him accused of is of plotting and conspiring with the King of England and Herr Hitler to restore the ex-Crown Prince of Germany and establish an autocratic monarchy.

Thomas Wolfe, novelist, letter of October 23, 1936, to Jonathan Daniels, quoted in Nowell, The Letters of Thomas Wolfe *(1956).*

It cannot be successfully denied that whatever the merits of the New Deal policies, they have, as a whole, caused an appreciable drift away from individual responsibility and self-reliance. They have brought about an excessive, utterly fallacious and dangerous reliance upon government as a substitute for private endeavor and obligation. Worst of all, they have been based upon the juvenile assumption that social betterment does not need to be grown from the roots of character and moral suasion, but can be imposed from the head downwards at a single happy-go-lucky stroke, by compulsory legislation or by administrative decree.

These, in sober fact, are among the very essentials of New Deal policy, and no voter can escape the serious responsibility of deciding whether American institutions really fit into such a pattern.

The Saturday Evening Post, *editorial of November 7, 1936.*

Like most great victories, the Roosevelt triumph raises more questions than it answers. It is easy to guess what the people voted against, but not what they voted for. The majority was reluctant to turn the country over to the same crowd that had been represented by Coolidge and Hoover, that had helped to bring on the depression and had done so little to end it or to relieve the distress it caused. Many voters feared what this crowd, if in power, might do to labor or to those on relief, or to the farmers, who pled so long and so vainly for a fair deal before Mr. Roosevelt was elected. . . .

But what did they vote for? . . . if Mr. Roosevelt has any mandate from the electorate, it is a mandate to remain President and do what he wishes.

The New Republic, *editorial of November 11, 1936.*

A President who thinks Communism a bugaboo today in the United States is as far out of touch with reality as the President who tried to rock us to sleep to the tune of the lullaby "Prosperity is just around the corner." Now, unfortunately, some of Mr. Roosevelt's closest companions have been playing around with the "Pinks" who in turn form a *liaison* with the real "Reds." Mr. Roosevelt's smart under-secretaries may not realize it, but to play with the Pinks and the Reds is to play with fire.

The Catholic World, *editorial of December 1936.*

At last I am able to say a few words of my own. . . . I have found it impossible to carry the heavy burden of responsibility . . . without the help and support of the woman I love. . . .

I now quit altogether public affairs, and I lay down my burden. . . .

And now we all have a new King. . . . God bless you all. God save the King.

King Edward VIII of Great Britain, announcing his abdication, radio address of December 11, 1936, quoted in Longford, The Royal House of Windsor *(1974).*

I saw an article in yesterday's paper stating that $3,600 a year was really the minimum on which an average family could lead a satisfactory existence. Most of us know that a very great percentage of our people see only from $200 to $600 cash in hand during the course of a year. Many others have incomes under $1,000 or ranging from $1,000 to $2,000 a year.

This problem involves so many people that we cannot just say, "Let the government solve it." We, as a people, must solve it by deciding on the type of social and economic philosophy we wish to see established in this country.

Eleanor Roosevelt, from her "My Day" newspaper column of December 15, 1936, quoted in Chadakoff, Eleanor Roosevelt's My Day *(1989).*

The forty-first annual convention of the National Association of Manufacturers was officially labeled "The New Horizons Sessions" . . . but perhaps the newest and most significant thing in the whole history of industrialism was the liberalism and social awareness which characterized every resolution and utterance throughout the convention. . . .

There was no yielding on questions of basic principle. The American system of government and the American theory of private enterprise were defended unequivocally. . . .

On the other hand, organized industry took a forthright stand in favor of social security, equitable labor relations, higher real wages, an advanced standard of living, and the abolition of child labor. It proposed not only to accept but to encourage and promote many such measures.

Business Week, *editorial of December 19, 1936.*

They play every night—clarinet, piano, vibra-phone, drums, and they make music you would not believe. No arrangements, not a false note, one finishing his solo and dropping into background support, then the other, all adding inspiration until with some number like "Stomping at the Savoy" they get going too strong to quit. . . . no two notes the same and no one note off the chord, the more they relax in the excitement of it the more a natural genius in preselection becomes evident and the more indeed the melodic line becomes rigorously pure. This is really composition on the spot, with the spirit of jazz strongly over all of them but the iron laws of harmony and rhythm never lost sight of; and it is a collective thing, the most beautiful example of men working together to be seen in public today.

Otis Ferguson, editor, commenting on the playing of Benny Goodman, Teddy Wilson, Lionel Hampton, and Gene Krupa at the Cafe Rouge in New York, in the New Republic *(December 30, 1936).*

6

Storms Gather Abroad
1937–1938

FDR PROPOSES JUDICIAL REFORM

Reinvigorated by his election triumph, President Roosevelt entered 1937 intent on pursuing an even stronger tack. In a January message to Congress he requested legislation authorizing the reorganization of the executive branch in an effort to streamline administrative functions and reduce their costs (opponents would see this request as a grab for increased power). In his inaugural address he promised to ask Congress for more New Deal types of programs designed to relieve the sufferings, still continuing despite the administration's four-year effort, of the "one-third of a nation ill-housed, ill-clad, ill-nourished," as he saw it. Roosevelt's intentions to reorganize the executive branch and to pursue an enhanced New Deal both foundered (although a revised executive reorganization act would eventually be approved in 1939). One reason for this was that events abroad demanded the government's increasing attention. By the end of 1938, the administration would be largely preoccupied with foreign policy issues. But the most immediate cause of the New Deal's derailment in 1937 lay in a fatal error of judgment by the president. The error probably resulted from overconfidence derived from his sense of the public's support.

In February, determined to overcome the Supreme Court's gutting of New Deal legislation and programs such as the Agricultural Adjustment Administration (AAA) and the National Recovery Administration (NRA), Roosevelt dropped a bomb. Surprising and perturbing public and politicians alike, he asked Congress for legislation mandating reform of the federal courts system. As was quickly evident, the clear target of this effort was the Supreme Court. Roosevelt proposed a plan devised by Attorney General Homer Cummings (but opposed by close advisers Thomas Corcoran and Benjamin Cohen) that contended the federal courts were overwhelmed with cases because they were understaffed or perhaps limited in capacity due to the age or infirmity of the judges—his case in point being that the Supreme Court had rejected 87 percent of the cases (717 out of 867) appealed to it in the previous year. To rectify this problem, the Roosevelt plan stipulated that if a federal judge who had served for 10 years or more did not resign or retire within six months after his 70th birthday, then the president could appoint a new judge to the bench on which he served. In all the president could appoint 44 judges to supplement the lower federal courts and a total of six to supplement the Supreme Court under this stipulation, meaning that the number of justices on the Supreme Court could increase from nine to 15. Although the administration's argument for this proposal stressed the issue of the federal courts' inefficiency in handling work loads, both Congress and the public soon realized that its real purpose was political: to pack the Supreme Court with new justices who could be counted on to uphold New Deal legislation.

Roosevelt suffered an enormous political loss as the significance of this proposal sunk in during the following months. Many saw his tactics as deeply cynical and politically self-serving. Some resented the apparent attack on Justice Louis Brandeis, who at 80 was among the Court's oldest justices and yet a consistent supporter of New Deal programs. Still others came to regard the proposal as a blatant attempt to undermine the constitutional separation of powers among the three branches of government and to degrade the Supreme Court as an institution generally held in honor. Even leaders of the president's own party in Congress were dismayed and irate because Roosevelt had failed to inform them of his intent to make such an extreme proposal. Among the more disgruntled was Montana's senator Burton K. Wheeler, a friend of Brandeis. With Brandeis's help, he elicited a letter from Chief Justice Charles Evans Hughes, which he read at the hearings on the court-packing bill before the Senate Judiciary Committee. In his letter Hughes declared the Court "fully abreast of its work." He explained that the number of cases heard in the previous year did not reflect on the efficiency or competence of the Court but only on the merits of the various cases. Hughes further argued that increasing the number of justices would actually cause inefficiency since the Court had to operate as a unit and noted that the views in his letter had the support of Justice Brandeis and Justice Willis Van Devanter, representing both the liberal and conservative wings of the Court. The letter's tone and content inspired those opposed to the bill. Senator Carter Glass and others took to the airwaves to berate the president's proposal. The Supreme Court aided its own cause by reversing earlier decisions or reaching new ones supporting New Deal programs, finding in *West Coast Hotel Co. v. Parrish* on March 29 that Washington State's minimum wage law (similar to New York's, earlier rejected) was constitutional and ruling in *NLRB v. Jones and Laughlin Steel* and two other cases on April 12 that the collective bargaining provision of the Wagner Act was constitutional. In May Justice Van Devanter, one of the Court's chief opponents to the New Deal, announced his decision to retire. And importantly, also during May, the Court upheld provisions of the Social Security Act.

COURT PACKING LOSES

As all of these developments unfolded, polls indicated that public support of the court-packing proposal and the resulting bill had consistently dwindled while opposition to the proposal was climbing to 50 percent or more. In mid-June the Senate Judiciary Committee issued a majority report excoriating the bill as a violation of judicial independence and democratic principle and recommending that it be "emphatically rejected." Nevertheless, Roosevelt, normally an astute politician, adamantly pursued congressional approval of his proposal. Majority leader Joe Robinson of Arkansas, whom the president had promised to appoint to the Supreme Court when a vacancy occurred, led the fight for the bill's approval in the Senate—a fight so grueling that the stress resulted in Robinson's suffering a fatal heart attack in mid-July. Finally, in the third week of July, following Alben Barkley's election to succeed Robinson as majority leader, the Senate voted to recommit the bill, strip it of any reference to the Supreme Court, and have it thoroughly revised to authorize some procedural reforms for the federal courts but not for the president to appoint additional judges. This revised legislation passed both houses and went to the president for his signature in late August. Thus the better part of the legislative year had focused on the court-packing dispute, resulting in anger and opposition toward the president even among Democratic legislators. The results were a derailment of any New Deal legislative initiatives (most of the submitted bills failed approval) and a very serious loss of public trust in the president. The New Deal as a program of social and economic reform lost its momentum.

The one bright spot for Roosevelt in the court controversy may have been his appointment and the subsequent confirmation in August of Senator Hugo Black to replace Van Devanter in the Supreme Court, but even this easy victory was clouded by brief controversy when it was revealed in September that Black had been a member of the Ku Klux Klan during the twenties. Roosevelt could also be pleased that some reform legislation did gain congressional approval, especially late in the session following disposal of the court-packing bill. The Bankhead-Jones Farm Tenancy Act extended easier credit so that small farmers could obtain federal loans. The Bituminous Coal Act reestablished some of the provisions of the Guffey Act that the Supreme Court had invalidated in spring 1936. The Wagner Housing Act authorized creation of the U.S. Housing Authority and the issuing of federal loans for building low-rent housing units. In addition, the Revenue Act of 1937 revised the tax code to eliminate some forms of tax evasion used by wealthy taxpayers. But these reforms, small-scale as their effects were, seemed inconsequential in the context of domestic labor and economic developments during 1937. Strikes, acrimony, and expanding unionization characterized the labor scene. And unfortunately the nation sank back again into serious economic depression, bringing renewed threats of unemployment, dispossession, and starvation.

LABOR SUCCESSES

The year 1937 opened with major strikes that had begun in late December 1936 still in progress at General Motors Corporation plants in Cleveland, Ohio, and Flint, Michigan. At Flint the workers staged a "sit-down strike," occupying the factory for six weeks. This new tactic—it had been introduced in France a year before—proved so effective that workers at other GMC facilities adopted it. On February 11, General Motors caved in and agreed to accept the United Auto Workers (UAW) union as the official bargaining agent for the corporation's factory workers. In March the United States Steel Corporation, a major opponent of unions, surrendered to pressure and accepted the Congress of Industrial Organizations' (CIO) Steel Workers' Organizing Committee (SWOC), headed by Philip Murray, as its workers' bargaining agent and also granted a wage increase and a 40-hour week.

These victories at GMC and U.S. Steel were major breakthroughs for the CIO unions and established the viability of industrial unionism—that is, organization of all workers in an industry as a whole rather than organization only by craft, as with the American Federation of Labor (AFL) unions (for example, the separate brotherhoods of railroad engineers, firemen, conductors, and brakemen). The union victories also provided the impetus for organizing most of the other automotive and steel manufacturers during 1937, except for Republic Steel and the Ford Motor Company. The aging Henry Ford bitterly fought all efforts to unionize his shops and hired agents to suppress the unionizers—a result of which was a bloody altercation at the River Rouge plant in May, when Ford's agents bludgeoned Walter Reuther and other UAW organizers. At the end of May a confrontation between strikers and policemen at the Republic Steel plant in south Chicago resulted in the deaths of 10 strikers—the so-called Memorial Day massacre. Elsewhere unionization proceeded fairly peaceably. In the spring Firestone Tire and Rubber accepted the United Rubber Workers union. Other giants that agreed to unionization during the year included General Electric and RCA. The numbers of union members increased by hundreds of thousands.

THE STATE OF THE ECONOMY

Some entrepreneurs and businessmen argued that this rapid growth in union strength contributed to the sudden economic decline that marred 1937. The year began promisingly: Some economic indicators even suggested the Great Depression might be nearing its end. The level of industrial production was less than 8 percentage points below that of 1929; stock prices had recovered, as had dividends; and wages had advanced by an average of 10 percent beyond their 1929 level. Yet significant problems clearly remained. Unemployment stood officially at about 11 percent, and about 4.5 million families were on the relief rolls. Industrialists registered their lack of confidence in the recovery by committing meager amounts of capital to expansion or renovation. Roosevelt found these continuing problems disturbing, and his response was to resurrect fiscal stringency. He requested a balanced budget for the 1938 fiscal year—he wanted to reduce the deficit. Doing so would entail cutting expenditures for relief and public works. Employers, he assumed, encouraged by an improving economy and goaded by a shortened workweek won in new union contracts, would carry the ball by hiring more workers. But the cutbacks in federal programs merely exposed the underlying weakness of the general economy, which showed signs of faltering in May and began to collapse in August, ushering in the "Roosevelt recession." The new Social Security program removed $2 billion in taxes from taxpayers' incomes to place in reserve, and the fiscal tightening removed another $4 billion. With less money circulating, consumer spending fell off. Without consumers buying products, production levels in

Unemployed men in the public
square of the Gateway district,
Minneapolis, Minnesota, June 1937
(Library of Congress)

major industries plummeted. Between August and October the Dow Jones
Industrial Average (DJIA) fell from 190 to 115—a 40 percent decline. In the
last four months of the year 2 million workers lost their jobs.

Alarmed, the Roosevelt administration struggled to devise an effective
response. Secretary of the Treasury Morgenthau, who had always advocated a
balanced budget, argued that the economy should now be allowed to rectify
itself. But Marriner Eccles, chairman of the Federal Reserve Board, with
presidential advisers Harry Hopkins and Secretary of the Interior Harold
Ickes, advocated abandoning fiscal tightness in favor of lavish government
spending that would generate deficits—as advocated by British economist
John Maynard Keynes—to stimulate recovery. (Although Eccles had not read
Keynes's work, his own view replicated Keynesian principles.) The advocates
of increased spending prevailed. In the meantime, the administration chose to
blame monopolists and plutocrats—"economic royalists," in the president's
terms—for the current economic problems. Assistant Attorney General
Robert Jackson, head of the Justice Department's Antitrust Division, publicly
advocated a government crackdown on monopolies. Roosevelt's own initial
reaction to the recession was to call a special session of Congress for November, although his statements about what the session's concerns should be
fudged the issue of the recession. The special session was called specifically to
enact legislation left in the doldrums during the travails of the regular

session—bills dealing with agriculture, regulation of wages and hours, creation of an agency for national planning and seven regional authorities (referred to as the "seven little TVAs"), and reorganization of the executive branch. But the president had lost his clout with legislators as a result of the court-packing battle, and they adjourned shortly before Christmas without passing a single piece of legislation he advocated.

Somewhat ironically, one of the problems that confronted Roosevelt early in the new year concerned a controversy among the three directors of the Tennessee Valley Authority (TVA). Chairman Arthur Morgan in March publicly accused his colleagues David Lilienthal and Harcourt Morgan, who opposed Morgan's views on the TVA's purposes, of official misconduct. When the three men were called into conference with the president at the White House, Morgan could provide no evidence to support his charges, and Roosevelt removed him from office. Such a public quarrel further jeopardized the president's credibility, as well as the image of the TVA.

Although 1937 included many distractions for Roosevelt, the recession remained his major domestic concern as 1938 began. The year opened with estimates of the rate of unemployment at 11 million and continuing to rise. Sales of automobiles, an indicator of consumer spending, dropped 50 percent in the early months of the year and production levels of the steel industry by nearly as much. Economic indices, including the stock market, indicated that about two-thirds of the recovery experienced since 1933 had been lost.

Saturday afternoon in Harrington, Delaware, June 1937; photo by Arthur Rothstein *(Library of Congress)*

CONGRESS AND THE PRESIDENT

Rural school near Tipler, Wisconsin, May 1937 *(Library of Congress)*

In its new session, Congress fortunately already exhibited some initiative, or at least less resistance. In February the legislators approved and sent to the president the agricultural legislation he had requested in the 1937 regular and special sessions, the Soil Conservation and Domestic Allotment Act, which empowered the secretary of agriculture to establish acreage allotments for major crops (wheat, corn, tobacco, rice, and cotton), "parity" adjustments and payments to farmers, and storage facilities for excess production. In late March the Senate approved the president's executive branch reorganization legislation, although by only one vote. The bill did not make it through the House of Representatives, however.

But it was not until April that Roosevelt, who had vacillated between supporting a balanced budget and supporting spending—something embracing

Farmers plowing near Tipler, Wisconsin, May 1937 *(Library of Congress)*

both at the same time—finally determined upon a course to tackle the continuing recession. Persuaded at last by Harry Hopkins, he committed himself to seeking an increased spending program from Congress in order to stimulate the economy. (The commitment caused Morgenthau to submit his resignation, which the president refused to accept.) On April 14, Roosevelt asked Congress to approve $2 billion in spending on public works and other programs and $1 billion for government loans. He also ordered the freeing up of gold reserves to put $2 billion more into public circulation. Congress, perhaps registering the fact that a congressional election loomed in the fall, quickly approved the president's requests. Since Congress had on its own granted the Reconstruction Finance Corporation $1.5 billion in additional funding for loans, the total of federal funds that would flood into the economy following enactment of the bills in June amounted to $6.5 billion. In addition, in mid-May, at the president's request, Congress approved an appropriation of $1.2 billion to expand the navy. By the latter months of 1938 signs of increased industrial production and general recovery were emerging, although the unemployment level stubbornly persisted near 11 million.

At the end of April the president had also requested that Congress appropriate funding for the study of monopolistic power in the economy. The study would examine pricing structures, distribution systems, antitrust laws, corporate taxes, and other factors that might affect the development of monopolies. Congress passed the legislation but provided for congressional rather than executive administration and oversight of the study. The resulting Temporary National Economic Committee (TNEC) was composed of representatives from both the executive and legislative branches and chaired by Senator Joseph O'Mahoney. Because the TNEC only began hearings in December and continued its inquiry for several years, any economic effects of its findings would not be revealed for some time.

The Revenue Act of 1938 that Congress approved opposed the president's desires. Wealthy Democratic entrepreneurs, such as Bernard Baruch and Joseph P. Kennedy, had helped persuade members of Congress that the tax on undistributed profits set up by the Revenue Act of 1936 but only nominally imposed had been a cause of the 1937–38 recession. Roosevelt threatened to veto the act, prodding Congress to make a modest change in the act's stipulations about capital gains taxes. The revenue act as passed repealed the tax on undistributed profits and decreased taxation of capital gains, setting a flat rate of 15 percent. In the end Roosevelt allowed the act to become law without his signature—a gesture of disapproval.

To the president's liking, however, Congress also passed the Fair Labor Standards Act. This act—a major piece of New Deal legislation and reform—created a minimum wage of 25 cents for one year, 30 cents for the following

American Indian family in a camp of blueberry pickers in Little Fork, Minnesota, August 1937 *(Library of Congress)*

six years, and then 40 cents; mandated a maximum 40-hour workweek after two years and time-and-a-half wages for overtime; and reaffirmed the ban on child labor. And finally, Congress approved the Food, Drug, and Cosmetics Act, which required adequate testing of new drugs before their marketing and a listing of ingredients on containers of foods, drugs, and cosmetics. The act originally established other consumer protections, but it was weakened by some serious legal loopholes created by compromises resulting from strong industry opposition. Overall, however, it appeared that the president's renewed sense of purpose had recouped much of his influence with the Congress—in domestic policy, at least.

THE GOOD NEIGHBOR

In foreign policy, the president succeeded quite well in pursuing the Good Neighbor policy of effectively treating other hemispheric nations as equals. A crisis seemed imminent when, in March 1938, President Lázaro Cárdenas of Mexico announced that his government would expropriate the properties in Mexico of U.S., British, and Dutch oil companies. With Roosevelt's approval, Secretary of State Cordell Hull instructed Ambassador Josephus Daniels to deliver a note to Cárdenas affirming the Mexican government's right to effect the expropriation but asserting that the U.S. oil companies deserved fair compensation. Cárdenas responded agreeably. In July, while Roosevelt was cruising in Mexican waters aboard the USS *Houston,* he cordially welcomed aboard the ship representatives sent by Cárdenas to convey the Mexican president's warm regards. One month later, in August, the president also personally sealed friendly relations with Canada's prime minister, William Mackenzie King, when the two men met to dedicate a bridge spanning the St. Lawrence River near Kingston, Ontario.

The eighth Pan-American Conference held in Lima, Peru, in December 1938 could also be regarded as a diplomatic success. Secretary of State Hull headed the U.S. delegation, which included Alf Landon. Twenty other American republics also sent representatives. Nearly three weeks in duration, the conference culminated with the issuing of the Lima Declaration, which reflected Hull's views and committed the assembled republics to consult one another on defensive measures to be taken in the event any of them was threatened by a power from outside the hemisphere. These various events suggested dependable and open relations among the American nations—a happy circumstance. But events outside the American hemisphere—aggression and repression in Asia and Europe—were not as readily manageable nor as easily influenced by personal diplomacy.

THE TRAGEDY OF SPAIN

In dealing with European and Asian events a significant element in the problems the Roosevelt administration faced was the president's indecisiveness. Although he apparently held determined views on what should be done, anxiety over the political opposition from isolationists and other partisans caused him to hesitate or waffle. His sense of what could be done, what was politically possible, became his overriding concern. The administration's response to the Spanish civil war largely exemplified this approach. Like the British and French leaders, Roosevelt, who personally supported the Loyalists, publicly advocated a staunch neutrality that regarded the civil war as if it were a struggle between two distinct nations. But the primary struggle of the Spanish civil war clearly merited some form of commitment. The Loyalists supported a democratically elected government officially recognized by the United States since 1931; the Nationalists, originating in an army revolt, had the direct military support of Germany and Italy. In January 1937, the war was essentially a stalemate, and intervention on the side of the Loyalists may well have decided the outcome. But Roosevelt, who the previous summer had imposed a "moral embargo" on the sale of arms to either side, now requested that Congress revise the Neutrality Act to provide for legal embargoes against nations involved in civil wars. Congress complied. In the spring, Congress again revised the act to allow the president to put into effect a "cash-and-carry" policy whereby belligerents could buy U.S. goods other than armaments for cash and transport them in their own vessels. The act left standing the embargo on Spain.

Subsequent events caused some legislators to change their minds, however. By April the Italians had 100,000 troops in Spain fighting for Franco's Nationalists, and the Germans had 6,000 men involved through the air units of the Condor Legion. On April 27 the Condor Legion bombed Guernica, occupied solely by civilians—the first bombing of an open city in the West. This horror and other atrocities committed by the Nationalists escalated pro-Loyalist sentiments in the United States, although two-thirds of those polled remained neutral. Hundreds of young American men (some 3,000 during 1937 and 1938) sailed for France, then made their way into Spain to fight for the Loyalists in what became known as the Abraham Lincoln Brigade. Many writers and intellectuals, such as Archibald MacLeish and E. E. Cummings, spoke out against Franco and the fascists. Ernest Hemingway and John Dos Passos went to Spain to report on the war, making quite clear their support for the Loyalists. Eleanor Roosevelt overtly and strongly supported the Loyalists.

But there were strong pressures against any official intervention. The neutral position taken by the governments of Great Britain and France, based largely on the fact that communists (especially detested by Neville Chamberlain) supported the Loyalist cause, meant the administration could expect no support from these nations. Secretary of State Hull, for much the same reason, adamantly opposed aiding the Loyalists in any way. On the other hand, Morgenthau and Ickes prodded the president to lift the embargo on arms shipments to the Loyalists. In May 1938, isolationist Republican senator Gerald Nye introduced a resolution in the Senate to remove the embargo from the Neutrality Act so that the United States could provide help to the Loyalists. Even Senator William Borah of Idaho, a staunch isolationist, objected to the embargo on grounds that the effect of U.S. neutrality favored the Nationalists. Roosevelt by this time appeared to be persuaded of the virtue of lifting the embargo, but he never took the necessary steps because of what for him was the decisive factor: The Roman Catholic Church hierarchy supported Franco, so the administration's siding with the Loyalists would cost Democratic congressmen the "loss of every Catholic voter" in the upcoming election, Roosevelt believed. The embargo stood.

INCREASING TENSIONS WITH JAPAN

Other events of 1937–38 likely impressed Roosevelt as evidence of a far greater long-term threat than the outcome of the Spanish civil war. In July 1937 an encounter between Japanese and Chinese troops at Marco Polo Bridge several miles west of Peiping (Beijing) resulted in gunfire, a three-day skirmish, and the onset of full-scale war. In August, after Chinese troops shot and killed purported infiltrators near Shanghai, the Japanese launched an attack on the city. Chinese pilots accidentally bombed the International Settlement in Shanghai while trying to attack Japanese warships in the city's harbor and killed 40 foreign residents, including three Americans. Roosevelt ordered 1,200 marines sent to Shanghai to protect American citizens. Hull appealed for a peaceful resolution of the Sino-Japanese conflict. In October the League of Nations censured Japan for violating the Nine-Power Treaty and the Pact of Paris and invoked a meeting of the signatories in November, which proved futile since the Japanese refused to attend. (Roosevelt had instructed the head of the American delegation to recommend that as a counter to Japan's aggression other nations make it easier for China to acquire arms—something he admitted the United States could not do because of the Neutrality Act, thus underscoring the total futility of the conference.) Also in October, Roosevelt traveled to Chicago, where he delivered a speech that garnered intense interest here and abroad. He said aggression was a "contagion" and an "epidemic" threatening the entire world; consequently, he proposed a "quarantine" of the aggressor nations. Although many in France and Great Britain believed this proposal was a sign that the United States might be prepared to join in a system of collective security (as the speech clearly indicated), isolationist congressmen expressed outrage at the abandonment of neutrality that the proposal implied. The next day in a press conference the president retreated.

On December 10, a day after the announcement that Joseph P. Kennedy would be appointed to the crucial post of ambassador to the Court of St. James (Great Britain), the Japanese launched a major offensive against Nanjing near Shanghai. The staff of the American embassy, journalists, and other Americans in Nanjing boarded the USS *Panay*, which steamed more than 20 miles upriver along with three U.S. oil tankers to seek safety. On December 12, Japanese planes deliberately bombed all the vessels, sinking the *Panay* and destroying two of the tankers. The bombings killed four people and wounded 74, including the captain of the *Panay*. It was a virtual act of war. Roosevelt and Secretary Hull both strenuously protested to the Japanese ambassador, and Foreign Minister Koki Hirota quickly apologized, describing the attack as a mistake. Then the day before Christmas the Japanese agreed to pay indemnities and to prevent future such "mistakes," and the incident was over. It did, however, suggest possible events to come. The incident also provided an excuse for a push in Congress to approve the Ludlow Amendment (so-called after its sponsor, Congressman Louis Ludlow of Indiana), which provided that, except when attacked, the United States could not declare war without the approval of a majority of voters in a national referendum—a means of slowing any movement toward war and also of impeding the president's initiatives. Under extremely strong opposition from the White House, the amendment failed to pass the House of Representatives in January 1938, but by only 21 votes.

HITLER'S SUCCESSES

Other events abroad promised still greater long-term menace. As the year unfolded, Nazi actions and British responses thrust the European nations inexorably toward war. In January Austrian officials discovered that Nazis, financed by Germany, planned a revolt and the overthrow of the Austrian government, even though a July 1936 agreement committed Germany to avoid involvement in Austria's internal affairs. Hitler reacted quickly to Austria's discovery, and, at the suggestion of recent ambassador to Austria Franz von Papen, as a subterfuge he invited Austrian chancellor Kurt von Schuschnigg to Berchtesgaden for diplomatic discussions in February. There Hitler browbeat the Austrian chancellor and tried to impose on him an agreement that would have legitimized the Nazis in Austria and even granted them ministerial posts, including control of the police. Hitler gave Schuschnigg four days to accept. The ploy worked. British prime minister Neville Chamberlain also accepted the agreement, causing Foreign Minister Anthony Eden, an opponent of appeasement (in this context, surrender to threats by the fascist powers), to resign—a fateful development, as the arch-appeaser Edward Frederick Lindley Wood, Lord Halifax, replaced him. Hitler then demanded "self-determination" for Germans living in Austria. Schuschnigg refused, but his government's ability to resist was crumbling. Schuschnigg called for a plebiscite, and an enraged Hitler ordered the occupation of Austria. On March 12, 1938, German troops crossed the border of Austria. Hitler followed after to a warm welcome—the Anschluss (annexation) of Austria was complete. Great Britain and France accepted the German occupation.

Next came the turn of Czechoslovakia. The crisis began in May as Germany massed troops in Saxony near the Czech border. Some members of the German general staff opposed invading Czechoslovakia, however, and the internal division within the general staff caused a lull in German military movement. Some of the general staff joined in a conspiracy to overthrow Hitler; they sent emissaries to the British government to try to persuade Chamberlain to stand fast against a German attack on Czechoslovakia—arguing that opposition would stymie and discredit Hitler and provide the opportunity for the army conspirators to remove him—but to no avail. Chamberlain requested a meeting with Hitler at Berchtesgaden on September 15. There Hitler demanded control of the Sudetenland, a Czech province inhabited mostly by Germans, but his real intention was to take control of the entire country. Further negotiations stumbled, and war appeared imminent between Germany and Czechoslovakia, the latter ostensibly supported by Great Britain and France.

THE MUNICH APPEASEMENT

Then at the last minute Chamberlain and French premier Édouard Daladier, whose governments were pledged to come to Czechoslovakia's defense, undermined and betrayed Czech president Eduard Beneš in order to reach an accommodation with Hitler. They gathered at a conference, which included Italy but not Czechoslovakia or Czech supporter the USSR, at Munich on September 29–30. The four powers agreed that the Sudetenland would be ceded to Germany by October 10, that they would guarantee the new Czech borders, and that an international commission would oversee plebiscites to determine the future of minorities in Czechoslovakia. Chamberlain returned to London and declared, "I believe it is peace in our time." The United States had long since made clear its intention to avoid involvement—in fact, Roosevelt approved of Chamberlain's decision to participate in the Munich conference.

Prime Minister Neville Chamberlain of Great Britain *(Library of Congress)*

Many believed the appeasement policy toward Germany would end in failure. Premier Daladier, who had originally urged Chamberlain to negotiate with Hitler and then had followed Chamberlain's lead, regarded the Munich agreement as a disaster. Winston Churchill rose in the British House of Commons to denounce Munich as "a total and unmitigated defeat" that marked only a beginning; Hitler would soon want more, Churchill declared. Following debate, the House of Commons voted to approve Chamberlain's policies. Roosevelt thoroughly disapproved of both Hitler and Mussolini, but he continued to adhere to what he perceived as the demands of domestic politics. In fact, his acquiescence in the appeasement of Hitler reflected the sentiments of the American public; 60 percent of Americans polled approved of the Munich agreement. Events in both Austria and Germany, however, evidenced the kinds of consequences that could be expected to follow such agreements.

SEEDS OF THE HOLOCAUST

In the first few weeks after the Anschluss, the Nazi militia the SS conducted a vicious pogrom against Viennese Jews and began construction of the concentration camp at Mauthausen, near Linz. In late October the Nazis rounded up 10,000 Polish Jews living in Germany, confiscated their property, and deported them. The night of November 9–10, 1938, in Germany offered the most telling evidence of what was to come. Using as an excuse the killing of a German consular official in Paris by a Jewish émigré, the Nazis staged riots throughout Germany, attacking and burning thousands of Jewish homes, shops, and temples, killing scores of Jews and arresting 20,000 to be sent to concentration camps. Kristallnacht (night of broken glass), as it was called, went unpunished; Hermann Göring decreed that Jews would pay for the damages and that all insurance payments would go to the government. Roosevelt recalled the U.S. ambassador from Berlin and granted permits for 15,000 refugees from Germany and Austria to remain in the United States. Even in this small gesture he took some risk; following Kristallnacht, public support for the current restrictive immigration laws actually rose to 83 percent. During the period from the completion of the Anschluss to the Japanese attack on Pearl Harbor in December 1941, only 150,000 refugees would be admitted; the United States would not become a haven for refugees.

That circumstance reflected a certain grim irony since, following the Anschluss, Roosevelt had at least made a gesture toward accommodating Jewish refugees who wished to flee Nazi persecution. In late March 1938, he sent invitations to 33 nations (not including Germany, of course) to attend a conference on planning for the acceptance of larger numbers of emigrants than current laws permitted, with the processing of the emigrants to be conducted by private agencies. Thirty-two nations accepted. The conference convened in Evian-les-Bains, France for 10 days in July, but the U.S. government, which should have provided the needed leadership as sponsor of the meeting, provided no direction at the conference. As a result the conference ended with most of the assembled nations' representatives voicing reluctance to accept more refugees. Their only concrete achievement was establishment of the Intergovernmental Committee on Refugees (IGC), but it failed to devise any means of resolving the refugee problem. The same failure occurred in the United States with the impotent President's Advisory Committee on Political Refugees, which Roosevelt had appointed in April 1938 in preparation for the international conference. In a nutshell, the Roosevelt administration lacked the will to tackle the refugee issue or even to help educate the American public about the seriousness of the problem.

THE IMPACT OF ISOLATIONISM

To a very large extent, it must be noted, Roosevelt's hands were tied by the conditions of domestic politics. Isolationists controlled enormous power in the Congress, although, as evidenced in Senator Nye's response to the Spanish civil war, they sometimes showed willingness to compromise. The isolationists also apparently had the support of the vast majority of the American public. As the president, however, Roosevelt had a pulpit from which to preach views that might help transform opinion—apprising the public of the serious menace in Asia and Europe, making it clear that the United States could not escape the consequences of fascist domination in these areas of the world (if only because of the realities of international trade), calling attention to Nazi and Japanese atrocities, underscoring the untrustworthiness of the dictators as evidenced by their treaty violations, and repeatedly stating the need for preparedness and for preventive measures that required U.S. involvement in pressuring Japan and Germany. Still, 1938 was a congressional election year, and the electoral outcome could either improve or impair the president's ability to lead domestically. The depression, after all, still persisted.

Billboard advertising primary election in Vincennes, Indiana, May 1938; photo by Arthur Rothstein *(Library of Congress)*

THE 1938 ELECTION

A rural family in Caruthersville, Missouri, August 1938 *(Library of Congress)*

Roosevelt decided to embark on a campaign journey to lend his support to liberal candidates and make known his opposition to conservatives within his own party. In truth, many liberals had actually quarreled with and moved away from the administration's views. Perhaps the most obvious manifestation of this disaffection was the founding in late April 1938 of the National Progressives of America by Wisconsin governor Phil La Follette, whose brother Senator Robert La Follette, Jr., had also abandoned the president over fiscal policy. In launching this centrist party for liberals, the governor blasted the inconsistencies of the administration, called for public ownership of the credit system, and denounced concentrations of power among the wealthy. A major tenet of the party's program was isolationism, a popular position throughout the Midwest. The National Progressives, however, never constituted a major threat to the president.

Roosevelt was apparently a sufficient detriment in himself: The majority of the candidates he supported in his national tour failed to be elected—a major blow to the president's morale. In the southern states especially the president fared badly. Although Alben Barkley won reelection in Kentucky, Roosevelt's support of him was not a decisive factor; more to the point, candidates he spoke against, such as Senator Cotton Ed Smith of South Carolina, Senator Walter George of Georgia, and Senator Millard Tydings of Maryland, all handily won reelection in the fall congressional elections. All were segregationists, and it is quite conceivable that Roosevelt's advocacy of antilynching legislation sponsored by Senator Wagner influenced the outcome. On the other hand, Roosevelt supported Texas congressman Maury Maverick, who had voted for the bill when it passed the House in April 1937, and Maverick won reelection. The southern senators Roosevelt opposed campaigned on the issue of states' rights, an understood appeal to distrust of outsiders.

SLOW PROGRESS FOR BLACKS

Eleanor Roosevelt speaking in Ashland, Kentucky, May 29, 1937 *(Mary Flanery Collection, courtesy of the Photographic Archives, Special Collections and Archives, University of Kentucky Libraries)*

The antilynching bill brought before the Senate in January 1938 died there in February as a result of southerners' filibustering. (Lynchings of blacks rose during the mid-thirties, exceeding 20 or more per year, but fell sharply to two in 1939, apparently as a result of southern states' efforts to forestall future demands for federal legislation.) Roosevelt's support for the antilynching bill was a

Sharecropper's family in New
Madrid, Missouri, May 1938
(Library of Congress)

unique instance of his public espousal of civil rights. Whatever he believed personally, his public position was very cautious, as he was always concerned to preserve the Democratic Party's strong base in the South. Or at least it was his consistent argument that there was little he could do on civil rights because he must avoid offending southern leaders in the Congress who controlled so many chairmanships of key committees; there were more important issues on which he needed their support. Eleanor Roosevelt, on the other hand, was outspoken in her advocacy of equal rights and integration. She had been persuaded of the justness of this position largely through her friendships with Mary McLeod Bethune, an educator and civil rights leader whom she first met in 1927, and with Walter White, the first black to hold the post of national secretary of the National Association for the Advancement of Colored People (NAACP). Bethune served on an advisory committee for the National Youth Administration and regularly visited the White House to confer with the president on civil rights issues. The president as a politician was not unaware of the importance of support among black voters, three-fourths of whom had supported him in the 1936 election in a massive shift away from the Republican Party. It would be their votes and the nation's sense of moral outrage that eventually secured approval of civil rights policies that in 1937 were just beginning to receive some attention from national leaders. In the meantime the New Deal provided the initial step through social programs that directly benefited blacks as well as whites by requiring nondiscriminatory application. It should be noted also that all African Americans experienced a symbolic triumph on June 22, 1937, when Joe Louis defeated James J. Braddock to become world heavyweight boxing champion.

One program in which blacks attained a new stature was the Federal Theatre Project (FTP). Even though the casts for the FTP productions were mostly segregated—16 "Negro Units" were created nationwide—black actors and actresses could perform genuine roles for once rather than stereotypical ones. Unfortunately, the FTP inspired widespread hostility among conservatives. Its demise occurred after only four years because of an investigation begun in 1938 into the program's activities by the House Un-American Activities Committee (HUAC), whose members charged that the FTP was communist oriented. During its four-year run, however, the FTP's productions attracted a total audience of nearly 30 million and boosted the careers of such talents as Orson Welles, E. G. Marshall, John Houseman, Arlene Francis, Arthur Miller, and John Huston. Congress would eliminate the FTP's budget from Works Progress Administration (WPA) funding in 1939. In 1938 HUAC also investigated the Federal Writers' Project, a boon to black writers Richard Wright and Ralph Ellison along with many white authors, which resulted in cuts in this program's funding. These and the music and art programs in the Federal One

Mary McLeod Bethune with her son at Bethune-Coleman College in Daytona Beach, Florida, January 1943 *(Courtesy of the Library of Congress)*

project at least served for a short time to make forms of art expression available to millions of Americans, many for the first time in their lives.

Through the influence of Eleanor Roosevelt modest but meaningful improvements for blacks appeared in other areas as well. The first lady persuaded the president to increase funding for Howard University and the Freedmen's hospital in Washington, D.C., and Harry Hopkins and Aubrey Williams to administratively effect greater equality in the WPA and other relief programs. Secretary of the Interior Harold Ickes, who had forbade segregation in his department's cafeterias and restrooms in 1933, compelled the Public Works Administration (PWA) to hire both skilled and unskilled African-American laborers for construction projects; he also made certain that a third of all the public housing units built by the PWA had black residents. Hopkins pressed similar improvements in the WPA's programs, insisting on equitable treatment of African Americans so that by 1939 the WPA provided earnings for more than 1 million black families, and more than 5,000 blacks had employment as teachers in the WPA's education program. Similarly the Civilian Conservation Corps (CCC) advanced enrollment of black youths from 6 percent in 1936 to 11 percent in 1938. Given such promising developments, black leaders abandoned their earlier criticisms of the New Deal and adopted new expectations.

Women also witnessed marginal changes that had long-term significance. The Roosevelt administration set a certain standard for elevating women with the appointments of Frances Perkins as secretary of labor, Florence Allen as a judge of the U.S. Court of Appeals for the Sixth Circuit, Marion Glass Banister as assistant U.S. treasurer, and Nellie Tayloe Ross as director of the U.S. Mint. Numerous other women held leadership positions in the Children's Bureau, the Women's Bureau, the NRA, and the Social Security Board. Women composed more than 40 percent of the enrollees in the Federal Arts Project, but elsewhere in the WPA's programs hundreds of thousands of women found themselves limited to employment in menial tasks, such as sewing apparel. Married women experienced restrictions on entering either government or private employment, as federal and many state regulations forbade hiring married couples and employers followed that lead. Nevertheless, during the thirties women gained over a 25 percent representation in the labor force, and married women's work involvement increased 50 percent. Many married women, of course, suffered broken homes as their husbands joined the ranks of the unemployed and in many cases abandoned their families. African-American women fared worst, with their employment outside the home declining significantly as white women displaced them in domestic service work, further exacerbating hardships for many black families.

FINE ARTS AND PLEASURES

The New Deal programs also had a significant impact on building and architecture. The PWA was responsible for building nearly 22,000 public housing units in cities throughout the United States. The TVA, in constructing dams whose development admirably combined the talents of both engineers and architects, provided the nation some grand examples of functional design. And the Greenbelt towns created in Maryland, Ohio, and Wisconsin along with the rural resettlement communities created by the Resettlement Administration

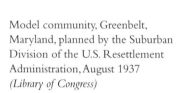

Model community, Greenbelt,
Maryland, planned by the Suburban
Division of the U.S. Resettlement
Administration, August 1937
(*Library of Congress*)

influenced town planning and the development of suburbs. Arguably the most important event in American architecture in these years, however, was the arrival of Walter Gropius. Having left Germany for England in 1934 to escape Nazism, Gropius came to the United States in 1937 to teach architecture at Harvard, where he would remain until 1952, with enormous effect in steering American architecture toward adopting the so-called International Style.

In the areas of arts and entertainment, movies and radio remained the favorites, as the final years of the decade proceeded. Fred Astaire and Ginger Rogers had another hit during 1937 with *Shall We Dance,* featuring the music of George Gershwin. The *Gold Diggers* series produced yet another musical in 1937. In January 1938, Walt Disney Studios released the company's first feature-length cartoon, one of the most popular animated films of all time, *Snow White and the Seven Dwarfs.* Also in 1938 the popular, zany comedy *Bringing Up Baby,* directed by Howard Hawks and starring Katharine Hepburn and Cary Grant was released. In addition these years produced adventure films such as *Captains Courageous,* starring Spencer Tracy, and *Adventures of Robin Hood.* Although William Wyler's *Dead End* (1937), starring Humphrey Bogart, depicted the legacies of slum life and crime, the more popular films, as the titles here suggest, provided moviegoers escape from serious issues raised by the recurrent depression at home and the triumphs of fascism abroad.

The Roosevelts as movie fans had some influence on the public's embrace of cinema as an art and entertainment form. Although they watched films in the privacy of the White House, Eleanor Roosevelt sometimes commented publicly in cinema magazines on her and her husband's enthusiasm for movies, endorsing the movies both as family entertainment and as a legitimate art medium. She let the public know that the president regularly enjoyed Mickey

Mouse films, and she noted other films that their entire family had liked. She also praised newsreels as an important source of information and advocated an educational role for the film industry. In her first lady role Eleanor Roosevelt visited the studios of Warner Brothers, MGM, and Twentieth Century–Fox in Hollywood. And she and FDR invited movie stars to the White House for both family and formal events; visiting stars included Ginger Rogers, Jean Harlow, Janet Gaynor, Robert Taylor, and Frederic March. No doubt as a consequence Hollywood, which became highly politicized during the thirties, joined the political campaigns. Some Hollywood moguls had already been involved during the twenties; Louis B. Mayer, for example, had worked in Coolidge's and Hoover's campaigns. Jack Warner supported FDR and persuaded William Randolph Hearst to join him. Among FDR's other Hollywood supporters were Helen and Melvyn Douglas, Paul Muni, and John Garfield; and in the 1940 election he would gain the support of Douglas Fairbanks, Jr., Henry Fonda, Joan Bennett, Alice Faye, Rosalind Russell, Humphrey Bogart, Lucille Ball, and Groucho Marx. Hollywood actors have been actively involved in politics ever since.

As for reading, the success ethic found reinforcement in Dale Carnegie's *How to Win Friends and Influence People,* which sold 750,000 copies in 1937, its first full year in print. The book ranked fifth among best sellers during the entire decade. Self-help books, however unlikely their relevance might seem,

A Polish miner listens to the radio after work at Westover on Scott's Run, Pennsylvania, September 1938. *(Library of Congress)*

sold well throughout the depression years. Among fictional works, 1936 Pulitzer Prize winner *Gone with the Wind* continued to sell well; it was joined in 1938 by Marjorie Rawlings's Pulitzer-winning *The Yearling,* a novel about backwoods Florida and a boy's relationship with an orphaned fawn. Other popular books during these years included mysteries by Erle Stanley Gardner, the humorous stories of Damon Runyon (later the basis for the 1952 musical *Guys and Dolls*), Kenneth Roberts's historical novel *Northwest Passage* set on the 18th-century frontier, and English novelist Daphne du Maurier's *Rebecca* about a woman haunted by the ghost of her husband's first wife. Such works might suggest an escape into the past and into fantasy—like many movies of the era, a means of not confronting an undesirable reality.

For sports fans at least the depression years afforded a positive development in the resurgence of horse racing, and 1938 witnessed the sport's premier event. The road to that event began in California, where gambling on horse racing had been illegal for more than two decades, until the fiscal crisis effected by the depression prodded the state's government to pursue sources of additional revenues. In 1933, consequently, California legalized gambling on horse races, with the stipulations that tracks would use pari-mutuel betting machines instead of bookmakers to limit corruption and that the betting be severely taxed. This move paved the way for the success of the new Santa Anita Park, which opened for racing at the end of 1934. And the park became the site for

Horse races, Hialeah Park, Florida, February 1939 *(Library of Congress, Prints and Photographs Division [USF 3301-030470-M2])*

launching the stellar career of Seabiscuit, whom Charles Howard acquired in August 1936 for his stable near San Francisco. Although it was not his first race, Seabiscuit debuted at the Santa Anita Handicap, with a winning purse of $100,000, on February 27, 1937, when he lost by a nose to Rosemont. But his greatness had been evident, and he would return to win a week later by seven lengths, setting a course record. Seabiscuit gained the rapt attention of the western public and media.

As the greatest race horse in the West, it appeared to Howard and his trainer Tom Smith, as well as the racing industry as a whole, that Seabiscuit must challenge the greatest horse in the East, War Admiral, sired by Man o' War, owned by Samuel Riddle, and winner of the Triple Crown for 1937. The approach to that encounter proved rocky. There were on-again, off-again efforts to have the two horses compete at Belmont Park, War Admiral's home track in New York. Finally, through the negotiations of Alfred Vanderbilt, the two owners reached a deal whereby Seabiscuit and War Admiral would race at the Pimlico Special in Maryland on November 1, 1938. And, in the most compelling of circumstances for race fans, the horses would meet, not in a field of entries, but one on one. In what some termed the race of the century, War Admiral, ridden by Charley Kurtsinger, and Seabiscuit, with jockey George Woolf (nicknamed the "Iceman") astride, surged into competition shortly after 4 o'clock on the appointed day. Seabiscuit and the "Iceman" proved victorious, winning by more than four lengths and achieving permanent fame in horse racing history.

A Clouded Future

At the end of 1938 the American people faced a threatening future of entanglement in deadly foreign events. The Munich agreement and the various other efforts to appease Mussolini and Hitler (most especially the latter) had failed, leaving Hitler convinced that he faced no real opposition to aggression. Appeasement sealed the fate of Europe: A second world war was now inevitable. Despite their disdain for becoming involved in foreign affairs and conflicts, Americans were destined to be drawn into the maelstrom of that war. It was unrealistic for a nation that bordered on the Earth's two great oceans and traded goods with nations across the vast expanses of those oceans to expect ultimately to avoid some kind of direct involvement in the wars of both Asia and Europe. Roosevelt reluctantly sensed America's inevitable involvement, but he was still, by his understanding, not in a favorable position to influence events either abroad or at home in such a way as to forestall war, and certainly not to preclude it. The British prime minister, Neville Chamberlain, had responded with indifference to the American president's efforts to foster peace; the fascist dictators had responded with contempt. Although domestically Roosevelt appeared to have regained lost momentum with Congress's approval of new programs, the resurgent recession was a reminder of how intractable were the economic and social problems the nation continued to experience.

The November 1938 elections also added a dispiriting note for Roosevelt. Not only were congressmen and senators he had opposed returned to office, but the Republicans also scored impressive gains: eight seats in the Senate and

Crowd at the South Louisiana State Fair, November 1938 *(Library of Congress)*

81 in the House. Republican candidates also took control of 11 governorships. The Democrats still held firm control of the Congress (69 to 23 in the Senate and 262 to 169 in the House) and retained the great majority (30 to 18) of the governorships. Nevertheless, the results indicated a substantial loss of political sway for the president, perhaps a growing disenchantment with the New Deal's management of the depression among middle-class voters. Conservatives gained strength in the new Congress; among the new class was Senator Robert Taft of Ohio, who would quickly gain prominence as a spokesman for isolationism and fiscal restraint. Roosevelt would enter the last two years of his second term with justifiable foreboding.

CHRONICLE OF EVENTS

1937

January 1: In Flint, Michigan, General Motors Corporation workers go on strike, closing down seven of the company's plants and idling more than 33,000 workers. The strikers demand the company recognize the United Auto Workers (UAW) as their collective bargaining agent to negotiate higher wages, shorter hours, and improved working conditions; they also employ a tactic first used a year earlier, the "sit-down strike," occupying two GM factories in Flint.

January 6: Roosevelt presents the State of the Union address to Congress. He requests legislation prohibiting the shipment of war matériel to Spain and advocates adopting an "increasingly enlightened" view of the Constitution, among other things.

January 8: Responding to the president's request, Congress passes the Spanish Embargo Act, placing an embargo on any shipments of arms to Spain.

January 12: In a special message to Congress the president proposes a reorganization of the executive branch of the government, based on the recommendations of an accompanying report from the President's Committee on Administrative Management, as a means of improving efficiency and saving money.

January 20: President Roosevelt is inaugurated for the second time. In his address the president observes that one-third of the nation remains "ill-housed,

This photo by Dorothea Lange shows four families, refugees from the dust bowl in Texas, at an overnight camp in Calipatria, Imperial Valley, California, March 1937. *(Library of Congress)*

ill-clad, ill-nourished" and promises more radical measures to attack the problems.

January 30: In a speech to the Reichstag, Hitler proclaims Germany's official repudiation of the Treaty of Versailles, already affected in practice.

February 5: Roosevelt presents to the Congress a proposal to "vitalize" the federal courts. He proposes that when a judge who has served for 10 years does not retire or resign within six months following his 70th birthday, then the president may appoint a new additional judge to the bench. The president would be empowered to appoint no more than six new members to the Supreme Court and 44 to lower federal courts under this guideline. The proposal is immediately viewed as an attempt by the president to pack the Supreme Court with justices favorable to New Deal legislation and programs.

February 11: General Motors Corporation capitulates to the strike begun as the year opened and offers terms to the United Automobile Workers (UAW) union.

March 2: United States Steel Corporation, threatened with a strike, gives in and accepts the Steel Workers' Organizing Committee (SWOC) of the Congress of Industrial Organizations (CIO) as its employees' bargaining agent, while also agreeing to raise wages and improve working conditions.

March 14: Pope Pius XI issues an encyclical accusing the Nazi government of violating the 1933 Reich Concordat between Germany and the Vatican and of generating hostility against the church.

March 22: Senator Burton K. Wheeler, a strong opponent of the court-packing proposal, in hearings before the Senate Judiciary Committee on the proposal, reads into the record a letter from Chief Justice Charles Evans Hughes that explains the Supreme Court's procedures for choosing lower court decisions for review and refutes charges of inefficiency in the high court's operations, describing the Court as "fully abreast of its work." The letter seriously undermines the president's arguments for legislation to "vitalize" the federal courts system.

March 29: The Supreme Court announces a decision, reversing its position of the previous year, that finds the minimum wage law of the state of Washington constitutional. Justice Owen Roberts crosses over to join Chief Justice Hughes and the Court's three liberal justices in the majority.

April 12: In the case of *National Labor Relations Board v. Jones and Laughlin Steel Corporation,* the Supreme Court decides by a vote of 5-4 that provisions of the Wagner Act are constitutionally valid.

April 13: During a press conference the president tells reporters (off the record) that, despite the recent Supreme Court decisions favoring New Deal programs, he is still committed to seeking legislation to reform the court system. Since publication of Chief Justice Hughes's letter and of statements by opponents of the legislation, such as Carter Glass, polls indicate that public support for the president's proposal is declining; opposition in Congress to the proposal is mounting.

April 26: Roosevelt signs into law the Guffey-Vinson Bituminous Coal Act, which restores the provisions of the Guffey-Snyder Act invalidated by the Supreme Court except for the wages and hours provisions that the Court had objected to.

April 27: In support of Francisco Franco in Spain, airplanes of the Condor Legion of the German Luftwaffe bomb Guernica into rubble.

April 29: Congress passes an act that continues the arms embargo and loan prohibition provisions of the earlier law, but in addition it prohibits Americans from traveling on the ships of belligerent nations and forbids the arming of American merchant ships, while also granting the president discretionary power to extend to any nations a "cash-and-carry" policy—they may buy anything but arms from the United States but must pay for them with cash and transport them in their own ships.

May 1: Roosevelt signs into law a revised Neutrality Act granting him power to decide whether the act's terms apply to any civil war except for that in Spain, where the January embargo resolution still is in effect; the president immediately signs a proclamation banning exports of American arms or ammunition to either side in the Spanish civil war.

May 6: At Lakehurst, New Jersey, the huge, year-old German dirigible *Hindenburg,* completing its first transatlantic flight of the year, bursts into flames at its mooring and disintegrates.

May 14: In a meeting at the White House a delegation of congressional leaders tells Roosevelt that the court-packing bill cannot be passed, but the president rejects their counsel, insisting, "The people are with me!"

A January 1937 photo by Arthur Rothstein shows a camp for migrant agricultural workers, near Belle Glade, Florida. *(Library of Congress, Prints and Photographs Division [USF 33-T01-2365-M2])*

May 18: Supreme Court justice Willis Van Devanter, a member of the Court's conservative bloc, announces his plans to retire.

May 24: The Supreme Court, in a series of decisions, validates the unemployment insurance and old-age pension provisions of the Social Security Act.

May 28: Neville Chamberlain becomes prime minister of Great Britain, replacing Stanley Baldwin.

May 30: In Chicago picketing strikers confront police at the Republic Steel Company mill. After a striker hurls a stick toward them, the police fire three shots into the air; the strikers react by throwing rocks and sticks at the police, who then open fire and chase and beat the fleeing strikers. Ten strikers die, 30 are wounded, and 28 are hospitalized with severe beating wounds, leading the press to refer to the event as the "Memorial Day massacre."

May 31: German warships shell the Spanish port of Almería.

June 5: Although General Hayashi Senjuro lost the April elections in Japan and his government was forced out of power, the military manipulates the installation of a new cabinet favorable to the military's policies, with Prince Konoye Fumimaro as premier.

June 14: The Senate Judiciary Committee releases a majority report condemning the court-packing bill as unjustifiable, unnecessary, and a threat to the Supreme Court's independence, urging its rejection by the Congress.

June 29: Norman Thomas, recently returned from a tour of Europe, meets with Roosevelt in the White House to advocate his support for the Loyalists in the Spanish civil war but to no avail.

July 1: In Berlin officials arrest and imprison Rev. Dr. Martin Niemoller, Protestant leader of the Confessional Church, which opposes Nazi racial concepts and Nazi efforts to subjugate the Protestant churches.

July 2: A substitute court reform bill is introduced in the Senate.

July 7: A clash occurs between Japanese forces and Chinese civilians at Wanping (Lugoujiao) near Peiping (Beijing). Known as the Marco Polo Bridge incident, the clash evolves into events forming the pretext for war between Japan and China.

July 14: Senator Joseph Robinson, majority leader and spearhead for the president of the court-packing bill in the Senate, exhausted and stressed by his efforts to win approval of the bill, dies of heart failure in his apartment.

July 21: Senator Alben Barkley, with the support of the White House, is elected majority leader of the Senate. A motion is introduced recommitting the court-packing bill to the Senate Judiciary Committee.

July 22: Roosevelt signs into law the Bankhead-Jones Farm Tenancy Act, which replaces the Resettlement Administration with the Farm Security Administration (FSA), mandated to provide loans to tenant farmers to buy their own farms and to aid poor farmers with efforts to improve their lands. The Senate votes (70-20) to recommit the court reform bill.

July 30: Japanese troops occupy Tianjin (Tientsin).

August 8: Japanese troops occupy Peiping.

August 9: Chinese guards shoot a Japanese naval officer and sailor who purportedly, acting as spies, have tried to enter a military air base near Shanghai.

August 13: Roosevelt nominates Senator Hugo Black to replace Van Devanter on the Supreme Court.

August 13: Fighting between Chinese and Japanese erupts in Shanghai.

August 14: While attempting to bomb Japanese warships in the harbor at Shanghai, Chinese aviators, by mistake, drop bombs on the International Settlement, killing 800 Chinese civilians and 40 foreigners, including three Americans. The U.S. government asks all Americans to leave the war zone.

August 17: Responding to fighting in Shanghai, the Japanese government orders a mobilization of troops; 15 divisions are to be deployed in northern and central China by the end of September.

A trailer home near Little Fork, Minnesota, in August 1937 *(Library of Congress, Prints and Photographs Division [USF-US33-011251-M3])*

August 17: The United States dispatches 1,200 marines from San Diego to Shanghai, where already 1,000 marines are stationed, to help protect and evacuate Americans.

August 17: Roosevelt signs into law the Miller-Tydings Act intended to enhance fair trade laws.

August 17: The Senate confirms Hugo Black's nomination to the Supreme Court by a vote of 63-16.

August 21: Congress adjourns.

August 23: Secretary of State Cordell Hull urges China and Japan to settle their conflict through peaceful means.

August 26: Roosevelt signs into law the Judicial Procedures Reform Act, a substitute for his reform proposal, which provides for minor procedural reforms in the lower federal courts but contains no provisions affecting the composition of the Supreme Court or any lower courts.

September 1: Roosevelt signs into law the Wagner-Steagall Housing Act, which creates the U.S. Housing Authority (USHA) within the Interior Department and provides $500 million for loans for low-cost housing.

September 3: In a public address John L. Lewis concedes that the CIO has failed in its efforts to organize Republic Steel and other firms referred to as Little Steel and blames Roosevelt for the failure.

September 14: Roosevelt issues an executive order banning shipment of war matériel to either China or Japan aboard ships owned by the U.S. government, but he does not implement the restrictions provided for in the Neutrality Act.

September 22: At Hyde Park the president boards the train to begin a national tour.

September 24: Japanese troops occupy Baoding (Pao-ting).

September 25: Mussolini begins a four-day visit to Germany—his first personal meeting with Hitler in three years.

September 28: A huge celebration in Berlin climaxes Mussolini's visit to Germany. Both he and Hitler address a massive gathering of a million people.

October 1: While Hugo Black and his wife have been vacationing in Europe, newspaper reports have revealed that Black had been a member of the Ku Klux Klan in Alabama; he had told the Senate during his confirmation hearings that he was not "now" a Klan member. The resulting controversy awaited

Black's return home. In a brief radio broadcast Black admits that he had belonged to the Klan but left it before becoming a senator and has had no dealings with it since—his final statement on the subject, closing the controversy.

October 5: While returning from his national tour, President Roosevelt advocates a "quarantine" of belligerent nations during a speech in Chicago that gains wide attention for implying that the United States should join in collective security measures with other nations against the spread of the "disease" of war, but he also voices his "determination to pursue a policy of peace."

October 6: Roosevelt arrives back at Hyde Park, ending his national tour that included numerous speeches in Iowa, Wyoming, Montana, Idaho, Oregon, North Dakota, and Minnesota. During a press conference he refuses to elaborate on what he meant by "quarantine" in his Chicago speech the day before, obscuring any suggestion about a policy for collective security.

October 10: Japanese troops occupy Shijiazhuang (Shih-chia-chuang).

October 11: Roosevelt signs a formal request for a special session of Congress to convene on November 15 to address budgetary issues. Heavy selling begins on the New York Stock Exchange.

October 19: More than 7 million shares are traded on the New York Stock Exchange, the largest volume since July 21, 1933, and prices collapse ominously—a reminder of 1929.

October 31: Japanese troops capture Anyang and Yucheng in China.

November 3: Representatives of the nations that signed the Nine-Power Treaty begin a conference in Brussels, sponsored by the League of Nations, to try to negotiate a settlement between China and Japan, but Japan refuses to send a delegate.

November 5: The Japanese stage amphibious landings in Hangzhou (Hangchow) Bay, disembarking four divisions to bolster the forces attacking Shanghai.

November 5: During a secret meeting at the Reich Chancellory in Berlin with several of his military leaders, including Commander in Chief General Werner von Blomberg and Minister of Aviation Hermann Göring, Hitler outlines a plan to take control of Czechoslovakia and Austria, making clear that he expects to go to war even if that means conflict with Great Britain and France. Blomberg opposes such a move on the grounds that the armed forces are inadequate to conduct a large war. Foreign Minister Baron Konstantin von Neurath and Commander in Chief of the Army General Baron Werner von Fritsch, also present, voice their opposition as well.

November 6: Japan rejects a second invitation to be represented at the Brussels conference, thus condemning the conference to failure.

November 9: Japanese troops occupy Taiyuan, effectively securing the conquest of Shanxi (Shansi) Province.

November 11: The Chinese begin the evacuation of Shanghai. The city's defense has cost the Chinese armies an estimated 270,000 casualties.

November 15: The special session of Congress opens with a message from the president acknowledging that since August an economic recession has occurred. He cites as his reason for calling the session the need to enact four New Deal bills dealing with wages and hours, agriculture, reorganization of the executive branch, and creation of seven regional authorities and a national planning authority that failed to attain consideration in the regular session of Congress.

November 19: With the approval of British prime minister Chamberlain, Edward Frederick Lindley Wood, Lord Halifax, meets with Hitler at Berchtesgaden, site of the German chancellor's mountaintop retreat in Bavaria and leaves Hitler with the impression that the British government seeks accommodation with Germany.

November 27: Roosevelt leaves the capital for Miami for a fishing holiday.

December 6: Having decided to cut short his holiday in Florida, Roosevelt arrives back in Washington, D.C.

December 9: Word leaks out through an article in the *New York Times* that Roosevelt has appointed Joseph P. Kennedy as ambassador to the Court of St. James (Great Britain) to replace Robert W. Bingham, who had returned home deathly ill.

December 10: Japan begins a full-scale offensive against Nanjing.

December 12: Japanese airplanes attack the U.S. gunboat *Panay* and an accompanying convoy of oil tankers that had moved upstream in the Yangzi River to escape involvement in the battle at Nanjing. The planes strafe (firing with machine guns) the ship's deck and a lifeboat carrying wounded men to shore,

killing three Americans and wounding 43. The *Panay* sinks.

December 13: Japanese troops occupy Nanjing, inflicting mass murder, torture, and rape upon the residents.

December 13: Roosevelt instructs Secretary of State Hull to inform the Japanese ambassador in Washington that the president is "deeply shocked" by the attack on the *Panay;* wishes the ambassador to so advise the emperor; and hopes that Japan will express regrets, offer compensation, and guarantee that no other such attacks will occur in the future.

December 14: The Japanese North China Area Army installs a puppet government in Peiping. They also have established a puppet government in eastern Inner Mongolia.

December 24: The Japanese government, already having formally apologized although describing the attack as a blunder (it was, in fact, deliberate), promises to pay indemnities for the *Panay* incident and to prevent any further such incidents.

December 26: Chinese general Chiang Kai-shek publicly rejects the possibility of negotiating any settlement with the Japanese. Jinan (Chinan) in Shandong (Shantung) Province falls to the Japanese advance.

1938

January 3: In his State of the Union message Roosevelt restates the government's commitment to New Deal programs, advocates a strong defense policy, and expresses his concern to balance the budget as soon as possible.

January 5: Japanese troops capture Jining (Tsining).

January 6: The Senate begins debate on an anti-lynching bill originally introduced by Senator Wagner in 1934.

January 10: By a vote of 209-188, the House of Representatives defeats adoption of the Ludlow Amendment to the Constitution, which would have given Congress the power to declare war by a simple majority vote only if the United States were invaded; in all other cases a declaration of war would have to be approved by the voters in a national referendum.

January 10: Japanese navy and army units in a combined attack take possession of Qingdao (Tsingtao).

January 16: The Japanese government announces that from now on Japan will conduct no dealings with Chiang Kai-shek and will eliminate the cause of the "disturbance" in China.

January 25: Hitler dismisses General von Blomberg. During a raid on the Nazi underground's headquarters in Vienna, Austrian police discover documents approved by Rudolf Hess describing a plot for a revolt in the spring that would entail the intervention of German troops.

January 26: Hitler forces out General von Fritsch as commander in chief of the army.

February 4: Hitler announces that henceforth he personally will be supreme commander of all the armed forces. He also dismisses Baron von Neurath as foreign minister, appointing Joachim von Ribbentrop in his place, and relieves Franz von Papen of his duties as ambassador to Austria. Hitler is now in total control of Germany's economic, military, and foreign policies.

February 10: As unemployment increases Roosevelt requests a $250 million appropriation from Congress to fund Works Progress Administration (WPA) programs until the end of June.

February 12: In a meeting at Berchtesgaden arranged by Papen (still serving Hitler's purposes despite his removal as ambassador to Austria), Hitler presents an ultimatum to Austrian chancellor Kurt von Schuschnigg that includes legalizing the Nazi Party in Austria and appointing pro-Nazis to head the ministry of interior (with control of police and internal security) and the ministry of war—in effect a demand that Schuschnigg relinquish the Austrian government's control of his nation's sovereignty. Both intimidated and beguiled, Schuschnigg signs a document agreeing to Hitler's demands.

February 16: Roosevelt signs into law a new act authorizing programs of the Agricultural Adjustment Administration. The terms of the new law provide for crop loans, "parity payments," insurance for wheat crops, a permanent soil conservation program, and authority for the secretary of agriculture to establish acreage allotments and subsidies for staple crops (wheat, corn, cotton, rice, and tobacco) nationwide.

February 16: Despite the initial opposition of President Wilhelm Miklas, the Austrian government puts into effect the terms Schuschnigg had agreed to at Berchtesgaden.

February 20: Advancing in Shanxi, Japanese troops capture Zhangzhi (Changchih).

February 20: In a speech to the Reichstag, Hitler declares that Germany will protect the rights of German people living in the states bordering Germany— that is, Austria and the Sudeten area of Czechoslovakia. Nazi demonstrations erupt throughout Austria.

February 20: In London, Anthony Eden resigns as foreign secretary in protest against Chamberlain's policy of appeasing Mussolini and Hitler. Chamberlain appoints Lord Halifax to take Eden's place.

February 21: After six weeks of filibustering by southern senators and two failures to vote cloture (closing the debate), Senator Wagner withdraws his antilynching bill.

February 24: Japanese troops capture Lishi.

February 24: During a speech to the Bundestag in defiance of Hitler, Schuschnigg declares that Austria will never willingly surrender its independence.

March 1: As a result of the so-called Roosevelt recession, unemployment has climbed back up to about 12.5 million, stock valuations have declined by nearly 50 percent from the prior year, automobile sales are down 50 percent, steel factories are operating at only half capacity, and other indicators of the economy's health have fallen.

March 3: Newspapers report charges by Arthur Morgan, chairman of the Tennessee Valley Authority (TVA), contending that his board colleagues David Lilienthal and Harcourt Morgan had mismanaged a claims case against TVA and impugning their honesty.

March 6: Japanese troops capture Yongji (Yung-chi).

March 8: It is announced on the New York Stock Exchange that the firm of Richard Whitney and Company, owned by the former president of the exchange, has been suspended from trading because of insolvency.

March 9: Japanese troops capture Binglu (Ping-lu). Their advances from the east and the north have now given them control over Shanxi, with a securely established front along the Yellow River.

March 9: Chancellor Schuschnigg announces a plebiscite to be held on March 13 to provide the people of Austria the chance to vote for or against a continuing free and independent Austria.

March 10: In New York City, under orders from District Attorney Thomas E. Dewey, police arrest Richard Whitney and charge him with larceny. Whitney, it is revealed, has for years been looting his clients' accounts.

March 10: Enraged by Schuschnigg's announcement of the plebiscite, Hitler decides to order the invasion of Austria. He sends an emissary to Rome to enlist Mussolini's acquiescence, as Italy is supposed to be a protector of Austria's sovereignty.

March 10: In Paris, Premier Camille Chautemps and his government resign, leaving France without an acting government.

March 11: Whitney is arrested a second time, now by orders of the New York State attorney general.

March 11: Roosevelt meets with Arthur Morgan, David Lithienthal, and Harcourt Morgan at the White House to discuss the conflicts among the three TVA administrators.

March 11: Under pressure from pro-Nazis in his government, Schuschnigg cancels the plebiscite, but Hitler has Göring deliver over the telephone a new ultimatum to Schuschnigg; He must resign and be replaced as chancellor by the pro-Nazi minister of security, Arthur Seyss-Inquart. Schuschnigg resigns, but Austrian president Miklas refuses to appoint Seyss-Inquart as his replacement. Late in the evening, Hitler receives word over the telephone that Mussolini is agreeable to Germany's takeover of Austria.

March 12: German troops invade Austria. Hitler enters Austria and is enthusiastically welcomed by crowds as he proceeds to Linz, his hometown. Schuschnigg is placed under house arrest.

March 13: In Linz and Vienna a quickly proclaimed law accomplishes the Anschluss (annexation) of Austria—the formerly independent nation becomes a province of Germany.

March 13: In Paris a new government is formed with Léon Blum as premier.

March 14: Hitler enters Vienna in triumph.

March 14: In an address to the House of Commons, Chamberlain in effect accepts the Anschluss as irreversible—something that could not have been prevented except by force, which the British government had not been prepared to employ.

March 17: The government of the Soviet Union proposes the calling of an international conference to discuss means of preventing any further aggressions by Germany.

March 18: Mexican president Lázaro Cárdenas announces that his government will expropriate all oil properties held in Mexico by U.S., British, and Dutch companies.

March 23: Roosevelt removes Arthur Morgan as chairman of TVA; he will appoint Harcourt Morgan as successor.

March 24: In a speech in the House of Commons, Chamberlain rejects the Soviet Union's proposal for an international conference and also states that Great Britain should offer no guarantee to come to the aid of Czechoslovakia or to support French assistance to Czechoslovakia, as mandated by treaty between the latter two nations, in the event that Czechoslovakia were to be attacked—in effect, giving Hitler a free hand.

March 25: Roosevelt announces at Warm Springs, Georgia, that the administration has initiated the calling together of 33 nations to participate in a conference on means of assisting Jewish emigration from Germany and Austria.

March 27: The U.S. ambassador delivers a message to President Cárdenas from Secretary of State Hull granting that Mexico has the sovereign right to expropriate the property of American oil companies but that the companies are entitled to expect fair compensation for the properties.

March 28: The Senate passes the executive reorganization bill but by only one vote. The bill would empower the president to appoint more executive assistants, reassign agencies to appropriate departments, and oversee the Bureau of the Budget.

April 8: The House of Representatives votes in favor of recommitting the executive reorganization bill to the Rules Committee—meaning, in effect, the bill is dead.

April 10: A plebiscite in both Germany and Austria reveals overwhelming support for the Anschluss.

April 11: At a White House conference of congressional leaders Roosevelt announces he plans to request major new funding for relief programs—$1.25 billion for WPA, $150 million for the Farm Security Administration, $50 million for the Civilian Conservation Corps (CCC) and National Youth Administration (NYA)—over the objections of Secretary of the Treasury Morgenthau, who believes such expenditures will increase the 1939 budget deficit by $3.5 billion.

April 13: Deeply concerned over the president's proposals for new relief expenditures, Morgenthau tells the president he is considering resigning; Roosevelt tells him he cannot do so.

April 14: Roosevelt sends a message to Congress requesting legislation authorizing $3.7 billion in new spending for public works and other programs.

April 16: In Rome, Great Britain and Italy sign a pact by which Great Britain legally recognizes Italy's possession of Ethiopia and Italy renounces any claims of territory or economic advantage in Spain.

April 21: Hitler summons General Wilhelm Keitel, chief of the Supreme Command, to the Reich Chancellory to discuss plans for the conquest of Czechoslovakia.

April 28: Governor Phil La Follette of Wisconsin announces the formation of a new political party, the National Progressives.

April 29: In a message to Congress, Roosevelt formally requests that Congress appropriate funds to finance an investigation of monopoly businesses and malpractices among American industries.

May 1: Jersey City's dictatorial mayor Frank Hague, vice chairman of the Democratic National Committee, has his police break up a public gathering that Norman Thomas is addressing in the city, abducting Thomas, his wife, and others and forcing them aboard the ferry to New York City.

May 2: Senator Gerald Nye introduces a resolution in the Senate to repeal the embargo on shipments of arms to Spain.

May 13: Congress approves legislation requested by the president authorizing $1.2 billion for increasing the strength of the navy.

May 18: Japanese troops capture Xuzhou (Suchow), effectively ending Chinese military resistance in the Shandong province. Chinese forces regroup to the west and along the coast.

May 20: General Keitel sends a draft of the plan for conquering Czechoslovakia to Hitler, who is staying in Obersalzberg. Reports that German troops are concentrating in Saxony (the state bordering Czechoslovakia to the north) generate a wave of anxiety throughout the capitals of Europe that Germany is planning another invasion. The government of Czechoslovakia, headed by President Eduard Beneš, orders a partial mobilization of the nation's armed forces. In Berlin the ambassador from Great Britain, Sir Neville Henderson, begins an urgent round of diplomatic visits to the German Foreign Office.

May 23: Under orders from Hitler, the Foreign Office in Berlin assures the envoy from Czechoslovakia that German troops are not being concentrated anywhere along the border and that Germany intends no acts of aggression against Czechoslovakia.

May 24: The House of Representatives passes the Fair Labor Standards Bill, moving the bill to conference with the Senate, which had passed a different version of the bill a year earlier.

May 26: The House of Representatives authorizes creation of the House Un-American Activities Committee (HUAC) to investigate the activities of profascist organizations. Martin Dies of Texas will serve as chairman.

May 27: The Revenue Act of 1938 becomes law without the president's signature. Roosevelt objects to the act's stipulations (despite a compromise worked out between the House and Senate versions in the final draft) because they lower the capital gains tax from a graduated rate to a flat 15 percent and, in effect, eliminate the tax on undistributed profits of corporations that had been authorized by the Revenue Act of 1936—thus, as he sees it, favoring the rich and corporations.

May 28: Having suddenly returned from his stay in Obersalzberg, Hitler meets with his military leaders and orders preparations for an invasion of the Sudetenland, a part of Czechoslovakia where German nationals are concentrated, to begin on October 1. He vows to wipe Czechoslovakia off the map.

June 1: Once again Mayor Hague's agents break up a gathering being addressed by Norman Thomas; this time in Newark.

June 7: Japanese troops capture Kaifeng.

June 10: Japanese troops capture Zhengzhou (Chengchow). Unable to prevent the Japanese from driving further south or west from the Yellow River, Chinese forces throw open the dikes on the Yellow, allowing the river to flow southward for hundreds of miles and join the waters of the Hwai River, thus stalling the Japanese advance but also causing the deaths of many Chinese civilians.

June 12: Japanese troops capture Anking on the north bank of the Yangzi River.

June 14: Both the House and the Senate approve the Fair Labor Standards Act resulting from the House-Senate conference on the bill. The act creates a minimum wage to rise from 25 cents an hour in the first year to 30 cents over the following six years and then to 40 cents, sets a maximum work week of 40 hours to go into effect in two years, provides that overtime work will be compensated at one and one-half times normal wages, and reinstitutes the outlawing of child labor.

Interior of prefabricated house intended for the reestablishment of farm laborers, New Madrid, Missouri, May 1938 *(Library of Congress)*

June 16: The Temporary National Economic Committee (TNEC), created by Congress in response to the president's April 29 request for an investigation of monopolies and business malpractices, holds its first meeting. Senator Joseph O'Mahoney of Wyoming is chairman.

June 16: Congress adjourns after approving acts appropriating funds for increased public works and relief expenditures and for investigating monopolies.

June 23: The Civil Aeronautics Act becomes law, establishing the Civil Aeronautics Authority to replace the Bureau of Air Commerce set up in 1926. The new authority is empowered to regulate economic and safety regulations affecting commercial aviation.

June 24: In a fireside chat, Roosevelt announces his intention to work for the nomination of liberal candidates and the defeat of conservative candidates

in the Democratic Party and denounces efforts to suppress free speech—a slap at Mayor Hague.

June 25: Roosevelt signs into law the Fair Labor Standards Act and the Food, Drug, and Cosmetics Act. The latter repeals and supersedes the Food and Drug Act of 1906 but lacks the former law's restrictions on false or misleading advertising. It establishes the policies of "adequate testing" before a new drug may be placed on the market and of listing ingredients and information on strength and purity on containers, along with warnings about habit-forming dangers of use.

July 2: Newspapers report that Amelia Earhart has made a crash landing somewhere between New Guinea and the Howland Islands after losing radio contact during the around-the-world flight she and her navigator were making.

July 4: Japanese troops continue their advance along the Yangzi, capturing Hukou (Hukow).

July 5: The conference on the emigration of Jewish and other political refugees that the president had initiated and announced on March 25 begins in Evian-les-Bains, France.

July 6: Roosevelt begins a railroad tour to speak in support of liberal candidates for national offices in Ohio, Kentucky, Oklahoma, Texas, and Nevada.

July 9: Supreme Court justice Benjamin Cardozo dies.

July 14: Roosevelt arrives in San Francisco and reviews the navy fleet at anchor in the harbor after a speech touting the Golden Gate International Exposition to be held in the city in 1939.

July 15: The conference at Evian-les-Bains ends, with only a few nations—the United States not among them—agreeing to increase the number of emigrants they will allow in. The conference's only concrete achievement is creation of an Intergovernmental Committee on Refugees (IGC), but its efforts prove inconsequential.

July 16: At the naval base in San Diego, Roosevelt boards the USS *Houston* to begin a vacation cruise of four weeks.

July 16: In Berlin, General Ludwig Beck, chief of the army general staff, brings a memorandum to Gen-

Steel mill workers in Midland, Pennsylvania, July 1938; photo by Arthur Rothstein *(Library of Congress)*

eral Walther von Brauchitsch, commander in chief of the army, in which he demands that plans to invade Czechoslovakia be abandoned and argues this view with the commander.

July 17: Roosevelt warmly welcomes aboard the USS *Houston* representatives sent personally by President Lázaro Cárdenas of Mexico and asks them to convey his regards to Cárdenas with assurances that he understands the Mexican president's political and economic goals.

July 26: Japanese troops take Jiujiang (Kiukang) on the Yangzi.

August 2: Japanese troops capture Huangmei (Hwangmei).

August 4: General Beck meets secretly with the senior army generals and urges them to oppose the invasion of Czechoslovakia and also to push for reforms in the government.

August 9: Ending his voyage aboard the USS *Houston,* Roosevelt disembarks at Pensacola, Florida.

August 12: The president arrives back in Washington, D.C.

August 13: The United States Film Service is established to foster and coordinate work on documentaries, such as those created for the U.S. Resettlement Administration by Pare Lorentz.

August 18: In Kingston, Ontario, President Roosevelt receives an honorary doctorate from Queens University, and, with Prime Minister William Lyon Mackenzie King, dedicates the International Bridge across the St. Lawrence River.

August 18: Having failed to persuade Brauchitsch and other generals to adopt his view and press it upon Hitler, Beck resigns as chief of the army general staff. Hitler orders that the resignation not be made public; he will secretly appoint General Franz Halder as Beck's successor. In London, Ewald von Kleist, an emissary from a group of military and civilian conspirators in Germany plotting the overthrow of Hitler, meets with Sir Robert Vansittart, an adviser to the Foreign Office. Kleist hopes to persuade the British government to stand firm against the threat of German aggression against Czechoslovakia in order to assist the conspirators' plans. Vansittart sends a report to Chamberlain and Lord Halifax.

August 28: Impressed by Vansittart's report, Chamberlain has recalled Ambassador Nevile Henderson to London for consultations and instructs the ambassador to begin personal contacts with Hitler and to warn Hitler against aggression in Czechoslovakia. The ambassador, however, persuades the prime minister to forgo the warning.

September 5: Another emissary from the German conspirators, Theodor Kordt, a counselor at the German embassy in London, meets secretly with Lord Halifax, tells him that Hitler plans to attack Czechoslovakia on October 1, and again urges French and British firmness to force Hitler to back down—but to no avail. In Prague, President Beneš of Czechoslovakia meets with leaders of the Sudetenland Germans and agrees to accept their demands—whatever form they take.

September 7: Alarmed that Beneš's acceptance of demands by the Sudetenland negotiators will abort the conquest of Czechoslovakia, the Hitler government orders the puppet leader of the Sudetenland Germans, Konrad Henlein, to break off negotiations with the Czech government.

September 12: In a speech to the Nuremberg Party Rally, Hitler demands that the Czech government grant "justice" to the Sudetenland Germans or Germany will intervene to secure such "justice."

September 13: After daylong deliberations, the French cabinet, headed by Premier Édouard Daladier, who succeeded Blum in April, fails to decide whether to honor France's treaty commitment to come to the support of Czechoslovakia if that nation is attacked. Daladier then confers with the British ambassador and urges that Chamberlain strike a bargain with Hitler.

September 15: At dawn Chamberlain leaves London by airplane—his first flight—to meet with Hitler at Berchtesgaden. Hitler harangues the prime minister and insists that the Sudetenland must be ceded to Germany and that to accomplish this end he is willing even to undergo a world war if necessary, if opposing nations thrust war upon him; he will not compromise on this issue. Chamberlain agrees to the cession of the Sudetenland but advises that he must confer with the government of France and his own cabinet before committing himself. In return Hitler promises that Germany will take no military action against Czechoslovakia before he and Chamberlain have met again.

September 16: Chamberlain returns to London.

September 18: Premier Daladier and Foreign Minister Georges Bonnet arrive in London to consult with the British. While Chamberlain confers with both the French and his own cabinet, Hitler meets with his generals to pursue military and political planning for the conquest of Czechoslovakia.

September 21: After initially rejecting an Anglo-French proposal and invoking France's treaty obligation to come to Czechoslovakia's defense, the Beneš government submits to pressure from the British and French governments and accepts a proposal in which Czechoslovakia agrees to cede all of its territory where Sudeten Germans are more than half of the inhabitants; in return France and Great Britain will support an international guarantee of the nation's resulting new boundaries.

September 22: Chamberlain leaves London for Germany to meet with Hitler at Godesberg, where he presents the proposal the French, British, and Czech governments have agreed to. Hitler rejects it, insisting now that Germany must be allowed to occupy the Sudetenland immediately.

September 23: Hitler presents Chamberlain with a demand that the Czechs must begin evacuating the Sudeten areas on the morning of September 26 but, following Chamberlain's protests, makes a "concession," postponing the evacuation date to October 1. Beneš orders a general military mobilization of Czechoslovakia.

September 24: In the early morning Chamberlain and Hitler part, with Hitler declaring that the Sudetenland is the last territorial gain Germany will demand. Chamberlain returns to London.

September 25: Premier Daladier and his ministers, again meeting with the British in London, state that they will honor France's treaty obligation to defend Czechoslovakia but want to know Britain's intentions. Chamberlain agrees to support the French but decides on one final appeal to Hitler.

September 27: Sir Horace Wilson, sent by Chamberlain with a letter from the prime minister, meets with Hitler but to no avail. Later in the day, after learning that France and Britain are partially mobilizing, Hitler sends a conciliatory letter by telegraph to Chamberlain offering to negotiate with the Czech government and suggesting that Chamberlain renew his efforts to persuade the Czechs to come to terms. Chamberlain responds with an offer to come to Germany to meet with German, French, Czech, and Italian representatives to resolve the issue.

September 28: Hitler agrees to a conference of representatives of France, Great Britain, Germany, and Italy—but not representatives from Czechoslovakia or the Soviet Union, which has supported the Czechs—to begin at noon in Munich the following day.

September 30: The national leaders conferring at Munich—Chamberlain, Daladier, Hitler, and Mussolini—sign an agreement reached the night before by which Germany will be allowed to occupy "predominantly German" areas in Czechoslovakia in stages from October 1 through October 10 as the Czechs evacuate them. Further, an international commission will conduct plebiscites and determine what additional areas should be conceded to Germany. Betrayed and pressured by Britain and France, the Beneš government accepts the agreement. Chamberlain returns to London and tells waiting crowds that the agreement will deliver "peace in our time."

October 2: With Czechoslovakia now helpless, Poland takes advantage of its neighbor by seizing the Teschen area.

October 5: At the insistence of Germany, President Beneš resigns.

October 5: During a debate in Parliament on the Munich agreement, Winston Churchill declares, "We have suffered a total and unmitigated defeat."

October 6: The House of Commons votes overwhelmingly in favor of a motion approving the Munich agreement and the Chamberlain government's policy.

October 13: The international commission established by the Munich agreement decides to abandon the plebiscites meant to determine the future disposition of disputed areas in Czechoslovakia as being unnecessary.

October 15: Brigadier General George C. Marshall becomes deputy chief of staff of the U.S. Army.

October 21: Japanese troops take control of Guangzhou (Canton), prompting Chiang Kai-shek to withdraw his troops to the safety of the mountains in Sichuan and set up his headquarters at Chongqing (Chungking).

October 26: Japanese troops capture Wuchang and Hanyang on the south bank of the Yangzi River.

October 28: German government agents round up and expel 10,000 Polish Jews living in Germany after confiscating their property.

October 30: Over CBS radio, a theatrical group headed by Orson Welles broadcasts an adaptation of H. G. Wells's *The War of the Worlds* containing "news"

Cowboys driving cattle in Dawson County, Nebraska, October 1938 (*Library of Congress*)

bulletins that Martian spaceships are landing in New Jersey and elsewhere. Thousands of listeners panic.

October 31: Japanese troops take Sienning to the south of the Yangzi.

November 7: In Paris a teenage German Jewish refugee, the son of a Polish family among those exiled from Germany, shoots the third secretary of the German embassy, Ernst vom Rath.

November 8: President Roosevelt suffers a humiliating rejection at the polls as most of the liberal Democratic candidates for whom he had campaigned lose their races for Congress or for governorships. Out of 33 contested governorships, the Republicans win 18, gaining 11 over their previous strength. The Republicans gain 81 seats in the House of Representatives and eight in the Senate, although Democrats still hold a majority in both houses: 262 to 169 in the House (with four seats held by other parties) and 69

to 23 in the Senate (with four seats held by members of other parties). Among the newly elected Republican senators is Robert Taft of Ohio.

November 9: Rath dies of his wounds.

November 10: In the early morning hours "spontaneous demonstrations" actually organized by SS leader Reinhard Heydrich erupt throughout Germany, supposedly in response to Rath's killing in Paris. The demonstrators attack thousands of synagogues and Jewish shops and homes, breaking windows, pillaging, and setting fires; dozens of Jews are killed or injured, and about 20,000 are arrested. Known as Kristallnacht (night of broken glass), the rioting and devastation mark the beginning of the worst Nazi campaign against the Jews to date.

November 12: In Berlin a government committee chaired by Hermann Göring declares the Jews responsible for the devastation of Kristallnacht. The government decrees that the Jews must pay for all the destruction and that all insurance payments will be turned over to the government; in addition, the government imposes a fine of 1 billion marks on the nation's half million Jews as an "atonement" for the killing of Rath.

December 1: The Temporary National Economic Committee (TNEC) begins public hearings on monopolies.

December 6: The foreign ministers of France and Germany, Bonnet and Ribbentrop, sign a pact in Paris guaranteeing the two nations' current boundaries and agreeing to settle all future disputes through consultations.

December 9: The eighth Pan-American Conference opens in Lima, Peru, with representatives of 21 American nations attending; Secretary of State Cordell Hull heads the U.S. delegation.

December 13: Accompanied by Undersecretary of State Summer Welles, Anthony Eden (former British foreign minister) visits the White House for a discussion with the president.

December 16: Accompanied in Washington by William C. Bullitt, the American ambassador to France, Jean Monnet visits Secretary of the Treasury Morgenthau, who is in charge of aircraft purchases for the army and navy, to discuss the purchase of 1,000 American airplanes for the French air force; Morgenthau asks the president to approve the purchase.

December 21: Roosevelt sends Morgenthau a written order authorizing the French to purchase American airplanes but cautioning that the deal has to be kept secret.

December 23: Roosevelt appoints Harry Hopkins to succeed Daniel Roper as secretary of commerce, with Hopkins resigning as WPA administrator.

December 23: Franco's Nationalist forces begin a drive toward Barcelona.

December 27: The Pan-American Conference adjourns, having accepted a modified version of the Lima Declaration suggested by Hull that commits the American nations to consult on using force to counteract any threat to the peace or territory of any American republic by an overseas power.

EYEWITNESS TESTIMONY

The developments of 1929–1933 brought about a radical change in our attitude. We found that all our technical ability and financial acumen were of little avail in the face of steadily shrinking demands for goods. . . . The first aspect of the problem of securing national economic well-being was suddenly thrust upon us in the form of widespread industrial stagnation and unemployment. We were, however, totally unprepared to grapple with it. Our first impulse was to apply the homely precepts applicable to our individual problems. There was talk of the importance of living within our means and of the importance of balancing the Federal budget by curtailing expenditures. There was talk of the necessity of getting back to the old virtues of thrift, economy, and hard work. It was not appreciated that in the face of shrinking money incomes and expenditures any course of action that led to a further curtailment of community expenditures, whether it ws increased saving or reduced government expenditures, merely intensified our difficulties and led to less utilization of our human and physical resources.

Marriner S. Eccles, chairman of the Board of Governors of the Federal Reserve System, from "Controlling Booms and Depressions," in Gayer, ed., The Lessons of Monetary Experience *(1937).*

The outbreak of the Manchurian affair and the abandonment by Great Britain of the gold standard in September, 1931, caused sharp falls in the prices of securities and staple commodities. Apprehension over the fate of the gold standard in this country [Japan] induced a heavy selling of the yen to acquire dollar as well as to invest in dollar securities. Naturally this was followed by a recurrence of substantial shipments of gold from this country. By this time it became evident that recourse was being had to borrowing at home to obtain funds wherewith to carry on speculative dealings in the yen. The Bank of Japan, therefore, raised its discount rate twice in October and November, 1931, to 6.57 per cent, while the demand for gold or foreign exchange was met freely to save the gold standard. This, however, was of no avail in stemming the tide of capital flight, to which this outward gold movement really amounted. Gold exports continued unabated.

Eigo Fukai, former governor of the Bank of Japan and member of the House of Peers, from "The Recent Monetary Policy of Japan," in Gayer, ed., The Lessons of Monetary Experience *(1937).*

I do advocate restoration of flexible interest rates. There is a time for cheap money and a time for dear money. The time for a firming of rates is in the advanced stages of a recovery cycle. What I object to is the primrose doctrine that a country ought to have easy money in extreme degree all the time. I object to the notion that recovery will collapse if interest rates are allowed to adjust themselves to midway position. . . .

Just as it was sound to fight deflation by cheap money, so it is sound to fight inflation by firm money. The national economy needs a non-rigid curve of money rates. . . . To promise the public easy money throughout a boom is, according to any standards of evaluation which I can understand, a dangerous and unwarranted procedure.

Lionel D. Edie, from his book Easy Money *(1937).*

The C.C.C. [Civilian Conservation Corps] has been as successful in alleviating unemployment as it has been in completing valuable conservation work. During the three years and a half that this new venture in social rehabilitation and conservation has been in operation, employment has been given for varying periods of time to almost 2,000,000 persons, the majority of them youngsters in their teens and early twenties. Records show that something like 1,287,000 young men have spent an average of nine months each in the healthful outdoor atmosphere of the C.C.C. camps. Of this number, approximately 325,000 . . . are now in the camps.

More than 135,000 war veterans have worked in the camps; approximately 25,000 are now enrolled. Employment has been given to some 170,000 persons in supervisory positions. . . .

The C.C.C. has brought about a spiritual and moral development of the men who have been given an opportunity to learn the value of a good day's work. Life in the camps provides the enrollees with many opportunities for self-development and improvement. . . . It has been estimated that the C.C.C. offers opportunities for enrollees to learn more than sixty major occupations.

Robert Fechner, director of the Civilian Conservation Corps, from Oliver and Dudley, This New America *(1937).*

The folklore of 1937 was expressed principally by the literature of law and economics. Here were found elaborately framed the little pictures which men had of society as it ought to be. Of course, this literature was not called folklore. No one thought of sound principles of law or economics as religion. They were considered as inescapable truths, as natural laws, as principles of justice, and as the only method of an ordered society. . . .

The effect of the peculiar folklore of 1937 was to encourage the type of organization known as industry or business and discourage the type known as government. Under the protection of this folklore the achievements of American business were remarkable. There was no questioning of myths which supported independent empires by those engaged in those enterprises. So-called private institutions like General Motors never lost their direction through philosophical debate.

Thurman Arnold, lawyer, future (1938) assistant attorney general in the Justice Department's Antitrust Division, The Folklore of Capitalism *(1937).*

"You know, honey, us colored folks is branches without roots and that makes things come round in queer ways. You in particular. Ah was born back due in slavery so it wasn't for me to fulfill my dreams of whut a woman oughta be and to do. Dat's one of de hold-backs of slavery. But nothing can't stop you from wishin'. You can't beat nobody down so low till you can rob 'em of they will. Ah didn't want to be used for a work-ox and a brood-sow and Ah didn't want mah daughter used dat way neither . . . Ah even hated de way you was born. But, all de same Ah said thank God, Ah got another chance. Ah wanted to preach a great sermon about colored women sittin' on high, but they wasn't no pulpit for me. Freedom found me with a baby daughter in mah arms . . . She would expound what Ah felt. But somehow she got lost offa de highway and next thing Ah knowed here you was in de world . . . Ah been waitin' a long time, Janie, but nothin' Ah been through ain't too much if you just take a stand on high ground lak Ah dreamed."

The grandmother character speaking to her granddaughter, in Zora Neale Hurston's novel Their Eyes Were Watching God *(1978, 1937).*

The unparalleled growth of cities has been accompanied by uncontrolled subdivision and speculative practices and by the most fantastic real estate booms, which have meant dramatic profits to a few but tragic personal losses to others and burdensome delinquent properties to the community. . . . We are now faced with the problem of arriving at a rational urban land policy which, while affording private owners and developers adequate opportunity for wise and profitable land uses, will curb the forms of speculation that prove calamitous to the investing and taxpaying public.

Report of the Urbanism Committee, in Our Cities: Their Role in the National Economy *(1937).*

Since 1925 the city of 36,500 has grown under the prodigal hand of prosperity to almost 50,000 and has experienced momentous impetus to social change. . . . During the first half of the decade, the good years of the late 1920's, men were talking of the arrival of "permanent prosperity"; here it seemed was America's "manifest destiny." . . . Middletown busily turned its wishes into horses—and then abruptly and helplessly rode them over a precipice. . . .

A city committed to faith in education as the key to its children's future has had to see many of its college-trained sons and daughters idle, and to face the question as to what education is really "worth." . . .

A city still accustomed to having its young assume largely the values of their parents has had to listen to an increasing number of its young speak of the world of their parents as a botched mess.

A city in which the "future" has always been painted in terms of its gayer-hued hopes has been forced to add to its pigments the somber dark tones of its fears.

Robert S. Lynd and Helen Merrell Lynd, sociologists, in Middletown in Transition *(1937).*

During the depression hundreds of thousands of young men road [sic] the rails [obtained free rides by secretively boarding freight cars]. . . . The government's paternalistic CCC [Civilian Conservation Corps] now has 340,000 under its wing. And Harry Hopkins announces the fact that this year there will be more than 6,500,000 unemployed to be provided for by the public. How persistent, then, in the face of so much evidence that an American should account himself lucky if he gets along at all, is the tradition that this is still the land of opportunity? To find out, *Fortune* asked the question above. The answers were:

Yes 39.6%
Yes, if he's lucky 18.0
No 34.7
Don't know 7.7

. . . Only a little more than a third of the people believe that opportunity to reach the goal is dead. And the goal here defined is a high one, for, although nearly half of the nation's families own their homes, very few have incomes of $5,000 or more—only 8 percent even in the boom year of 1929.

Fortune, quarterly survey results, January 1937.

A new strike technique [the sit-down strike] has swept the country, arousing enthusiasm among workers and bewilderment among employers. In industry after industry, in state after state, the workers remain at their posts but refuse to work. No longer is it possible to introduce strikebreakers, for ther workers are in possession. Nor are the workers readily dispersed, for they can barricade themselves in a strong defensive position. If strikebreakers or police storm the factory gate, they are clearly responsible in the eyes of the public for whatever violence may occur. The employer cannot too easily afford to alienate public opinion nor risk damage to his machinery.

Joel Seidman, labor leader in New Frontiers
(January 1937).

One might wish that the TVA, as an experiment in regional government, in cooperation with local and state governments and with private industry, could endeavor to work out the irrelation of these various problems, and by a process of research, cooperation, coordination and encouragement, stimulate an enduring and prosperous economy in a region that has great natural resources and a fine native population. Industry should be related to agriculture. Forestry, industry and agriculture cannot well be separated. The greatest check to soil erosion would be an increase of industrial opportunity which would . . . result in taking some marketable land out of cultivation. The low educational level of some regions, with all of the bad social consequences which follow, is largely a result of inadequate economic opportunity. In some areas vigorous activity is checked by the prevalence of malaria.

Arthur E. Morgan, Tennessee Valley Authority chairman,
in the New Republic *(January 6, 1937).*

But if the Republican party can hope nothing from a patient and patriotic term as His Excellency's [FDR's] Opposition and if it can hope even less from a decision to change its spots and come out a blushing pink, what can it hope to do? . . .

They can make the Era of Good Feeling unanimous by doing what the Federalists did a hundred years ago. They can disappear.

Fortune, editorial of February 1937.

Much is being heard of the illegality of the sit-down strike. . . . The debate over legality seems to us entirely off the point. The real objection to the sit-down is that it is effective; the employers are willing to grant to labor any weapon except one that works. It is perfectly plain that General Motors' objection to the sit-down is that they don't want to settle with the union.

The *New Republic, article of February 3, 1937.*

Acting by the direction of Bishop Molloy, of Brooklyn, and the Board of Diocesan Consultors, the Brooklyn *Tablet,* the official organ of the great Brooklyn diocese, has opened a Spanish Relief Fund.

The Commonweal rejoices that at last the appalling indifference of American Catholics to the horrible sufferings of the Catholic people of Spain has been broken. It hopes and believes that now an authorized movement to help the Spanish people, not to wage war, but to bind up their wounds . . . has been made, the diocesan press in general . . . will follow the lead of the Brooklyn *Tablet.*

The *Commonweal, editorial of February 5, 1937.*

The United Automobile Workers' union has not yet, of course, won a complete victory. . . . But it has without question established itself in a sense in which no union independent of employers was ever before established in this great industry. The first step has been made, and it looks like a decisive one. The CIO, in its first important battle in the campaign to organize the mass-production industries, has broken through the enemy lines at one of the strongest salients, and has consolidated its position. Workers everywhere in the country recognize the fact clearly enough.

The *New Republic, article of February 24, 1937,*
about the United Automobile Workers' victory in
organizing General Motors workers.

This February 1937 photo by Arthur Rothstein shows a sign in Birmingham, Alabama. *(Library of Congress, Prints and Photographs Division [USF 33-T01-2393-M2])*

Don't take chances. "Just sniffles" may turn out to be a long siege. It all depends on your body's resistance.

That's why today's physicians believe in helping the body's natural defense when a cold comes. They recommend two important steps:

1. Cleanse the intestinal tract.

2. Help Nature combat the acidity that frequently accompanies a cold.

You can do both those things at once by taking Sal Hepatica. For that's what this bubbling mineral salt laxative does.

Advertisement for Sal Hepatica, sponsor of Fred Allen's NBC radio show Town Hall Tonight, *in* Life *(March 8, 1937).*

The Court, in addition to the proper use of its judicial function, has improperly set itself up as a third House of the Congress—a superlegislature, as one of the justices has called it—reading into the Constitu-

tion words and implications which are not there and which were never intended to be there.

We have, therefore, reached the point as a nation where we must take action to save the Constitution from the Court and the Court from itself. We must find a way to take an appeal from the Supreme Court to the Constitution itself. We want a Supreme Court which will do justice under the Constitution—not over it. In our courts we want a government of laws and not of men.

President Franklin D. Roosevelt, radio address of March 9, 1937, advocating his court-packing bill, in Senate Report No. 711, the Congressional Record *(1937).*

[I]n 1932 the number of concerts had dropped to 2,600—to 69 per cent of the 1929–30 total. This was the low year of the depression, when according to Federal Reserve figures the production of manufactures and minerals had fallen to 50 per cent of the

1929 level. During the present season (1936–37), concert bookings have risen to a total of 3,900—exactly 104 per cent of the 1929–30 figures . . . the production of manufacturers and minerals has reached only 91.6 per cent of its 1929 level. . . .

Since 1929 the number of major symphony orchestras in our principal cities has jumped from ten to seventeen—not only despite the fact that concerts may be heard at home over the radio, but also despite the competition offered during the past two years by the . . . concerts of the WPA's Music Project.

The magnitude of this latter understanding has been colossal. On December 1, 1936, 15,382 musicians were on the Federal payroll, their services extending into forty-two States and the District of Columbia.

John Tasker Howard, musicologist, author of Our American Music *(1931), in* Harper's *(April 1937).*

Wendell Willkie's liberalism, however, being of the strictly Jeffersonian type now espoused by so many enemies of the Administration, is not what makes him a formidable spokesman of the private-ownership forces of this country. . . . For one thing, he has as quick witted and resourceful a legal mind—as cagey, in short—as his principal antagonist, David Lilienthal himself. For another, he . . . runs too clean and up-to-date a company of his own to be inhibited by the errors of the Insull era . . . Finally, he is so manifestly candid, sharp, and unaffected that many Congressmen have probably been reminded unconsciously of the traditional American type . . . cracker-barrel simplifier of national issues in the style of Abe Martin and Will Rogers. . . . "I am in business personally to make a living," says Wendell Willkie, who has never even owned an automobile. . . . There is . . . nothing bogus or staged about Willkie's picturesque Americanism.

Fortune, *article of May 1937.*

On her first transatlantic crossing of the 1937 season, the huge, grey German Zeppelin [hydrogen blimp] *Hindenburg* nosed into the U.S. Naval Air Station at Lakehurst, N.J., at dusk on May 6. A severe thunderstorm had just subsided. Inside the dirigible were 36 passengers, 61 officers and men, a ton of mail and baggage and 6,700,000 cubic ft. of explosive hydrogen. Landing lines had been dropped and the ground crew was pulling the big ship towards the mooring

mast when a sheet of fire burst from her tail. In a twinkling the whole rear half of the *Hindenburg* was aflame . . . Spectators 200 ft. below saw the huge ship buckle near the middle and settle slowly to earth. As the blazing stern smacked the ground several sharp explosions shook the ship. Passengers and crew, caught in an inferno, started to jump for their lives and the tiny men on the mooring mast were silhouetted against a cloud of living fire. . . . Then the flames rushed forward and belched through the *Hindenburg's* nose. . . . In five minutes the fire had burned itself out, leaving 35 dead and one more twisted wreck to add to the dismal history of lighter-than-air craft.

Life, *text of a photographic essay of May 17, 1937.*

He [Roosevelt], in effect, served notice on the Vice President that he might be found in open opposition to members of the House and the Senate who have been fighting his Court bill during this session. The President's position is that it was he who was elected by an overwhelming vote, a vote so large that a lot of Representatives and Senators managed to ride through on his coat tails. He doesn't like it that men who owe their election to him should all of a sudden discover that they are statesmen in their own right.

Secretary of the Interior Harold L. Ickes, diary entry of May 22, 1937, in The Secret Diary of Harold L. Ickes, *vol. 2 (1954).*

1. The reports herewith presented reveal the imminence of a few very important inventions that may soon be widely used with resultant social influences of significance. . . . it is recommended that a series of studies be undertaken by the planning agencies herein recommended or by existing planning boards, with the aid of such natural and social scientists as may be needed, on the following inventions: the mechanical cotton picker, air conditioning equipment, plastics, the photoelectric cell, artificial cotton and woolenlike fibres made from cellulose, synthetic rubber, prefabricated houses, television, facsimile transmission, the automobile trailer, gasoline produced from coal, steep-flight aircraft planes, and tray agriculture.

From "Technological Trends and National Policy, Including the Social Implications of New Inventions," June 1937, Report of the Subcommittee on Technology to the National Resources Committee *(Washington, D.C., 1937), pp. 1–14.*

This photo by Dorothea Lange shows those bound for the wheat harvest in southwestern Oklahoma, June 1937. *(Library of Congress, Prints and Photographs Division [604355 LC-USF34-017090-C])*

I have scanned the papers with great anxiety since Friday evening, when I first heard over the radio that Amelia Earhart and her navigator were missing. I never feel like giving up hope for anyone who has courage until every possible chance for rescue is over. . . . I feel sure that if she comes through safely, she will feel that what she has learned has made it all worth while [sic]. But her friends will wish science could be served without quite so much risk to a fine person, whom many people love as a person and not as a pilot or adventurer.

Eleanor Roosevelt, from her "May Day" newspaper column of July 7, 1937, quoted in Chadakoff, Eleanor Roosevelt's My Day *(1989).*

Tom Corcoran came to see me on Tuesday late in the afternoon. Senator Barkley had called him out of bed very early in the morning to tell him of [Senator Joseph] Robinson's death. Tom at once called Miss Le Hand to suggest to her that she get to the President right away with the news and also to warn him that his telephone would soon begin to ring with messages advising him on account of Robinson's death to drop the Court bill. In ten or fifteen minutes after Miss Le Hand had reached the President, Bernie Baruch called him up from New York. He was on a ship prepared to sail for Europe when he got a flash of Robinson's death. He hastened ashore, canceling his passage, and called the President to tell him that he hoped he would now drop the Court bill and not kill any more Senators.

Secretary of the Interior Harold L. Ickes, diary entry of July 16, 1937, in The Secret Diary of Harold L. Ickes, *vol. 2 (1954).*

You must be tired and I shall not trouble you with a long letter of congratulations, but I must write a line, at least, to tell you that no one else could have led that fight as you led it. Your name is now fixed in the history books. Moreover, above the obvious victory which has been won, in my opinion you have saved not only the Court and the conception of constitutional government, but the soul of American progressivism itself. On the line that Roosevelt began to travel last February, the end could only have been the blackest kind of reaction.

Walter Lippman, newspaper columnist, letter of July 23, 1937, to Senator Burton K. Wheeler, main opponent of the court-packing proposal, in Blum, Public Philosopher: Selected Letters of Walter Lippmann *(1985).*

The New Dealers have conceived that they can adapt a part of the European systems of coercive planned economy and at the same time preserve our spiritual and intellectual liberties and allow us the moral stature of free men. They assert that this is the only humanitarian road and the only road to cure of abuse and greater security for the less fortunate groups.

The trouble is that coercive, planned economy, with its necessary accompaniment of personal government, does not and cannot remain half and half. It spawns daily new compulsions in order to make it work. Like all drugs, it requires increasing doses.

Former president Herbert Hoover, in the Atlantic Monthly *(September 1937).*

I had an appointment with the President on Thursday. I found him very much absorbed in his fight to reform the judiciary. This fight has been waged at white heat ever since he sent his special message on the subject to Congress. A number of men, especially in the Senate, who ought to be with him on this issue, have gone over to the enemy and it looks as if the fight would be a very close one indeed. The President expressed confidence that he would win but he looks for a long, drawn-out fight.

Secretary of the Interior Harold L. Ickes, diary entry of September 27, 1937, concerning Roosevelt's court-packing attempt, in The Secret Diary of Harold L. Ickes, *vol. 2 (1954).*

It seems to be unfortunately true that the epidemic of world lawlessness is spreading. When an epidemic of physical disease starts to spread, the community approves and joins in a quarantine of the patients in order to protect the health of the community against the spread of the disease.

It is my determination to pursue a policy of peace and to adopt every practicable measure to avoid involvement in war.

President Franklin D. Roosevelt, speech delivered in Chicago, October 5, 1937, in the Congressional Record.

During the worst of the depression many of the farmers had to deny their families butter, eggs, meat etc. and sell it to pay their taxes and then had to stand by and see the dead-beats carry it home to their families by the arm load, and they knew their tax money was helping pay for it. . . . The crookedness, shelfishness [sic], greed and graft of the crooked politicians is making one gigantic racket out of the new deal and it is making this a nation of dead-beats and beggars and if it continues the people who will work will soon be nothing but slaves for the pampered poverty rats.

Anonymous woman in Columbus, Indiana, letter of December 14, 1937, to Eleanor Roosevelt, quoted in McElvaine, Down and Out in the Great Depression: Letters from the "Forgotten Man" *(1983).*

A crisis and the disorganization that accompanies it are highly charged with emotion, a reaction to be expected when habits become ineffective and new modes of response must be found and adopted. In the case of the depression the emotion tends to be fear—fear of loss of status, of loss of money reserves, of failure to have needed food and clothing, of the necessity to go on relief. When re-employment is not found, worry, discouragement, and depression follow. Some people become resentful or angry, but most of them are simply afraid of a moneyless existence for which they have no habitual conduct and no philosophy. For many people the condition of unemployment continues over many months, even over several years.

Ruth Shonle Cavan and Katherine Howland Ranck, in
The Family and the Depression *(1938).*

The annual meeting of the American bishops was held in Washington late in November, with eighty-two members of the hierarchy present. A letter signed by His Eminence Dennis Cardinal Dougherty, Archbishop of Philadelphia, who presided, was sent to the German hierarchy to assure them of the genuine sympathy, sincere admiration and deep affection of our bishops and pledging their continued prayers. The letter stressed the fact that the sense of all religious minded men and women throughout the world has been outraged "by the satanic resourcefulness of these leaders of modern paganism and by the incredible excesses committed by them in their attempt to exterminate religion and to blot out from the minds of the German people all true knowledge and love of God."

The Catholic Word, *news article of January 1938.*

Join the President in Founding the New National Foundation for Infatile Paralysis. Your dollars will help stamp out this dread disease.

Advertisement to raise money to be used in fighting polio (also called infantile paralysis), the disease that struck Roosevelt at age 39, in the Atlantic Monthly *(January 1938).*

Founded in 1919, the Radio Corporation of America has completed 18 years of pioneering effort to develop and improve the use of radio.

. . . RCA has created a world-wide communications system with direct circuits between the United States and 42 foreign countries, and with ships at sea. It has created a nation-wide broadcasting system of endless cultural possibilities. . . . It has created essential instruments for the radio transmission and reception of sound, of code messages, and of facsimile reproductions, and for the recording and reproduction of sound on records and on motion picture films. It has created countless radio devices indispensable to modern science, industry, medicine, telephony, and public safety. It has created the basis for a system of electronic television.

Advertisement for Radio Corporation of America (RCA), in Business Week *(January 1, 1938).*

Man of two years (1932 & 1934) was Franklin Delano Roosevelt, but certainly he has not been Man of 1937. For 1937 is the first year since he became President of the U.S. that Franklin Roosevelt has not clearly been the dominant figure in U.S. public life: In his one big political battle of the year, over the Supreme Court, he was worsted. Had any one man been primarily responsible for that defeat, he would be a towering figure of politics, but in fact . . . Franklin Roosevelt largely wrought his own defeat by antagonizing opinion in Congress and out.

Time, *article of January 3, 1938.*

"Rhapsody in Blue" is the way Paul Whiteman, King of Jazz, describes the Gillette Blade. "I work the night life week in and week out," says Whiteman. "My face has to be clean shaven. . . . So I use a Gillette Blade in a Gillette Razor. There's close harmony! . . ." Next time you see Paul Whiteman, notice how well-groomed his face looks. . . . Gillette shaves *really* last!

Advertisement for Gillette, in Time *(January 3, 1938).*

On Manhattan's 69th Street last week, in a white-tiled studio which was once a garage, a rangy man who looks a little like Abraham Lincoln and more like the Pied Piper ran his fingers through his long grey hair, folded his arms, grinned, yelled, gestured, strode to & fro, swinging his spectacles. On this occasion Photographer Edward Steichen was . . . helping several assistants dismantle his studio for good. As of Jan. 1, 1938, Edward Steichen was through with commercial photography.

Time, *article of January 10, 1938 on Steichen, major photographer famed for his portraits of such movie stars as Greta Garbo and Charlie Chaplain.*

About four miles from Spring Green, Wisc., the hills splay into two soft ranges to let a fast stream flow toward the Wisconsin River. Facing southeast over this valley a big, long house folds around the summit of one hill, its roof lines parallel to the line of ridges, its masonry the same red-yellow sandstone that crops out in ledges along the stream. . . . Its name is Taliesin, a Welsh word meaning "shining brow." Its history is one of tragic irony. Its character is one of extraordinary repose. It is the home of Frank Lloyd Wright, the greatest architect of the 20th Century.

Time, *article of January 17, 1938, on Frank Lloyd Wright.*

Hearing—apparently with great surprise—that the western world was horrified at the slaughter of hundred of thousands of innocent men, women and children in Shanghai and all along the Yangtse-Kiang, the Japs, as a concession to our peculiar western prejudices about cruelty, commenced to make excuses. They tried three or four that didn't go very well. But finally they hit upon one that sounded good: Anti-Communism! It is the mission of Nippon, they explained, to save Asia and the rest of the world from the malign influence of Leninism and Stalinism. Shrewd enough! Germany and Italy applaud. England and the United States dare not object for fear of seeming to favor Russia.

The Catholic World *editorial of February 1938.*

Advocates of the equal-rights amendment sometimes argue that restrictions on women's work prevent them from getting jobs. Every time a proposal comes up in a state legislation [sic] for a prohibition on night work by women, or for a limited working day or a minimum wage, opponents bring forward some woman who tells the committee tearfully that she will lose her job if the bill is passed. Careful nationwide studies of the Women's Bureau at Washington show, however, that this is not true. Women do not lose their jobs because of restrictive legislation; on the contrary, the states with the most drastic laws show the highest proportion of employed women.

The New Republic *article of February 16, 1938, on women's rights.*

Last week the administration visibly suffered under its inability to heave a cobblestone at Herr Hitler. The more tumultuous became his triumphs in Austria and again in Germany, the greater became the administration's impulse to show that all the world did not agree. But since Austria had been made an integral part of the German Reich, State Department experts

This photo by Arthur Rothstein shows a tenement in Pittsburgh, Pennsylvania, 1938. *(Library of Congress)*

appeared stumped in their search for a way of expressing disapproval. . . .

The administration's current European policy is a tenuous affair, but one definite factor in it is the German-Italian-Japanese anti-Comintern pact [pact against the Soviets]. The United States, according to officials, finds itself in opposition to Japan's actions in China, and is obliged to take into account that Japan—at least for the moment—is linked to Germany and Italy by an alliance the full terms of which have not been disclosed. Officials then explain that, although the State Department has a European policy, it has no tangible means of executing it.

T.R.B., an editor, in the New Republic
(March 30, 1938).

To find . . . a "solution" for the problems which have been created by revolution, civil war, political and racial persecutions, arbitrary decrees repealing guaranteed civil rights, and propaganda carried out by powerful governments, is neither our expectation nor even our hope. In particular, the historic Jewish problem . . . will never be solved by emigration. What can be hoped now is that it will be mitigated. . . . The attempt must be made, if only as a testimony to the vitality of our faith in the democratic principles we profess to live by . . . the attempt must be made not out of pity for the exiles, actual and potential, but as reaffirmation of our own beliefs, lest they become hollow dogmas to which, eventually, not even lip service will be given anywhere.

Dorothy Thompson, journalist, supporting rescuing Jewish refugees, in Foreign Affairs *(April 1938).*

We are a rich nation; we can afford to pay for security and prosperity without having to sacrifice our liberties into the bargain.

President Franklin D. Roosevelt, from his fireside chat of April 14, 1938, in Buhite and Levy,
FDR's Fireside Chats *(1992).*

A dinner was given last night to celebrate the fifth birthday of the CCC [Civilian Conservation Corps] camps and I went to read a message from the President. . . .

Aside from the fact that it has taken boys who might have drifted into evil ways and kept them busy, it has given them better health and skill with which

to face the world. Someday we will have fewer floods because of the trees which the CCC has planted, better soil because of the soil erosion program which they have helped to carry on, and innumerable improvements which can be seen everywhere throughout the country.

Eleanor Roosevelt, from her "My Day" newspaper column of April 16, 1938, quoted in Chadakoff,
Eleanor Roosevelt's My Day *(1989).*

To most people the Administration's new spending program is probably very appealing, there being so many temptations to regard it as proper medicine for an emergency. But the country should beware of continuing and aggravating its unbalanced budget, or piling too high its bonded debt, pledging the next generation to pay too large a part of the national income for interest on borrowed funds.

Business is bad now; but it would be infinitely better for us—assuming no further decline, which seems unlikely—to rattle along as we are for a few months, and let the upward restoration of business come in the slow and hard way, by a restoration of confidence. True, we have an unemployment problem, and we must assure food and shelter to millions. But we should do that in such a manner as to produce the most actual sustenance out of the fewest dollars . . .

Business Week, *editorial of April 16, 1938, on Roosevelt's decision to increase government spending.*

In the three months from August 15 to November 15, 1937, the market value of securities listed on the New York Stock Exchange declined by more than $25,000,000,000. This loss of values was, with one exception, the greatest ever suffered in any comparable period of time. But, considered in relation to the small volume of liquidation that brought it about, it was by far the worst break in history.

Clifford B. Reeves, in the Atlantic Monthly
(May 1938).

New Mobilgas signs are going up by the thousands—because the demand for Mobilgas is growing bigger every day! In the 60 seconds it takes you to read this page, over 1,000 car owners have stopped for Mobilgas.

Would you like to know the reason for this swing to America's favorite?

One tankful will tell you! Next time "fill 'er up"—at the sign of the Flying Red Horse.

Advertisement for Socony-Vacuum Oil Company, in the
Saturday Evening Post (June 11, 1938).

In the last installment the answers showed the impact of the depression. . . . Here is the change after three months:

Economic conditions are—

	April, 1938	July, 1938
Better	25.3%	16.3%
Same	17.2	18.1
Worse	51.0	60.2
Don't know	6.5	5.4

People are—

	April, 1938	July, 1938
More secure	28.2%	22.4%
Same	34.7	32.0
Less	34.2	43.4
Don't know	2.9	2.2

Here is an increase of pessimism during three months of about 9 percent, both as to economic conditions and personal security. . . .

The tide of pessimism has risen to various new levels in each section of the country, but most spectacular have been the freshets in the Southwest and the Mountain States.

Fortune, quarterly survey results, July 1938.

We rode that train all day and night and most of the next day. It was a thrill seeing the wonderful scenery as we went along. At night Slim and Daddy Joe showed us how to roll up in the paper that lined the boxcar walls and stay warm.

Later the next afternoon we arrived at Nampa, Idaho. We had to change trains to go northwest. Irene and I waited in the [hobo] jungle, while our friends went uptown to beg for food. When we'd eaten we went to join other hoboes sitting on a grassy amphitheater opposite the one empty boxcar that was going to Le Grande, Oregon. We were the only women among the group of fifty men.

As darkness came we saw railroad detectives patrolling the track with lanterns and rifles. When the train started and the boxcar rolled forward, the fifty hoboes rose up as one person and rushed to the door.

Somebody grabbed me by the seat of my pants and the nape of my neck and pitched me into the train. Irene was right behind me. I heard Daddy Joe call my name in the dark. They came over and sat protectively in front of us but I didn't sleep much that night.

Reminiscence of Phoebe Eaton Dehart, who, with her
friend Irene Willis, left her family's homestead near
Glendo, Wyoming, in July 1938, aged 18;
they were befriended by two hoboes, Slim (aged 37)
and Daddy Joe (aged 60); quoted in Uys,
Riding the Rails *(1999).*

Movies of every fascinating phase of baby's progress now cost less than a dime a shot—if you make them with Cine-Kodak Eight, the specially designed "economy movie maker."

A "shot" runs as long on your screen as the average scene in the newsreels, and the Eight makes 20 to 30 such shots on a roll of film costing you only $2.25, black-and-white, *finished, ready to show.*

Advertisement for the Eastman Kodak Company, in
Time *(September 5, 1938).*

Born of the boom and orphaned in 1929, network radio grew up lustily through the lean decade without ever having to go to a foundling home. In only one year, 1933, did it fail to pile up gross revenues to top all previous years. In 1934, gross incomes exceeded 1933's by 35.4%, 1932's by 9%. Radio's 1933 depression was not only brief, it was also noteworthy for being tardy, for other industries were near bottom as early as 1932. So network sales experts have derived from that experience their characteristically optimistic axiom that in times of slump radio is the last industry to slip in, the first to scramble out.

Time, *article of September 19, 1938.*

Mark "urgent" on your grocery list: Order Heinz DeLuxe Tomato Juice, nature's most colorful, refreshing beverage! Serve a chilly glass at breakfast. . . . And at bedtime, remember that this famous member of the 57 Varieties will relax and refresh you; send you off to deep slumber and pleasant dreams!

Advertisement for Heinz tomato juice, in
Time *(September 19, 1938).*

A homemade swimming pool for the children of steel mill workers in Pittsburgh, Pennsylvania, July 1938; photo by Arthur Rothstein *(Library of Congress)*

Of course, this is probably not too great a price to pay if it will insure a permanent European peace. But will it? I doubt it very much, Hitler being the maniac he is. That he should stop now, even if he has announced that he has no further territorial aspirations in Europe, is more than I am willing to believe. Perhaps his next move will be for the return of the lost German colonies, but this will be at the expense largely of Great Britain and France. After that no one knows what may happen.

Secretary of the Interior Harold L. Ickes, diary entry of September 30, 1938, commenting on the Munich agreement, in The Secret Diary of Harold L. Ickes, *vol. 2 (1954).*

A fabulous place, this Rockefeller Center. It is not simply the biggest non-governmental building project in American history; it has become virtually a principality. It has its own United States Post Office

and a passport office. . . . Rockefeller Center has also two big theaters; the NBC broadcasting studios; shops, restaurants, tearooms, bars, night-clubs, a Museum of Science and Industry, a Museum of Modern Art. . . . Rugged individualism? This is twentieth-century organized large-scale operation . . . a characteristic manifestation of an era in which, if big things are to be done, they apparently must be done either by a multi-millionaire, a super-corporation, or a government.

Frederick Lewis Allen, editor of Century *and author of* Only Yesterday *(1931), in* Harper's *(October 1938).*

Nearly the whole world last week undertook to pass judgment in one form or another on Britain's Prime Minister. That Neville Chamberlain will be awarded the Nobel Peace Prize was taken for granted by the Norwegian press. . . .

The triumph of Germany was enormous, but not without limits. . . . If the crisis proved anything with finality, it proved that modern communication and enlightenment of the peoples reduce the chances of an outbreak of war . . . And while all men of goodwill deplored the dismemberment of central Europe's one island of democracy and were saddened for the painful uprooting of the minorities which will leave the ceded territories, realists took heart from one fact. Unlike the rapes of Manchukuo and Ethiopia, the Czechoslovak rape had at least set a precedent, which might flower into a great influence for peace, for aggressors being persuaded to follow legal-diplomatic forms.

> Time, *article of October 10, 1938, discussing the Munich agreement.*

My point about the Munich peace is that the power to intimidate Great Britain by the aerial threat to London has immobolized the British Navy, and that there no longer is in Europe an effective balance of power, as there is no longer one in the Far East. How soon we shall feel the practical consequences in this hemisphere I don't know, but that there has been a radical change in the conditions of our security I feel certain.

> *Walter Lippmann, newspaper columnist, letter of October 25, 1938, to Jerome N. Frank of the Securities Exchange Commission, in Blum,* Public Philosopher: Selected Letters of Walter Lippman *(1985).*

The supreme reason for keeping America out of war is not, however, our own safety. That, also, is an honorable cause. But the supreme reason for peace is the fact that only in an America spared from war can we develop for ourselves and for mankind the new tech-

nics of conflict against the system which breeds poverty, tyranny, and war, without the wholesale murder, the mass insanity, and bitter frustration which are war's inescapable heritage.

> *Norman Thomas, Socialist leader, arguing against the United States entering a war, in* Harper's *(November 1938).*

For Those Celebrating Days—that call for the choicest of gifts, Cartier has the inexpensive whims of fashion as well as important pieces. Jewelled clips from $150.00; bracelets from $40; broaches from $16; the exceptional Cartier watches, from $32.

> *Advertisement for Cartier, Inc., of New York, in* Fortune *(December 1938).*

But Coca-Cola sweeps steadily on. Last year's net income of $24,680,000 just about doubled the net for 1929. This year the net will be larger still. August, 1938, was the biggest month of Coca-Cola's history, and the third quarter was Coca-Cola's biggest third quarter ever. . . . It would be hard to name any company comparable in size to Coca-Cola and selling, as Coca-Cola does, an unchanged product that can point to a ten-year record anything like Coca-Cola's.

> Fortune, *article of December 1938, on the profitability of the Coca-Cola Company.*

Wrap her up in Jaeckel furs and she'll be all wrapped up in you. Give her this lovely coat in tipped Russian sable $8500, or blended Hudson Bay sable $2750, or sable dyed Baum Marten $2350. . . . just one of the many models you may select in either our Los Angeles or New York shop.

> *Advertisement for Jaeckel furs, in* Fortune *(December 1938).*

7

The Emerging War
1939–1941

A FOCUS ON FOREIGN EVENTS

Like the year 1929 that concluded the preceding decade, 1939 became a fateful, pivotal year. The events that year encompassed and those that it later spawned would prove far more momentous and cataclysmic than even the Great Depression. World War II, the cold war, Communist domination in Eastern Europe and China, and finally the collapse of communism in Europe can all be traced back to events in 1939. No one could possibly have foreseen this long-term chain of events as the year opened, but it required no great

Father and son, idle workers, in Bridgeton, New Jersey, in a photo by Dorothea Lange *(Library of Congress)*

prescience at least to predict the coming of world war. President Roosevelt, according to Harry Hopkins's recollection, already understood, as the negotiations leading to the September 1938 Munich conference developed, that the United States would end up at war. Yet the isolationists, if anything, had grown in strength as the threat of war increased, and Roosevelt could sustain little optimism about persuading them to compromise. In addition, he faced a less malleable Congress than in 1938, with a larger representation of conservatives and isolationists and including a number of legislators he had tried to "purge" through his involvement in the 1938 election campaigns.

As the year began, the stern reality persisted: After six years of trying, the New Deal had been unable to end the Great Depression and restore the prosperity of the twenties. The unemployment level remained at 17 percent of the workforce, with almost 10 million still lacking work. And now the New Deal's momentum dissolved, largely because Roosevelt's political muscle had withered. During the previous two years the New Deal had endured strong opposition, even with a commanding Democratic majority in Congress. Now, with the power of Republicans and conservative Democrats augmented in the new Congress, slight hope existed for the possibility of strengthening the New Deal's reform programs and even less hope of creating new ones. Congress in fact seemed intent on unravelling the New Deal—at least some of it.

Roosevelt began 1939 with the evident determination simply to hold fast. One of his first acts (January 2) was to appoint the liberal reformer Frank

Blizzard (coal miner) family in Kempton, West Virginia, May 1939
(Library of Congress)

Salvation Army band and preacher on a street in San Francisco, California, April 1939; photo by Dorothea Lange *(Library of Congress)*

Murphy—former governor of Michigan who had refused to interfere with the sit-down strikes against the auto companies and lost his bid for reelection in 1938—as attorney general. A few days later Roosevelt nominated liberal Harvard law professor Felix Frankfurter to fill the Supreme Court vacancy created by the death of Benjamin Cardozo the previous July. At the end of March the president would nominate another liberal to the court, William O. Douglas, chairman of the Securities and Exchange Commission and a former Yale law professor, to succeed Louis Brandeis, who announced his resignation in February.

In his State of the Union address presented on January 4, the president advocated maintaining the budgets of the New Deal programs, enhancing the Social Security program, devising a plan to provide medical care for the poor, resolving management-labor disputes peacefully, and reorganizing the executive branch of government—nothing new in these proposals. He also requested increased funding for national defense and revision of the Neutrality Act. In fact, the major emphasis of the first half of his speech concerned the threat to the democracies by aggressor nations in Europe and Asia and the means of responding to that threat. That emphasis revealed the new dominance of foreign affairs in Roosevelt's perspective.

A French Faux Pas

A mishap in January drew nearly everyone's attention to concerns abroad and what they might portend. In late December the president had directed Secretary of the Treasury Morgenthau, who had final authority over buying aircraft for the army and navy, to arrange the sale of as many as 1,000 warplanes to France—the result of a deal arranged by Jean Monnet. The sale, however, was to remain confidential in order to avoid diplomatic problems or congressional opposition. Unfortunately, one of the French aviation experts authorized by Morgenthau and the president to examine bombers being developed by the Douglas Aircraft Company in California prior to purchasing them was injured when one of the planes crashed during a test flight. The mishap exposed the secret, newspapers reported it, and fierce controversy followed.

Roosevelt tried to defuse the controversy in a January 27 press conference; Morgenthau and others also tried while testifying before the Senate Military Affairs Committee. Roosevelt invited the entire committee to the White House for a confidential conference on the last day of January. His explanation for the aircraft sale as a means of helping prevent Nazi domination of Europe and potentially of South America, thereby imperiling the United States, alarmed several of the senators and generated probing questions. The answers increased the senators' suspicions about the president's intentions. An interview given by North Dakota senator Gerald Nye after the conference, though largely guarded, led to headlines reporting that the president regarded France, or even the Rhine River, as the United States' "first line of defense." Although polls indicated that two-thirds of the American public believed we should support France and Great Britain in the event of their being engaged in war with Germany—support them, that is, short of joining in the war—Roosevelt backpedaled in his February 3 news conference, obscured the truth, accused the newspapers of lying, and did his best to divorce the administration from a stance that clearly favored the Allies. But isolationists in Congress publicly blasted him for pursuing an "unneutral" policy. Thus Roosevelt's hedging gutted another opportunity for him to educate the public, to spur Americans toward a realistic view of European events.

Such a mishandled episode was unlikely to enhance the president's stature among members of Congress. After all, the senators who had met with him at the White House conference knew he was actually lying to the press and therefore to the public about what he had told them in private. Nor was his waffling likely to generate confidence in the president's policies among British and French leaders. (Despite the furor and dismay over the incident and the president's responses, however, the administration carried out the agreement to sell planes to France.) Perhaps the worst effect for the long term was that, as part of his effort to quiet the controversy, Roosevelt offered no leadership, not even taking an official position when Senator Elbert Thomas of Utah introduced legislation to revise the Neutrality Act. The revisions would allow the president to embargo shipments of all goods of any kind to belligerent nations and *also,* with congressional approval, to authorize shipments of arms and other materials to any nation besieged by an aggressor—exactly the revision the president favored. Without Roosevelt's support, Thomas's proposed amendment died.

CONGRESS BALKS, THEN RELENTS

Other measures Roosevelt favored or advocated suffered defeat or cutbacks imposed by the revitalized opposition in Congress. The House killed off Roosevelt's request for $800 million in additional funding of loans by the Federal Housing Administration (FHA). Congress substantially cut the president's request for funding of the Works Progress Administration (WPA) programs intended to generate employment for 3 million people. As part of the WPA cutback, at the end of June the budget of the Federal Theatre Project, under attack from the House Un-American Activities Committee (HUAC), was eliminated. In addition, under the Reorganization Act of 1939, the WPA was renamed the Works *Projects* Administration within the newly created Federal Works Agency. The appropriations that the Congress approved for the agricultural program omitted funds for parity payments. Yet Congress did approve increases in the number of people covered by Social Security and in old-age benefit payments.

Congress' version in 1939 of the executive reorganization act was greatly revised. Roosevelt's original proposal of 1937 had fallen by the wayside during the court-packing controversy and subsequently in 1938 incurred scorching attack by congressional opponents who accused Roosevelt of seizing power. Still, the final law, representing the president's only real legislative victory of the year, gave him broad authority to reform the executive branch by reducing or regrouping its various independent agencies, as was the case with the WPA. Perhaps the most significant outcome of the reorganization was moving the Bureau of the Budget from the Treasury Department to the Executive Office of the President. Various agencies were consolidated under a single authority— for example, the Social Security Board, the U.S. Employment Service, the

Works Progress Administration (WPA) parade on Market Street, San Francisco, California, protesting reductions in relief voted by Congress, February 1939; photo by Dorothea Lange *(Library of Congress)*

Public Health Service, the Office of Education, the National Youth Administration, and the Civilian Conservation Corps would all now be consolidated under a new executive office authority called the Federal Security Agency. In addition, the president could appoint six assistants to his staff. The reorganization saved money and also improved administrative efficiency at the White House.

THE END FOR SPAIN AND CZECHOSLOVAKIA

Most of this legislative work was achieved in March (although it did not go into effect until July 1939). By then the last links in the chain of events leading to war were being forged. The final tragedy of the Spanish civil war occurred as Nationalist troops captured Madrid (March 28), securing the entire nation for General Franco. The British and French governments had already officially recognized the Franco regime in February. At the beginning of March, Roosevelt recalled Ambassador Claude Bowers, a strong Loyalist sympathizer, and pressed Franco for a pledge not to inflict reprisals on his opponents. The fascist leader responded evasively. As soon as Madrid was in his control, Franco ordered the executions of hundreds of Loyalists. Ironically, on the first day of April, Roosevelt signed a proclamation ending the embargo against Spain; on April 4, the administration announced recognition of the Franco government.

Even before the final triumph of Franco, the debacle implicit in the agreement signed at Munich the previous September exploded into view. On March 15, mechanized units of the German army invaded Bohemia and Moravia and by the end of the day occupied all of Czechoslovakia. The German government cunningly rationalized that the occupation was necessary to quell disturbances, their source being that the Slovaks, encouraged by the Germans, had ostensibly split away from the republic. Simultaneously, of course with Hitler's prior approval, Hungarian troops occupied Ruthenia, the eastern tip of Czechoslovakia. In the evening Hitler arrived in Prague to announce that Czechoslovakia had become a German protectorate.

How would British prime minister Chamberlain and French premier Daladier react? They simply accepted the German occupation. Chamberlain explained that the Slovaks' secession had rendered the Munich agreement null and void: Since Czechoslovakia no longer existed, neither in effect did the Allies' commitment to guarantee its borders against aggression. In fact, since the republic had been sundered, "No such aggression has taken place," the prime minister asserted in response to his critics in the House of Commons. By March 18, however, following outraged reaction in the Commons and in British newspapers, Chamberlain had seen the light. He declared that Hitler had deceived him and had violated the Munich agreement. Hitler proceeded to add further to his domain by forcing Lithuania to cede the coastal enclave of Memel to Germany on March 23. Then on the last day of the month Chamberlain publicly and unequivocally committed Great Britain to protect the independence of Poland. By now British commitments mattered little to the fascists. More impressed by Hitler's easy successes and the Allies' obvious weakness, Mussolini sent troops over the Adriatic Sea to conquer Albania on Good Friday (April 7). A few days later Chamberlain offered guarantees to Greece and Romania. Subsequently, on May 22, at the Reich Chancellery in Berlin the Germans and Italians signed a military alliance known as the Pact of Steel.

FDR FINDS FEW OPTIONS

The Roosevelt administration searched for some way to respond to these events without overstepping the limits imposed by the Neutrality Act or evoking the wrath of the isolationists. Roosevelt returned to publicly advocating revision of the Neutrality Act but without effect. Congressional debate ended in stalemate and insufficient votes even to extract a bill from the Senate Foreign Relations Committee by the time Congress adjourned in August. During the critical days following the sudden demise of Czechoslovakia no direct communication occurred between Roosevelt and Chamberlain, evidencing once again the British prime minister's indifference toward the U.S. president's views. Since Secretary of State Cordell Hull was on vacation, Undersecretary of State Sumner Welles, with Roosevelt's approval, issued an innocuous statement condemning Czechoslovakia's loss of independence as a nation. The State Department, with Welles presiding at discussions, decided not to break off diplomatic relations with Germany, although Ambassador Hugh Wilson, called home following Kristallnacht, would never return to Berlin. The department also protested Italy's takeover of Albania. The administration maintained official recognition of the Czech and Albanian ministers and ambassadors and terminated trade agreements with the former Czechoslovakian republic.

In mid-April, Roosevelt launched an effort to prevent further aggression. He sent personal messages, largely drafted by Adolf Berle, to both Hitler and Mussolini requesting that Germany and Italy pledge not to invade 33 European and Middle Eastern nations—all listed by name, including Poland, Greece, the Netherlands, France, Great Britain, and the USSR—for a period of at least 10 years. In return, Roosevelt agreed to elicit similar assurances to Germany and Italy from each of the listed nations. During a news conference, the president read the text of the statements and commented at length on what they meant. The Allies expressed approval of his effort. Mussolini ignored the message and ridiculed the president. Hitler sent telegrams to each of the nations listed and asked whether they felt threatened by Germany and had authorized Roosevelt's proposal. He received negative answers from all except Switzerland and Romania. Then in a long and cunning speech to the Reichstag, he used the answers not only to heap sarcasm on Roosevelt's proposal but also to assure each of the nations listed that, if it desired, he would provide assurances that Germany would not invade. Some isolationists expressed appreciation for Hitler's speech, suggesting the president had made a false step and deserved the rebuff. Roosevelt had not expected positive responses from Hitler and Mussolini, but he had hoped at least that the responses would expose the dictators' disregard of international law while his proposal would claim a role for the United States in influencing future events.

THE UNITED STATES AND JAPAN

The Roosevelt administration had better luck in securing Japan's attention. For one thing the general public, some congressional isolationists, and prominent leaders like Henry Stimson supported a tougher approach toward Japan, giving the administration a freer hand to at times pursue a somewhat more forceful diplomacy with the Japanese government than with the Europeans. In addition, the United States was a major supplier to Japan of steel and other materials used for building ships and weapons, and this commerce provided a means of exerting pressure. In January the Japanese had seized Hainan, and in February they occupied the Spratly Islands, placing their forces within 400 miles of the Philippines. Members of Congress proposed sanctions against Japan, and to that end Senator Arthur Vandenberg in July introduced a resolution requesting that the president cancel the 1911 commercial treaty with Japan. Roosevelt instructed Hull to inform the Japanese government that the United States would terminate the treaty at the end of six months—a move that created consternation among Japanese officials.

AMERICAN NAZI SYMPATHIZERS

The difficulties of dealing with foreign affairs were to some extent compounded by the existence of divisive movements within the United States. Hitler's charisma and policies appealed to a number of Americans, who joined such fascist groups as the Ku Klux Klan, the Knights of the White Camelia, and the Silver Shirts. (The House Un-American Activities Committee had been created in 1938 to investigate these groups but instead turned its full attention on communists and even New Dealers.) The quasi-military, pro-Nazi organization the German-American Bund attracted thousands of supporters to its rallies. William Dudley Pelley's Silver Shirts (deliberately using the initials SS) made use of arm bands and other Nazi-style regalia and preached virulent anti-Semitism; Pelley continually railed against "the international Jewish conspiracy." Anti-Semitism was the common theme of such groups, including the Christian Front that Father Coughlin supported in these years. Many denounced Roosevelt as a "Jew" or a tool of the "Jewish conspiracy." Fortunately, these groups never mounted a serious national threat, but their numbers and protestations could not be ignored. At the very least, they represented a challenge to the principle of free speech.

THE NAZI-SOVIET PACT

To the dismay of both American fascists and communists, on August 24, 1939, in Moscow, the foreign ministers of Germany and the Soviet Union, Joachim von Ribbentrop and V. M. Molotov, respectively, signed a nonaggression pact that bound the two nations to avoid armed conflict with each other and to resolve disagreements by arbitration over the next 10 years. Unknown at the time, secret protocols in the pact awarded spheres of influence to each nation—Finland, Estonia, and Latvia to the Soviets, Lithuania to Germany—and provided for the partition of Poland. Thus the Nazi-Soviet Pact secured Hitler's plan to invade Poland. Contrary to Hitler's expectations, in the afternoon following the announcement of the pact, Chamberlain restated Britain's commitment to Poland. Hoping to dislodge Great Britain and France from their support of Poland, Hitler offered to guarantee the security of Britain and her empire in exchange for a free course in dealing with Poland. Chamberlain refused the offer. Europe once again verged on war.

THE WAR BEGINS

On September 1, 1939, at dawn German forces stormed into Poland to launch a blitzkrieg (a rapid and massive air and ground attack). As the day passed the Chamberlain government offered no reaction. Finally, in the evening, the British ambassador in Berlin delivered the message that unless immediate assurances were received that the German aggression had ceased, Great Britain would honor its commitment to Poland. The French government had faltered, accepting a proposal by Mussolini to convene a conference on Poland, but the British pressured the French to meet their obligation and deliver an identical ultimatum. Mussolini, desperate to avoid Italian involvement in a full-scale war, persisted with his proposal of a September 2 conference; the British agreed to one only if German troops were withdrawn to Germany's border. Hitler made no response. The French hesitated to take the final step. On Sunday, September 3, Chamberlain announced that a state of war existed with Germany. The French government followed. Both France and Great Britain had already begun general mobilizations of their armed forces. On following days the blitzkrieg raced forward, smashing Polish forces, and on September 17 the Soviet Union invaded its stricken neighbor as well. Warsaw surrendered 10 days later. Germany and the USSR divided the conquered nation, with the latter taking eastern Poland.

Roused from bed in the early hours of September 1 to be informed of the German attack, Roosevelt in the afternoon issued an appeal to Germany and Poland to avoid the bombing of civilians—reports to the president indicated that Luftwaffe bombers were over Warsaw. On September 3, following the declarations of war by Great Britain and France, the president presented a fireside chat, expressing his hope that the United States "will keep out of this war" and his assurance that the administration would do everything possible to avoid involvement. He acknowledged, however, that individual Americans could not "remain neutral in thought" but must exercise their consciences. His meaning was clear. As a Gallup poll indicated, 84 percent of those questioned favored a victory by the Allies, with only 2 percent favoring Germany. Only a few hours before the president's talk a German submarine sank the British liner *Athenia* off the Scottish coast, killing 112, including 28 Americans. On September 5, invoking the terms of the Neutrality Act, Roosevelt authorized an embargo on sales of war materials to the belligerents (Germany, France, and Great Britain). Three days later, on September 8, Roosevelt declared a "limited national emergency," allowing him to call an additional modest number of navy and army reserve personnel into active duty, and he arranged for navy patrols to prevent ships of belligerent nations from entering U.S. waters (although the navy lacked enough vessels to carry out the patrols). He also considered establishing bases of operation for aircraft or navy vessels in the Caribbean and the Gulf of St. Lawrence. On September 13 FDR called for a special session of Congress. In mid September, Ambassador Joseph Kennedy, who had tried for weeks to convince the Roosevelt administration to prod Poland into making concessions to Hitler, sent word from London that the Chamberlain government believed the embargo imposed by Roosevelt would hinder Great Britain and France. A few days later, on September 21, the president once again requested that Congress, now convened in special session, revise the Neutrality Act.

REVISING THE NEUTRALITY ACT

In making his request to amend the Neutrality Act, Roosevelt attempted to conciliate his isolationist opponents by arguing that as part of the revision U.S. ships should be banned from waters within the zones of warfare so that they would avoid "incidents" (meaning attacks) that might involve the nation in hostilities—the purpose of the revision supposedly being, then, not to aid the Allies but to keep the United States out of the war. In conjunction with this ban, the president argued, the revision should also provide that belligerent nations could buy U.S. goods only on a cash-and-carry basis: They would have to pay in cash and transport the goods in their own ships, or at least in non-American ships. Isolationists in Congress refused the bait. They denounced the president's proposal as the work of European warmongers and insisted it would open the gates to providing credit, then outright gifts, and finally U.S. troops. Father Coughlin's followers joined the fray, excoriating the president and the British. Charles Lindbergh, back in the States after a four-year self-imposed exile in Europe, broadcast radio speeches advocating neutrality that some interpreted as favoring the Germans. The National Keep America Out of Foreign War Committee, which New York congressman Hamilton Fish had set up, and the Women's National Committee to Keep the United States Out of War joined the chorus. But this time the president had majority public opinion on his side—polls indicated that 60 percent supported outright repeal of the Neutrality Act—as well as public advocates such as Henry Stimson and respected newspaper editor William Allen White, both Republicans. He also had more forceful support in Congress; even Robert Taft advocated repeal on the grounds that the Neutrality Act worked in favor of the aggressors. On November 3, 1939, sizable majorities of both houses of Congress approved a revised Neutrality Act that ended the arms embargo while forbidding Americans to travel on ships of belligerent nations or to enter their ports. On the following day Roosevelt declared all of the Baltic Ocean and the Atlantic Ocean from southern Norway to northern Spain war zones to be avoided by U.S. ships.

HEMISPHERIC SECURITY

The administration also pursued diplomatic and collective security arrangements in the Western Hemisphere. At Roosevelt's behest, the First Meeting of the Foreign Ministers of the American Republics convened in Panama to confer on ways to protect the hemisphere against involvement in the war. On October 3 the delegates unanimously adopted the Declaration of Panama, which defined a zone between the southern border of Canada and the tip of South America and extending from 300 to 1,000 miles into the Atlantic and Pacific Oceans in which belligerents were warned not to engage in any naval actions. Although Hitler responded by secretly ordering his naval commanders not to initiate hostilities in this zone, he had in August—preparatory to the invasion of Poland—ordered 21 submarines and a pocket battleship to move into positions off the British Isles and another pocket battleship, the *Admiral Graf Spee,* into position off the coast of Brazil to prey upon merchant ships of the Allies. The *Admiral Graf Spee* sank nine cargo vessels in the waters off Latin America. But in mid-December three British cruisers surprised the German ship off the coast of Uruguay and opened fire. After a 14-hour battle, the *Admiral Graf Spee* sought refuge in the harbor at Montevideo. The Uruguayan government ordered the German ship to leave; the captain, aware that the three British cruisers awaited his exit, had the German ship blown up in the Río de la Plata. The crew was interned in Argentina, where the captain committed suicide.

THE PHONY WAR AND THE WINTER WAR

Following the Allies' declaration of war, a hiatus in the conduct of the war between the Allies and Germany settled in during the winter of 1939–40. Neither side attacked throughout this so-called Phony War (a term taken from a statement by Idaho senator Borah). They simply waited. By mid-October the British had four divisions, a total of only 158,000 troops, in France. The French High Command, in control of one of Europe's largest armies, suffered from a malaise of defeatism that stymied initiative. At the end of September, Hitler proposed a peace conference. The majority of the French cabinet favored the proposal, but Daladier and Chamberlain demanded proof of Hitler's peaceful intentions. No proof was forthcoming. At the same time that he was offering peace, Hitler actually ordered preparations for an attack in the west—that is, through the Low Countries and into France—to begin in November, but as the date approached he postponed the attack. In November two plots to overthrow Hitler failed, including an assassination attempt in Munich. The Phony War would continue into May 1940.

It was the Soviets who pursued the war on the ground during these winter months. In October 1939 the Soviets began negotiations with Finland to elicit concessions that would protect approaches to Leningrad in the Gulf of Finland, restore the 18th-century border on the Karelian Isthmus (the neck of land that lies between Lake Ladoga and the Gulf of Finland), and conclude a mutual assistance pact. In return they offered to cede eastern Karelia to Finland. The Finns were unyielding, and the negotiations ended in mid-November without agreement. The Soviets then launched the so-called Winter War, invading Finland. They reached the Finns' defensive Mannerheim Line by December 5, where they encountered defeat and withdrew. The Soviets launched a second offensive in February 1940, culminating in a March victory that gained them larger territorial concessions than originally demanded but at a huge cost in casualties. The Winter War was not simply a sideline. France and Great Britain had promised help to Finland but could not provide it because the Scandinavian nations, intent on preserving their neutrality, denied them access to ports. This failure to aid Finland caused the downfall of the Daladier government in March 1940, adding to instability in France at a critical juncture.

The Winter War intensified American sympathies for Finland, consistently well regarded in the United States for being the only nation never to miss a payment on its World War I debt. Still, the Americans were not prepared to transform their sympathies into overt action and become directly involved.

Roosevelt, who in private referred to the Soviet attack as the "rape of Finland," in public denounced the USSR for violating international law, invoked a "moral embargo" against the USSR, and extended $10 million in credits to Finland for purchases of surplus U.S. agricultural products. Later the president condemned the Soviets' bombing of civilians, but he did not embargo shipments of war materials to the USSR. A bill had been introduced in Congress to provide a $60 million loan for Finland to buy arms, but by the time it received final approval (reduced to only $20 million and earmarked for agricultural purchases rather than arms), the Soviets had already attained victory. However sympathetic, the Americans, in their insistence on neutrality, proved as ineffectual in helping Finland as the League of Nations, which expelled the USSR in mid-December 1939 and empowered remaining League members to offer Finland assistance of any kind.

THREE IMPORTANT LETTERS

Unknown to the public, the events of autumn 1939 generated the creation of a personal relationship between Roosevelt and a prominent British official, Winston Churchill, that would nurture the president's strong inclination to side with the Allies. On the very day that Great Britain declared war, Chamberlain, although most reluctantly, returned Churchill to the cabinet after a 10-year absence by appointing him first lord of the admiralty, a post Churchill had held during World War I. Roosevelt wrote Churchill a note applauding the appointment and stating his desire to be in personal touch with Churchill and the prime minister. The president also wrote to Chamberlain, but the letter to Churchill began an intimate correspondence that would last the rest of the president's life and would slowly but surely spur Roosevelt toward involving the United States in assisting the British war effort. In responding to Roosevelt in October, Churchill expressed the British government's intention to honor the noncombat zone defined by the Declaration of Panama. This exchange initiated thousands of letters and phone calls to follow; the two men would always be in close touch as the war proceeded.

Another piece of correspondence that reached Roosevelt in October would also have significant long-term consequences. This letter was carried personally by economist Alexander Sachs, who had been seeking a private meeting with the president for two months. The letter he carried had been composed in early August and was signed by the physicist Albert Einstein. Meeting with Roosevelt on October 11, Sachs supposedly read aloud the letter's content. It apprised the president of successful experiments in Europe, replicated in this country, to unleash the uranium atom in a chain reaction (nuclear fission) that, Einstein said, provided the potential for creating "extremely powerful bombs of a new type." Einstein appealed to Roosevelt to involve the government in supporting these experiments and in securing uranium supplies. (Czechoslovakia, now in Germany's control, had the world's largest known uranium deposits.) Roosevelt reacted hesitantly. He did appoint an Advisory Committee on Uranium, headed by Lyman J. Briggs, that met with some of the scientists—Leo Szilard, Edward Teller, and Eugene Wigner—but no sense of urgency or pursuit of adequate funding resulted until months later.

WORLD'S FAIRS AND OTHER ATTRACTIONS

While the momentous events of 1939 occupied the newspaper headlines, Americans busied themselves with their daily lives—worried at times no doubt over what the events might mean, but mostly absorbed with continuing efforts to make a living or find work or enjoy entertaining distractions. During the summer months Americans could enjoy visiting two world's fairs, one on each coast. President Roosevelt himself, accompanied by Eleanor and his mother, formally opened the New York World's Fair at Flushing Meadow on April 30, the 150th anniversary of George Washington's first inauguration as president. There, among other things, they could view "Democracity," a model planned city of the future. And there also Roosevelt became the first president to speak and appear on television, a new, not yet viable broadcasting tool. In June the president accompanied Great Britain's king George VI and queen Elizabeth on a brief visit to the fair before their sojourn with his family at Hyde Park. At the opposite end of the nation, San Francisco hosted the other world's fair, the Golden Gate International Exposition.

Unlike some previous expositions, neither fair generated a significant influence on American architecture, but the buildings for the General Motors Company and Ford Motor Company exhibits at New York attracted much attention and reflected increased emphasis on stylistic simplicity combined with economy and efficiency of construction. Most of the buildings were streamlined and severe in form. Perhaps in the long run the most significant building was Alvar Aalto's Finnish Pavilion, which exemplified a more flexible use of space than most modern designs. Actually, the legacy of earlier fairs continued, as revealed in John Russell Pope's classical design for the Jefferson Memorial in Washington, D.C., completed in 1939. Pope also designed the National Gallery, completed in 1941. Among significant architectural events of the years 1939 through 1941 was a one-man exhibit of Frank Lloyd Wright's work that opened at the Museum of Modern Art in New York City in November 1940. In these years, however, Wright's influence was confined almost entirely to residential design. The International Style promoted by resident European immigrants such as Walter Gropius and Ludwig Mies van der Rohe, who arrived in this country in 1939 as political refugees, was attaining increased recognition in the design of industrial and commercial buildings.

Of far greater interest to the vast majority of Americans was the Hollywood film scene. Still in its golden age, Hollywood movies continued to improve in content and execution. It was during this time that many groundbreaking films were made. Frank Capra continued to celebrate the little guy who succeeds through pluck and decency in his 1939 film *Mr. Smith Goes to Washington,* starring James Stewart. Comedies, such as *My Little Chickadee* (1939), starring W. C. Fields and Mae West, and Howard Hawks's *His Girl Friday* (1940), with Cary Grant and Rosalind Russell, thrived during these years. Walt Disney Studios released the classic *Fantasia* in 1940. The western attained added dimensions with John Ford's *Stagecoach* (1939), which made John Wayne a star. In the same year, Ford produced *Young Mr. Lincoln,* celebrating both an American hero and democracy. Two enduring blockbuster films, totally different in content, filled screens for the first time in 1939. One was *Gone With the Wind,* starring Clark Gable and Vivien Leigh; the other was *The Wizard of Oz,*

Children and farmers waiting to enter a movie theater on a Saturday afternoon in Littleton, New Hampshire *(Library of Congress)*

with Judy Garland playing the lead role. Two of John Steinbeck's novels, *The Grapes of Wrath* and *Of Mice and Men,* were transformed into movies in 1940. In that same year, Charlie Chaplin made a satire of Hitler entitled *The Great Dictator.* Some of Alfred Hitchcock's best suspense films, *Rebecca* (1940) and *Suspicion* (1941), appeared during this time. John Huston's *The Maltese Falcon,* starring Humphrey Bogart, was released in 1941, the same year as Orson Welles's pathbreaking film based on the life of William Randolph Hearst, *Citizen Kane.* Although some of these films suggest fantasy and escape, others reflect a serious view of contemporary realities.

A similar comment might pertain to what Americans were reading. The best-selling novel of 1939 was Steinbeck's *The Grapes of Wrath.* It told the epic story of the Joad family as exemplars of the Okies—poor farm families from Oklahoma who were forced from their homes by the dustbowl—dispossession from their land and their travails in California (as noted, made into a film the year after its publication). Ernest Hemingway's novel based on the Spanish civil war, *For Whom the Bell Tolls* (1940), sold well, as did journalist William Shirer's *Berlin Diary* (1941), a chronicle of the Nazi ascendancy. These works were joined as solid sellers by such books as Eric Knight's *Lassie Come Home* (1940), Osa Johnson's African tale *I Married Adventure* (1940), and Mary O'Hara's *My Friend Flicka* (1941). Ellery Queen mysteries continued to sell well in these years, as did those of Leslie Charteris, Raymond Chandler, and Agatha Christie. Two of Thomas Wolfe's giant novels, *The Web and the Rock* (1939) and *You Can't Go Home Again* (1940), appeared, published posthumously. Also in 1940, Richard Wright's powerful *Native Son,* a harrowing tale of an African-American youth's alienation and accidental slide into brutality, appeared in print. Van Wyck Brooks's *The Flowering of New England* (1940) generated a new interest in the history and legacy of American literature. As for recent history, the chronicler of the Jazz Age, F. Scott Fitzgerald, died of a heart attack at age 44 in Hollywood in December 1940—not one of his books was still in print, an ironic testament that made the twenties now seem archaic.

A most interesting and significant constituent dropped from the American art scene in late May 1939 with the death of Joseph Duveen, an English citizen and a baron. His enterprise headquartered on Fifth Avenue in Manhattan, Duveen was probably the greatest art dealer in history. His career as buyer and seller of art, mostly Renaissance paintings, had begun prior to World War I so that by 1914 he held a virtual monopoly on the transatlantic trade in works by Frans Hals, Rembrandt, Thomas Gainesborough, Johannes Vermeer, Raphael, Leonardo da Vinci, and other great masters. Duveen had been almost single-handedly responsible for the representation of works by such old masters in the world-class collections of Henry E. Huntington, Henry Clay Frick, John D. Rockefeller, William C. Whitney, John Pierpont Morgan, Benjamin Altman, and other titans of American business and finance. Duveen had even chosen the architectural firm Carrere & Hastings (architects of the main New York Public Library building on 42nd Street and Fifth Avenue) and worked with Thomas Hastings on the room designs and decor for the great mansion that steel magnate Frick built on Fifth Avenue during World War I. Frick died in

Easter morning on Chicago's South Side, April 1941 *(Library of Congress, Prints and Photographs Division [PPMSC 00256])*

1919, bequeathing his mansion to New York City, and it became one of the city's major art museums following his wife's death in 1931.

Not surprisingly, Duveen continued to acquire master paintings for his wealthy American clients through the affluent twenties, but the apex of his career actually occurred during the financially bleak years of the Great Depression, suggesting that during this crisis the wealthiest Americans pursued their lives mostly as they did in any other year. From 1931 on, the art dealer cultivated the man who became his foremost client, Andrew W. Mellon, whom Duveen first met in 1921 but with whom he had conducted no business. Through the 1930s their relationship solidified, as Duveen helped Mellon to complete his imposing collection at a cost of many millions of dollars. Most important, Duveen persuaded Mellon to undertake a project that became the financier's and the art dealer's greatest legacy. And so Mellon wrote to President Roosevelt offering to build a gallery and donate it along with his collection and an endowment fund of $5 million to the nation. In March 1937 the president and Congress accepted the offer. Duveen chose John Russell Pope, who also designed the Jefferson Memorial (1939), as the architect for the building to be erected in Washington, D.C. Since the taciturn Mellon, who died in 1937, had refused to have his name on the building, thereby precluding frayed sensibilities among lesser collectors, Duveen was able to persuade another major client, the dime store tycoon Samuel H. Kress, a bachelor, to bequeath his collection to the gallery as well. The National Gallery of Art opened to the public in 1941.

ROOSEVELT PURSUES DEFENSE

As 1940 began Roosevelt's primary concern was the course the European war would take and its effect on the security of the United States. In his annual message to Congress on January 3, he observed that the world would become "a shabby and dangerous place to live in" if, as his words implied, it were ruled by the fascist dictators. He requested renewal of the act providing for reciprocal trade agreements and an increased defense budget. The following day in his budget message he requested a total of $1.8 billion for defense, only a modest increase. His new budget even countered this request by seeking reduced appropriations for agricultural programs, public works, old-age assistance programs, and work relief (to be cut by $500 million even though unemployment remained high). Despite his concern over the nation's security, the president assumed that to placate his opponents he had to opt for reducing the deficit. Roosevelt's opposition was potent. Extending the act on reciprocal trade for three years won congressional approval by only small majorities after caustic debate. The defense budget bill that emerged from committee in the House in April revealed substantial cuts in the president's requests. But spring events in Europe would have a decisive impact on the outcome of the fight over defense appropriations.

GERMANY INVADES SCANDINAVIA AND FRANCE

Although an independent Finland tottered through the 1939–40 winter months, it was the Phony War that set the tone of uneasy waiting as the spring of 1940 approached. The suspense intensified in early April. Aware that the Allies had plans to seize Narvik and perhaps other ports in Norway—the plans originated ostensibly as a means of helping Finland—Hitler determined in March to occupy the Scandinavian countries. The operation was set to begin on April 9, and a German naval task force approached the coast of Norway two nights before, at the very time the British were mining the waters.

Unfortunately, Great Britain had moved too slowly. Although fighting occurred between the German and British naval forces, with the British destroying 10 German destroyers and nine other ships, air support favored the Germans, and their attack on Norway proceeded as planned. Following Norwegian rejection of an ultimatum on April 9, German forces captured Narvik and took control of the airfields at Sola and Oslo. At the same time a helpless Denmark submitted to the Germans' ultimatum and was immediately occupied. In mid-April the British landed forces at Namsos and Andalsnes to try to halt the German advance in Norway, but they were unsuccessful and had to be evacuated. By the end of the first week of May the Germans were in control of most of the strategic areas in southern and central Norway, and any serious effort by Britain to dislodge them in northern Norway had to be abandoned after the Germans launched their major offensive against the Low Countries (modern Belgium, Luxembourg, and the Netherlands) and France.

On May 10 the Phony War suddenly ended. Hitler sent his massed armies against the Low Countries, with France their destination. When the attack began, the Allies actually held a sizable superiority in numbers of troops, tanks, and artillery but not, as it turned out, in their effectiveness. In a blitzkrieg the German land forces smashed rapidly ahead, aided in part by the Luftwaffe (German air force). As the Germans raced through Luxembourg, the British and French moved troops into the Netherlands and Belgium to confront them. By the end of the first day of fighting the Germans had already broken through major Belgian defenses and reached the Meuse River. By mid-May they had smashed the supposedly impregnable French defenses along the Maginot Line in Lorraine, traversed the Ardennes Forest, and crossed the Meuse. Within a week of the attack's beginning the Germans captured Brussels and Antwerp. A few days later they had driven deep into northern France, conquered the Netherlands, and reached the English Channel, threatening to annihilate British, Belgian, and French forces which were effectively surrounded, with no exit but the channel, near Dunkirk. Unexpectedly, at this critical moment, Hitler called a halt to the advance against Dunkirk. Belgium capitulated on May 28, two days after the British began a desperate operation to evacuate the troops ensnared at Dunkirk, making use of not only naval vessels but small private craft. By June 4 the operation succeeded in transporting more than 338,000 men to England; about 190,000 more were also withdrawn from other French ports. On June 10 the French government abandoned Paris for Orléans and then Tours. On June 14, German troops marched into Paris. On the 16th, Marshal Philippe Pétain, French hero of World War I, replaced Paul Reynaud as premier. And on the 22nd the new government signed an armistice with the Germans at Compiègne in the same railroad car in which the Germans had been compelled to sign the Treaty of Versailles ending World War I. The armistice ceded most of France outright to the Germans and allowed the French to set up a government headed by Pétain (known as the

Vichy government) at Vichy in nominal control of the southern half of France. Great Britain now stood alone. Fortunately, on the day the invasion in the west began, May 10, 1940, Neville Chamberlain had been forced from office, succeeded as prime minister by the indomitable Winston Churchill.

A FEEBLE AMERICAN RESPONSE

Reynaud had futilely appealed to the U.S. government to declare war on Germany. But that was simply not possible, and the French army's collapse occurred so rapidly that, even if the United States had intervened by sending supplies, they could not have reached France in time. Roosevelt did appeal to Mussolini to remain on the sidelines; Mussolini responded by attacking southern France on June 10. The president probably knew his appeal was pointless. In February he had sent Sumner Welles as his personal emissary to converse with leaders in Great Britain, France, Germany, and Italy and to evaluate "present conditions." The president fruitlessly hoped that Welles's mission might forestall further German aggression while the Allies rearmed and also somehow promote peace. Welles, who returned to the United States in late March, had conveyed no cause for optimism. He reported that his conversations with German and Italian leaders, including Hitler and Mussolini, led him to conclude that Mussolini had no influence with his German ally—that Hitler would do whatever he decided to do and Mussolini would be obliged to acquiesce.

Churchill had also appealed to the president in mid-May, warning that Great Britain expected to be attacked and might not be able to endure without American aid. The prime minister asked the president to provide a "loan of forty or fifty of your older destroyers," several hundred airplanes, antiaircraft weapons and ammunition, expedited sales of American steel and other materials to England, a U.S. squadron to be sent to an Irish port to discourage the Germans from an airborne attack, and a fleet to visit Singapore or other Pacific ports to discourage a Japanese attack. Roosevelt responded cautiously, agreeing only to expedite shipments of antiaircraft weapons and sales of materials while declaring that a decision to provide destroyers would have to be made by Congress. But at the end of May, with his original defense budget now approved, Roosevelt requested a greater increase in the military budget than he had asked from Congress in January—an additional $1.4 billion for expanding both the army and the navy. Churchill wrote again to underscore the danger facing the Allies and to warn Roosevelt of the possible consequences to the United States if the Churchill government fell and was replaced by officials who negotiated a peace that gave control of the British fleet to the Germans. Roosevelt and the War Department discussed the possibility of providing more planes and war materials to the Allies; he received scant encouragement but ordered the job done, and, through U.S. Army chief of staff George Marshall's organizing, additional armaments channeled from War Department reserves were being loaded aboard British ships at New York City and other ports by early June.

ROOSEVELT MOVES TO PREPARE THE UNITED STATES

Roosevelt became deeply concerned over the potential danger to the United States if Germany gained control not only of the British fleet but also of the

French fleet in the Mediterranean: American military planners estimated that the Germans would need only six months following the defeat of France and Great Britain to man these fleets and send them against the United States. This concern was partly alleviated when, on July 3, the British attacked and destroyed much of the French fleet stationed in Oran, Algeria, after the French agreed to turn over the fleet to the Germans; the British also seized or destroyed French ships in other ports. But the threat that Great Britain's fleet could still be lost remained. The president believed that maintaining control of the Atlantic Ocean was imperative to defending the United States and that some form of mobilization was necessary to ensure American security. Roosevelt decided to pursue the kind of cooperative effort involving both government and private industry employed during World War I to spur weapons production for the defense of the United States. On the day of Belgium's surrender he announced reestablishment of the Council of National Defense, a committee of Cabinet officers including the secretaries of war, agriculture, commerce, labor, the interior, and the navy, to meet weekly with the president. At this time, he also appointed an executive committee, the Advisory Committee of the Council, to oversee implementation of plans for mobilizing industries for arms production. Edward Stettinius, chairman of the board of United States Steel, and William Knudsen, president of General Motors, served the council in a full-time capacity.

Roosevelt also went on the offensive in his public speeches in an effort to rally the American people to face up to the perceived danger. In asking Congress to authorize increasing U.S. airplane production from 12,000 to 50,000 per year, he pointed out that the oceans could not protect the United States from airborne attack. During an address at the University of Virginia at Charlottesville on June 10, he denounced the Italian attack on France, launched the same day, as a stab in the back and declared that the United States would provide more materials to the Allies while increasing production for defense. He also sent a secret message of support to Premier Reynaud, but, despite Churchill's urgent pleas that a public commitment by the United States to France might save Britain's ally, Roosevelt believed he dare not make such a move—authority to make a final commitment rested with Congress. The president did authorize the sale of 12 B-17 bombers to Great Britain, but Secretary of War Harry Woodring refused to approve the sale. On June 19, consequently, Roosevelt asked for Woodring's resignation and appointed Henry L. Stimson, a Republican who had served as secretary of war in the Taft administration and secretary of state in the Hoover administration, to replace Woodring. At the same time he appointed Frank Knox, also a Republican, as secretary of the navy. In addition, in mid-June the president made another decision of long-term significance: He ordered creation of the National Defense Research Committee and appointed Vannevar Bush, former dean of electrical engineering at the Massachusetts Institute of Technology and current president of the Carnegie Institute, as its chairman. The committee would have responsibility for furthering research projects that might have military applications, including experiments with nuclear fission.

The German success in overrunning the Low Countries and France may have appeared ominous yet still only a distant threat to most Americans. But to others it served as a catalyst. At the beginning of June the leaders of the

Military Training Camp Association (MTCA) organized a National Emergency Committee of 1,000 members representing its nationwide chapters in order to publicly campaign for conscription. They were joined in their campaign by other groups who now believed that the United States must prepare for becoming a participant in the war. Perhaps surprisingly, their cause gained a focus when, on June 20 and 21, Senator Edward Burke and Congressman James Wadsworth introduced a "selective service" bill in the Congress. Despite his desire for preparedness, the president refused to support the bill—1940, after all, was an election year, and he was wary of how the public might react to the idea of peacetime conscription.

THE THIRD-TERM QUESTION AND THE CONVENTIONS

The approach of the presidential election had raised the question of whether Roosevelt would run for a third term. The answer might, among other things, determine the success of a Republican candidate. Whoever the Democratic nominee would be—and Roosevelt had misgivings about all the potential candidates—the president wished to contribute to a Democratic victory in order to secure the future of the programs his administration had instituted. Well aware that the subdued economy continued as a major political issue, Roosevelt recognized that sales of armaments to the Allies could prove helpful. In fact, in March, well before Churchill's furtive appeals, the president had already eased War Department resistance to sales of advanced-model airplanes to Great Britain, authorizing that the sales proceed—orders for 5,000 airplane frames and 10,000 engines had been received—and noting to members of his staff that the sales could generate some prosperity and thus be beneficial to the Democrats in the fall election. During 1940, however, the sales of armaments were inadequate to have any major impact on the economy. Industrialists, in fact, resisted accepting orders for armaments because of concerns that they would boost production only to learn the orders would not be repeated and that they might be labeled as "merchants of death" since the stench of discredit created by the Nye Committee hearings on World War I munitions profiteers still lingered.

The Republican National Convention officially opened in Philadelphia on June 24. The front-runners for the presidential nomination entering the convention were Senators Robert Taft and Arthur Vandenberg and also Thomas E. Dewey, the famed racket-busting district attorney of New York City who had run unsuccessfully for governor against Herbert Lehman in 1938. The senators represented the isolationist wing of the party; Dewey described himself as a "New Deal Republican." The front-runners all lost out to a dark horse candidate, Wendell Willkie from Indiana. An attorney for the Commonwealth & Southern Corporation utility who had fought against creation of the Tennessee Valley Authority (TVA), Willkie was a registered Democrat until 1938 and had never held any public office. He lacked any substantive political backing yet won the nomination on the sixth ballot on June 28. The crucial issue on everyone's mind was the American role in the war. Willkie's opponents for the nomination either adamantly opposed any form of American involvement or hedged their answers. Willkie vigorously advocated full-scale aid to Great Britain (to both Allies before the fall of France), although not armed participa-

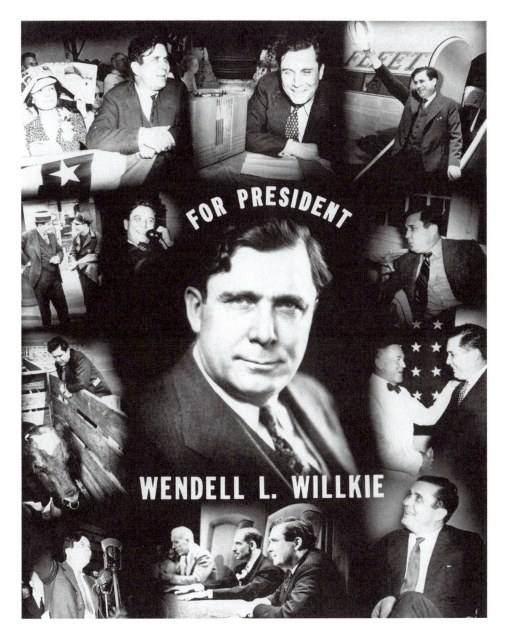

Wendell Willkie *(Library of Congress)*

tion in the conflict—actually a popular stand with the public. His running mate was Senate minority leader Charles McNary.

When the Democratic National Convention opened in Chicago on July 15, the question of whether Roosevelt would be a candidate for an unprecedented third term remained unanswered—for everyone but the president's closest advisers, that is. The president had, apparently quite sincerely, not wanted to run but rather to retire to Hyde Park. After numerous and lengthy consultations, he had decided, however, also apparently quite sincerely, that there was no viable alternative to his candidacy. He had also decided his nomination should appear to be a popular "draft" by the convention delegates that it would be irresponsible for him to reject. To this end, he had the convention's permanent chairman, Senate Majority Leader Alben Barkley, read to the delegates a short note from the president in which Roosevelt declared that he had never

President Franklin D. Roosevelt
(Library of Congress)

had "any wish or purpose to remain in the office of President . . . after next January." In his address Barkley recounted the achievements of the New Deal, finally mentioning Roosevelt by name and evoking a huge, spontaneous floor demonstration. When the delegates calmed down, Barkley read the president's statement and added that the president, "in all earnestness and sincerity," desired the delegates to vote for the candidate of their choice. Silence followed. Then from the basement of the stadium, as prearranged by Harry Hopkins, the city's superintendent of sewers blared over a microphone, "We want Roosevelt." Music, cheering, and tumult ensued. The next night, July 17, the convention chose Roosevelt as its nominee for president. The following night, against their own desires, their preference being Speaker of the House William Bankhead, the delegates acquiesced to Roosevelt and chose Henry Wallace as his runningmate.

THE BATTLE OF BRITAIN

The overriding issue of the campaign was U.S. involvement in the war. Roosevelt chose to concentrate his energies on fulfilling his presidential duties, leaving the campaign trail to Willkie. The capitulation of France and subsequent events in Europe and Asia revealed the imperativeness of trying to ensure Great Britain's survival. Encouraged by France's surrender, the Japanese in late

June demanded the right to send troops into France's Indochinese colonies. At the end of June the Germans occupied Britain's Channel Islands off the coast of France. In July the Battle of Britain began. Hitler, believing that Great Britain's situation was hopeless after the fall of France, was astonished when the British refused to come to terms. On July 7, 1940, Hitler sent the Luftwaffe in air attacks that were meant to cripple the Royal Air Force (RAF) and British shipping while also conducting bombing raids of airfields in preparation for the launch of Operation Sea Lion—the invasion of England.

In truth, Hitler was correct in thinking that Great Britain's situation was nearly hopeless: So much equipment had been left behind during the evacuation of Dunkirk that the British had minimal defensive capabilities, but the RAF prevented the invasion. From July 7 to August 23, the RAF destroyed nearly 600 German planes while losing a little more than 350 planes. Thereafter, however, the destruction came nearly into balance, and by early September the RAF's Fighter Command faced destruction. Then the Luftwaffe changed tactics. The Germans had accidentally bombed London in late August, and the British, believing the bombing deliberate, had retaliated by bombing Berlin. This raid induced the Luftwaffe to concentrate on bombing London, in a weeklong series of raids that began on September 7, instead of continuing to batter airfields and radar stations. The respite gave the RAF a chance to muster its forces once again to inflict heavy destruction on the Luftwaffe. By September 15 the Luftwaffe's losses had risen to 1,116 planes; the RAF's, to 779. The Luftwaffe's losses convinced the Germans that the Battle of Britain could not be won, and on September 16, Hitler ordered that Operation Sea Lion be postponed. Throughout the fall of 1940 and into the winter the Luftwaffe continued to bomb English cities, but the tide had been stemmed and England for the moment knew there would be no invasion. The Roosevelt administration had feared that Great Britain would succumb to Germany's might and worried whether, if the United States supplied Britain with ships and armaments, these supplies would fall into the hands of the Germans following Britain's surrender. The British success in the Battle of Britain and Churchill's forceful public declarations of Britain's determination to prevail assuaged these fears and encouraged the administration to pursue ways of providing aid.

BOLSTERING DEFENSE AND THE 1940 ELECTION

After the Battle of Britain began, Roosevelt, on July 10, asked Congress to provide $5 billion more for the defense budget on top of the increases already approved. With this request, the president foresaw greatly expanded aircraft production, shipbuilding, and recruitment of troops. In late July, he signed into law an act appropriating $4 billion to construct 400 ships, including seven battleships, for the two-ocean navy. Now well aware of the dangers, Congress voted approval of FDR's requested increase in early October, bringing the total defense appropriations voted since June to nearly $17.7 billion. In September both houses also would pass the Selective Service Act, which the president signed into law on September 16; it authorized the first peacetime draft in U.S. history. At the end of July, the president received a message from Churchill renewing the request for a loan, this time for "50 or 60 of your oldest destroyers," needed to bolster convoys in the Atlantic defending merchant vessels against submarine attacks. How to grant the request presented a quandary because Congress had specified the restriction that destroyers could be furnished to Britain only if the navy attested that they were not needed to defend the United States. Secretary of the Navy Knox and the British ambassador, Philip Kerr, Lord Lothian, devised the solution: The United States would provide the destroyers in exchange for British bases in the Caribbean and Newfoundland. The final deal, announced on September 3, provided that Britain would give the United States bases in Bermuda and Newfoundland and lease other bases in the Caribbean in exchange for the destroyers.

Willkie, who had agreed beforehand not to attack the deal after it was made, a few days later repudiated it as a "dictatorial and arbitrary act" by the

CIO leader John L. Lewis (left)
(Library of Congress)

president as Congress had not been asked to approve the deal. The election campaign was now in full swing, and the nature of Willkie's statements had shifted from an evenhandedness to a certain shrillness. Polls showed him running behind the president. Willkie now charged that if Roosevelt won reelection the United States would be at war by April 1941. The charge stung the president into open campaigning in the last few weeks before the election. He gave his first campaign speech in Philadelphia on October 23, pledging his administration to the pursuit of peace. Two days later, Congress of Industrial Organizations (CIO) leader John L. Lewis excoriated Roosevelt in a radio address, asserting that his policies would result in American sons' becoming "cannon fodder." Although even CIO members denounced Lewis afterward, Roosevelt felt obliged to respond. During a speech in New York he defended his policies as sustaining neutrality. Almost ironically, he also presided at the first drawing of numbers for selective service on October 29, although Stimson did the actual drawing (more than 16 million men had registered). Then in a speech delivered in Boston on October 30, Roosevelt made a statement that would later haunt him: "I have said this before, but I shall say it again and again and again: Your boys are not going to be sent into any foreign wars." Roosevelt won reelection, receiving 27 million popular votes to Willkie's 22 million and 449 electoral votes to Willkie's 82.

WORLDWIDE CONCERNS

The chain of events that would undo the president's promises to keep the nation out of war had proceeded along with the election campaign. In mid-July 1940, Prince Fumimaro Konoye became premier of Japan; he chose General Hideki Tojo as his minister of war. During the first week of August, the USSR seized Latvia, Lithuania, and Estonia. At the beginning of August, Italian troops invaded British Somaliland from East Africa (Ethiopia). Near the end of July, concerned over increasing Japanese purchases of airplane gasoline and lubricants, the Roosevelt administration had imposed an embargo on exports of top-grade scrap iron and aviation gasoline to Japan. Although the embargo served as a warning, it was largely ineffectual, and in September the Japanese sent troops into Indochina. The United States imposed an embargo on exports of all types of scrap iron to any nation outside the Western Hemisphere except Britain—the Japanese government called the embargo an unfriendly act. In mid-September Italian troops invaded Egypt from Libya. Near the end of September Germany, Italy, and Japan formed the Tripartite Pact, committing each to come to the aid of any other of the three that became involved in war with the United States. In October Roosevelt sent two squadrons of planes and two submarines to the Philippines—he had already authorized the Flying Tigers' support of Chiang Kai-shek's air force—and in December he extended the embargo against Japan to include iron ore, steel, and other items. Near the end of October, Italian troops stationed in Albania attacked Greece. In late-November Hungary and Romania joined the Axis alliance. And in December, with the invasion of Britain on hold, Hitler issued secret orders to his top commanders to prepare for Operation Barbarossa, the invasion of the USSR.

The Roosevelt administration also had to worry about the effects of the European war on hemispheric relations. Hitler warned the Latin American nations that they would have to depend on Germany for markets because Great Britain would be defeated by autumn. This threat caused several governments to back out of the July Pan-American conference in Havana that was organized by the United States to prepare a hemispheric defense plan. Their withdrawal forced the Roosevelt administration to negotiate defense agreements with each nation separately (these agreements were accomplished by the end of the year, with the exception of Argentina). Nevertheless, the participants in the conference agreed to the Act of Havana, which authorized a "collective trusteeship" over European territories in the Caribbean and gave the United States the power to occupy Atlantic islands threatened by outside control or to take other actions deemed necessary to protect the sovereignty of Latin American states. The Roosevelt administration provided armaments and ships to safeguard the region and persuaded Congress to increase loans through the Export-Import Bank to stimulate exports to the region. Roosevelt also created (in August) an Office for Co-ordination of Commercial and Cultural Relations between the American Republics, headed by Nelson Rockefeller, whose purpose was to counteract German influence in the hemisphere. In addition, Roosevelt met with Canada's prime minister, William Mackenzie King, at Ogdensburg, New York, to set up a Permanent Joint Board of Defense that established ongoing consultations between U.S. and Canadian military personnel—a clearcut American link with the British Commonwealth, of which Canada was a member.

AMERICAN AID FOR BRITAIN

While aboard a cruise liner in the Caribbean on December 9, 1940, Roosevelt received a message from Churchill warning of Great Britain's desperate need for aid to prevent the nation's collapse and advising that by the following June, Britain would no longer be able to pay for American supplies. Roosevelt made clear in a December 17 press conference that he believed the United States' best defense was the success of Great Britain in defending herself. Consequently, Roosevelt tried to convince Congress that the United States needed to develop a means of helping the British. Britain's dollar holdings and lines of credit were, as Churchill had made clear, nearly exhausted, while the Neutrality Act forbade loans by the federal government to belligerents and the Johnson Act forbade loans to nations that had defaulted on repaying World War I loans, as Britain had. The president already had devised a means of aid that sidestepped these hindrances: a lend-lease system based on an earlier agreement to lend cargo vessels to the British on the condition that they be returned after the war. As the year ended Roosevelt presented a fireside chat in which he reiterated this lend-lease concept and defined the United States' war role as the provider of ships, airplanes, and armaments for Britain and the Free French (commanded from England by General Charles de Gaulle) to use in defeating the Axis powers. "We must be the great arsenal of democracy," Roosevelt asserted. The Lend-Lease Bill, H.R. 1776, was introduced on January 10, 1941: It gave the president broad discretion to make exchanges of or lease or lend materials to any nation whose defense he deemed vital to protecting the United States and to arrange for repayment as he saw fit. The House passed the bill in February by a 250-165 vote, and the Senate passed it in March by 60 votes to 31—wide margins of approval in both houses. Roosevelt signed the act into law on March 11. Congress then quickly appropriated $7 billion to fulfill the program, and Roosevelt appointed Commerce Secretary Harry Hopkins to carry it out as head of the Lend-Lease Administration. Roosevelt, anticipating the bill's approval, had already sent diplomat Averell Harriman to Great Britain at the end of February to help expedite the flow of lend-lease aid.

Congress's quick and substantial passage of lend-lease despite bitter disapproval from the America First Committee, isolationists in Congress, and other outspoken opponents of intervention (including Joseph Kennedy, who had opposed Roosevelt's reelection bid and resigned as ambassador after the election), indicated that the clout of congressional isolationists had withered before public support of the argument that aiding Britain in the long term would help to preclude U.S. involvement in the war. The president may also have won congressional converts to his views with his annual message, delivered January 6, in which he reiterated his goals for the nation, described the benefits that might accrue from aiding the Allies, and envisioned a future in which all peoples of the world would be blessed with "freedom of speech and expression . . . freedom of every person to worship God in his own way . . . freedom from want . . . freedom from fear." The clear-cut idealism and vision of the speech enhanced the public's support of Roosevelt's position on aiding Great Britain.

From abroad Churchill helped solidify that support in an eloquent speech addressed to the American people, asserting that Great Britain did not need American troops to achieve ultimate victory but only American material aid: "Give us the tools and we will finish the job." The fact is, however, that by the end of 1941 lend-lease provided only 1 percent of Britain's total armaments for the year, with another 7 percent deriving from already existing contracts that obliged the British to pay cash. Nevertheless, lend-lease was of major significance. It assured Britain of future American financial and military support at a critical juncture, committed the United States to securing Great Britain's survival, and bound the two nations into a working partnership. The liaisons established by Harriman and Hopkins, sent earlier to London by the president, and secret discussions between U.S. and British military personnel begun at the end of January 1941 helped further an ever-increasing cooperation between the two nations.

BATTLE FOR THE ATLANTIC AND AFRICA

In the early months of 1941 an especially major challenge to the British war effort was German U-boat (submarine) and Luftwaffe (air force) operations in the Atlantic, which threatened massive destruction of British ships transporting war materials to England, and in the Mediterranean, which menaced Great Britain's supply of oil from the Middle East. With the U-boats and "tonnage warfare" (sinking many tons of merchant ships to prevent them from resupplying Britain), Hitler hoped to starve the British into submission. During the first year of the war the Germans had lacked sufficient numbers of submarines in the Atlantic—many had been diverted to support the occupation of Norway and Denmark—to thoroughly disrupt shipping. From the beginning of 1941 until May, however, the Luftwaffe destroyed 269 British merchant ships in the Atlantic and the Mediterranean. In March the Germans reached a monthly level of more than a half million tons of destroyed vessels. By June German U-boats had sunk 848 merchantmen since the beginning of the war while only 43 U-boats were lost. But in July, when U.S. troops occupied Iceland (by diplomatic agreement), American ships began escorting convoys of British merchant ships to and from Iceland, helping reduce losses. Radar, improved depth charges, and the diversion of German planes and submarines to other operations also helped. American occupation of Greenland on April 7—agreed to by Danish officials in Washington, D.C., but not in Copenhagen—increased protection of merchant shipping, as did Roosevelt's April 18 establishment of a "neutrality patrol" to report locations of U-boats, alerting both merchantmen and British warships. (Roosevelt remained reluctant to authorize naval escorts for convoys, even though a May Gallup poll revealed that three-fourths of the American public supported supplying Great Britain even if it meant risking war.) The Germans had hoped to establish a base for raiding operations by warships in the North Atlantic at Brest, a seaport in the Brittany region of France, and dispatched the battleship *Bismarck* for this purpose. But on May 27, British ships and planes sank the German battleship and effectively eliminated the threat of surface raids in the future.

The threat to Britain's oil supply line in the Middle East remained. Hitler had hoped to persuade Franco to allow access to attack the British colony of Gibraltar in southern Spain, which could have made possible German control of French North Africa and the Mediterranean Sea, but Franco refused. In the early months of the year, the British, attacking from bases in Kenya and Sudan, experienced success against the Italians, forcing them into retreat. By February 7 the British had captured Tobruk and Benghazi on the coast of Libya; by the end of March they had destroyed the Italian fleet in the Battle of Cape Matapan; and by April 7, they captured all of Italian East Africa (Ethiopia and Somaliland) and restored Haile Selassie to the throne of Ethiopia in Addis Ababa. From Libya they sent troops to Greece in early March. But a German offensive in Libya in late-March by the Afrika Korps under command of General Erwin Rommel quickly sent the British falling back toward Egypt and forced the British to relinquish the Libyan coast. In addition, the Germans came to the aid of Italy in Albania and Greece after securing control of Bulgaria and Yugoslavia in March and April, thereby effecting control over the Balkans. By the end of April, the British evacuated their positions in mainland Greece, although still holding the island of Crete, and Greece surrendered to Germany. This intervention, however, had cost Hitler a fateful delay in pursuing his then highest priority, Operation Barbarossa, on the eastern front. In May the British invaded Iraq to prevent its being seized by Germany.

AMERICAN NAVAL ESCORTS

On May 27, 1941, reacting to sightings of the *Bismarck* in the North Atlantic, Roosevelt declared an "unlimited national emergency," although exactly what this meant was never made clear. In a speech to the Pan-American Union the same day, he explained that the German threat to the Americas was not simply military but also economic. If the Germans defeated Great Britain and took control of Africa, they would be within airplane range: Bombers could fly round-trip without refueling between Britain and New England or between

Dakar, Senegal, and Brazil. Moreover, Germany and Italy would use the resources of all the regions they controlled to wage economic war against the Americas. By using the native people of those regions as "slave labor" Germany and Italy could undersell U.S. goods. With a huge internal market and planned economies, they would be able to subjugate the Americas economically, forcing the United States to radically alter its methods and principles of doing business. As a means of protecting U.S. commerce for the time being, Roosevelt in April authorized naval patrols in the Atlantic as far as the 25th parallel (later extended to the 26th), but he wavered on providing escorts for convoys, as the navy planned, because it was considered a controversial move that increased risks of U.S. ships being attacked. The president asked the army and navy to prepare plans for seizing the Azores and the Cape Verde Islands in the event that the Germans invaded Spain and Portugal, but Chief of Staff General George C. Marshall and Chief of Naval Operations Admiral Harold Stark professed that U.S. forces simply were not prepared to fulfill such an undertaking. Clearly, Roosevelt was trying to devise defensive measures, but he assured cabinet members at the end of May that he was unwilling "to fire the first shot."

In June events pushed the United States toward deeper involvement. On the 12th, Americans learned that a German submarine, whose commander believed the U.S. freighter *Robin Moor* to be a disguised British ship, had sunk the ship in the South Atlantic. (Hitler had ordered that U.S. ships were not to be attacked.) Although there was no loss of life and the public reacted calmly, the Roosevelt administration protested the act as a violation of international law, froze all assets of the Axis nations in the United States, and ordered German consuls to leave the country—but did not break off diplomatic relations.

GERMANY INVADES THE USSR

One of the war's most cataclysmic events, the event that would determine the ultimate outcome of the war in Europe, occurred on June 22. The Germans launched Operation Barbarossa. Along a 2,000-mile front from the Baltic Sea to the Black Sea, the Germans sent into battle 148 divisions (3.2 million men) to conquer the Soviet Union. Despite warnings from the British and a German defector, the Soviets were unprepared and totally surprised, and the Germans smashed rapidly ahead toward Leningrad, Moscow, and Kharkov.

The unexpected invasion created a quandary for the American public and president. Should the United States support the USSR, ally of Germany in dismembering Poland and ravager of Finland, a Communist nation ruled by the brutal dictator Joseph Stalin, as ruthless and inhumane as Hitler in condemning millions to imprisonment and death in the gulags (labor camps)? Churchill, pleased to have any ally against the Germans, immediately pledged the British government to aid the Soviets in whatever way possible. Initially, Roosevelt reacted cautiously, advised by army officials that it would take the Germans perhaps three months to conquer the USSR. Supporters of the America First Committee and isolationist congressmen voiced the hope that the Soviets and Germans might destroy each other. The Roosevelt administration issued a statement condemning the invasion and expressing the belief that opposition to Hitler from any opponent would help sustain American security. Then in a press conference on June 24 the president pledged that the United States would "give all the aid that we possibly can to Russia," but it would be months before the promise resulted in any substantial aid. What appeared more immediately pressing for the president was his concern that the attack on the USSR might inspire the Japanese to make a move in Southeast Asia.

AMERICAN-BRITISH TIES STRENGTHEN

In July, concerned for the safety of Iceland and the North Atlantic sealanes, Roosevelt completed an agreement with Iceland approved by Great Britain that extended U.S. protection to Iceland—4,400 marines landed on July 7—and authorized naval protection of convoys en route to Iceland. The president also sent Harry Hopkins to Moscow as his personal envoy. Hopkins returned with an optimistic assessment based on Stalin's assertions of the Soviet Union's ability to withstand German aggression if provided with antiaircraft weapons, fuel, and aluminum. Hopkins's assessment would provide the basis for advocating extension of lend-lease to the Soviets, which Congress approved in November. Initially, however, the administration obliged the Soviets to pay mostly in cash or gold, and the Soviets received only a very modest amount of aid through the remainder of 1941. The German invasion of the USSR also prodded the administration to request revisions in the selective service program. These revisions involved an extension in the duration of time draftees would serve (the original act had limited the time of service to one year) and eliminated the restriction that the draftees could not serve outside the Western Hemisphere. In requesting the revisions, Roosevelt asked Congress to agree that a national emergency existed and warned that the armed forces were faced with "disintegration" if Congress did not extend the service period. In August Congress approved an extension to 17 months but retained the restriction against service outside the hemisphere.

August brought a strengthening of ties between Roosevelt and Churchill. On August 3 the president boarded the *Potomac,* supposedly for a holiday of cruising, but at sea he transferred to the cruiser *Augusta* and sailed to Newfoundland. Those accompanying the president included General Marshall, Admiral Stark, and Undersecretary of State Welles, but not Secretary of State Hull, Secretary of the Navy Knox, or Secretary of War Stimson. On August 9, in the harbor at Argentia in the Placentia Bay, they began four days of discussions with Churchill and his staff, brought to Newfoundland by the battleship *Prince of Wales.* The two leaders agreed that defeating Germany must remain the primary focus of the war effort and that war with Japan must be postponed as long as possible.

At the end of their meeting Roosevelt and Churchill issued a public joint declaration that became known as the Atlantic Charter. It was a statement of war aims that committed the two nations to such goals as seeking no territories, supporting the right of all peoples to have the governments of their choice, promoting equal access to international trade, upholding freedom of the seas, and establishing universal peace "after the final destruction of the Nazi tyranny." The charter virtually bound the United States and Great Britain as allies in pursuing the defeat of Germany and other goals in a war that the United States had not yet even entered. It rallied worldwide support and hope.

For many people, including Churchill, the Newfoundland meeting suggested the eventual participation of the United States in the war. For the time being, however, Hitler had issued standing orders to avoid any "incident" that might provoke U.S. involvement because he wished to secure the conquest of the USSR before encountering another enemy. No attacks were to be made on American ships, even though patrols and convoy escorts (ordered quietly by the president) extending all the way to Iceland certainly increased the potential for such an "incident" to occur. In early September, as the destroyer USS *Greer* approached Iceland, it was warned by a British plane that a U-boat lay ahead. When the *Greer*'s sounding devices located the submarine, a British plane dropped depth charges. The U-boat fired a torpedo that the *Greer* dodged. Then the *Greer* dropped depth charges, followed by another torpedo and more depth charges before it proceeded unharmed to Reykjavík. The president in a September 11 news conference deviously described the incident as an unprovoked German attack, cited the sinking of two other U.S. vessels, and announced that he was ordering American ships to "shoot on sight" at any German submarines or cruisers in United States' "defensive waters." He then announced that U.S. naval ships were escorting American merchant ships and that since the incident in fact navy ships had begun escorting British convoys.

As sinkings of American ships continued, Roosevelt asked Congress to revise the Neutrality Act again to allow the arming of merchant ships and to lift the ban on American ships entering war zones. In mid-October a U-boat torpedo damaged the destroyer USS *Kearney,* killing 11 men. Then on the last day of October, a U-boat torpedoed and sank the destroyer USS *Reuben James,* escorting a convoy 600 miles west of Iceland, with a loss of 100 men. During the first two weeks of November both houses of Congress approved repealing the Neutrality Act restrictions, freeing the president to send armed convoys all the way across the Atlantic. He chose to authorize sending unarmed ships to Lisbon, Portugal, and armed ships to Arkhangel'sk, USSR; ships flying the American flag would join convoys to Great Britain. But the president announced only the Lisbon crossings. The United States was now fully involved in transporting armaments and supplies directly to Great Britain and the Soviet Union to uphold their resistance to Germany. The United States was technically not at war, but the risk of provocation was heightened, increasing the potential for entering the war.

Japan Forces the Issue

It was not Germany, however, but Japan that generated the final impetus to the American full-scale entry into war. In February 1941, the Japanese sent a new ambassador, Kichisaburo Nomura, to Washington, D.C. By April he had established ongoing personal discussions with Secretary of State Hull. Nomura sincerely desired to maintain peace between the two nations, and he pressed Hull to agree to restore commerce, pressure Chiang Kai-shek to make peace on Japanese terms, and support Japan in other ways in exchange for which the Japanese would pursue more peaceable policies in Southeast

Asia while supporting Germany only if it were attacked. Hull never rejected these proposals outright but pursued alternatives, including a Japanese withdrawal from Southeast Asia. In April representatives of Japan and the USSR, meeting in Moscow, signed a nonaggression pact. In July, following the German invasion of the Soviet Union, the Japanese decided not to intervene on Germany's side but to pursue their own efforts to dominate Southeast Asia. By now American cryptographers had deciphered Japan's diplomatic code and could inform the Roosevelt administration of Japan's real intentions in Southeast Asia.

On July 2, the Japanese took control of all of French Indochina. In late July, reacting to Japan's dispatch of troops to Saigon, the administration froze Japanese assets in the United States, ordered General Douglas MacArthur to assume command of Filipino forces, and stationed B-17 bombers in the Philippines. Defenses on Guam also were strengthened. The State Department inadvertently embargoed shipments of oil to Japan—an embargo the administration decided in September to let stand—shutting off 60 percent of Japan's oil imports; the British and Dutch shut off another 30 percent. Equally threatening to the Japanese, the British massed planes and ships at Singapore. The freezing of Japanese assets terminated trade of any kind between the two nations. Prime Minister Konoye proposed a personal meeting with Roosevelt, but Hull persuaded the president not to agree. In September Ambassador Nomura offered a modified agreement by which Japan would take an "independent" view of the Tripartite Pact and withdraw from China after a peace treaty was signed. Hull wanted assurances that Japan would withdraw early from China and Southeast Asia. If Japan took control of British possessions in Malaya, Burma, and Singapore and threatened India, Australia, and New Zealand, then British survival in the war against Germany would be further jeopardized. The Japanese wanted a satisfactory conclusion to what they called the "China incident." Negotiations between Japan and the United States continued.

Militants gained power in Japan during September. In mid-October, his diplomatic tactics having borne no fruit, Konoye and his government resigned; General Tojo became prime minister. The military leaders, concerned that Japan's economy was foundering, planned to capture the Malayan Peninsula, Java, Sumatra, and Borneo and their rich stores of bauxite, rubber, tin, iron ore, and other natural resources. To succeed in this venture, they judged, they must first destroy the U.S. fleet stationed in Hawaii. With the American fleet wiped out, the Japanese could also occupy the Solomons, the Philippines, the Gilberts, and other islands as well as the planned targets in Southeast Asia and the Dutch East Indies. On November 5 the Japanese government decided that if negotiations with the United States government did not succeed by November 25, then this plan would be carried out—before Japanese oil reserves were used up and the British and Americans gained more time to bolster their forces in the Pacific. In a communication that was intercepted and interpreted by American cryptographers, the Japanese government advised Nomura of the November 25 deadline and instructed him to continue negotiating. Knowing the significance of this communiqué, Hull and his staff tried to work out a modus vivendi (a temporary arrangement) that would revive the pre-July goals of having Japan withdraw from Indochina and the United States unfreeze Japanese funds. But Japan's condition that the United States cease supporting Chiang Kai-shek

doomed any genuine hope of agreement. In addition, the Roosevelt administration learned on November 26 that Japanese ships transporting troops had
been sighted south of Formosa (present-day Taiwan), leading the president to
accuse the Japanese of duplicity and to cancel the modus vivendi proposal. In
any event, Japanese military leaders were intent on fulfilling their plan of
attack. U.S. commanders were sent a "final alert" and advised to expect "an
aggressive move by Japan within the next few days."

But where would the "aggressive move" occur? Japanese leaders received
assurances of support from the Axis nations and, on December 1, Emperor
Hirohito's acquiescence in a plan to attack Hawaii. They decided to maintain
the secrecy of the plan by continuing the Washington negotiations to within
20 minutes of the attack. American cryptographers decoded a final message to
Nomura on the morning of December 7 that indicated a strike was imminent.
General Marshall sent a warning to San Francisco, the Philippines, the Canal
Zone, and Hawaii. Atmospheric interference prevented its reception in Hawaii,

Prime Minister Winston Churchill
addressing the U.S. Congress,
December 1941. Behind him sit
Congressman William P. Cole (left)
and Vice President Henry Wallace
(right); to his right sits Senator Alben
W. Barkley. *(Alben W. Barkley
Collection, Courtesy of Wendell H. Ford
Research Center and Public Policy
Archives, Special Collections and Archives,
University of Kentucky Libraries)*

and switched to Western Union dispatch, it arrived too late. As dawn rose over Pearl Harbor, 183 aircraft launched from six Japanese carriers attacked ships of the U.S. Pacific Fleet in the harbor and airplanes parked at the army base at Wheeler Field. The Japanese attack left 2,403 dead, two battleships destroyed, six battleships badly damaged, numerous other ships lost, and 188 planes destroyed. Japanese losses amounted to 28 airplanes, five midget submarines, and fewer than 100 men.

THE UNITED STATES ENTERS THE WAR

On the following day, December 8, the president appeared before Congress and asked for a declaration of war. Roosevelt spoke briefly. "Yesterday, December 7, 1941—a date which will live in infamy—the United States of America was suddenly and deliberately attacked by the naval and air forces of Japan," he declared. The attack, he said, was "unprovoked and dastardly"; he asserted that "the American people in their righteous might will win through to absolute victory." On this very day the Japanese continued their attack, bombing Guam and Wake Island while also sending troops into Thailand and Malaya. Two days later they extended the attack to the Philippines. At the same time, Germany and Italy, fulfilling the Tripartite Pact, declared war on the United States. On December 22, Churchill arrived in Washington, D.C., for discussions with the president and administration officials on the joint conduct of the war. The administration moved quickly to address war planning, but it would be many months before armaments production and military recruitment and training met needed levels for effective prosecution of the war in both Europe and Asia. Full-scale mobilization, transforming the American economy to war status and inducting millions into service with the armed forces, would at last bring an end to the Great Depression, but the final cure exacted a terrible ultimate cost in lost lives and wasted material resources.

CHRONICLE OF EVENTS

1939

January 2: Roosevelt appoints Frank Murphy as attorney general.

January 2: Italian physicist Enrico Fermi, who had taken his family with him to Stockholm in December to accept the Nobel Prize in physics, arrives in New York City to assume an appointment at Columbia University.

January 4: Roosevelt presents the annual State of the Union address to Congress, expressing his concern that the peace of the world is under threat and advocating a program for an "adequate defense" that includes social and economic reforms.

January 5: Roosevelt nominates Felix Frankfurter as associate justice of the Supreme Court to succeed Benjamin Cardozo, who died in July 1938.

January 6: A German scientific journal publishes a report by physicists Otto Hahn and Fritz Strassmann that by bombarding uranium with neutrons they have released a radioisotope of barium.

January 11: Despite the Italian involvement in the Spanish civil war, British prime minister Chamberlain and foreign minister Lord Halifax arrive in Rome for discussions with Mussolini.

January 12: Roosevelt sends to Congress a special message on national defense, but his proposals have been greatly altered, with the program for an expanded air force and increased airplane production being dropped.

January 13: Having secured no concessions of any sort from Mussolini, Chamberlain and Lord Halifax leave Rome to return to London.

January 14: By applying Albert Einstein's equation on mass and energy, physicist Lise Meitner, conducting an experiment in Stockholm, corroborates the findings of Hahn and Strassmann.

January 16: President Roosevelt issues an order that French air force personnel be allowed to inspect bombers being manufactured by the Douglas Aircraft Company to ascertain whether they are suitable for purchase by the French.

January 16: Swedish physicist Niels Bohr arrives in New York to assume a post at the Institute for Advanced Study at Princeton University, in nearby New Jersey, where Einstein has worked since leaving Germany in 1932.

January 17: Meitner and her nephew in Copenhagen, physicist Otto Frisch, with whom she has collaborated by telephone, send papers to London to be published in *Nature* that confirm the process of splitting atoms. They term the process "nuclear fission."

January 20: Two French aviation experts sent by diplomat Jean Monnet arrive at the Douglas plant to inspect the bombers; one of them is injured in a crash when the test pilot, killed in the accident, makes a false maneuver, and the secret of the French experts' visit to the plant is revealed, generating heated controversy.

January 25: At Columbia University, following the suggestion of Fermi, Herbert Anderson conducts an experiment confirming nuclear fission. Neither physicist yet knows of the findings by Meitner and Frisch.

January 25: Barcelona falls to the Nationalist forces, destroying any hope that the Loyalists can attain victory in the civil war.

January 26: At a conference on theoretical physics at George Washington University, Fermi and Bohr announce and explain to the assembled physicists the discovery of nuclear fission.

January 31: Roosevelt meets at the White House with the members of the Senate Military Affairs Committee to discuss the policy of selling airplanes to France. He expresses his deep concern over the potential threat to the United States and Latin America posed by Germany and Japan and the nation's need to support the America's "first line of defense"—unspecified islands in the Pacific and the still independent nations of Europe—as justification for selling airplanes on a "cash-and-carry" basis. The senators voice strong objections.

February 2: Despite a pledge of secrecy regarding the discussion at the White House on the last day of January, stories appear in the press stating that the president had declared America's "frontier" to be "on the Rhine."

February 3: Through dissembling and denial during a press conference, the president attempts to defuse the controversy over the sale of airplanes to France and to discredit the news stories about the nation's frontier being on the Rhine as "lies." Surprisingly, polls indicate that nearly two-thirds of the public approve sales of airplanes to Great Britain and France.

February 9: Following the uproar over the issue of selling airplanes to France, Roosevelt is rumored to want to replace Joseph Kennedy, ambassador to the Court of St. James (Great Britain), whose views on appeasing Hitler the president abhors. Kennedy nonetheless cuts short a lengthy holiday in Florida and boards the *Queen Mary* in New York City to sail to England, at Roosevelt's suggestion.

February 13: Senator Elbert D. Thomas introduces a resolution in the Senate that would grant the president the power to ban sales of not only arms but all raw materials to belligerent nations and also to remove, with congressional approval, the embargo on sales to nations victimized by aggression. Opposition from Senator Gerald Nye and other isolationists dooms the resolution.

February 14: Associate Justice Louis Brandeis submits his letter of resignation from the Supreme Court to the president.

February 16: Acting on reports from the Natural Resources Committee, Roosevelt recommends legislation to Congress creating grants and a regulatory agency to combat water pollution and the establishment of a comprehensive national energy policy.

March 13: Brigadier General Edwin M. ("Pa") Watson becomes presidential secretary.

March 15: German troops take control of the Bohemia and Moravia regions of Czechoslovakia, while, with Hitler's approval, Hungarian forces take over Ruthenia.

March 15: In Parliament, Chamberlain expresses his regret over the German seizure of Bohemia and Moravia but declares that Britain is not obligated to intervene because the Slovaks have declared their independence, so that the Czechoslovakian republic, whose boundaries were guaranteed by the Munich agreement, no longer exists.

March 17: The Roosevelt administration issues a statement signed by Undersecretary of State Sumner Welles (Hull is on vacation in Florida) deploring the takeover of Czechoslovakia as a threat to world peace.

March 17: Fermi, aware that the largest deposits of uranium in Europe are found in Czechoslovakia, visits the Navy Department in hopes of convincing the chief of naval operations that the military should be interested in nuclear fission's potential, but he is shunted off to talk with junior officers.

March 18: Responding to protests and expressions of outrage in reaction to his acceptance of German occupation of Czechoslovakia, Chamberlain rejects Hitler's claims that the occupation was necessary because of disorder within the Czech republic.

March 20: Senator Key Pittman, chairman of the Senate Foreign Relations Committee and a Roosevelt supporter, introduces a bill to revise the neutrality law by providing the president authority to limit shipments of goods to belligerent nations to a cash-and-carry basis and also to bar U.S. ships from areas the president has determined to be dangerous—in effect, a loosening of the neutrality law's embargo stipulations. Senator Borah and other isolationist senators denounce the proposal.

March 20: The administration announces the nomination of William O. Douglas to succeed Brandeis in the Supreme Court.

March 20: Germany demands that Lithuania return Memel, a seaport on the Baltic Sea that had been ceded to Lithuania in 1923.

March 23: Lithuania surrenders Memel to Germany. Hitler himself accepts the surrender in the port city.

March 30: Franco's Nationalist troops complete the occupation of Madrid begun on March 28. From his headquarters in Burgos, Franco issues orders to begin executions of Loyalists in the capital and other cities throughout Spain.

March 31: In a speech in Parliament, Chamberlain, who has been trying to create new collective security arrangements since March 17, publicly commits Great Britain to come to the defense of Poland if that nation's independence is threatened. France would be obligated to support Great Britain in such a response.

April 1: Roosevelt, at Warm Springs, Georgia, signs a proclamation ending the arms embargo against Spain.

April 1: The Spanish Loyalists capitulate; the Nationalists have complete control of Spain.

April 3: Roosevelt signs into law the Administrative Reorganization Act and an act appropriating funds for national defense. He also agrees to a de jure (legal) recognition of the Franco government to be announced officially on April 4.

April 7: On this Good Friday, Mussolini sends his troops into Albania to occupy the Balkan state.

April 9: Roosevelt leaves Warm Springs, Georgia, by train for Washington, D.C.

April 14: In a speech before the governing board of the Pan-American Union, Roosevelt pledges to

Produce peddler's truck in San Antonio, Texas, March 1939 *(Library of Congress, Prints and Photographs Division [604355 LC-USF33-012065-M4])*

defend the peace and sovereignty of the American nations. He also sends messages to Hitler and Mussolini offering to serve as an intermediary to disseminate a policy statement from the dictators assuring that their armed forces will not attack 33 nations in Europe and the Middle East listed by name: Roosevelt pledges to deliver this statement to the governments of these nations and to seek reciprocal assurances from each.

April 15: During a press conference Roosevelt announces that he has sent dispatches to Hitler and Mussolini offering to serve as an intermediary.

April 17: While Mussolini treats Roosevelt's April 14 message with contempt, Hitler sends telegrams to each of the nations listed in the message asking them whether they feel threatened by Germany and whether they had authorized Roosevelt to make his proposal.

April 17: In Moscow, Commissar of Foreign Affairs Maxim Litvinov presents a proposal to the British ambassador to create an alliance among Great Britain, France, and the Soviet Union which would pledge each to come to the aid of any other under attack and also to the aid of eastern European nations between the Baltic Ocean and the Black Sea that might be attacked.

April 26: Roosevelt sends to Congress his Reorganization Plan Number 1, which is intended to reduce the number of agencies that report directly to the president and to streamline management of the executive branch.

April 27: The British government imposes the first peacetime draft in the nation's history.

April 28: Having received answers to his telegrams from most of the affected nations, Hitler delivers a speech before the Reichstag sarcastically responding to Roosevelt's April 14 proposal and promising to give assurances to any nation that requests such assurances that Germany will not attack or invade its territory. Hitler also nullifies a nonagressions treaty with Poland and naval treaties with Great Britain.

April 30: President Roosevelt officially opens the New York World's Fair.

May 3: In the USSR, Litvinov is removed as foreign minister and replaced by V. M. Molotov.

May 8: Predisposed against Litvinov's proposal for an alliance—Chamberlain regards the Soviet Communists with greater concern than the fascists—the British government only now responds.

May 9: Roosevelt sends to Congress his second executive reorganization plan, which is intended to make still more reductions in the number of government agencies and to realign agencies into more logical groupings.

May 13: Molotov rejects Chamberlain's response to the Litvinov proposal as unfavorable to the Soviet Union since it would obligate the Soviets to aid Britain and France if they became involved in war due to their support of Poland or Romania but would not commit them to come to the Soviet Union's aid if it were involved in war because of its support of an eastern European state. Molotov's counter offer is the original Litvinov proposal, but no agreement will result.

May 19: Since Senator Pittman's efforts to seek a revision of the neutrality law have proven ineffectual, Roosevelt calls Speaker of the House William Bankhead, Majority Leader Sam Rayburn, and other leaders of the House of Representatives to the White House and announces to them that he personally intends to fight for a bill that will repeal the arms embargo.

May 22: At the Reich Chancellery in Berlin the foreign ministers of Germany and Italy, Joachim von Ribbentrop and Count Galeazzo Ciano, sign a military alliance, to be known as the Pact of Steel, that commits each country to come to the other's defense in the event of attack by a third country.

June 7: King George VI and Queen Elizabeth of Great Britain begin a five-day visit to the eastern United States.

June 10: President Roosevelt entertains King George VI and Queen Elizabeth as his house guests at Hyde Park, in New York State.

June 13: The House Foreign Affairs Committee reports out a bill for consideration by the entire House that revises the Neutrality Act and repeals the arms embargo.

June 30: Following floor debate and narrow approval of an amendment that restores the arms embargo, the House passes the neutrality bill. Congress terminates funding for the Federal Theatre Project. Roosevelt signs into law the Relief Act of 1939, which stipulates that all those who have worked on Works Progress Administration (WPA) projects for 18 consecutive months be let go.

July 1: The Roosevelt reorganization plans for the executive branch go into effect: The Bureau of the Budget moves from the Treasury Department to the president's office; the National Resources Committee (now named the National Resources Planning Board), joined with the Employment Stabilization Office, also becomes part of the president's office. Three new agencies, each consolidating various formerly disparate agencies into one, are created in the president's office: the Federal Security Agency, the Federal Works Agency (which includes the renamed Works Projects Administration), and the Federal Loan Agency.

July 12: The neutrality bill, passed by the House and sent on to the Senate, dies in the Senate Foreign Relations Committee.

July 18: Senator Arthur Vandenberg introduces a resolution in the Senate requesting that the president notify Japan that the 1911 commercial treaty between the two nations will be terminated. In an effort to resurrect the neutrality bill from burial by the Senate Foreign Relations Committee, Roosevelt meets with leaders of the Senate, including Majority Leader Alben Barkley and Minority Leader Charles L. McNary, to try to persuade them of the bill's necessity—to no avail.

July 26: Secretary of State Hull notifies the Japanese government that the 1911 commercial treaty will expire in six months.

August 2: Einstein writes a letter (actually composed by his former assistant Leo Szilard) to the president, for delivery by economist Alexander Sachs, that appeals to Roosevelt to keep informed on the experiments with nuclear fission and to do what he can to accelerate those experiments because of fission's potential military uses.

August 2: Roosevelt signs into law the Hatch Act, which prohibits political activity by employees of the federal government.

August 5: Congress adjourns.

August 24: Meeting in Moscow, Molotov and German foreign minister Joachim von Ribbentrop sign the so-called Nazi-Soviet Pact, which pledges each country for a period of 10 years to avoid any aggressive acts against the other and to submit mutual disputes to arbitration. The pact contains a secret protocol whereby eastern Europe is divided into German and Soviet spheres of influence, with Poland split between the two powers, Germany given Lithuania, and the Soviet Union given Finland, Latvia, Estonia, and Bessarabia (a province of Romania).

September 1: German troops invade Poland from the north, south, and west. The governments of Great Britain and France order general mobilization of their armed forces.

September 1: During a press conference Roosevelt attempts to calm public concern over the invasion of Poland and says he believes the United States can avoid involvement in the war.

September 3: In a fireside chat, Roosevelt again sounds a note of reassurance and declares that the United States will remain neutral, adding that he recognizes it cannot be expected that every American will remain neutral in thought and conscience.

September 3: The Chamberlain government issues an ultimatum to Germany demanding an announcement by 11:00 A.M. that Germany will begin an immediate withdrawal of forces from Poland; otherwise Great Britain will declare war. At 11:15 A.M., having received no response to his ultimatum, Chamberlain announces over the radio that "this country is now at war . . ." Chamberlain appoints Winston Churchill as first lord of the admiralty and declares a naval blockade of Germany. Its own ultimatum to Germany also unanswered, France declares war. During the evening a German U-boat torpedoes the British liner *Athenia,* crossing the Atlantic for Canada; 112 passengers die, including 28 Americans.

A photo by Arthur Rothstein shows four cowboys dressed alike in front of a bar in Billings, Montana. *(Library of Congress, Prints and Photographs Division [604355 LC-USF33-003092-M3])*

September 4: In the first air raid of the war, Great Britain's Royal Air Force (RAF) planes bomb ships in the harbor at Wilhelmshaven, Germany.

September 5: German troops cross the Vistula River and occupy Kraków, Poland; German planes begin bombing Warsaw, Poland.

September 8: Roosevelt issues Executive Order 8248, creating the Executive Office of the President staffed by six administrative assistants to oversee the agencies moved to the president's office—including, most important, the Bureau of the Budget—under the stipulations of the Reorganization Act. During a press conference he announces a presidential proclamation placing the nation in a state of "limited national emergency," by which he will call up army and navy reserves, recommission 30 moth-balled destroyers, and beef up investigative agencies of the government to prevent subversive acts.

September 10: A British Expeditionary Force begins disembarking in France.

September 13: Roosevelt issues a formal summons to the Congress to convene in special session beginning September 21.

September 13: In Paris, Premier Édouard Daladier announces formation of a war cabinet.

September 15: Charles A. Lindbergh, back in the United States from a self-imposed exile to Europe that began in April 1935, makes a national radio broadcast in which he advocates avoiding American involvement in the European war and expresses a seemingly pro-German view.

September 17: Troops of the Soviet Union invade Poland from the east. Polish government leaders flee to Romania to establish a government-in-exile.

September 18: German and Soviet troops capture Brest-Litovsk in Poland.

September 21: In an address to the just-convened Congress, Roosevelt advocates legislation to make major revisions in the Neutrality Act, including a repeal of the embargo on arms and a revision to treat both munitions and raw materials as cash-and-carry transactions (that is, the purchasers would have to pay in cash and to provide their own transports for shipment of the goods purchased).

September 27: Meeting with his military commanders, Hitler announces his decision for an attack in the west, specifying that it should begin on November 12.

September 28: Warsaw surrenders to German troops; the conquest of Poland is complete. In Moscow, Molotov and Ribbentrop sign a treaty partitioning possession of Poland between their two countries; the USSR receives nearly half of Poland's territory.

October 2: In a radio broadcast, prominent Republican newspaperman William Allen White announces formation of the Non-Partisan Committee for Peace through Revision of the Neutrality Act (referred to as the White Committee).

October 3: At the behest of the United States, the delegates to the First Meeting of Foreign Ministers of the American Republics, held in Panama, unanimously approve the Declaration of Panama, which designates a zone between the southern border of Canada and the tip of South America and extending from 300 to 1,000 miles into the Atlantic and Pacific Oceans wherein belligerent nations are warned to avoid any naval actions.

October 3: British forces in France take up positions along the border with Belgium.

October 5: With the approval of the Chamberlain government, Churchill sends a message to Roosevelt via the U.S. embassy in London declaring Great Britain's intention to respect the neutral zone established by the Declaration of Panama.

October 6: In a speech before the Reichstag, Hitler makes an appeal for peace, insisting Germany has no quarrel with Great Britain and France, listing problems that need to be resolved, and proposing a European peace conference to tackle these problems.

October 7: Premier Daladier replies to Hitler's proposal for a peace conference that France will maintain its mobilization unless Germany provides guarantees of genuine peace.

October 11: The long-delayed meeting of Alexander Sachs with the president occurs at the White House. Supposedly, Sachs reads aloud the letter from Einstein concerning the potential military applications of nuclear fission. As a result of their meeting, Roosevelt appoints an Advisory Committee on Uranium within the National Bureau of Standards with Lyman J. Briggs as chairman.

October 12: Chamberlain, speaking in the House of Commons, describes Hitler's proposal of October 6 as "vague" and insists on actions that prove Hitler wants peace.

October 12: The Soviet Union begins negotiations with Finland seeking a treaty that would include concessions to protect approaches to Leningrad in the

Gulf of Finland, a 30-year lease on the port of Hangö, and restoration of an 18th-century border in the Karelian Isthmus in return for the cession of territory in Karelia.

October 13: Germany declares that Great Britain has rejected Hitler's proposal and thereby chosen war.

October 14: A German U-boat slips undetected into the British naval base at Scapa Flow and torpedoes the battleship *Royal Oak.*

October 21: Alexander Sachs, Leo Szilard, Edward Teller, and Eugene P. Wigner meet with the Advisory Committee on Uranium.

November 1: In his report to the president about the October 21 meeting, Lyman Briggs recommends that the government fund research into the possibility of using nuclear fission to power submarines; the research, he says, might result in development of a bomb capable of inflicting far greater devastation "than anything now known."

November 4: Roosevelt signs into law the new Neutrality Act, passed by both houses of Congress the day before, which applies cash-and-carry restrictions to shipments of goods in the North Atlantic, with shipments even to belligerents in the South Atlantic and the Pacific to be processed under normal trade standards; it also stipulates that U.S. citizens must not travel aboard ships of belligerent nations and that U.S. ships must not enter the ports of belligerent nations. Under authority granted him by the new law, the president also designates the whole of the Baltic Sea and the Atlantic Ocean extending between southern Norway and northern Spain as a combat zone from which American ships will be excluded.

November 7: Hitler decides to postpone the offensive in the west.

November 8: Hitler, speaking at a Munich commemoration of the 1923 Beer Hall Putsch, escapes assassination, as a bomb planted near the speaker's platform explodes after he has finished his speech and, with other Nazi leaders, left the beer hall. The explosion kills seven persons and wounds 36.

November 13: Negotiations between the Soviet Union and Finland end without any agreement.

November 18: Edwin Watson, the presidential secretary, informs Lyman Briggs that Roosevelt has read his November 1 report and wants to keep it on file.

November 30: Troops of the Soviet Union invade Finland while Soviet airplanes bomb Helsinki and Viipuri (Vyborg).

December 1: Roosevelt issues a statement expressing shock over the Soviet attack on Finland and urging both sides not to bomb civilians. He also emphasizes Americans' high regard for Finland, the only nation to consistently repay its debts to the United States resulting from World War I.

December 5: Advancing Soviet troops in the Karelian Isthmus reach the Mannerheim Line, the major defensive position of the Finns.

December 8: Having received reports from an attaché in Norway that the Allies plan landings in that nation, Admiral Erich Raeder advises Hitler that Germany should occupy Norway.

December 11: In Berlin, Admiral Raeder meets with Major Vidkun Quisling of the Norwegian army, who plans a coup in Norway and offers to help the Germans secure bases there to forestall any prospect that the Allies might try to land their forces.

December 13: The German pocket battleship *Admiral Graf Spee,* which has sunk nine British cargo ships in the South Atlantic during the previous three months, enters the harbor at Montevideo, Uruguay, seeking safety after being damaged during a surprise encounter with three British cruisers off the Río de la Plata.

December 14: The League of Nations expels the Soviet Union and empowers League members to provide assistance of any sort they choose to Finland.

December 14: Admiral Raeder and Major Quisling meet with Hitler at the Reichs Chancellory, after which Hitler orders the German High Command to work out plans for occupying Norway with Quisling's assistance.

December 17: After the *Admiral Graf Spee* is ordered to leave Montevideo harbor by the Uruguayan government, Captain Hans Langsdorff, knowing that British cruisers wait to destroy his ship if it emerges into the estuary of the Río de la Plata, has his crew blow up the German battleship in the river while a crowd of 300,000 watches from the river's banks. The captain and crew are taken into custody by Argentine authorities.

December 19: Captain Langsdorff commits suicide.

December 22: Finnish troops counterattack at the Mannerheim Line and force back the Soviets.

December 26: Having suffered substantial losses, the Soviets discontinue the attack in Finland in order to reorganize their invading armies.

1940

January 3: In his annual message to Congress, Roosevelt, while deploring the prospect of a world "ruled by force in the hands of a few," commits the government once again to a course of peace. He does request increased funding for defense and renewal of the Trade Agreements Act of 1934 but proposes no new programs.

January 4: In his budget message to Congress, Roosevelt requests a modest increase in spending for defense (a total of $1.8 billion) along with decreases in appropriations for work relief, agriculture, public works, and other government assistance programs.

January 8: The Chamberlain government mandates food rationing.

January 10: Plagued by bad weather, a Luftwaffe major flying from Münster to Bonn becomes lost and is forced to land in Belgium; among his secret papers the Belgian authorities find copies of the operations plans for a German attack on France to be launched through the Low Countries (Netherlands, Belgium, and Luxembourg) on January 17. They send the plans to Paris and London.

January 13: Following presumed exposure of the operations plans for the attack in the west, Hitler postpones the offensive again and orders that new plans be prepared.

January 16: Following appeals for aid from Finland, Roosevelt urges Congress to approve credits for the beleaguered nation from the Reconstruction Finance Corporation (RFC) and the Export-Import Bank for purchases of agricultural products and other goods, excluding armaments.

January 20: Soviet troops attack Finnish positions in the Lake Lagoda region.

January 24: During a speech in Columbus, Ohio, Congress of Industrial Organization (CIO) leader John L. Lewis denounces the president, accusing the administration of not keeping faith with labor and asserting that if Roosevelt runs for a third term he will be defeated.

January 26: The 1911 commercial treaty between Japan and the United States expires, and Secretary of

During the Great Depression, many people left home in search of employment. In a photograph taken by Dorothea Lange in 1939, these two men walk down a dirt road toward Los Angeles, California. *(Library of Congress)*

Many families were uprooted by the Great Depression. This family, in a photograph by Dorothea Lange, takes a break from traveling by freight train in Washington State in August 1939. *(Library of Congress)*

State Hull informs the Japanese government that trade between the two nations may continue on a day-to-day basis.

January 29: Finland opens secret negotiations with the Soviet Union.

February 9: At a press conference, Roosevelt announces that Undersecretary of State Sumner Welles will soon depart for Europe for visits to Great Britain, France, Germany, and Italy as the president's personal emissary in order to gather information on "present conditions in Europe."

February 11: The Soviet Union launches a second major attack in Finland, capturing Summa on the Mannerheim Line. In Moscow representatives of Germany and the Soviet Union sign a trade agreement by which the Soviets will receive German machinery and armaments, including a cruiser and 30 airplanes, in exchange for grains, oil, phosphates, and other raw materials.

February 23: Appearing before the House Appropriations Committee, George C. Marshall argues for funding of the president's budget request ($1.8 billion) for defense and for a well-ordered program to create military preparedness.

February 23: Welles arrives in Rome to begin his visits to the capitals of Italy, Germany, France, and Great Britain.

February 25: Pushed back from the Mannerheim Line, Finnish troops regroup at their third and final line of defense at Viipuri.

February 29: Finnish troops destroy an entire Soviet division—the fourth division destroyed since the fighting began—on the northern shore of Lake Lagoda.

March 1: Hitler issues orders to the military to prepare for the occupation of Norway and Denmark.

March 2: Welles arrives in Berlin for discussions with German leaders. Soviet forces begin their final attack in Finland.

March 11: Welles arrives in London.

March 12: Finland accepts the Soviet Union's terms for peace.

March 13: The Treaty of Moscow ends the war between Finland and the Soviet Union (known as the Winter War); by its terms, the Soviets win even more territorial concessions than they had originally demanded, including cession of the Karelian Isthmus, Viipuri, and islands in the Gulf of Finland. The Soviets also receive the lease of a military base at Hangö.

The Great Depression was particularly difficult on children as they traveled with their parents in search of work and food. This photograph of children of migrant workers was included in a Farm Security Administration panel in 1939. *(Library of Congress)*

March 18: Hitler and Mussolini meet at Brenner Pass. The German dictator persuades the Italian dictator to commit Italy to support Germany in the war—arguing that once Germany has defeated France the Mediterranean Sea will be under Italian control.

March 20: Brought down by failure to assist Finland, the Daladier government leaves office, replaced by new premier Paul Reynaud, who commits the French government to winning the war.

March 20: Following his discussions with European government leaders, including Chamberlain, Hitler, and Mussolini, Welles sails from Naples for New York City.

March 29: Roosevelt issues a public statement concerning Welles's visit to Europe, declaring that there is "scant immediate prospect" for peace but that the information Welles has gathered will prove useful when the time comes for a peace settlement.

March 30: The Japanese establish a new puppet regime at Nanjing.

April 2: Hitler orders that the occupation of Norway and Denmark begin on April 9.

April 3: The House Appropriations Committee reports out a bill to the House for defense appropriations that underfunds Roosevelt's request by 10 percent.

April 3: The British cabinet approves a proposal by Churchill to mine waters off Norway.

April 4: Chamberlain reluctantly assigns responsibility for Great Britain's defenses to Churchill.

April 8: During the night of April 7 and 8, the Allies set mines in the waters off Narvik, Norway, to interrupt access and iron-ore shipments to Germany. They announce this action on the 8th.

April 9: As German forces move into place for the invasions, in the early morning German envoys in Copenhagen, Denmark, and Oslo, Norway, present ultimatums demanding that each country accept German "protection" against possible occupation by French and British forces. Denmark has no choice but to accept; Norway rejects the ultimatum. German troops occupy Denmark. German ships and airplanes attack Norway, with raids at key sites from Oslo to Narvik, and capture Narvik, Trondheim, and Bergen and the airfield at Sola (Norway's largest), near Stavenger. The royal family and members of parliament flee Oslo, which falls to the Germans, and arrive by train in Hamar. In the evening Nazi collaborator Vidkun Quisling announces over the radio that he

has become head of the Norwegian government and orders that resistance to the Germans cease.

April 14: Having devastated 10 German destroyers in engagements off Narvik, the British land troops at Namsos in an effort to protect northern Norway. They will be reinforced by French troops.

April 18: British troops land at Andalsnes, Norway.

April 21: At Lillehammer, north of Hamar, German troops attack the British—the first engagement of the war for troops from the two nations.

April 30: Allied troops fall back after being decisively defeated by the Germans near Trondheim. British troops begin to evacuate Andalsnes.

May 1: Hitler orders that plans for the attack in the west be completed by May 5.

May 2: British and French troops are evacuated from Namsos.

May 7: Parliament begins a three-day debate on the Chamberlain government's war policies.

May 9: Anti-Nazis in the German High Command warn Belgian intelligence operatives of an impending German attack on the Low Countries; the Belgians pass on the information to London and Paris, but few, if any, preparations result.

May 10: At 4:00 A.M., under Hitler's orders and command, the German attack in the west begins; troops and tanks surge across the borders into the Low Countries, while the Luftwaffe bombs rail lines, airfields, ports, and communication centers. Several hours after the invasion begins, the British and French rush troops into Belgium to help defend the line along the Meuse and Dyle Rivers to the east of Brussels.

May 10: Following three days of stinging criticism in the House of Commons, Neville Chamberlain and his cabinet resign. In the evening King George VI summons Winston Churchill to Buckingham Palace and commissions him to serve as prime minister and to form a new government.

May 11: German forces complete the occupation of Luxembourg. In Belgium the Germans capture Fort Eben Emael, the key strongpoint in the Belgian defensive line stretching along the Albert Canal.

May 13: German panzer (armored) divisions plunge into the Ardennes region of France, capturing Sedan and establishing bridgeheads on the Meuse River.

May 13: In his first address to Parliament as prime minister, Churchill makes the memorable declaration,

"I have nothing to offer but blood, toil, tears and sweat . . ." but insists that he is assuming his task with "bouyancy and hope."

May 14: The Luftwaffe bombs Rotterdam, Netherlands, an open city, even while German officers are involved in negotiating the city's surrender. More than 800 residents die, and thousands are wounded. Queen Wilhelmina and members of the government embark for London aboard a British destroyer. The commander of the Dutch armed forces orders his troops to lay down their arms. In the Ardennes the German panzer units smash French forces and speed toward the English Channel, threatening to cut off the British, French, and Belgian troops to the north in Belgium.

May 15: Roosevelt receives a telegram from Churchill, stating that he expects Great Britain to be attacked by air and requesting that the United States loan Great Britain 40 to 50 old destroyers, hundreds of planes, and anti-aircraft equipment and ammunition; expedite sales of steel and other materials; send a squadron of naval vessels to an Irish port to discourage German parachute landings in Ireland; and have the U.S. Navy move about in the Pacific, including visiting Singapore, in order to forestall Japanese military actions there.

May 15: The Netherlands officially surrenders to the Germans.

May 16: Roosevelt sends Churchill a noncommittal reply to his request, leaving the door open for steel purchases but stating that the U.S. Pacific Fleet will remain at Hawaii and that the loan of destroyers would have to be approved by Congress. In an address before Congress, the president requests that the legislators increase expenditures for defense and proposes that production of airplanes for the army and navy be increased to 50,000 per year from the current level of 12,000.

May 17: German forces capture Antwerp and Brussels.

May 20: Driving westward from the Ardennes, German panzer units reach Abbeville at the mouth of the Somme River, encircling and trapping British, Belgian, and French forces.

May 24: German panzer units have captured Boulogne, encircled Calais, and reached Gravelines, forcing the British, French, and Belgian armies into a triangular area. Now only 20 miles from Dunkirk, the panzer division receives totally unexpected orders to halt.

May 26: In a broadcast over CBS radio, Charles Lindbergh debunks Roosevelt's proposed production of 50,000 military planes per year.

May 26: In the evening, Hitler rescinds the order halting the panzer division at Gravelines, but the two-day hiatus has given the Allies time to improve their defenses and to assemble hundreds of vessels, including sailboats manned by civilians, to mount a massive evacuation of troops from Dunkirk.

May 28: During a press conference, Roosevelt announces that he has reinstituted the Council of National Defense (originally authorized by a 1916 law)—a committee composed of the secretaries of agriculture, labor, the interior, commerce, war, and the navy—and that he has also appointed an Advisory Commission of the Council, an executive committee with the responsibility of largely planning and fulfilling the mobilization of American industry for defense preparedness. The latter's two full-time members are Edward R. Stettinius, Jr., chairman of United States Steel, and William S. Knudsen, president of General Motors.

May 28: Against the unanimous judgment of the Belgian government and without consulting the British and French, King Leopold III surrenders Belgium to the Germans.

May 30: By now the British flotilla has managed to evacuate more than 125,000 troops from Dunkirk and disembark them in England before the Germans finally realize what is happening.

June 3: Under a directive from Roosevelt, General Marshall approves a list of armaments—rifles, ammunition, machine guns, TNT, and bombs—for shipment to Great Britain. Members of the Military Training Camp Association establish the National Emergency Committee, a nationwide organization of 1,000 members chaired by Wall Street lawyer Grenville Clark, to advocate creating a conscription system and providing armaments and other forms of aid to the Allies.

June 4: Working throughout the night, when the Luftwaffe is not operative, the British flotilla has succeeded in evacuating a total of more than 338,000 British and French soldiers from Dunkirk, which is still defended by 40,000 French troops.

June 4: In a stirring speech before Parliament, Churchill pledges that the British will fight to the end: "We shall never surrender. . . ."

June 5: German forces capture Dunkirk.

June 6: The Germans unleash a massive attack along the Somme River.

June 7: At Tromso the king of Norway and his government board the British cruiser *Devonshire* and set sail for exile in London.

June 10: The French government leaves Paris for Orléans; residents and others flee southward in a mass exodus from the city. Mussolini declares war on Great Britain and France and launches an invasion of the French Riviera with an attack force of 400,000 troops.

June 10: Presenting the commencement address for the University of Virginia at Charlottesville, Roosevelt, referring to Mussolini's attack on France, declares "the hand that held the dagger has struck it into the back of its neighbor." He pledges to provide materials to the "opponents of force" (France and Britain) and to expedite industrial productivity.

June 12: Vannevar Bush, president of the Carnegie Institute, meets in the Oval Office with the president and presents a memorandum proposing creation of a council to oversee and coordinate research projects with potential military applications. Roosevelt approves the memorandum.

June 14: German forces occupy Paris.

June 14: The SS officially opens the newly completed concentration camp at Auschwitz for the incarceration of Polish political prisoners.

June 15: By executive order, Roosevelt establishes the National Defense Research Committee to coordinate research projects that may have military significance, including research on nuclear fission; he appoints Bush chairman.

June 16: In the early morning Brigadier General Charles de Gaulle arrives in London to work with Great Britain to pursue the war as representative of the French government, which Premier Paul Reynaud intends to continue in exile in Algiers.

June 16: In the evening, with the French government now ensconced in Bordeaux, a majority of the cabinet overrides the opposition of Premier Reynaud and votes to ask the Germans for an armistice. Reynaud resigns and is replaced by General Philippe Pétain, hero of World War I.

June 17: Contacting the Germans through the Spanish ambassador, General Pétain requests an armistice.

June 18: In a radio broadcast from London, General de Gaulle, with Churchill's approval, appeals to

French people throughout the world to continue the fight against Germany.

June 19: Roosevelt requests that Secretary of War Harry Woodring resign. Two days earlier Woodring had refused to approve the sale of a dozen B-17 bombers to Great Britain despite the president's agreement to the sale.

June 20: Roosevelt announces two major appointments: Henry L. Stimson as secretary of war and Frank Knox as secretary of the navy, both Republicans. Senator Edward R. Burke introduces a bill in the Senate to set up a conscription system.

June 21: Congressman James W. Wadsworth introduces a conscription bill in the House.

June 21: In the forest near Compiègne, in the same railway carriage in which the French forced the Germans to sign the 1918 armistice ending World War I, with Hitler, Göring, and other prominent Nazis looking on, General Keitel presents the Germans' terms for surrender to the French delegates: Over half of France, including Paris and the entire Atlantic coastal area will become a German province; the remainder, unoccupied France, will be governed by officials who are willing to cooperate with Germany; France will pay the costs of German occupation; the French fleet will be disarmed and demobilized; France will surrender to Germany all anti-Nazi German refugees on French soil.

June 22: With the approval of the Pétain government, the French delegates at Compiègne sign the armistice.

June 24: The Republican National Convention officially opens in Philadelphia.

June 25: The Japanese government demands from France the right to send troops into French Indochina.

June 28: On the sixth ballot, the Republican National Convention nominates Wendell Willkie as the party's candidate for the presidency; he has overcome the early leads of Thomas E. Dewey, New York City district attorney, and Senator Robert Taft of Ohio. The convention nominates Senator Charles L. McNary of Oregon, Senate minority leader, as vice presidential candidate.

June 28: The British government officially recognizes de Gaulle as the leader of the Free French.

June 28: Pope Pius XII sends messages to Hitler, Churchill, and Mussolini offering to be a mediator in arranging "a just and honorable peace" among the three nations.

July 2: General Pétain, head of the government of unoccupied France establishes the government's headquarters at Vichy in the Bourbon region.

July 3: In order to prevent Germany from gaining control of French warships, British ships attack the French fleet in Oran harbor in Algeria, destroying three battleships and a carrier. In Alexandria, Egypt, the British force the French commander to render the fleet there incapable of fighting.

July 4: The British take possession of all French ships in British ports in order to prevent their takeover by Vichy France and thus their falling under German control.

July 4: Mussolini begins an offensive in East Africa. Italian troops occupy border towns in Sudan.

July 7: The Luftwaffe launches massive attacks on southern ports in England and on British shipping in the English Channel, the beginning of the Battle of Britain.

July 10: Following his confirmation by the Senate the day before, Stimson assumes the duties of secretary of war. Roosevelt requests that Congress appropriate $5 billion in additional funding for defense.

July 14: The Soviet Union stages elections in Estonia, Latvia, and Lithuania in which only Communists are legal candidates.

July 15: The Democratic National Convention begins in Chicago.

July 15: Italian troops invade Kenya.

July 16: Hitler issues orders to prepare for Operation Sea Lion, the invasion of Great Britain.

July 17: The Democratic National Convention nominates Roosevelt as the party's presidential candidate.

July 18: Despite major opposition, the Democratic Convention nominates Roosevelt's choice as vice presidential candidate, Henry A. Wallace.

July 20: Roosevelt signs into law an act that will double the size of the U.S. Navy, creating a "two-ocean navy."

July 26: Concerned over increased Japanese purchases of gasoline and lubricants for airplanes, Roosevelt declares that the United States needs to conserve supplies for its own stockpiles and therefore imposes an embargo on sales of top-grade scrap iron and aviation gasoline to Japan. At the request of the president, Louis Johnson resigns as assistant secretary of war and is replaced by Robert P. Patterson, Stimson's choice.

July 30: Roosevelt's special assistant Harry Hopkins arrives in Moscow for discussions with Joseph Stalin.

August 3: Crossing the border from East Africa, Italian troops invade British Somaliland.

August 3: The Soviet Union takes possession of Lithuania.

August 4: In a radio broadcast, General John J. Pershing, commander of the American Expeditionary Force in World War I, speaks out in favor of the proposal to provide 50 over-age destroyers to Great Britain, declaring that the United States must immediately give any possible aid to the British "before it is too late."

August 5: The Soviet Union takes possession of Latvia.

August 6: The Soviet Union takes possession of Estonia.

August 15: The Luftwaffe attacks with 2,000 planes in an effort to destroy the RAF in the skies over England and the Channel in preparation for the invasion of Great Britain.

August 18: Roosevelt meets with Canadian prime minister William Mackenzie King at Ogdensburg, New York, on the St. Lawrence River; the two leaders establish a Permanent Joint Board of Defense to consider plans for defending the northern half of the hemisphere.

August 23: Due to navigational error, German bombers, intending to attack oil tanks and aircraft factories on the edges of London, mistakenly drop their bombs in the heart of the city. The British assume the bombing is deliberate.

August 25: Retaliating for the bombing of London, RAF planes bomb Berlin—the first time bombs have ever fallen on the German capital.

September 3: Roosevelt issues a special message announcing that the United States is sending 50 old destroyers to Great Britain in exchange for the grant of leases to British bases in Newfoundland and the Caribbean.

September 4: Secretary of State Hull issues a warning to Japan not to pursue aggression in Indochina.

September 4: After a summer of organizing, the America First Committee announces its formation, with headquarters set up in Chicago. Dedicated to lobbying against intervention in foreign conflicts, the organization is headed by General Robert E. Wood, chairman of Sears, Roebuck and Company.

September 7: More than 1,200 Luftwaffe bombers and fighters attack London during the night, the first intended and major German bombing of the city. It marks the beginning of the "London Blitz," bombings that will continue for 57 consecutive nights.

September 13: Italian forces cross the border from Libya and invade Egypt; their orders are to drive the British out of Egypt and to capture the Suez Canal.

September 14: Both houses of Congress approve the Burke-Wadsworth Bill creating a conscription system, known as selective service.

September 15: In attempting a daytime bombing raid on London, the Luftwaffe suffers crippling losses from RAF attacks; the RAF also attacks ports along the coast of France and the Low Countries where German ships have assembled for the invasion of England.

September 16: Roosevelt signs into law the Selective Training and Service Act. The law establishes the Selective Service System under the control of the president. Under the law's terms, all men between the ages of 21 and 36 are to register on October 16 for military training; the first drawing of lots is scheduled for October 29.

September 17: Because of heavy losses endured by the Luftwaffe since the beginning of the Battle of Britain—1,116 airplanes to the RAF's 779 losses—difficulties in assembling the needed ships, and controversies over strategy, Hitler decides to indefinitely postpone Operation Sea Lion, the invasion of England.

September 19: Hitler reverses himself and orders that the fleet for the invasion of England should continue assembling.

September 26: Roosevelt declares an embargo on exporting scrap iron and steel to all nations not located in the Western Hemisphere except for Great Britain.

September 26: Japanese troops invade Indochina.

September 27: Representatives of Germany, Italy, and Japan meeting in Berlin sign the Tripartite Pact, which recognizes Europe as the Germans' and Italians' sphere of influence and East Asia as Japan's and pledges each to come to the support of any of the others that is attacked by any nation not currently involved in the European war or in the conflict between Japan and China (that is, the United States, although not specifically named).

September 29: U.S. Marines land on Midway Island to begin building new defense installations.

October 4: Hitler and Mussolini meet at Brenner Pass, with Hitler trying to convince Il Duce (Mussolini) to avoid action in the Balkans but telling him nothing about German intentions toward Romania.

October 7: German troops occupy Romania, seizing that nation's oil fields—a surprise to Mussolini.

October 12: After postponements, changes of orders, and long delays during which RAF planes have wreaked destruction on the fleet assembling for Operation Sea Lion, Hitler officially orders that the invasion of England be postponed until the spring of 1941.

October 16: The Selective Service System registers about 16.5 million men.

October 23: In his first campaign speech for the election, Roosevelt denies Republican accusations that he intends to lead the nation into war. The president also issues orders that two squadrons of pursuit planes and two submarines be sent to the Philippines to bolster American defenses there. He has already promised aid to Chiang Kai-shek and approved Colonel Claire Chennault's leading of a group of American volunteers known as the Flying Tigers in support of Chiang Kai-shek's air force.

October 25: In a radio broadcast, C10 head John L. Lewis castigates Roosevelt, accuses him of wanting dictatorial powers, and announces his support of Willkie.

October 28: Hitler and Mussolini meet in Florence, where Il Duce informs the German dictator that Italian troops have crossed the border from Albania and invaded Greece.

October 29: Roosevelt personally officiates at the first drawing of conscription numbers; Stimson, wearing a blindfold, draws the lot from a glass bowl. Some 900,000 inductees may be drafted each year to serve in the armed forces for a year and then to become reservists; under the terms of the law, they will serve only within the United States or its territories.

October 30: During a campaign speech in Boston, addressing himself specifically to American parents, Roosevelt asserts, "I have said this before, but I shall say it again and again and again: Your boys are not going to be sent into any foreign wars."

November 1: Italian planes bomb Athens and Salonika.

November 2: During a campaign speech in Buffalo, New York, Roosevelt states, "Your President says this country is not going to war."

President Roosevelt's New Deal programs helped some people keep their homes by allowing them to borrow money from the federal government. The children in this September 1940 photograph taken in Saint Mary's County, Maryland, belong to one of the families this policy aided. *(Library of Congress, Prints and Photographs Division [LC-USF34-014501-D])*

November 2: British troops occupy Crete.

November 4: Roosevelt wins reelection to a third term, carrying 38 states with a total electoral college vote of 449 to Willkie's winning of 10 states with 82 electoral votes. The popular vote is much closer: more than 27.2 million for FDR to more than 22.3 million for Willkie.

November 9: Neville Chamberlain dies, a victim of cancer.

November 11: RAF planes launched from carriers bomb the Italian fleet in harbor at Taranto, Italy, destroying three battleships.

November 12: Foreign Minister V. M. Molotov of the USSR meets in Berlin with Foreign Minister Joachim von Ribbentrop of Germany and Hitler, but they reach no agreements on issues related to the Baltic and eastern European countries.

November 14: Luftwaffe bombers devastate Coventry, England.

November 19: Counterattacks by Greek forces send Italian troops into retreat.

November 20: Hungary officially joins the Axis alliance.

November 23: Romania and Slovakia officially join the Axis alliance.

December 3: Driving the Italians ever backward into Albania, Greek forces capture Porto Edda and tens of thousands of prisoners.

December 7: Mussolini requests German help in Albania and Greece.

December 9: While on a cruise in the Caribbean, Roosevelt receives a telegraphed message from Churchill warning that Great Britain is in desperate peril and might fail entirely without aid from the United States.

December 9: Commanded by General Archibald Wavell, the British Army of the Nile attacks the Italian forces invading Egypt.

December 18: Hitler issues a directive ordering preparations for Operation Barbarossa, the invasion and conquest of the Soviet Union. The military plans are to be completed by May 15, 1941.

December 29: During a fireside chat Roosevelt contends that the Nazis intend to "enslave" all of Europe and to use Europe's resources to achieve world domination. He asserts that the United States must produce the armaments the Allies need to defeat the Axis powers: "We must be the great arsenal of democracy."

1941

January 6: In his annual message to Congress, Roosevelt outlines his domestic goals and his aspirations for a future world in which "four essential human freedoms prevail": the freedoms of speech and worship and the freedoms from want and fear. He asks Congress to approve legislation authorizing lend-lease forms of aid to the Allies.

January 10: The Lend-Lease Bill is introduced in the House of Representatives.

January 15: British forces in Kenya and Sudan invade Italian East Africa, beginning a drive into Ethiopia.

January 17: Roosevelt issues orders for the navy to make preparations to provide convoys for American shipping in the Atlantic.

January 19: In a meeting with Mussolini at Berchtesgaden, Hitler agrees to support the Italians in Albania and North Africa.

January 20: Roosevelt is inaugurated for a third term as president.

January 22: Great Britain's Army of the Nile, steadily driving the Italians westward in Libya, captures the port city of Tobruk.

January 29: Secret talks between staff representatives of the U.S. and British armies and navies begin in Washington, D.C., to discuss preparations for joint action in the event the United States is drawn into the war.

February 5: The Army of the Nile encircles and destroys Italian forces in Cyrenaica.

February 7: The Army of the Nile captures Benghazi.

February 8: The House passes the Lend-Lease Bill by a vote of 250-165.

February 12: General Erwin Rommel arrives in Tripoli, Libya, to assume command of German and Italian forces in North Africa.

February 14: German armored (panzer) units arrive in Tripoli to shore up Italian operations in North Africa.

February 17: In a unanimous decision in the case of *United States v. Darby Lumber Company,* the Supreme Court upholds the constitutionality of the 1938 Fair Labor Standards Act.

February 18: Roosevelt announces that W. Averell Harriman will serve as the president's representative in expediting defense aid to Great Britain and will leave for that nation by the end of the month.

March 1: Bulgaria, occupied by German troops, joins the Axis alliance.

March 5: British Army of the Nile troops shipped from North Africa arrive in Greece.

March 9: The Senate passes the Lend-Lease Bill by a vote of 60–31.

March 11: Roosevelt signs into law the Lend-Lease Act, which empowers the president to arrange for the sale, lease, or loan of armaments to nations whose defense is vital to U.S. interests and authorizes $7 billion in appropriations for this purpose. Roosevelt appoints Harry Hopkins as administrator of the lend-lease program.

March 24: The Afrika Korps commanded by General Erwin Rommel begins operations against the British in Libya.

March 25: Yugoslavia joins the Axis alliance.

March 27: With broad public support, a military coup overthrows the government of Yugoslavia; the leaders intend to renounce the Axis alliance.

March 28: In the Battle of Cape Matapan (Tainaron), Greece, the British destroy the remaining ships of the Italian navy.

April 1: United Automobile Workers (UAW) organizers stage a strike at the Ford Motor Company's River Rouge plant, closing it down.

April 3: Having been weakened by the redeployment of troops to Greece, the Army of the Nile abandons Benghazi and falls back under attack by the Afrika Korps.

April 6: British forces occupy Addis Ababa, Ethiopia, completing their seizure of Italian East Africa; they will restore Haile Selassie to the Ethiopian throne.

April 6: German forces invade Greece and Yugoslavia, a diversion that forces Hitler to postpone Operation Barbarossa.

April 9: Roosevelt signs an agreement with the Danish representative in Washington, D.C., that permits the United States to occupy Greenland if necessary for defensive purposes.

April 13: German troops capture Belgrade.

April 13: In Moscow representatives of Japan and the USSR. sign a treaty committing each country to remain neutral if the other country becomes involved in the war.

April 17: The Yugoslavian army and government officially capitulate to the Germans.

April 18: Concerned about losses of ships to German submarine torpedoes, Roosevelt decides to enhance navy patrols in the Atlantic, extending their range to the 25th parallel (later to the 26th and including Iceland). Within this expanded zone, which overlaps the combat zone announced by the Germans on March 25, naval vessels on "neutrality patrol" will flash warnings to merchant ships whenever a U-boat (German submarine) is spotted and signal the U-boat's location (British naval vessels might also take advantage of these signals).

April 20: Units of Rommel's Afrika Korps encircle and lay siege to Tobruk.

April 23: King George II and members of the Greek government leave for Crete.

April 24: British and Greek forces begin to evacuate the mainland, heading for Crete.

April 27: German forces occupy Athens.

April 29: Having moved too far beyond its supply lines, the Afrika Korps' advance across North Africa comes to a halt at the Egyptian border.

April 30: German forces secure the occupation of Greece.

April 30: Hitler orders that Operation Barbarossa begin on June 22.

May 2: Following a coup in Iraq on April 1 that brought pro-Axis leaders to power and a request by the new government that the Germans send military aid, British forces move into Iraq.

May 8: RAF planes bomb Bremen and Hamburg.

May 10: Hitler's trusted confidant and deputy leader of the Nazi Party Rudolf Hess flies solo across the North Sea and parachutes into Scotland; he intends to present a peace plan to the British government that would result in a pact between Great Britain and Germany to fight Bolshevism. After talks with British officials, Hess is imprisoned.

May 20: The Germans stage an airborne attack on Crete, landing paratroopers and equipment.

May 21: Finally forced to compromise with the union movement because of the strike at the River Rouge plant, Henry Ford has agreed to an election overseen by the National Labor Relations Board in which the Ford workers can choose who will bargain for them. The ballot results indicate that 70 percent of the workers favor the UAW, 27 percent the AFL, and less than 3 percent the nonunion representatives proposed by Ford.

May 21: A German U-boat torpedoes and sinks the American merchant ship *Robin Moor,* bound for Capetown, South Africa, in the south Atlantic. It is the first American ship to be torpedoed during the war. The U-boat had the crew and passengers board lifeboats before the attack; all eventually were rescued.

May 22: Roosevelt issues orders to the army and navy to make preparations for seizing the Azores and the Cape Verde Islands in the event that Germany invades Spain and Portugal.

May 24: After being sighted by British reconnaissance planes off the coast of Norway, the *Bismarck,* the world's largest battleship, duels with the *Hood* and the *Prince of Wales,* sent with other ships from the British Home Fleet to intercept the German ship. The *Bismarck* sinks the *Hood* and escapes into the open seas.

May 26: British reconnaissance planes again sight the *Bismarck,* now racing for the coast of France. A torpedo from a British ship knocks out the battleship's rudder.

May 27: In response to the *Bismarck*'s appearance in the Atlantic, Roosevelt issues a declaration that the United States is in an "unlimited national emergency"—what the term means is left unclear.

May 27: British planes and ships bombard the *Bismarck* for hours and finally sink it.

May 27: German forces complete the conquest of Crete. All British troops are evacuated.

May 31: British troops enter Baghdad, Iraq.

June 4: Kaiser Wilhelm II, monarch of Germany during World War I, dies in the Netherlands, where he had been exiled following the war.

June 8: Free French troops, supported by the British, invade Syria in a challenge to the Vichy government.

June 16: Since it took weeks for the survivors to be rescued, Roosevelt had not learned of the sinking of the *Robin Moor* until June 12. He accused Germany of violating international law and now orders all assets of the Axis nations held within the United States to be frozen; he also orders the German consuls and their staffs to leave the United States.

June 22: Operation Barbarossa begins. German forces—190 divisions supported by 3,000 aircraft—attacking from Poland and Prussia smash into the USSR along a 2,000-mile front that stretches from the Black Sea to the Baltic Sea.

June 24: During a press conference Roosevelt responds to a question about a State Department statement issued on June 22 condemning the German invasion of the USSR by stating, ". . . we are going to give all the aid that we possibly can to Russia."

July 1: German forces capture Riga, the capital of Latvia.

July 2: A high-level conference of Japanese military and political leaders, including Emperor Hirohito, concludes that Japan should stay out of Germany's attack on the Soviet Union, unless the Germans appear obviously to be winning, and to concentrate instead on Southeast Asia.

July 7: Following negotiations in which Iceland has agreed to accept American protection, 4,400 U.S. Marines land in Iceland and relieve the British garrison there.

July 12: Representatives of the Soviet Union and Great Britain conclude a pact for mutual assistance in fighting Germany.

July 12: Vichy forces in Syria capitulate to the Free French.

July 16: German forces capture Smolensk on their drive toward Moscow.

July 21: In a message to Congress, Roosevelt requests revision of the Selective Service Act to extend the time of service for draftees, presently limited to one year, and to end the restriction against draftees' serving outside the Western Hemisphere.

July 23: Japan announces the creation of a joint protectorate with France over French Indochina and the occupation of bases around Saigon by Japanese troops. Japan pressures Vichy France for bases in southern Indochina, from which invasions could be launched against all of Southeast Asia.

July 25: In response to the Japanese occupation of French Indochina, the Roosevelt administration imposes a total embargo on trade with Japan, except for oil, and freezes all Japanese assets in the United States. (Since, by administrative oversight, no licenses are issued for the export of oil in the coming months, the embargo effectively covers oil also.)

July 27: Roosevelt issues orders placing the Philippines' armed forces under U.S. command.

August 3: At New London, Connecticut, Roosevelt boards the yacht *Potomac,* supposedly for a fishing cruise; once at sea he transfers to the cruiser *Augusta* to steam to Newfoundland. With him are General George C. Marshall, General H. H. Arnold,

Admiral Harold Stark, and Sumner Welles; Stimson, Knox, and Hull have been left in Washington, unapprised of Roosevelt's destination and purposes.

August 7: The Senate votes approval for the revision of the Selective Service Act and extends draftees' required service period to 17 months, providing them with a raise after one year's service. The ban on serving outside the Western Hemisphere remains intact.

August 9: The *Prince of Wales,* carrying Churchill and his staff, arrives in Argentia Harbor, Newfoundland; Churchill boards the *Augusta* to begin four days of meetings with Roosevelt.

August 12: The House passes the revision to the Selective Service Act already approved by the Senate but by only a one-vote margin.

August 14: Concluding their meetings, Roosevelt and Churchill issue a joint declaration of war aims known as the Atlantic Charter. The declaration pledges that the two nations, among other things, seek no territorial acquisitions; advocate self-determination for all peoples; intend to see Nazism destroyed; and support creation of an international organization following the war's conclusion to secure disarmament, freedom of the seas, and other peacekeeping measures.

August 25: By mutual agreement, British and Soviet forces invade Iran—the British from the south, the Soviets from the north—in order to prevent Nazi control of this key oil nation.

September 4: In the open sea, about 200 miles southwest of Iceland, the U.S. destroyer *Greer* encounters a German U-boat. The *Greer's* sounding mechanism alerts a British airplane that drops depth charges. The U-boat responds by launching a torpedo toward the *Greer,* which maneuvers out of the torpedo's path and drops depth charges. The U-boat fires another torpedo that misses; after dropping a few more depth charges, the *Greer* heads for Iceland.

September 4: German forces begin to lay siege to Leningrad (St. Petersburg).

September 11: Citing the U-boat attack on the Greer as an act of aggression—asserting that the U-boat fired first—Roosevelt issues orders to U.S. ships providing escorts in the Atlantic to "shoot on sight" after spotting an Axis submarine or cruiser within American "defensive waters," now extending to within 400 miles of the coast of Scotland. U.S. naval vessels begin escorting British merchant convoys within these waters.

September 16: The shah of Iran abdicates, giving control of Iran to the British and Soviet forces.

September 19: German forces cross the Dnieper River and capture Kiev, capital of Ukraine.

September 24: Stalin announces his acceptance of the provisions of the Atlantic Charter.

September 29: Following mutual agreement between Roosevelt and Churchill to assist the Soviets, Averell Harriman and William Maxwell Aitken, Lord Beaverbrook, arrive in Moscow for discussions with Stalin on providing American and British war supplies.

October 1: Discussions involving Harriman, Lord Beaverbrook, and Stalin result in a protocol under which the United States and Great Britain will provide war supplies to the Soviets for nine months.

October 2: German forces launch a massive frontal push toward Moscow.

October 9: Roosevelt asks that Congress authorize the arming of American merchant ships.

October 12: German forces capture Bryansk on their march to Moscow. Stalin orders that most government operations be relocated to Kuibyshev on the Volga River.

October 14: German forces push to within 60 miles of Moscow.

October 16: Japanese prime minister Fumimaro Konoye and his government resign. General Hideki Tojo replaces Konoye while also retaining the post of minister of war.

October 17: A German U-boat torpedoes the U.S. destroyer *Kearney,* damaging the ship's hull and killing 11 seamen.

October 20: The defensive strategy prepared by General Georgi Zhukov halts the German advance upon Moscow, but Stalin declares the city to be in a state of siege.

October 31: About 600 miles west of Iceland, a German U-boat torpedoes the American destroyer *Reuben James,* escorting a convoy. The destroyer sinks; more than 100 seamen die.

November 5: Japanese military and political leaders confer and decide to set November 25 as a deadline for reaching a diplomatic agreement with the United States that would restore trade in oil; if no agreement is reached, they will ask the emperor's permission to attack Hawaii.

November 7: The Senate approves by a 50-37 vote the removal of restrictions from the Neutrality Act that Roosevelt has requested be eliminated, in particular those prohibiting American ships from entering "danger zones" and the arming of American merchant ships.

November 10: Ambassador Kichisaburo Nomura presents to Roosevelt and Hull his government's proposal that the United States restore normal trade with Japan and pressure Chiang Kai-shek to accept Japanese terms for peace in China—a proposal made several times previously. In return the Japanese would agree not to attack the United States in the event of Germany's and Italy's going to war with the United States; instead Japan would interpret the Tripartite Pact "independently." Japan would also agree to withdraw troops from China, but only after an interval of years, and from Indochina, but only after settlement of the China conflict.

November 13: By a vote of 212-94, the House approves the removal of restrictions from the Neutrality Act.

November 15: The Roosevelt administration officially rejects the proposal submitted by Ambassador Nomura.

November 15: German forces renew their drive toward Moscow.

November 20: Ambassador Nomura submits a new proposal to Roosevelt and Hull: Japan will agree to halt the advance in Southeast Asia and the Western Pacific and withdraw from Indochina after a settlement in China if, in return, the United States agrees to release Japanese frozen assets, supply oil to Japan, pressure the Dutch to reopen trade with the East Indies, and cease assisting Chiang Kai-shek.

November 25: The Roosevelt administration decides to allow unarmed ships to cross the Atlantic to Lisbon; armed ships, to Arkhangel'sk; and ships flying the U.S. flag, to Great Britain. But only the decision about Lisbon is publicly announced.

November 25: Under orders from Admiral Yamamoto Isokuru, a Japanese task force of two battleships, six carriers, three cruisers, and nine destroyers steams out of harbor at Tankan Bay in the Kurile Islands and heads toward Hawaii. Preceding the fleet by 200 miles are three submarines that also carry midget submarines that can be operated by only two men.

November 26: Roosevelt learns that ships transporting Japanese troops have been sighted south of Formosa (present-day Taiwan). He concludes that the

effort to negotiate a modus vivendi (temporary arrangement) that would have included some of the concessions the Japanese have requested is futile.

December 2: Japanese leaders decide to carry out the plan to attack Hawaii and to keep it a surprise by maintaining diplomatic relations with the United States until the last minute. They send a coded order to the fleet that is en route.

December 6: Roosevelt sends a direct appeal to Emperor Hirohito suggesting means of compromising American-Japanese differences and arriving a modus vivendi.

December 6: Forces commanded by General Zhukov counterattack after again halting the German advance toward Moscow.

December 7: Shortly after dawn, 183 Japanese fighters, torpedo planes, and bombers attack U.S. Pacific Fleet ships anchored at the naval base at Pearl

President Roosevelt signs the declaration of war, December 1941
(Library of Congress, Prints and Photographs Division [CPH 3C28756])

Harbor and airplanes at the army air base on the island of Oahu. They destroy or severely damage eight battleships, three light cruisers, four other ships, and 188 airplanes, leaving 2,403 people dead and 1,000 wounded. The attack costs the Japanese 28 airplanes, five midget submarines, and fewer than 100 dead. Japanese planes bomb American military bases on Guam and Wake Island; Japanese troops invade Malaya, Thailand, and Hong Kong.

December 8: Citing the Japanese attack on Pearl Harbor the previous day—"a date which will live in infamy"—President Roosevelt asks Congress to declare war on Japan. Congress promptly obliges, with one dissenting vote—that of Republican representative Jeanette Rankin of Montana.

December 9: Japanese forces invade the Gilbert Islands.

December 10: Japanese forces attack airfields in the Philippines, land on Bataan Island, and capture Guam. U.S. Marines thwart the invasion of Wake Island.

December 10: Germany and Italy declare war on the United States.

December 11: The U.S. Congress declares war on Germany and Italy.

December 17: Roosevelt appoints Admiral Chester Nimitz commander of the U.S. Pacific Fleet.

December 18: Congress approves the War Powers Act, granting to the president broad authority to exercise direct control over government agencies involved in conducting the war and over production of armaments, censorship of the press, and other areas to facilitate mobilization and policy.

December 19: Congress passes legislation extending conscription to men between the ages of 20 and 44.

December 20: Roosevelt appoints Admiral Ernest King commander of the U.S. Navy.

December 21: Meeting in Washington, D.C., U.S. and British military representatives prepare plans for jointly waging war, with a combined chiefs of staff.

December 22: Prime Minister Winston Churchill arrives in Washington for discussions with Roosevelt.

December 22: Japanese troops land on Luzon and force defending American and Filipino troops commanded by General Douglas MacArthur to fall back.

December 23: Japanese forces capture Wake Island. MacArthur's troops retreat into Bataan.

December 26: Churchill addresses Congress.

December 27: The Roosevelt administration begins a rationing program.

December 31: Admiral Nimitz arrives at Pearl Harbor to assume command of the Pacific Fleet.

Eyewitness Testimony

I do not for a moment doubt that my Negro descent and narrow group culture have in many cases predisposed me to interpret my facts too favorably for my race; but there is little danger of long misleading here, for the champions of white folk are legion. The Negro has long been the clown of history; the football of anthropology; and the slave of industry. I am trying to show here why these attitudes can no longer be maintained.

W. E. B. DuBois, author, educator, and one of the founders of the National Association for the Advancement of Colored People (NAACP), in Black Folk: Then and Now *(1939).*

Through the Arts Projects, free and popular-priced dramatic and musical entertainment—most of it good, and some of excellent, quality—and free class instruction in scores of cultural branches incidental to the musical, dramatic, and graphic arts, have been brought to millions of American citizens of the economic stratum generally described as "underprivileged." . . .

[T]he 4 million persons who, within two years, participated in activities of the new federally sponsored Community Art Centers . . . the 25 million to 30 million persons who attended 1,700 performances by the Federal Theatre between February 1936—the date of its first play—and the beginning of 1938 . . . the stupendous audience total of 92 million, to whom, it is estimated, the Federal Music Project, through more than 100,000 programs, brought "living music" between October 1935 and January 1938.

Grace Overmyer, author, reporting on the four Works Progress Administration (WPA) arts projects, in Government and the Arts *(1939).*

But not even the soft wash of dusk could help the houses. Only dynamite would be of any use against the Mexican ranch houses, Samoan huts, Mediterranean villas, Egyptian and Japanese temples, Swiss chalets, Tudor cottages, and every possible combination of these styles that lined the slopes of the canyon.

When he noticed that they were all of plaster, lath and paper, he was charitable and blamed their shape on the materials used. . . .

It is hard to laugh at the need for beauty and romance, no matter how tasteless, even horrible, the results of that are. But it is easy to sigh. Few things are sadder than the truly monstrous.

Nathanael West, novelist, commenting on Hollywood architecture, in The Day of the Locust *(1939).*

And then the dispossessed were drawn west—from Kansas, Oklahoma, Texas, New Mexico; from Nevada and Arkansas families, tribes, dusted out, tractored out. Carloads, caravans, homeless and hungry . . . They streamed over the mountains, hungry and restless—restless as ants, scurrying to find work. . . .

They were hungry, and they were fierce. And they had hoped to find a home, and they found only hatred. Okies—the owners hated them because the owners knew they were soft and the Okies strong, that they were fed and the Okies hungry.

John Steinbeck, novelist, in The Grapes of Wrath *(1939).*

It was well within the circle of factual description to say that in his numerous discourses Franklin D. Roosevelt discussed the basic human and economic problems of American society with a courage and range displayed by no predecessor in his office; that he thrust their challenges into spheres hitherto indifferent or hostile; that he set in swift circulation, through the use of the radio, ideas once confined to groups more or less esoteric; that he both reflected and stirred the thought of the nation to the uttermost borders of the land. And in doing this he carried on the tradition of humanistic democracy which from colonial times had been a powerful dynamic in the whole movement of American civilization and culture—economic, political, literary, scientific, and artistic.

Charles A. Beard and Mary R. Beard, historians, in America in Midpassage *(1939).*

Following the recent "radio terror" broadcast, commentators and editorial writers did a pretty thorough job of plumbing the reasons for the public's unreasoning, instant credulity. Largely it was assigned to a jittery state of nerves brought on by the war crisis through which the world had just passed. . . .

Yet in all our wide reading about the unfortunate incident, we recall not one hint of certain broader implications. . . .

Shopping and visiting on main street of Pittsboro, North Carolina; photo by Dorothea Lange, July 1939 *(Library of Congress, Prints and Photographs Division [604355 LC-USF34-019846-E])*

The lesson that seems to be taught . . . is that a few words over the radio, dramatized just so, exert a powerful influence over millions of our people. With a given set of conditions, a psychosis carefully built up by radicals, reformers, politicians, or "revolutionaries" of whatever stripe, it would appear that only a few suave promises, hysterical diatribes, or epithets hurled at this or that would set the people off.

F. D. McHugh, commenting on Orson Welles's Halloween radio broadcast of "The War of the Worlds," in Scientific American *(January 1939).*

With the fall of Barcelona in January 1939 and the imminent triumph of Franco forces, I was summoned home, ostensibly for consultation. . . .

My sympathy had been wholly with the legal, constitutional, democratic government of Spain. The nonintervention trickery, cynically dishonest, was supplemented by us with our embargo denying the Spanish government, which we recognized, its right under international law to buy arms and ammunition to defend itself. My government stood militantly behind this embargo, thus placing us in collaboration with the Axis in one of the moves in its campaign to wipe out democracy in Europe.

> *Claude Bowers, U.S. ambassador to Spain, in* My Life: The Memoirs of Claude Bowers *(1962).*

But this country has been profoundly affected by the destruction of the balance of power in Europe. So great a shift portends . . . a shift in the balance of power in the world. The results for the United States—economic, political, and strategic—in both of the bordering oceans and in Latin America are incalculable. So also are the results for international law, the observance of treaties, and the concept of sovereignty in a world of which the United States, much as it wishes the contrary, is more and more inexorably shown to be a part.

> *Hamilton Fish Armstrong, editor, in* Foreign Affairs *(January 1939).*

Have you realized your hopes? Are the better things of life always just beyond your reach? . . .

It takes no greater mental effort to *achieve results*—when you know how. Successful living is the oldest art in the world. . . . The knowledge of the art was acquired in centuries past through the personal sacrifices of the ancient sages, who *dared to investigate* life's mysteries. Their discoveries of the secret functionings of man's mind have been preserved by the Rosicrucians, an age-old, world-wide fraternity (not a religious organization).

> *Advertisement by the Rosicrucians (AMORC), a worldwide occult order whose symbol combines a rose and a cross, in* Scientific American *(February 1939).*

There are, according to West Coast production statistics, two great dates in Southern history. One is the Civil War and the other is the day on which an actress was named to play Scarlett O'Hara.

> *Katharine Best, film critic, in* Stage *(February 1939).*

Industrial wastes . . . may remain potent over long periods of time and may affect both aquatic life and domestic water supplies at relatively long distances from the source of pollution.

While this subject is only one phase of the broad problem of water pollution, it is important, since it deals with a direct effect on public health in that shellfish have been involved more or less frequently in the spread of disease. It deals with an indirect effect on public health in that trade wastes and sewage tend to make certain valuable sea foods scarcer and more expensive, thus depriving a portion of the population of benefits of foods rich in iodine, iron, copper, and other essential food elements and vitamins.

> *L. M. Fisher, senior sanitary engineer with the U.S. Public Health Service in Washington, D.C., in* Scientific American *(March 1939).*

That pale, pasty, inefficient, indoor look is a business and social handicap. Why put yourself at such an unforgivable disadvantage when you can get that *handsome, healthy,* TAN *everybody admires so much* in your home? Within ten days you can improve your appearance remarkably—look like a million dollars—*as if you had just returned from a vacation in Palm Beach!*

Palm Beach Sun Lamps furnish an abundance of the vital Ultra-Violet Rays that produce Vitamin D.

> *Advertisement for the U. V. R. Laboratories of New York City, in* Scientific American *(March 1939).*

Laughter is completely out of the picture Lillian Hellman paints of a Southern family. Tallulah Bankhead as one of *The Little Foxes,* "the little foxes that spoil the vines," returns to Broadway in an effective part. Miss Hellman's Hubbard family is indeed a menace to the vineyards of the world, preying upon society and tearing at each other. Clever, voracious, and utterly without principle . . . The result of this is exciting melodrama which leaves behind it the conviction that it is not so much the vicious capitalistic system which is to blame for the evils of the world, as the fact that man is still largely unregenerated, still at heart a beast of prey.

> *Rosamond Gilder, associate editor, in* Theatre Arts Monthly *(April 1939).*

A lunchroom near Belle Glade, Florida, January 1939 *(Library of Congress, Prints and Photographs Division [PPMSC 00215])*

In view of these developments one may say that at present the special theory of relativity is one of the most thoroughly accepted and most firmly established doctrines of modern physics. It has permeated the fields of mechanics, electromagnetism (including optics) and atomic physics; while it may appear desirable to have further direct checks on the validity of its mechanical aspects, a deviation from the predicted effects would constitute a most puzzling—and, at least temporarily, distressing—jolt for modern physics.

H. P. Robertson, professor of mathematical physics at Princeton University, in Scientific American *(June 1939).*

I mean by this that although the New York World's Fair has glaring deficiencies—even some cases of bad faith and bad taste which cry to heaven for correction—nevertheless . . . it abundantly justifies the faith of the people who first conceived and organized it. It is a better fair than the American people deserve, and probably a better one than they wanted. It really has a unified plan, not merely in its glamorous exterior but in the triumph of a spirit of intelligence and order in the control it has exercised over the greatest individualists of all time, the business men and industrialists of the United States.

Gardner Harding, newspaper correspondent with service in Europe, China, and Latin America, commenting on the 1939 New York World's Fair, in Harper's *(July 1939).*

The Wizard of Oz (M.G.M.) should settle an old Hollywood controversy: whether fantasy can be presented on the screen as successfully with human actors as with cartoons. It can. As long as *The Wizard of Oz* sticks to whimsey and magic, it floats in the same rare atmosphere of enchantment that distinguished Walt Disney's *Snow White and the Seven Dwarfs.* When it descends to earth it collapses like a scarecrow in a cloudburst.

Review of the movie The Wizard of Oz, *in* Time *(August 21, 1939).*

How can you feel kindly toward a man [Hitler] who tells you that German minorities have been brutally treated, first in Czechoslovakia and then in Danzig, but that never can Germany be accused of being unfair to a minority? I have seen evidence with my own eyes of what this same man has done to people belonging to a minority group—not only Jews, but Christians, who have long been German citizens.

Eleanor Roosevelt, from her "My Day" newspaper column of September 2, 1939, quoted in Chadakoff, Eleanor Roosevelt's My Day *(1989).*

The nation will remain a neutral nation, but I cannot ask that every American remain neutral in thought as well. Even a neutral has a right to take account of facts. Even a neutral cannot be asked to close his mind or close his conscience.

I have said not once, but many times, that I have seen war and that I hate war. I say that again and again.

President Franklin D. Roosevelt, from his fireside chat of September 3, 1939, in Buhite and Levy, FDR's Fireside Chats *(1992).*

World War II began last week at 5:20 A.M. (Polish time) Friday, September 1, when a German bombing plane dropped a projectile on Puck. . . . It was a grey day, with gentle rain.

Time, *news article of September 11, 1939.*

In the fall of 1938, Joe Kennedy worked with the appeasers, and although his faith was badly shaken during the Munich crisis, hoped settlement would be made, told Americans there would be no war in 1938. Last winter he changed tunes. With William Christian Bullitt, U.S. Ambassador to France, he became a prophet of doom, a skeleton at the feast. Again & again he croaked warnings that 1939 was a year of war.

Time, *article of September 18, 1939.*

It may or may not be significant that, since early spring, no accounts of research on nuclear fission have been heard from Germany—not even from discoverer Hahn. It is not unlikely that the German government, spotting a potential powerful weapon of war, has imposed military secrecy on all recent German investigations. A larger concentration of isotope 235, sub-

jected to neutron bombardment, might conceivably blow up all London or Paris.

It has been impossible, even in this long article, to mention all the thousand aspects of this fascinating phenomenon, or name many of the able contributors to the sum of information amassed since last January. But the fact remains that nuclear fission is the most important scientific discovery of the year, and holds who knows what promise for the future.

Jean Harrington, in Scientific American *(October 1939).*

"Business is stymied," murmured the Doctor. "Almost half the population is in dire want. Sixty millions of people cannot buy the products of industry." The Doctor's statistics were staggering and loose jointed, but his tone was quietly authoritative. There could be small room for doubt.

He spoke disparagingly of the New Deal and knocked all the alphabetical schemes for employing idle men. "Do you want to be taxed for these useless and futile activities?"

His audience shook their heads.

And all the while he spoke, the plan was unfolding—simply, logically. A child could have understood

Farmers at a filling station near Chapel Hill, North Carolina, July 1939; Farm Security Administration photo by Dorothea Lange *(Library of Congress)*

it. Levy a two percent tax on the gross business of the country and divide the revenue among persons over sixty years of age.

E. B. White, journalist and author, describing a talk by Dr. Francis E. Townsend, in Harper's *(October 1939).*

American isolationists, long in the saddle, are fighting to stave off the disaster, as they see it, of a swing in American public opinion back from the direction it began following in 1919. True, they won a major victory in preventing revision of the Neutrality Act at the last session of Congress. But on every hand they see evidence of a deep tide of American sympathy for the democracies and against the totalitarian Powers—a tide which might lead us to give moral and material support to the democracies, engaged in a life and death struggle, or even to our eventually becoming their partners.

John Crosby Brown, lawyer and public relations counsel for universities and other institutions, discussing the propaganda for and against U.S. isolation, Foreign Affairs *(October 1939).*

In the course of the last four months it has been made probable . . . that it may become possible to set up a nuclear chain reaction in a large mass of uranium, by which vast amounts of power and large quantities of new radium-like elements would be generated. Now it appears almost certain that this could be achieved in the immediate future.

This new phenomenon would also lead to the construction of bombs, and it is conceivable—though much less certain—that extremely powerful bombs of a new type may thus be constructed. A single bomb of this type, carried by a boat and exploded in a port, might very well destroy the whole port together with some of the surrounding territory. However, such bombs might very well prove to be too heavy for transportation by air.

Albert Einstein letter of August 2, 1939, delivered to President Roosevelt on October 11, in Grodzin and Rabinowitz, The Atomic Age *(1963).*

Walt Disney's second full-length cartoon, *Pinocchio,* expected for Christmas release, is another film which seems destined to elude the cataloguer. The famous Italian fairy tale is seen here in a Disneyesque adaptation, with a Mae West fish introduced, whose boy friend is Figaro the cat, and a chorus of Ubangi savage

Woman with chauffeur on Fifth Avenue, New York City, July 1939; Farm Security Administration photo by Dorothea Lange *(Library of Congress)*

girls for good measure . . . but it is Jiminy Cricket, Pinocchio's conscience, who is said to steal the show in much the same blatant manner as Dopey did in *Snow White.* The cartoon is, of course, in "gorgeous Technicolor," as the publicists insist on describing it. . . .

Also on the Disney schedule . . . is the full-length musical *Fantasia,* on which Leopold Stokowski and Deems Taylor are collaborating with Disney, and eighteen shorts, twelve of which star that already swellheaded character, Donald Duck.

Allen Bishop, in Theatre Arts *(November 1939).*

Last week the cinema event for which the U.S. has palpitated for three years took place in Atlanta, Ga.—the premiere of *Gone With the Wind.* . . .

Belle of the ball was Vivien Leigh, who nearly everyone agreed looked right like Scarlett O'Hara. Darkly grinning Clark Gable's head was a whirl. Hundreds of the prettiest little girls he had ever seen had surrounded him earlier. . . . An eleven-year-old girl, given a choice of getting a Christmas present or meeting Clark Gable, chose Gable. When Gable kissed her, she asked, "Now am I a woman?"

. . . Whatever it was not, *Gone With the Wind* was a first-rate piece of Americana, and Americans in the mass knew what they wanted before the critics had got through telling them they should not want it.

Time, article of December 25, 1939.

Sport's No. 1 hero of 1939 is dimple-cheeked, piano-legged Lou Gehrig. Last spring, when a rare form of paralysis compelled First Baseman Gehrig to give up his beloved post after 15 years with the New York Yankees, U.S. sportswriters wreathed their columns with encomiums seldom bestowed on the living. Skimming over the Iron Horse's unrivaled feat of playing in 2,130 consecutive major-league games and casually reviewing his extraordinary batting records (some surpassing those of Babe Ruth), they crowned Lou Gehrig's Honesty, Modesty, Courage. Practically canonized, 36-year-old Lou Gehrig became the idol of U.S. youth.

. . . Last week the Baseball Writers Association of America, waiving the rule that a candidate must be out of play for at least a year, unanimously voted Lou Gehrig in Baseball's Hall of Fame at Cooperstown, N.Y.

Time, article of December 25, 1939.

They stood in the mouth of the cave and watched them. The bombers were high now in fast, ugly arrow-heads beating the sky apart with the noise of their motors. They *are* shaped like sharks, Robert Jordan thought, the wide-finned, sharp-nosed sharks of the Gulf Stream. But these, wide-finned in silver, roaring, the light mist of their propellers in the sun, these do not move like sharks. They move like no thing there has ever been. They move like mechanized doom.

Ernest Hemingway, writer, in his novel set in Spain during the Spanish civil war, For Whom the Bell Tolls *(1940).*

In our moments of sober thought we all realize that booms are bad things, not good. But nearly all of us have a secret hankering for another one. "Another little orgy wouldn't do us any harm," is the feeling that persists both downtown and up. This is quite human, because in the last boom we acted so silly. If we are old enough we probably acted silly in the last three. We either got in too late, or out too late, or both. But

now that we are experienced, just give us one more shot at a good reliable runaway boom!

Fred Schwed, Jr., from his book Where Are the Customers' Yachts? *(1940).*

Yet in the long run we know that our only permanent defense is to create a democracy which works. . . . Our first and our last line of defense is the proof to the rest of the world that under democracy we can do a better job to promote the social security, the economic opportunity, and the human dignity of all people, than can those nations which we pity or condemn for their system of social regimentation. . . . A working American democracy can dissolve opposition and induce our rivals to imitate our methods in order to share our benefits, but a working totalitarianism may have the same fascination for us if we cannot make democracy give our people food as well as liberty.

That is why the political decisions of the next few years may determine whether we shall survive. It is comparatively easy to die in battle for democracy. . . . It is not so easy for the victors to arrange their post-war lives with such wisdom as to ensure the survival of popular sovereignty and democratic nationalism. We have traveled a long way from Gettysburg, and today it is doubtful that the Negroes as a whole are better off than they were under slavery or that the victorious Union has made life worth living for the heirs of the Grand Army of the Republic.

Jay Franklin, newspaper columnist and an organizer of Time *magazine, from his book* 1940 *(1940).*

History . . . will have one question to ask of our generation, people like ourselves. It will be asked of the books we have written. . . . The question will be this: Why did the scholars and writers of our generation in this country, witnesses as they were to the destruction of writing and of scholarship in great areas of Europe and to the exile and the imprisonment and murder of men whose crime was scholarship and writing—witnesses also to the rise in their own country of the same destructive forces with the same impulses, the same motives, the same means—why did the scholars and the writers of our generation in America fail to oppose those forces [totalitarian governments] while they could—while there was still time and still place to oppose them with the arms of scholarship and writing?

Archibald MacLeish, poet and librarian of congress, in The Irresponsibles *(1940).*

I think the true discovery of America is before us. I think the true fulfillment of our spirit, of our people, of our mighty and immortal land, is yet to come. I think the true discovery of our own democracy is still before us. And I think that all these things are certain as the morning, as inevitable as noon. I think I speak for most men living when I say that our America is Here, is Now, and beckons on before us, and that this glorious assurance is not only our living hope, but our dream to be accomplished.

Credo of character George Webber, in Thomas Wolfe's novel You Can't Go Home Again *(1940).*

[T]he appalling[ly] low earnings available for this type of labor [migrant farm labor] at present make workers desperate. The bitterness which these conditions create among workers is just as intense as the bitterness felt by growers during a labor dispute. Fear is the element that has created the appalling bitterness, which in the past has too frequently resulted in riots, bloodshed, and murder—a fear of the loss of crops on the part of growers—fear of starvation on the part of workers. As long as this psychological tension exists—and it exists in California today—the problem of maintaining civil liberties is inherently difficult . . .

The townspeople themselves become active partisans, usually on the side of the grower interests, and the entire community is divided into hostile camps. Many townspeople in the rural areas have slight sympathy for migratory labor. During the peak labor periods, their hospitals are overcrowded, their schools are overrun with new pupils, and their various social agencies are

Mexican workers on strike in California *(Library of Congress)*

burdened with the problems incident to this annual influx of nonresident workers.

Governor Culbert L. Olsen of California, speech to a Senate subcommittee of the Committee on Education and Labor, in the Congressional Record *(1940).*

It is my opinion that the most artistically successful American opera thus far is Louis Gruenberg's *Emperor Jones.* . . . And the work which, for all its structural shortcomings, most strongly suggests what the nature and character of *the* great American opera will be, when it finally bursts upon us, is George Gershwin's *Porgy and Bess.* Had Gershwin possessed, together with his musical zest and fine lyrical equipment, a greater technical skill and a sense of self-criticism, he might have produced for us a work that would

remain a prototype of what a successful American opera should be.

David Ewen, musicologist, author, biographer, in Theatre Arts *(January 1940).*

Second, so long as the Church pretends, or assumes to preach, absolute values, but actually preaches relative and secondary values, it will merely hasten this process of disintegration. We are asked to turn to the Church for our enlightenment, but when we do so we find that . . . the voice of the Church today . . . is the echo of our own voices. And the result of this experience, already manifest, is disillusionment. . . . The effect of this experience on the present generation has been profound. It is the effect of a vicious spiral, like the spiral the economists talk about that

The Lansing family, Farm Security Administration (FSA) borrowers, in Ross County, Ohio, October 1940 *(Library of Congress)*

leads into depression. But in this spiral there is at stake, not merely prosperity, but civilization.

Fortune, *editorial of January 1940 on the church's failure to teach absolute moral values.*

Mr. Smith Goes to Washington drops Senatorial courtesy onto the cutting-room floor and points an accusing finger at those members of the Congress who are, to put it mildly, not without dishonor; *Ninotchka* makes fun of the whole Russian experiment and suggests, audaciously, that Communists have just as many frailties as capitalists and that their way of life is far less attractive—unconventional themes for an industry tuned to the strict "dos and don'ts" of the Hays office. As additional virtues, both films have a sense of humor, not only about themselves, but about the whole human race, and an engaging tolerance which gives a warm glow to their satire.

Allen Bishop, movie review in Theatre Arts *(February 1940).*

The American economic system . . . works better than any other in the world—for the 77 per cent who belong to it. This story is about the other 23 per cent—the unemployed and their dependents, the unemployables and other members of the dispossessed. In all they total about thirty million—seven times the population of Finland. . . .

There are no official figures on the number of unemployed. Estimates for unemployment are derived by taking the April, 1930 census figure for the unemployed, adding to it the losses in employment since then and allowing for net growth in the working population. . . . The American Federation of Labor estimate, which is usually in the middle, has been used throughout this article. A. F. of L. estimates [of unemployment] for the last eleven years are:

1929	1,864,000
1930	4,735,000
1931	8,568,000
1932	12,870,000
1933	13,271,000
1934	11,424,000
1935	10,652,000
1936	9,395,000
1937	8,282,000
1938	10,936,000
1939	10,450,000

Fortune, *article of February 1940 on the unemployed or "dispossessed" people in the United States.*

This collective bargaining development is unparalleled in American industrial and labor history. A great change has taken place in management's attitude toward its workers. In view of the fact that the character of industrial relations, by and large, is determined by the attitude of management, this new and changed attitude is a healthy sign. It is a bulwark to our democratic form of government. I am happy to report that not a single company that embarked upon contractual relations with the SWOC [Steel Workers' Organizing Committee] beginning in 1937 has severed relations with SWOC . . . and others have since signed SWOC contracts. The part the industrial-relations policy of the federal government, as administered by the National Labor Relations Board, played in this development, and continues to play in it, is indeterminable. But to the credit and glory of our political democracy, it has been substantial, and rightly so.

Philip Murray, leader of the Steel Workers Organizing Committee (SWOC) of the Congress of Industrial Organizations (CIO), testimony of February 1940 before the Senate Committee on Education and Labor, in the Congressional Record *(1940).*

Just about a year ago, two German physicists who had been gunning at the metal uranium with neutron bullets . . . suddenly found that they had caused the biggest explosion in atomic history. . . .

Now, a year after the original discovery, word comes from Paris that we don't have to worry—at least, probably not. Frederic Joliot, son-in-law of Mme. Curie, and three co-workers . . . finally traced to its end the tumultuous course of the uranium fission chain reaction. They found that, instead of building up to a grand climax, it runs down and stops like an unwound clock.

Jean Harrington, in Scientific American *(May 1940).*

If Hitler wins in Europe—if the strength of the British and French armies and navies is forever broken—the United States will find itself alone in a barbaric world—a world ruled by Nazis, with "spheres of influence" assigned to their totalitarian allies. However different the dictatorships may be, racially, they all agree on one primary objective: *"Democracy must be wiped from the face of the earth."*

Advertisement entitled "STOP HITLER NOW!" written by Robert E. Sherwood, playwright, for the Committee to Defend America by Aiding the Allies, in the New York Times *(June 10, 1940).*

Some, indeed, still hold to the now somewhat obvious delusion that we of the United States can safely permit the United States to become a lone island in a world dominated by the philosophy of force.

Such an island may be the dream of those who still talk and vote as isolationists. Such an island represents to me and to the overwhelming majority of Americans today a helpless nightmare, the helpless nightmare of a people without freedom; yes, the nightmare of a people lodged in prison, handcuffed, hungry, and fed through the bars from day to day by the contemptuous, unpitying masters of other continents.

President Franklin D. Roosevelt, commencement address at the University of Virginia on June 10, 1940, following Italy's invasion of France, in the Congressional Record Appendix *(1940).*

Eleanor Roosevelt and New York City mayor Fiorello La Guardia in the latter's office in Washington, D.C., on the occasion of Mrs. Roosevelt's being sworn in as La Guardia's assistant in the Office of Civilian Defense. Mrs. Roosevelt's title was assistant director of the Office of Civilian Defense. The ceremony took place on the morning of September 29, 1941. *(Library of Congress, Prints and Photographs Division [USE6-D-001357])*

Something curious is happening to us in this country and I think it is time we stopped and took stock of ourselves. Are we going to be swept away from our traditional attitude toward civil liberties by hysteria about "Fifth Columnists," or are we going to keep our heads and rid ourselves of "Fifth Columnists" through the use of properly constituted government officials?

If we violate the rights of innocent people or even of guilty people, we lose our long established liberties because of our desire to curtail the activities of those who are dangerous as groups or as individuals, by trying to curtail them in unconstitutional and ill considered ways.

> *Eleanor Roosevelt, from her "My Day" newspaper column of June 23, 1940, quoted in Chadakoff,* Eleanor Roosevelt's My Day *(1989).*

Eyes of the scientific world . . . widened the first week in May at the startling news that work of a 28-year-old physicist at the University of Minnesota in isolating the explosive uranium isotope, U-235, had been corroborated, marking a significant advance toward shackling atomic energy.

The physicist is Dr. Alfred O. C. Niers, who modestly expressed dismay at the extravagant reports which blossomed on front pages everywhere, to the effect that the incalculable forces of the atom were on the verge of being pressed into the service of mankind.

There were fabulous predictions that this discovery made feasible bombs of unheard-of strength.

> *Roy H. Copperud, professor at the University of Minnesota, in* Scientific American *(July 1940).*

On him lay the responsibility that no other President had faced—that of explaining why he believed it wise and necessary to break a tradition that had lasted through 151 turbulent years of U.S. political life. . . . His task was to answer the historic objection to the Third Term—the tenet of democracy which holds that the great reservoir of democratically trained citizens can always yield new leaders; that one danger of democracy is that an ambitious Executive may use the power of his office to keep himself in power. . . .

So the 32nd President scrapped the Third Term tradition. Few who heard his acceptance speech did not believe that before doing so he had convinced himself that his decision was for the best interest of the nation. If in the coming campaign voters are also convinced, the tradition will be scrapped for good; if not it will be Franklin Roosevelt who is scrapped.

> Time, *article of July 29, 1940.*

As to the third term, it is all very well for conservative Democrats and regular Republicans to use this as a talking point. But there is a kickback in it for your real supporters. It is that many of them would have supported Roosevelt for a third term if you had not been nominated. Moreover, I believe, you would never have been nominated had Roosevelt withdrawn before Philadelphia and left the Republicans with no one to defeat but Hull, Jackson, etc., etc. The spearpoint of the Willkie movement was composed of people who were so concerned about American security (external and internal) that no other political consideration seemed important. People of this sort will not vote against Roosevelt because of the third term principle but they will vote for you if they believe you will do better than he in making the country strong. These people are a minority of the voters but they supply the driving energy of the Willkie movement. The only way to state the third term issue to them is to say that with you in the field, Roosevelt is not indispensable. If Taft were the candidate, these people would, however reluctantly, go to Roosevelt.

> *Walter Lippmann, newspaper columnist, letter of July 30, 1940, to Wendell Willkie, the Republican Party's nominee for president, in Blum,* Public Philosopher: Selected Letters of Walter Lippmann *(1985).*

I believe that the forces of free enterprise must be regulated. I am opposed to business monopolies. I believe in collective bargaining, by representatives of labor's own free choice, without any interference and in full protection of those obvious rights. I believe in the maintenance of minimum standards for wages and of maximum standards for hours. I believe that such standards should constantly improve. I believe in the federal regulation of interstate utilities, of securities markets, and of banking. I believe in federal pensions, in adequate old-age benefits, and in unemployment allowances.

> *Wendell Willkie, Republican Party nominee for president, speech of August 17, 1940, in* This is Wendell Willkie: A Collection of Speeches and Writings on Present-Day Issues *(1940).*

Presently we learned that anxiety was felt in the United States about the air and naval defense of their Atlantic seaboard, and President Roosevelt has recently made it clear that he would like to discuss with us, and with the Dominion of Canada and with New-foundland, the development of American naval and air facilities in Newfoundland and in the West Indies. There is, of course, no question of any transference of sovereignty . . . but for our part, His Majesty's Government are entirely willing to accord defense facilities to the United States on a 99 years' leasehold basis . . . Undoubtedly this process means that these two great organizations of the English-speaking democracies, the British Empire and the United States, will have to be somewhat mixed up together in some of their affairs for mutual and general advantage. For my own part, looking out upon the future, I do not view the process with any misgivings. I could not stop it if I wished; no one can stop it. Like the Mississippi, it just keeps rolling along. Let it roll on full flood, inexorable, irresistible, benignant, to broader lands and better days.

Prime Minister Winston S. Churchill of Great Britain, speech to the House of Commons, August 20, 1940, quoted in his Blood, Sweat, and Tears *(1941).*

Propaganda is a wondrous thing. It has made of Hitler, according to welcoming phrases of German newspapers when he recently returned from the Battle of France: "A Genius for Commanding," "The Lord of Battle," "Leader from Darkness to Light." . . .

Hitler is not the secret. . . . It is German planning and doing and sacrificing that the world must beat. So far as American national defense is concerned, we can beat it hands down—and a dozen times over. Are we going to do it, or sit back, play politics, and say "What's the use? Hitler is invincible"?

F. D. McHugh, editor, in Scientific American *(September 1940).*

The whole future of the white man in the Far East is confused and no glass can show it otherwise than darkly. And the darkest of all is the possibility envisaged by Nazi leaders of an Asia united against Europe. It is the old familiar nightmare of the Yellow Peril; but it may be used again as an excuse for a new conquest of the Far East by the white man. If it is, the Yellow Peril will be a peril indeed, especially if Russia decides not to be white. Then war, now destroying

mankind separately in the West and East, will complete the destruction in a last gigantic struggle of East against West.

Where is the voice in the world today to speak for the simple and practical wisdom of peace and good will among men?

Pearl Buck, author, in Foreign Affairs *(October 1940).*

[T]his week the Book of the Month judges, of whom I am one, chose a book called "Out of the Night" by a German who signs his name Jan Valtin. It is a marvelous story of a communist agitator of international scope who fell into the hands of the Nazi Gestapo, was taken to a concentration camp, and, of course, treated rough, turned Nazi spy, went into Russia and Norway, and escaped and came to America.

I am sending you the book. It's a most remarkable document—remarkable psychologically, remarkable as a revelation of a kind of work in continental Europe that will interest you. I wish you would read it.

William Allen White, journalist, letter of November 18, 1940, to FBI director J. Edgar Hoover, in Selected Letters of William Allen White, 1899–1943 *(1947).*

We must be the great arsenal of democracy. For us this is an emergency as serious as war itself. We must apply ourselves to our task with the same resolution, the same sense of urgency, the same spirit of patriotism and sacrifice as we would show were we at war.

We have furnished the British great material support and we will furnish far more in the future.

President Franklin D. Roosevelt advocating support of the forthcoming lend-lease program in his fireside chat of December 29, 1940, in Buhite and Levy, FDR's Fireside Chats *(1992).*

Meanwhile, the purple mountains of our own land look down upon a different army of refugees: 4,000,000 of them. They are refugees . . . from the silent gnawing of depression, from the inexorable constriction of a retarded economy. For ten years this army has been growing. Today it is growing still. These are America's Refugees. Not clipper-flown titled exiles; not Old World economic aristocrats. Just plain Americans, mostly young, mostly families; more whites and fewer aliens than in the rest of the population; 1,300,000 of them children. Poor in pocket, but pioneers in spirit. Exiles in the land of their birth—4,000,000 of them.

. . . Not only are no economic classes immune from the ravages of being uprooted (although the poor, of course, are hit the hardest), but no other division of population is secure from the threat of forcible migration. Protestant, Catholic and Jew alike share the discomforts of the transient camp. Negro and white pass and repass each other's tattered flivvers in search of employment. Italian, Norwegian and Pole and the descendants of these and half a hundred other nationalities face equally the noonday sun of the cotton field and the daylong rain filtering through a shanty's leaky roof. As neither creed, color nor country is exempt from a roving existence, so the evil genius of migrancy ignores neither age nor sex.

From naturalist and author Henry Hill Collins's book America's Own Refugees *(1941).*

In the conduct of relations with foreign governments, the policies of the New Deal reflected the contradictory sentiments of the country and the turbulent course of events in other parts of the world. After following for a time the traditional policy of recognizing *de facto* governments and doing business with "good" and "evil" governments under a positive conception of the national interest, President Roosevelt and the State Department set out on a course of lecturing and condemning governments out of line with the American way. By 1940 they had brought the United States into the position of practical isolation, in a world of powerful enemies, excepting perhaps Great Britain. Hammered by national indignation at Hitler and all his works, hammered by the incessant demands of what appears to be an overwhelming majority of the people for abstention from wars in Asia and Europe, engaged in a furious expansion of military preparations, President Roosevelt rendered aid to Great Britain short of armed action and, after openly repudiating the foreign policy enunciated in the platform of his party, endorsed its declaration: "We will not participate in foreign wars, and we will not send our Army, Naval, and Air forces to fight in foreign lands outside of the Americas, except in case of attack."

Historians Charles A. Beard and George H. E. Smith, from their book The Old Deal and the New *(1941).*

If we register under the act, even as conscientious objectors, we are becoming part of the act. . . . If a policeman (or a group of vigilantes) stops us on the street, our possession of the government's card shows that we are "all right"—we have complied with the act for the militarization of America. If that does not hurt our Christian consciences, what will? If we try to rationalize on the theory that we must go along with the act in order to fight the fascism and militarism of which it is part, it seems to us that we are doing that very thing which all pacifist Christians abhor: we are consciously employing bad means on the theory that to do so will contribute to a good end.

Seven students of Union Theological Seminary, court statement of 1941 on their refusal to register for conscription as required by the Selective Service and Training Act, in Lynd, Nonviolence in America: A Documentary History *(1966).*

He knew there were many stories about Russia, not to mention The Story, and he had employed a squad of writers and research men for over a year, but all the stories involved had the wrong feel. He felt it could be told in terms of the American thirteen states, but it kept coming out different, in new terms that opened unpleasant possibilities and problems. He considered he was very fair to Russia—he had no desire to make anything but a sympathetic picture, but it kept turning into a headache.

The character Monroe Stahr, film producer, in F. Scott Fitzgerald's novel The Last Tycoon *(1941).*

People under thirty in this country have a moral sense just as people over thirty do, just as both age groups speak the same language. . . . But if our moral sense is strong enough to make us feel guilty, but not strong enough to make us civilize ourselves, we may drive the next generation, who also have a moral sense and also want to be right—at least part of the time—into the fold of totalitarian leaders. The totalitarian leaders will not make the mistake of blaming and blackening those who by an accident of age are going to have to take it on the chin. They will praise them, encourage them, and give them work to do.

Margaret Mead, anthropologist, in Harper's *(January 1941).*

In public speeches I have warned the American people that if Britain is defeated, we ought then to be fully prepared to repel attempts by Germany to seize bases on this side of the Atlantic. Germany would use these bases either to attack us directly or else first to establish herself solidly in South America. Many of our people and many of the speakers who have opposed giving ample aid to Great Britain apparently believe it fantastic to think that there is any real danger of invasion. I disagree with such people and believe that a victorious Germany would move over to this hemisphere just as soon as she could accumulate the strength to do so, and certainly very soon unless we now take the steps to check her career of reckless aggression.

Secretary of the Navy Frank Knox, testifying before the Senate Foreign Relations Committee in January 1941, in support of the Lend-Lease Bill, in the Congressional Record *(1941).*

In the future days, which we seek to make secure, we look forward to a world founded upon four essential human freedoms.

The first is freedom of speech and expression everywhere in the world.

The second is freedom of every person to worship God in his own way everywhere in the world.

The third is freedom from want, which, translated into world terms, means economic understandings which will secure to every nation a healthy peacetime life for its inhabitants everywhere in the world.

The fourth is freedom from fear—which, translated into world terms, means a worldwide reduction of armaments to such a point and in such a thorough fashion that no nation will be in a position to commit an act of physical aggression against any neighbor—anywhere in the world.

That is no vision of a distant millennium. It is a definite basis for a kind of world attainable in our time and generation. That kind of world is the very antithesis of the so-called new order of tyranny which the dictators seek to create with the crash of a bomb.

President Franklin D. Roosevelt, annual State of the Union speech to Congress, January 6, 1941, in the Congressional Record *(1941).*

If the American people want a dictatorship—if they want a totalitarian form of government and if they want war—this bill should be steam-rollered through Congress, as is the wont of President Roosevelt.

Approval of this legislation means war, open and complete warfare. I, therefore, ask the American peo-

ple before they supinely accept it—Was the last World War worthwhile?

Senator Burton K. Wheeler of Montana, speech of January 12, 1941, opposing the Lend-Lease Bill, in Congressional Record Appendix *(1941).*

The probability is that the United States is about to collide with Hitler face to face. And the U.S. will either have to back down or fight.

In making this momentous decision there are two points of which we Americans must be aware. First, if we choose to back down and follow our isolationist line, we shall certainly have to fight anyway. It is almost inconceivable that Americans . . . could live in a world almost entirely totalitarian without clashing with those hostile forces . . . to suppose that Hitler will leave the Western Hemisphere alone is naive. . . . But if they [Americans] fight at that later time they will fight alone.

Secondly, it is necessary to remember that in this choice we are being presented with the last chance in our time to make the international view effective. . . . If we do not choose international democracy this time, *we* shall not have the opportunity to choose again.

Editorial, Fortune, *April 1941.*

This week's coal stoppage and the strike against Ford do not change the business outlook materially. The tieups impede the smooth flow of production, they tend to increase the operating costs of industry and so cut down profits, but they do not—they cannot for long—change the tidal wave of industrial expansion that started when the United States embarked on an all-out defense program last spring, following the capitulation of France.

Business Week, article of April 5, 1941.

A way to speed production and defense

America can't rearm with machines shut down. Isn't it practical patriotism as well as good business to buy equipment that will subject you to fewer delivery delays?

Advertisement for B. F. Goodrich, in Business Week *(April 5, 1941).*

While we should have been concentrating on American defense we have been forced to argue over foreign quarrels. We must turn our eyes and our faith back to our own country before it is too late. And when we do this a different vista opens before us. Practically every difficulty we would face in invading Europe becomes an asset to us in defending America. Our enemy, and not we, would then have the problem of transporting millions of troops across the ocean and landing them on a hostile shore. They, and not we, would have to furnish the convoys to transport guns and trucks and munitions and fuel across 3,000 miles of water. Our battleships and submarines would then be fighting close to their home bases. We would then do the bombing from the air and the torpedoing at sea.

Charles A. Lindbergh, radio broadcast of April 23, 1941, arguing against American intervention in the war and for support of the America First Committee, in the Congressional Record Appendix *(1941).*

Joe Louis *(Library of Congress)*

In Washington's Griffith Stadium one night last week 25,000 fight fans yelled themselves limp. It was the first round of Washington's first world-championship heavyweight fight, and there, hanging over the ropes, was Joe Louis, the champ. The boxer who had dumped him onto the ring apron was 25-year-old Buddy Baer, baby brother of one-time champion Max Baer.

Baby Baer in the fifth round brought the crowd to its feet again when he opened a gash over Louis' left eye. With blood streaming down his cheek for the first time in his career, the champion went after Baer with the savageness for which he is famed. In the sixth round he weakened the giant with chopping rights & lefts, and then felled him as though he were a redwood tree. At the count of seven, Baer staggered to his feet, only to be toppled again with another right to the jaw.

Time, sports article of June 2, 1941, on the world championship heavyweight boxing match between Joe Louis and Buddy "Baby" Baer.

Although the television industry in the United States appears to be on the edge of a boom, triggered off by the final consent of the Federal Communications Commission to permit commercial operation, it is still too early to forecast a wide-spread trend. Frequency modulation has now entered the picture. . . . This, of course, will make necessary major operations on, if not complete replacements of, those television receivers already in the hands of the public. Then, too, the national defense program looms large, taking precedence in essential materials that are necessary both to its needs and to the construction of television receivers. Thus any large-scale production in this field may be a long time coming, despite the enormous technical strides that have been made in the laboratories where television has been gestating for years.

Scientific American, article of July 1941.

We all listened breathlessly yesterday when the radio from England gave us a statement of the peace aims drawn up by the President and Mr. Winston Churchill. There was nothing new, nothing which I had not heard many times before in conversation about our foreign policy. Yet, stated this way to the people of the world, one felt it was an important moment in the history of world progress.

Eleanor Roosevelt on the Atlantic Charter, from her "My Day" newspaper column of August 16, 1941, quoted in Chadakoff, Eleanor Roosevelt's My Day *(1989).*

We have wished to avoid shooting. But the shooting has started. And history has recorded who fired the first shot. In the long run, however, all that will matter is who fired the last shot.

America has been attacked. The U.S.S. *Kearny* is not just a Navy ship. She belongs to every man, woman, and child in this nation....

The forward march of Hitler and of Hitlerism can be stopped—and it will be stopped. Very simply and very bluntly, we are pledged to pull our own oar in the destruction of Hitlerism. And when we have helped to end the curse of Hitlerism, we shall help to establish a new peace.

> *President Franklin D. Roosevelt, Navy Day speech of October 27, 1941, 10 days following the torpedoing of the* Kearny, *in the* Congressional Record Appendix *(1941).*

The repeal of Sections 2 and 3 of the Neutrality Act would mean the dispatch of American ships into British ports through the submarine blockade of the Germans. It cannot be doubted that many of those ships would be sunk and that many Americans would be drowned. It cannot be doubted that that would be the first result of our vote here to repeal the Neutrality Act and authorize Americans and American ships, not only authorize them but perhaps order them, to proceed into the battlefields of Europe.

> *Senator Robert A. Taft, speech before the Senate of October 28, 1941, opposing revision of the Neutrality Act to allow American ships to enter ports of belligerent nations, in the* Congressional Record *(1941).*

You can operate a Mimeograph duplicator in the privacy of your own office. Its speed ranges up to 150 copies in a minute. Those copies can be small tickets, simple bulletins or complicated forms.

America has found thousands of uses for this easy, economical method of duplication. America likes its neatness and legibility, its permanence and honesty, the way it works through the years and laughs at those years.

> *Advertisement for Mimeograph duplicators by A. B. Dick Company of Chicago, in* Fortune *(December 1941).*

The Japs came in from the southeast over Diamond Head. They could have been U.S. planes shuttling westward from San Diego.... They whined over Waikiki, over the candy-pink bulk of the Royal Hawaiian Hotel. All that they met as they came in was a tiny private plane in which Lawyer Ray Buduick was out for a Sunday morning ride. They riddled the lawyer's plane with machine-gun bullets, but the lawyer succeeded in making a safe landing. By the time he did, bombs were thudding all around the city.

Torpedoes launched from bombers tore at the dreadnoughts in Pearl Harbor. Dive-bombers swooped down on the Army's Hickam and Wheeler Fields. Shortly after the attack began, radio warnings were broadcast. But people who heard them were skeptical until explosions wrenched the guts of Honolulu. All the way from Pacific Heights to the center of town the planes soared, leaving a wake of destruction.

> Time, *reporting on the Japanese attack on Pearl Harbor, December 7, 1941 (December 15, 1941).*

We are now in this war. We are all in it—all the way. Every single man, woman, and child is a partner in the most tremendous undertaking of our American history. We must share together the bad news and the good news, the defeats and the victories—the changing fortunes of war.

> *President Franklin D. Roosevelt, fireside chat of December 9, 1941, in the* Congressional Record Appendix *(1941).*

APPENDIX A
Documents

1. The Eighteenth Amendment, ratified January 16, 1919
2. The Nineteenth Amendment, ratified August 18, 1920
3. The Senate resolution of ratification of the Treaty of Peace with Germany and the League of Nations, March 19, 1920
4. The Pact of Paris, August 27, 1928
5. The Stimson Doctrine, February 6, 1931
6. President Herbert Hoover's State of the Union Message to Congress, December 8, 1931
7. The Twentieth Amendment, ratified January 23, 1933
8. The Twenty-first Amendment, ratified December 5, 1933
9. First Inaugural Address of Franklin Delano Roosevelt, March 4, 1933
10. The Tennessee Valley Authority Act, signed into law May 18, 1933
11. The National Industrial Recovery Act, June 16, 1933
12. President Franklin D. Roosevelt's letter to Maxim Litvinov, Envoy of the USSR, November 16, 1933
13. The Johnson Act, April 13, 1934
14. Treaty between the United States and Cuba, signed May 29, 1934
15. Anti-War Treaty of Non-Aggression and Conciliation, ratified June 15, 1934
16. Emended text of the Supreme Court Opinion for *A. L. A. Schechter Poultry Corporation et al. v. United States,* May 27, 1935
17. Emended text of the Social Security Act, signed into law August 14, 1935
18. The Neutrality Act of 1937, signed into law May 1, 1937
19. President Franklin D. Roosevelt's State of the Union message to Congress, delivered January 6, 1941
20. The Lend-Lease Act, March 11, 1941
21. Executive Order 8802, establishing the President's Committee on Fair Employment Practices, issued June 25, 1941
22. The Atlantic Charter, August 12, 1941
23. President Franklin D. Roosevelt's request to Congress for a declaration of war on Japan, December 8, 1941
24. Declaration of War on Germany, December 11, 1941

1. THE EIGHTEENTH AMENDMENT, RATIFIED JANUARY 16, 1919

Section 1. After one year from the ratification of this article the manufacture, sale, or transportation of intoxicating liquors within, the importation thereof into, or the exportation thereof from the United States and all territory subject to the jurisdiction thereof for beverage purposes is hereby prohibited.

Section 2. The Congress and the several States shall have concurrent power to enforce this article by appropriate legislation.

Section 3. This article shall be inoperative unless it shall have been ratified as an amendment to the Constitution by the legislatures of the several States, as provided in the Constitution, within seven years from the date of the submission hereof to the States by the Congress.

2. THE NINETEENTH AMENDMENT, RATIFIED AUGUST 18, 1920

The right of the citizens of the United States to vote shall not be denied or abridged by the United States or by any State on account of sex.

Congress shall have power to enforce this article by appropriate legislation.

3. THE SENATE RESOLUTION OF RATIFICATION OF THE TREATY OF PEACE WITH GERMANY AND THE LEAGUE OF NATIONS, MARCH 19, 1920

The PRESIDENT pro tempore. Upon agreeing to the resolution of ratification the yeas are 49 and the nays are 35. Not having received the affirmative votes of two-thirds of the Senators present and voting, the resolution is not agreed to, and the Senate does not advise and consent to the ratification of the treaty of peace with Germany.

The resolution of ratification voted upon and rejected is as follows:

Resolution of Ratification

Resolved (two-thirds of the Senators present concurring therein), That the Senate advise and consent to the ratification of the treaty of peace with Germany concluded at Versailles on the 28th day of June, 1919, subject to the following reservations and understandings, which are hereby made a part and condition of this resolution of ratification, which ratification is not to take effect or bind the United States until the said reservations and understandings adopted by the Senate have been accepted as a part and a condition of this resolution of ratification by the allied and associated powers . . .:

1. The United States so understands and construes article I that in case of notice of withdrawal from the League of Nations, as provided in said article, the United States shall be the sole judge as to whether all its international obligations and all its obligations under the said covenant have been fulfilled, and notice of withdrawal by the United States may be given by a concurrent resolution of the Congress of the United States.

2. The United States assumes no obligation to preserve the territorial integrity or political independence of any other country by the employment of its military or naval forces, its resources, or any form of economic discrimination, or to interfere in any way in controversies between nations, including all controversies relating the territorial integrity or political independence . . . or to employ the military or naval forces of the United States . . . unless . . . the Congress, which under the Constitution, has the sole power to declare war or authorize the employment of the military or naval forces of the United States, shall, in the exercise of full liberty of action, by act or joint resolution so provide.

. . .

4. The United States reserves to itself exclusively the right to decide what questions are within its domestic jurisdiction and declares that all domestic and political questions relating wholly or in part to its internal affairs, including immigration, labor, coastwise traffic, the tariff, commerce, the suppression of traffic in women and children and in opium and other dangerous drugs, and all other domestic questions, are solely within the jurisdiction of the United States and are not under this treaty to be submitted in any way either to arbitration or to the consideration of the council or assembly of the League of Nations, or any agency thereof, or to the decision or recommendation of any other power.

5. The United States will not submit to arbitration or to inquiry by the assembly or by the council of the League of Nations, provided for in said treaty of peace, any questions which in the judgment of the United States depend upon or relate to its long-

established policy, commonly known as the Monroe Doctrine; said doctrine is to be interpreted by the United States alone.

. . .

7. No person is or shall be authorized to represent the United States, nor shall any citizen of the United States be eligible, as a member of any body or agency established or authorized by said treaty of peace with Germany, except pursuant to an act of the Congress of the United States providing for his appointment and defining his powers and duties.

8. The United States understands that the reparation commission will regulate or interfere with exports from the United States to Germany, or from Germany to the United States, only when the United States by act or joint resolution of Congress approves such regulation or interference.

9. The United States shall not be obligated to contribute to any expenses of the League of Nations, or of the secretariat, or of any commission, or committee, or conference, or other agency, organized under the League of Nations or under the treaty or for the purpose of carrying out the treaty provisions, unless and until an appropriation of funds available for such expenses shall have been made by the Congress of the United States: *Provided,* That the foregoing limitation shall not apply to the United States' proportionate share of the expense of the office force and salary of the secretary general.

10. No plan for the limitation of armaments proposed by the council of the League of Nations under the provision of article 8 shall be held as binding the United States until the same shall have been accepted by Congress, and the United States reserves the right to increase its armament without the consent of the council whenever the United States is threatened with invasion or engaged in war.

11. The United States reserves the right to permit, in its discretion, the nationals of a covenant-breaking State, as defined in article 16 of the covenant of the League of Nations, residing within the United States or in countries other than such covenant-breaking State, to continue their commercial, financial, and personal relations with the nationals of the United States.

. . .

14. Until Part I, being the covenant of the League of Nations, shall be so amended as to provide that the United States shall be entitled to cast a number of votes equal to that which any member of the league

and its self-governing dominions, colonies, or parts of empire, in the aggregate shall be entitled to cast, the United States assumes no obligation to be bound, except in cases where Congress has previously given its consent, by any election, decision, report, or finding of the council or assembly in which any member of the league and its self-governing dominions, colonies, or parts of empire, in the aggregate have cast more than one vote.

The United States assumes no obligation to be bound by any decision, report, or finding of the council or assembly arising out of any dispute between the United States and any member of the league if such member, or any self-governing dominion, colony, empire, or part of empire united with it politically has voted.

15. In consenting to the ratification of the treaty with Germany the United States adheres to the principle of self-determination and to the resolution of sympathy with the aspirations of the Irish people for a government of their own choice adopted by the Senate June 6, 1919, and declares that when such government is attained by Ireland, a consummation it is hoped at hand, it should promptly be admitted as a member of the League of Nations.

4. The Pact of Paris, August 27, 1928

The President of the German Reich, the President of the United States of America, His Majesty the King of the Belgians, the President of the French Republic, His Majesty the King of Great Britain, Ireland and the British Dominions beyond the Seas, Emperor of India, His Majesty the King of Italy, His Majesty the Emperor of Japan, the President of the Republic of Poland, the President of the Czechoslovak Republic,

Deeply sensible of their solemn duty to promote the welfare of mankind;

Persuaded that the time has come when a frank renunciation of war as an instrument of national policy should be made to the end that the peaceful and friendly relations now existing between their peoples may be perpetuated;

Convinced that all changes in their relations with one another should be sought only by pacific means and be the result of a peaceful and orderly process, and that any signatory power which shall hereafter seek to promote its national interests by resort to war should be denied the benefits furnished by this treaty;

Hopeful that, encouraged by their example, all the other nations of the world will join in this humane endeavor and by adhering to the present treaty as soon as it comes into force bring their peoples within the scope of its beneficent provisions, thus uniting the civilized nations of the world in a common renunciation of war as an instrument of their national policy;

Have decided to conclude a treaty and for that purpose have appointed as their respective plenipotentiaries: . . .

Who, having communicated to one another their full powers found in good and due form have agreed upon the following articles:

ART. 1. The high contracting parties solemnly declare in the names of their respective peoples that they condemn recourse to war for the solution of international controversies, and renounce it as an instrument of national policy in their relations with one another.

ART. 2. The high contracting parties agree that the settlement or solution of all disputes or conflicts of whatever nature or of whatever origin they may be, which may arise among them, shall never be sought except by pacific means.

ART. 3. The present treaty shall be ratified by the high contracting parties named in the preamble in accordance with their respective constitutional requirements, and shall take effect as between them as soon as all their several instruments of ratification shall have been deposited at Washington.

This treaty shall, when it has come into effect as prescribed in the preceding paragraph, remain open as long as may be necessary for adherence by all the other powers of the world. Every instrument evidencing the adherence of a power shall be deposited at Washington and the treaty shall immediately upon such deposit become effective as between the power thus adhering and the other powers parties hereto. . . .

5. THE STIMSON DOCTRINE, FEBRUARY 6, 1931

[Abbreviated text of an address by Secretary of State Henry L. Stimson to the Council on Foreign Relations]

. . . The practice of this country as to the recognition of new governments has been substantially uniform from the days of the administration of Secretary of State Jefferson in 1792 to the days of Secretary of State Bryan in 1913. There were certain slight departures from this policy during the Civil War, but they were manifestly due to the exigencies of warfare and were abandoned immediately afterwards. This general policy, as thus observed, was to base the act of recognition not upon the question of the constitutional legitimacy of the new government but upon its *de facto* capacity to fulfill its obligations as a member of the family of nations. This country recognized the right of other nations to regulate their own internal affairs of government and disclaimed any attempt to base its recognition upon the correctness of their constitutional action.

Said Mr. Jefferson in 1792:

We certainly cannot deny to other nations that principle whereon our own Government is founded, that every nation has a right to govern itself internally under what forms it pleases, and to change these forms at its own will; and externally to transact business with other nations through whatever organ it chooses, whether that be a king, convention, assembly, committee, president, or whatever it be.

In these essentials our practice corresponded with the practice of the other nations of the world.

The particular considerations upon which our action was regularly based were well stated by Mr. Adee, long the trusted Assistant Secretary of State of this Government, as follows:

Ever since the American Revolution entrance upon diplomatic intercourse with foreign states has been *de facto,* dependent upon the existence of three conditions of fact: the control of the administrative machinery of the state; the general acquiescence of its people; and the ability and willingness of their government to discharge international and conventional obligations. The form of government has not been a conditional factor in such recognition; in other words, the *de jure* element of legitimacy of title has been left aside.

With the advent of President Wilson's administration this policy of over a century was radically departed from in respect to the Republic of Mexico, and, by a public declaration on March 11, 1913, it was announced that

Cooperation (with our sister republics of Central and South America) is possible only when supported at every turn by the orderly processes of just government based upon law, not upon arbitrary or irregular force. We hold, as I am sure that all thoughtful leaders of republican government everywhere hold, that just government rests always upon the consent of the governed, and that there can be no freedom without order based upon law and upon the public conscience and approval. We shall look to make these principles the basis of mutual intercourse, respect, and helpfulness between or sister republics and ourselves.

Mr. Wilson's government sought to put this new policy into effect in respect to the recognition of the then Government of Mexico held by President Victoriano Huerta. Although Huerta's government was in *de facto* possession, Mr. Wilson refused to recognize it, and he sought through the influence and pressure of his great office to force it from power. Armed conflict followed with the forces of Mexico, and disturbed relations between us and that republic lasted until a comparatively few years ago.

In his sympathy for the development of free constitutional institutions among the people of our Latin American neighbors, Mr. Wilson did not differ from the feelings of the great mass of his countrymen . . ., but he differed from the practice of his predecessors in seeking actively to propagate these institutions in a foreign country by the direct influence of this Government and to do this against the desires of the authorities and people of Mexico.

The present administration had declined to follow the policy of Mr. Wilson and has followed consistently the former practice of this Government since the days of Jefferson. As soon as it was reported to us, through our diplomatic representatives, that the new governments in Bolivia, Peru, Argentina, Brazil, and Panama were in control of the administrative machinery of the state, with the apparent general acquiescence of their people, and that they were willing and apparently able to discharge their international and conventional obligations, they were recognized by our Government. And, in view of the economic depression, with the consequent need for prompt measures of financial stabilization, we did this with as little delay as possible in order to give those sorely pressed countries the quickest possible opportunities for recovering their economic poise.

6. President Herbert Hoover's State of the Union Message to Congress, December 8, 1931

It is my duty under the Constitution to transmit to the Congress information on the state of the Union and to recommend for its consideration necessary and expedient measures.

The chief influence affecting the state of the Union during the past year has been the continued world-wide economic disturbance. Our national concern has been to meet the emergencies it has created for us and to lay the foundations for recovery.

If we lift our vision beyond these immediate emergencies we find fundamental national gains even amid depression. In meeting the problems of this difficult period, we have witnessed a remarkable development of the sense of cooperation in the community. For the first time in the history of our major economic depressions there has been a notable absence of public disorders and industrial conflict. Above all there is an enlargement of social and spiritual responsibility among the people. The strains and stresses upon business have resulted in closer application, in saner policies, and in better methods. Public improvements have been carried out on a larger scale than even in normal times. The country is richer in physical property, in newly discovered resources, and in productive capacity than ever before. There has been constant gain in knowledge and education; there has been continuous advance in science and invention; there has been distinct gain in public health. Business depressions have been recurrent in the life of our country and are but transitory. The Nation has emerged from each of them with increased strength and virility because of the enlightenment they have brought, the readjustments and the larger understanding of the realities and obligations of life and work which come from them.

. . .

The Domestic Situation

Many undertakings have been organized and forwarded during the past year to meet the new and changing emergencies which have constantly confronted us.

Broadly the community has cooperated to meet the needs of honest distress, and to take such emergency measures as would sustain confidence in our financial system and would cushion the violence of liquidation in industry and commerce, thus giving time for orderly readjustment of costs, inventories, and credits without panic and widespread bankruptcy. These measures have served those purposes and will promote recovery.

In these measures we have striven to mobilize and stimulate private initiative and local and community responsibility. There has been the least possible Government entry into the economic field, and that only in temporary and emergency form. Our citizens and our local governments have given a magnificent display of unity and action, initiative and patriotism in solving a multitude of difficulties and in cooperating with the Federal Government.

For a proper understanding of my recommendations to the Congress it is desirable very briefly to review such activities during the past year.

The emergencies of unemployment have been met by action in many directions. The appropriations for the continued speeding up of the great Federal construction program have provided direct and indirect aid to employment upon a large scale. By organized unity of action, the States and municipalities have also maintained large programs of public improvement. Many industries have been prevailed upon to anticipate and intensify construction. Industrial concerns and other employers have been organized to spread available work amongst all their employees, instead of discharging a portion of them. A large majority have maintained wages at as high levels as the safe conduct of their business would permit. This course has saved us from industrial conflict and disorder which have characterized all previous depressions. Immigration has been curtailed by administrative action. Upon the basis of normal immigration the decrease amounts to about 300,000 individuals who otherwise would have been added to our unemployment. The expansion of Federal employment agencies under appropriations by the Congress has proved most effective. Through the President's organization for unemployment relief, public and private agencies were successfully mobilized last winter to provide employment and other measures against distress. Similar organization gives assurance against suffering during the coming winter. Committees of leading citizens are now active at practically every point of unemployment. In the large majority they have been assured the funds necessary which together with local government aids, will meet the situation.

A few exceptional localities will be further organized. The evidence of the Public Health Service shows an actual decrease of sickness and infant and general mortality below normal years. No greater proof could be adduced that our people have been protected from hunger and cold and that the sense of social responsibility in the Nation has responded to the need of the unfortunate.

To meet the emergencies in agriculture the loans authorized by Congress for rehabilitation in the drought areas have enabled farmers to produce abundant crops in those districts. The Red Cross undertook and magnificently administered relief for over 2,500,000 drought sufferers last winter. It has undertaken this year to administer relief to 100,000 sufferers in the new drought area of certain Northwest States. The action of the Federal Farm Board in granting credits to farm cooperatives saved many of them from bankruptcy and increased their purpose and strength. By enabling farm cooperatives to cushion the fall in prices of farm products in 1930 and 1931 the Board secured higher prices to the farmer than would have been obtained otherwise, although the benefits of this action were partially defeated by continued world overproduction. Incident to this action the failure of a large number of farmers and of country banks was averted which could quite possibly have spread into a major disaster. The banks in the South have cooperated with the Farm Board in creation of a pool for the better marketing of accumulated cotton. Growers have been materially assisted by this action. Constant effort has been made to reduce overproduction in relief of agriculture and to promote the foreign buying of agricultural products by sustaining economic stability abroad.

To meet our domestic emergencies in credit and banking arising from the reaction to acute crises abroad the National Credit Association was set up by the banks with resources of $500,000,000 to support sound banks against the frightened withdrawals and hoarding. It is giving aid to reopen solvent banks which have been closed. Federal officials have brought about many beneficial unions of banks and have employed other means which have prevented many bank closings. As a result of these measures the hoarding withdrawals which had risen to over $250,000,000 per week after the British crisis have substantially ceased.

Further Measures

The major economic forces and weaknesses at home and abroad have now been exposed and can be appraised, and the time is ripe for forward action to expedite our recovery.

Although some of the causes of our depression are due to speculation, inflation of securities and real estate, unsound foreign investments, and mismanagement of financial institutions, yet our self-contained national economy, with its matchless strength and resources, would have enabled us to recover long since but for the continued dislocations, shocks, and setbacks from abroad.

Whatever the causes may be, the vast liquidation and readjustments which have taken place have left us with a large degree of credit paralysis, which, together with the situation in our railways and the conditions abroad, are now the outstanding obstacles to recuperation. If we can put our financial resources to work and can ameliorate the financial situation in the railways, I am confident we can make a large measure of recovery independent of the rest of the world. A strong America is the highest contribution to world stability.

One phase of the credit situation is indicated in the banks. During the past year banks, representing 3 per cent of our total deposits have been closed. A large part of these failures have been caused by withdrawals for hoarding, as distinguished from the failures early in the depression where weakness due to mismanagement was the larger cause of failure. Despite their closing, many of them will pay in full. Although such withdrawals have practically ceased, yet $1,100,000,000 of currency was previously withdrawn which has still to return to circulation. This represents a large reduction of the ability of our banks to extend credit which would otherwise fertilize industry and agriculture. Furthermore, many of our bankers, in order to prepare themselves to meet possible withdrawals, have felt compelled to call in loans, to refuse new credits, and to realize upon securities, which in turn has demoralized the markets. The paralysis has been further augmented by the steady increase in recent years of the proportion of bank assets invested in long-term securities, such as mortgages and bonds. These securities tend to lose their liquidity in depression or temporarily to fall in value so that the ability of the banks to meet the shock of sudden withdrawal is greatly lessened and the restric-

tion of all kinds of credit is thereby increased. The continuing credit paralysis has operated to accentuate the deflation and liquidation of commodities, real estate, and securities below any reasonable basis of values.

All of this tends to stifle business, especially the smaller units, and finally expresses itself in further depression of prices and values, in restriction on new enterprise, and in increased unemployment.

The situation largely arises from an unjustified lack of confidence. We have enormous volumes of idle money in the banks and in hoarding. We do not require more money or working capital—we need to put what we have to work.

The fundamental difficulties which have brought about financial strains in foreign countries do not exist in the United States. No external drain on our resources can threaten our position, because the balance of international payments is in our favor; we owe less to foreign countries than they owe to us; our industries are efficiently organized; our currency and bank deposits are protected by the greatest gold reserve in history.

Our first step toward recovery is to reestablish confidence and thus restore the flow of credit which is the very basis of our economic life. We must put some steel beams in the foundations of our credit structure. It is our duty to apply the full strength of our Government not only to the immediate phases, but to provide security against shocks and the repetition of the weaknesses which have been proven.

The recommendations which I here lay before the Congress are designed to meet these needs by strengthening financial, industrial, and agricultural life through the medium of our existing institutions, and thus to avoid the entry of the Government into competition with private business.

Federal Government Finance

The first requirement of confidence and of economic recovery is financial stability of the United States Government. I shall deal with fiscal questions at greater length in the Budget message. But I must at this time call attention to the magnitude of the deficits which have developed and the resulting necessity for determined and courageous policies. These deficits arise in the main from the heavy decrease in tax receipts due to the depression and to the increase in expenditure on construction in aid to unemployment, aids to agriculture, and upon services to veterans.

During the fiscal year ending June 30 last we incurred a deficit of about $903,000,000, which included the statutory reduction of the debt and represented an increase of the national debt by $616,000,000. Of this, however, $153,000,000 is offset by increased cash balances.

In comparison with the fiscal year 1928 there is indicated a fall in Federal receipts for the present fiscal year amounting to $1,683,000,000, of which $1,034,000,000 is in individual and corporate income taxes alone. During this fiscal year there will be an increased expenditure, as compared to 1928, on veterans of $255,000,000, and an increased expenditure on construction work which may reach $520,000,000. Despite large economies in other directions, we have an indicated deficit, including the statutory retirement of the debt, of $2,123,000,000, and an indicated net debt increase of about $1,711,000,000.

The Budget for the fiscal year beginning July 1 next, after allowing for some increase of taxes under the present laws and after allowing for drastic reduction in expenditures, still indicates a deficit of $1,417,000,000. After offsetting the statutory debt retirements this would indicate an increase in the national debt for the fiscal year 1933 of about $921,000,000.

Several conclusions are inevitable. We must have insistent and determined reduction in Government expenses. We must face a temporary increase in taxes. Such increase should not cover the whole of these deficits or it will retard recovery. We must partially finance the deficit by borrowing. It is my view that the amount of taxation should be fixed so as to balance the Budget for 1933 except for the statutory debt retirement. Such Government receipts would assure the balance of the following year's budget including debt retirement. It is my further view that the additional taxation should be imposed solely as an emergency measure terminating definitely two years from July 1 next. Such a basis will give confidence in the determination of the Government to stabilize its finance and will assure taxpayers of its temporary character. Even with increased taxation, the Government will reach the utmost safe limit of its borrowing capacity by the expenditures for which we are already obligated and the recommendation here proposed. To go further than these limits in either

expenditures, taxes, or borrowing will destroy confidence, denude commerce and industry of its resources, jeopardize the financial system, and actually extend unemployment and demoralize agriculture rather than relieve it.

Federal Land Banks

I recommend that the Congress authorize the subscription by the Treasury of further capital to the Federal land banks to be retired as provided in the original act, or when funds are available, and that repayments of such capital be treated as a fund available for further subscriptions in the same manner. It is urgent that the banks be supported so as to stabilize the market values of their bonds and thus secure capital for the farmers at low rates, that they may continue their services to agriculture and that they may meet the present situation with consideration to the farmers.

Deposits in Closed Banks

A method should be devised to make available quickly to depositors some portion of their deposits in closed banks as the assets of such banks may warrant. Such provision would go far to relieve distress in a multitude of families, would stabilize values in many communities, and would liberate working capital to thousands of concerns. I recommend that measures be enacted promptly to accomplish these results and I suggest that the Congress should consider the development of such a plan through the Federal Reserve Banks.

Home Loan Discount Banks

I recommend the establishment of a system of home loan discount banks as the necessary companion in our financial structure of the Federal Reserve Banks and our Federal Land Banks. Such action will relieve present distressing pressures against home and farm property owners. It will relieve pressures upon and give added strength to building and loan associations, savings banks, and deposit banks, engaged in extending such credits. Such action would further decentralize our credit structure. It would revive residential construction and employment. It would enable such loaning institutions more effectually to promote home ownership. I discussed this plan at some length in a statement made public November 14, last. This plan has been warmly indorsed by the recent

National Conference upon Home Ownership and Housing, whose members were designated by the governors of the States and the groups interested.

Reconstruction Finance Corporation

In order that the public may be absolutely assured and that the Government may be in position to meet any public necessity, I recommend that an emergency Reconstruction Finance Corporation of the nature of the former War Finance Corporation should be established. It may not be necessary to use such an instrumentality very extensively. The very existence of such a bulwark will strengthen confidence. The Treasury should be authorized to subscribe a reasonable capital to it, and it should be given authority to issue its own debentures. It should be placed in liquidation at the end of two years. Its purpose is that by strengthening the weak spots to thus liberate the full strength of the Nation's resources. It should be in position to facilitate exports by American agencies; make advances to agricultural credit agencies where necessary to protect and aid the agricultural industry; to make temporary advances upon proper securities to established industries, railways, and financial institutions which can not otherwise secure credit, and where such advances will protect the credit structure and stimulate employment. Its functions would not overlap those of the National Credit Corporation.

Federal Reserve Eligibility

On October 6th I issued a statement that I should recommend to the Congress an extension during emergencies of the eligibility provision in the Federal reserve act. This statement was approved by a representative gathering of the Members of both Houses of the Congress, including members of the appropriate committees. It was approved by the officials of the Treasury Department, and I understand such an extension has been approved by a majority of the governors of the Federal reserve banks. Nothing should be done which would lower the safeguards of the system.

The establishment of the mortgage-discount banks herein referred to will also contribute to further reserve strength in the banks without inflation.

Banking Laws

Our people have a right to a banking system in which their deposits shall be safeguarded and the flow of credit less subject to storms. The need of a sounder system is plainly shown by the extent of bank failures. I recommend the prompt improvement of the banking laws. Changed financial conditions and commercial practices must be met. The Congress should investigate the need for separation between different kinds of banking; an enlargement of branch banking under proper restrictions; and the methods by which enlarged membership in the Federal reserve system may be brought about.

...

Conclusion

It is inevitable that in these times much of the legislation proposed to the Congress and many of the recommendations of the Executive must be designed to meet emergencies. In reaching solutions we must not jeopardize those principles which we have found to be the basis of the growth of the Nation. The Federal Government must not encroach upon nor permit local communities to abandon that precious possession of local initiative and responsibility. Again, just as the largest measure of responsibility in the government of the Nation rests upon local selfgovernment, so does the largest measure of social responsibility in our country rest upon the individual. If the individual surrenders his own initiative and responsibilities, he is surrendering his own freedom and his own liberty. It is the duty of the National Government to insist that both the local governments and the individual shall assume and bear these responsibilities as a fundamental of preserving the very basis of our freedom.

Many vital changes and movements of vast proportions are taking place in the economic world. The effect of these changes upon the future can not be seen clearly as yet. Of this, however, we are sure: Our system, based upon the ideals of individual initiative and of equality of opportunity, is not an artificial thing. Rather it is the outgrowth of the experience of America, and expresses the faith and spirit of our people. It has carried us in a century and a half to leadership of the economic world. If our economic system does not match our highest expectations at all times, it does not require revolutionary action to bring it into accord with any necessity that experience may prove. It has successfully adjusted itself to changing conditions in the past. It will do so again. The mobility of our institutions, the richness of our resources, and the abilities of our people enable us to meet them unafraid. It is a distressful time for many of our people, but they have shown qualities as high in fortitude, courage, and resourcefulness as ever in our history. With that spirit, I have faith that out of it will come a sounder life, a truer standard of values, a greater recognition of the results of honest effort, and a healthier atmosphere in which to rear our children. Ours must be a country of such stability and security as can not fail to carry forward and enlarge among all the people that abundant life of material and spiritual opportunity which it has represented among all nations since its beginning.

7. THE TWENTIETH AMENDMENT, RATIFIED JANUARY 23, 1933

Section 1. The terms of the President and Vice-President shall end at noon on the 20th day of January, and the terms of Senators and Representatives at noon on the 3d day of January, of the years in which such terms would have ended if this article had not been ratified; and the terms of their successors shall then begin.

Section 2. The Congress shall assemble at least once in every year, and such meeting shall begin at noon on the 3d day of January, unless they shall by law appoint a different day.

Section 3. If, at the time fixed for the beginning of the term of the President, the President elect shall have died, the Vice-President elect shall become President. If a President shall not have been chosen before the time fixed for the beginning of his term, or if the President elect shall have failed to qualify, then the Vice-President elect shall act as President until a President shall have qualified; and the Congress may by law provide for the case wherein neither a President elect nor a Vice-President shall have qualified, declaring who shall then act as President, or the manner in which one who is to act shall be selected, and such person shall act accordingly until a President or Vice-President shall have qualified.

Section 4. The Congress may by law provide for the case of the death of any of the persons from whom the House of Representatives may choose a President whenever the right of choice shall have devolved upon them, and for the case of the death of any of the persons from whom the Senate may choose a Vice-President whenever the right of the choice shall have devolved upon them.

Section 5. Sections 1 and 2 shall take effect on the 13th day of October following the ratification of this article.

Section 6. This article shall be inoperative unless it shall have been ratified as an amendment to the Constitution by the legislatures of three-fourths of the several States within seven years from the date of its submission.

8. THE TWENTY-FIRST AMENDMENT, RATIFIED DECEMBER 5, 1933

Section 1. The eighteenth article of amendment to the Constitution of the United States is hereby repealed.

Section 2. The transportation or importation into any State, Territory, or possession of the United States for delivery or use therein of intoxicating liquors, in violation of the laws thereof, is hereby prohibited.

Section 3. This article shall be inoperative unless it shall have been ratified as an amendment to the Constitution by convention in the several States, as provided in the Constitution, within seven years from the date of the submission hereof to the States by the Congress.

9. FIRST INAUGURAL ADDRESS OF FRANKLIN DELANO ROOSEVELT, MARCH 4, 1933

I am certain that my fellow Americans expect that on my induction into the presidency I will address them with a candor and a decision which the present situation of our nation impels. This is preeminently the time to speak the truth, the whole truth, frankly and boldly. Nor need we shrink from honestly facing conditions in our country today. This great nation will endure as it has endured, will revive and will prosper.

So, first of all, let me assert my firm belief that the only thing we have to fear is fear itself—nameless, unreasoning, unjustified terror which paralyzes needed efforts to convert retreat into advance. In every dark hour of our national life a leadership of frankness and vigor has met with that understanding and support of the people themselves which is essential to victory. I am convinced that you will again give that support to leadership in these critical days.

In such a spirit on my part and on yours we face our common difficulties. They concern, thank God, only material things. Values have shrunken to fantastic levels; taxes have risen; our ability to pay has fallen; government of all kinds is faced by serious curtailment of income; the means of exchange are frozen in the currents of trade; the withered leaves of industrial enterprise lie on every side; farmers find no markets for their produce; the savings of many years in thousands of families are gone.

More important, a host of unemployed citizens face the grim problem of existence, and an equally great number toil with little return. Only a foolish optimist can deny the dark realities of the moment.

Yet our distress comes from no failure of substance. We are stricken by no plague of locusts. Compared with the perils which our forefathers conquered because they believed and were not afraid, we have still much to be thankful for. Nature still offers her bounty, and human efforts have multiplied it. Plenty is at our doorstep, but a generous use of it languishes in the very sight of the supply. Primarily this is because the rulers of the exchange of mankind's goods have failed, through their own stubbornness and their own incompetence, have admitted their failure, and have abdicated. Practices of the unscrupulous money changers stand indicted in the court of public opinion, rejected by the hearts and minds of men.

True they have tried, but their efforts have been cast in the pattern of an outworn tradition. Faced by failure of credit, they have proposed only the lending of more money. Stripped of the lure of profit by which to induce our people to follow their false leadership, they have resorted to exhortations, pleading tearfully for restored confidence. They know only the rules of a generation of selfseekers. They have no vision, and when there is no vision the people perish.

The money changers have fled from their high seats in the temple of our civilization. We may now restore that temple to the ancient truths. The measure of the restoration lies in the extent to which we apply social values more noble than mere monetary profit.

Happiness lies not in the mere possession of money; it lies in the joy of achievement, in the thrill of creative effort. The joy and moral stimulation of work no longer must be forgotten in the mad chase of evanescent profits. These dark days will be worth all they cost us if they teach us that our true destiny is not to be ministered unto but to minister to ourselves and to our fellowmen.

Recognition of the falsity of material wealth as the standard of success goes hand in hand with the abandonment of the false belief that public office and high political position are to be valued only by the standards of pride of place and personal profit; and there must be an end to a conduct in banking and in business which too often has given to a sacred trust the likeness of callous and selfish wrongdoing. Small wonder that confidence languishes, for it thrives only on honesty, on honor, on the sacredness of obligations, on faithful protection, on unselfish performance; without them it cannot live.

Restoration calls, however, not for changes in ethics alone. This nation asks for action, and action now.

Our greatest primary task is to put people to work. This is no unsolvable problem if we face it wisely and courageously. It can be accomplished in part by direct recruiting by the government itself, treating the task as we would treat the emergency of a war, but, at the same time, through this employment, accomplishing greatly needed projects to stimulate and reorganize the use of our natural resources.

Hand in hand with this we must frankly recognize the overbalance of population in our industrial centers and, by engaging on a national scale in a redistribution, endeavor to provide a better use of the land for those best fitted for the land. The task can be helped by definite efforts to raise the values of agricultural products and with this the power to purchase the output of our cities. It can be helped by preventing realistically the tragedy of the growing loss through foreclosure of our small homes and our farms. It can be helped by insistence that the federal, state, and local governments act forthwith on the demand that their cost be drastically reduced. It can be helped by the unifying of relief activities which today are often scattered, uneconomical, and unequal. It can be helped by national planning for and supervision of all forms of transportation and of communication and other utilities which have a definitely public character. There are many ways in which it can be helped, but it can never be helped merely by talking about it. We must act and act quickly.

Finally, in our progress toward a resumption of work, we require two safeguards against a return of the evils of the old order: there must be a strict supervision of all banking and credits and investments; there must be an end to speculation with other people's money, and there must be provision for an adequate but sound currency.

These are the lines of attack. I shall presently urge upon a new Congress in special session detailed measures for their fulfillment, and I shall seek the immediate assistance of the several states.

Through this program of action we address ourselves to putting our own national house in order and making income balance outgo. Our international trade relations, though vastly important, are in point of time and necessity secondary to the establishment of a sound national economy. I favor as a practical policy the putting of first things first. I shall spare no effort to restore world trade by international economic readjustment, but the emergency at home cannot wait on that accomplishment.

The basic thought that guides these specific means of national recovery is not narrowly nationalistic. It is the insistence, as a first consideration, upon the interdependence of the various elements in and parts of the United States—a recognition of the old and permanently important manifestation of the American spirit of the pioneer. It is the way to recovery. It is the immediate way. It is the strongest assurance that the recovery will endure.

In the field of world policy I would dedicate this nation to the policy of the good neighbor—the neighbor who resolutely respects himself and, because he does so, respects the rights of others—the neighbor who respects his obligations and respects the sanctity of his agreements in and with a world of neighbors.

If I read the temper of our people correctly, we now realize as we have never realized before our interdependence on each other; that we cannot merely take but we must give as well; that if we are to go forward, we must move as a trained and loyal army willing to sacrifice for the good of a common discipline, because with out such discipline no progress is made, no leadership becomes effective. We are, I know, ready and willing to submit our lives and property to such discipline, because it makes possible a leadership which aims at a larger good. This I propose to offer, pledging that the larger purposes will bind upon us all as a sacred obligation, with a unity of duty hitherto evoked only in time of armed strife.

With this pledge taken, I assume unhesitatingly the leadership of this great army of our people dedicated to a disciplined attack upon our common problems.

Action in this image and to this end is feasible under the form of government which we have inherited from our ancestors. Our Constitution is so simple and practical that it is possible always to meet extraordinary needs by changes in emphasis and arrangement without loss of essential form. That is why our constitutional system has proved itself the most superbly enduring political mechanism the modern world has produced. It has met every stress of vast expansion of territory, of foreign wars, of bitter internal strife, of world relations.

It is to be hoped that the normal balance of executive and legislative authority may be wholly adequate to meet the unprecedented task before us. But it may be that an unprecedented demand and need for undelayed action may call for temporary departure from that normal balance of public procedure.

I am prepared under my constitutional duty to recommend the measures that a stricken nation in the midst of a stricken world may require. These measures, or such other measures as the Congress may build out of its experience and wisdom, I shall seek, within my constitutional authority, to bring to speedy adoption.

But in the event that the Congress shall fail to take one of these two courses, and in the event that the national emergency is still critical, I shall not evade the clear course of duty that will then confront me. I shall ask the Congress for the one remaining instrument to meet the crisis—broad executive power to wage a war against the emergency, as great as the power that would be given to me if we were in fact invaded by a foreign foe.

For the trust reposed in me I will return the courage and the devotion that befit the time. I can do no less.

We face the arduous days that lie before us in the warm courage of national unity; with the clear consciousness of seeking old and precious moral values; with the clean satisfaction that comes from the stern performance of duty by old and young alike. We aim at the assurance of a rounded and permanent national life.

We do not distrust the future of essential democracy. The people of the United States have not failed. In their need they have registered a mandate that they want direct, vigorous action. They have asked for discipline and direction under leadership. They have made me the present instrument of their wishes. In the spirit of the gift I take it.

In this dedication of a nation we humbly ask the blessing of God. May He protect each and every one of us. May He guide me in the days to come.

10. THE TENNESSEE VALLEY AUTHORITY ACT, SIGNED INTO LAW MAY 18, 1933

AN ACT to improve the navigability and to provide for the flood control of the Tennessee River; to provide for reforestation and the proper use of marginal lands in the Tennessee Valley; to provide for the agricultural and industrial development of said valley; to provide for the national defense by the creation of a corporation for the operation of Government properties at and near Muscle Shoals in the State of Alabama, and for other purposes. . . .

Be it enacted, That for the purpose of maintaining and operating the properties now owned by the United States in the vicinity of Muscle Shoals, Alabama . . . there is hereby created a body corporate by the name of the "Tennessee Valley Authority." . . .

Sec. 2. . . .

(f) No director shall have a financial interest in any public-utility corporation engaged in the business of distributing and selling power to the public nor in any corporation engaged in the manufacture, selling, or distribution of fixed nitrogen or fertilizer, or any ingredients thereof, nor shall any member have any interest in any business that may be adversely affected by the success of the Corporation as a producer of concentrated fertilizers or as a producer of electric power. . . .

Sec. 3. . . .

All contracts to which the Corporation is a party and which require the employment of laborers and mechanics in the construction, alteration, maintenance, or repair of buildings, dams, locks, or other projects shall contain a provision that not less than the prevailing rate of wages for work of a similar nature prevailing in the vicinity shall be paid to such laborers or mechanics. . . .

Sec. 4. Except as otherwise specifically provided in this Act, the Corporation—

. . .

(f) May purchase or lease and hold such real and personal property as it deems necessary or convenient in the transaction of its business, and may dispose of any such personal property held by it. . . .

(h) Shall have power in the name of the United States of America to exercise the right of eminent domain, and in the purchase of any real estate or the acquisition of real estate by condemnation proceedings, the title of such real estate shall be taken in the name of the United States of America. . . .

(i) Shall have power to acquire real estate for the construction of dams, reservoirs, power houses, power structures, transmission lines, navigation projects, and incidental works in the Tennessee River and its tributaries, and to unite the various power installations into one or more systems by transmission lines.

Sec. 5. The board is hereby authorized—

. . .

(b) To arrange with farmers and farm organizations for large-scale practical use of the new forms of fertilizers under conditions permitting an accurate measure of the economic return they produce.

(c) To cooperate with National, State, district, or county experimental stations or demonstration farms, for the use of new forms of fertilizer or fertilizer practices during the initial or experimental period of their introduction.

(d) The board in order to improve and cheapen the production of fertilizer is authorized to manufacture and sell fixed nitrogen, fertilizer, and fertilizer ingredients at Muscle Shoals by the employment of existing facilities, by modernizing existing plants, or by any other process or processes that in its judgment shall appear wise and profitable for the fixation of atmospheric nitrogen or the cheapening of the production of fertilizer.

(e) Under the authority of this Act the board may make donations or sales of the product of the plant or plants operated by it to be fairly and equitably distributed through the agency of county demonstration agents, agricultural colleges, or otherwise as the board may direct, for experimentation, education, and introduction of the use of such products in cooperation with practical farmers so as to obtain information as to the value, effect, and best methods of their use.

. . .

(h) To establish, maintain, and operate laboratories and experimental plants, and to undertake experiments for the purpose of enabling the Corporation to furnish nitrogen products for military purposes, and nitrogen and other fertilizer products for agricultural purposes in the most economical manner and at the highest standard of efficiency. . . .

. . .

(l) To produce, distribute, and sell electric power, as herein particularly specified.

(m) No products of the Corporation shall be sold for use outside of the United States, its Territories and possessions, except to the United States Government for the use of its Army and Navy, or to its allies in case of war.

Sec. 10. The board is hereby empowered and authorized to sell the surplus power not used in its operations, and for operation of locks and other works generated by it, to States, counties, municipalities, corporations, partnerships, or individuals, according to the policies hereinafter set forth; and to carry out said authority, the board is authorized to enter into contracts for such sale for a term not exceeding twenty years, and in the sale of such current by the board it shall give preference to States, counties, municipalities, and cooperative organizations of citizens or farmers, not organized or doing business for profit, but primarily for the purpose of supplying electricity to its own citizens or members. . . . In order to promote and encourage the fullest possible use of electric light and power on farms within reasonable distance of any of its transmission lines the board in its discretion shall have power to construct transmission lines to farms and small villages that are not otherwise supplied with electricity at reasonable rates, and to make such rules and regulations governing such sale and distribution of such electric power as in its judgment may be just and equitable: *Provided further,* That the board is hereby authorized and directed to make studies, experiments, and determinations to promote the wider and better use of electric power for agricultural and domestic use, or for small or local industries, and it may cooperate with State governments, or their subdivisions or agencies, with educational or research institutions, and with cooperatives or other organizations, in the application of electric power to the fuller and better balanced development of the resources of the region.

Sec. 11. It is hereby declared to be the policy of the Government so far as practical to distribute and sell the surplus power generated at Muscle Shoals equitably among States, counties, and municipalities within transmission distance. This policy is further declared to be that the projects herein provided for shall be considered primarily as for the benefit of the people of the section as a whole and particularly the domestic and rural consumers to whom the power can economically be made available, and accordingly that sale to and use by industry shall be a secondary purpose, to be utilized principally to secure a sufficiently high load factor and revenue returns which will permit domestic and rural use at the lowest possible rates and in such manner as to encourage increased domestic and rural use of electricity. It is further hereby declared to be the policy of the Government to utilize the Muscle Shoals properties so far as may be necessary to improve, increase and cheapen the production of fertilizer and fertilizer ingredients. . . .

11. THE NATIONAL INDUSTRIAL RECOVERY ACT, JUNE 16, 1933

AN ACT to encourage national industrial recovery, to foster fair competition, and to provide for the construction of certain useful public works, and for other purposes.

Title I—Industrial Recovery

DECLARATION OF POLICY

Sec. 1. A national emergency productive of widespread unemployment and disorganization of industry, which burdens interstate and foreign commerce, affects the public welfare, and undermines the standards of living of the American people, is hereby declared to exist. It is hereby declared to be the policy of Congress to remove obstructions to the free flow of interstate and foreign commerce which tend to diminish the amount thereof; and to provide for the general welfare by promoting the organization of industry for the purpose of cooperative action among trade groups, to induce and maintain united action of labor and management under adequate governmental sanctions and supervision, to eliminate unfair competitive practices, to promote the fullest possible utilization of the present productive capacity of industries, to avoid undue restriction of production (except as may be temporarily required), to increase the consumption of industrial and agricultural products by increasing purchasing power, to reduce and relieve unemployment, to improve standards of labor, and otherwise to rehabilitate industry and to conserve natural resources.

12. President Franklin D. Roosevelt's Letter to Maxim Litvinov, Envoy of the USSR, November 16, 1933

Formalizing the terms of their agreement securing official United States recognition of the USSR and the exchange of ambassadors

I am glad to have received the assurance expressed in your note to me of this date that it will be the fixed policy of the government of the Union of Soviet Socialist Republics:

1. To respect scrupulously the indisputable right of the United States to order its own life within its own jurisdiction in its own way and to refrain from interfering in any manner in the internal affairs of the United States, its territories, or possessions.

2. To refrain and to restrain all persons in government service and all organizations of the government or under its direct or indirect control, including organizations in receipt of any financial assistance from it, from any act overt or covert liable in any way whatsoever to injure the tranquility, prosperity, order, or security of the whole or any part of the United States, its territories, or possessions, and, in particular, from any act tending to incite or encourage armed intervention, or any agitation or propaganda having as an aim the violation of the territorial integrity of the United States, its territories, or possessions, or the bringing about by force of a change in the political or social order of the whole or any part of the United States, its territories, or possessions.

3. Not to permit the formation or residence on its territory of any organization or group—and to prevent the activity on its territory of any organization or group, or of representatives or officials of any organization or group—which makes claim to be the government of, or makes attempt upon the territorial integrity of, the United States, its territories, or possessions; not to form, subsidize, support, or permit on its territory military organizations or groups having the aim of armed struggle against the United States, its territories, or possessions, and to prevent any recruiting on behalf of such organizations and groups.

4. Not to permit the formation or residence on its territory of any organization or group—and to prevent the activity on its territory of any organization or group, or of representatives or officials of any organization or group—which has as an aim the overthrow or the preparation for the overthrow of, or the

bringing about by force of a change in, the political or social order of the whole or any part of the United States, its territories or possessions.

It will be the fixed policy of the Executive of the United States within the limits of the powers conferred by the Constitution and the laws of the United States to adhere reciprocally to the engagements above expressed.

13. The Johnson Act, April 13, 1934

AN ACT to prohibit financial transactions with any foreign government in default on its obligations to the United States.

Be it enacted, That hereafter it shall be unlawful within the United States or any place subject to the jurisdiction of the United States for any person to purchase or sell the bonds, securities, or other obligations of, any foreign government or political subdivision thereof or any organization or association acting for or on behalf of a foreign government or political subdivision thereof, issued after a passage of this Act, or to make any loan to such foreign government, political subdivision, organization, or association, except a renewal or adjustment of existing indebtedness while such government, political subdivision, organization, or association, is in default in the payment of its obligations, or any part thereof, to the Government of the United States. Any person violating the provisions of this Act shall upon conviction thereof be fined not more than $10,000 or imprisoned for not more than five years, or both.

Sec. 2. As used in this Act the term "person" includes individual, partnership, corporation, or association other than a public corporation created by or pursuant to special authorization of Congress, or a corporation in which the Government of the United States has or exercises a controlling interest through stock ownership or otherwise.

14. Treaty between the United States and Cuba, Signed May 29, 1934

[Abrogating the Platt Amendment that appropriated for the United States the right to intervene in Cuba's internal affairs]

Article I

The Treaty of Relations which was concluded between the two contracting parties on May 22, 1903, shall cease to be in force, and is abrogated from the date on which the present Treaty goes into effect.

Article II

All the acts effected in Cuba by the United States of America during its military occupation of the island, up to May 20, 1902, the date on which the Republic of Cuba was established, have been ratified and held as valid; and all the rights legally acquired by virtue of those acts shall be maintained and protected.

Article III

Until the two contracting parties agree to the modification or abrogation of the stipulations of agreement in regard to the lease to the United States of America of lands in Cuba for coaling and naval stations signed by the president of the Republic of Cuba on February 16, 1903, and by the President of the United States of America on the 23rd day of the same month and year, the stipulations of that agreement with regard to the naval station of Guantanamo shall continue in effect. The supplementary agreement in regard to naval or coaling stations signed between the two governments on July 2, 1903, also shall continue in effect in the same form and on the same conditions with respect to the naval station of Guantanamo. So long as the United States of America shall not abandon the said naval station of Guantanamo or the two governments shall not agree to a modification of its present limits, the station shall continue to have the territorial area that it now has, with the limits that it has on the date of the signature of the present Treaty.

Article IV

If at any time in the future a situation should arise that appears to point to an outbreak of contagious disease in the territory of either of the contracting parties, either of the two governments shall, for its own protection, and without its act being considered unfriendly, exercise freely and at its discretion the right to suspend communications between those of its ports that it may designate and all or part of the territory of the other party, and for the period that it may consider to be advisable.

Article V

The present Treaty shall be ratified by the contracting parties in accordance with their respective constitutional methods; and shall go into effect on the date of the exchange of their ratifications, which shall take place in the city of Washington as soon as possible.

15. Anti-War Treaty of Non-Aggression and Conciliation, Ratified June 15, 1934

The states designated below, in the desire to contribute to the consolidation of peace, and to express their adherence to the efforts made by all civilized nations to promote the spirit of universal harmony;

To the end of condemning wars of aggression and territorial acquisitions that may be obtained by armed conquest, making them impossible and establishing their invalidity through the positive provisions of this treaty, and in order to replace them with pacific solutions based on lofty concepts of justice and equity;

Convinced that one of the most effective means of assuring the moral and material benefits which peace offers to the world, is the organization of a permanent system of conciliation for international disputes, to be applied immediately on the violation of the principles mentioned;

Have decided to put these aims of non-aggression and concord in conventional form, by concluding the present treaty, to which end they have appointed the undersigned plenipotentiaries, who, having exhibited their respective full powers, found to be in good and due form, have agreed upon the following:

ART. I. The High Contracting Parties solemnly declare that they condemn wars of aggression in their mutual relations or those with other states, and that the settlement of disputes or controversies of any kind that may arise among them shall be effected only by the pacific means which have the sanction of international law.

ART. II. They declare that as between the High Contracting Parties, territorial questions must not be settled by violence, and that they will not recognize any territorial arrangement which is not obtained by pacific means, nor the validity of the occupation or acquisition of territories that may be brought about by force of arms.

ART. III. In case of non-compliance by any state engaged in a dispute, with the obligations contained in the foregoing articles, the contracting states undertake to make every effort for the maintenance of peace. To that end they will adopt in their character as neutrals a common and solidary attitude; they will exercise the political, juridical or economic means authorized by international law; they will bring the influence of public opinion to bear but will in no case resort to intervention either diplomatic or armed; subject to the attitude that may be incumbent on them by virtue of other collective treaties to which such states are signatories.

ART. IV. The High Contracting Parties obligate themselves to submit to the conciliation procedure established by this treaty, the disputes specially mentioned and any others that may arise in their reciprocal relations, without further limitations than those enumerated in the following article, in all controversies which it has not been possible to settle by diplomatic means within a reasonable period of time.

ART. V. The High Contracting Parties and the states which may in the future adhere to this treaty, may not formulate at the time of signature, ratification or adherence, other limitations to the conciliation procedure than those which are indicated below:

(a) Differences for the solution of which treaties, conventions, pacts or pacific agreements of any kind whatever may have been concluded, which in no case shall be considered as annulled by this agreement, but supplemented thereby in so far as they tend to assure peace, as well as the questions or matters settled by previous treaties;

(b) Disputes which the parties prefer to solve by direct settlement or submit by common agreement to an arbitral or judicial solution;

(c) Questions which international law leaves to the exclusive competence of each state, under its constitutional system, for which reason the parties may object to their being submitted to the conciliation procedure before the national or local jurisdiction has decided definitely; except in the case of manifest denial or delay of justice, in which case the conciliation procedure shall be initiated within a year at the latest;

(d) Matters which affect constitutional precepts of the parties to the controversy. In case of doubt, each party shall obtain the reasoned opinion of its respective tribunal or supreme court of justice, if the latter should be invested with such powers.

The High Contracting Parties may communicate, at any time and in the manner provided for by Article XV, an instrument stating that they have abandoned wholly or in part the limitations established by them in the conciliation procedure.

The effect of the limitations formulated by one of the contracting parties shall be that the other parties shall not consider themselves obligated in regard to that party save in the measure of the exceptions established.

ART. VI. In the absence of a permanent Conciliation Commission or of some other international organization charged with this mission by virtue of previous treaties in effect, the High Contracting Parties undertake to submit their differences to the examination and investigation of a Conciliation Commission which shall be formed as follows, unless there is an agreement to the contrary of the parties in each case; ...

ART. X. It is the duty of the Commission to secure the conciliatory settlement of the disputes submitted to its consideration.

After an impartial study of the questions in dispute, it shall set forth in a report the outcome of its work and shall propose to the Parties bases of settlement by means of a just and equitable solution. ...

16. EMENDED TEXT OF THE SUPREME COURT OPINION FOR *A. L. A. SCHECHTER POULTRY CORPORATION ET AL. V. UNITED STATES,* MAY 27, 1935

[This unanimous decision of the Supreme Court, rendered by Chief Justice Charles Evans Hughes, found the National Industrial Recovery Act's provisions legally invalid.]

Petitioners in no. 854 were convicted in the District Court of New York on eighteen counts of an indictment charging violation of what is known as the "Live Poultry Code," and on an additional count for conspiracy to commit such violations. By demurrer to the indictment and appropriate motions on the trial, the defendants contended: (1) that the Code had been adopted pursuant to an unconstitutional delegation by Congress of legislative power; (2) that it attempted to regulate intrastate transactions which lay outside the authority of Congress; and (3) that in certain provisions it was repugnant to the due process clause of the Fifth Amendment. ...

The "Live Poultry Code" was promulgated under Section 3 of the National Industrial Recovery Act. That section ... authorizes the President to approve "codes of fair competition." Such a code may be approved for a trade or industry upon application by one or more trade or industrial associations or groups if the President finds: (1) that such associations or groups "impose no inequitable restrictions on admission to membership therein and are truly representative"; and (2) that such codes are not designed "to promote monopolies or to eliminate or oppress small enterprises and will not operate to discriminate against them, and will tend to effectuate the policy" of Title I of the act. Such codes "shall not permit monopolies or monopolistic practices."

As a condition of his approval, the President may "impose such conditions (including requirements for the making of reports and the keeping of accounts) for the protection of consumers, competitors, employees, and others, and in furtherance of the public interest, and may provide such exceptions to and exemptions from the provisions of such code as the President in his discretion deems necessary to effectuate the policy herein declared." Where such a code has not been approved, the President may prescribe one, either on his own motion or on complaint. Violation of any provision of a code (so approved or prescribed) "in any transaction in or affecting interstate or foreign commerce" is made a misdemeanor punishable by a fine of not more than $500 for each offense, and each day the violation continues is to be deemed a separate offense.

The "Live Poultry Code" was approved by the President on April 13, 1934. Its divisions indicate its nature and scope. The Code has eight articles entitled (1) purposes, (2) definitions, (3) hours, (4) wages, (5) general labor provisions, (6) administration, (7) trade practice provisions, and (8) general.

The declared purpose is "To effect the policies of Title I of the National Industrial Recovery Act." The Code is established as "a code of fair competition for the live poultry industry of the metropolitan area in and about the city of New York." ...

The "industry" is defined as including "every person engaged in the business of selling, purchasing for resale, transporting, or handling and/or slaughtering live poultry, from the time such poultry comes into the New York metropolitan area to the time it is sold in slaughtered form," and such "related branches" as may from time to time be included by amendment. ...

The Code fixes the number of hours for workdays. It provides that no employee, with certain exceptions, shall be permitted to work in excess of forty (40) hours in any one week, and that no employee, save as stated, "shall be paid in any pay period less than at the rate of fifty (50) cents per hour." The article containing "general labor provisions" prohibits the employment of any person under sixteen years of age, and declares that employees shall have the right of "collective bargaining," and freedom of choice with respect to labor organizations, in the terms of Section 7(a) of the act. ...

Provision is made for administration through an "industry advisory committee," to be selected by trade associations and members of the industry, and a "code supervisor" to be appointed, with approval of the committee, by agreement between the secretary of agriculture and the administrator for industrial recovery ...

The 7th Article, containing "trade practice provisions," prohibits various practices which are said to constitute "unfair methods of competition." The final article provides for verified reports, such as the secretary or administrator may require, "(1) for the protection of consumers, competitors, employees, and others, and in furtherance of the public interest; and (2) for the determination by the secretary or administrator of the extent to which the declared policy of the act is being effectuated by this code." The members of the industry are also required to keep books and records which "will clearly reflect all financial transactions . . .," and to submit weekly reports showing the range of daily prices and volume of sales for each kind of produce.

. . .

Of the eighteen counts of the indictment upon which the defendants were convicted, aside from the count for conspiracy, two counts charged violation of the minimum wage and maximum hour provisions of the Code, and ten counts were for violation of the requirement (found in the "trade practice provisions") of "straight killing." This requirement was really one of "straight" selling. The term "straight killing" was defined in the Code as "the practice of requiring persons purchasing poultry for resale to accept the run of any half coop, coop, or coops, as purchased by slaughterhouse operators, except for culls." The charges in the ten counts, respectively, were that the defendants in selling to retail dealers and butchers had permitted "selections of individual chickens taken from particular coops and half coops."

Of the other six counts, one charged the sale to a butcher of an unfit chicken; two counts charged the making of sales without having the poultry inspected or approved in accordance with regulations or ordinances of the city of New York; two counts charged the making of false reports or the failure to make reports relating to the range of daily prices and volume of sales for certain periods, and the remaining count was for sales to slaughterers or dealers who were without licenses required by the ordinance and regulations of the city of New York.

First, two preliminary points are stressed by the government with respect to the appropriate approach to the important questions presented. We are told that the provisions of the statute authorizing the adoption of codes must be viewed in the light of the grave national crisis with which Congress was confronted. Undoubtedly, the conditions to which power is addressed are always to be considered when the exercise of power is challenged. Extraordinary conditions may call for extraordinary remedies. But the argument necessarily stops short of an attempt to justify action which lies outside the sphere of constitutional authority. Extraordinary conditions do not create or enlarge constitutional power.

The Constitution established a national government with powers deemed to be adequate, as they have proved to be both in war and peace, but these powers of the national government are limited by the constitutional grants. Those who act under these grants are not at liberty to transcend the imposed limits because they believe that more or different power is necessary. Such assertions of extra-constitutional authority were anticipated and precluded by the explicit terms of the Tenth Amendment—"The powers not delegated to the United States by the Constitution, nor prohibited by it to the states, are reserved to the states respectively, or to the people."

The further point is urged that the national crisis demanded a broad and intensive cooperative effort by those engaged in trade and industry, and that this necessary cooperation was sought to be fostered by permitting them to initiate the adoption of codes. But the statutory plan is not simply one for voluntary effort. It does not seek merely to endow voluntary trade or industrial associations or groups with privileges or immunities. It involves the coercive exercise of the lawmaking power. The codes of fair competi-

tion which the statute attempts to authorize are codes of laws. If valid, they place all persons within their reach under the obligation of positive law, binding equally those who assent and those who do not assent. Violations of the provisions of the codes are punishable as crimes.

Second, . . . The Constitution provides that "all legislative powers herein granted shall be vested in a Congress of the United States, which shall consist of a Senate and a House of Representatives." . . . And the Congress is authorized "To make all laws which shall be necessary and proper for carrying into execution" its general powers . . . The Congress is not permitted to abdicate or to transfer to others the essential functions with which it is thus vested.

. . .

The Federal Trade Commission Act (Section 5) introduced the expression "unfair methods of competition," which were declared to be unlawful. That was an expression new in law . . . [the phrase] does not admit of precise definition, its scope being left to judicial determination as controversies arise. . . .

What are "unfair methods of competition" are thus to be determined in particular instances, upon evidence, in the light of particular competitive conditions and of what is found to be a specific and substantial public interest. . . . To make this possible, Congress set up a special procedure. A commission, a quasi-judicial body, was created. Provision was made for formal complaint, for notice and hearing, for appropriate findings of fact supported by adequate evidence, and for judicial review to give assurance that the action of the commission is taken within its statutory authority. . . .

In providing for codes, the National Industrial Recovery Act dispenses with this administrative procedure and with any administrative procedure of an analogous character. But the difference between the code plan of the Recovery Act and the scheme of the Federal Trade Commission Act lies not only in procedure but in subject matter . . . the "fair competition" of the codes has a much broader range and a new significance. The Recovery Act provides that it shall not be construed to impair the powers of the Federal Trade Commission, but, when a code is approved, its provisions are to be the "standards of fair competition" for the trade or industry concerned, and any violation of such standards in any transaction in or affecting interstate or foreign commerce is to be deemed "an unfair method of competition" within the meaning of the Federal Trade Commission Act . . .

The question, then, turns upon the authority which Section 3 of the Recovery Act vests in the President to approve or prescribe. If the codes have standing as penal statutes, this must be due to the effect of the executive action. But Congress cannot delegate legislative power to the President to exercise an unfettered discretion to make whatever laws he thinks may be needed or advisable for the rehabilitation and expansion of trade or industry. . . .

Accordingly, we turn to the Recovery Act to ascertain what limits have been set to the exercise of the President's discretion.

First, the President, as a condition of approval, is required to find that the trade or industrial associations or groups which propose a code, "impose no inequitable restrictions on admission to membership" and are "truly representative." That condition, however, relates only to the status of the initiators of the new laws and not to the permissible scope of such laws.

Second, the President is required to find that the code is not "designed to promote monopolies or to eliminate or oppress small enterprises and will not operate to discriminate against them." And, to this is added a provision that the code "shall not permit monopolies or monopolistic practices." But these restrictions leave virtually untouched the field of policy envisaged by Section 1, and, in that wide field of legislative possibilities, the proponents of a code, refraining from monopolistic designs, may roam at will and the President may approve or disapprove their proposals as he may see fit. That is the precise effect of the further finding that the President is to make—that the code "will tend to effectuate the policy of this title." While this is called a finding, it is really but a statement of an opinion as to the general effect upon the promotion of trade or industry of a scheme of laws. These are the only findings which Congress has made essential in order to put into operation a legislative code having the aims described in the "Declaration of Policy."

Nor is the breadth of the President's discretion left to the necessary implications of this limited requirement as to his findings. As already noted, the President in approving a code may impose his own conditions, adding or taking from what is proposed, as "in his discretion" he thinks necessary "to effectuate the policy" declared by the act. Of course, he has no less liberty when he prescribes a code on his own motion or on complaint, and he is free to prescribe one if a code has not been approved.

The act provides for the creation by the President of administrative agencies to assist him, but the action or reports of such agencies, or of his other assistants— their recommendations and findings in relation to the making of codes—have no sanction beyond the will of the President, who may accept, modify, or reject them as he pleases. Such recommendations or findings in no way limit the authority which Section 3 undertakes to vest in the President with no other conditions than those there specified. And this authority relates to a host of different trades and industries, thus extending the President's discretion to all the varieties of laws which he may deem to be beneficial in dealing with the vast array of commercial and industrial activities throughout the country.

Such a sweeping delegation of legislative power finds no support in the decisions upon which the government especially relies. . . .

To summarize and conclude upon this point: Section 3 of the Recovery Act is without precedent . . . In view of the scope of that broad declaration, and of the nature of the few restrictions that are imposed, the discretion of the President in approving or prescribing codes, and thus enacting laws for the government of trade and industry throughout the country, is virtually unfettered. We think that the code-making authority thus conferred is an unconstitutional delegation of legislative power.

Third, the question of the application of the provisions of the Live Poultry Code to intrastate transactions. . . . This aspect of the case presents the question whether the particular provisions of the Live Poultry Code, which the defendants were convicted for violating and for having conspired to violate, were within the regulating power of the Congress.

These provisions relate to the hours and wages of those employed by the defendants in their slaughterhouses in Brooklyn and to the sales there made to retail dealers and butchers.

Were these transactions "in" interstate commerce? Much is made of the fact that almost all the poultry coming to New York is sent there from other states. But the code provisions, as here applied, do not concern the transportation of the poultry from other states to New York, or the transactions of the commission men or others to whom it is consigned, or the sales made by such consignees to defendants. When defendants had made their purchases . . . the poultry was trucked to their slaughterhouses in Brooklyn for local disposition. The interstate transactions in relation to that poultry then ended. . . . Neither the slaughtering nor the sales by defendants were transactions in interstate commerce. . . .

The undisputed facts thus afford no warrant for the argument that the poultry handled by defendants at their slaughterhouse markets was in *"current"* or *"flow"* of interstate commerce and was thus subject to congressional regulation. The mere fact that there may be a constant flow of commodities into a state does not mean that the flow continues after the property has arrived and has become commingled with the mass of property within the state and is there held solely for local disposition and use. So far as the poultry here in question is concerned, the flow in interstate commerce had ceased. The poultry had come to a permanent rest within the state. It was not held, used, or sold by defendants in relation to any further transactions in interstate commerce and was not destined for transportation to other states. Hence, decisions which deal with a stream of interstate commerce—where goods come to rest within a state temporarily and are later to go forward in interstate commerce—and with the regulations of transactions involved in that practical continuity of movement, are not applicable here. . . .

. . . . .

If the commerce clause were construed to reach all enterprises and transactions which could be said to have an indirect effect upon interstate commerce, the federal authority would embrace practically all the activities of the people and the authority of the state over its domestic concerns would exist only by sufferance of the federal government. Indeed, on such a theory, even the development of the state's commercial facilities would be subject to federal control. . . .

The distinction between direct and indirect effects has been clearly recognized in the application of the Antitrust Act. Where a combination or conspiracy is formed, with the intent to restrain interstate commerce or to monopolize any part of it, the violation of the statute is clear. . . . But where that intent is absent, and the objectives are limited to intrastate activities, the fact that there may be an indirect effect

upon interstate commerce does not subject the parties to the federal statute. . . .

The distinction between direct and indirect effects of intrastate transactions upon interstate commerce must be recognized as a fundamental one, essential to the maintenance of our constitutional system. Otherwise, as we have said, there would be virtually no limit to the federal power and for all practical purposes we should have a completely centralized government. We must consider the provisions here in question in the light of this distinction.

The question of chief importance relates to the provisions of the Code as to the hours and wages of those employed in defendants' slaughterhouse markets. . . . The persons employed in slaughtering and selling in local trade are not employed in interstate commerce. Their hours and wages have no direct relation to interstate commerce. . . .

. . . . .

The argument of the government proves too much. If the federal government may determine the wages and hours of employees in the internal commerce of a state because of their relation to cost and prices and their indirect effect upon interstate commerce, it would seem that a similar control might be exerted over other elements of cost also affecting prices, such as the number of employees, rents, advertising, methods of doing business, etc. All the processes of production and distribution that enter into cost would likewise be controlled. If the cost of doing an intrastate business is in itself the permitted object of federal control, the extent of the regulation of cost would be a question of discretion and not of power.

The government also makes the point that efforts to enact state legislation establishing high labor standards have been impeded by the belief that unless similar action is taken generally, commerce will be diverted from the states adopting such standards, and that this fear of diversion has led to demands for federal legislation on the subject of wages and hours. The apparent implication is that the federal authority under the commerce clause should be deemed to extend to the establishment of rules to govern wages and hours in intrastate trade and industry generally throughout the country, thus overriding the authority of the states to deal with domestic problems arising from labor conditions in their internal commerce.

It is not the province of the Court to consider the economic advantages or disadvantages of such a centralized system. It is sufficient to say that the federal Constitution does not provide for it. Our growth and development have called for wide use of the commerce power of the federal government in its control over the expanded activities of interstate commerce and in protecting that commerce from burdens, interferences, and conspiracies to restrain and monopolize it. But the authority of the federal government may not be pushed to such an extreme as to destroy the distinction, which the commerce clause itself establishes, between commerce "among the several states" and the internal concerns of a state. The same answer must be made to the contention that is based upon the serious economic situation which led to the passage of the Recovery Act—the fall in prices, the decline in wages and employment, and the curtailment of the market for commodities. Stress is laid upon the great importance of maintaining wage distributions which would provide the necessary stimulus in starting "the cumulative forces making for expanding commercial activity." Without in any way disparaging this motive, it is enough to say that the recuperative efforts of the federal government must be made in a manner consistent with the authority granted by the Constitution.

We are of the opinion that the attempt through the provisions of the Code to fix the hours and wages of employees of defendants in their intrastate business was not a valid exercise of federal power.

The other violations for which defendants were convicted related to the making of local sales. Ten counts, for violation of the provision as to "straight killing," were for permitting customers to make "selections of individual chickens taken from particular coops and half coops." Whether or not this practice is good or bad for the local trade, its effect, if any, upon interstate commerce was only indirect. The same may be said of violations of the Code by intrastate transactions consisting of the sale "of an unfit chicken" and of sales which were not in accord with the ordinances of the city of New York. The requirement of reports as to prices and volumes of defendants' sales was incident to the effort to control their intrastate business.

In view of these conclusions, we find it unnecessary to discuss other questions which have been raised as to the validity of certain provisions of the Code under the due process clause of the Fifth Amendment.

On both the grounds we have discussed, the attempted delegation of legislative power and the attempted regulation of intrastate transactions which affect interstate commerce only indirectly, we hold the code provisions here in question to be invalid and that the judgment of conviction must be reversed.

17. Emended Text of the Social Security Act, Signed into law August 14, 1935

AN ACT to provide for the general welfare by establishing a system of Federal old-age benefits, and by enabling the several States to make more adequate provision for aged persons, blind persons, dependent and crippled children, maternal and child welfare, public health, and the administration of their unemployment compensation laws; to establish a Social Security Board; to raise revenue; and for other purposes.

Be it enacted by the Senate and House of Representatives of the United States of America in Congress assembled,

Title I—Grants to States for Old Age Assistance

Appropriation

Section 1. For the purpose of enabling each State to furnish financial assistance, as far as practicable under the conditions in such State, to aged needy individuals, there is hereby authorized to be appropriated for the fiscal year ending June 30, 1936, the sum of $49,750,000, and there is hereby authorized to be appropriated for each fiscal year thereafter a sum sufficient to carry out the purposes of this title. The sums made available under this section shall be used for making payments to States which have submitted, and had approved by the Social Security Board established by Title VII, State plans for old-age assistance.

State Old-age Assistance Plans

Sec. 2 (a) A State plan for old-age assistance must (1) provide that it shall be in effect in all political subdivisions of the State, and, if administered by them, be mandatory upon them; (2) provide for financial participation by the State; (3) either provide for the establishment or designation of a single State agency to administer the plan, or provide for the establishment or designation of a single State agency to supervise the administration of the plan; (4) provide for granting to any individual, whose claim for old-age assistance is denied, an opportunity for a fair hearing before such State agency; (5) provide such methods of administration (other than those relating to selection, tenure of office, and compensation of personnel) as are found by the Board to be necessary for the efficient operation of the plan; (6) provide that the State agency will make such reports, in such form and containing such information, as the Board may from time to time require, and comply with such provisions as the Board may from time to time find necessary to assure the correctness and verification of such reports; and (7) provide that if the State or any of its political subdivisions collects from the estate of any recipient of old-age assistance any amount with respect to old-age assistance furnished him under the plan, one-half of the net amount so collected shall be promptly paid to the United States. Any payment so made shall be deposited in the Treasury to the credit of the appropriation for the purposes of this title.

(b) The Board shall approve any plan which fulfills the conditions specified in subsection (a), except that it shall not approve any plan which imposes, as a condition of eligibility for old-age assistance under the plan—

(1) An age requirement of more than sixty-five years, except that the plan may impose, effective until January 1, 1940, an age requirement of as much as seventy years; or

(2) Any residence requirement which excludes any resident of the State who has resided therein five years during the nine years immediately preceding the application for old-age assistance and has resided therein continuously for one year immediately preceding the application; or

(3) any citizenship requirement which excludes any citizen of the United States.

PAYMENT TO STATES

Sec. 3. (a) From the sums appropriated therefor, the Secretary of the Treasury shall pay to each State which has an approved plan for old-age assistance, for each quarter, beginning with the quarter commencing July 1, 1935, (1) an amount, which shall be used exclusively as old-age assistance, equal to one-half of the total of the sums expended during such quarter as old-age assistance under the State plan with respect to each individual who at the time of such expenditure is sixty-five years of age or older

and is not an inmate of a public institution, not counting so much of such expenditure with respect to any individual for any month as exceeds $30, and (2) 5 per centum of such amount, which shall be used for paying the costs of administering the State plan or for old-age assistance, or both, and for no other purpose: *Provided,* That the State plan, in order to be approved by the Board, need not provide for financial participation before July 1, 1937 by the State, in the case of any State which the Board, upon application by the State and after reasonable notice and opportunity for hearing to the State, finds is prevented by its constitution from providing such financial participation.

(b) The method of computing and paying such amounts shall be as follows:

(1) The Board shall, prior to the beginning of each quarter, estimate the amount to be paid to the State for such quarter under the provisions of clause (1) of subsection (a), such estimate to be based on (A) a report filed by the State containing its estimate of the total sum to be expended in such quarter in accordance with the not more than $3,000, the old-age benefit shall be at a monthly rate of one-half of 1 per centum of such total wages;

(2) If such total wages were more than $3,000, the old-age benefit shall be at a monthly rate equal to the sum of the following:

(A) One-half of 1 per centum of $3,000; plus

(B) One-twelfth of 1 per centum of the amount by which such total wages exceeded $3,000 and did not exceed $45,000; plus

(C) One-twenty-fourth of 1 per centum of the amount by which such total wages exceeded $45,000.

(b) In no case shall the monthly rate computed under subsection (a) exceed $85 . . .

PAYMENTS UPON DEATH

Sec. 203. (a) If any individual dies before attaining the age of sixty-five, there shall be paid to his estate an amount equal to 3½ per centum of the total wages determined by the Board to have been paid to him, with respect to employment after December 31, 1936 . . .

PAYMENTS TO AGED INDIVIDUALS NOT QUALIFIED FOR BENEFITS

Sec. 204. (a) There shall be paid in a lump sum to any individual who, upon attaining the age of sixty-five, is not a qualified individual, an amount equal to 3½ per centum of the total wages determined by the Board to have been paid to him, with respect to employment after December 31, 1936, and before he attained the age of sixty-five.

(b) After any individual becomes entitled to any payment under subsection (a), no other payment shall be made under this title in any manner measured by wages paid to him, except that any part of any payment under subsection (a) which is not paid to him before death shall be paid to his estate....

Sec. 210 ...

(b) The term "employment" means any service, of whatever nature, performed within the United States by an employee for his employer, except—

(1) Agricultural labor;

(2) Domestic service in a private home;

(3) Casual labor not in the course of the employer's trade or business;

(4) Service performed as an officer or member of the crew of a vessel documented under the laws of the United States or of any foreign country;

(5) Service performed in the employ of the United States Government or of an instrumentality of the United States;

(6) Service performed in the employ of a State, a political subdivision thereof, or an instrumentality of one or more States or political subdivisions;

(7) Service performed in the employ of a corporation, community chest, fund, or foundation, organized and operated exclusively for religious, charitable, scientific, literary, or educational purposes, or for the prevention of cruelty to children or animals, no part of the net earnings of which inures to the benefit of any private shareholder or individual....

Title III—Grants to States for Unemployment Compensation Administration

APPROPRIATION

Section 301. For the purpose of assisting the States in the administration of their unemployment compensation laws, there is hereby authorized to be appropriated, for the fiscal year ending June 30, 1936, the sum of $4,000,000, and for each fiscal year thereafter the sum of $49,000,000, to be used as hereinafter provided.

PAYMENTS TO STATES

Sec. 302. (a) The Board shall from time to time certify to the Secretary of the Treasury for payment to each State which has an unemployment compensation approved by the Board under Title IX, such amounts as the Board determines to be necessary for the proper administration of such law during the fiscal year in which such payment is to be made. The Board's determination shall be based on (1) the population of the State; (2) an estimate of the number of persons covered by the State law and of the cost of proper administration of such law; and (3) such other factors as the Board finds relevant....

Title IV—Grants to States for Aid to Dependent Children

APPROPRIATION

Section 401. For the purpose of enabling each State to furnish financial assistance, as far as practicable under the conditions in such State, to needy dependent children, there is hereby authorized to be appropriated for the fiscal year ending June 30, 1936, the sum of $24,750,000, and there is hereby authorized to be appropriated for each fiscal year thereafter a sum sufficient to carry out the purposes of this title. The sums made available under this section shall be used for making payments to States which have submitted, and had approved by the Board, State plans for aid to dependent children....

DEFINITIONS

Sec. 406. When used in this title—

(a) The term "dependent child" means a child under the age of sixteen who has been deprived of parental support or care by reason of the death, continued absence from the home, or physical or mental incapacity of a parent, and who is living with his father, mother, grandfather, grandmother, brother, sister, stepfather, stepmother, stepbrother, stepsister, uncle, or aunt, in a place of residence maintained by one or more of such relatives as his or their home....

Title V—Grants to States for Material and Child Welfare

PART 1—MATERNAL AND CHILD HEALTH SERVICES

APPROPRIATION

Section 501. For the purpose of enabling each State to extend and improve, as far as practicable under the conditions in each State, services for promoting the health of mothers and children, especially in rural areas and in areas suffering from severe economic distress, there is hereby authorized to be appropriated for each fiscal year, beginning with the fiscal year ending June 30, 1936, the sum of $3,800,000. The sum made available under this section shall be used for making payments to States which have submitted, and had approved by the Chief of the Children's Bureau, State plans for such services.

ALLOTMENTS TO STATES

Sec. 502. (a) Out of the sums appropriated pursuant to section 501 for each fiscal year the Secretary of Labor shall allot to each State $20,000, and such part of $1,800,000 as he finds that the number of live births in such State bore to the total number of live births in the United States, in the latest calendar year for which the Bureau of the Census has available statistics.

PART 2—SERVICES FOR CRIPPLED CHILDREN

APPROPRIATION

Sec. 511. For the purpose of enabling each State to extend and improve (especially in rural areas and in areas suffering from severe economic distress), as far as practicable under the conditions in such State, services for locating crippled children, and for providing medical, surgical, corrective, and other services and care, and facilities for diagnosis, hospitalization, and aftercare, for children who are crippled or who are suffering from conditions which lead to crippling, there is hereby authorized to be appropriated for each fiscal year, beginning with the fiscal year ending June 30, 1936, the sum of $2,850,000. The sums made available under this section shall be used for making payments to States which have submitted, and had approved by the Chief of the Children's Bureau, State plans for such services . . .

PART 3—CHILD-WELFARE SERVICES

Sec. 521. (a) For the purpose of enabling the United States, through the Children's Bureau, to cooperate with State public-welfare agencies in establishing, extending, and strengthening, especially in predominantly rural areas, public-welfare services (hereinafter in this section referred to as "child-welfare services") for the protection and care of homeless, dependent, and neglected children, and children in danger of becoming delinquent, there is hereby authorized to be appropriated for each fiscal year,

beginning with the fiscal year ending June 30, 1936, the sum of $1,500,000. Such amount shall be allotted by the Secretary of Labor for use by cooperating State public-welfare agencies on the basis of plans developed jointly by the State agency and the Children's Bureau, to each State, $10,000, and the remainder to each State on the basis of such plans, not to exceed such part of the remainder as the rural population of such State bears to the total rural population of the United States. The amount so allotted shall be expended for payment of part of the cost of district, county or other local child-welfare services in areas predominantly rural, and for developing State services for the encouragement and assistance of adequate methods of community child-welfare organization in areas predominantly rural and other areas of special need. . . .

PART 4—VOCATIONAL REHABILITATION

Sec. 531. (a) In order to enable the United States to cooperate with the States and Hawaii in extending and strengthening their programs of vocational rehabilitation of the physically disabled, and to continue to carry out the provisions and purposes of the Act entitled "An Act to provide for the promotion of vocational rehabilitation of persons disabled in industry or otherwise and their return to civil employment," approved June 2, 1920, . . . there is hereby authorized to be appropriated for the fiscal years ending June 30, 1936, and June 30, 1937, the sum of $841,000 for each such fiscal year in addition to the amount of the existing authorization, and for each fiscal year thereafter the sum of $1,938,000.

Title VI—Public Health Work

APPROPRIATION

Section 601. For the purpose of assisting states, counties, health districts, and other political subdivisions of the States in establishing and maintaining adequate public-health services, including the training of personnel for State and local health work, there is hereby authorized to be appropriated for each fiscal year, beginning with the fiscal year ending June 30, 1936, the sum of $8,000,000 to be used as hereinafter provided.

STATE AND LOCAL PUBLIC HEALTH SERVICES

Sec. 602. (a.) The Surgeon General of the Public Health Service, with the approval of the Secretary of the Treasury, shall, at the beginning of each fiscal year, allot to the States the total of (1) the amount appropriated for each year pursuant to section 601; and (2) the amounts of the allotments under this section for the preceding fiscal year remaining unpaid to the States at the end of such fiscal year. The amounts of such allotments shall be determined on the basis of (1) the population; (2) the special health problems; (3) the financial needs of the respective States. Upon making such allotments the Surgeon General of the Public Health Service shall certify the amounts thereof to the Secretary of the Treasury. . . .

INVESTIGATION

Sec. 603. (a) There is hereby authorized to be appropriated for each fiscal year, beginning with the fiscal year ending June 30, 1936, the sum of $2,000,000 for expenditure by the Public Health Service for investigation of disease and problems of sanitation. . . .

Title VII—Social Security Board

ESTABLISHMENT

Section 701. There is hereby established a Social Security Board to be composed of three members to be appointed by the President, by and with the advice and consent of the Senate. During his term of membership on the Board, no member shall engage in any other business, vocation, or employment. Not more than two of the members of the Board shall be members of the same political party. Each member shall receive a salary at the rate of $10,000 a year and shall hold office for a term of six years. . . .

DUTIES OF THE SOCIAL SECURITY BOARD

Sec. 702. The Board shall perform the duties imposed upon it by this Act and shall also have the duty of studying and making recommendations as to the most effective methods of providing economic security through social insurance, and as to legislation and matters of administrative policy concerning old-age pensions, unemployment compensation, accident compensation, and related subjects. . . .

Title VII—Taxes with Respect to Employment

INCOME TAX ON EMPLOYEES

Section 801. In addition to other taxes, there shall be levied, collected, and paid upon the income of every individual a tax equal to the following percentages of wages . . . received by him after December 31, 1936, with respect to employment . . . after such date:

(1) With respect to employment during the calendar years 1937, 1938, and 1939, the rate shall be 1 per centum.

(2) With respect to employment during the calendar years 1940, 1941, and 1942, the rate shall be 1½ per centum.

(3) With respect to employment during the calendar years 1943, 1944, and 1945, the rate shall be 2 per centum.

(4) With respect to employment during the calendar years 1946, 1947, and 1948, the rate shall be 2½ per centum.

(5) With respect to employment after December 31, 1948, the rate shall be 3 per centum.

DEDUCTION OF TAX FROM WAGES

Sec. 802. The tax imposed by section 801 shall be collected by the employer of the taxpayer, by deducting the amount of the tax from the wages as and when paid. . . .

EXCISE TAX ON EMPLOYERS

Sec. 804. In addition to other taxes, every employer shall pay an excise tax, with respect to having individuals in his employ, equal to the following percentages of the wages . . . paid by him after December 31, 1936, with respect to employment . . . after such date:

(1) With respect to employment during the calendar years 1937, 1938, and 1939, the rate shall be 1 per centum. . . .

Title IX—Tax on Employers of Eight or More

IMPOSITION OF TAX

Section 901. On and after January 1, 1936, every employer shall pay for each calendar year an excise tax, with respect to having individuals in his employ, equal to the following percentages of the total wages payable by him with respect to employment during such calendar year:

(1) With respect to employment during the calendar year 1936 the rate shall be 1 per centum;

(2) With respect to employment during the calendar year 1937 the rate shall be 2 per centum. . . .

UNEMPLOYMENT TRUST FUND

Sec. 904. (a) There is hereby established in the Treasury of the United States a trust fund to be known as the "Unemployment Trust Fund . . ."

(b) It shall be the duty of the Secretary of the Treasury to invest such portion of the Fund as is not, in his judgment, required to meet current withdrawals. Such investment may be made only in interest bearing obligations of the United States or in obligations guaranteed as to both principal and interest by the United States . . .

Title X—Grants to States for Aid to the Blind

APPROPRIATION

Section 1001. For the purpose of enabling each State to furnish financial assistance, as far as practicable under the conditions in such State, to needy individuals who are blind, there is hereby authorized to be appropriated for the fiscal year ending June 30, 1936, the sum of $3,000,000, and there is hereby authorized to be appropriated for each fiscal year thereafter a sum sufficient to carry out the purposes of this title. The sums made available under this section shall be used for making payments to States which have submitted, and had approved by the Social Security Board, State plans for aid to the blind. . . .

18. THE NEUTRALITY ACT OF 1937, SIGNED INTO LAW MAY 1, 1937

EXPORT OF ARMS, AMMUNITION, AND IMPLEMENTS OF WAR

Section 1. (a) Whenever the President shall find that there exists a state of war between, or among, two or more foreign states, the President shall proclaim such fact, and it shall thereafter be unlawful to export, or attempt to export, or cause to be exported, arms, ammunition, or implements of war from any place in the United States to any belligerent state named in such proclamation, or to any neutral state for transshipment to, or for the use of, any such belligerent state.

(b) The President shall, from time to time, by proclamation, extend such embargo upon the export of arms, ammunition, or implements of war to other states as and when they may become involved in such war.

(c) Whenever the President shall find that a state of civil strife exists in a foreign state and that such civil strife is of a magnitude or is being conducted under such conditions that the export of arms, ammunition, or implements of war from the United States to such foreign state would threaten or endanger the peace of the United States, the President shall proclaim such fact, and it shall thereafter be unlawful to export, or attempt to export, or cause to be exported, arms, ammunition, or implements of war from any place in the United States to such foreign state, or to any neutral state for transshipment to, or for the use of, such foreign state.

(d) The President shall, from time to time by proclamation, definitely enumerate the arms, ammunition, and implements of war, the export of which is prohibited by this section. . . .

(e) Whoever, in violation of any of the provisions of this Act, shall export, or attempt to export, or cause to be exported, arms, ammunition, or implements of war from the United States shall be fined not more than $10,000, or imprisoned not more than five years, or both. . . .

EXPORT OF OTHER ARTICLES AND MATERIALS

Sec. 2. (a) Whenever the President shall have issued any proclamation under the authority of section 1 of this Act and he shall thereafter find that the placing of restrictions on the shipment of certain articles or materials in addition to arms, ammunition, and implements of war from the United States to belligerent states, or to a state wherein civil strife exists, is necessary to promote the security or preserve the peace of the United States, he shall so proclaim, and it shall thereafter be unlawful, for any American vessel to carry such articles or materials to any belligerent state, or to any state wherein civil strife exists, named in such proclamation issued under the authority of section 1 of this Act, or to any neutral state for transshipment to, or for the use of, any such belligerent state or any such state wherein civil strife exists. The President shall by proclamation from time to time definitely enumerate the articles and materials which it shall be unlawful for American vessels to so transport. . . .

(c) The President shall from time to time by proclamation extend such restrictions as are imposed under the authority of this section to other states as and when they may be declared to become belligerent states under proclamations issued under the authority of section 1 of this Act.

(d) The President may from time to time change, modify, or revoke in whole or in part any proclamations issued by him under the authority of this section.

(e) Except with respect to offenses committed, or forfeitures incurred, prior to May 1, 1939, this section and all proclamations issued there under shall not be effective after May 1, 1939.

FINANCIAL TRANSACTIONS

Sec. 3. (a) Whenever the President shall have issued a proclamation under the authority of section 1 of this Act, it shall thereafter be unlawful for any person within the United States to purchase, sell, or exchange bonds, securities, or other obligations of the government of any belligerent state or of any state wherein civil strife exists, named in such proclamation, or of any political subdivision of any such state, or of any person acting for or on behalf of the government of any such state, or of any faction or asserted government within any such state wherein civil strife exists, or of any person acting for or on behalf of any faction or asserted government within any such state wherein civil strife exists, issued after the date of such proclamation, or to make any loan or extend any credit to any such government, political subdivision, faction, asserted government, or person, or to solicit or receive any contribution for any such government, or person: *Provided,* That if the President shall find that such action will serve to protect the commercial or other interests of the United States or its citizens, he may, in his discretion, and to such extent and under such regulations as he may prescribe, except from the operation of this section ordinary commercial credits and short-time obligations in aid of legal transactions and of a character customarily used in normal peacetime commercial transactions. Nothing in this subsection shall be construed to prohibit the solicitation or collection of funds to be used for medical aid and assistance, or for food and clothing to relieve human suffering, when such solicitation or collection of funds is made on behalf of and for use by any person or organization which is not acting for or on behalf of any such government, political subdivision, faction, or asserted government, but all such solicitations and collections of funds shall be subject to the approval of the President and shall be made under such rules and regulations as he shall prescribe . . .

(c) Whoever shall violate the provisions of this section or of any regulations issued hereunder shall, upon conviction thereof, be fined not more than $50,000 or imprisoned for not more than five years, or both. Should the violation be by a corporation, organization, or association, each officer or agent thereof participating in the violation may be liable to the penalty herein prescribed. . . .

EXCEPTIONS—AMERICAN REPUBLICS

Sec. 4. This Act shall not apply to an American republic or republics engaged in war against a non-American state or states, provided the American republic is not cooperating with a non-American state or states in such war.

NATIONAL MUNITIONS CONTROL BOARD

Sec. 5. (a) There is hereby established a National Munitions Control Board . . . to carry out the provisions of this Act. The Board shall consist of the Secretary of State, who shall be chairman and executive officer of the Board, the Secretary of the Treasury, the Secretary of War, the Secretary of the Navy, and the Secretary of Commerce. Except as otherwise provided in this Act, or by other law, the administration of this Act is vested in the Department of State. The Secretary of State shall promulgate such rules and regulations as he may deem necessary to carry out its provisions. The Board shall be convened by the chairman and shall hold at least one meeting a year.

(d) It shall be unlawful for any person to export, or attempt to export, from the United States to any other state, any of the arms, ammunition, or implements of war referred to in this Act, or to import, or attempt to import, to the United States from any other state, any of the arms, ammunition, or implements of war referred to in this Act, without first having obtained a license therefor. . . .

(k) The President is hereby authorized to proclaim upon recommendation of the Board from time to time a list of articles which shall be considered arms, ammunition, and implements of war for the purposes of this section.

AMERICAN VESSELS PROHIBITED FROM CARRYING ARMS TO BELLIGERENT STATES

Sec. 6. (a) Whenever the President shall have issued a proclamation under the authority of section 1 of this Act, it shall thereafter be unlawful, until such proclamation is revoked, for any American vessel to carry any arms, ammunition, or implements of war to any belligerent state, or to any state wherein civil strife exists, named in such proclamation, or to any neutral state for transshipment to, or for the use of, any such belligerent state or any such state wherein civil strife exists. . . .

Use of American Ports as Base of Supply

Sec. 7. (a) Whenever, during any war in which the United States is neutral, the President, or any person thereunto authorized by him, shall have cause to believe that any vessel, domestic or foreign, whether requiring clearance or not, is about to carry out of port of the United States, fuel, men, arms, ammunition, implements of war, or other supplies to any warship, tender, or supply ship of a belligerent state . . . and if, in the President's judgment, such action will serve to maintain peace between the United States and foreign states, or to protect the commercial interests of the United States and its citizens, or to promote the security or neutrality of the United States, he shall have the power and it shall be his duty to require the owner, master, or person in command thereof, before departing from a port of the United States, to give a bond to the United States, with sufficient sureties, in such amount as he shall deem proper, conditioned that the vessel will not deliver the men, or any part of the cargo, to any warship, tender, or supply ship of a belligerent state.

(b) If the President, or any person thereunto authorized by him, shall find that a vessel, domestic or foreign, in a port of the United States, has previously cleared from a port of the United States during such war and delivered its cargo or any part thereof to a warship, tender, or supply ship of a belligerent state, he may prohibit the departure of such vessel during the duration of the war.

Submarines and Armed Merchant Vessels

Sec. 8. Whenever, during any war in which the United States is neutral, the President shall find that special restrictions placed on the use of the ports and territorial waters of the United States by the submarines or armed merchant vessels of a foreign state, will serve to maintain peace between the United States and foreign states, or to protect the commercial interests of the United States and its citizens, or to promote the security of the United States, and shall make proclamation thereof, it shall thereafter be unlawful for any such submarine or

armed merchant vessel to enter a port or territorial waters of the United States or to depart therefrom, except under such conditions and subject to such limitations as the President may prescribe. Whenever, in his judgment, the conditions which have caused him to issue his proclamation have ceased to exist, he shall revoke his proclamation and the provisions of this section shall cease to apply.

Travel on Vessels of Belligerent States

Sec. 9. Whenever the President shall have issued a proclamation under the authority of section 1 of this Act it shall thereafter be unlawful for any citizen of the United States to travel on any vessel of the state or states named in such proclamation, except in accordance with such rules and regulations as the President shall prescribe . . .

Arming of American Merchant Vessels Prohibited

Sec. 10. Whenever the President shall have issued a proclamation under the authority of section 1, it shall thereafter be unlawful, until such proclamation is revoked, for any American vessel engaged in commerce with any belligerent state, or any state wherein civil strife exists, named in such proclamation, to be armed or to carry any armament, arms, ammunition, or implements of war, except small arms and ammunition therefor which the President may deem necessary and shall publicly designate for the preservation of discipline aboard such vessels.

Regulations

Sec. 11. The President may, from time to time, promulgate such rules and regulations, not inconsistent with law, as may be necessary and proper to carry out any of the provisions of this Act; and he may exercise any power of authority conferred on him by this Act through such officer or officers, or agency or agencies, as he shall direct. . . .

19. President Franklin D. Roosevelt's State of the Union Message to Congress, Delivered January 6, 1941

[Known as the Four Freedoms Speech]

Just as our national policy in internal affairs has been based upon a decent respect for the rights and dignity of all our fellowmen within our gates, so our national policy in foreign affairs has been based on a decent respect for the rights and dignity of all nations, large and small. And the justice of morality must and will win in the end.

Our national policy is this:

First, by an impressive expression of the public will and without regard to partisanship, we are committed to all inclusive national defense.

Second, by an impressive expression of the public will and without regard to partisanship, we are committed to full support of all those resolute peoples, everywhere, who are resisting aggression and are thereby keeping war away from our Hemisphere. By this support, we express our determination that the democratic cause shall prevail, and we strengthen the defense and security of our own nation.

Third, by an impressive expression of the public will and without regard to partisanship, we are committed to the proposition that principles of morality and considerations for our own security will never permit us to acquiesce in a peace dictated by aggressors and sponsored by appeasers. We know that enduring peace cannot be bought at the cost of other people's freedom.

In the recent national election there was no substantial difference between the two great parties in respect to that national policy. No issue was fought out on this line before the American electorate. Today it is abundantly evident that American citizens everywhere are demanding and supporting speedy and complete action in recognition of obvious danger. Therefore, the immediate need is a swift and driving increase in our armament production.

Leaders of industry and labor have responded to our summons. Goals of speed have been set. In some cases these goals are being reached ahead of time; in some cases we are on schedule; in other cases there are slight but not serious delays; and in some cases— and I am sorry to say very important cases—we are all concerned by the slowness of the accomplishment of our plans. The Army and Navy, however, have made substantial progress during the past year. Actual experience is improving and speeding up our methods of production with every passing day. And today's best is not good enough for tomorrow.

I am not satisfied with the progress thus far made. The men in charge of the program represent the best in training, ability, and patriotism. They are not satisfied with the progress thus far made. None of us will be satisfied until the job is done.

No matter whether the original goal was set too high or too low, our objective is quicker and better results.

To give two illustrations:

We are behind schedule in turning out finished airplanes; we are working day and night to solve the innumerable problems and to catch up.

We are ahead of schedule in building warships; but we are working to get even further ahead of schedule.

To change a whole nation from a basis of peacetime production of implements of peace to a basis of wartime production of implements of war is no small task. And the greatest difficulty comes at the beginning of the program, when new tools and plant facilities and new assembly lines and shipways must be constructed before the actual materiel begins to flow steadily and speedily from them.

The Congress, of course, must rightly keep itself informed at all times of the progress of the program. However, there is certain information, as the Congress itself will readily recognize, which, in the interests of our own security and those of the nations we are supporting, must of needs be kept in confidence. New circumstances are constantly begetting new needs for our safety. I shall ask this Congress for greatly increased new appropriations and authorizations to carry on what we have begun. I also ask this Congress for authority and for funds sufficient to manufacture additional munitions and war supplies of many kinds to be turned over to those nations which are now in active war with aggressor nations.

Our most useful and immediate role is to act as an arsenal for them as well as for ourselves. They do not need manpower. They do need billions of dollars' worth of the weapons of defense.

The time is near when they will not be able to pay for them in ready cash. We cannot, and will not, tell them they must surrender merely because of present inability to pay for the weapons which we know they must have. I do not recommend that we make them a loan of dollars with which to pay for these weapons—a loan to be repaid in dollars. I recommend that we make it possible for those nations to continue to obtain war materials in the United States, fitting their orders into our own program. Nearly all of their materiel would, if the time ever came, be useful for our own defense.

Taking counsel of expert military and naval authorities, considering what is best for our own security, we are free to decide how much should be kept here and how much should be sent abroad to our friends who, by their determined and heroic resistance, are giving us time in which to make ready our own defense. For what we send abroad we shall be repaid, within a reasonable time following the close of hostilities, in similar materials or, at our option, in other goods of many kinds which they can produce and which we need.

Let us say to the democracies: "We Americans are vitally concerned in your defense of freedom. We are putting forth our energies, our resources, and our organizing powers to give you the strength to regain and maintain a free world. We shall send you, in ever increasing numbers, ships, planes, tanks, guns. This is our purpose and our pledge."

In fulfillment of this purpose we will not be intimidated by the threats of dictators that they will regard as a breach of international law and as an act of war our aid to the democracies which dare to resist their aggression. Such aid is not an act of war, even if a dictator should unilaterally proclaim it so to be. When the dictators are ready to make war upon us, they will not wait for an act of war on our part. They did not wait for Norway or Belgium or the Netherlands to commit an act of war. Their only interest is in a new one-way international law, which lacks mutuality in its observance and, therefore, becomes an instrument of oppression.

The happiness of future generations of Americans may well depend upon how effective and how immediate we can make our aid felt. No one can tell the exact character of the emergency situations that we may be called upon to meet. The nation's hands must not be tied when the nation's life is in danger. We must all prepare to make the sacrifices that the emergency—as serious as war itself—demands. Whatever stands in the way of speed and efficiency in defense preparations must give way to the national need.

A free nation has the right to expect full cooperation from all groups. A free nation has the right to look to the leaders of business, of labor, and of agriculture to take the lead in stimulating effort, not among other groups but within their own groups.

The best way of dealing with the few slackers or troublemakers in our midst is, first, to shame them by patriotic example; and if that fails, to use the sovereignty of government to save government.

As men do not live by bread alone, they do not fight by armaments alone. Those who man our defenses and those behind them who build our defenses must have the stamina and courage which come from an unshakable belief in the manner of life which they are defending. The mighty action which we are calling for cannot be based on a disregard of all things worth fighting for.

The nation takes great satisfaction and much strength from the things which have been done to make its people conscious of their individual stake in the preservation of democratic life in America. Those things have toughened the fiber of our people, have renewed their faith and strengthened their devotion to the institutions we make ready to protect.

Certainly this is no time to stop thinking about the social and economic problems which are the root cause of the social revolution which is today a supreme factor in the world. There is nothing mysterious about the foundations of a healthy and strong democracy. The basic things expected by our people of their political and economic systems are simple. They are: Equality of opportunity for youth and for others; jobs for those who can work; security for those who need it; the ending of special privilege for the few; the preservation of civil liberties for all; the enjoyment of the fruits of scientific progress in a wider and constantly rising standard of living. These are the simple and basic things that must never be lost sight of in the turmoil and unbelievable complexity of our modern world. The inner and abiding strength of our economic and political systems is dependent upon the degree to which they fulfill these expectations.

Many subjects connected with our social economy call for immediate improvement. As examples:

We should bring more citizens under the coverage of old-age pensions and unemployment insurance.

We should widen the opportunities for adequate medical care.

We should plan a better system by which persons deserving or needing gainful employment can obtain it.

I have called for personal sacrifice. I am assured of the willingness of almost all Americans to respond to that call. A part of the sacrifice means the payment of more money in taxes. In my budget message I recommend that a greater portion of this great defense program be paid for from taxation than we are paying today. No person should try, or be allowed, to get rich out of this program; and the principle of tax payments in accordance with ability to pay should be constantly before our eyes to guide our legislation. If the Congress maintains these principles, the voters, putting patriotism ahead of pocketbooks, will give you their applause.

In the future days, which we seek to make secure, we look forward to a world founded upon four essential human freedoms.

The first is freedom of speech and expression everywhere in the world.

The second is freedom of every person to worship God in his own way everywhere in the world.

The third is freedom from want, which, translated into world terms, means economic understandings which will secure to every nation a healthy peacetime life for its inhabitants everywhere in the world.

The fourth is freedom from fear—which, translated into world terms, means a worldwide reduction of armaments to such a point and in such a thorough fashion that no nation will be in a position to commit an act of physical aggression against any neighbor—anywhere in the world.

That is no vision of a distant millennium. It is a definite basis for a kind of world attainable in our own time and generation. That kind of world is the very antithesis of the so-called new order of tyranny which the dictators seek to create with the crash of a bomb.

To that new order we oppose the greater conception—the moral order. A good society is able to face schemes of world domination and foreign revolutions alike without fear.

Since the beginning of our American history, we have engaged in change—in a perpetual peaceful revolution—a revolution which goes on steadily, quietly adjusting itself to changing conditions—without the concentration camp or the quicklime in the ditch. The world order which we seek is the cooperation of free countries, working together in a friendly, civilized society.

This nation has placed its destiny in the hands and hearts of its millions of free men and women, and its faith in freedom under the guidance of God. Freedom means the supremacy of human rights everywhere. Our support goes to those who struggle to gain those rights or keep them. Our strength is in our unity of purpose. To that high concept there can be no end save victory.

20. THE LEND-LEASE ACT, MARCH 11, 1941

Be it enacted, That this Act may be cited as "An Act to Promote the Defense of the United States." . . .

Section 3.

(a) Notwithstanding the provisions of any other law, the President may, from time to time, when he deems it in the interest of national defense, authorize the Secretary of War, the Secretary of the Navy, or the head of any other department or agency of the Government—

(1) To manufacture in arsenals, factories, and shipyards under their jurisdiction, or otherwise procure, to the extent to which funds are made available therefor, or contracts are authorized from time to time by the Congress, or both, any defense article for the government of any country whose defense the President deems vital to the defense of the United States.

(2) To sell, transfer title to, exchange, lease, lend, or otherwise dispose of, to any such government any defense article, but no defense article not manufactured or procured under paragraph (1) shall in any way be disposed of under this paragraph, except after consultation with the Chief of Staff of the Army or the Chief of Naval Operations of the Navy, or both. The value of defense articles disposed of in any way under authority of this paragraph, and procured from funds heretofore appropriated, shall not exceed $1,300,000,000. The value of such defense articles shall be determined by the head of the department or agency concerned or such other department, agency or officer as shall be designated in the manner provided in the rules and regulations issued hereunder. Defense articles procured from funds hereafter appropriated to any department or agency of the Government, other than from funds authorized to be appropriated under this Act, shall not be disposed of in any way under authority of

this paragraph except to the extent hereafter authorized by the Congress in the Acts appropriating such funds or otherwise.

(3) To test, inspect, prove, repair, outfit, recondition, or otherwise to place in good working order, to the extent to which funds are made available therefor, or contracts are authorized from time to time by the Congress, or both, any defense article for any such government, or to procure any or all such services by private contract.

(4) To communicate to any such government any defense information, pertaining to any defense article furnished to such government under paragraph (2) of this subsection.

(5) To release for export any defense article disposed of in any way under this subsection to any such government,

(b) The terms and conditions upon which any such foreign government receives any aid authorized under subsection (a) shall be those which the President deems satisfactory, and the benefit to the United States may be payment or repayment in kind or property, or any other direct or indirect benefit which the President deems satisfactory.

(c) After June 30, 1943, or after the passage of a concurrent resolution by the two Houses before June 30, 1943, which declares that the powers conferred by or pursuant to subsection (a) are no longer necessary to promote the defense of the United States, neither the President nor the head of any department or agency shall exercise any of the powers conferred by or pursuant to subsection (a); except that until July 1, 1946, any of such powers may be exercised to the extent necessary to carry out a contract or agreement with such a foreign government made before July 1, 1943, or before the passage of such concurrent resolution, whichever is the earlier.

(d) Nothing in this Act shall be construed to authorize or to permit the authorization of convoying vessels by naval vessels of the United States.

(e) Nothing in this Act shall be construed to authorize or to permit the authorization of the entry of any American vessel into a combat area in violation of section 3 of the Neutrality Act of 1939. . . .

Section 8

The Secretaries of War and of the Navy are hereby authorized to purchase or otherwise acquire arms, ammunition, and implements of war produced within the jurisdiction of any country to which section 3 is applicable, whenever the President deems such purchase or acquisition to be necessary in the interests of the defense of the United States.

Section 9

The president may, from time to time, promulgate such rules and regulations as may be necessary and proper to carry out any of the provisions of this Act; and he may exercise any power or authority conferred on him by this Act through such department, agency, or officer as he shall direct.

21. EXECUTIVE ORDER 8802, ESTABLISHING THE PRESIDENT'S COMMITTEE ON FAIR EMPLOYMENT PRACTICES, ISSUED JUNE 25, 1941

[This order established the principle of nondiscriminatory hiring in government and in the defense industries.]

Reaffirming policy of full participation in the defense program by all persons, regardless of race, creed, color, or national origin, and directing certain actions in furtherance of said policy.

Whereas it is the policy of the United States to encourage full participation in the national defense program by all citizens of the United States, regardless of race, creed, color, or national origin, in the firm belief that the democratic way of life within the nation can be defended successfully only with the help and support of all groups within its borders; and

Whereas there is evidence that available and needed workers have been barred from employment in industries engaged in defense production solely because of considerations of race, creed, color, or national origin to the detriment of workers' morale and of national unity;

Now, Therefore, by virtue of the authority vested in me by the Constitution and the statutes, and as a prerequisite to the successful conduct of our national defense production effort, I do hereby reaffirm the policy of the United States that there shall be no discrimination in the employment of workers in defense industries or government because of race, creed, color, or national origin; and I do hereby declare that it is the duty of employers and of labor organizations, in furtherance of said policy and of this order, to provide for the full and equitable participation of all workers in defense industries, without discrimination because of race, creed, color, or national origin;

And it is hereby ordered as follows:

1. All departments and agencies of the government of the United States concerned with vocational and training programs for defense production shall take special measures appropriate to assure that such programs are administered without discrimination because of race, creed, color, or national origin.

2. All contracting agencies of the government of the United States shall include in all defense contracts hereafter negotiated by them a provision obligating the contractor not to discriminate against any worker because of race, creed, color, or national origin.

3. There is established in the Office of Production Management a Committee on Fair Employment Practice, which shall consist of a chairman and four other members to be appointed by the President. The chairman and members of the committee shall serve as such without compensation but shall be entitled to actual and necessary transportation, subsistence, and other expenses incidental to performance of their duties. The committee shall receive and investigate complaints of discrimination in violation of the provisions of this order and shall take appropriate steps to redress grievances which it finds to be valid. The committee shall also recommend to the several departments and agencies of the government of the United States and to the President all measures which may be deemed by it necessary or proper to effectuate the provisions of this order.

22. THE ATLANTIC CHARTER, AUGUST 12, 1941

[A declaration of British and U.S. goals issued by Prime Minister Winston Churchill and President Franklin D. Roosevelt following their three-day meeting aboard ship in harbor at Newfoundland]

Joint declaration of the President of the United States of America and the Prime Minister, Mr. Churchill, representing His Majesty's government in the United Kingdom, being met together, deem it right to make known certain common principles in the national policies of their respective countries on which they base their hopes for a better future for the world.

First, their countries seek no aggrandizement, territorial or other.

Second, they desire to see no territorial changes that do not accord with the freely expressed wishes of the peoples concerned.

Third, they respect the right of all peoples to choose the form of government under which they will live; and they wish to see sovereign rights and self-government restored to those who have been forcibly deprived of them.

Fourth, they will endeavor, with due respect for their existing obligations, to further the enjoyment by all states, great or small, victor or vanquished, of access, on equal terms, to the trade and to the raw materials of the world which are needed for their economic prosperity.

Fifth, they desire to bring about the fullest collaboration between all nations in the economic field with the object of securing, for all, improved labor standards, economic advancement, and social security.

Sixth, after the final destruction of the Nazi tyranny, they hope to see established a peace which will afford to all nations the means of dwelling in safety within their own boundaries, and which will afford assurance that all the men in all the lands may live out their lives in freedom from fear and want.

Seventh, such a peace should enable all men to traverse the high seas and oceans without hindrance.

Eighth, they believe that all of the nations of the world, for realistic as well as spiritual reasons, must come to the abandonment of the use of force. Since no future peace can be maintained if land, sea, or air armaments continue to be employed by nations which threaten, or may threaten, aggression outside of their frontiers, they believe, pending the establishment of a wider and permanent system of general security, that the disarmament of such nations is essential. They will likewise aid and encourage all other practicable measures which will lighten for peaceloving peoples the crushing burden of armaments.

23. PRESIDENT FRANKLIN D. ROOSEVELT'S REQUEST TO CONGRESS FOR A DECLARATION OF WAR ON JAPAN, DECEMBER 8, 1941

Yesterday, December 7, 1941—a day which will live in infamy—the United States of America was suddenly and deliberately attacked by naval and air forces of the Empire of Japan.

The United States was at peace with that nation, and, at the solicitation of Japan, was still in conversation with its government and its emperor looking toward the maintenance of peace in the Pacific. Indeed, one hour after the Japanese air squadron had commenced bombing in Oahu, the Japanese ambassador to the United States and his colleague delivered to the secretary of state a formal reply to a recent American message. While this reply stated that it seemed useless to continue the existing diplomatic negotiations, it contained no threat or hint of war or armed attack.

It will be recorded that the distance of Hawaii from Japan makes it obvious that the attack was deliberately planned many days or even weeks ago. During the intervening time the Japanese government has deliberately sought to deceive the United States by false statements and expressions of hope for continued peace.

The attack yesterday on the Hawaiian Islands has caused severe damage to American naval and military forces. Very many American lives have been lost. In addition, American ships have been reported torpedoed on the high seas between San Francisco and Honolulu.

Yesterday the Japanese government also launched an attack against Malaya.

Last night Japanese forces attacked Hong Kong.

Last night Japanese forces attacked Guam.

Last night Japanese forces attacked the Philippine Islands.

Last night the Japanese attacked Wake Island.

This morning the Japanese attacked Midway Island.

Japan has, therefore, undertaken a surprise offensive extending throughout the Pacific area. The facts of yesterday speak for themselves. The people of the United States have already formed their opinions and well understand the implications to the very life and safety of our nation.

As commander in chief of the Army and Navy I have directed that all measures be taken for our defense.

Always will we remember the character of the onslaught against us. No matter how long it may take us to overcome this premeditated invasion, the American people, in their righteous might, will win through to absolute victory. I believe I interpret the will of the Congress and of the people when I assert that we will not only defend ourselves to the uttermost but will make very certain that this form of treachery shall never endanger us again.

Hostilities exist. There is no blinking at the fact that our people, our territory, and our interests are in grave danger.

With confidence in our armed forces—with the unbounded determination of our people—we will gain the inevitable triumph—so help us God.

I ask that the Congress declare that since the unprovoked and dastardly attack by Japan on Sunday, December 7, a state of war has existed between the United States and the Japanese Empire.

24. DECLARATION OF WAR ON GERMANY, DECEMBER 11, 1941

The President's Message

To the Congress of the United States:

On the morning of Dec. 11 the Government of Germany, pursuing its course of world conquest, declared war against the United States.

The long-known and the long-expected has thus taken place. The forces endeavoring to enslave the entire world now are moving toward this hemisphere.

Never before has there been a greater challenge to life, liberty and civilization.

Delay invites great danger. Rapid and united effort by all of the peoples of the world who are determined to remain free will insure a world victory of the forces of justice and of righteousness over the forces of savagery and of barbarism.

Italy also has declared war against the United States.

I therefore request the Congress to recognize a state of war between the United States and Germany, and between the United States and Italy.

FRANKLIN D. ROOSEVELT.

The War Resolution

Declaring that a state of war exists between the Government of Germany and the government and the people of the United States and making provision to prosecute the same.

Whereas the Government of Germany has formally declared war against the government and the people of the United States of America:

Therefore, be it

Resolved by the Senate and House of Representatives of the United States of America in Congress assembled, that the state of war between the United States and the Government of Germany which has thus been thrust upon the United States is hereby formally declared; and the President is hereby authorized and directed to employ the entire naval and military forces of the United States and the resources of the government to carry on war against the Government of Germany; and, to bring the conflict to a successful termination, all of the resources of the country are hereby pledged by the Congress of the United States.

Appendix B
Biographies of Major Personalities

Addams, Jane (1860–1935) *social worker, reformer, author*
Addams was born in Cedarville, Illinois. She graduated from Rockford College (Illinois) in 1881. After a visit to Toynbee Hall in London, she and Ellen Gates Starr established Hull-House in Chicago in September 1889 to provide educational and other opportunities to working-class, mostly immigrant neighborhood residents. Addams advocated the eight-hour workday for women, factory inspections, workers' compensation, women's suffrage, and other reforms. In 1910 she became the first woman president of the National Conference of Social Work. She opposed U.S. entry into World War I, was president of the Women's International League for Peace (1919 to 1935), and received the Nobel Peace Prize in 1931. Addams's best-known book is her memoir *Twenty Years at Hull-House* (1910).

Agee, James (1909–1955) *poet, novelist, film critic*
Agee was born in Knoxville, Tennessee. He graduated from Harvard University in 1932 and thereafter wrote film reviews for *Time*, the *Nation*, and *Fortune* magazines. In 1934 he published a collection of poems, *Permit Me Voyage*. In 1936 he and photographer Walker Evans lived among sharecroppers in Alabama for six weeks to gather materials for an article for *Fortune*, which formed the basis of his book *Let Us Now Praise Famous Men* (1941). During the last seven years of his life, Agee worked mostly as a scriptwriter for films, including *The African Queen* (1951) and *The Night of the Hunter* (1955). His other works include the novel *A Death in the Family* (1957), adapted for the stage as *All the Way Home* (1960).

Aldrich, Winthrop W. (1885–1974) *banker*
Born in Providence, Rhode Island, Aldrich graduated from Harvard University (1907) and Harvard Law School (1910). He began practicing law in 1912, served in the naval reserve during World War I, then was a partner in the Murray, Aldrich and Webb law firm until 1929, when he became president of Equitable Trust Co. In 1930 he became president of Chase National Bank, and in 1933 he joined the Business Advisory Council. During that time, he supported New Deal programs, including the National Recovery Administration. But he opposed the Banking Act of 1935 and the court-packing proposal. In 1935 he became chairman of the Chase board, serving until 1953, when he was named ambassador to Great Britain.

Alexander, Will W. (1884–1956) *clergyman, administrator, head of the Farm Security Administration*
Born in Morrisville, Missouri, Alexander graduated from Scarrett Morrisville College (1908) and entered the Methodist ministry, with parishes in Tennessee. In 1919 he became executive director of the Commission on Interracial Cooperation. He opposed the Ku Klux Klan in the 1920s and served as chairman of the Social Science Research Council's Advisory Commission on Racial Problems. In 1930 he became president of Dillard University in New Orleans, leaving in 1935 to become assistant administrator of the Resettlement Administration. In 1937, President Franklin D. Roosevelt named him head of the Farm Security Administration, which absorbed the Resettlement Administration. He retired in 1940.

Anderson, Marian (1902–1993) *opera singer*
Born in Philadelphia, Anderson studied voice with Guiseppi Boghetti. She appeared with the New York Philharmonic after winning a contest. She debuted in Europe in 1930 in Berlin, then toured Europe under Sol Hurok's management, winning acclaim. Anderson returned to the United States in 1935 and performed

at Carnegie Hall. A 1939 scheduled performance at Constitution Hall in Washington, D.C., was canceled by the Daughters of the American Revolution (DAR), owners of the hall, prompting Eleanor Roosevelt to resign from the DAR and arrange for the recital at the Lincoln Memorial, where Anderson sang for an audience estimated at 75,000. In 1955, Anderson became the first black to perform at the Metropolitan Opera.

Anderson, Mary (1872–1964) *director of the Women's Bureau*
Anderson was born in Lynhoping, Sweden, and came to the United States in 1889; the family settled in Chicago. In 1902, Anderson joined the Women's Trade Union League. In 1919, President Woodrow Wilson appointed her as director of the new Women's Bureau in the Department of Labor; she served until retiring in 1944. She supported the National Recovery Administration, Social Security, the Fair Labor Standards Act, and other New Deal programs. *Woman at Work: The Autobiography of Mary Anderson as Told to Mary N. Winslow* appeared in 1951.

Anderson, Sherwood (1876–1941) *novelist*
Born in Camden, Ohio, Anderson served in the Spanish-American War. He moved to Cleveland in 1906, living there for five years with successful ventures in manufacturing and advertising. He moved to Chicago in 1913 and began writing fiction while working in a paint factory. His first two novels were *Windy McPherson's Son* (1916) and *Marching Men* (1917). The acclaimed and influential collection of short stories *Winesburg, Ohio* appeared in 1919. His only popular novel, *Dark Laughter,* was published in 1925. Through his works and encouragement Anderson influenced major writers, such as William Faulkner and F. Scott Fitzgerald. In 1927 he moved to Marion, Virginia, where he owned and edited two newspapers.

Armstrong, Louis (1900–1971) *renowned jazz trumpeter and bandleader*
Armstrong, popularly known as "Satchmo," was born and raised in New Orleans, where he imbibed Dixieland music. In 1922 bandleader Joe "King" Oliver invited him to Chicago to play second trumpet in his Creole Street Band, which produced a series of popular recordings. With the Hot Five and Hot Seven ensembles he created, Armstrong showcased his solo virtuosity in recordings produced from 1925 to 1928. Armstrong invented improvisational "scat" singing, later perfected by Ella Fitzgerald. After 1930 he was not only widely popular as a bandleader but also as a composer, movie star, and comedian. His best-known compositions include "I Wish That I Could Shimmy Like My Sister Kate" and "Dipper Mouth Blues."

Astaire, Fred (1899–1987) *most popular and proficient dancer of his time*
Astaire, born Frederick Austerlitz in Omaha, was dancing by age seven in vaudeville with his sister, Adele. Their act moved to Broadway in 1917, achieving world renown with such hits as *Funny Face* (1927) and *The Bandwagon* (1931). In 1933 Astaire appeared in two films, the more important being *Flying Down to Rio,* where he was teamed with Ginger Rogers; the two thereafter appeared in a series of highly popular films that revolutionized the movie musical. These include *The Gay Divorcee* (1934), *Roberta* (1935), *Top Hat* (1935), *Swing Time* (1936), and *The Story of Vernon and Irene Castle* (1939). Astaire retired in 1946 but returned to film in 1948 in *Easter Parade,* with Judy Garland. In 1949 he received a special Academy Award.

Baldwin, Roger Nash (1884–1981) *head of the American Civil Liberties Union*
Baldwin was born in Wellesley, Massachusetts. He received bachelor's (1904) and master's (1905) degrees from Harvard University. From 1910 to 1917 he was executive secretary of the St. Louis Civic League. In 1917 he became director of the American Union Against Militarism. As its offshoot he established the American Civil Liberties Union (ACLU) in 1920. Baldwin was imprisoned for a year during 1918 for refusing to register for the draft. He headed the ACLU until 1950. Baldwin worked to defend Sacco and Vanzetti, to lift the censorship of James Joyce's *Ulysses,* and to pay Clarence Darrow's fees for the Scopes trial, among other causes.

Baldwin, Stanley (1867–1947) *British prime minister, Conservative Party leader*
Baldwin served as a member of the House of Commons from 1908 to 1937. In fall 1922 he and Andrew Bonar Law forced the end of the wartime

coalition government under David Lloyd George, with Law becoming prime minister. When Law became ill, Baldwin succeeded him as prime minister in May 1923. Although unseated by Ramsay MacDonald in January 1924, he resumed the prime ministership in November of that year and served until 1929, when MacDonald again became prime minister, with Baldwin serving in a coalition government. Baldwin once again became prime minister in June 1935, serving until May 1937.

Ballantine, Arthur A. (1883–1960) *undersecretary of the treasury*
Ballantine was born in Oberlin, Ohio. He graduated from Harvard University (1904) and earned a Harvard law degree (1907). He practiced law in Boston and in 1918 became federal solicitor of internal revenue. In 1930, President Herbert Hoover appointed him as assistant secretary of the treasury; he became undersecretary in 1932. Ballantine advised Hoover and later President Franklin D. Roosevelt on the banking crisis, successively urging FDR to declare a bank holiday and to support a law allowing the government to invest in troubled private banks.

Barkley, Alben W. (1877–1956) *legislator, vice president*
Barkley was born in Graves County, Kentucky, and began practicing law in Paducah in 1898. Active in Democratic politics, he was elected county attorney and county judge, and, in 1912, U.S. congressman. He served in the House of Representatives until 1927. Elected U.S. senator in 1926, he served until 1949 and was majority leader from 1937 to 1947. Barkley helped secure passage of laws establishing the Agricultural Adjustment Administration, the Farm Security Administration, Social Security, and other New Deal programs. A major Democratic power broker from 1932 on, he served as Harry Truman's vice president from 1949 to 1953. Barkley was reelected to the Senate in 1954.

Bankhead, John H. (1872–1946) *Democratic senator*
Born in Moscow, Alabama, Bankhead, whose father was a U.S. senator, graduated from University of Alabama (1891) and earned a law degree at Georgetown University (1893). He practiced law in Alabama and served in the state legislature (1903–07).

In 1930, Bankhead was elected to the Senate, where he served until his death. He coauthored the Soil Conservation and Domestic Allotment Act (1936), the Bankhead-Jones Farm Tenancy Act (1937), and the Agricultural Adjustment Act of 1938. Though a supporter of President Franklin D. Roosevelt, he opposed the court-packing proposal.

Bankhead, William B. (1874–1940) *congressman*
Bankhead was born in Moscow, Alabama, and was the brother of Senator John Bankhead. He graduated from the University of Alabama (1893), where he also earned a master's degree (1896), and received a law degree from Georgetown University (1895). He practiced law in Alabama from 1895 until he was elected to Congress in 1917, where he served until his death. As chairman of the House Rules Committee, Bankhead aided passage of New Deal programs. In 1935 he became majority leader.

Barton, Bruce (1886–1967) *editor, advertising executive, congressman*
Barton was born in Robbin, Tennessee, and graduated from Amherst College (1907). He began working for the *Home Herald* in Chicago and became editor of *Housekeeper.* In 1912 he joined P. F. Colliers Sons as an editor. He was editor of *Everyweek* (1914–18) and, in 1919, organized the advertising firm Barton, Durstine, and Osborne, which created the Betty Crocker symbol for General Mills. Also a freelance writer, Barton published the enormously popular *The Man Nobody Knows* in 1925. In 1936 he was elected to Congress as a Republican. A strong opponent of Franklin D. Roosevelt, Barton left Congress in 1941.

Baruch, Bernard M. (1870–1965) *financier, investor, head of the War Industries Board during World War I, staunch Democrat*
Baruch graduated from the College of the City of New York in 1889, worked in stock brokerage firms, and became extremely wealthy speculating in stocks. He served on the Supreme Economic Council at Versailles and advised President Woodrow Wilson on proposals for the peace treaty. A reluctant supporter of Franklin D. Roosevelt in 1932, he later became an adviser to the president, although in no significant way except for counsel on economic policies during World War II. Baruch staffers such as Hugh Johnson and George Peek served FDR as administrators.

Beard, Charles A. (1874–1948) *influential historian*
A native of Knightstown, Indiana, Beard graduated from DePauw University in 1898 and then studied at Oxford University until 1904, returning home in 1900 to marry Mary Ritter. In 1904 he joined the political science faculty at Columbia University. Influenced by John Ruskin, E. R. A. Seligman, and the progressive movement, Beard wrote his seminal *An Economic Interpretation of the Constitution of the United States* (1913). In 1917 Beard resigned from Columbia to protest dismissal of faculty members charged as subversives, and in 1919 he became cofounder of the New School for Social Research. His classic history, *The Rise of American Civilization,* which he coauthored with his wife, Mary, appeared in 1927. Between 1934 and 1945, Beard wrote critiques of Franklin D. Roosevelt's foreign policy.

Bellows, George W. (1882–1925) *painter, portraitist*
Born in Columbus, Ohio, Bellows graduated from Ohio State University (1903) and studied painting with Robert Henri in New York. He became part of the realistic movement known as the Ash Can school and gained fame especially for his paintings of fight scenes, such as *Stag at Sharkey's* (1909) and *Dempsey and Firpo* (1924). Bellows taught at the Art Students League in New York City and at the Art Institute of Chicago.

Benny, Jack (1894–1974) *comedian*
Born Benjamin Kubelsky in Chicago and raised in Waukegan, Illinois, Benny studied violin and then entered vaudeville. He returned to the circuit after service in World War I and took the stage name Jack Benny. In 1929 he appeared in his first movie, *Hollywood Review of 1929.* In 1932 he began his own radio program on NBC. Among the most popular shows on radio, his program endured until 1955. Benny also began a television program in 1950 that lasted until 1960.

Bergen, Edgar (1903–1978) *ventriloquist*
Born in Chicago (original name Bergren), Bergen studied with a professional ventriloquist and had a dummy made that he named Charlie McCarthy. He toured on the Chautauqua circuit, studied at Northwestern University (1924), and then entered vaudeville (1926), touring for 10 years. In 1936

Bergen was a hit on the Rudy Vallee program, and in 1937 he got his own show, which became one of the most popular shows on radio for the next 10 years. He and Charlie also appeared in several movies.

Berle, Adolf Augustus, Jr. (1895–1971) *member of Roosevelt's "Brains Trust" (with Moley and Tugwell)*
Berle was born in Boston and earned bachelor's (at age 18) and law (at age 21) degrees from Harvard University. In the twenties, Berle practiced corporate law in New York, forming his own firm in 1924. In 1927 he joined the Columbia University Law School faculty. In 1932 he published *The Modern Corporation and Private Property,* written with Gardiner Means, and became an adviser to President Franklin D. Roosevelt. He returned to New York City to help Fiorello LaGuardia win the 1933 mayoral election and then served as city chamberlain, while continuing to advise FDR and write speeches for him. In 1938, FDR persuaded Berle to become assistant secretary of state. Berle helped negotiate with Canada to create the St. Lawrence Seaway. During the war he coordinated State Department intelligence activities.

Berlin, Irving (1888–1989) *composer*
Born in Russia (real name Israel Baline), Berlin was brought to the United States while an infant. Early on, he worked as a singing waiter in New York. Berlin created songs encompassing virtually the entire history of American popular music in the first half of this century. His popular musical comedies during the depression years included *Face the Music* (1932), *As Thousands Cheer* (1936), and *Louisiana Purchase* (1940), his greatest success was *Annie Get Your Gun* (1946). Among Berlin's most popular songs are "God Bless America," "Blue Skies," "Everybody's Doin' It," and "White Christmas."

Bethune, Mary McLeod (1875–1955) *educator, civil rights leader*
Bethune was born to former slaves in Mayesville, South Carolina. She graduated from Moody Bible Institute in Chicago in 1895, taught in Presbyterian schools in the South, and in 1905 founded a girls' primary school in Daytona Beach, Florida. In 1923 the school and a men's school merged to become Bethune-Cookman College, with Bethune as president. In 1935 she founded the National Council on Negro Women. A friend of Eleanor Roosevelt—they

first met in 1927—Bethune became head of the Division of Negro Affairs of the National Youth Administration (NYA) in 1935. Through meetings with President Franklin D. Roosevelt, she was the New Deal's chief adviser on African-American issues and led the so-called Black Cabinet of federal officials.

Biddle, Francis B. (1886–1968) *U.S. attorney general*
Born in Paris, France, while his parents were traveling, Biddle attended Groton School (Groton, Massachusetts) and graduated with honors from Harvard Law School in 1911. He served as secretary to Justice Oliver Wendell Holmes, entered the family's law firm in Philadelphia, and founded a law partnership in 1917. Until 1934 he was counsel for the Pennsylvania Railroad and other corporations. He broke with the Republicans to support the Progressive Party's Robert La Follette in 1924 and Democrat Alfred Smith in 1928 for president. In 1932 he supported Franklin D. Roosevelt, who appointed him chairman of the National Labor Relations Board in 1934, but the Supreme Court's *Schechter* decision ended this agency in 1935. In 1939, Biddle became solicitor general, and in September 1941 he became attorney general, serving until 1945.

Black, Hugo L. (1886–1971) *senator, associate justice of the Supreme Court*
Black was born and raised in Alabama and graduated from University of Alabama law school in 1906. He practiced law and served in county prosecutorial posts; he won election to the Senate in 1926, serving until 1937. Black helped secure passage of the 1935 Wheeler-Rayburn Act. Black supported President Franklin D. Roosevelt's plans to increase the size of the Supreme Court, and FDR appointed him to the Court in 1937. His opinions favored New Deal views on economic regulations, labor relations, and other programs. He supported protection of civil liberties, especially First Amendment rights. In failing health, he resigned from the Court in September 1971.

Bogart, Humphrey (1899–1957) *actor*
Born in New York City, Bogart served in the navy during World War I. He played juvenile roles on the stage and debuted in film in *Broadway's Like That* (1930). He played the role of murderer Duke Mantee in *The Petrified Forest* both on Broadway (1935) and in the movie (1936). Bogart appeared in gangster movies with Edward G. Robinson and James Cagney and became a star in 1941 with lead roles in *High Sierra* and *The Maltese Falcon,* in the latter portraying Dashiell Hammett's hard-boiled detective Sam Spade.

Borah, William Edgar (1865–1940) *senator from Idaho*
Born in Illinois, Borah began practicing law in Kansas in 1889, then moved to Boise, Idaho. In 1892 he became chairman of the Republican State Central Committee. In 1906 he was elected to the Senate from Idaho and served for 33 years. He supported creation of the Department of Labor and the Children's Bureau, but as an isolationist, he opposed ratifying the Peace of Paris and recognizing the League of Nations. In 1924, Borah became chairman of the Senate Committee on Foreign Relations. He supported the Pact of Paris, diplomatic recognition of the USSR, and the Good Neighbor policy. Though favoring economic reform, he opposed the National Industrial Recovery Act. Borah rejected U.S. involvement in World War II.

Bourke-White, Margaret (1906–1971) *photographer, photojournalist*
Born in New York City, Bourke-White was hired in 1929 by Henry Luce as a photographer for *Fortune.* She became one of the first staff photographers for *Life,* begun in 1936. During World War II, she accompanied U.S. troops in North Africa and Italy, covered the German siege of Moscow, and went with American forces advancing into Germany. After the war, she shot photoessays in India, including famous portraits of Mohandas Gandhi, South Africa, and Korea (during the war there). She published several books, including *You Have Seen Their Faces* (1937) with her second husband, writer Erskine Caldwell.

Bow, Clara (1905–1965) *film actor known as the "It girl" for her vivacious, sensual portrayals, symbol of the flapper*
Born in Brooklyn, New York, Bow won a beauty contest at 17 and went on to appear in her first movie, *Beyond the Rainbow* (1922). Madame Elinor Glyn chose her to star in the movie version of her novel *It* (1927), a box office hit, and for the rest of the decade, Bow was among the highest-paid stars in

Hollywood. A decline in popularity after the advent of sound and a scandalous lifestyle caused her to retire in the 1930s.

Brandeis, Louis D. (1856–1941) *associate justice of the Supreme Court*
Brandeis was born in Louisville, Kentucky, graduated from Harvard Law School in 1877, prachced law briefly in St. Louis, and in 1879 formed a law firm with a Harvard friend in Boston. An active Zionist and political reformer, he supported Woodrow Wilson in 1912. In 1916, Wilson appointed him to the Supreme Court, the first Jew ever to serve on the Court. With Professor Felix Frankfurter of the Harvard Law School, Brandeis supported liberal causes. Both recommended appointees for New Deal posts and influenced proposed legislation. But Brandeis opposed the National Recovery Administration, the Agricultural Adjustment Administration, and Franklin D. Roosevelt's attempt to increase the size of the Supreme Court. He retired from the Court in 1939.

Browder, Earl R. (1891–1973) *leader of the Communist Party*
Browder was imprisoned in 1919–20 for opposing U.S. entry into World War I. He joined the Communist Party in 1921, served as general secretary from 1933 to 1944, and was a presidential candidate in 1936 and 1940. In 1940 he was sentenced to prison for a passport violation. In 1944 he was forced out as party leader for advocating peaceful coexistence between capitalism and communism, a heretical view referred to as "Browderism," for which he was expelled from the party in 1946. Browder was the author of numerous books.

Bryan, William Jennings (1860–1925) *political leader, statesman*
Raised in Illinois, Bryan practiced law (1883–87) in Jacksonville and then moved to Lincoln, Nebraska, where his speeches in support of Democratic candidates earned him public recognition. He was elected to Congress in 1890, where he argued against imposing tariffs and repealing the Sherman Act's silver purchase clause, earning him leadership of the free silver movement. Defeated in a run for the Senate in 1894, Bryan became editor of the *Omaha World-Herald*. In 1896 his impassioned "Cross of Gold" speech at the Democratic National Convention won him nomination as the party's presidential candidate, but he lost the race, repeating the loss in 1900 and 1908. In 1900 he established and edited a political journal entitled *Commoner*, which inspired his epithet "the Great Commoner." As Bryan helped to secure Woodrow Wilson's nomination in 1912, the president appointed him secretary of state. He campaigned for preventing wars through arbitration. A pacifist, Bryan resigned from office following Wilson's reprimand of Germany after the sinking of the *Lusitania* in 1915, but he supported the later war effort. Bryan's achievements as a political leader included advocacy of such reforms as popular election of senators, an income tax, women's suffrage, and creation of the Department of Labor; he also supported Prohibition. Bryan's involvement in the Scopes trial in Dayton, Tennessee, led to his death there from overexertion.

Buck, Pearl (1892–1973) *author*
Born in Hillsboro, West Virginia, but raised in China, where her parents were Presbyterian missionaries, Buck was educated in Shanghai and at Randolph-Macon Woman's College, graduating in 1914. She returned to China and taught in Nanjing. She married missionary John L. Buck in 1917. In the early 1920s, she began publishing articles and stories about China in American magazines. Her popular novel *The Good Earth* (1931) won the Pulitzer Prize in 1932. She expanded this work into a trilogy with *Sons* (1932) and *A House Divided* (1935). Divorced in 1934, she married New York publisher Richard J. Walsh in 1935 and resided in the United States thereafter. She received the Nobel Prize in literature in 1938. After World War II she founded the Pearl S. Buck Foundation to assist children fathered by U.S. servicemen in Asian nations.

Byrnes, James F. (1879–1972) *senator, justice, secretary of state*
Byrnes was born in Charleston, South Carolina. Admitted to the bar in 1903, he was elected congressman in 1910. He failed in a run for the Senate in 1924 but succeeded in 1930. A supporter of Franklin D. Roosevelt, he helped pass the Agricultural Adjustment Act, the Securities Act, and other New Deal legislation. Byrnes supported the court-packing proposal and the Reorganization Act

of 1939. Roosevelt appointed him to the Supreme Court in June 1941, but he resigned in 1942 to head the Office of Economic Stabilization and later the Office of War Mobilization. He served as secretary of state (1945–47) and governor of South Carolina (1951–55).

Cagney, James (1899–1986) *dancer, actor*
Cagney was born in New York City and debuted as a dancer (self-taught) on Broadway in *Pitter Patter* (1920). He performed in vaudeville and in a series of Broadway productions during the 1920s, including *Grand Street Follies* (1928), which gained him a film contract with Warner Brothers. In Hollywood, Cagney starred in gangster movies, notably *The Public Enemy* (1931), and in musicals. His *Yankee Doodle Dandy* (1942), based on the life and music of George M. Cohan, remains popular today. Cagney appeared in films through the 1960s; his last film was *Ragtime* (1983).

Cantor, Eddie (1892–1964) *vocalist, comedian*
Cantor was born Edward Israel Iskowitz in New York. He performed on Broadway during the years of World War I and in the *Ziegfield Follies* during the 1920s. In the 1930s, he began to star in films, such as *Palmy Days* (1931) and *Roman Scandal* (1933). In February 1931, he made his radio debut on Rudy Vallee's popular *Fleischmann Hour,* and in September he began his own program on NBC, *The Chase and Sanborn Hour,* which soon became the most popular show on radio. Cantor introduced the use of live audiences. Dinah Shore and George Burns and Gracie Allen debuted on Cantor's show. Cantor moved to Hollywood in 1950 to begin a television show.

Capone, Alphonse (1899–1947) *archetype of the 1920s gangster*
Capone was raised in Brooklyn, New York, left school at age 14, and worked as a bartender and bouncer. A knife wound suffered in a scrape earned him the nickname "Scarface." In 1920 Capone moved to Chicago and joined Johnny Torrio to create a gang that by 1924 controlled much of the city's gambling, prostitution, and bootlegging. Capone's men killed rival Dion O'Banion in 1924 and eliminated the remnants of his gang in the 1929 St. Valentine's Day Massacre. In 1930 Capone was sentenced to a year in prison for carrying

a concealed weapon in Philadelphia, and in 1931 the federal government prosecuted him for income tax evasion; he was sentenced to 11 years in prison. He was released in 1939.

Cardozo, Benjamin N. (1870–1938) *associate justice of the Supreme Court*
Cardozo was the son of a justice of the New York Supreme Court and a member of an accomplished Sephardic Jewish family. He earned undergraduate, master's, and law degrees from Columbia University. Cardozo began his distinguished career as a jurist in 1914, when he was appointed to the New York Court of Appeals; in 1926 he became chief judge. When Oliver Wendell Holmes resigned from the U.S. Supreme Court in January 1932, President Herbert Hoover appointed Cardozo as his replacement. On the Court, he supported Social Security and other New Deal programs, but he and the other liberal members of the Court were consistently outvoted by the majority.

Cermak, Anton Joseph (Tony Cermak) (1873–1933) *mayor of Chicago*
An immigrant from Bohemia, Cermak mastered Chicago's ethnic-centered politics and helped found the local Democratic organization that dominated the city's politics to the end of the century. He began as a pushcart peddler in Cook County and became secretary of a saloon keepers' league while learning the ins and outs of ward politics. He rose to president of the county board in the early 1920s. Cermak won election as mayor in 1931. He created deftly balanced candidates and platforms to appeal to Chicago's ethnic, business, and labor constituencies. Cermak also opposed Prohibition. His brief term as mayor ended in 1933, when he was killed during an assassination attempt against Franklin D. Roosevelt in Miami.

Chamberlain, Neville (1869–1940) *prime minister of Great Britain*
Chamberlain had been lord mayor of Birmingham and had served in David Lloyd George's coalition government during World War I. A Conservative member of Parliament after 1918, he served in various posts, including chancellor of the exchequer (1923–24 and 1931–37). As prime minister from 1937 to 1940, he pursued appeasement of Adolf Hitler

(acceding to Hitler's demands), climaxing in the infamous 1938 Munich agreement that paved the way for Hitler's conquest of Czechoslovakia. Although he initiated rearmament and committed the nation to war after Germany invaded Poland in September 1939, Chamberlain lost party support following a failed British expedition to Norway. He resigned and was succeeded by Winston Churchill.

Chaplin, Charles (1889–1977) *actor, comedian*

Chaplin was born in London, England, and began stage work with a pantomime group in 1897. On a tour of the United States in 1913, he was offered a job by a representative of Keystone Films and joined the company in 1914, quickly attaining film success. In 1919, with Mary Pickford, Douglas Fairbanks, and D. W. Griffith, he founded United Artists Films. During the 1920s, he became the first international media star with film portrayals of his little tramp character, as in *The Gold Rush* (1925). Chaplin produced two notable movies in the 1930s: *City Lights* (1931) and *Modern Times* (1936), the latter depicting depression-era life. His only full sound film, *The Great Dictator* (1940), satirized Hitler.

Chiang Kai-shek (Jiang Jieshi) (1887–1975) *ruler of China*

Chiang graduated from Tokyo Military Academy in 1907 and became involved in Chinese nationalist revolutionary movements. In 1917 he became military aide to Sun Yat-sen and his Guomindang (Kuomintang; Nationalist Party) attempting to overthrow the Qing dynasty and unite China as a republic. Chiang became supreme commander of the revolutionary army after Sun Yat-sen's death in 1925. He staged a coup d'état in 1927, rejected the Communists who had belonged to the Guomindang, subdued many of the warlords, captured Peiping (Beijing) and other major cities, and set up a central government in Nanjing in 1928. After 1937, Chiang tried to repulse the Japanese invasion of China, soliciting U.S. aid. When the Communists seized control of China in 1949, Chiang moved his forces to Formosa (Taiwan), where he remained the rest of his life.

Churchill, Winston S. (1874–1965) *prime minister of Great Britain*

Churchill served as a member of Parliament after his election in 1900, representing both the Liberal and Conservative parties at different times. During World War I he filled varied cabinet posts, including first lord of the admiralty during the ill-fated Gallipoli campaign. Churchill served in three cabinet posts during the 1920s, including chancellor of the exchequer (1924–29). Although continuing in Parliament, he held no government post from 1929 to 1939. With the collapse of Poland in September 1939, Chamberlain reappointed Churchill, an outspoken opponent of Hitler, as first lord of the admiralty. Following the defeat of France and Chamberlain's resignation, Churchill became prime minister in May 1940.

Cohen, Benjamin V. (1894–1983) *adviser to Franklin D. Roosevelt*

Born and raised in Muncie, Indiana, Cohen earned bachelor's (1914) and law (1915) degrees from the University of Chicago and an S.J.D. (doctor of juridical science) from Harvard Law School (1916). He was counsel for the U.S. Shipping Board during World War I. From 1919 to 1921, he was counsel for the American Zionists. In private practice during the 1920s, he amassed considerable wealth in the stock market. In 1933, Cohen and Thomas Corcoran drafted the Securities Act of 1933. Known as "the Gold Dust Twins," they drafted such other laws as the Securities and Exchange Act (1934), the Public Utilities Holding Company and Rural Electrification Acts of 1935, and the Fair Labor Standards Act (1938). Cohen supported aiding the Allies in World War II and helped draft lend-lease legislation.

Collier, John (1888–1968) *commissioner of Indian affairs*

Born in Atlanta, Collier studied at Columbia University and Collège de France. He became secretary of the People's Institute in New York in 1907; he resigned in 1919 when federal funds dried up. In 1922 he became a researcher for the Indian Welfare Committee of the General Federation of Women's Clubs, and in 1923 he organized and headed the American Indian Defense Association. In 1933 he was named commissioner of Indian affairs in the Interior Department. His "Indian New Deal" resulted in the Johnson-O'Malley Act (1934), the Indian Reorganization Act (1934), and the Indian Arts and Crafts Board (1935). Collier resigned in 1945 and taught at City College of New York and Knox College.

Connally, Thomas T. (1877–1963) *Democratic senator*

Born on a farm in McLennan County, Texas, Connally graduated from Baylor College (1896) and earned a law degree from the University of Texas (1898). He served in the state legislature (1900–04) and was elected congressman in 1916. In 1928, Connally was elected senator. He supported Franklin D. Roosevelt in 1932 and the early New Deal but disliked the Wealth Tax Act (1935) and the Public Utility Holding Company Act (1935). He opposed the court-packing proposal and the Reorganization Act (1939). For two years he and Roosevelt did not speak to each other.

Coolidge, (John) Calvin (1872–1933) *president of the United States*

Coolidge was born in Vermont but settled in Northampton, Massachusetts, to pursue a law career after graduating from Amherst College. Elected to the city council in 1899, he later served in varied posts, including mayor, state senator, and governor. As governor he gained national attention in opposing the 1919 Boston police strike and was nominated for the vice presidency at the 1920 Republican National Convention. He became president upon Warren G. Harding's death in 1923 and easily won election in 1924. He encouraged businesses through tax and tariff policies, opposed a bonus for World War I veterans, vetoed legislation granting financial relief to farmers, and avoided any significant involvement in international affairs.

Corcoran, Thomas G. (1900–1981) *adviser to Roosevelt*

"Tommy the Cork" Corcoran was born and raised in Pawtucket, Rhode Island. He earned bachelor's (1921) and master's (1922) degrees at Brown University and a law degree (1925) from Harvard Law School. In 1926 he became law clerk for Justice Oliver Wendell Holmes. From 1927 he practiced law in New York. In 1932, President Herbert Hoover appointed him to the legal staff of the Reconstruction Finance Corporation (RFC), where he remained until 1940, advising Franklin D. Roosevelt. With Benjamin Cohen, he drafted the Securities Act of 1933 and other important laws. One of the president's intimates, Corcoran recommended many lawyers for posts in New Deal agencies. He wrote speeches for

FDR in the 1936 campaign. He returned to private law practice in New York in 1941.

Coughlin, Charles E. (Father Coughlin) (1891–1979) *influential religious leader*

A native of Canada, Coughlin studied theology at the University of Toronto and became a Roman Catholic priest. Transferred to the Shrine of the Little Flower in Detroit in 1926, he began broadcasting commentaries over WJR radio and after 1930 in a weekly national spot on CBS radio. Known as the "radio priest," he had an enormous following (perhaps 45 million listeners) by 1934. Initially supportive of Franklin D. Roosevelt, he then turned against him and expressed admiration for Adolf Hitler and Benito Mussolini. In 1936, with Gerald L. K. Smith and Dr. Francis Townsend, Coughlin created the Union Party. His popularity declined in the late thirties. Increasingly reactionary, he founded the Christian Front, a protofascist, anti-Semitic organization, and *Social Justice* magazine.

Cox, James M. (1870–1957) *journalist, governor of Ohio*

Born in Jacksonburg, Ohio, Cox began his career as a teacher, became a reporter for the *Cincinnati Enquirer,* and finally was owner and publisher of the *Dayton Daily News.* In 1908 he won election to Congress, serving until 1912, when he was elected governor of Ohio. In 1920 he was nominated as Democratic candidate for president, with Franklin D. Roosevelt as his running mate. Following the loss of the election, he resumed his newspaper career. In 1933 Roosevelt appointed Cox as a delegate to the London World Monetary and Economic Conference.

Cullen, Countee (1903–1946) *poet associated with the Harlem Renaissance*

Cullen was born in New York City and adopted by Frederick Cullen, minister of an African Methodist Episcopal church in Harlem. He graduated with honors from New York University in 1925 and earned a master's degree from Harvard University in 1926. Cullen spent two years on fellowships studying in France and England. His first book of poems, *Color,* appeared in 1925. *Copper Sun* (1927), *The Ballad of the Brown Girl* (1928), and *The Black Christ and Other Poems* (1929) followed quickly. *The Medea and Some Poems* appeared in 1935. In 1934 Cullen began teaching in the New York City public school system; he continued teaching the rest of his brief life.

Cummings, E. E. (1894–1962) *poet, painter*

Born in Cambridge, Massachusetts, Cummings graduated from Harvard University in 1915 and earned an M.A. in 1916. He served in the French ambulance corps during World War I and was imprisoned by the French army for three months for writing "treasonable" letters, the source for his autobiographical *The Enormous Room* (1922). During the 1920s and 1930s, Cummings alternately lived in Paris and in New York. His first collection of poems, *Tulips and Chimneys,* appeared in 1923. In 1925 he published two works, *XLI Poems* and *&.* Numerous other collections—a total of 12 volumes—followed into the 1960s. In 1928 the Provincetown Players produced Cummings' play *Him.*

Cummings, Homer S. (1870–1956) *attorney general of the United States*

Cummings grew up in Chicago, graduated from Yale, where he also received his law degree (1893), and practiced law in Stamford, Connecticut, where he served as mayor in the early 1900s and as state's attorney from 1914 to 1924. A supporter of Franklin D. Roosevelt in 1932, he was chosen by the president as attorney general to head the Justice Department in 1933. Cummings devoted much of his time to defending New Deal programs in the federal courts. In 1936 the president obliged Cummings to draft the controversial proposal to increase the size of the Supreme Court. Cummings resigned in 1939 and returned to the practice of law, in Washington, D.C.

Daladier, Édouard (1884–1970) *premier of France*

Daladier was elected to the Chamber of Deputies in 1919, representing the Radical Party. As governments quickly rose and fell from 1925 to 1933, he served in seven different ministries. He became premier at the end of January 1933, his administration lasting until October of that year. He again became premier in January 1934 but was brought down within a month by the Stavisky Affair. In 1935 his party joined the Popular Front coalition government. Daladier once more became premier in 1938. An appeaser of Adolf Hitler, he agreed to the terms of the Munich agreement of 1938. In 1940 he was arrested by the Vichy regime after the fall of France. From 1942 until the end of the war, he was a German prisoner.

Daniels, Josephus (1862–1948) *secretary of the navy*

Daniels grew up in North Carolina and was editor and publisher of two Raleigh newspapers, the *State Chronicle* (1885–1904) and the *News and Observer* (1904–48). A supporter of Woodrow Wilson in 1912, he gained appointment as secretary of the navy, holding this post until 1921. He appointed Franklin D. Roosevelt as his assistant secretary. Daniels instituted numerous reforms, including competitive bidding for navy contracts, enhancement of the U.S. Naval Academy, and expansion of the fleet. In 1932 Daniels supported Roosevelt for the presidential nomination. Roosevelt appointed him ambassador to Mexico in 1933, a post he held until 1941, supporting the social and economic programs of the Mexican Revolution.

Darrow, Clarence S. (1857–1938) *exceptional defense lawyer*

Born near Kinsman, Ohio, Darrow attended Allegheny College and the University of Michigan but never earned a degree. He passed the Ohio bar exam in 1878. In 1887 he moved to Chicago and was lawyer for the Haymarket Riot defendants. He was attorney for the Chicago and Northwestern Railroad, resigning in 1894 to defend Eugene V. Debs against charges arising from the Pullman Strike. In the 1924 trial of Richard Loeb and Nathan Leopold, he saved the murders from execution through a plea of mental illness. In 1925 Darrow opposed William Jennings Bryan at the Scopes trial in Dayton, Tennessee. In 1926 he successfully defended Dr. Ossian Sweet's family, blacks whose Detroit home was attacked by a mob, causing one death.

Debs, Eugene V. (1855–1926) *union organizer, presidential candidate*

Debs was born and raised in Terre Haute, Indiana. A railroad laborer, Debs became national secretary and treasurer of the Brotherhood of Locomotive Firemen in 1880 and president of the American Railway Union, which he helped organize, in 1893. After imprisonment for involvement in the 1894 Pullman Strike, Debs became a Socialist. In 1898 he helped organize the Socialist Party of America; he was the party's presidential candidate in 1900, 1908, 1912, and 1920. In 1905 he helped organize the Industrial

Workers of the World (IWW) but opposed its growing radicalism and left. Imprisoned for sedition during World War I, he was set free by President Warren G. Harding in 1921.

DeMille, Cecil B. (1881–1959) *film producer-director*
Born in Ashfield, Massachusetts, DeMille studied at Pennsylvania Military College and the American Academy of Dramatic Arts in New York (1898–1900) and became an actor. He produced his first Hollywood film in 1913. Between 1914 and 1956 he made 100 films. His biblical spectaculars—such as *The Ten Commandments* (1923) and *The King of Kings* (1927)—were enormously popular. DeMille's films of the depression era included *The Sign of the Cross* (1932) and *Cleopatra* (1934).

Dewey, John (1859–1952) *educator, philosopher, psychologist*
Born in Burlington, Vermont, Dewey graduated from the University of Vermont and earned a Ph.D. from Johns Hopkins University (1884). He taught at the University of Michigan. In 1894 he became chairman of the department of philosophy, psychology, and pedagogy at the University of Chicago. His works on philosophy, psychology, and education from 1899 to 1903 gained national attention. In 1904, Dewey joined the faculty at Columbia University. Over the next 25 years, he published numerous works, including his monumental *Experience and Nature* (1925) that brought international fame. Dewey's ideas formed the basis of the progressive movement in education. He helped found the American Association of University Professors and the New School for Social Research (1919) with Charles Beard.

Dillinger, John (1902–1934) *criminal*
Born in Indianapolis, Dillinger began his crime career in Mooresville, Indiana, with a grocery store robbery and was sent to prison. Paroled in 1933, he formed a gang and robbed banks. Caught in Dayton, Ohio, Dillinger escaped by killing a sheriff. Named "public enemy number one" by the FBI, he was captured in Arizona but escaped from prison while awaiting trial in Chicago. Trapped in Little Bohemia, Wisconsin, Dillinger fought his way free, killing two policemen. With a $50,000 reward for his capture, the "Lady in Red" betrayed him, and FBI agents shot him dead as he left the Biograph Theatre in Chicago.

DiMaggio, Joseph (1914–1999) *baseball player*
Born in Martinez, California, DiMaggio began his career in the minor leagues in San Francisco and then played for the New York Yankees from 1936 until retiring in 1951—during these years the Yankees won 10 American League pennants and nine World Series. DiMaggio was nicknamed "Joltin' Joe" and "The Yankee Clipper." In 1939 and 1940 his batting average was the highest in the American League. In 1941 he set a major league record, hitting safely in 56 consecutive games. He was chosen Most Valuable Player in the American League in 1939, 1941, and 1947. In 1954 he was married for nine months to actress Marilyn Monroe, his second marriage. In 1955, DiMaggio was elected to the Baseball Hall of Fame.

Divine, Father (George Baker) (ca. 1880–1965) *founder, leader of the Peace Mission movement*
Father Divine was born to sharecroppers near Savannah, Georgia. In 1899 he moved to Baltimore and in 1914 to Valdosta, Georgia, where he proclaimed himself to be God. He moved his group to Harlem and founded a church in Brooklyn. Gaining many followers in the 1920s, his movement remained nondenominational and interracial, advocating integration, celibacy, industry, cleanliness, and honesty. He took the name Father Divine in 1930. His Peace Mission movement eventually owned many properties throughout the United States and abroad and numbered perhaps 2 million members; it also published a weekly newspaper, *New Day*. In 1938 Father Divine acquired the Krum Estate at Hyde Park. In 1941 he moved to Philadelphia.

Dos Passos, John (1896–1970) *novelist, historian*
Dos Passos was born in Chicago, Illinois, graduated from Harvard University in 1916, and studied architecture in Spain. In World War I, he served in a French ambulance unit, with the Red Cross in Italy, and then in the U.S. Army medical corps. These wartime experiences formed the basis for two novels, *One Man's Initiation—1917* (1920) and the antiwar *Three Soldiers* (1921). Dos Passos worked as a journalist, traveling extensively in Europe. His first social history novel, *Manhattan Transfer,* appeared in 1925. Then followed the monumental trilogy of American life entitled *U.S.A.—The 42nd Parallel* (1930), *1919* (1932), and *The Big Money* (1936). He completed another trilogy, *District of Columbia,* between 1939

and 1949. His nonfiction works include *The Ground We Stand On* (1941) and *The Head and Heart of Thomas Jefferson* (1953).

Douglas, William O. (1898–1980) *associate justice of the Supreme Court*
Douglas was born in Maine, Minnesota, but grew up in Washington State. He graduated from Whitman College and Columbia University Law School and became professor of law at Yale University, specializing in corporate law. In 1936 Franklin D. Roosevelt appointed him to the Securities and Exchange Commission (SEC); he became chairman in 1937. When Louis Brandeis retired from the Supreme Court in 1939, Roosevelt appointed Douglas to the vacancy. On the court, Douglas supported New Deal economic programs. In the 1960s, with Earl Warren as chief justice, Douglas supported decisions favoring civil rights. He retired from the court in 1975 following a stroke. He wrote numerous books, including two autobiographical volumes.

Dreiser, Theodore (1871–1945) *journalist, novelist*
Born and raised in Terre Haute, Indiana, Drieser's stature endures through his major works *Sister Carrie* (1900) and *An American Tragedy* (1925)—the latter, a popular success translated into stage and film productions—and two novels based on the life of unscrupulous entrepreneur Charles T. Yerkes. He suffered financial losses from the 1929 Great Stock Market Crash; became a severe critic of capitalism's inequities, which were exacerbated by the depression; and advocated social and economic reforms, especially in *Tragic America* (1932) and *America Is Worth Saving* (1941). Dreiser participated in the investigation of the 1931 Harlan County, Kentucky, coal miners' strike. He also supported the Loyalists in the Spanish civil war.

Dubinsky, David (1892–1982) *president of the International Ladies Garment Workers' Union*
Dubinsky grew up in Poland and immigrated to the United States in 1911, working in the garment trade in New York City. Elected chairman of his International Ladies Garment Workers' Union (ILGWU) local chapter in 1920, he became vice president of the national union in 1922 and president in 1932. From 1933 to 1935, he was a labor adviser for the National Recovery Administration. In 1935 he became a vice president of the American Federation of Labor (AFL); he joined John L. Lewis and others to found the Congress of Industrial Organizations (CIO). Dubinsky supported Franklin D. Roosevelt in 1936 and helped organize the NonPartisan League. In 1936, with Sidney Hillman and others, he organized the American Labor Party. In 1947 he helped organize Americans for Democratic Action (ADA).

DuBois, W. E. B. (1868–1963) *sociologist, historian, journalist, foremost African-American protest leader*
DuBois was born in Great Barrington, Massachusetts, graduated from Fisk University (1888), studied at the University of Berlin (1892–94), and earned a Ph.D. from Harvard University (1895). A professor of economics and history at Atlanta University (1897–1910), he published *The Souls of Black Folk* in 1903. DuBois helped found the Niagara Movement (1905) and, in 1909, the National Association for the Advancement of Colored People (NAACP). He served on the NAACP board and as editor of *Crisis* until 1934. In 1919 DuBois helped organize the first Pan-African movement. In the late twenties, he was a leader of the Harlem Renaissance. In 1934 he became chairman of sociology at Atlanta University, retiring in 1944.

Duveen, Joseph (1869–1939) *international art dealer*
The son of Sir Joseph Joel Duveen, who was a descendant of Dutch Jews, Duveen entered his family's London furniture and art business, established by his father in 1877, and began buying and selling art on a lavish scale. By 1914 he had created an effective monopoly on trade in old master Italian, Dutch, French, and English paintings on both sides of the Atlantic, as he established his principle headquarters in New York City. In the United States he became responsible for the foundation of major art collections for such clients as John D. Rockefeller, Henry Clay Frick, and Andrew Mellon. In reward of his services to the Tate Gallery and the British Museum, Duveen received a knighthood in 1919, and he was made baron Duveen of Millbank in 1926.

Earhart, Amelia (1897–1937) *aviator, first woman to fly solo across the Atlantic Ocean*
Earhart was born and raised in Kansas; she served as a military nurse in Canada during World War I and thereafter as a social worker in Boston. On June

17–18, 1928, she became the first woman to fly across the Atlantic as a passenger. In 1931 she married George P. Putnam of the publishing firm but continued to pursue her career as an aviator. On May 20–21, 1932, she flew across the Atlantic alone. In January 1935, Earhart became the first person to fly solo from Hawaii to California. In 1937, with navigator Fred Noonan, she began an around-the-world flight but disappeared on July 2 in the South Pacific. Putnam wrote and published a biography of her, *Soaring Wings,* in 1939.

Early, Stephen Tyree (1889–1951) *press secretary for FDR*
Early was born in Virginia and raised in the District of Columbia after age 9. He graduated from high school and joined the staff of United Press. As a reporter for the Associated Press, he met Franklin D. Roosevelt in 1912. Early served in World War I as an infantry officer and writer for *Stars and Stripes.* He entered the field of public relations and assisted Roosevelt's 1920 campaign for the vice presidency. He worked again for the Associated Press and, after 1927, for Paramount News. In 1933 Roosevelt appointed Early as assistant secretary in charge of press relations, managing White House communications and holding daily press conferences. In 1937 Roosevelt gave him the title of press secretary. Early retained his post under Truman but resigned in July 1945 to become vice president of the Pullman Company.

Eccles, Marriner S. (1890–1977) *chairman of the Federal Reserve Board*
Eccles was born and raised in Utah. He developed an inheritance into a banking and industrial empire, including 28 banks, Utah Construction Company, and Amalgamated Sugar Company. After an appearance before a Senate committee in February 1933 to discuss banking policy, he met Rexford Tugwell, who helped him gain his appointment as special assistant to Treasury Secretary Henry Morgenthau in February 1934. Eccles helped draft a bill that created the Federal Housing Authority. In the fall of 1934, he accepted chairmanship of the Federal Reserve Board in exchange for Franklin D. Roosevelt's support of a law taking control of the Federal Reserve System away from New York bankers and giving it to the board. Eccles stepped down to vice chairman in 1948 and served until 1951.

Edison, Charles (1890–1969) *secretary of the navy, governor of New Jersey*
Edison was born in West Orange, New Jersey, the son of the famous inventor Thomas Alva Edison. A graduate of MIT, Edison first met Franklin D. Roosevelt in 1917 when his father was chairman of the Navy Consulting Board. Roosevelt appointed him assistant secretary of the navy in 1936; he became acting secretary on July 7, 1939 and secretary the following January. Roosevelt encouraged him to run for the governorship of New Jersey, which he won in 1940.

Edward VIII (1894–1972) *king of Great Britain and Ireland, later duke of Windsor*
For nearly one year he served as King Edward VIII of Great Britain, then abdicated the throne in 1936 to marry Wallis Warfield Simpson, an American divorcée he had met in 1931. As the eldest son of George V, Edward became prince of Wales in 1911. He served as a staff officer in the British Army during World War I and then traveled widely, including a visit to the United States in 1924, earning much goodwill. Popular at home for his support for laborers, he succeeded to the throne in January 1936 but abdicated in December to marry Simpson, who had divorced her second husband in October. The affair and abdication created a crisis for Prime Minister Stanley Baldwin and an international scandal. Edward's brother, who succeeded him as George VI, created the title duke of Windsor for him. He and Simpson married in June 1937.

Einstein, Albert (1879–1955) *prominent mathematician, physicist*
Born in Ulm, Germany, and raised in Munich, Einstein moved to Milan at age 15, then pursued schooling in Switzerland and later studied physics for four years at the Polytechnic Academy in Zurich. He became a Swiss citizen in 1900 and accepted employment at the patent office in Bern. A thesis published in a monthly physics journal earned him a Ph.D. from the University of Zurich. He continued publishing articles, including one positing the concept of photons (a term applied later) that revolutionized the theory of light and others beginning to define his theory of relativity. Einstein began teaching at universities and assumed a position in 1914 at the Prussian Academy of Sciences in Berlin. A pacifist, Einstein opposed World

War I and German militarism. He polished the final version of his theory of relativity for publication in 1916. Following the war's end, he received worldwide acclaim in November 1919, when experiments by the Royal Society verified the validity of his theory of relativity. He traveled and lectured widely and also became an ardent supporter of the Zionist movement. Awarded the Nobel Prize in physics in 1921, Einstein continued his research. In 1933, following Adolf Hitler's appointment as chancellor, Einstein renounced his German citizenship and later accepted a post at the Institute for Advanced Studies in Princeton, New Jersey, where he remained the rest of his life. His warnings to President Franklin D. Roosevelt about the potential of an atomic bomb eventually led to the Manhattan Project, in which Einstein himself was not personally involved.

Eliot, Thomas Stearns (T. S. Eliot) (1888–1965) *poet, playwright, literary critic*
Eliot was born in St. Louis. He studied at Harvard, earning an M.A. in 1910, and at the University of Paris (1910). In 1915 he studied at Oxford University and married the daughter of a British artist. His first book of poems, *Prufrock and Other Observations*, appeared in 1917. From 1918 till 1924, he worked for Lloyd's Bank in London; and in 1922 he published his most famous work, *The Wasteland*. In 1925 Eliot became a director for the publisher Faber and Faber. Eliot became a British subject in 1927. He published numerous works through the twenties and thirties, including his best-known play *Murder in the Cathedral* (1935). Eliot was awarded the Nobel Prize in literature in 1948.

Ellington, Duke (1899–1974) *jazz musician, composer, pianist, band leader*
Ellington was born in Washington, D.C. He began studying the piano at age 7 and performing professionally at age 17. In 1923 at the Kentucky Club in New York, he organized a band that grew into a larger group under his leadership. Ellington's band performed at the Cotton Club from 1927 to 1932. His popularity spread during the 1930s on the basis of the band's recordings and tours, including European jaunts. Among Ellington's most famous compositions are "Mood Indigo," "Sophisticated Lady," and "It Don't Mean a Thing If It Ain't Got That Swing."

Evans, Walker (1903–1975) *photographer noted for his pictures of rural victims of the Great Depression*
Evans was born in St. Louis. In 1934 his photos of 19th-century New England buildings comprised the first one-man photographic show held at the Museum of Modern Art. In 1935 he began photographing for the Rural Resettlement Administration, publishing a collection of this work, *American Photographs,* in 1938. Evans then collaborated with author James Agee on a study of Southern sharecroppers, *Let Us Now Praise Famous Men* (1941). After World War II, he became associate editor of *Fortune*.

Farley, James A. (1888–1976) *astute campaign manager, postmaster general, chairman of the Democratic National Committee*
Farley was born in Grassy Point, New York, and worked his way up in politics to become secretary of the Democratic State Committee in 1928, when he helped Franklin D. Roosevelt win the governorship. A close political adviser to Roosevelt, Farley distributed patronage and managed the president's landslide victory in 1936. Opposed to Roosevelt's running for a third presidential term, he left the national chairmanship in 1940 to work for the Coca-Cola Export Corporation in New York.

Faulkner, William (1897–1962) *novelist*
Born in New Albany, Mississippi, Faulkner worked for a while in a New York bookstore and as postmaster for the University of Mississippi in Oxford, where he spent most of his life. He had dropped out of school at the end of his sophomore year in high school and spent only one year studying at the University of Mississippi. His first book, a collection of poems entitled *The Marble Faun*, appeared in 1924; his first novel, *Soldier's Pay*, in 1926. Thereafter he published the widely admired novels *The Sound and the Fury* (1929), *As I Lay Dying* (1930), *Light in August* (1932), and *Absalom, Absalom!* (1936). He received the Nobel Prize in literature in 1949 and the Pulitzer Prize in 1955.

Fechner, Robert (1876–1939) *director of the Civilian Conservation Corps*
Fechner was born in Chattanooga, Tennessee, and attended schools in Macon and Griffin, Georgia, until age 15. He worked as a machinist for the Georgia Central Railroad and then in Mexico and Central

and South America. He moved to Savannah, Georgia, in late 1890. Fechner was as an officer of the International Association of Machinists (1913–33). In 1933 Franklin D. Roosevelt appointed him head of the Civilian Conservation Corps (CCC). He served until his death.

Fitzgerald, F. Scott (1896–1940) *novelist*
Born in St. Paul, Minnesota, Fitzgerald studied at Princeton University but left without a degree in 1917 to join the army. In 1920 he published his first novel, *This Side of Paradise,* which earned him fame and wealth. That same year he married Zelda Sayre. Two collections of short stories, *Flappers and Philosophers* (1920) and *Tales of the Jazz Age* (1922), established him as a chronicler of the 1920s. His second novel, *The Beautiful and Damned,* appeared in 1922 also. In 1924 he and Zelda moved to Paris, France, where he wrote his masterpiece *The Great Gatsby* (1925). Plagued by alcoholism and Zelda's mental illness, he was slow to produce *Tender Is the Night* (1934). In 1937 he became a screenwriter in Hollywood, where he lived with columnist Sheila Graham and died leaving incomplete a final novel, *The Last Tycoon,* begun in 1939.

Flynn, Edward J. (1891–1953) *chairman of the Democratic Party*
Flynn was born in New York, educated in Catholic schools and at Fordham University, admitted to the bar in 1913, and elected to the New York state assembly in 1917. In 1922 he became chairman of the Democratic Party in the Bronx; in 1928 he worked in Franklin D. Roosevelt's campaign for governor and then was appointed secretary of state. He assisted James Farley in the 1932 and 1936 presidential campaigns. Roosevelt appointed him regional administrator for the National Recovery Administration in 1933. When Farley refused to support a third term for Roosevelt in 1940, Flynn replaced him as national chairman of the Democratic Party.

Ford, Henry (1863–1947) *industrialist, automobile manufacturer*
Ford was born to Irish immigrant parents on a farm in Wayne County, Michigan. A machinist, he became chief engineer of the Edison Company in Detroit in 1888. In 1899 he organized the Detroit Automobile Company with a group of associates. In 1903 he and

other partners launched the Ford Motor Company, which began manufacturing the Model T in 1908 and instituted assembly line mass production in 1913. By the mid-1920s, the company was producing over 1.25 million cars a year and Ford was a billionaire. Although he increased his workers' wages and provided profit sharing, Ford strongly resisted unionization until 1941 after an election conducted by the National Labor Relations Board. Ford introduced the V-8 engine in 1932. He ran unsuccessfully for a Michigan seat in the U.S. Senate in 1918, supported the James M. Cox–Franklin D. Roosevelt ticket in the 1920 presidential election, and was a dark horse candidate for the presidency in 1924. Ford was a staunch opponent of the New Deal.

Fosdick, Harry Emerson (1878–1969) *Protestant minister*
Born in Buffalo, New York, Fosdick graduated from Colgate University (1900) and Union Theological Seminary (1904) and earned a master's degree from Columbia University (1908). He was minister at First Baptist Church in Montclair, New Jersey (1904–15), and then served on the faculty of Union Theological Seminary until 1934 while serving also as minister of Riverside Church. His sermons were broadcast nationally after 1922, and he filled the role of spokesman for liberal Protestantism.

Foster, William Z. (1881–1961) *leader of the Communist Party*
The self-educated Foster, born in Taunton, Massachusetts, was an active union organizer from 1894 on. In 1909 he joined the Industrial Workers of the World (IWW), and in 1919 he was a leader of the American Federation of Labor steel strike. In 1920 he founded the Trade Union Educational League, which became part of the Communist Party in 1921. As general secretary of the party, he was its presidential candidate in 1924, 1928, and 1932. Ill health forced his replacement by Earl Browder, whose policies he opposed; he returned as the party's leader in 1945. In 1948 he was indicted under terms of the Smith Act's definition of subversive behavior but was never tried.

Franco, Francisco (1892–1975) *dictator of Spain*
Franco joined the Spanish army in 1907 and earned renown for his success in quelling rebels in Morocco.

He became chief of the general staff in 1935. In 1936 Franco joined the military rebellion against the republican government, becoming head of the Nationalists and the government in that year. In 1937 he became head of the fascist Falange Party. With the help of the Germans and Italians, he won the civil war in 1939. Franco maintained Spain's neutrality during World War II. In 1947 he declared Spain a kingdom, with himself as regent. In 1969 he named Juan Carlos his successor but retained ultimate power until his death in 1975.

Frankfurter, Felix (1882–1965) *associate justice of the Supreme Court*
Frankfurter was born in Vienna; when he was 12, his family moved to the United States. He graduated from City College of New York and Harvard Law School. From 1906 to 1909, he was assistant to Henry L. Stimson, federal attorney for the Southern District of New York; and also served as Stimson's assistant from 1911 to 1913 when Stimson was secretary of war. A faculty member of the Harvard Law School from 1914 until 1939, he was legal adviser to Wilson at the Paris Peace Conference. He was a founder of the American Civil Liberties Union in 1920 and an active Zionist during the twenties. During Franklin D. Roosevelt's term as governor of New York, Frankfurter served as an adviser; after Roosevelt became president, Frankfurter served as an adviser on New Deal programs and recruited lawyers for the president's staff. Frankfurter influenced drafting of the Securities Act of 1933, the Public Utility Holding Company Act of 1935, and the Social Security Act. Roosevelt appointed him to the Supreme Court in January 1939; he retired from the bench in August 1962.

Frost, Robert (1874–1963) *major poet*
Born in San Francisco but raised in Massachusetts and New Hampshire after 1885, Frost studied briefly at Dartmouth College in 1892. He married in 1895, studied at Harvard from 1897 to 1899, leaving because of illness, and took up farming in Derry, New Hampshire. He sold the farm in 1911 and moved his family to England intending to write full time. His first two books of poems, *A Boy's Will* and *North of Boston,* were published there in 1913 and 1914 to critical acclaim. In 1915 the Frosts returned to the United States, settling on a farm in Franconia,

New Hampshire. Frost taught or occupied poetry posts at various times at Amherst, Dartmouth, Harvard, and the University of Michigan. From 1923 on, he lived in Vermont. Among his other major collections of poems are *Mountain Interval* (1916), *New Hampshire* (1923), *West-Running Brook* (1928), *Collected Poems* (1930), *A Further Range* (1936), and *A Witness Tree* (1942). Frost twice won the Pulitzer Prize.

Gable, (William) Clark (1901–1960) *film actor, exemplar of the M.G.M. star system*
Gable was born in Cadiz, Ohio. After working at odd jobs, he joined the Ed Lilly stock company doing repertory and had bit parts in films in the mid-1920s. His first lead role on Broadway was in *Machinal* in 1928. He returned to Hollywood in 1930, becoming popular portraying gangsters in two 1931 films. From 1931 to 1954, he was under contract to M.G.M., one of Louis B. Mayer's major stars. He won the Academy Award for his role in *It Happened One Night* in 1934. His most famous role was as Rhett Butler in *Gone With the Wind* (1939). Gable served in the Air Force in World War II, winning an Air Medal. His last film was *The Misfits* (released in 1961 after his death) with Marilyn Monroe.

Garbo, Greta (1905–1990) *film actor*
Born in Stockholm, Sweden, Garbo attended the Royal Dramatic Theatre School in Stockholm (1922–24) and moved to Hollywood in 1925 under contract with Metro-Goldwyn-Mayer. She portrayed the emancipated (or modern) woman. Her major films included *The Temptress* (1926), *The Divine Woman* (1928), *Anna Christie* (1930), *Grand Hotel* (1932), *Camille* (1937), and *Ninotchka* (1939). When her performance in a 1941 film was critically panned, she went into exile in Europe.

Garland, Judy (1922–1969) *star of movie musicals*
Born in Grand Rapids, Michigan, into a vaudeville family, Garland made her stage debut at age three. Her screen debut occurred in 1936, and she gained attention the following year with *Broadway Melody of 1938.* She then did several films costarring Mickey Rooney, and she achieved international fame in 1939 with *The Wizard of Oz.* She starred in several popular movie musicals during the forties and later returned to con-

cert hall and nightclub performing while also doing dramatic film roles in the 1950s and 1960s.

Garner, John Nance (1868–1967) *legislator, vice president of the United States*
Born in western Texas, Garner was a conservative Democrat known as "Cactus Jack." Admitted to the Texas bar in 1890, Garner served in the state legislature from 1898 to 1902, when he was elected to the House of Representatives, where he served until 1933. Influential in passing legislation during the Wilson administration, he became minority leader in 1928 and Speaker of the House in 1931. Initially an opponent of Franklin D. Roosevelt, he threw the Texas delegation's support to FDR at the 1932 convention and was rewarded with a nomination for the vice presidency. As vice president he had little influence, as his opposition to the New Deal was well known. Garner's conservatism hindered his attempt to win the 1940 presidential nomination.

Garvey, Marcus (1887–1940) *founder and head of the Universal Negro Improvement Association*
Garvey was born in Jamaica. In 1912–14 he lived in London, returning to Jamaica and founding the Universal Negro Improvement Association (UNIA) on August 1, 1914. He moved to the United States in 1916, settling in Harlem. Known as the "Black Moses," he developed the UNIA into the largest black organization up until that time. Garvey advocated "the new Negro" (exhibiting pride and determination), and his newspaper *Negro World* touted the virtues of black culture. He encouraged economic achievement as the means to independence, founding the Negro Factories Corporation and the Black Star Line. He also promoted pan-Africanism and separatism, calling for a black-ruled nation in Africa to which blacks could migrate. Garvey was indicted for mail fraud in 1922 over the sale of stock in the Black Star Line and was sentenced to five years in prison. In 1927, President Calvin Coolidge commuted his sentence; he was deported to Jamaica.

Gehrig, Henry Louis (1903–1941) *outstanding baseball player*
Gehrig was born in New York City and attended Columbia University (1921–22), where he played on the school team until it was discovered he had played with Hartford (minor league) in the Eastern League.

Ineligible for Columbia's team, he signed with the New York Yankees. He played for Hartford until 1924, when the Yankees called him up. A regular in the Yankee's lineup from 1925 till 1939, he played a record 2,130 consecutive games. Called the "Iron Horse," Gehrig hit 493 career home runs, had a .340 lifetime batting average, and served as team captain. In June 1939, it was discovered that he had amyotrophic lateral sclerosis, also known today as Lou Gehrig's disease.

Gershwin, George (1898–1937) *composer*
Born in Brooklyn, New York, Gershwin began piano studies at age 12. He started composing songs in 1916. His song "Swanee," composed for *Sinbad* (1918) and sung by Al Jolson, was his first success. He composed the score for *La, La Lucille* (1919) and from 1920 to 1924 contributed songs and operas to the annual productions of *George White's Scandals.* One of the operas, *Blue Monday,* gained notice by bandleader Paul Whiteman, who commissioned Gershwin to compose *Rhapsody in Blue* (1924). In 1924, with his brother Ira, Gershwin produced his first major Broadway success, *Lady Be Good.* The brothers subsequently created *Tip-Toes* (1925), *Oh, Kay!* (1926), *Strike Up the Band* (1927), and *Girl Crazy* (1930). *Of Thee I Sing* (1931) was their biggest Broadway success. Gershwin's greatest work is the opera *Porgy and Bess* (1935), based on a novel by Dubose Heyward, who wrote the libretto. Other major works include *Piano Concerto in F Major* (1925) and *An American in Paris* (1928).

Goddard, Robert Hutchings (1882–1945) *scientist, inventor*
Born in Worcester, Massachusetts, Goddard entered that city's Clark University in 1908 and earned a doctoral degree there. Goddard taught physics at Clark and also conducted experiments in rocketry at the university. From 1914 through the mid-1940s he received more than 200 patents on methods of propulsion through space. In 1919 Goddard published *A Method of Reaching Extreme Altitudes,* which eventually became a classic treatise on rocketry. In 1925–26 he successfully tested liquid-propelled rockets, and in 1935 he successfully launched a liquid-fueled rocket that surpassed the speed of sound—a first in the field. On the basis of his 1919 book and his experiments Goddard is generally regarded as the father of modern rocketry. He died in Baltimore, Maryland.

Goodman, Benny (1909–1986) *musician, band leader*
A native of Chicago, Goodman began studying clarinet at Hull-House and sitting in with local jazz bands. He toured with Ben Pollack's band (1925–29), then freelanced in New York. In 1934 he organized his own band. One year later, in 1935 at the Palomar Ballroom in Los Angeles, his band gained popularity with their new brand of big band jazz called "swing." Goodman was crowned "King of Swing" and had his own radio program, *Let's Dance.* In 1937 he returned to New York, successfully introducing jazz to Carnegie Hall in 1938. Goodman wrote an autobiography, *The Kingdom of Swing* (1939).

Green, William (1873–1952) *president of the American Federation of Labor*
Born in Coschochton, Ohio, Green became a coal miner in 1889. From 1900 to 1906, he was a subdistrict president of the United Mine Workers of America (UMWA), and from 1912 to 1924, he served as UMWA international secretary-treasurer. Appointed to the American Federation of Labor (AFL) executive committee in 1913, Green succeeded Samuel Gompers as president in 1924, holding the post until his death. He broke with John L. Lewis over the founding of the Congress of Industrial Organizations (CIO) in 1935 and helped achieve the CIO's expulsion from the AFL in 1936. Although Green opposed Franklin D. Roosevelt's appointment of Frances Perkins as secretary of labor, the president appointed Green to several posts, including the National Labor Board (1933–34) and the Labor Advisory Board of the National Recovery Administration (1933–35). Thereafter Green lost influence with the Roosevelt administration to Lewis and the CIO.

Gropius, Walter (1883–1969) *architect, teacher*
Born in Berlin, Germany, Gropius studied at the technical institutes in Munich (1903–04) and Berlin (1905–07). He worked with Peter Behrens and Adolph Meyer. In 1919 Gropius became director of the Staatliches Bauhaus in Weimar, which moved to Dessau in 1925. He resigned in 1928. (Adolf Hitler closed the Bauhaus in 1933.) Gropius, a Nazi opponent, moved to England in 1934. In 1937 Gropius came to the United States to be professor of architecture at Harvard University, serving as department chairman from 1938 to 1952. He collaborated on designs with Marcel Breuer. In 1946 he founded The Architects Collaborative (TAC).

Guthrie, Woody (1912–1967) *guitarist, singer, composer*
Raised in Oklahoma, Guthrie left home at 15, traveling by freight train, staying in hobo camps. He composed over 1,000 songs, most of them espousing working men's and populist views. Among his most famous songs are "So Long (It's Been Good to Know Yuh)" and "This Land Is Your Land."

Hammett, Samuel Dashiell (1894–1961) *mystery writer*
Born in Baltimore, Hammett quit school in 1908. He worked at varied jobs, became an investigator with the Pinkerton National Detective Agency, served in the army in World War I, returned to the agency for three years, and then began to write. He created the "hard-boiled" detective in fiction; during the 1920s and 1930s, he was the nation's most popular mystery writer. Among his best works were *Red Harvest* (1929), *The Maltese Falcon* (1930), which introduced Sam Spade, and *The Thin Man* (1932). From 1930 until his death, he and playwright Lillian Hellman were lovers.

Harding, Warren Gamaliel (1865–1923) *president of the United States*
Born in Blooming Grove (Corsica), Ohio, Harding launched his political career based on the success of his daily newspaper the *Star* (attributed to his wife Florence DeWolfe's efforts) in Marion, Ohio, and his involvement with the state Republican political machine. He was elected state senator, lieutenant governor, and U.S. senator from Ohio, serving in the latter post from 1915 to 1921. At the 1920 Republican National Convention, backroom politicos secured his nomination as the presidential candidate after the convention became deadlocked. Harding won a landslide victory, gaining more than 60 percent of the popular vote. As president he introduced a federal budget system, supported high tariffs and restrictions on immigration, and arranged the Washington Conference to negotiate reductions in naval forces. He died suddenly and unexpectedly in 1923 during a transcontinental tour at a time when exposure of the

corruption involving members of his administration was at hand.

Hearst, William Randolph (1863–1951)
newspaper publisher, politician

Hearst was born in San Francisco into a wealthy family—his father George owned gold mines and was a U.S. senator from California (1886–91). Hearst attended St. Paul's School in New Hampshire and studied at Harvard University for two years. In 1887 he acquired control of the San Francisco *Examiner,* owned by his father. In 1895 he bought the New York *Morning Journal;* Hearst built the newspaper (later renamed the *Journal-American*) into the newspaper with the largest circulation in New York. Hearst served in the House of Representatives from 1903 to 1907 and ran for mayor of New York City in 1904 and for New York governor in 1906. Hearst advocated isolationism and opposed American entry into World War I and the League of Nations. By 1925 he owned newspapers throughout the nation and the palatial San Simeon in California. He helped secure Franklin D. Roosevelt's 1932 nomination but later turned against the New Deal, which after 1935 his newspapers called the "Raw Deal."

Hellman, Lillian (1905–1984) *playwright*

Born in New Orleans, Hellman attended public schools in New York City, New York University, and Columbia University. She worked as a book reviewer and press agent before beginning to write plays. Her best-known dramas include *The Children's Hour* (1934), *The Little Foxes* (1939), *Another Part of the Forest* (1946), and *Toys in the Attic* (1960). In the play *Watch on the Rhine* (1941) she derided the generation that produced the Treaty of Versailles.

Hemingway, Ernest (1899–1961) *novelist, short story writer*

Born in Oak Park, Illinois, Hemingway became a reporter for the Kansas City *Star* in 1917 following graduation from high school. He participated in World War I as an ambulance driver in France and was severely wounded in combat in Italy. After his recovery, he returned to journalism and became a correspondent in Paris, where Gertrude Stein befriended him. His first book, a collection of short stories entitled *In Our Time,* was published in 1925. In 1926 his first novel appeared—*The Sun Also Rises,* a portrayal of American expatriates. *A Farewell to Arms,* based on his war experiences in Italy, appeared in 1929. His *For Whom the Bell Tolls* (1940), concerned the Spanish civil war in which he supported the Loyalist government. *Death in the Afternoon* (1932) focused on bull fighting, and *The Green Hills of Africa* (1935) ritualized big game hunting. After publication of *The Old Man and the Sea* (1952), Hemingway was awarded the Pulitzer Prize (1953) and the Nobel Prize in literature (1954).

Hitler, Adolf (1889–1945) *chancellor, dictator of Germany*

Hitler was born and raised in Austria. He moved to Munich in 1913. He was wounded and gassed while serving in the German army during World War I. In 1919 he joined the German Workers Party and became its leader in 1921, transforming it into the Nazi Party. After an abortive attempt to seize power in Munich in 1923 (known as the Beer Hall Putsch), he was sentenced to Landsberg prison, where he wrote *Mein Kampf.* After his release, he built up the Nazi Party, ran for the presidency of Germany in 1932, and was appointed chancellor in 1933 by President Paul von Hindenburg. Hitler immediately curtailed civil liberties, eliminated opposition parties, and consolidated power. He secured merging of the offices of chancellor and president in 1934 and as dictator remilitarized Germany, pursuing policies that caused World War II. With Germany's defeat imminent, Hitler committed suicide in 1945.

Holmes, Oliver Wendell (1841–1935) *associate justice of the Supreme Court*

Holmes was born in Boston and educated at Harvard. He served in the Civil War with the 20th Massachusetts Regiment of Volunteers (1861–64) and then entered Harvard Law School. Admitted to the bar in 1867, he served as editor of the *American Law Review* from 1870 to 1873. In 1881 he published *The Common Law,* and in 1882 he became Weld Professor of Law at Harvard Law School. Holmes became a justice of the Massachusetts Supreme Judicial Court in 1883 and chief justice in 1899. President Theodore Roosevelt appointed him to the Supreme Court in 1902. Known as "the Great Dissenter," Holmes was a consistent advocate of judicial restraint, leaving the making of laws to the legislators. He also originated the concept of "clear and present danger" as the sole criterion for limiting freedom of speech. He retired from the Court on January 12, 1932.

Hood, Raymond (1881–1934) *architect*
Born in Pawtucket, Rhode Island, Hood studied at Brown University, the Massachusetts Institute of Technology (MIT), and the Ecole des Beaux-Arts in Paris. In 1914 he moved to New York and formed a partnership with J. Andre Fouilhoux. With Mead Howells, they submitted the competition-winning neo-Gothic design for the Chicago Tribune Building (1922) that won Hood national attention. Later he abandoned revival styles to design the unornamented Daily News Building (1930) and McGraw-Hill Building (1932), both in New York. He was on the Board of Design for the Century of Progress Exposition in Chicago (1933). At his death, he was involved in designing Rockefeller Center, the 14-building complex in New York City that includes Radio City Music Hall. Begun in 1929, the complex was completed in 1940.

Hoover, Herbert Clark (1874–1964) *president of the United States*
Hoover was born in Iowa, orphaned at eight, and raised by an uncle in oregon thereafter. He received a bachelor's degree in mining engineering from Stanford University in 1895 (the school's first graduating class). Hoover pursued an engineering career worldwide and became a millionaire by the time he was 40. When World War I began in 1914, he became head of the Allies' relief operations in London. He also headed the Commission for Relief in Belgium and became American food administrator when the United States entered the war. His success earned him high regard as a humanitarian and an efficient administrator. In 1921 Warren G. Harding appointed Hoover secretary of commerce, a post he held through Calvin Coolidge's administration. Hoover reorganized his department, adding new divisions, while aiding efforts to construct the St. Lawrence Seaway and Boulder Dam. In the 1928 presidential race, Hoover defeated Democrat Alfred E. Smith. As president his theme was a "New Day," but the depression marred his tenure in office. Reluctant to establish relief programs, he finally gave in somewhat, creating the Reconstruction Finance Corporation (RFC) and the Federal Farm

Board; but he continued to oppose aid to the unemployed. After losing the 1932 election to Franklin D. Roosevelt, he assumed the role of public critic of New Deal policies. During the late 1940s and early 1950s, Hoover chaired federal commissions to devise plans to eradicate government waste and inefficiency. He also wrote his *Memoirs*.

Hoover, J(ohn) Edgar (1895–1972) *director of the Federal Bureau of Investigation*
Hoover spent his entire life in Washington, D.C. After earning law degrees from George Washington University in 1916 and 1917, he joined the staff of the Department of Justice, becoming Attorney General A. Mitchell Palmer's special assistant in 1919. He was appointed acting head of the Bureau of Investigation (later the Federal Bureau of Investigation, or FBI) in 1924 and confirmed as permanent head the following year. He reorganized the bureau, establishing rigorous hiring policies, and set up a fingerprints file, a scientific laboratory, and the FBI National Academy for training special officers. Hoover devoted the FBI to crusades against organized crime, communists, and civil rights activists from the 1930s through the 1960s.

Hopkins, Harry L. (1890–1946) *one of Roosevelt's closest advisers and ablest administrators*
Hopkins was raised in Iowa and educated at Grinnell College. He was a social worker in New York City during the 1920s. Franklin D. Roosevelt, then governor, appointed him administrator of the New York Temporary Emergency Relief Administration in 1931. In 1933 he moved to Washington to head the Federal Emergency Relief Administration and then the Works Progress Administration (WPA, largely his creation). He served on several committees and headed the Federal Surplus Relief Corporation. Roosevelt appointed him secretary of commerce in 1938. During World War II, Hopkins served as the president's liaison in Britain and the USSR, headed the lend-lease program, and was a member of both the War Production Board and the Pacific War Council. He was among the president's advisers at the Allied conferences in Cairo, Teheran, and Casablanca during 1942–43. In 1945 he served as adviser at the Yalta Conference and was instrumental in arranging the Potsdam and San Francisco Conferences.

Howe, Louis (1871–1936) *close adviser and staff member for Roosevelt*

Howe was born in Indianapolis but grew up in Saratoga Springs, New York. Following graduation from high school, he worked in his father's print shop, helping produce the *Sun,* a Democratic newspaper. In 1906 he joined the staff of the mayor of Auburn, New York, to handle political affairs but was let go in 1909. Eleanor Roosevelt enrolled him to run Franklin D. Roosevelt's 1912 campaign for the New York General Assembly, and he stayed on. He managed Roosevelt's 1920 campaign for the vice presidency and remained as an adviser after Roosevelt was stricken with polio in August 1921, helping keep alive FDR's hope of a future in politics. When Roosevelt became governor in 1928, Howe handled his political affairs in New York City. He moved with Roosevelt to the White House in 1932, but declining health limited his responsibilities.

Hughes, Charles Evans (1862–1948) *associate justice and chief justice of the Supreme Court*

Hughes was born in Glen Falls, New York, and earned degrees from Brown University and Columbia University Law School. After graduation he joined a law firm in New York City. In 1906 he defeated William Randolph Hearst in the election for governor; he won reelection in 1908. President William Howard Taft appointed him associate justice of the Supreme Court, where he served from October 10, 1910, to June 10, 1916, when he was nominated for the presidency by the Republican Party—he lost the election to Woodrow Wilson. Hughes served as secretary of state from March 4, 1921 to March 3, 1925, when he returned to private practice. In 1930 President Hoover appointed him chief justice of the Supreme Court; he served from February 24, 1930, until retiring July 1, 1941. He wrote several books on foreign relations and on the Supreme Court.

Hull, Cordell (1871–1955) *secretary of state*

Hull was born in Pickett County, Tennessee. He was a staunch Democrat and supporter of Woodrow Wilson's views. He served in the House of Representatives from 1907 to 1921 and again from 1923 to 1931. From 1931 until Franklin D. Roosevelt appointed him secretary of state, in 1933, he served in the Senate. He served longer as secretary of state than anyone else in history. He supported trade agreements allowing lower tariffs, the Good Neighbor policy toward Latin America, and formation of the United Nations. Hull resigned following the 1944 election. In 1945 he received the Nobel Peace Prize for his role in organizing the United Nations.

Ickes, Harold LeClair (1874–1952) *secretary of the interior*

Ickes was born in Pennsylvania, moved alone to Chicago at age 16, graduated with honors from the University of Chicago in 1897, worked as a reporter for Chicago newspapers, earned a law degree from the University of Chicago Law School in 1907, and thereafter practiced law in Chicago with Donald R. Richberg. In progressive politics before World War I, he worked in the liberal wing of the Republican Party during the twenties and headed the Western Independent Republican Committee for Franklin D. Roosevelt in 1932. Scrupulously honest, an outstanding administrator, but petulant and tyrannical, Ickes was a strong advocate of conservation and the rights of minorities. Roosevelt appointed him secretary of the interior in 1933 and put Ickes in charge of several agencies, notably the Public Works Administration (PWA) from 1933 to 1939. He distributed some $5 billion, with not a single instance of graft by anyone involved, for PWA projects. During World War II, Ickes administered the allocation of petroleum and other fuels and headed the War Relocation Authority. He resigned as secretary of the interior in early 1946.

Insull, Samuel (1859–1938) *head of Middle West Utilities*

Insull was a preeminent empire builder. A native of London, England, he became assistant to Thomas Edison's London agent and then to Edison, moving to the United States in 1881. He helped Edison develop the General Electric Company, later sold to J. P. Morgan. In 1892 Insull became president of Chicago Edison Company. He began building an empire, employing the nation's first steam turbines to create cheap electricity and pyramiding his holdings rapidly during the 1920s. By 1928 Middle West Utilities controlled more than 200 electric utilities and 27 other holding companies in 32 states. In 1931 and 1932, his utilities holding companies went into receivership, and in 1932 he fled to Europe to escape prosecution. Extradited in 1934 to stand trial in Chicago on fraud and other charges, he won acquittal three times.

Jackson, Robert H. (1892–1954) *solicitor general, attorney general, associate justice of the Supreme Court*
Jackson, born in Spring Creek, Pennsylvania, studied law for a year at Albany Law School and clerked for a lawyer in Jamestown, New York. Active in New York Democratic politics, he became general counsel for the Bureau of Internal Revenue in 1934; he successfully prosecuted former secretary of the treasury Andrew W. Mellon for tax evasion. Thereafter Jackson worked in the Treasury Department, the Securities and Exchange Commission, and the Justice Department. Franklin D. Roosevelt appointed Jackson as solicitor general in 1938 and attorney general in 1940. When Associate Justice Harlan Fiske Stone became chief justice of the Supreme Court in 1941, Roosevelt appointed Jackson as his successor. In 1945 Truman appointed him chief prosecutor for the Nuremberg trials; in 1946 he returned to the Supreme Court, serving until his death.

Johnson, Hiram (1866–1945) *Republican senator*
Johnson was born in Sacramento, California. After gaining statewide attention for his crusading work as a prosecuting attorney in San Francisco, he was elected governor on a reform ticket in 1910 and reelected in 1914. Johnson helped form the Progressive Party in 1912, running as vice presidential candidate with Theodore Roosevelt on the Bull Moose ticket that year. He was elected to the Senate in 1916 and served until his death. Johnson supported progressive programs, including relief for farmers and New Deal legislation to alleviate unemployment. An isolationist, he opposed the Treaty of Versailles and American participation in the League of Nations and the World Court. He also sponsored the Neutrality Acts and opposed efforts to prepare for war in the late thirties.

Johnson, Hugh Samuel (1882–1942) *first head of the National Recovery Administration*
Johnson was raised in Oklahoma; he attended Oklahoma Northwestern Teachers College and in 1903 graduated from West Point. He served in the army in various western states and the Philippines and also studied law at the University of California. During World War I, he helped set up the conscription system, organized a supply system along with the War Industries Board, and became a brigadier general. In 1919 he became general counsel for the Moline Plow Company. That same year he also helped George Peek create farm relief plans. In 1927 he became an assistant to Bernard Baruch and, in 1932, an adviser to Franklin D. Roosevelt. Johnson helped draft the National Industrial Recovery Act. Roosevelt appointed him head of the National Recovery Administration (NRA) in 1933 but replaced him in 1934 with an administrative board. He became a newspaper columnist, wrote his memoirs, supported Roosevelt in 1936 but fell out with the New Deal and backed Wendell Willkie in 1940. Johnson also helped organize the isolationist America First Committee.

Johnson, James Weldon (1871–1938) *lawyer, poet, major advocate of African-American causes*
Johnson was born in Jacksonville, Florida, received B.A. and M.A. degrees from Atlanta University, and studied at Columbia University. Admitted to the Florida bar in 1897, he practiced law and, with his brother, composed songs, including "Lift Every Voice and Sing," considered the "Negro national anthem." In 1901 he and his brother went to New York; they composed 200 songs for Broadway musicals. Johnson was appointed consul to Venezuela (1906) and to Nicaragua (1909). His *Autobiography of an Ex-Coloured Man* (anonymous, 1912) won wide attention when republished under his own name in 1927. He became field secretary for the National Association for the Advancement of Colored People (NAACP) in 1916 and executive secretary in 1930. From 1917 to 1930 he published works of his own poetry and anthologies of other black poets, interpreting blacks' contributions to American letters and music and in 1933, his autobiography *Along This Way*.

Jones, Jesse H. (1874–1956) *banker, chairman of the Reconstruction Finance Corporation*
Jones was born in Robertson County, Tennessee. The family moved to Dallas in 1883. Jones graduated from Hill's Business School in Dallas. He entered his uncle's lumber business and finally became manager. Jones built a huge fortune in lumber, real estate, construction, and banking in Houston. He supported Woodrow Wilson in 1912 and during World War I headed the American Red Cross's Military Relief Section. In 1926 he and his wife acquired the *Houston Chronicle.* Herbert Hoover appointed him to the board of the Reconstruction Finance Corporation (RFC) in 1932, and in 1933 Franklin D. Roosevelt

appointed him chairman. Over time the RFC became the major funding agency for many New Deal programs. In 1939 Roosevelt appointed Jones head of the Federal Loan Agency, with control of the RFC and other agencies. In 1940 he became secretary of commerce. He resigned in 1945, returning to Houston.

Kaltenborn, Hans V. (1878–1965) *journalist*
Born in Milwaukee, Wisconsin, Kaltenborn began work with the *Merrill News* (Wisconsin) at 15. He served as a war correspondent in the Spanish-American War and then in Europe, returning to the United States to earn a degree from Harvard University (1909). In 1910 he joined the staff of the *Brooklyn Eagle*. In 1922 Kaltenborn began making news broadcasts, and in 1929 he joined CBS as chief news commentator. His most famous news coup was continuous broadcasting of the Munich conference (1938). In 1940 he became commentator for NBC. Kaltenborn published several books, including an autobiography, *Fifty Fabulous Years* (1950).

Kellogg, Frank B. (1856–1937) *secretary of state*
Kellogg was born in St. Paul, Minnesota. With little formal education, he achieved prominence prosecuting antitrust cases for the federal government. He served in the Senate from 1917 until 1923, when he was appointed ambassador to England, serving until 1925. Calvin Coolidge appointed him as secretary of state in 1927, a post he held until 1929. He helped organize the 1927 Geneva Conference to limit naval armaments and joined French foreign minister Aristide Briand in devising the Pact of Paris (also called the Kellogg-Briand Pact) of 1928 outlawing war, for which he received the Nobel Peace Prize in 1929. From 1930 until 1935, he served as a member of the International Court of Justice at The Hague.

Kennedy, Joseph P. (1888–1969) *financier, fundraiser for Roosevelt*
Kennedy was born in East Boston. He attended Boston Latin School and graduated from Harvard University in 1912. over the next 20 years, Kennedy amassed a fortune through banking, finance, and the movie industry. He met Franklin D. Roosevelt in 1917 and backed him in 1932, raising funds for the campaign and engineering William Randolph Hearst's support for FDR's nomination at the Democratic Convention. Roosevelt appointed him chairman of the Securities and Exchange Commission in 1934. He resigned in 1935 to return to private business. In 1937 Roosevelt appointed him chairman of the Maritime Commission and, in 1938, ambassador to Great Britain. Kennedy resigned in 1940. He was the father of President John F. Kennedy.

Keynes, John Maynard (1883–1946) *economist, journalist*
Born in Cambridge, England, Keynes was educated at Eton and at Cambridge University. He served in the India Office, lectured at Cambridge, and was economic adviser during the Paris Peace Conference— an experience that generated *The Economic Consequences of the Peace* (1919). Thereafter he was a financier in London. His unorthodox works—*The Means to Prosperity* (1933) and *The General Theory of Employment, Interest and Money* (1935), which advocated government deficit spending and redistribution of incomes to stimulate private investment, consumption, and employment—influenced New Deal policies. Keynes met with Franklin D. Roosevelt in 1934 to advocate his views but with no clear effect. Later economic advisers to the administration, including Paul Samuelson, advocated Keynesian concepts.

King, W. L. Mackenzie (1874–1950) *prime minister of Canada*
Born in Berlin (Kitchener), Ontario, King studied at the universities of Toronto and Chicago and at Harvard. He did settlement work, living at Jane Addams's Hull House. He became Canadian deputy minister of labor in 1900 and edited the *Labour Gazette*. Elected to Parliament in 1908, he became minister of labor in 1909. He lost his Parliament seat in 1911, won reelection in 1917 and became head of the Liberal Party in 1919. At the end of 1921, he became prime minister; he resigned in the summer of 1926 but returned in September, serving until 1930. King became prime minister again after the Liberals won a majority in the 1935 election, and he served until 1948.

Knox, William Franklin (1874–1944) *secretary of the navy*
Born in Boston, Massachusetts, Knox left school in 1898 to become a Rough Rider (a volunteer in the Spanish-American War serving under Theodore

Roosevelt). He became a newspaperman, supported the Bull Moose ticket in 1912, served in World War I, and joined the Hearst newspaper chain. He became editor of the *Chicago Daily News* in 1931. In 1936 he was the Republican Party's candidate for the vice presidency. In 1939 Franklin D. Roosevelt asked him to serve as secretary of the navy; he accepted the post in 1940 and served until his sudden death in 1944. He organized the agreement with Great Britain to exchange destroyers for bases and was vocal in urging the United States to oppose the Axis powers and to provide American naval escorts of lend-lease convoys to Great Britain.

Konoye, Fumimaro (1891–1946) *prime minister of Japan*

Konoye attended Tokyo Imperial University and earned a law degree from Kyoto Imperial University, acquiring wide knowledge of Western literature, philosophy, sociology, and social problems. Following World War I, he was an attendant for the Japanese delegation to the Paris Peace Conference. Konoye entered politics in about 1920 under the aegis of an elder statesman. As a prince, he entered the upper house of the parliament, where he advocated reforms, including renovations to the military to restrict its political power, especially after war broke out in Manchuria in 1931. Konoye served as vice president of the upper house and was appointed president in 1933. Declining to form a cabinet in 1936, he acquiesced to establishing a nonpartisan cabinet in June 1937, serving as prime minister. While accepting the army's more reasonable demands, he sought to control its extreme elements while promoting international reconciliation. But in July 1937 war erupted between Japan and China, and in January 1939 his government fell. Konoye was appointed to the privy council and given a cabinet post by the new prime minister, Hiranuma Kiichiro. In June 1940 he resigned from the privy council, intent on forming a popular, national political movement to restrain the military, but he was then persuaded to form another cabinet. Japan joined in the Tripartite Pact and a nonaggression treaty with the Soviet Union. Konoye worked diligently to foster negotiations with the United States and formed a new cabinet in July 1941 in order to displace Foreign Minister Matsuoka Yosuke, who opposed the negotiations, from office. But his efforts finally failed, and he resigned from office in October 1941 as a result of opposition by the army's minister, Hideki Tojo. Suspected by the military, Konoye was driven from major political involvement. He helped bring down the Tojo government in 1944. Following World War II, he served as minister of national affairs, but an arrest warrant issued by the occupation army alleging that he might have been a war criminal precipitated his suicide in January 1946.

Krock, Arthur (1887–1974) *premier journalist of his time*

Krock was born in Glasgow, Kentucky. He studied at Princeton University (1904), left for financial reasons, and earned an associate of arts degree at Chicago's Lewis Institute (1906). Upon graduation he became a reporter for the *Louisville Herald*. Krock became Washington correspondent for the *Louisville Times* in 1910 and editor in chief in 1919. In 1923 he joined the staff of the *New York World* and, in 1927, at Adolph Ochs's invitation, joined the *New York Times*. In 1931 Krock became the *Times*'s Washington correspondent. In 1937 Franklin D. Roosevelt granted him an exclusive interview, confirming his preeminent journalistic stature.

La Follette, Robert M., Jr. (1895–1953) *Democratic senator*

Son of Senator Robert M. La Follette, he attended the University of Wisconsin (1913–1915) and served as his father's secretary from 1919 until his father's death in 1925, when he was elected to serve the remainder of his father's term in the Senate. La Follette advocated public works and relief measures during the Herbert Hoover presidency and supported the New Deal, although advocating more extreme measures than Franklin D. Roosevelt accepted. From 1936 till 1940, he chaired the Civil Liberties Committee investigating antiunion activities by business. An isolationist, La Follette opposed the Lend-Lease Act and advocated neutrality; following the attack on Pearl Harbor, however, he supported the war effort. He lost his Senate seat in 1946 to Republican Joseph McCarthy.

La Guardia, Fiorello (1882–1947) *mayor of New York City, congressman*

Known as the "Little Flower," La Guardia was born in New York. Educated at army posts and at his mother's home in Trieste, Austria, he returned to New York in

1906, graduated from New York University Law School, and began practicing law in 1910. La Guardia was elected to Congress as a Republican in 1916 but took a leave of absence in 1917 to serve as an air force pilot in Europe, where he met Franklin D. Roosevelt. He returned to Congress in 1918 and was reelected in 1922, despite supporting Robert M. La Follette of the Progressive Party for the presidency. A backer of organized labor, he cosponsored the Norris–La Guardia Act in 1932. He lost his congressional seat in 1932 but was elected mayor of New York City in 1933. Roosevelt appointed him director of the office of Civilian Defense in 1941. He retired as mayor in 1945 and served as director of the United Nations Relief and Rehabilitation Administration in 1946.

Landon, Alfred M. (1887–1987) *governor of Kansas, presidential candidate*
Landon was born in Pennsylvania and raised in Ohio. His family moved to Kansas in 1904. Landon earned a law degree from the University of Kansas in 1908 and then became involved in oil production. In 1912 he supported Bull Moose candidate Theodore Roosevelt for president. Landon served in World War I in the chemical warfare service. He was elected governor of Kansas in 1932 and reelected in 1934. Landon advocated tax and financial reforms, regulation of banks, and government reorganization; he supported New Deal unemployment, farm, and conservation programs. He was the Republican Party candidate for the presidency in 1936. In 1938 Roosevelt appointed him as vice chairman of the Inter-American Conference held in Lima, Peru.

Lange, Dorothea (1895–1965) *documentary photographer*
Lange was born in Hoboken, New Jersey, studied photography with Clarence White, and settled in San Francisco, opening a studio in 1916. During the Great Depression, she began making documentary photographs of the homeless and was hired by the state to photograph migrant farm workers. The effectiveness of these works led the state to establish camps for the workers and the federal government to establish the Rural Resettlement Administration. Lange was a photographer for the RRA, making classic photos of the poor, many of them appearing in *An American Exodus: A Record of Human Erosion* (1939). Lange received a Guggenheim Fellowship in 1941 and was one of the

few photographers who recorded the evacuation of Japanese Americans after the attack on Pearl Harbor. Lange later shot photo essays for *Life* magazine.

LeHand, Marguerite (1898–1944) *secretary to Roosevelt*
Known as "Missy," LeHand was born in Potsdam, New York, but grew up in Massachusetts. A high school graduate, she worked at various clerical jobs until joining the staff of the Democratic National Headquarters in 1920. She became Franklin D. Roosevelt's personal secretary following the 1920 election and remained in this post until suffering a stroke in 1941. She had great influence with the president, who sought her advice. With Eleanor Roosevelt she shared the role of acting as the conscience of the administration.

Lehman, Herbert H. (1878–1963) *governor of New York, U.S. senator*
Lehman was born in New York City. He graduated from Williams College in 1899 and later joined his brother in the investment banking firm Lehman Brothers. He supported the Henry Street Settlement and, during World War I, the Joint Distribution Committee, a charity serving Jews in Europe and Palestine. During World War I, he worked at the Navy Department, where he began a lifelong friendship with Franklin D. Roosevelt. In 1928 he supported Alfred E. Smith, served as finance chairman for the Democratic National Committee, and ran successfully for the lieutenant governorship of New York. Roosevelt was the candidate for governor. Both won reelection in 1930. Lehman succeeded Roosevelt in 1932 and was reelected three times. In 1943 Lehman became director of the United Nations Relief and Rehabilitation Administration. He lost a 1946 election for the Senate but succeeded in a 1949 special election. He left the Senate in 1957.

Lewis, John L. (1880–1969) *coal miner, union leader*
Born near Lucas, Iowa, Lewis headed the United Mine Workers of American (UMWA) from 1920 to 1960 and was an organizer of the Congress of Industrial Organizations (CIO) in 1935. As first president of the CIO from 1936 to 1940, he was an effective leader of sometimes strident campaigns to unionize the steel, automobile, tire, and rubber industries. Lewis broke from the Republican Party to

support Franklin D. Roosevelt in the 1936 election; the UMWA provided sizable funding to the Democratic Party. He resigned as CIO president in 1940 after Roosevelt's election to a third term, which he opposed.

Lewis, (Harry) Sinclair (1885–1951) *novelist, satirist*

Lewis was born in Sauk Centre, Minnesota. He graduated from Yale University in 1907. He worked in New York as a publisher's reader, publishing his first novel, *Our Mr. Wrenn,* in 1914. The novel that established his stature, *Main Street* (1920), satirized life in a midwestern town. *Babbitt* (1922) also won wide readership—it satirized small businessmen. *Arrowsmith* (1925) concerned the medical profession. *Elmer Gantry* (1927) satirized evangelical preachers, and *Dodsworth* (1929) focused on the big businessman. These five novels earned him the Nobel Prize in literature in 1930—the first American to receive the prize. A later work, *It Can't Happen Here* (1935), concerned the possibility of fascist rule in the United States. Lewis's reputation declined after 1930, and he lived most of the time in Europe. Two marriages, the second to journalist Dorothy Thompson, ended in divorce.

Lilienthal, David E. (1899–1981) *member and chairman of the Tennessee Valley Authority*

Lilienthal was born in Morton, Illinois. He graduated from DePauw University and Harvard Law School. After his graduation Felix Frankfurter recommended him to Daniel Richberg, and Lilienthal joined Richberg's law firm in Chicago. He was appointed chairman of the Wisconsin Public Service Commission in 1931. Franklin D. Roosevelt appointed him to the first Tennessee Valley Authority (TVA) board in 1933; he served until 1945, the last four years as chairman. In 1945 he became chairman of the Atomic Energy Commission, serving until 1950.

Lindbergh, Charles A. (1902–1974) *aviator*

Born in Detroit, Michigan, Lindbergh studied for two years at the University of Wisconsin and at the U.S. Army flying schools in Texas (1924–25). In 1926 he became an airmail pilot flying from St. Louis to Chicago. Backed by St. Louis businessmen, he entered the competition for a $25,000 prize for the first solo flight across the Atlantic. In May 1927, Lindbergh flew alone from New York to Paris in a monoplane christened *The Spirit of St. Louis,* winning the prize, becoming an American hero, and earning the Congressional Medal of Honor. He then worked as an adviser to airlines. Lindbergh married Anne Morrow in 1930; in 1932 their son was kidnapped and murdered—a celebrated crime. The Lindberghs lived in Europe (1935 to 1939) and visited Germany in 1936 and 1938. Lindbergh joined the America First Committee in 1941, but during the war he flew combat missions in the Pacific. After the war, he was a director with Pan American World Airways. His *The Spirit of St. Louis* (1953) won the Pulitzer Prize.

Lippmann, Walter (1889–1974) *influential newspaper columnist*

Lippmann was born in New York City. He graduated from Harvard University in 1909. He helped found *The New Republic* in 1914 and served as assistant editor. His writings influenced Woodrow Wilson, who in 1919 appointed him as a delegate to the Paris Peace Conference. From 1921 to 1929, Lippmann was editorial writer for the New York *World* and then served as editor until 1931, when he joined the *New York Herald-Tribune*. His column "Today and Tomorrow" became syndicated in over 250 papers, including those in two dozen other nations. In 1928 Lippmann supported Alfred E. Smith for president and Franklin D. Roosevelt for governor of New York. He supported the First New Deal but not the Second and backed Alf Landon in 1936. During the war, Lippmann supported the administration's policies. His column, "Today and Tomorrow," won the Pulitzer Prize in 1958 and 1962. He wrote several books, perhaps the most influential being *Public Opinion* (1922).

Long, Huey P. (1893–1935) *governor of Louisiana, U.S. senator*

Long was born near Winnfield, Louisiana. Largely self-educated, he passed the bar exam in 1915. In 1918 he was elected to the state railroad commission; he served for eight years on the Louisiana Public Service Commission. In 1928 Long was elected governor. Known as the "Kingfish," Long aggrandized power through a dominant political machine. He won election to the Senate in 1930 but remained governor until 1932, then resigned to assume his Senate seat while maintaining control over the governorship. He criticized Herbert Hoover's policies, advocated redistribution of wealth, and supported Franklin D. Roosevelt for the presidency. By the end of 1933, however, Long had become a Roosevelt opponent. He organized his own political base through his Share Our Wealth Society. Long advocated confiscatory taxes on income and inheritances and a guaranteed annual income—his slogan was "every man a king." He was assassinated in Baton Rouge by Dr. Carl Austin Weiss, who was immediately killed by Long's bodyguards.

Louis, Joe (1914–1981) *world heavyweight boxing champion*
Louis was born Joseph Louis Barrow in Lexington, Alabama. He began boxing in Detroit, won a Golden Gloves title and in 1934 the U.S. Amateur Athletic Union 175-pound championship. He began fighting professionally on July 4, 1934. He defeated several previous heavyweight title holders. He lost his first professional fight to Max Schmeling in 1936 on a technical knockout, but on June 22, 1937, he knocked out James J. Braddock to win the heavyweight title, which he held until retiring on March 1, 1949—a record reign. Known as the "Brown Bomber," Louis was elected to the Boxing Hall of Fame in 1954.

Luce, Henry R. (1898–1967) *publisher, editor*
Luce was born to Presbyterian missionaries in China. He attended Yale and Oxford Universities, then worked as a newspaper reporter in Chicago and Baltimore. In 1922 he and Yale classmate Briton Hadden came up with the idea of publishing a weekly newsmagazine, borrowed money, and began *Time.* Its first issue was March 3, 1923. Hadden died in March 1929, and Luce became sole head of Time, Inc., and editor in chief of the magazine. In 1930 Luce founded *Fortune;* in 1936, *Life;* in 1954, *Sports Illustrated.* He was editor in chief of all four magazines until 1964. In 1931 Luce began the radio series *March of Time* and in 1935 newsreels of the same title. In 1935 he married playwright Clare Boothe.

MacArthur, Douglas (1880–1964) *general*
Born on an army base near Little Rock, Arkansas, MacArthur graduated from West Point (1903). He served in the Philippines and Mexico and with the Rainbow Division in World War I. He became commandant of West Point and was promoted to general in 1930. In 1932, as army chief of staff, he command-

ed the troops that dispersed the Bonus Army, World War I veterans who had gathered in Washington, D.C., to pressure Congress for early payment on service certificates. In 1935 he became military adviser in the Philippines. MacArthur retired in 1937, but Franklin D. Roosevelt recalled him in 1941 to be commander in the Philippines and later appointed him as commander in chief in the Pacific. MacArthur was commander of the Japanese occupation (1945–51) and of United Nations forces in Korea (1950–51) but was relieved of command by Truman.

McCormick, Robert R. (1880–1955) *newspaper publisher*
Born in Wheaton, Illinois, McCormick was the grandson of Joseph Medill, editor and publisher of the *Chicago Tribune.* He graduated from Groton School and Yale University (1903), served as a Chicago alderman for a year, and was president of the Chicago Sanitary District Board from 1905 to 1910. He became president of the *Chicago Tribune* in 1911. Though against American entry into World War I, he served in France and became a colonel. In 1925 he became sole editor and publisher of the *Tribune,* holding both posts until his death. He was a fierce opponent of Prohibition, Wall Street, and Great Britain and a proponent of isolationism. He opposed the entire New Deal, except for the Securities and Exchange Commission. McCormick advocated appeasing Germany and Japan, until the attack on Pearl Harbor.

MacDonald, (James) Ramsay (1866–1937) *British prime minister*
Born in Scotland, MacDonald moved to London in 1886 and joined the Fabian Society (a socialist group). In 1894 he joined the new Independent Labour Party. In 1900 he became first secretary of the Labour Representation Committee, which evolved into the Labour Party in 1906—the year MacDonald won election to the House of Commons. He became leader of the party in 1911 but was forced out after opposing war with Germany. He lost reelection in 1918, returned to the Commons in 1922, and again became party leader. MacDonald became the first Labour prime minister in January 1924 with support of the Liberal Party, but a Conservative Party win in the November elections forced his resignation. MacDonald again became prime minister in June 1929, retaining the post after 1931 as head of a

coalition government. In June 1935 he was succeeded by Conservative Stanley Baldwin.

McIntyre, Marvin (1878–1943) *secretary to Roosevelt*

McIntyre was born in La Grange, Kentucky, and attended Vanderbilt University. A career newspaperman, he became head of press relations for the Navy Department in 1917. He was in charge of publicity for Franklin D. Roosevelt during his 1920 vice presidential campaign. Afterwards he joined the staff of *Army and Navy Journal* until 1932, when he took charge of publicity for Franklin D. Roosevelt's presidential campaign. As part of the White House staff, he was among FDR's closest associates, insiders known as the "Cufflinks Gang" that also included Stephen Early, Louis Howe, and Marguerite ("Missy") LeHand.

McPherson, Aimee Semple (1890–1944) *evangelist*

Born in Ingersoll, Ontario, McPherson began preaching at age 17, inspired by her mother and evangelist Robert Semple. Semple became her husband; in 1908 they went to China, where Semple was a missionary. After his death, she moved to the United States and, in 1912, married Harold McPherson. They divorced, and she became an itinerant evangelist and healer, ending up in Los Angeles, where her followers built the Angelus Temple for her. By the end of the 1920s, she had tens of thousands of followers, a radio station, a publishing firm, about 200 missions, and a Bible school. She founded the International Church of the Four Square Gospel. Her movement peaked in the 1930s and early 1940s. McPherson died of an overdose of barbiturates, and her son Rolf McPherson succeeded her. Among her many books are *In the Service of the King* (1927) and *Give Me My Own God* (1936).

Madden, Joseph W. (1890–1972) *chairman of the National Labor Relations Board*

Madden was born in Damascus, Illinois. He graduated from the University of Illinois (1911), earned a law degree at the University of Chicago (1914), and served on the law faculties of the University of Oklahoma and Ohio State University. In 1927 he became professor of law at the University of Pittsburgh. Appointed chairman of the National Labor Relation Board (NLRB) in 1935, he served until 1940, cementing the NLRB's stature. In 1941 Franklin D. Roosevelt appointed him to the U.S. Court of Claims in Washington.

Marshall, George C. (1880–1959) *chief of staff of the U.S. Army, secretary of state*

Marshall was born in Uniontown, Pennsylvania. He graduated from Virginia Military Academy in 1901 and was commissioned a second lieutenant in the army in 1902. He served twice in the Philippines and both studied and taught at Fort Leavenworth, Kansas, before World War I, when he served in France. Marshall was General John J. Pershing's chief aide until 1923 and then served in China and as head of instruction at the Infantry School, Fort Benning, Georgia. He also commanded army units involved with the Civilian Conservation Corps. In 1938 he became chief of the War Plans Division in Washington and then, deputy chief of staff. In 1939 Franklin D. Roosevelt appointed him chief of staff. He accompanied Roosevelt to all the major Allied war conferences during World War II. Marshall served as secretary of state in 1947–49 and devised the Marshall Plan for aiding European nations' recovery from the war. He was awarded the Nobel Peace Prize in 1953.

Mayer, Louis B. (1885–1957) *movie mogul archetype*

Born in Minsk, Russia (his family emigrated to the United States), Mayer went to work at 14 in his father's scrap iron firm. In 1907 he opened a nickelodeon in Haverhill, Massachusetts, which he expanded into the largest chain of cinemas in New England by 1918, when he founded Louis B. Mayer Pictures in Hollywood. In 1924 his firm joined Metro Pictures Corporation (owned by Marcus Loew, deviser of the merger) and Goldwyn Pictures Corporation (Samuel Goldwyn had left to work independently) to form Metro-Goldwyn-Mayer (M.G.M), with Mayer as studio head—the beginning of his nearly 30 years as the preeminent executive in the industry. Considered the "czar of Hollywood" from 1924 to 1949, Mayer created the star system during the 1930s and 1940s, with leading actors and actresses under contract to M.G.M. He retired in 1951.

Mellon, Andrew W. (1855–1937) *secretary of the treasury*

Mellon was born in Pittsburgh, where his father owned a banking firm. He graduated from the

University of Pittsburgh and worked for the family firm, eventually becoming president. He had financial interests in the aluminum, coal, and oil industries and amassed one of the largest fortunes in the nation. In 1921, Warren G. Harding appointed him secretary of the treasury, a post he retained nearly to the end of Herbert Hoover's administration. He was responsible for lowering tax rates and federal indebtedness resulting from World War I. In 1932 Hoover appointed him ambassador to England, a post he relinquished in 1933. In 1937 Mellon gave a major part of his art collection to the federal government with a gift of $15 million to build the National Gallery of Art to house it. The gallery opened in 1941.

Mencken, Henry L. (1880–1956) *journalist, literary critic, author*
Born in Baltimore, Maryland, Mencken graduated from Baltimore Polytechnic Institute at age 16 and then studied privately. At 19 he joined the staff of the Baltimore *Morning Herald,* and in 1905 he joined the *Sun* syndicate, working first for the *Evening Herald* and then the Baltimore *Sun,* continuing some work for the latter until 1941. In 1914 Mencken and George Jean Nathan became coeditors of *The Smart Set,* an influential literary magazine for which Mencken had written book reviews since 1908. In 1917 Mencken became a literary adviser to Alfred A. Knopf publishing firm and published a collection of critical pieces, *A Book of Prefaces.* In 1919 appeared *Prejudges: First Series,* the first of a series of six works completed in 1926. In 1924 Mencken and Nathan founded *The American Mercury,* which Mencken edited until 1933. In these years, Mencken was also a contributing editor for the liberal *Nation.* He published numerous other books, including autobiographical works and *The American Language.*

Meyer, Eugene, Jr. (1875–1959) *financier*
Born in Los Angeles, Meyer graduated from Yale University (1895) and worked in banking houses in European capitals. He formed his own firm in 1901, with a seat on the New York Stock Exchange. Bernard Baruch made him head of a division of the War Industries Board; in 1918 Woodrow Wilson appointed him managing director of the War Finance Corporation, which he headed until it was dissolved in 1925. Herbert Hoover appointed him governor of the Federal Reserve Board in 1930 and chairman of

the Reconstruction Finance Corporation in 1932. In 1933 Meyer bought the *Washington Post.* In 1941 Franklin D. Roosevelt appointed him to the National Defense Mediation Board. In 1946 Meyer became president of the World Bank.

Millay, Edna St. Vincent (1892–1950) *poet, librettist*
Millay was born in Rockland, Maine, and began wring verse as a child, publishing in *St. Nicholas.* She graduated from Vassar College in 1917, moved to Greenwich Village (Manhattan), and supported herself by selling poems and stories to magazines. Associated as an actress and playwright with Provincetown Players, she wrote several poetic dramas. Her first collection *Renascence and Other Poems* appeared in 1917. *A Few Figs from Thistles* (1920) was the poetic equivalent of Fitzgerald's prose works for youths of the 1920s. Millay received the Pulitzer Prize in 1923 for the title poem of *The Harp Weaver and Other Poems.* She wrote the libretto for Deems Taylor's opera *The King's Henchman,* produced by the Metropolitan Opera in 1927. Later works include *Fatal Interview* (1931), *Wine from These Grapes* (1934), and *Conversation at Midnight* (1937). In some works of the late 1930s and early 1940s, she protested against the European fascist regimes.

Miller, Glenn (1904–1944) *composer, band leader*
Miller was born in Clarinda, Iowa, and educated at the University of Colorado-Boulder. In 1926 he joined Ben Pollack's band as trombonist, then began to freelance in New York. He helped organize the Dorsey brothers' band in 1934 and Ray Noble's band in 1935. He organized his own band in 1938, achieving great popular and commercial success within a year. Among his best-known compositions were "Moonlight Serenade" and "In the Mood." His band appeared in two films, *Sun Valley Serenade* (1941) and *Orchestra Wives* (1942). During World War II, Miller was a captain and leader of the U.S. Air Force Band in Europe. On a flight from England to Paris (December 16, 1944), his plane disappeared.

Mitchell, Margaret (1900–1949) *author*
Born in Atlanta, Georgia, Mitchell attended Washington Seminary and Smith College. She became a writer for the *Atlanta Journal* in 1922, leaving the newspaper after suffering a severe ankle injury in 1926.

She then devoted herself to writing her only book, *Gone with the Wind,* a novel about the Civil War and Reconstruction eras in the South. Published in 1936, the novel won the Pulitzer Prize in 1937. The most popular novel in American history, *Gone with the Wind* sold 2 million copies in the United States by 1939 and continues to sell; by the time of Mitchell's death, 8 million copies had been sold in 40 countries. She sold the movie rights for $50,000; the 1939 film held the record for gross receipts well into the 1960s.

Moley, Raymond (1886–1975) *member of Roosevelt's "Brains Trust" (with Berle and Tugwell)*
Moley served as the president's main adviser on economic policy as assistant secretary of state. Born in Berea, Ohio, he earned a B.A. degree from Baldwin-Wallace College (1906) and, after three years in the southwest being cured of tuberculosis, an M.A. from Oberlin College (1913) and a Ph.D. from Columbia University (1918). He taught at Western Reserve University. From 1919 to 1923, he served as director of the Cleveland Foundation, an organization for civic reform and philanthropy. He also served on crime commissions of several states, including New York. In 1923 he joined the Columbia University faculty. He volunteered to advise Franklin D. Roosevelt before the 1932 campaign, helped draft speeches, and coined the term "New Deal." He was Roosevelt's principal adviser on cabinet choices. Roosevelt sent him to oversee the American delegation to the 1933 World Economic and Monetary Conference in London, then moved him to a post in the Justice Department. Moley resigned in the fall to become editor of *Today;* later he was editor of *Newsweek.* He opposed the New Deal after 1939, regarding its policies as antibusiness.

Molotov, Vyacheslav M. (1890–1986) *diplomat, statesman of the USSR*
Born in Kukarka, Russia, Molotov participated in the Russian Revolution of 1905 when a student at the gymnasium level. He assumed the pseudonym Molotov in 1906 (his original surname was Skryabin) and became a Bolshevik. Molotov was arrested in 1909 and sent into exile in the Vologda region until 1911, when he enrolled in the Polytechnic Institute in St. Petersburg. He continued working as a Bolshevik organizer and as editor of the party's newspaper *Pravda,* founded in St. Petersburg in 1912.

Arrested again in 1915, he was deported to Irkutsk province, escaping in 1916. Following the Bolsheviks' seizure of power in 1917, Molotov worked in various provincial positions and then in 1921 became secretary of the Central Committee and a candidate member of the Politburo. After Vladimir Lenin's death in 1924, Molotov strongly supported Joseph Stalin during the ensuing power struggle. In December 1925 he received full membership in the Politburo and became head of the Moscow Party Committee purging the Moscow organization of Stalin's opponents. In 1930, Molotov became chairman of the Council of People's Commissars—that is, prime minister of the USSR—serving in this capacity until 1941. In May 1939 he also assumed the post of foreign minister, which he held until March 1949. After Stalin's death in 1953, Molotov again became foreign minister. Nikita Khrushchev dismissed him in 1956. A participant in the unsuccessful coup attempt against Khrushchev in 1957, Molotov lost his party and governmental offices. Thereafter he served as ambassador to Mongolia and as the permanent Soviet delegate to the International Atomic Energy Agency in Vienna until retiring in 1961. He died November 8, 1986.

Morgan, Arthur E. (1878–1975) *chairman of the Tennessee Valley Authority*
Born in Cincinnati, Ohio, Morgan was a self-trained engineer. He gained recognition in 1913 when Dayton, Ohio hired him to build the Miami Conservancy flood prevention system. In 1920 he became president of Antioch College, which he transformed into a leader in educational reform. In 1933 Franklin D. Roosevelt appointed Morgan as the first chairman of the Tennessee Valley Authority (TVA), which Morgan envisioned as an agency for social and economic planning. Thwarted in this vision by the other two members of the TVA board, he made public charges of malfeasance against H.A. Morgan and David Lithienthal in 1938. When Morgan could not substantiate the charges, FDR removed him from the TVA board.

Morgan, John Pierpont, Jr. (1867–1943) *banker, financier*
Morgan was born in Irvington-on-Hudson, New York. He graduated from Harvard University (1889) and entered banking in Boston. In 1891 he joined his father's firm, Drexel, Morgan and Company, in New

York. He worked in London (1898–1905) as a partner of J.P. Morgan and Company. His business prospered in the 1920s. An expert on government debt, Morgan helped with the Dawes and Young plans. He tried to stabilize the stock market after the 1929 crash. Initially a New Deal supporter, Morgan quickly became an opponent as the Banking Act of 1933 forced his firm to separate its banking and investment operations into two firms, J.P. Morgan Company and Morgan, Stanley and Company, respectively.

Morgenthau, Henry T., Jr. (1891–1967) *secretary of the treasury*
Morgenthau was born into a wealthy family in New York City and attended Phillips Exeter Academy and Cornell University but graduated from neither. After a year in Texas (1911–12) recovering from typhoid fever, he purchased land in Dutchess County, New York, becoming a neighbor of the Roosevelts at Hyde Park, and succeeded at farming. He and Franklin D. Roosevelt first met in 1915 and became lifelong friends. In 1922 Morgenthau began publishing *American Agriculturist,* which continued until 1933. As governor in 1928, Roosevelt appointed Morgenthau chairman of the state Agricultural Advisory Commission, and in 1930 as conservation commissioner. In 1933 Roosevelt appointed Morgenthau as head of the Federal Farm Board. In November 1933, when Secretary of the Treasury William Woodin was ill, Roosevelt appointed Morgenthau as assistant secretary; when Woodin could not resume his duties, in January 1934, Morgenthau became secretary of the treasury. He served until July 1945.

Murphy, Francis (Frank) W. (1893–1949) *associate justice of the Supreme Court*
Murphy was born in Harbor Beach, Michigan. He earned a law degree from the University of Michigan in 1914. He served as an army officer in Europe in 1918 and then studied law at Lincoln's Inn, London and Trinity College, Dublin. He lost a bid for Congress in 1920 but won election to the Detroit Recorder's Court in 1923. Murphy was elected mayor of Detroit in 1930. In 1932 he supported Franklin D. Roosevelt, who appointed him as governor general of the Philippines in 1933. He served until 1936, when he agreed to Roosevelt's request that he run for governor of Michigan. As governor he supported union efforts to organize the auto workers. After his defeat

for reelection in 1938, Roosevelt appointed him as attorney general. In 1940 Roosevelt appointed him associate justice of the Supreme Court; he served until his death.

Murray, Philip (1886–1952) *labor leader, organizer of the United Steelworkers of America*
Murray was born in Blantyre, Scotland, and immigrated to the United States in 1902. He became a coal miner in Pennsylvania and joined the United Mine Workers of America (UMWA). After 1912 he was a member of the UMWA's international board; he served as vice president from 1920 till 1942. In 1936, when John L. Lewis helped form the Congress of Industrial organizations (CIO), he assigned Murray to organize the steelworkers. Murray was chairman of the Steelworkers Organizing Committee from 1936 until 1942, when it was replaced by the United Steelworkers of America (USWA), of which he became president. In November 1940 he succeeded Lewis as president of the CIO, serving in that post until his death.

Murrow, Edward R. (1908–1965) *broadcast journalist*
Born in Greensboro, North Carolina, Murrow graduated from Washington State University (1930). He was president of the National Student Association (1930–32), assistant director of the Institute of International Education (1932–35), and secretary of the Emergency Commission of Displaced German Scholars (1933–34). In 1935 he joined CBS; in 1937 he became head of the network's European Bureau in London. Murrow covered the German takeover of Austria, the 1938 Munich Conference, the 1939 German occupation of Czechoslovakia, and events in Great Britain. After the war, Murrow returned to the United States to be a CBS vice president in charge of news and education programming. From 1947 on, he had a weeknight newscast. In 1951 he moved to television with *See It Now.* He also became producer and host of *Person to Person* and *Small World.* In 1961 President John F. Kennedy appointed Murrow director of the U.S. Information Agency.

Mussolini, Benito (1883–1945) *prime minister, dictator of Italy*
Mussolini was born near Predappio, earned a teacher's diploma, and embraced socialism as a young man. He

gained some prominence as a Socialist speaker and journalist. He opposed Italy's entry into World War I but fought in the army. Abandoning socialism, in 1919 he organized the Fascist Party in Milan. In 1922 his Fascist militia's march on Rome secured his appointment as prime minister. Calling himself Il Duce (the leader), he aggrandized power, becoming effective dictator within two years. In October 1935, Mussolini began the Italian invasion and conquest of Abyssinia (Ethiopia). He allied Italy with Germany in October 1936 and supported Francisco Franco in the Spanish civil war. In April 1939, Mussolini sent his troops into Albania. In June 1940, Italy invaded France. Following the Allied invasion of Italy, Mussolini was removed from power in 1943 and was shot by his countrymen in 1945.

Norris, George W. (1861–1944) *congressman, senator*

Born in Sandusky, Ohio, Norris studied a year (1877–78) at Baldwin University (Baldwin Wallace). He taught school and studied law at Northern Indiana Normal School (Valparaiso University), earning a law degree in 1883. Admitted to the bar in 1883, he moved to Nebraska in 1885 and began to practice law. Norris was elected to Congress in 1902 as a Republican. He served as a representative until 1912, when he was elected to the Senate. He opposed American entry into World War I and ratification of the Treaty of Versailles. Norris was author of the 20th Amendment (setting the president's date of inauguration) and a proponent of presidential primaries and direct popular election of senators. His long-term fight for public ownership and development of Muscle Shoals finally succeeded with the Tennessee Valley Authority Act, which he introduced. He also coauthored the Norris–La Guardia Act. Though a Republican, Norris supported Robert La Follette in 1924, Alfred E. Smith in 1928, and Roosevelt in all his campaigns for the presidency. Norris left the Senate in 1943; in 1945 he published *Fighting Liberal*.

Nye, Gerald P. (1892–1971) *Republican senator*

Born in Hortonville, Wisconsin, Nye graduated from high school in 1911 and moved to Iowa and then to North Dakota pursuing a career in journalism. In North Dakota he bought the *Fryburg Pioneer* (1919) and the *Griggs County Sentinel-Courier* (1920). In 1925 the governor appointed him to fill the seat of the deceased Senator Edwin F. Ladd. Nye won election in 1926 and served in the Senate until defeated for reelection in 1944. Nye was highly critical of New Deal programs. An ardent isolationist, he supported passage of the Neutrality Act, opposed the armaments industry, and accused Franklin D. Roosevelt of leading the nation to war.

Ochs, Adolph S. (1858–1935) *newspaper publisher*

Born in Cincinnati, Ohio, Ochs began working for the Knoxville *Chronicle* in 1869. At age 19 he moved to Chattanooga and in 1878 bought a controlling interest in the failing *Chattanooga Times,* which he revived. In 1896 he bought the *New York Times* for $75,000 and made it a success. In 1901–02, Ochs bought the Philadelphia *Public Ledger* and *Times* and merged them—he sold them to Cyrus H.K. Curtis in 1912. By 1920, the *New York Times* was among the most respected newspapers in the nation. Ochs introduced rotogravure printing of photographs and a separate book review supplement.

O'Keeffe, Georgia (1887–1986) *painter*

Born on a farm near San Prairie, Wisconsin, O'Keeffe studied at the Art Institute of Chicago (1904–05) with William Merritt Chase and at the Art Students League in New York (1907–08). She met photographer and gallery-owner Alfred Stieglitz in 1916; he arranged the first one-woman exhibit of her watercolors and photographs at his gallery in 1917. O'Keeffe and Stieglitz married in 1924. O'Keeffe's work during the 1920s was modernist and abstract—she began painting large flower forms in 1924; then she turned to realistic views of the city. In the 1930s she began spending winters in Santa Fe, New Mexico. She moved there in 1946.

O'Neill, Eugene (1888–1953) *playwright*

Born in New York City, in a Broadway hotel, his father being a popular actor, O'Neill was educated by tutors and in private schools. He attended Princeton University (1906–07) but was obliged to leave after a prank. He joined the crew of a Norwegian freighter, sailed to Buenos Aires, and caroused in Latin American port towns. Upon returning home, he helped his father as an advance agent and then became a reporter for the New London (Connecticut) *Telegraph*. While recuperating from tuberculosis in 1912, O'Neill read the classic theater repertoire, and during the winter of 1914 he studied in George Baker's renowned drama workshop at Harvard University. In 1915 he joined the Provincetown Players on Cape Cod, writing one-act plays for the troupe that attracted the attention of George Jean Nathan and H. L. Mencken, who published some of the plays in their magazine *The Smart Set* in 1917–18. In 1920, O'Neill's first full-length play to be produced, *Beyond the Horizon,* won the Pulitzer Prize. Over the next two years he produced *The Emperor Jones, Anna Christie,* and *The Hairy Ape.* From 1924 to 1931 O'Neill created nine plays, including *Desire Under the Elms* (1924), *Strange Interlude* (1928), and *Mourning Becomes Electra* (1931). *Ah, Wilderness,* produced in 1933, was O'Neill's only domestic comedy. Diagnosed with a fatal neurological disease in 1944, O'Neill won the Nobel Prize in 1936 and continued to write plays, including some of his greatest, *The Iceman Cometh* (1939, first produced in 1946), *A Moon for the Misbegotten* (1943, produced in 1952), and *Long Day's Journey into Night* (1941, produced in 1956).

Owens, Jesse (1913–1981) *outstanding track and field athlete*
Born in Danville, Alabama, Owens attended high school in Cleveland, Ohio. As a track star at Ohio State University, he matched or set world records in 100-yard and 220-yard dash, the 220-yard low hurdles, and the broad jump during a Big Ten meet. At the 1936 Olympic Games held in Berlin, Owens set world records in the 200-meter run and the running broad jump (this record stood until 1960) while winning four gold medals—to the obvious displeasure of Adolf Hitler. After his athletic career, Owens worked in child guidance and served as a goodwill ambassador for the Department of State and as secretary of the Illinois Athletic Association.

Paley, William S. (1901–1990) *broadcasting executive*
Born in Chicago, Paley graduated from the University of Pennsylvania's Wharton School of Finance (1922) and entered the family's La Palina cigar business. He became interested in radio and in 1928 bought a failing network of 16 stations, changing its name in 1929 to Columbia Broadcasting System (CBS). The network offered free programming to affiliates in exchange for their airing network programs earning advertising fees. By the end of the 1930s, CBS had 114 stations. It aired such stars as Frank Sinatra, Bing Crosby, Kate Smith, and Eddie Cantor and offered dramas on *Columbia Workshop* and *Mercury Theatre.* Paley also revolutionized broadcast journalism after 1935, with a team led by Edward R. Murrow. After World War II, he transformed CBS into a major television network.

Parker, Dorothy (1893–1967) *writer, poet, reviewer*
Parker was born in West End, New Jersey, grew up in New York City, graduated from Miss Dana's School, and went to work for *Vanity Fair.* She was one of the talented and witty group known as the Algonquin Round Table. Dismissed from *Vanity Fair,* she worked as a freelance writer. From 1927 to 1933, she did book reviews for the *New Yorker* as "Constant Reader." Her first collection of poems, *Enough Rope,* a best seller, appeared in 1926. It was amalgamated with two later volumes into *Collected Poems: Not So Deep as a Well* (1936). One of her short stories won the O. Henry Award in 1929. In 1933 she and second husband Alan Campbell moved to Hollywood to collaborate on writing film scripts. They wrote the scripts for 15 films, including *A Star Is Born* (1937). Parker covered the Spanish civil war as a correspondent. After 1945, she wrote two plays and did book reviews for *Esquire.*

Pecora, Ferdinand (1882–1971) *original member of the Securities and Exchange Commission*
Pecora was born in Nicosia, Sicily, and came to the United States in 1887. He graduated from City College of New York and from New York Law School (1906). He practiced law and was assistant district attorney in New York County (1918–22) and chief assistant district attorney (1922–30). In January 1933, the Senate Banking and Currency Committee appointed him as legal counsel in the investigation of banking and securities fraud; he gained fame exposing illegal practices by J. P. Morgan, Jr., Richard Whitney, Thomas Lamont, and others. Pecora helped draft the Securities Exchange Act (1934), and Franklin D. Roosevelt appointed him to the first Securities and Exchange Commission (SEC). He resigned in 1935 after Herbert H. Lehman appointed him justice of the New York Supreme Court.

Peek, George N. (1873–1943) *administrator of the Agricultural Adjustment Administration*
Peek was born in Polo, Illinois. He attended Northwestern University for a year (1891–92) and then worked for the John Deere Plow Company in Omaha, Nebraska. In December 1917, he was appointed to the War Industries Board. In 1921 Peek published *Equality for Agriculture;* it advocated that the federal government buy surplus agricultural products and sell them abroad, charging farmers an equalization fee, to drive up prices. Peek's ideas infused the contents of the Agricultural Adjustment Act (March 1933). Peek was appointed as the first administrator of the Agricultural Adjustment Administration (AAA), but he and Secretary of Agriculture Henry Wallace had major disagreements. In December 1933, Franklin D. Roosevelt requested Peek's resignation but made him special adviser on foreign trade. Peek resigned in November 1935 and became publicly critical of the New Deal. He joined the isolationist America First Committee, formed in July 1940 to oppose U.S. entry into war.

Pelley, William Dudley (1890–1965) *newspaperman, screenwriter, real estate agent in California*
Pelley in 1928 claimed to have died and gone to heaven for seven minutes, when he learned of Adolf Hitler's imminent rise. The day following Hitler's assumption of the chancellorship in 1933, Pelley formed the Silver Shirts (SS), headquartered in Asheville, North Carolina. His organization's magazine, *Liberation,* denounced the New Deal as communistic, advocated Nazism, and espoused anti-Semitism. Convicted of sedition in 1942, Pelley spent eight years in prison. During his incarceration, the Silver Shirts disbanded.

Pendergast, Thomas J. (1872–1945) *political boss of Kansas City, Missouri*
Pendergast was born in St. Joseph, Missouri, and attended Roman Catholic schools. Through ward politics, he gained control of Kansas City's Democratic machine. At the 1932 party convention, Pendergast supported Roosevelt. He was given control over dispersal in Missouri, of funds from the Civil Works Administration and the Works Progress Administration, augmenting his power in the state. In 1934 the Pendergast machine helped elect Harry S. Truman to the Senate. New Deal patronage to Pendergast ceased in 1938, and in 1939 he was sentenced to prison for 15 months for income tax evasion.

Penney, James Cash (1875–1971) *retail chain store magnate*
Penney worked in dry goods stores in his hometown of Hamilton, Missouri, and in Ohio and Colorado after graduating from high school in 1893. In 1899 he moved to Wyoming, and in 1902 he bought an interest in a store in Kemmerer he managed. He began to buy other small stores and set up headquarters in Salt Lake City in 1904. By 1917 he owned 48 stores; he bought out his partners and moved the headquarters to New York City. By 1929 the J. C. Penney chain had 1,450 stores nationwide and by 1940, more than 1,600. It was the most successful retail store chain in the United States in the 1930s and 1940s.

Perkins, Frances (1882–1965) *secretary of labor, first woman cabinet member*
Perkins was raised in Massachusetts. She graduated from Mount Holyoke College in 1902, worked in settlement houses, participated in the women's suffrage movement, and served with Alfred E. Smith and others on the commission investigating the Triangle shirtwaist factory fire (1911) that killed 146 women garment workers. Smith, elected governor of New York in 1918, appointed her to the state's industrial board. Franklin D. Roosevelt, elected governor in 1928, appointed her as the industrial commissioner and then in 1933 made her U.S. secretary of labor, a post she held to the end of his presidency. Perkins set up the department's Division of Labor Standards, cleaned up the corrupt Immigration and Naturalization Service, and expanded the Bureau of Labor Statistics. She helped draft the Social Security Act of 1935. In 1945 Truman appointed her to the Civil Service Commission. In 1946 she published an autobiography, *The Roosevelt I Knew.*

Pittman, Key (1872–1940) *Democratic senator*
Born in Vicksburg, Mississippi, orphaned at 12, and raised by his grandmother in Louisiana, Pittman attended Southwestern Presbyterian University in Tennessee for three years. In 1890 he moved to Seattle, read law, and was admitted to the bar. In 1897 he joined the Alaska gold rush; in 1901 he moved to Nevada. He became a Democrat in 1908, ran unsuc-

cessfully for the Senate in 1910, but was appointed to the Senate in 1912 after George Nixon's death. He served as senator from Nevada until the end of his life. In the 1930s he advocated inflationary spending and the Silver Purchase Act (1934). As chairman of the Senate Foreign Relations Committee, he had influence over lend-lease and other efforts to aid the Allies.

Porter, Cole (1892–1964) *composer, lyricist*
Porter was born in Peru, Indiana, studied violin and piano, and began composing at age 10. While at Yale University he composed musical reviews and football songs. He also studied at Harvard Law School (1914) and at Harvard Graduate School of Arts and Sciences (1915–16). His Broadway debut was *See America First* in 1916. He entertained French troops in North Africa during World War I and then served in the American army. After the war, he traveled widely in Europe and studied at the Schola Cantorum in Paris. His first Broadway hit was *Fifty Million Frenchmen* in 1929. Other popular shows included *The Gay Divorcee* (1932), *Anything Goes* (1934), *Dubarry Was a Lady* (1939), and *Panama Hattie* (1940). Porter's later major shows were *Kiss Me Kate* (1948), *Can-Can* (1953), and *Silk Stockings* (1955). He also composed songs for several movies.

Randolph, A(sa) Philip (1889–1979) *civil rights leader, president of the Brotherhood of Sleeping Car Porters*
Randolph was born in Crescent City, Florida, attended high schools in Jacksonville, and, in 1911, moved to New York City. He attended the City College of New York and lectured at the Rand School. In 1917 Randolph helped found *The Messenger*. He became organizer and president of the Brotherhood of Sleeping Car Porters in 1925. After the Railway Labor Act of 1934 outlawed company unions, the BSCP attained success and a contract with the Pullman Company. Randolph pressured the Roosevelt administration to adopt nondiscriminatory policies, until his organizing of a march on Washington scheduled for July 1, 1941 resulted in Executive Order 8802, creating the Fair Employment Practices Committee and a policy of nondiscrimination in government and defense industry employment. Randolph's civil rights activities continued into the 1960. He was an organizer of the 1963 March on Washington.

Raskob, John Jacob (1879–1950) *corporate executive, Democratic Party chairman*
Born in Lockport, New York, Raskob left school after his father's death and worked as a stenographer for Worthington Pump Co. In 1902 he became Pierre S. du Pont's secretary. He rose to treasurer and finally director and vice-president of E.I. du Pont de Nemours & Co. and also became a major stockholder in General Motors Corporation. In 1928 Raskob became chairman of the Democratic National Committee. He aided Franklin D. Roosevelt's election in 1932 but fell out with the New Deal and became an organizer of the American Liberty League.

Rayburn, Samuel T. (1882–1961) *Speaker of the House of Representatives*
Rayburn was born in Tennessee but raised on a farm in east Texas. He worked as a teacher and lawyer in Bonham, Texas, and was elected to the state legislature in 1907, serving as speaker of the house from 1911 to 1913. In 1912 Rayburn won election as congressman; he was reelected 24 times. A strong supporter of New Deal legislation, he served as chairman of the Committee on Interstate and Foreign Commerce from 1931 to 1937 and coauthored many important bills, including the Securities Exchange Act, the Federal Communications Act, and the Public Utility Holding Company Act. Elected Democratic leader of the House in 1937, Rayburn became Speaker in 1940 and held the post for 17 years—a record. His long service and his influence won him the appellation "Mr. Democrat."

Reed, Stanley F. (1884–1980) *Supreme Court associate justice*
Reed was born in Mason County, Kentucky, graduated from Kentucky Wesleyan University (1902) and Yale University (1906), and studied law at the University of Virginia, Columbia University, and the Sorbonne. He practiced law in Maysville, Kentucky, and served in the legislature and also in World War I. Herbert Hoover appointed him general counsel of the Federal Farm Board in 1929 and of the Reconstruction Finance Corporation in 1932. In 1933 he helped draft the Agriculture Adjustment Act and also helped establish the Commodity Credit Corporation. In 1935 Franklin D. Roosevelt appointed him special assistant to Attorney General Homer Cummings and then solicitor general. He brought

Robert H. Jackson, Alger Hiss, and others to the Justice Department staff. In 1938 Roosevelt appointed him to the Supreme Court; he served until 1957.

Ribbentrop, Joachim von (1893–1946) *foreign minister of Germany*

Born in Wesel to an army officer, Ribbentrop schooled in Germany, France, Switzerland, and England before moving to Canada in 1910. When World War I broke out in August 1914, he returned to Germany and served on the Eastern Front as a hussar before being stationed with the German military mission in Turkey. Ribbentrop returned to Germany following the war and became a champagne salesman. His marriage to the daughter of a wealthy champagne maker brought him financial independence. Ribbentrop met Adolf Hitler and became a member of the National Socialist (Nazi) Party in 1932. When Hitler assumed the chancellorship in January 1933, Ribbentrop served as his main foreign affairs adviser. Appointed commissioner of disarmament at Geneva in 1934, Ribbentrop negotiated the Anglo-German Naval Agreement of 1935 that allowed Germany to rebuild its navy. He became ambassador to Great Britain in 1936 but failed in efforts to establish rapprochement with the British government as Nazi Germany's aggressiveness burgeoned. Ribbentrop negotiated the anti-Comintern pact with Japan in 1936. He returned to Germany in 1938 and advised Hitler that Great Britain would not come to Poland's aid in any effective way. Appointed minister of foreign affairs, he signed the so-called Pact of Steel with Italy in May 1939. In August of the same year he signed the nonaggression treaty with the USSR that opened the way for invasion of Poland. Ribbentrop also signed the Tripartite Pact with Japan and Italy in September 1940, but his star faded thereafter. At the end of World War II the Allies captured him in Hamburg, tried him at Nürnberg for war crimes, and had him hanged. Ribbentrop left a memoir published in English in 1954 as *The Ribbentrop Memoirs.*

Richberg, Donald R. (1881–1960) *New Deal legal adviser*

Born in Knoxville, Tennessee, Richberg graduated from the University of Chicago (1901) and Harvard Law School (1904) and joined the family firm of Richberg and Richberg in Chicago. He worked for the Progressive Party but left in 1916 to campaign for Woodrow Wilson. He helped draft the Railway Labor Act (1926), supported Alfred Smith in 1928, and in 1933 helped set up the National Progressive League and worked with Raymond Moley during the campaign. In 1933 he served as assistant to Hugh Johnson and helped draft the National Industrial Recovery Act. In 1934 Franklin D. Roosevelt appointed him to the National Recovery Administration board. He resigned in 1935 after the *Schechter* decision invalidating the NRA.

Roberts, Owen J. (1875–1955) *Supreme Court associate justice*

Owens was born in Germantown, Pennsylvania. He graduated from the University of Pennsylvania and its law school, then joined the latter's faculty. He was first assistant district attorney for Philadelphia (1903–06). In the 1920s he won prominence as special counsel in the Teapot Dome case. Herbert Hoover appointed him to the Supreme Court in 1930. During the New Deal, he sided with the court's conservative wing in *Schechter* and other cases, but in 1937 he joined the liberals. He resigned in 1945.

Robeson, Paul B. (1898–1976) *actor, singer*

Born in Princeton, New Jersey, and of African and Indian descent, Robeson graduated from Rutgers University (1919) and Columbia University Law School (1923). In 1922 Eugene O'Neill offered him a role in *The Emperor Jones.* His performances in this play and *All God's Chillun Got Wings* with the Provincetown Players in 1923 established his career as an actor. Though he never had a voice lesson, he also became a prominent singer. He sang in *Showboat* (1926) and gave numerous concerts. Robeson had roles in *Black Boy* (1926) and *Porgy* (1928). He went to England in 1930 and performed in *Othello, The Hairy Ape,* and other productions. He returned to Broadway in 1934. Until 1939 he also toured widely in Europe. Robeson had roles in numerous movies from the 1930s to the 1950s.

Robinson, Bill ("Bojangles") (1878–1949) *tap dancer, actor*

Born Luther Robinson in Richmond, Virginia, Robinson began performing as a child and moved to vaudeville. During World War I, he performed in cabarets on the black theater circuit, including the Cotton Club and the Apollo Theatre in New York. During the 1920s, he appeared in several Broadway hits, such as *Lew Leslie's Blackbirds of 1927.* Robinson achieved national popularity and stardom through four films he made with Shirley Temple: *The Little Colonel* (1935), *The Little Rebel* (1935), *Rebecca of Sunnybrook Farm* (1938), and *Just Around the Corner* (1938).

Robinson, Joseph T. (1872–1937) *Democratic senator*
Born in Lonoke County, Arkansas, Robinson attended the University of Arkansas and the University of Virginia law school. He passed the bar exam in 1895 and began practicing law in Lonoke. He was elected congressman in 1902, serving until 1913, when he was elected governor of Arkansas but then immediately (January 28, 1913) became senator; he was reelected four times. He supported Woodrow Wilson, the League of Nations, and the Dawes Plan. Robinson was chairman of the Democratic National Conventions in 1920, 1928, and 1936. He was the vice presidential candidate in 1928, with Alfred E. Smith. He became Senate majority leader in 1933, supported the New Deal, and worked tirelessly for Franklin D. Roosevelt's court-packing proposal.

Rodgers, Richard (1902–1979) *composer*
Born in New York City, Rodgers enrolled at Columbia University in 1918. At Columbia he met Lorenz Hart; they collaborated on the university's 1920 variety show. Rodgers studied composition for two years at the Juilliard School of Music while continuing to collaborate with Hart. *The Garrick Gaieties* (1925) was their first professional success. Other successes during the twenties included *A Connecticut Yankee* (1927), based on Mark Twain's novel. In 1936 Rodgers and Hart had a major success with *On Your Toes,* which contained the ballet *Slaughter on Tenth Avenue,* choreographed by George Balanchine. *I Married an Angel* and *The Boys from Syracuse* appeared in 1938. *Pal Joey* (1940) succeeded as a revival in 1952. Rodgers and Hart's last collaboration was *By Jupiter* in 1942 (Hart died in 1943). With Oscar Hammerstein II, Rodgers had major successes in *Oklahoma!* (1943), *Carousel* (1945), *South Pacific* (1949), *The King and I* (1951), and *The Sound of Music* (1959).

Rogers, Will (1879–1935) *humorist, columnist, film actor*
Rogers was born and raised on a ranch in the Indian Territory (now Oklahoma). Skilled with the rope, he worked as a cowboy in steer-roping contests, Wild West shows, and vaudeville. In Florenz Ziegfeld's *Midnight Frolic* (1915), he began to make humorous political comments, resulting in a syndicated weekly newspaper column in 1922 (it became a daily column in 1926). Rogers wrote several books, including *Illiterate Digest* (1924) and *Will Rogers's Political Follies* (1929). He starred in such films as *A Connecticut Yankee* (1931), *State Fair* (1933), and *David Harum* (1934). He and pilot Wiley Post died in a plane crash in Alaska.

Roosevelt, Anna Eleanor (1886–1962) *first lady, social reformer*
Born in New York City, Roosevelt was the daughter of Theodore Roosevelt's younger brother. Her parents died when she was eight, and she and her brothers went to live with their maternal grandmother. She was educated at Allenwood, a finishing school in England. She became involved in settlement house and other philanthropic work in New York City. On March 17, 1905, she and Franklin, then a law student at Columbia University, were married. She became involved in politics as her husband attained election to state offices; she served as financial chairman of the women's division of the state Democratic Party (1924 to 1928). She worked in Alfred E. Smith's campaigns for the governorship and the presidency. From 1927 to 1933, she was vice principal and teacher at the Todhunter School in New York City. As first lady, she supported a variety of social reform efforts, traveled extensively gathering information for the president, held press conferences and a regular radio broadcast, and after 1936 wrote a newspaper column entitled "My Day." She guided creation of the National Youth Administration and advocated civil rights for blacks. Harry S. Truman appointed her as a delegate to the United Nations. She served in 1945, 1949-52, and 1961.

Roosevelt, Franklin Delano (1882–1945) *president of the United States*
Roosevelt was born at his family's home at Hyde Park, New York. After age 14, he was educated at the Groton School and at Harvard University (1900–04); he studied law at Columbia University but passed the

bar exam before taking a degree and began working in a New York City law firm. He and Eleanor Roosevelt, niece of Theodore Roosevelt, wed on March 17, 1905. In 1910 Roosevelt was elected to the state senate to represent Dutchess County; he was reelected in 1912 while supporting Woodrow Wilson. In 1913 Wilson appointed him assistant secretary of the navy. Roosevelt held this post until 1920, when he was Democratic Party nominee for the vice presidency, running with James M. Cox. After the election, which the Democrats lost, he became vice president of the Fidelity and Deposit Company of Maryland. In August 1921, while vacationing at Campobello Island, Roosevelt contracted crippling polio, limiting his political pursuits. In 1924 and 1928 at the Democratic conventions, he nominated Alfred E. Smith for the presidency. At Smith's urging, he ran successfully for the governorship of New York in 1928 and won reelection in 1930. Chosen Democratic nominee for the presidency in 1932, Roosevelt won an overwhelming victory against incumbent President Herbert Hoover. Roosevelt was reelected three times—the only president in history to be elected to four terms—and died in office. During Roosevelt's tenure in office, he instituted the New Deal and entered the United States into World War II.

Roper, Daniel C. (1867–1943) *secretary of commerce*
Roper was born in Marlboro County, South Carolina. He graduated from Trinity College (now Duke University) in 1888 and earned a law degree at Washington National University (1901). He served in two posts in the Woodrow Wilson administration: postmaster general (1913–16) and commissioner of internal revenue (1917–20). Franklin D. Roosevelt appointed him secretary of commerce in 1933. He was also chairman of the cabinet committee that oversaw the National Recovery Administration. Roper resigned in December 1938.

Rosenman, Samuel I. (1896–1973) *adviser to Roosevelt*
Rosenman was born in San Antonio, Texas, but raised in New York City. He graduated from Columbia University (1915), entered the university's law school, and left in 1917 to join the army. After the war he earned his LL.B. (bachelor of laws degree) and began practicing law in 1920. He was elected to the New

York Assembly in 1921. An associate of Alfred E. Smith, he served in Franklin D. Roosevelt's 1928 campaign for governor, writing speeches for FDR, who appointed him governor's counsel. Not friendly with Roosevelt's closest adviser Louis Howe, he remained in New York after FDR won the presidency. Before leaving the governorship, Roosevelt appointed him to the state supreme court; Herbert Lehman reappointed him in 1933. In this post, Rosenman continued as an adviser and speech writer for FDR. He left the bench in 1943 to be the president's special counsel, holding the post under Truman also. He resumed the practice of law in New York in 1946.

Ruth, George Herman ("Babe" Ruth) (1895–1948) *archetypal baseball player known as the "Sultan of Swat"*
Ruth was born in Baltimore, where he began his professional career in 1914. In 1915 he joined the Boston Red Sox. In 1916 and 1918 he set a pitching record of over 29 consecutive scoreless innings that stood until 1960. Ruth won 94 games out of 140. He became an outfielder in 1918. In 1920 he was sold to the New York Yankees and played outfield for them through 1934. Ruth led the American League in home runs for 12 years, set the longstanding season record of 60 home runs in 1927, and had a lifetime record of 714 home runs that stood until 1974. His last year as a player (1935) was with the Boston Braves. In 1938 he served as coach of the Brooklyn Dodgers. In 1936 Ruth was among the first five players elected to the Baseball Hall of Fame.

Sanger, Margaret (1879–1966) *leading advocate of birth control*
Born in Corning, New York, Sanger married in 1902, moved to New York City, and became active in the International Workers of the World (IWW). She campaigned for sexual reform and in 1914 founded the journal *Woman Rebel* to advocate birth control. Accused of violating the postal code while sending information on birth control, Sanger fled to England to avoid prosecution but returned in 1914 to campaign for opening contraceptive advice centers, setting up the first one in Brooklyn. In 1921, Sanger founded the American Birth Control League (in 1942 it became the Planned Parenthood Federation of America). In 1923 she set up the Birth Control

Clinical Research Bureau of New York, the first U.S. contraceptive clinic staffed by doctors. By 1938 Sanger had established 300 clinics nationwide.

Sarnoff, David (1891–1971) *broadcasting executive*
Born in Uzlian, Russia, Sarnoff came to New York City in 1900. He began work in 1906 as an office boy at the Marconi Wireless Telegraph Co. In 1912, operating Marconi's station atop the Wanamaker's Department Store, he reported messages on the sinking of the *Titanic*. In 1916 he wrote a memo about making radio sets and broadcasting to households. In 1919, when Radio Corporation of America (RCA) acquired Marconi, RCA head Owen Young embraced Sarnoff's idea. In 1921 RCA began to make sets and broadcasts, with Sarnoff as general manager. In September 1926, RCA launched the National Broadcasting Company (NBC), headed by Sarnoff. In 1928 Sarnoff set up a station to experiment with television. The first broadcast was at the 1939 New York World's Fair. Sarnoff served as NBC's president from 1930 to 1966.

Schneiderman, Rachel R. (1882–1972) *labor leader*
Born in Savin, Russian Poland, Schneiderman came to the United States in 1890. She attended public schools till age 13, then worked in hat factories. In 1903 she helped set up Local 23 of the United Cloth Hat and Cap Makers of North America. She was appointed to its board in 1904. In 1905 she joined the Women's Trade Union League (WTUL) and was appointed to its board in 1911. After the Triangle Shirtwaist fire (1911), she campaigned for safe working conditions. Schneiderman was elected president of the New York branch of WTUL in 1918. She served as WTUL national vice president (1919–26) and president (1926–50). Though a Socialist Party member, she supported Democratic presidential candidates.

Sheeler, Charles (1883–1965) *painter, photographer*
Born in Philadelphia, Sheeler attended the School of Industrial Arts (1900–03) and Pennsylvania Academy of Fine Arts (1903–06). After travels in Europe, he began painting in Philadelphia in 1910. In 1913 he had six paintings in the famous Armory Show. In the 1920s and 1930s, he painted mostly cityscapes and industrial subjects. An accomplished photographer,

Sheeler joined Edward Steichen in 1923 in doing fashion photos for *Vogue*. In 1927 he was commissioned to do photos of the Ford Motor Company's River Rouge plant, resulting in several paintings as well. In 1939 *Fortune* commissioned him to do paintings of industrial sites. A 1939 show at the Museum of Modern Art won his work wide acclaim.

Sinatra, Frank (1917–1998) *singer, actor*
Born in Hoboken, New Jersey, Sinatra debuted on radio with the Hoboken Four in Major Bowes's "Original Amateur Hour," begun in 1935. Band leader Harry James discovered Sinatra singing in a cafe in 1939, and Sinatra began recording with the James band in July 1939. In 1940–42, Sinatra sang with the Tommy Dorsey Orchestra. He made his solo debut the last day of 1942, quickly attaining world fame thereafter.

Sinclair, Upton (1878–1968) *novelist, reformist*
Sinclair was born in Baltimore, Maryland. He graduated from the City College of New York, where he began writing novels, in 1897. His best-selling novel-exposé of the Chicago meatpacking industry, *The Jungle* (1906), resulted from an assignment for the Socialist weekly *Appeal to Reason* and helped gain passage of laws for meat inspection. His book *Oil!* (1927) was based on the Teapot Dome scandal; and *Boston* (1928), on the Sacco-Vanzetti case. In 1933 Sinclair organized a campaign for the governorship of California based on his program End Poverty in California (EPIC). He lost the election in November 1934. Sinclair wrote about 80 books, including autobiographical works.

Sloan, Alfred P., Jr. (1875–1966) *head of General Motors Corporation*
Born in New Haven, Connecticut, Sloan graduated from the Massachusetts Institute of Technology (1895). He joined the Hyatt Roller Bearing Company, becoming president in 1898. In 1909 the firm became a GMC supplier and in 1916 a GMC holding company, renamed United Motors Corporation, to buy parts and supplies, with Sloan as president of it and as vice president and director of GMC. During his tenure, Sloan created GMC's autonomous divisions. He became president and chief executive officer (CEO) in 1923. Sloan served on the Business Advisory Council in 1933 but resigned in 1934 and helped found the American

Liberty League. He became president of the GMC board in 1937, retiring as CEO in 1946 and from the board in 1956.

Smith, Alfred E. (1873–1944) *governor of New York*
Smith was born in poverty in New York City. After his father's death, he left school and worked in the Fulton Fish Market to support his family. He began working for Tammany Hall (Democratic Party organization) in 1895. In 1903 he was elected to the state assembly, serving through 1915, the last two years as speaker. In 1915 Tammany Hall appointed him sheriff of New York County, and in 1917 he was elected president of the Board of Aldermen of Greater New York. Smith was elected governor of New York in 1918, lost his bid for reelection in 1920 but won again in 1922. He was reelected twice more, serving through 1928. As governor he supported factory labor laws, improved child welfare, creation of state parks, government reorganization, and other reforms. Smith was chosen Democratic candidate for the presidency in 1928. Referred to by Franklin D. Roosevelt, who nominated him, as the "Happy Warrior," Smith was the nation's first Roman Catholic presidential candidate. He fell out with Roosevelt after 1932, helped found the Liberty League in 1934, and in 1936 and 1940 supported the Republican candidates.

Smith, Bessie (ca. 1898–1937) *outstanding jazz singer*
Born in Chattanooga, Tennessee, Smith began singing early and was backed by "Ma" Rainey, the first great blues singer. She sang in theaters throughout the South, was discovered by Clarence Williams of Columbia Records and produced her first recording in 1923. During her career, she recorded over 150 songs with such renowned musicians as Louis Armstrong, Fletcher Henderson, and Benny Goodman, earning the sobriquet "the Empress of the Blues."

Smith, Gerald L. K. (1898–1976) *founder of the Union Party*
Born in Pardeeville, Wisconsin, Smith graduated from Valparaiso University (1917); he was active in the Ku Klux Klan in Indiana. In 1928 he became minister at the King's Highway Christian Church in Shreveport, Louisiana. A populist, he influenced Huey Long and became his assistant when Long went to the U.S.

Senate in 1930. Smith wrote speeches and organized Share Our Wealth clubs. In 1936 he joined Father Coughlin's National Union for Social Justice in forming the Union Party but was expelled for his anti-Catholic, anti-Semitic, profascist views. He formed the America First Party in 1942 and was its candidate for the presidency in 1944. In 1947 he formed the Christian Nationalist Crusade.

Stalin, Joseph (1879–1953) *dictator of the USSR*
Stalin was born in Georgia (later incorporated into the USSR). In 1903 he joined the Bolshevik faction of the Russian Socialists. After the 1917 Revolution, he was commissar for nationalities until 1923 and commissar for state control (1919–23). In 1922 he became secretary-general of the Communist Party. After Vladimir Lenin died in 1924, Stalin fought Leon Trotsky and others for control of the government, which he effectively secured by 1926. In 1928 he collectivized agriculture, and in the 1930s he purged the Communist Party of all rivals for power. In 1939 Stalin signed a nonaggression pact with Hitler that allowed the USSR to divide conquered Poland with Germany. After Germany invaded Russia in 1941, Stalin was both head of the government and supreme commander in chief throughout the war.

Steichen, Edward J. (1879–1973) *photographer*
Born in Luxembourg, Steichen came to the United States at age three; his family settled in Milwaukee in 1889. He left school at 15 to be an apprentice lithographer, bought his first camera at age 16, and had works exhibited in Chicago in 1900. In 1900 he met Alfred Stieglitz and traveled to Europe, where he photographed artists such as sculptor Auguste Rodin. He opened a studio in New York in 1902 at 291 Fifth Avenue, site of the 291 Gallery he and Stieglitz and others opened in 1905. He spent 1906–14 in France and was a U.S. aerial photographer during World War I. He returned to New York in 1923, becoming head of photography for Condé Nast Publications, doing portraits of Greta Garbo, Charlie Chaplin, and other stars for *Vanity Fair*. Steichen served in the navy (1941–46) and, in 1947, became director of photography at the Museum of Modern Art.

Steinbeck, John (1902–1968) *novelist*
Born in Salinas, California, Steinbeck attended Stanford University off and on from 1920 to 1926,

never earning a degree. He worked as a laborer while writing. The popularity of his short novel *Tortilla Flat* (1935) permitted him to write full time. His next novel, *In Dubious Battle* (1936) focused on organizing migrant workers. His novella *Of Mice and Men* (1937) was transformed into film and play versions; the play won the Drama Critics' Circle Award. In 1939 his monumental work *The Grapes of Wrath,* the classic of the Great Depression, won the Pulitzer Prize and was transformed into a major film. During World War II, Steinbeck worked as a war correspondent and wrote a propagandistic novel *The Moon Is Down* (1942). These works followed: *Cannery Row* (1945), *The Pearl* (1947), *The Wayward Bus* (1947), and *East of Eden* (1952). Steinbeck received the Nobel Prize in literature in 1962.

Stettinius, Edward R., Jr. (1900–1949) *administrator, secretary of state*
Born in Chicago, Stettinius attended the University of Virginia. He worked for the General Motors Corporation and U.S. Steel, becoming board chairman of the latter in 1938. In 1933 Franklin D. Roosevelt appointed him to the Industrial Advisory Board as liaison to the National Recovery Administration. In 1939 Roosevelt appointed him chairman of the War Resources Board. Stettinius served in the Advisory Council of National Defense (1940) and the Office of Production Management (1941). In 1941 he became head of the Lend-Lease Administration; in 1943 he was appointed undersecretary of state; and in 1944 appointed secretary of state.

Still, William Grant (1895–1978) *composer, conductor*
Born in Woodville, Mississippi, and raised in Little Rock, Arkansas, Still studied medicine at Wilberforce University and then composition at Oberlin Conservatory of Music and New England Conservatory. In the 1920s, he arranged music for Paul Whiteman and W. C. Handy and began to compose orchestral works. His best-known work, *Afro-American Symphony* (1931), incorporated black motifs. His other depression-era works included the ballets *Sahdji* (1930) and *Lenox Avenue* (1937) and the opera *Troubled Island* (1938), with a libretto by Langston Hughes. After 1935 Still served as an arranger and program director for the CBS and Mutual radio networks.

Stimson, Henry L. (1867–1950) *secretary of war, secretary of state*
Born in New York City, Stimson attended Phillips Academy (Andover) and graduated from Yale University (1888). Admitted to the New York bar in 1891, he served as U.S. attorney for the state's southern district (1906–09). President William Howard Taft appointed him as secretary of war in 1911; he served until 1913. Stimson was an artillery officer in France during World War I. President Calvin Coolidge appointed him as special commissioner to Nicaragua in 1927, and from 1927 until 1929 he served as governor general of the Philippines. During the Herbert Hoover administration, Stimson served as secretary of state (1929–33). He opposed Japanese aggression in China, advocated U.S. intervention in World War II, and was a member of the Committee to Defend America by Aiding the Allies. In 1940 Franklin D. Roosevelt appointed him as secretary of war, a post he held until the war ended.

Stone, Harlan Fiske (1872–1946) *associate justice and chief justice of the Supreme Court*
Stone was born in Chesterfield, New Hampshire. He graduated from Amherst College (1894) and Columbia University Law School (1898). He began teaching at Columbia in 1899 and became dean in 1910. Calvin Coolidge appointed him U.S. attorney general in 1924. Stone began to reform the prison system and the Federal Bureau of Investigation (FBI), appointing J. Edgar Hoover as acting director of the FBI. Coolidge appointed Stone associate justice of the Supreme Court in 1925. He was in the court's liberal wing, with Brandeis, Holmes, and (after 1932) Cardozo. In 1941, following the resignation of Charles Evans Hughes, Franklin D. Roosevelt appointed Stone chief justice; he served until his death.

Sunday, Billy (William A.) (1863–1935) *evangelist*
Born in Ames, Iowa, Sunday grew up an orphan. He became a professional baseball player in 1883 but in 1891 went to work for the YMCA. In 1896 he began conducting religious revivals. In 1903 Sunday was ordained as a Presbyterian minister. He held revivals in major cities throughout the nation, supported by a choir and several assistants. During his career Sunday held more than 300 revivals that attained an overall

estimated attendance of 100 million. He was an outspoken advocate of Prohibition.

Swanson, Claude A. (1862–1939) *legislator, governor of Virginia, secretary of the navy*

Swanson was born in Swansonville, Virginia. He graduated from Randolph-Macon College (1885) and earned a law degree from the University of Virginia (1886). He was elected congressman from Virginia, serving from 1893 to 1906, when he was elected governor of Virginia. Swanson served as governor until 1910, when he was appointed senator. He served in the Senate until 1933, when Roosevelt appointed him as secretary of the navy—a post he held until his death. Wary of Japanese aggression, Swanson in 1937 proposed strengthening the naval base at Pearl Harbor and creating a major base on Guam, but Congress would not agree.

Swope, Gerard (1872–1957) *president of General Electric*

Swope was born in St. Louis, Missouri. He graduated from the Massachusetts Institute of Technology (1895) with a degree in electrical engineering and then worked for Western Electric Co., becoming vice president in 1913. He was appointed president of General Electric in 1919, holding this post until 1939. An associate of Jane Addams and Herbert Hoover, Swope supported national economic planning. His ideas were incorporated in the National Industrial Recovery Act. During the New Deal he served on the Business Advisory Council, the Coal Arbitration Board, and the Committee on Economic Security.

Taft, Robert A. (1889–1953) *Republican senator*

Born in Cincinnati, son of William Howard Taft, president and Supreme Court justice, Taft was admitted to the Ohio bar in 1913. During World War I, he served as assistant to the U.S. Food Administration and counsel to the American Relief Administration. Elected to the Ohio House of Representatives in 1920, he served until 1926; he also served in the Ohio Senate in 1931–32. In 1938 he won election to the U.S. Senate, where he served until his death. Influential in the Senate, he was called "Mr. Republican." He opposed New Deal "socialistic" policies and intervention abroad.

Thomas, Lowell (1892–1981) *broadcast journalist*

Born in Woodington, Ohio, Thomas graduated from Valparaiso University (1911) and received B.A. and M.A. degrees from the University of Denver (1912) and an M.A. from Princeton University (1915). His lectures on a 1915 trip to Alaska caused President Woodrow Wilson to have him make an onscene historical record of World War I, the subject of postwar lectures. Thomas toured the world in 1923 and published his first book, *With Lawrence in Arabia,* in 1924. In 1930 he became network newscaster for CBS, beginning the longest-running program in radio history—*Lowell Thomas and the News,* which ended in May 1976. In 1935 Thomas began filming and narrating travelogues for Twentieth Century–Fox. During World War II, he broadcast reports from all of the war zones.

Thomas, Norman (1884–1968) *Socialist Party leader*

Thomas was born in Marion, Ohio. He graduated from Union Theological Seminary (1911) and became minister of a church and chairman of a settlement house in East Harlem. A pacifist, Thomas joined the Socialist Party and became secretary of the Fellowship of Reconciliation in 1918. He was a founder of the American Civil Liberties Union in 1920. In 1921 he became associate editor of *The Nation* and, in 1922, codirector of the League for Industrial Democracy. In 1924 Thomas was the Socialist Party candidate for governor of New York; in 1925 and 1929, the party's candidate for mayor of New York City. In 1928 and for every national election thereafter through 1948, Thomas was the Socialist Party candidate for the presidency. He advocated such reforms as unemployment insurance, a shortened work week, public works projects, and an end to child labor. Thomas ended his connection with the *New Leader* in favor of the new *Socialist Call* in 1935. He opposed American involvement in World War II. Thomas wrote more than 50 books, including *America's Way Out* (1931), *The Choice before Us* (1934), and *Socialism on the Defensive* (1938).

Thompson, Dorothy (1894–1961) *journalist*

Born in Lancaster, New York, Thompson graduated from Syracuse University (1914) and became a social worker in New York. In 1920 she went to Europe, serving as foreign correspondent first for the *Philadelphia Ledger* and then the *New York Post*. She was the *Post*'s Berlin chief (1924–28). In 1928 she married Sinclair Lewis and returned to the United States (they divorced in 1942). Thompson had a syndicated column, "On the Record," for the *New York Herald Tribune* (1936–41). She also was a columnist for *Ladies' Home Journal* after 1937. Thompson wrote many books, including *I Saw Hitler* (1932), *Refugees* (1938), and *Let the Record Speak* (1939).

Thomson, Virgil G. (1896–1989) *composer*
Born in Kansas City, Missouri, Thomson studied music from age five. He graduated from Kansas City Polytechnic Institute and enlisted in the army (1917). At Harvard University in 1920, he composed his first work, based on a poem by Amy Lowell. He graduated from Harvard (1923), studied at the Mannes Music School, and moved to Paris (1925–35). There he composed *Sonata de Chiesa* (1926); *Symphony on a Hymn Tune* (1928) and *Symphony Number 2* (1931), using American folk themes; and, with Gertrude Stein as librettist, the opera *Four Saints in Three Acts* (1928). Thomson composed numerous other works into the 1960s, including scores for films such as *The Plow That Broke the Plains* (1936) and *The River* (1937). He was also music critic for the *New York Herald Tribune* (1940–54).

Tobin, Daniel J. (1875–1955) *union leader*
Born in County Clare, Ireland, Tobin came to the United States in 1890 and began work in a sheet metal factory. In 1894 he was a driver for a Boston street railway company. In 1895 he became a truck driver for a meat packing firm and joined the International Brotherhood of Teamsters, Chauffeurs, Warehousemen and Helpers of America. In 1904 Tobin became the Teamsters Union business manager; in 1907 he was elected president, holding this post until 1952.

Townsend, Francis E. (1867–1960) *physician, reformer*
Townsend was born on a farm in Illinois. He worked as a farm laborer and teacher before entering Omaha Medical College in 1900. He earned his medical degree at age 36 and practiced medicine in the Black Hills of South Dakota until 1919, when he moved his family to Long Beach, California. From 1930 to 1933,

he served as Los Angeles County health officer. In 1934 he founded Old Age Revolving Pensions, Ltd., to promote his program for ending the depression. Its primary tenet was a monthly government payment to the elderly. By 1936 there were more than 2 million members. In 1936 Congress began investigating his movement, and he was jailed for contempt of Congress in 1938 but pardoned by Franklin D. Roosevelt. In 1936 Townsend had joined Gerald L. K. Smith and Father Charles Coughlin in the Union Party challenge to Roosevelt.

Truman, Harry S. (1884–1972) *president of the United States*
Born in Lamar, Missouri, Truman served in the army in World War I and then studied law at night in Kansas City. With the support of the Pendergast machine, he won election as Jackson County judge (1923), Jackson County presiding judge (1926), and U.S. senator (1934). In 1941 he chaired the Senate Select Committee to Investigate the National Defense Program. He was elected vice president in 1944 and succeeded to the presidency after Roosevelt's death in 1945.

Tugwell, Rexford Guy (1891–1979) *member of Roosevelt's "Brains Trust" (with Berle and Moley)*
Tugwell was raised in western New York in towns on Lakes Erie and Ontario. He earned bachelor's (1915), master's (1917), and Ph.D. (1922) degrees from the Wharton School of Finance and Commerce at the University of Pennsylvania. From 1920 to 1932, he taught economics at Columbia University. In 1932 he became an adviser to Franklin D. Roosevelt. Appointed assistant secretary of agriculture, he became the major contributor to drafting the Agricultural Adjustment Act. Roosevelt appointed Tugwell to the new post of under secretary of agriculture in 1934; in 1935 Roosevelt made him head of the Resettlement Administration. Tugwell resigned in 1937 to be vice president of the American Molasses Company. He was governor of Puerto Rico (1941–46), professor of political science at the University of Chicago (1946–57), and a fellow and associate at the Center for the Study of Democratic Institutions (1964–79). He published 33 books, including a prize-winning biography of Roosevelt, *The Democratic Roosevelt* (1957), and a three-volume autobiography.

392   The Great Depression

Vallee, Rudolph (Rudy Vallee) (1901–1986)
singer, radio star
Born Hubert Prior Vallee in Island Pond, Vermont, Vallee grew up in Westbrook, Maine. He studied music at the University of Maine and Yale University. An accomplished saxophonist, Vallee toured with Vincent Lopez's band and then formed his own band, the Connecticut Yankees, and performed at the Heigh-Ho Club in New York, broadcasting over WABC radio. *The Fleischmann Hour,* a variety show with Vallee as host, premiered on NBC radio in October 1929. Vallee's program soon became the most popular show on radio, remaining popular throughout the 1930s. The show introduced such stars as Kate Smith, Bob Hope, Eddie Cantor, and Edgar Bergen.

Vandenberg, Arthur H. (1884–1951) *Republican senator*
Vandenberg was born in Grand Rapids, Michigan. He studied for one year at the University of Michigan Law School. He became a staff member of the *Grand Rapids Herald* in 1902 and was editor from 1906 until 1928, when he was appointed to the U.S. Senate to fill a vacancy; repeatedly reelected, he served until his death. Vandenberg supported most of the First New Deal, except for the Agricultural Adjustment Act and the National Industrial Recovery Act. In 1935 he became Republican minority leader in the Senate, where he was a staunch opponent of the Second New Deal. As a member of the Foreign Relations Committee, he supported isolationism and the Neutrality Acts and opposed the Lend-Lease Act. After the bombing of Pearl Harbor, his views changed; he supported the war effort, a bipartisan approach to foreign affairs, and American participation in the United Nations.

Van Devanter, Willis (1859–1941) *Supreme Court associate justice*
Van Devanter was born in Marion, Indiana, studied at Indiana Asbury University (DePauw) (1875–78), and earned a law degree from University of Cincinnati (1881). After practicing law in Cheyenne, Wyoming, he served in the Wyoming legislature and was appointed to the state supreme court. A member of the Republican National Committee (1892–94), Van Devanter became assistant attorney general (1900–03) under William McKinley. In 1903

Theodore Roosevelt appointed him as a circuit judge; in 1910 William Howard Taft appointed him to the U.S. Supreme Court. During the New Deal, he voted with the conservatives, but he resigned in May 1937 in the hope of defusing the court-packing issue.

Wagner, Robert F. (1877–1953) *Democratic senator*
Wagner was born in Germany; his family immigrated to the United States in 1886 and settled in New York City. Wagner graduated from City College of New York (1898) and from New York Law School (1900). Supported by Tammany Hall (Democratic Party organization), he won election to the state house of representatives in 1904 and to the state senate in 1908, becoming president pro-tem in 1911. In response to the famous 1911 Triangle Shirtwaist Factory fire, he joined Alfred E. Smith, then leader of the house, in organizing and serving on a commission to investigate factory conditions, which led to reforms. Wagner was elected to the state supreme court in 1918. He became U.S. senator in 1926. Wagner persuaded the Senate to support public works and relief during the Herbert Hoover administration. He supported the New Deal and drafted and mustered support for the National Labor Relations Act. He was also an advocate for anti-lynching and public housing laws. Wagner retired from the Senate in 1949.

Walker, James J. (1881–1946) *mayor of New York City*
Walker was born in Greenwich Village in New York City. He wrote songs for Tin Pan Alley for years, attended New York Law School, and worked for Tammany Hall (Democratic Party organization) as a district captain. Walker won election in 1909 to the state assembly, where he served for 16 years. As Tammany's choice in 1925, Walker was elected mayor of New York. Among his few achievements was creation of a city sanitation department. Walker became best known for his flamboyant life, stylish clothes, mistress, and partying. An official investigation forced an inquiry by Governor Franklin D. Roosevelt in 1932, but FDR did not want to remove Walker from office for fear of alienating Tammany Hall during his presidential campaign. Walker obligingly resigned on September 1.

Wallace, Henry A. (1888–1965) *secretary of agriculture, and vice president*
Wallace was born on a farm in Adair County, Iowa, but grew up mostly in Ames and Des Moines. He graduated from Iowa State College (1910) and went to work for the family newspaper *Wallaces' Farmer.* (His father, Henry C. Wallace, served as secretary of agriculture in the Warren G. Harding and Calvin Coolidge administrations, 1921 to 1924.) Wallace became a Democrat and supported Alfred E. Smith in 1928 and Franklin D. Roosevelt in 1932. Roosevelt appointed him as secretary of agriculture in 1933; he held this post until 1940. Wallace had major responsibility for drafting the Agricultural Adjustment Act and other farm bills. In 1940 Roosevelt chose Wallace to be his running mate. As vice president he served as an advocate of New Deal causes, but party conservatives forced him out as the vice presidential candidate in 1944. He served as secretary of commerce in 1945–46 and then became editor of the *New Republic,* leaving that post in 1947 to help form a new Progressive Party; he received a million votes as presidential candidate in 1948. Wallace was the author of numerous books.

Watson, Edwin M. ("Pa" Watson) (1883–1945) *military aide, secretary to Roosevelt*
Born in Eufala, Alabama, Watson graduated from West Point Military Academy (1908), served as an artillery commander in World War I, and was chief of the military in Woodrow Wilson's delegation at the Paris Peace Conference. He became Franklin D. Roosevelt's military aide in June 1933 and also his secretary in 1939. Watson died on board a cruiser while returning from the Yalta Conference.

Welles, Benjamin Sumner (1892–1961) *assistant secretary and undersecretary of state*
Born in New York City, a graduate of the Groton School and Harvard University, Welles entered the Foreign Service in 1915. He became acting head of the Division of Latin American Affairs in the State Department but left in 1925. In 1928 he published a book on the Dominican Republic. Franklin D. Roosevelt appointed Welles as assistant secretary of state and then ambassador to Cuba in 1933; he was the president's chief adviser on Latin American affairs and was responsible for the treaty with Cuba abrogating the Platt Amendment. Welles also had a major role at the 1936 Inter-American Conference held in Buenos Aires and the 1942 Rio de Janeiro Conference. Roosevelt appointed him under secretary of state in 1937. Cordell Hull's personal animosity toward him forced Welles's resignation in 1944. Thereafter he wrote several books on foreign affairs.

Welles, (George) Orson (1915–1985) *radio broadcaster, film actor, director*
Born in Kenosha, Wisconsin, Welles studied violin, piano, and painting and briefly attended the Art Institute of Chicago before going to Ireland. He made his acting debut in Dublin in 1931. He debuted in New York in *Romeo and Juliet* in 1934, when his radio career began with the *March of Time,* sponsored by *Time.* In 1937 Welles assumed the radio role of Lamont Cranston in *The Shadow.* In 1938 he began "Mercury Theatre," presenting radio dramas. The program's most famous broadcast aired on October 30, 1938—an adaptation of H. G. Wells's *The War of the Worlds,* it depicted an invasion by Martians that created panic among listeners. Welles went to Hollywood in 1940. He directed and played the title role in *Citizen Kane* (1941), regarded by many cinema historians as the finest film ever made. His *The Magnificent Ambersons* (1942) is also highly regarded.

Wheeler, Burton K. (1882–1975) *Democratic senator*
Wheeler was born in Hudson, Massachusetts. He earned a law degree from the University of Michigan (1910) and practiced law in Butte, Montana. He served in the state legislature and as district attorney and, in 1922, won election to the U.S. Senate, serving until 1947. Wheeler was Senate prosecutor in the investigation of the Teapot Dome scandal. In 1924 he was the vice-presidential candidate of the Progressive Party. Wheeler supported most of the New Deal legislation, and he managed the floor battle for the Public Utility Holding Company Act of 1935. He vehemently opposed Franklin D. Roosevelt's effort to pack the Supreme Court. An isolationist, Wheeler opposed American involvement in World War II and the Lend-Lease Act. He lost the primary election for senator in 1946.

White, Walter F. (1893–1955) *head of the National Association for the Advancement of Colored People*
Born in Atlanta, Georgia, White graduated from Atlanta University (1916) and worked for the Atlanta

Life Insurance Co. After his success in establishing an Atlanta chapter of the National Association for the Advancement of Colored People (NAACP), he was made national assistant secretary in New York in 1918. In 1931 White succeeded James Weldon Johnson as secretary of the NAACP, serving until 1955. He advocated the antilynching bill, voting rights laws, a ban on poll taxes, nondiscrimination in the armed forces, and integration of public schools. Though in frequent contact with Eleanor Roosevelt, he was granted only one conference with Franklin D. Roosevelt.

White, William Allen (1868–1944) *newspaper editor, author*
Born in Emporia, Kansas, White studied journalism at the University of Kansas. In 1895 he became owner and editor of the *Emporia Daily and Weekly Gazette.* Through his role as editor and author of books on politics, he gained national stature and influence. Among his many books were works on Woodrow Wilson and Calvin Coolidge written in the 1920s and a second book on Coolidge entitled *A Puritan in Babylon* (1938). Although a Republican, White supported many New Deal programs. An internationalist, he chaired the Committee to Defend America by Aiding the Allies formed in 1940.

Whitney, Richard (1888–1974) *president of the New York Stock Exchange*
Whitney was born in Beverly, Massachusetts, attended Groton, and graduated from Harvard University (1911). He worked for J.P. Morgan and Co. and his family's securities business, becoming president of Richard Whitney and Co. In 1929, after the Great Wall Street Crash, he became president of the New York Stock Exchange. He opposed the Securities Act (1933) and the Securities Exchange Act (1934). He resigned in 1935 to return to private business. In 1938 a Securities and Exchange Commission investigation exposed his embezzlement of funds from the New York Stock Exchange and the New York Yacht Club. Convicted of fraud, Whitney spent three years in prison.

Williams, Aubrey W. (1890–1965) *deputy administrator of the Works Progress Administration, administrator of the National Youth Administration*
Born in poverty in Alabama, Williams had to leave school at age seven but later attended Maryville College and the University of Cincinnati. During World War I, he served with the YMCA in Europe, the French Foreign Legion, and, after 1917, the U.S. Army. He earned a degree from the University of Bordeaux. Williams became executive secretary of the Wisconsin Conference of Social Work in 1922. In 1932–33 he served the Franklin D. Roosevelt administration in the Reconstruction Finance Corporation. He became southwest regional director of the Federal Emergency Relief Administration and then deputy to Harry Hopkins, with effective control of the Works Progress Administration (WPA). In 1938 he was prevented from succeeding Hopkins as head of the WPA by congressmen opposed to his strong civil rights advocacy. He became director of the National Youth Administration (NYA), which was disbanded in 1943. Williams went to Montgomery, Alabama, where he edited *Southern Farmer.*

Willkie, Wendell L. (1892–1944) *lawyer, corporate executive, presidential candidate*
Willkie was born in Elwood, Indiana. He earned bachelor's (1913) and law (1916) degrees from Indiana University and began practicing law with his father. He served in the U.S. Army during World War I. Willkie then took up corporate law in Akron, Ohio. In 1924 he unsuccessfully fought for endorsement of the League of Nations and the rebuke of the Ku Klux Klan at the Democratic National Convention. He moved to New York City in 1929 to join the legal department of Commonwealth and Southern Corporation, becoming president of the utility firm in 1933. He opposed competition from power generation by the Tennessee Valley Authority (TVA), to which in 1939 his company sold its Tennessee holdings. In 1938 Willkie left the Democratic Party and became a Republican. His criticisms of the New Deal and his "We, the People" article gained him nomination as the Republican candidate for the presidency in 1940. Willkie favored support of the Allies and of Franklin D. Roosevelt's war policies. His book *One World* (1943) advocated international cooperation.

Wilson, Edmund (1895–1972) *writer, critic*
Wilson was born in Red Bank, New Jersey. He graduated from Princeton University (1916) and became a reporter for the New York *Sun.* He worked in a

French hospital and in the U.S. intelligence forces during World War I. Wilson became editor of *Vanity Fair,* and in 1926 he became book review editor for the *New Republic,* for which he later was editor. Wilson left that position in 1931 to pursue his writing. His first book of criticism, *Axel's Castle* (1931) discussed the Symbolist poets; his second, *American Jitters* (1932), the nation's slide into depression. *To the Finland Station* (1940) discussed the background of the Russian Revolution. *The Wound and the Bow* (1941) discussed art and neurosis. Wilson published numerous works—travel discussions, novels, short stories, poems, plays, critical essays—during the remainder of his life, including a work about the Great Depression, *The American Earthquake* (1958). He also edited for publication Fitzgerald's uncompleted novel (*The Last Tycoon* [1941]) and notebooks (*The Crack-Up* [1945]).

Wilson, (Thomas) Woodrow (1856–1924)
president of the United States
Born in Staunton, Virginia, Wilson grew up in Georgia and South Carolina. He graduated from Princeton University in 1879 and earned a Ph.D. degree from Johns Hopkins University in 1886. In 1888 he joined the faculty of Wesleyan University. In 1890 he began teaching at Princeton University, where he became president in 1902. Wilson was elected governor of New Jersey in 1910. In 1912 he was elected president; he won reelection in 1916. He appointed Franklin D. Roosevelt as assistant secretary of the navy in 1913 as a reward for his support in the 1912 election. Wilson failed to persuade the Allies to adopt his proposals at the Paris Peace Conference, except for the League of Nations, which he could not persuade the U.S. Senate to accept. He suffered a crippling stroke in 1919.

Winchell, Walter (1897–1972) *journalist*
Born in New York City, Winchell worked on the vaudeville stage for 12 years and, about 1920, began contributing gossip to *Billboard* and *Vaudeville News.* For the latter, in 1922, he began his own column. In 1924 he began a column, "On Broadway," about show business for the *New York Evening Graphic.* In 1929 Winchell began a syndicated column for the *New York Daily Mirror* that ran until 1963. In 1932 he began a weekly radio show that ran until the 1950s. A strong supporter of Franklin D. Roosevelt and the New Deal, Winchell broke the story on FDR's decision to run for a third term in 1940.

Woodring, Harry H. (1890–1967) *secretary of war*
Woodring was born in Elk City, Kansas. He attended Lebanon University for one year and became a successful banker. Woodring was elected governor of Kansas in 1930, and Franklin D. Roosevelt appointed him as assistant secretary of war in 1933. He became secretary of war in 1936, holding the post until 1940. An outsider in the administration, Woodring supported war readiness but insisted on upholding the Neutrality Acts and on not providing war materiel to the Allies. Roosevelt requested his resignation in June 1940.

Woodward, Ellen Sullivan (unknown–1971)
New Deal director of women's programs
Woodward was born in Oxford, Mississippi, but raised in Washington, D.C. (her father was in Congress). She married Albert Young Woodward (1906), succeeding him in the Mississippi legislature when he died (1926). She headed the State Board of Development (1929–33). Harry Hopkins appointed her director of the Women's Division of the Federal Emergency Relief Administration, which in 1935 became the Division of Women's and Professional Projects in the Works Progress Administration (WPA). In 1936 Woodward became director of the WPA Federal Artists and Writers' Projects. In 1938 Franklin D. Roosevelt appointed her to the three-member Social Security Board; she served until 1946. Next to Frances Perkins, Woodward was the most powerful woman in the government.

Wright, Frank Lloyd (1867–1959) *architect, writer*
Born in Richland Center, Wisconsin, but raised in varied locales, Wright studied engineering briefly at the University of Wisconsin (1885–86) and went to work as an architectural apprentice with J. L. Silbee in Chicago and later with Louis Sullivan in the firm of Adler and Sullivan. On his own after 1893, Wright developed his Prairie school of residential design. After 1909 he spent much of his time in Europe and Japan, living in Japan from 1916 until his return to this country in 1922. Among his major works during the Great Depression years were Falling Water (1936) in Mill Run, Pennsylvania; Taliesin West (1938), his winter home in Scottsdale, Arizona; and

Hanna House (1938) in Palo Alto, California. Wright published two important books in these years: *Autobiography* (1932) and *An Organic Architecture* (1939).

Wright, Richard (1908–1960) *author*

The son of a tenant farmer who abandoned his family, Wright was born on a plantation in Natchez, Mississippi; migrations throughout Mississippi, Tennessee, and Arkansas characterized his childhood years, with his mother working as a cook or a maid. Graduating from the ninth grade after a brief stay in Memphis, Wright left home in 1927 and went to Chicago, where he held several menial jobs. There by chance he read some of H. L. Mencken's writings and thus discovered the novels of Sinclair Lewis and Theodore Dreiser. During the depression years he worked in the Federal Negro Theatre and the Illinois Writers' Project and began attending meetings of the John Reed Club, which was supported by the Communist Party. Wright wrote for *New Masses* and *The Daily Worker;* he moved to New York City in 1937 to be Harlem editor for the latter. During these years he also produced a volume of short stories entitled *Uncle Tom's Children* (1938), which won a Guggenheim Fellowship that allowed him to complete his powerful novel *Native Son* (1940), which gained immediate acclaim and large sales and was transformed into a play. In 1944 Wright quit the Communist Party following a bitter fight. He published an autobiography, *Black Boy,* in 1945. Increasingly disaffected with racism in the United States, he moved to France in 1947. His collection of stories, *Eight Men,* was published posthumously in 1961.

APPENDIX C
Graphs and Charts

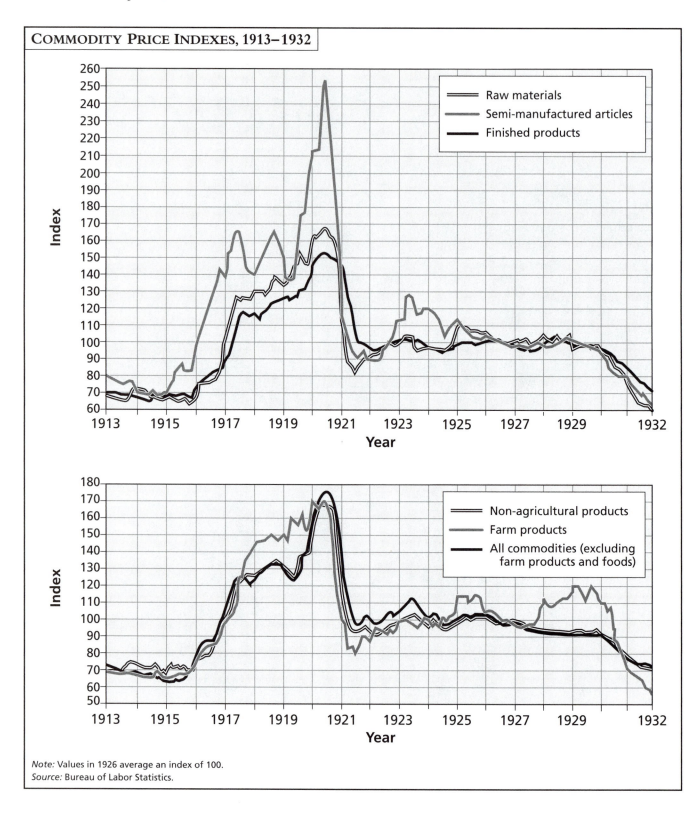

COMMODITY PRICE INDEXES, 1913–1932

Note: Values in 1926 average an index of 100.
Source: Bureau of Labor Statistics.

STOCK PRICE INDEXES, 1913–1932

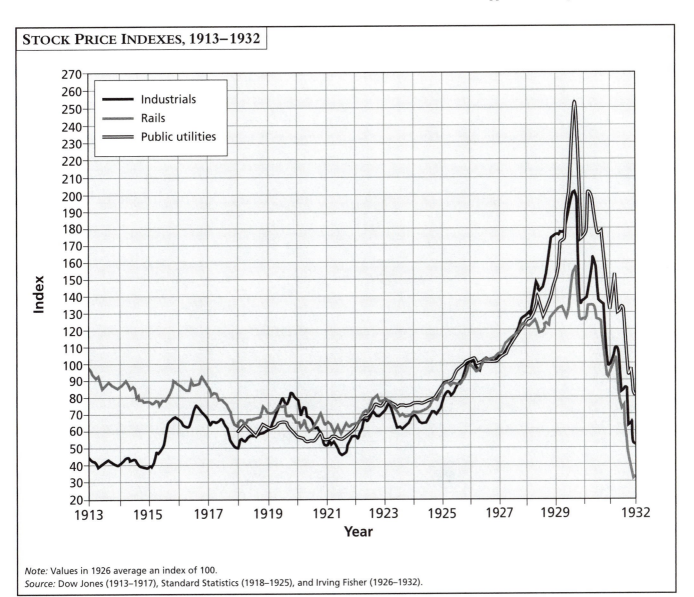

Note: Values in 1926 average an index of 100.
Source: Dow Jones (1913–1917), Standard Statistics (1918–1925), and Irving Fisher (1926–1932).

SUMMARY OF FINANCIAL AND BUSINESS STATISTICS, 1929–1938

Type of Statistics	1938 Oct.	1938 Sept.	1938 Aug.	1937 Oct.	1937 Sept.	1937 Aug.	Annual Averages 1937	1936	1935	1934	1933	1929
MEMBER BANK RESERVES, RESERVE BANK CREDIT, AND RELATED ITEMS	*Averages of daily figures; in millions of dollars*											
Reserve bank credit outstanding—total	2,598	2,610	2,590	2,583	2,584	2,573	2,554	2,481	2,475	2,502	2,429	1,459
Bills discounted	8	8	7	22	24	17	14	6	7	36	283	952
Bills bought	1	1	1	3	3	3	3	4	5	25	83	241
U.S. Government securities	2,564	2,572	2,564	2,527	2,526	2,527	2,540	2,430	2,431	2,432	2,052	208
Gold stock	13,940	13,441	13,057	12,782	12,653	12,512	12,162	10,578	9,059	7,512	4,059	3,996
Treasury currency outstanding	2,745	2,733	2,724	2,603	2,590	2,576	2,567	2,503	2,478	2,381	2,271	2,015
Currency in circulation	6,668	6,570	6,482	6,566	6,558	6,500	6,475	6,101	5,585	5,403	5,576	4,476
Treasury cash holdings	2,782	2,717	2,392	3,636	3,618	3,655	3,225	2,474	2,791	2,798	288	207
Treasury deposits with F. R. banks	665	704	774	95	190	212	158	446	128	81	55	22
Nonmember deposits and other accounts	622	598	606	717	607	592	595	551	507	438	497	406
Member bank reserve balances:												
Total	8,546	8,196	8,119	6,954	6,854	6,701	6,830	5,989	5,001	3,676	2,343	2,358
Excess	3,143	ʳ2,920	2,955	1,043	900	750	1,220	2,512	2,469	1,564	528	43
REPORTING MEMBER BANKS	*Averages of Wednesday figures; in millions of dollars*											
Total loans and investments	21,323	21,078	20,675	21,889	22,187	22,332	22,198	22,064	19,997	18,672	17,505	22,599
Loans—total	8,282	8,268	8,215	9,890	10,026	9,929	9,546	8,462	8,028	8,491	9,156	16,887
Commercial, industrial and agricultural	3,904	3,893	3,886	4,828	4,733	4,558	(¹)	(¹)	(¹)	(¹)	(¹)	(¹)
To brokers and dealers in securities	669	675	636	1,103	1,317	1,362	1,226	1,181	990	981	777	ᵉ2,208
Other loans for purchasing or carrying securities	576	578	577	669	687	698	(¹)	(¹)	(¹)	(¹)	(¹)	(¹)
All other loans	3,133	3,122	3,116	3,290	3,289	3,311	(¹)	(¹)	(¹)	(¹)	(¹)	(¹)
Investments—total	13,041	12,810	12,460	11,999	12,161	12,403	12,652	13,602	11,969	10,181	8,349	5,712
U.S. Government direct obligations	8,084	7,957	7,702	7,914	8,068	8,229	8,394	9,080	7,989	6,856	5,228	2,865
Obligations fully guaranteed by U.S. Govt.	1,682	1,668	1,646	1,132	1,131	1,160	1,164	1,250	928	ᵉ325	——	——
Other securities	3,275	3,185	3,112	2,953	2,962	3,014	3,094	3,272	3,052	3,000	3,121	2,847
Reserve with Federal Reserve banks	7,005	6,712	6,602	5,384	5,313	5,149	5,307	4,799	4,024	2,875	1,822	1,725
Cash in vault	425	416	387	326	305	296	337	383	326	271	240	248
Balances with domestic banks	2,446	2,413	2,416	1,781	1,703	1,683	1,884	2,358	2,112	1,688	1,322	1,142
Demand deposits—adjusted	15,688	15,377	15,118	14,756	14,843	14,918	15,097	14,619	12,729	(¹)	(¹)	(¹)
Time deposits (excluding interbank)²	5,164	5,213	5,206	5,278	5,283	5,245	5,202	4,999	4,883	4,937	4,946	6,788
Deposits of domestic banks³	6,122	5,974	5,920	5,088	4,990	4,979	5,298	5,810	4,938	3,814	2,822	2,787
Borrowings	1	——	1	5	11	36	12	5	6	8	115	674
MONEY RATES AND BOND YIELDS	*Averages of daily figures; percent per annum*											
Commercial paper	69	.69	.75	1.00	1.00	1.00	.95	.75	.76	1.02	1.72	5.85
Stock exchange call loans	1.00	1.00	1.00	1.00	1.00	1.00	1.00	.91	.56	1.00	1.16	7.61
U.S. Treasury bills (91 days)	.05	.08	.06	.20	.31	.29	.28	.17	.17	.28	——	——
U.S. Treasury bonds, long-term⁴	2.48	2.58	2.51	2.76	2.77	2.72	2.68	2.65	2.79	3.12	3.31	3.60
Corporate high grade bonds (Moody's Aaa)	3.15	3.21	3.18	3.27	3.28	3.24	3.26	3.24	3.60	4.00	4.49	4.73

Type of Statistics	1938			1937			Annual Averages					
	Oct.	Sept.	Aug.	Oct.	Sept.	Aug.	1937	1936	1935	1934	1933	1929
CAPITAL ISSUES	*Amounts per month; in millions of dollars*											
All issues—total	763	r237	415	203	221	187	323	518	392	180	89	959
New	165	r144	180	96	154	79	173	164	121	116	60	841
Refunding	598	r92	235	107	67	109	150	354	270	64	29	118
Domestic corporate issues—total	337	r150	336	136	152	107	198	382	189	41	32	781
New	64	r85	125	67	113	51	99	99	34	15	13	667
Refunding	273	r65	211	70	39	56	99	282	155	26	18	115
PRICES	*Index numbers*											
Common stocks (1926=100)	91	86	90	91	106	121	112	111	78	72	63	190
Wholesale commodity prices (1926=100):												
All commodities	78	78	78	85	87	88	86	81	80	75	66	95
Farm products	67	68	67	80	86	86	86	81	79	65	51	105
Foods	74	75	73	86	88	87	86	82	84	71	61	100
Other commodities	81	81	81	85	86	86	85	80	78	78	71	92
Retail food prices (1923–25=100)	78	79	78	85	86	86	85	82	80	74	66	105
BUSINESS INDEXES	*Index numbers, adjusted for seasonal variation, 1923–25=100*											
Industrial production	p96	91	88	102	111	117	110	105	90	79	76	119
Manufactures	p95	89	87	101	110	117	109	105	90	78	75	119
Minerals	p100	97	95	113	116	113	115	105	91	86	82	115
Construction contracts awarded—total	p86	78	66	52	56	62	59	55	37	32	25	117
Residential	p57	56	53	36	37	40	41	37	21	12	11	87
All other	p110	96	77	65	71	81	74	70	50	48	37	142
Factory employment	p88	87	85	105	107	109	106	98	91	86	73	106
Factory payrolls (unadjusted)	p84	81	77	105	104	108	102	86	74	65	50	110
Freight-car loadings	68	64	62	76	78	79	78	75	64	62	58	107
Department store sales	84	86	83	93	94	93	92	88	79	75	67	111
MERCHANDISE EXPORTS AND IMPORTS	*Amounts per month; in millions of dollars*											
Exports, including re-exports	p278	246	231	333	297	277	279	205	190	178	140	437
General imports	p178	168	166	224	233	246	257	202	171	138	121	367

pPreliminary.   rRevised.   ePartly estimated.
[1]Figures not available.
[2]Includes time deposits of banks, domestic and foreign, 1929–1934.
[3]Does not include time deposits 1929–1934.
[4]Revised series. Averages of yields of all outstanding bonds due or callable after 12 years.

Source: Federal Reserve System

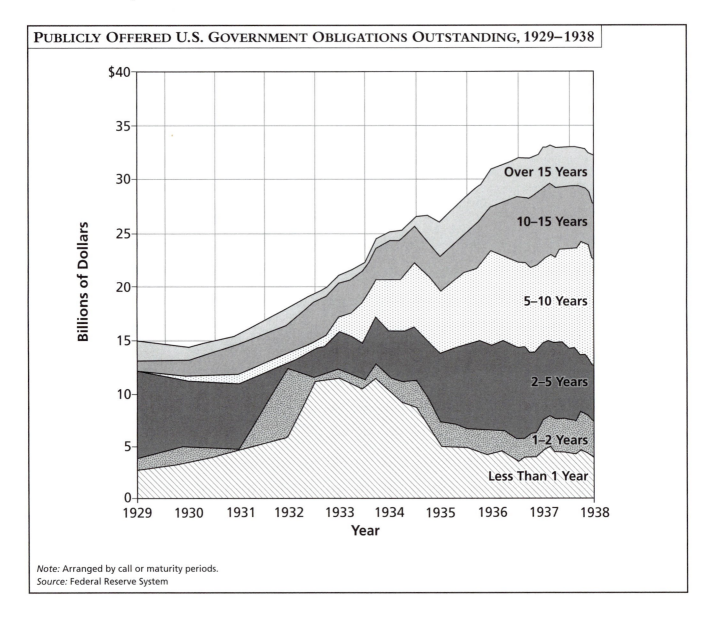

PUBLICLY OFFERED U.S. GOVERNMENT OBLIGATIONS OUTSTANDING, 1929–1938

Note: Arranged by call or maturity periods.
Source: Federal Reserve System

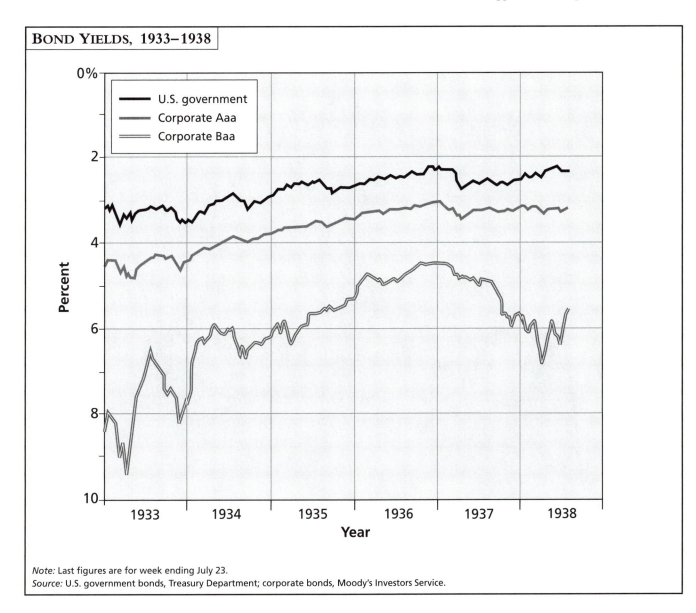

BOND YIELDS, 1933–1938

Note: Last figures are for week ending July 23.
Source: U.S. government bonds, Treasury Department; corporate bonds, Moody's Investors Service.

STOCK PRICES, 1933–1938

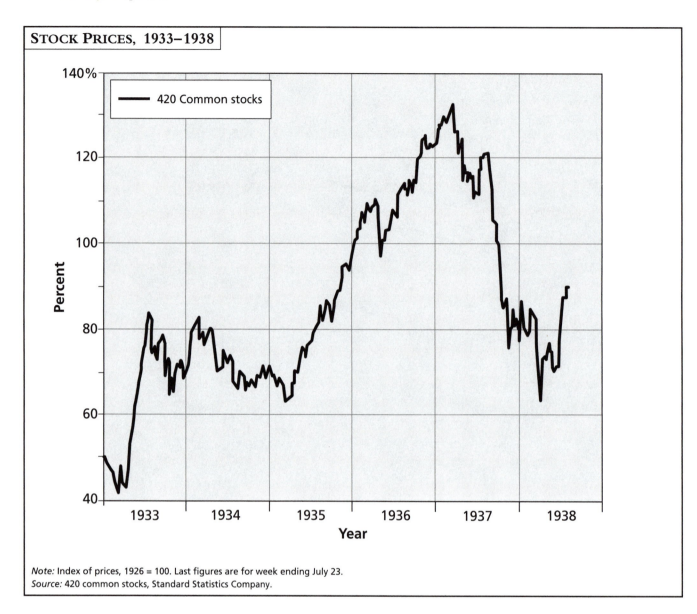

Note: Index of prices, 1926 = 100. Last figures are for week ending July 23.
Source: 420 common stocks, Standard Statistics Company.

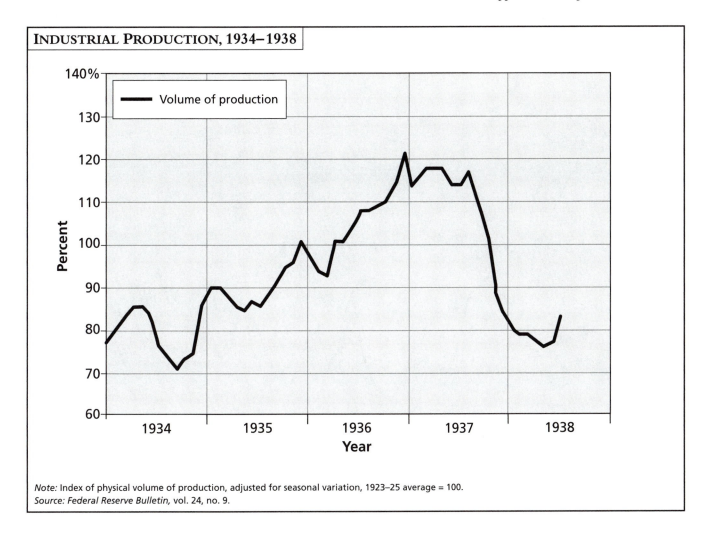

INDUSTRIAL PRODUCTION, 1934–1938

Note: Index of physical volume of production, adjusted for seasonal variation, 1923–25 average = 100.
Source: Federal Reserve Bulletin, vol. 24, no. 9.

CONSTRUCTION CONTRACTS AWARDED, 1929–1938

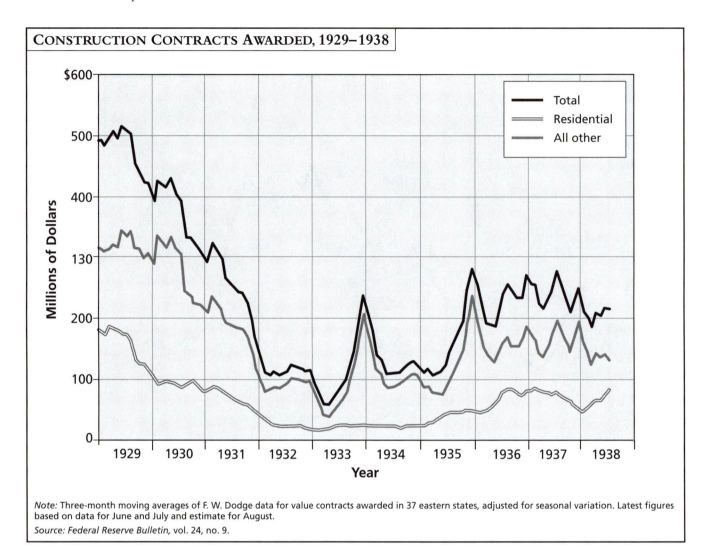

Note: Three-month moving averages of F. W. Dodge data for value contracts awarded in 37 eastern states, adjusted for seasonal variation. Latest figures based on data for June and July and estimate for August.

Source: Federal Reserve Bulletin, vol. 24, no. 9.

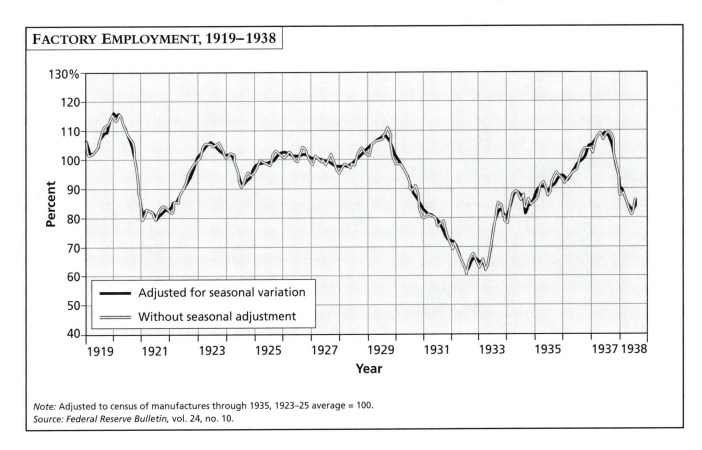

FACTORY EMPLOYMENT, 1919–1938

Note: Adjusted to census of manufactures through 1935, 1923–25 average = 100.
Source: Federal Reserve Bulletin, vol. 24, no. 10.

MEMBER BANK RESERVES AND RELATED ITEMS, 1918–1938

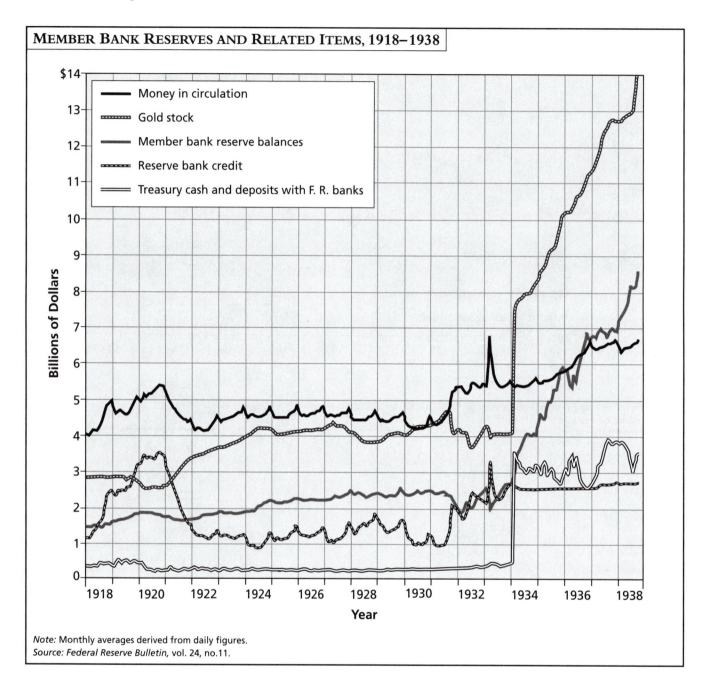

Legend:
- Money in circulation
- Gold stock
- Member bank reserve balances
- Reserve bank credit
- Treasury cash and deposits with F. R. banks

Y-axis: Billions of Dollars

X-axis: Year (1918, 1920, 1922, 1924, 1926, 1928, 1930, 1932, 1934, 1936, 1938)

Note: Monthly averages derived from daily figures.
Source: Federal Reserve Bulletin, vol. 24, no.11.

RESERVE BANK CREDIT, 1918–1938

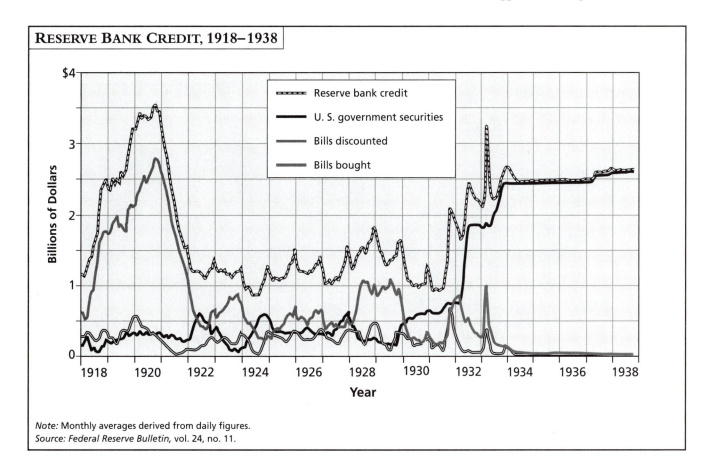

Note: Monthly averages derived from daily figures.
Source: Federal Reserve Bulletin, vol. 24, no. 11.

BIBLIOGRAPHY

Adamic, Louis. *My America, 1928–1938.* New York: Harper, 1938.

Allen, Fred. *Treadmill to Oblivion.* Boston: Little, Brown, 1954.

Allen, Frederick Lewis. *The Lords of Creation.* New York and London: Harper & Brothers Publishers, 1935.

———. *Only Yesterday: An Informal History of the Nineteen-Twenties.* New York: Harper & Row, 1964.

———. *Since Yesterday: The Nineteen-Thirties in America.* New York: Bantam, Books, 1961.

Angell, James W. *The Behavior of Money.* New York: McGraw-Hill, 1936.

Arnold, Thurman. *The Folklore of Capitalism.* New Haven, Conn.: Yale University Press, 1937.

Badger, Anthony J. *The New Deal: The Depression Years, 1933–40.* Basingstoke, U.K.: Macmillan, 1989.

Baker, Ray S., and William E. Dodd, eds. *The Public Papers of Woodrow Wilson.* New York: Harper & Brothers, 1925–27.

Baker, Russell. *Growing Up.* New York: New American Library, 1983.

Balderston, Theo, ed. *The World Economy and National Economies in the Interwar Slump.* New York: Palgrave Macmillan, 2003.

Barnhart, Michael A. *Japan Prepares for Total War: The Search for Economic Security, 1919–1941.* Ithaca, N.Y.: Cornell University Press, 1987.

Barnouw, Erik. *A History of Broadcasting in the United States.* 3 vols. New York: Oxford University Press, 1966–1970.

Beard, Charles A., ed. *America Faces the Future.* Boston and New York: Houghton Mifflin, 1932.

Beard, Charles A., and Mary R. Beard. *America in Midpassage.* New York: Macmillan, 1939.

Beard, Charles A., and George H. E. Smith. *The Old Deal and the New.* New York: Macmillan, 1941.

Becker, Stephen D. *Comic Art in America: A Social History of the Funnies, the Political Cartoons, Magazine Humor, Sporting Cartoons and Animated Cartoons.* New York: Simon & Schuster, 1959.

Behrman, S. N. *Duveen.* 1952. Reprint, New York: Little Bookroom, 2002.

Beito, David T. *Taxpayers in Revolt: Tax Resistance during the Great Depression.* Chapel Hill and London: University of North Carolina Press, 1989.

Bemis, Samuel Flagg, and Robert H. Ferrell. *The American Secretaries of State and Their Diplomacy.* 18 vols., new series. New York: Cooper Square, 1963.

Bendiner, David H. *Just Around the Corner: A Highly Selective History of the Thirties.* New York: Dutton, 1987.

Bennett, David H. *Demagogues in the Depression: American Radicals and the Union Party, 1932–1936.* New Brunswick, N.J.: Rutgers University Press, 1969.

Bergman, Andrew. *We're in the Money: Depression America and Its Films.* New York: New York University Press, 1971.

Berle, Adolf A., and Gardiner Means. *The Modern Corporation and Private Property.* 1932. Reprint, New York: Harcourt, Brace & World, 1968.

Bernays, Edward L. *Crystallizing Public Opinion.* New York: Liveright Publishing, 1923.

Bernstein, Irving. *The Lean Years: A History of the American Worker, 1920–1933.* Boston: Houghton Mifflin, 1960.

———. *Turbulent Years: A History of the American Worker, 1933–1941.* Boston: Houghton Mifflin, 1970.

Best, Gary Dean. *The Retreat from Liberalism: Collectivists versus Progressives in the New Deal Years.* Westport, Conn. and London: Praeger, 2002.

Bierman, Harold, Jr. *The Great Myths of 1929 and the Lessons to Be Learned.* New York and Westport, Conn.: Greenwood Press, 1991.

Biles, Roger. *A New Deal for the American People.* DeKalb: Northern Illinois University Press, 1991.

Blum, John Morton, ed. *Public Philosopher: Selected Letters of Walter Lippmann.* New York: Ticknor & Fields, 1985.

Boorstin, Daniel J. *The Americans: The Democratic Experience.* New York: Random House, 1973.

Bowers, Claude. *My Life: The Memoirs of Claude Bowers.* New York: Simon & Schuster, 1962.

Brinkley, Alan. *Voices of Protest: Huey Long, Father Coughlin, and the Great Depression.* New York: Knopf, 1982.

Brown, Harry Gunnison. *The Economic Basis of Tax Reform.* Columbia, Mo.: Lucas Brothers, 1932.

Brunner, Karl, ed. *The Great Depression Revisited.* Boston: Martinus Nijhoff, 1981.

Buhite, Russell D., and David W. Levy, eds. *FDR's Fireside Chats.* Norman: University of Oklahoma Press, 1992.

Bunche, Ralph J. *The Political Status of the Negro in the Age of FDR.* Chicago: University of Chicago Press, 1973.

Burchard, John, and Albert Bush-Brown. *The Architecture of America: A Social and Cultural History.* London: Victor Gollancz, 1966.

Burgess, W. Randolph. *The Reserve Banks and the Money Market.* New York: Harper & Brothers, 1927.

Burner, David. *Herbert Hoover: A Public Life.* New York: Knopf, 1979.

Burns, James MacGregor. *Roosevelt: The Lion and the Fox.* New York: Harcourt, Brace & World, 1956.

Bustard, Bruce I. *A New Deal for the Arts.* Washington, D.C.: National Archives & Records Administration and University of Washington Press, 1997.

Buxton, Frank, and Bill Owen. *Radio's Golden Age: The Programs and the Personalities.* New York: Easton Valley Press, 1966.

Cantor, Eddie. *Caught Short! A Saga of Wailing Wall Street.* New York: Simon & Schuster, 1929.

Carmichael, Hoagy, with Stephen Longstreet. *Sometimes I Wonder: The Story of Hoagy Carmichael.* New York: Farrar, Straus & Giroux, 1965.

Carver, Thomas Nixon. *The Present Economic Revolution in the United States.* Boston: Little, Brown, 1925.

Cash, W. J. *The Mind of the South.* New York: Alfred A. Knopf, 1941.

Cavan, Ruth Shonle, and Katherine Howland Ranck. *The Family and the Depression: A Study of One Hundred Chicago Families.* Chicago: University of Chicago Press, 1938.

Chadakoff, Rochelle, ed. *Eleanor Roosevelt's My Day: Her Acclaimed Columns, 1936–1945.* New York: Pharos Books, 1989.

Chafe, William H. *The Achievement of American Liberalism: The New Deal and Its Legacies.* New York: Columbia University Press, 2003.

Chase, Stuart. *Men and Machines.* New York: Macmillan, 1929.

———. *Prosperity: Fact or Myth.* New York: Albert and Charles Boni, 1930.

Choate, Jean. *Disputed Ground: Farm Groups That Opposed the New Deal Agricultural Program.* Jefferson, N.C., and London: McFarland, 2002.

Churchill, Winston S. *Blood, Sweat, and Tears.* New York: Putnam, 1941.

Cochran, Thomas C. *The Great Depression and World War II.* New York: Scott, Foresman, 1968.

Coffman, Edward M. *The War to End All Wars: The American Military Experience in World War I.* Madison: University of Wisconsin Press, 1986.

Cohen, Warren I. *America's Response to China: A History of Sino-American Relations.* New York: Columbia University Press, 1990.

Cole, Wayne S. *Roosevelt and the Isolationists, 1932–1945.* Lincoln: University of Nebraska Press, 1983.

Collins, Henry Hill, Jr. *America's Own Refugees: Our 4,000,000 Homeless Migrants.* Princeton, N.J.: Princeton University Press, 1941.

Commager, Henry Steele. *Documents of American History.* 8th ed. New York: Appleton-Century-Crofts, 1968.

Dallek, Robert. *Franklin D. Roosevelt and American Foreign Policy, 1932–1945.* New York: Oxford University Press, 1979.

Davis, Joseph S. *The World Between the Wars, 1919–1939: An Economist's View.* Baltimore, Md.: Johns Hopkins University Press, 1975.

Davis, Kenneth S. *FDR: Into the Storm, 1937–1940.* New York: Random House, 1993.

———. *FDR: The New Deal Years, 1933–1937.* New York: Random House, 1986.

Davis, Maxine. *The Lost Generation: A Portrait of American Youth Today.* New York: Macmillan, 1936.

Daynes, Bryan W., et al., eds. *The New Deal and Public Policy.* New York: St. Martin's Press, 1998.

De Conde, Alexander. *Herbert Hoover's Latin-American Policy.* Stanford, Calif.: Stanford University Press, 1970.

Dewey, John. *Human Nature and Conduct.* New York: Henry Holt, 1922.

Doenecke, Justus D., and John E. Wily. *From Isolation to War, 1931–1941.* 2d ed. Arlington Heights, Ill.: Harlan Davidson, 1991.

Dooley, Roger. *From Scarface to Scarlet: American Film in the 1930s.* New York: Harcourt Brace, 1981.

Douglas, Paul H. *Controlling Depressions.* New York: W. W. Norton, 1935.

Dreiser, Theodore. *Tragic America.* New York: Horace Liveright, 1931.

Driskell, David, David Levering Lewis, and Deborah Willis Ryan. *Harlem Renaissance: Art of Black America.* New York: Harry N. Abrams, 1994.

Dubofsky, Melwyn, and Stephen Burwood, eds. *Agriculture During the Great Depression: Selected Articles.* Vol. 4 of *The Great Depression and the New Deal.* New York: Garland, 1990.

———. *The American Economy During the Great Depression: Selected Articles.* Vol. 3 of *The Great Depression and the New Deal.* New York: Garland, 1990.

———. *American Foreign Policy in the 1930s: Selected Articles on the Depression, the New Deal, and Foreign Relations.* Vol. 5 of *The Great Depression and the New Deal.* New York: Garland, 1990.

———. *Labor and the New Deal: Selected Articles on Workers and Unions During the Great Depression.* Vol. 2 of *The Great Depression and the New Deal.* New York: Garland, 1990.

———. *The Law and the New Deal: Selected Articles on Legal Issues Surrounding the Depression and Roosevelt's Policies.* Vol. 7 of *The Great Depression and the New Deal.* New York: Garland, 1990.

———. *The New Deal: Selected Articles on the Political Response to the Great Depression.* Vol. 1 of *The Great Depression and the New Deal.* New York: Garland, 1990.

———. *Women and Minorities During the Great Depression: Selected Articles on Gender, Race, and Ethnicity.* Vol. 6 of *The Great Depression and the New Deal.* New York: Garland, 1990.

Edie, Lionel D. *Dollars.* New Haven, Conn.: Yale University Press, 1934.

————. *Easy Money.* New Haven, Conn.: Yale University Press, 1937.

Edsforth, Ronald. *The New Deal: America's Response to the Great Depression.* Malden, Mass.: Blackwell Publishers, 2000.

Elder, Glen H. *Children of the Great Depression.* Chicago: University of Chicago Press, 1974.

Elias, Robert H., ed. *Letters of Theodore Dreiser.* 3 vols. Philadelphia: University of Pennsylvania Press, 1959.

Ellis, Jack C. *A History of Film.* Englewood Cliffs, N.J.: Prentice-Hall, 1985.

Epstein, Ralph C. *The Automobile Industry: Its Economic and Commercial Development.* Chicago and New York: A. W. Shaw, 1928.

Fausold, Martin L. *The Presidency of Herbert Hoover.* Lawrence: University Press of Kansas, 1985.

Ferrell, Robert H., ed. *The American Secretaries of State and Their Diplomacy.* Vols. 11–13. New York: Cooper Square, 1963–64.

————. *Woodrow Wilson and World War I, 1917–1921.* New York: Harper & Row, 1985.

Fisher, Irving. *Booms and Depressions: Some First Principles.* New York: Adelphi Company, 1932.

————. *The Money Illusion.* New York: Adelphi Company, 1928.

Fitch, James Marston. *American Building: The Historical Forces That Shaped It.* New York: Schocken Books, 1973.

Fitzgerald, F. Scott. *The Crack-Up.* Ed. Edmund Wilson. New York: New Directions, 1945.

Forman, Henry James. *Our Movie Made Children.* New York: Macmillan, 1935.

Fowke, Edith, and Joe Glazer. *Songs of Work and Freedom.* Garden City, N.Y.: Dolphin Books, 1961.

Fraenkel, Osmond K. *The Sacco-Vanzetti Case.* New York: Alfred A. Knopf, 1931.

Franklin, Jay [pseud. of John Franklin Carter]. *1940.* New York: Viking Press, 1940.

Freidel, Frank. *Franklin D. Roosevelt: Launching the New Deal.* Boston: Little, Brown, 1973.

―――. *Franklin D. Roosevelt: A Rendezvous with Destiny.* Boston: Little, Brown, 1990.

Galbraith, John Kenneth. *The Great Crash, 1929.* Boston: Houghton Mifflin, 1961.

Garraty, John A. *The American Nation Since 1865: A History of the United States.* New York: Harper & Row, 1966.

―――. *The Great Depression: An Inquiry into the Causes, Course, and Consequences of the Worldwide Depression of the Nineteen-Thirties as Seen by Contemporaries and in the Light of History.* New York: Harcourt Brace Jovanovich, 1986.

Gayer, A. D., ed. *The Lessons of Monetary Experience: Essays in Honor of Irving Fisher.* New York: Farrar & Rinehart, 1937.

Gelderman, Carol. *Henry Ford: The Wayward Capitalist.* New York: Dial, 1981.

Gellman, Irwin F. *Good Neighbor Diplomacy: United States Policies in Latin America, 1933–1945.* Baltimore, Md.: Johns Hopkins University Press, 1979.

Gilbert, Martin. *The First World War: A Complete History.* New York: Henry Holt, 1994.

―――. *The Second World War.* New York: Holt, 1989.

Ginger, Ray. *The Bending Cross: A Biography of Eugene Victor Debs.* New Brunswick, N.J.: Rutgers University Press, 1949.

Goldman, Eric. *Rendezvous with Destiny: A History of Modern American Reform.* New York: Knopf, 1956.

Goldston, Robert. *The Great Depression: The United States in the Thirties.* Indianapolis, Ind.: Bobbs-Merrill, 1968.

Graham, Benjamin, and David L. Dodd. *Security Analysis: Principles and Technique.* New York and London: McGraw-Hill, 1934.

Graham, Otis L., Jr. *An Encore for Reform: The Old Progressives and the New Deal.* New York: Oxford University Press, 1967.

Graham, Otis L., Jr., and Meghan Robinson Wander, eds. *Franklin D. Roosevelt: His Life and Times, an Encyclopedic View.* Boston: Hall, 1985.

Guinsburg, Thomas N. *The Pursuit of Isolationism in the United States Senate from Versailles to Pearl Harbor.* New York: Garland, 1982.

Hamilton, David E., ed. *New Deal.* Boston: Houghton Mifflin, 1999.

Hawtrey, Ralph G. *The Gold Standard in Theory and Practice.* London, New York, and Toronto: Longmans, Green, 1933.

————. *Trade and Credit.* London, New York, and Toronto: Longmans, Green, 1928.

Hayek, Friedrich A. *Prices and Production.* 2d ed. London: George Routledge & Sons, 1932.

Hearn, Charles R. *The American Dream in the Great Depression.* Westport, Conn.: Greenwood Press, 1977.

Henderson, Amy. *On the Air: Pioneers of American Broadcasting.* Washington, D.C.: Smithsonian Institution Press, 1988.

Hicks, John D. *Republican Ascendancy, 1921–1933.* New York: Harper & Row, 1960.

Hillenbrand, Laura. *Seabiscuit: An American Legend.* New York: Ballantine Books, 2001.

Himmelberg, Robert F. *The Great Depression and the New Deal.* Westport, Conn.: Greenwood Press, 2001.

Hoffman, Frederick J. *The Twenties: American Writing in the Postwar Decade.* New York: Free Press, 1965.

Hoover, Herbert. *Memoirs: The Cabinet and the Presidency, 1920–1933.* New York: Macmillan, 1952.

————. *Memoirs: The Great Depression, 1929–1941.* New York: Macmillan, 1952.

————. *The New Day: Campaign Speeches of Herbert Hoover.* Stanford, Calif.: Stanford University Press, 1928.

Howard, John Tasker, and George Kent Bellows. *A Short History of Music in America.* New York: Crowell, 1967.

Ickes, Harold L. *The Secret Diary of Harold L. Ickes.* 3 vols. New York: Simon & Schuster, 1953–54.

Iriye, Akira. *The Origins of the Second World War in Asia and the Pacific.* New York: Longman, 1987.

Israel, Fred L., ed. *The State of the Union Messages of the Presidents.* Vol. 3: *1905–1966.* New York: Chelsea House–Robert Hector, 1966.

Jablon, Howard. *Crossroads of Decision: The State Department and Foreign Policy, 1933–1937.* Lexington: University Press of Kentucky, 1983.

James, Harold. *The End of Globalization: Lessons from the Great Depression.* Cambridge, Mass.: Harvard University Press, 2001.

Johnson, Hugh S. *The Blue Eagle from Egg to Earth.* Garden City, N.Y.: Doubleday, Doran, 1935.

Johnson, Walter, ed. *Selected Letters of William Allen White, 1899–1943.* New York: Holt, 1947.

Jonas, Manfred. *Isolationism in America, 1935–1941.* Ithaca, N.Y.: Cornell University Press, 1966.

———. *The United States and Germany: A Diplomatic History.* Ithaca, N.Y.: Cornell University Press, 1984.

Jones, Joseph M., Jr. *Tariff Retaliation: Repercussions of the Hawley-Smoot Bill.* Philadelphia: University of Pennsylvania Press, 1934.

Kallen, Horace M. *The Decline and Rise of the Consumer.* New York: D. Appleton-Century, 1936.

Kennedy, David M. *Freedom from Fear: The American People in Depression and War, 1929–1945.* New York and Oxford: Oxford University Press, 1999.

Keynes, John Maynard. *A Treatise on Money: The Applied Theory of Money.* Vol. 6 of *The Collected Writings of John Maynard Keynes.* Cambridge, U.K.: Cambridge University Press, 1971.

Kindleberger, Charles P. *The World in Depression, 1929–1939.* Rev. ed. Berkeley: University of California Press, 1986.

Kirby, John B. *Black Americans in the Roosevelt Era: Liberalism and Race.* Knoxville: University of Tennessee Press, 1980.

Klein, Maury. *Rainbow's End: The Crash of 1929.* Oxford, U.K.: Oxford University Press, 2001.

Komarovsky, Mira. *The Unemployed Man and His Family.* New York: Dryden, 1940.

Laux, James M. *The Great Depression in Europe.* St. Charles, Mo.: Forum Press, 1974.

Lawrence, Joseph Stagg. *Wall Street and Washington.* Princeton, N.J.: Princeton University Press, 1929.

Leff, Mark H. *Limits of Symbolic Reform: The New Deal and Taxation, 1933–1939.* New York: Cambridge University Press, 1984.

Leighton, Isabel, ed. *The Aspirin Age, 1919–1941.* New York: Simon & Schuster, 1976.

Leuchtenburg, William E. *Franklin D. Roosevelt and the New Deal, 1932–1940.* New York: Harper & Row, 1963.

———. *The Perils of Prosperity, 1914–1932.* Chicago: University of Chicago Press, 1958.

Lichtenberg, Bernard, and Bruce Barton. *Advertising Campaigns.* New York: Alexander Hamilton Institute, 1930.

Lippmann, Walter. *Interpretations, 1933–1935. Ed. Allan Nevins. New York: Macmillan, 1936.*

———. *A Modern Reader: Essays on Present-Day Life and Culture.* New York: Heath, 1936.

———. *Notes on the Crisis.* New York: John Day, 1931.

———. *A Preface to Morals.* New York: Macmillan, 1929.

Longford, Elizabeth. *The Royal House of Windsor.* New York: Alfred A. Knopf, 1974.

Lowitt, Richard. *America in Depression and War.* St. Louis, Mo.: Forum Press, 1979.

Lowitt, Richard, and Maurine Beasley. *One Third of a Nation: Lorena H ickok's Reports on the Great Depression.* Champaign: University of Illinois Press, 1981.

Lynd, Robert S., and Helen Merrell Lynd. *Middletown: A Study in American Culture.* New York: Harcourt, Brace & World, 1929.

———. *Middletown in Transition: A Study in Cultural Conflicts.* 1936. Reprint, New York: Harcourt, Brace, Jovanovich, 1965.

Lynd, Staughton. *Nonviolence in America: A Documentary History.* Indianapolis: Bobbs-Merrill, 1966.

Lynes, Russell. *The Tastemakers: The Shaping of American Popular Taste.* New York: Dover, 1980.

MacDonald, C. A. *The United States, Britain, and Appeasement, 1936–1939.* New York: St. Martin's Press, 1981.

MacDonald, J. Fred. *Don't Touch That Dial: Radio Programming in American Life from 1920 to 1960*. Chicago: Nelson-Hall, 1979.

MacLeish, Archibald. *The Irresponsibles: A Declaration*. New York: Duell, Sloan & Pearce, 1940.

MacMillan, Margaret. *Paris 1919: Six Months That Changed the World*. New York: Random House, 2001.

Maddox, Thomas R. *Years of Estrangement: American Relations with the Soviet Union, 1933–1941*. Gainesville: University Presses of Florida, 1980.

Manchester, William. *The Glory and the Dream: A Narrative History of America, 1932–1972*. Boston: Little, Brown, 1974.

Mangione, Jerre. *The Dream and the Deal: The Federal Writers Project, 1935–1943*. Boston: Little, Brown, 1972.

Marchand, Roland. *Advertising the American Dream: Making Way for Modernity, 1920–1940*. Berkeley: University of California Press, 1985.

Marks, Frederick W., III. *Wind Over Sand: The Diplomacy of Franklin Roosevelt*. Athens: University of Georgia Press, 1988.

Marquis, Alice Goldfarb. *Hopes and Ashes: The Birth of Modern Times, 1929–1939*. New York: Free Press, 1986.

Marshall, S. L. A. *World War I*. Boston: Houghton Mifflin, 1964.

Marshall, Thomas R. *Recollections of Thomas R. Marshall*. Indianapolis: Bobbs-Merrill Company, 1925.

McCoy, Donald R. *Coming of Age: The United States During the 1920's and 1930's*. Baltimore, Md.: Penguin Books, 1973.

McElvaine, Robert S., ed. *Down and Out in the Great Depression: Letters from the "Forgotten Man."* Chapel Hill: University of North Carolina Press, 1983.

———. *The Great Depression: America, 1929–1941*. New York: Times Books, 1984, 1993.

McKinzie, Richard D. *The New Deal for Artists*. Princeton, N.J.: Princeton University Press, 1973.

McLanathan, Richard. *The American Tradition in the Arts*. New York: Harcourt, Brace & World, 1968.

Mellon, Andrew W. *Taxation: The People's Business*. New York: Macmillan, 1924.

Meltzer, Milton. *Brother, Can You Spare a Dime? The Great Depression, 1929–1933.* New York: New American Library, 1969.

Metter, Suzanne. *Dividing Citizens: Gender and Federalism in New Deal Public Policy.* Ithaca, N.Y.: Cornell University Press, 1998.

Mitchell, Broadus. *Depression Decade: From New Era through New Deal, 1929–1941.* Armonk, N.Y.: M. E. Sharpe, 1989.

Moley, Raymond. *The First New Deal.* New York: Harcourt, Brace & World, 1966.

Montgomery, David. *Workers' Control in America: Studies in the History of Work, Technology, and Labor Struggle.* New York: Cambridge University Press, 1979.

Muscio, Giuliana. *Hollywood's New Deal.* Philadelphia: Temple University Press, 1997.

Myers, William Starr, ed. *The State Papers and Other Writings of Herbert Hoover.* 2 vols. New York: Kraus Reprint, 1970.

Nash, Gerald D. *The Great Depression and World War II: Organizing America, 1933–1945.* New York: St. Martin's Press, 1979.

Neu, Charles E. *The Troubled Encounter: The United States and Japan.* New York: Wiley, 1975.

Niebuhr, H. Richard. *The Church Against the World.* Chicago: Willett, Clark, 1935.

Nowell, Elizabeth, ed. *The Letters of Thomas Wolfe.* New York: Charles Scribners' Sons, 1956.

O'Connor, Harvey. *Mellon's Millions: The Biography of a Fortune, the Life and Times of Andrew W. Mellon.* New York: John Day, 1933.

Offner, Arnold A. *American Appeasement: United States Foreign Policy and Germany, 1933–1938.* Cambridge, Mass.: Belknap Press of Harvard University Press, 1969.

———. *The Origins of the Second World War: American Foreign Policy and World Politics, 1917–1941.* New York: Praeger, 1975.

Oliver, Alfred C., and Harold M. Dudley. *This New America: The Spirit of the Civilian Conservation Corps.* London, New York, and Toronto: Longmans, Green, 1937.

Olson, James, ed. *Historical Dictionary of the New Deal, 1933–1941.* Westport, Conn.: Greenwood Press, 1985.

———. *Historical Dictionary of the 1920s, 1919–1933*. Westport, Conn.: Greenwood Press, 1988.

Parrington, Vernon Louis. *Main Currents in American Thought*. New York: Harcourt, Brace, 1930.

Parrish, Michael E. *Anxious Decades: America in Prosperity and Depression, 1920–1941*. New York: Norton, 1992.

Paschall, Rod. *The Defeat of Imperial Germany, 1917–1918*. Chapel Hill, N.C.: Algonquin Books of Chapel Hill, 1989.

Paxton, Robert O. *Europe in the Twentieth Century*. New York: Harcourt Brace Jovanovich, 1975.

Pease, Otis. *The Responsibilities of American Advertising: Private Control and Public Influence, 1920–1940*. New Haven, Conn.: Yale University Press, 1958.

Pecora, Ferdinand. *Wall Street under Oath: The Story of Our Modern Money Changers*. New York: Simon & Schuster, 1939.

Pells, Richard H. *Radical Visions and American Dreams: Culture and Social Thought in the Depression Years*. New York: Harper & Row, 1973.

Perrett, Geoffrey. *America in the Twenties: A History*. New York: Simon & Schuster, 1982.

Phillips, Cabell. *From the Crash to the Blitz, 1929–1939*. New York: Macmillan, 1969.

Potter, Claire Bond. *War on Crime: Bandits, G-men, and the Politics of Mass Culture*. New Brunswick, N.J.: Rutgers University Press, 1998.

Questions on German History. Bonn, Germany: German Bundestag Press, 1984.

Ransom, John Crowe, et al. *I'll Take My Stand: The South and the Agrarian Tradition*. New York: Harper & Brothers, 1930.

Reynolds, David. *The Creation of the Anglo-American Alliance, 1937–1941: A Study of Competitive Cooperation*. Chapel Hill: University of North Carolina Press, 1982.

Robbins, Lionel. *The Great Depression*. New York: Macmillan, 1936.

Rock, Donald Cameron. *How War Came: The Immediate Origins of the Second World War*. New York: Pantheon Books, 1989.

Rogers, Will. *Ether and Me or "Just Relax."* New York: Putnam, 1929.

————. *How We Elect Our Presidents.* Ed. Donald Day. Boston: Little, Brown, 1949.

Romasco, Albert U. *The Politics of Recovery: Roosevelt's New Deal.* New York: Oxford University Press, 1983.

————. *The Poverty of Abundance: Hoover, the Nation, the Depression.* New York: Oxford University Press, 1965.

Roosevelt, Franklin D. *The Public Papers and Addresses of Franklin D. Roosevelt.* Vols. 2–9. Comp. Samuel I. Rosenman. New York: Russell & Russell, 1969.

Rose, Barbara. *American Art Since 1900: A Critical History.* New York: Praeger, 1968.

Rosen, Elliott A. *Hoover, Roosevelt, and the Brains Trust: From Depression to New Deal.* New York: Columbia University Press, 1977.

Russell, Francis. *The Shadow of Blooming Grove: Warren G. Harding and His Times.* New York: McGraw-Hill, 1968.

Saloutos, Theodore. *The American Farmer and the New Deal.* Ames: Iowa State University Press, 1982.

Santayana, George. *Character and Opinion in the United States.* New York: Charles Scribner's Sons, 1921.

Scharf, Lois. *To Work and to Wed: Female Employment, Feminism, and the Great Depression.* Westport, Conn.: Greenwood Press, 1980.

Scharf, Lois, and Joan M. Jensen. *Decades of Discontent: The Women's Movement, 1920–1940.* Boston: Northeastern University Press, 1987.

Schlesinger, Arthur M., Jr. *The Coming of the New Deal.* Boston: Houghton Mifflin, 1958.

————. *The Crisis of the Old Order, 1919–1933.* Boston: Houghton Mifflin, 1957.

————. *The Politics of Upheaval.* Boston: Houghton Mifflin, 1960.

Schlup, Leonard C., and Donald W. Whisenhunt, eds. *It Seems to Me: Selected Letters of Eleanor Roosevelt.* Lexington: University Press of Kentucky, 2001.

Schwartz, Jordan A. *The Interregnum of Despair: Hoover, Congress, and the Depression.* Urbana: University of Illinois Press, 1970.

————. *The New Dealers: Power Politics in the Age of Roosevelt.* New York: Alfred A. Knopf, 1993.

Schwed, Fred, Jr. *Where Are the Customers' Yachts? Or a Good Hard Look at Wall Street.* New York: Simon & Schuster, 1940.

Seldes, Gilbert. *The Seven Lively Arts.* New York and London: Harper & Brothers, 1924.

Sheehan, Marion Turner, ed. *The World at Home: Selections from the Writings of Anne O'Hare McCormick.* New York: Alfred A. Knopf, 1956.

Shirer, William L. *The Rise and Fall of the Third Reich.* New York: Simon & Schuster, 1960.

Sinclair, Andrew. *Prohibition: The Era of Excess.* New York: Atlantic–Little Brown, 1962.

Sitkoff, Harvard. *A New Deal for Blacks: The Emergence of Civil Rights as a National Issue.* Vol. 1: *The Depression Decade.* New York: Oxford University Press, 1978.

Smiley, Gene. *Rethinking the Great Depression.* Chicago: I. R. Dee, 2002.

Smith, Page. *Redeeming the Time: A People's History of the 1920s and the New Deal.* New York: McGraw-Hill, 1986.

Sontag, Raymond J. *A Broken World, 1919–1939.* New York: Harper & Row, 1971.

Southern, Eileen. *The Music of Black Americans: A History.* New York: Norton, 1971.

Spiller, Robert E., et al., eds. *Literary History of the United States.* 3d ed. New York: Macmillan, 1963.

Stearns, Marshall. *The Story of Jazz.* New York: Oxford University Press, 1958.

Steffens, Lincoln. *The Autobiography of Lincoln Steffens.* New York: Literary Guild, 1931.

Steindl, Frank G. *Monetary Interpretations of the Great Depression.* Ann Arbor: University of Michigan Press, 1995.

Sternsher, Bernard. *Hitting Home: The Great Depression in Town and Country.* Chicago: Quadrangle Books, 1970.

Sullivan, Louis H. *The Autobiography of an Idea.* 1924. Reprint, New York: Dover Publications, 1956.

Sulzberger, C. L. *World War II.* Boston: Houghton Mifflin, 1966.

Tawa, Nicholas. *Serenading the Reluctant Eagle: American Musical Life, 1925–1945*. New York: Schirmer Books, 1984.

Terkel, Studs. *Hard Times: An Oral History of the Great Depression*. New York: Pocket Books, 1970.

Thomas, Norman. *After the New Deal, What?* New York: Macmillan Company, 1936.

Tugwell, Rexford. *The Brains Trust*. New York: Viking, 1968.

Turnbull, Andrew, ed. *The Letters of F. Scott Fitzgerald*. New York: Charles Scribner's Sons, 1963.

Uys, Errol Lincoln. *Riding the Rails: Teenagers on the Move During the Great Depression*. New York: TV Books, 1999.

Walworth, Arthur. *Woodrow Wilson*. 3d ed. New York: Norton, 1978.

Ware, Susan. *Beyond Suffrage: Women in the New Deal*. Cambridge, Mass.: Harvard University Press, 1981.

White, David Manning, and Robert H. Abel, eds. *The Funnies: An American Idiom*. New York: Free Press, 1963.

White, G. Edward. *The Constitution and the New Deal*. Cambridge, Mass.: Harvard University Press, 2000.

Williams, T. Harry. *Huey Long*. New York: Knopf, 1969.

Willkie, Wendell. *This Is Wendell Willkie: A Collection of Speeches and Writings on Present-Day Issues*. New York: Dodd, Mead, 1940.

Willmott, H. P. *The Great Crusade: A New Complete History of the Second World War*. New York: Free Press, 1989.

Wilson, Elena, ed. *Edmund Wilson: Letters on Literature and Politics, 1912–1972*. New York: Farrar, Straus & Giroux, 1977.

Wolfskill, George. *Happy Days Are Here Again! A Short Interpretive History of the New Deal*. Hinsdale, Ill.: Dryden, 1974.

Woofter, T. J., Jr. *Races and Ethnic Groups in American Life*. New York and London: McGraw-Hill, 1933.

Young, Peter. *The Marshall Cavendish Illustrated Encyclopedia of World War I*. Vol. 11: 1919–21. New York: Marshall Cavendish, 1986.

Zieger, Robert H. *Republicans and Labor, 1919–1929.* Lexington: University of Kentucky Press, 1969.

Zinn, Howard, ed. *New Deal Thought.* Indianapolis: Bobbs-Merrill, 1966.

INDEX

Locators in *italic* indicate illustrations. Locators in **boldface** indicate main entries and biographies. Locators followed by *m* indicate maps. Locators followed by *g* indicate graphs. Locators followed by *c* indicate charts.

A

AAA. *See* Agricultural Adjustment Administration
Aalto, Alvar 253
Abbott, Grace 100
A. B. Dick Company 312
Abraham Lincoln Brigade 197
Absalom, Absalom! (William Faulkner) 160, 178
abstractionism 12
Acheson, Dean 117
ACLU (American Civil Liberties Union) 24
acreage 110, 193
Act of Havana 266
Adamic, Louis 89
Adams, Charles Francis 81
Adams, Grace 141
Adams, James Truslow 38, 57
Addams, Jane **349**
Addis Ababa, Ethiopia 168
Adjusted Compensation Act 23, 82
Adkins v. Children's Hospital 22
Administrative Reorganization Act 276
Admiral Graf Spee (ship) 251, 281
advertising *231*
Advertising Campaigns (Bernard Lichtenberg and Bruce Barton) 88
AFL. *See* American Federation of Labor
Africa 268, 287, 290, 291
African Americans xvii, 82
at 1936 Olympics 163
Mary McLeod Bethune 205, *206,* **352–353**

black section of Tupelo, Mississippi *163*
Chicago's South Side *255*
and Civilian Conservation Corps 106, 115, 207
under Coolidge administration 7
demobilized troops of 2–3
W. E. B. DuBois **360**
and education 207
and Federal Theater Project 205–206
Marcus Garvey 2, **365**
Harlem Renaissance 12, 50
Herbert Clark Hoover and 43
hopelessness of 115
internal migration of 115
and jazz 12, 13
Joe Louis 205, 311, *311,* **375**
lynchings 204
NAACP 70, 205
and New Deal **115**
and race riots 2–3
and Anna Eleanor Roosevelt 115
"the Scottsboro boys" 70, 86
sharecropper family *205*
slow progress for **204–207**
Eddie Tolan 72
Walter F. White 205, **393–394**
Afrika Korps 268, 291
After the New Deal, What? (Norman Thomas) 177
Agee, James **349**
Agricultural Adjustment Act 106, 128–129, 147–148, 151
Agricultural Adjustment Administration (AAA) 106, 111, 129, 219

Agricultural Export Corporation 23
Agricultural Marketing Act 53, 62
agricultural price supports 5, 6. *See also* subsidies for farmers
agricultural workers *180, 184, 215, 283*
agriculture. *See* farming and farmers
Ah, Wilderness! (Eugene O'Neill) 129
"*Aimee Semple McPherson: Prima Donna of Revivalism*" (Sarah Comstock) 37
airplanes 283–285, 288, 295
for France 227, **243–244,** 275
for Great Britain 260, 275, 286
interest in 9
production of 259
from United States 266
A.L.A. Schechter Poultry Corporation v. United States 146–147, 151, 166, 329–334
Alabama Supreme Court 86
Albania 247, 268, 276, 288, 290
alcohol 2–3, 106, 125. *See also* Prohibition
Aldrich, Winthrop W. **349**
Alexander (king of Yugoslavia) 68, 133
Alexander, Will W. **349**
Algeria 287
Allen, Florence 207
Allen, Fred 95, 125, 161
Allen, Frederick Lewis 96, 172, 239
Allen, Gracie 70, 125, 161
Allen, Robert S. 134

Allies 22, 82, 85, 251, 259, 267, 281, 290. *See also specific headings, e.g.:* Great Britain
allotment program (for farmers) 110, 151
Almería 215
America First Committee 267, 287
America in Midpassage (Charles A. Beard and Mary R. Beard) 296
American Civil Liberties Union (ACLU) 24
American Federation of Labor (AFL) 3–4, 106, 190
American Indians 43, 132, *195*
American Liberty League 118, 133, 155, 156, 168
American Telephone and Telegraph Company (AT&T) 25, 44, 46, 47, 53
America's Own Refugees (Henry Hill Collins, Jr.) 309
Ameringer, Oscar 96
Amos 'n' Andy (radio program) 10, 51
Anderson, Marian **349–350**
Anderson, Mary **350**
Anderson, Sherwood 89, **350**
Angell, James W. *See The Behavior of Money*
Animal Crackers (film) 71
Anna Christie (play) 71, 125
antiaircraft weapons 258
Anti-Comintern Pact 170–171
antilynching legislation 204, 205
anti-Semitism 153, 248. *See also* Nazism and Nazis
antitrust laws 107, 114